D1523715

The Biological Aspects
of Rare Plant
Conservation

PROCEEDINGS OF AN INTERNATIONAL CONFERENCE
HELD AT KING'S COLLEGE, CAMBRIDGE, ENGLAND

14–19 July 1980

Convened by

G. Ll. Lucas, F. H. Perring, S. M. Walters and T. C. E. Wells

and Sponsored by

The Linnean Society of London

and

The Botanical Society of the British Isles

The Biological Aspects of Rare Plant Conservation

Edited by
Hugh Synge
IUCN Threatened Plants Committee Secretariat,
c/o The Herbarium, Royal Botanic Gardens, Kew, Surrey, England

A Wiley–Interscience Publication

JOHN WILEY & SONS

Chichester · New York · Brisbane · Toronto

British Library Cataloguing in Publication Data:

The biological aspects of rare plant conservation
  1. Rare plants – Congresses
  2. Plant conservation – Congresses
  I. Synge, Hugh   II. Linnean Society
  of London   III. Botanical Society of the
  British Isles
  639.9′9   QK86.A1   80-42067

ISBN 0 471 28004 6

Typeset in Great Britain by
Pintail Studios Ltd., Ringwood, Hants.
Printed and bound in Great Britain at
The Pitman Press, Bath, Avon

085845

List of contributors

ASHTON, P. S.   *The Arnold Arboretum of Harvard University, The Arborway, Jamaica Plain, Massachusetts 02130, USA.*

AYENSU, E. S.   *Office of Biological Conservation, Smithsonian Institution, Washington, DC 20560, USA.*

BELOUSSOVA, L.   *All-Union Research Institute of Nature Conservation and Reserves, Znamenskoye–Sadki, 142790, P/O Vilar, Moscow Region, USSR.*

BOUCHER, C.   *Botanical Research Institute, PO Box 471, Stellenbosch 7600, South Africa.*

BRADSHAW, M. E.   *Department of Adult and Continuing Education, University of Durham, 32 Old Elvet, Durham DH1 3JB, England.*

BRÅKENHIELM, S.   *The National Swedish Environment Conservation Protection Board, Box 1302, S-171 25 Solna, Sweden.*

BRATTON, S. P.   *Uplands Field Research Laboratory, Twin Creeks Area, Great Smoky Mountains National Park, Gatlinburg, Tennessee 37738, USA.*

BRIGHTMAN, F. H.   *British Museum (Natural History), Cromwell Road, London SW7 5BD, England.*

BROOKES, B. S.   *The Scottish Field Studies Association, Kindrogan Field Centre, Enochdhu, Blairgowrie, Perthshire PH10 7PG, Scotland.*

BUCKLEY, R.   *Department of Biogeography and Geomorphology, The Australian National University, PO Box 4, Canberra, ACT 2600, Australia.*

CROMPTON, G.   *University Botanic Garden, Cambridge CB2 1JF, England.*

DAVY, A. J.   *School of Biological Sciences, University of East Anglia, Norwich NR4 7TJ, England.*

DENISSOVA, L.   *All-Union Research Institute of Nature Conservation and Reserves, Znamenskoye–Sadki, 142790 P/O Vilar, Moscow Region, USSR.*

DRANSFIELD, J.   *The Herbarium, Royal Botanic Gardens, Kew, Richmond, Surrey TW9 3AE, England.*

FAY, J. J.   *Office of Endangered Species, US Fish and Wildlife Service, Washington, DC 20240, USA.*

FEARN, G. M.   *Department of Biological Sciences, Sheffield City Polytechnic, Pond Street, Sheffield, England.*

FROST, L. C.   *Department of Botany, University of Bristol, Woodland Road, Bristol BS8 1UG, England.*

GIVEN, D. R.   *Botany Division, DSIR, Private Bag, Christchurch, New Zealand.*

GODICL, L.   *University of Maribor, PA-Koroška 160, YU-62000 Maribor, Yugoslavia.*

GOOD, R. B.   *Division of Plant Industry, CSIRO, PO Box 1600, Canberra City, ACT 2601, Australia.*

GREEN, B. H.   *Department of Environmental Studies and Countryside Planning, Wye College (University of London), Nr Ashford, Kent TN25 5AH, England.*

GREIG-SMITH, J.   *c/o School of Plant Biology, University College of North Wales, Memorial Buildings, Bangor LL57 2UW, Wales.*

GUBB, A. A.   *McGregor Museum, Kimberley, South Africa.*

HALL, J. B.   *20 Fishergate, Ripon, North Yorkshire, England.*

HARE, A. D. R.   *Department of Plant Biology and Microbiology, Queen Mary College, University of London, Mile End Road, London E1 4NS, England.*

HARPER, J. L.   *School of Plant Biology, University College of North Wales, Memorial Buildings, Bangor LL57 2UW, Wales.*

HARTMANN, H. E. K.   *Institut für Allgemeine Botanik, Universität Hamburg, Jungiusstrasse 6–8, D-2000 Hamburg 36, FRG.*

HARVEY, H. J.   *Department of Applied Biology, University of Cambridge, Pembroke Street, Cambridge CB2 3DX, England.*

HENDERSON, D. M.	*Royal Botanic Garden, Edinburgh EH3 5LR, Scotland.*
HERNÁNDEZ BERMEJO, J. E.	*Escuela Técnica Superior de Ingenieros Agrónomos, Universidad de Córdoba, Spain.*
JAIN, S. K.	*Botanical Survey of India, PO Botanic Garden, Howrah 711103, India.*
JAMES, P.	*British Museum (Natural History), Cromwell Road, London SW7 5BD, England.*
JARVIS, C. E.	*Threatened Plants Committee Secretariat, c/o The Herbarium, Royal Botanic Gardens, Kew, Richmond, Surrey TW9 3AE, England.*
JEFFERIES, R. L.	*Department of Botany, University of Toronto, Toronto, Ontario M5S 1A1, Canada.*
JERMY, A. C.	*British Museum (Natural History), Cromwell Road, London SW7 5BD, England.*
JOHN, D. M.	*British Museum (Natural History), Cromwell Road, London SW7 5BD, England.*
LAVARACK, P. S.	*National Parks and Wildlife Service, Pallarenda, Townsville, Queensland 4810, Australia.*
LEON, C.	*Threatened Plants Committee Secretariat, c/o The Herbarium, Royal Botanic Gardens, Kew, Richmond, Surrey TW9 3AE, England.*
LUCAS, G. LL.	*The Herbarium, Royal Botanic Gardens, Kew, Richmond, Surrey TW9 3AE, England.*
MEDWECKA-KORNAŚ, A.	*Institute of Botany, Jagiellonian University, ul. Lubicz 46, 31-512 Krakow, Poland.*
MEREDITH, T. C.	*Department of Geography, McGill University, 805 Sherbrooke Street West, Montreal, PQ, H3A 2K6, Canada.*
MOLL, E. J.	*Botany Department, University of Cape Town, P Bag Rondebosch 7700, South Africa.*
MORSE, L. E.	*The Nature Conservancy, 1800 North Kent Street, Arlington, Virginia 22209, USA.*
MYERS, N.	*PO Box 48197, Nairobi, Kenya.*
NILSSON, Ö.	*Botanical Garden, University of Uppsala, Villavägan 8, S-752 36 Uppsala, Sweden.*

OLDFIELD, S.   *The Herbarium, Royal Botanic Gardens, Kew, Richmond, Surrey TW9 3AE, England.*

PARKER, D. M.   *University of Liverpool Botanic Gardens, Ness, Neston, Wirral, Cheshire L64 4AY, England.*

PIGOTT, C. D.   *Department of Biological Sciences, University of Lancaster, Lancaster LA1 4YG, England.*

POWELL, H. T. and POWELL, G.   *Scottish Marine Biological Association, Dunstaffnage Marine Research Laboratory, PO Box 3, Oban, Argyll PA34 4AD, Scotland.*

PRINCE, S. D.   *Department of Plant Biology and Microbiology, Queen Mary College, University of London, Mile End Road, London E1 4NS, England.*

RABINOWITZ, D.   *Division of Biological Sciences, University of Michigan, Ann Arbor, Michigan 48109, USA.*

RABOTNOV, T. A.   *Department of Geobotany, M. V. Lomonosov State University of Moscow, 117234 Moscow, USSR.*

RANWELL, D. S.   *School of Biological Sciences, University of East Anglia, Norwich NR4 7TJ, England.*

RATCLIFFE, D. A.   *Nature Conservancy Council, Godwin House, George Street, Huntingdon PE18 6BG, England.*

RATCLIFFE, D.   *Department of Botany, University of Leicester, University Road, Leicester LE1 7RH, England.*

RICHARDS, P. W.   *14 Wootton Way, Cambridge CB3 9LX, England.*

SAGAR, G. R.   *School of Plant Biology, University College of North Wales, Memorial Buildings, Bangor LL57 2UW, Wales.*

SÁINZ OLLERO, H.   *Escuela Técnica Superior de Ingenieros Agrónomos, Universidad de Córdoba, Spain.*

SASTRY, A. R. K.   *Botanical Survey of India, PO Botanic Garden, Howrah 711103, India.*

SUKOPP, H.   *Institute of Ecology, Technical University of Berlin, Schmidt-Ott-Strasse 1, 1000 Berlin 41, FRG.*

SWAINE, M. D.   *Department of Botany, University of Aberdeen, St Machar Drive, Aberdeen AB9 2UD, Scotland.*

SYNGE, A. H. M.	*IUCN Threatened Plants Committee Secretariat, c/o The Herbarium, Royal Botanic Gardens, Kew, Richmond, Surrey TW9 3AE, England.*
TAMM, C. O.	*Department of Ecology and Environmental Research, The Swedish University of Agricultural Sciences, S-750 07 Uppsala, Sweden.*
TIKHOMIROV, V. N.	*Botanical Garden, Moscow State University, Moscow 117234, USSR.*
TRACEY, J. G.	*CSIRO Division of Forest Research, PO Box 273, Atherton, Queensland 4883, Australia.*
TRAUTMANN, W.	*Bundesforschungsanstalt für Naturschutz und Landschaftsökologie, Institut für Vegetationskunde, Konstantinstrasse 110, 5300 Bonn 2, FRG.*
WALTERS, S. M.	*University Botanic Garden, Cambridge CB2 1JF, England.*
WARD, L. K.	*Institute of Terrestrial Ecology, Monks Wood Experimental Station, Abbots Ripton, Huntingdon PE17 2LS, England.*
WATKINSON, A. R.	*School of Biological Sciences, University of East Anglia, Norwich NR4 7TJ, England.*
WELLS, D. A.	*Nature Conservancy Council, Godwin House, George Street, Huntingdon PE18 6BU, England.*
WELLS, T. C. E.	*Institute of Terrestrial Ecology, Monks Wood Experimental Station, Abbots Ripton, Huntingdon PE17 2LS, England.*
WEST, R. G.	*The Botany School, University of Cambridge, Downing Street, Cambridge CB2 3EA, England.*
WHITE, P. S.	*Uplands Field Research Laboratory, Twin Creeks Area, Great Smoky Mountains National Park, Gatlinburg, Tennessee 37738, USA.*
WILLIAMS, O. B.	*Division of Land Use Research, CSIRO, PO Box 1666, Canberra City, ACT 2601, Australia.*
WILLIAMS, V.	*Department of Plant Science, University College, Cardiff, Wales.*
WOODINGS, T. L.	*Department of Botany, University of Leicester, University Road, Leicester LE1 7RH, England.*

Contents

Preface

Principles of nature conservation were clearly set forth in 1947 in the Report of the Wild Life Conservation Special Committee, a report entitled *Conservation of Nature in England and Wales*. The main purposes which nature reserves should serve were stated to be: conservation and maintenance, survey and research, experiment, education and amenity. The close connection between observational and experimental science and nature conservation was described, with reference, for example, to the autecology of species, community studies and population biology. Since that time it has become increasingly evident that for conservation to be effective, a knowledge of the biology of species and communities and of the ecosystems in which they occur is absolutely essential. The problems which rare plants pose to the ecologist and conservationist may in the final analysis be much the same, though the stimulus for the solution of the problems may be different.

There is no doubt that the need for a scientific basis for conservation has stimulated fundamental ecological research. We become concerned with the intimate daily lives of particular species, how they are affected by their neighbours, and how their survival can be supported. The investigation of the nature of the rarity of a species requires an analysis of a complex of biological and environmental factors. It requires seemingly simple operations such as monitoring of populations and observations on life-cycles, together with ecological experiment. These subjects and many other relevant studies are described and discussed in the collection of conference papers which follow. They show the very active and growing field of research which is necessarily involved in rare plant conservation, with examples of achievements, problems and methods from many parts of the world.

It may be useful in a preface to place the subject of this book against a more general botanical background. The papers are concerned with the state of plant populations at present and how these populations can be retained in future. The environment is continually changing on a short time scale, perhaps with fluctuations imperceptible to us, and on a longer time scale with more obvious fluctuations. Nothing can be stable in the long-term history of vegetation, but knowledge of the origin and scientific basis of rarity must be an integral part of the study of evolution of plants and plant communities, especially with the self-evident necessity for the conservation of all 'created' species.

Botany School
Cambridge

R. G. WEST, FRS

Introduction

Between 14 and 19 July 1980, about 160 botanists gathered at King's College, Cambridge, to discuss and explore how the many varied disciplines of the biological sciences can be translated into practical conservation management to save rare and threatened plants. The papers presented at the meeting form the basis of this book and illustrate the many expanding activities available in plant conservation.

First one needs to identify which species are under threat, a subject covered in the first section of the book, backed up by a bibliography of Red Data Books and threatened plant lists (Appendix 2). Chapters review the programmes being undertaken in the United States (E. S. Ayensu), in India (S. K. Jain and A. R. K. Sastry), in New Zealand (D. R. Given), in Australia (R. B. Good and P. S. Lavarack), in the USSR (L. Beloussova and L. Denissova, V. N. Tikhomirov) and in Sweden (Ö. Nilsson). Each author emphasizes a different aspect: Dr Given, for example, concentrates on the type of documentation required to help conservation managers and convince decision-makers. Dr Beloussova and Dr Denissova describe how a Red Data Book is compiled. Professor Tikhomirov stresses the value of regional schemes to complement national programmes in identifying and protecting rare plant sites on the ground. Dr Nilsson analyses the habitats and distributions of threatened plants in Sweden and shows how this affects plans for their conservation – under Project Linnaeus detailed studies in the field have been made on all their threatened plants. It is necessary to analyse precisely why species are threatened, as shown by H. Sukopp's and W. Trautmann's study in West Germany.

For a very different flora Dr Jain and Dr Sastry outline the great difficulties rare plant conservation faces in many parts of the world – lack of taxonomists combined with a rich flora and extensive threats to vegetation. In some countries, such as Australia, it is still possible to protect large areas of intact ecosystems and Dr Good and Dr Lavarack suggest that, in this respect, Australia is in a position reached by the United States in the 1800s. In the Cape York Peninsula, a centre for rare plants, the area reserved for conservation has increased from 125 000 hectares in 1974 to a staggering 1.57 million hectares today. But the future for Australia's rain forests is less than rosy, as J. G. Tracey shows; only 20 per cent now remain and in future only those areas protected in national parks and reserves are likely to survive intact. Here the emphasis is on classifying the rain forest types and trying to conserve intact samples of each, but data on species are being built up too.

Assessing which species are threatened is only the beginning. As P. White and S. Bratton explain, there are several stages to practical conservation: (1) assessment of threatened species; (2) locating sites from herbarium specimens, notebooks, published literature; (3) verifying those sites on the ground and adding new ones; and (4) monitoring the populations. Steps (2) and (3) are the subject of G. Crompton's chapter on surveying rare plant sites in Eastern England. Dr Bratton and Dr White themselves describe the practical difficulties in tackling these four steps, especially in monitoring small rare plant sites in a big national park – the Great Smokies of the Appalachian Mountains – and outline similar programmes in other US parks. In their later chapter they show how changes, both natural and man-made, continue in national parks after protection. These can present theoretical dilemmas as well as practical problems for the conservation manager.

Their fourth step is the subject of the next two sections of the book, a major part of which covers the application of population biology to rare and threatened species. Theoretical papers by J. Harper and D. Rabinowitz explore the concept of rarity as a biological phenomenon. A. J. Davy and R. L. Jefferies outline the many different approaches now available to the student of plant populations, and O. B. Williams shows their application in desert environments. Both show how population monitoring can provide an understanding of the biology of a rare species and can serve as a basis for conservation management. The results are often surprising: Dr Williams describes an experiment in which lucerne pellets, simulating seedlings, were scattered over a large paddock where grazing intensity was low; the sheep soon found virtually all the pellets, showing how efficient a grazing animal can be in eliminating a rare species, even if that species is only an apparently insignificant portion of the vegetation and even if the vegetation is not being noticeably degraded. The practical papers by M. Bradshaw on monitoring the rare plants at Upper Teesdale and by A. R. Watkinson on winter annuals underline one of the secrets of this science: the experimenter monitors the fate of individual 'labelled' plants within the population rather than counts populations, and so can pinpoint the stage in the life cycle where losses and gains take place. As a result, in Professor Harper's words, we now have the tools to make some rare species common!

The concept of rarity itself is an elusive one, as Professor Harper explains. Everyone has a different idea of what is a 'rare plant'. Yet in practical conservation, there must be some standard terminology to indicate rarity, or at least the degree of threat. The different criteria used for rare plant lists and the range of conflicting definitions of the word 'endangered' are a source of great confusion, as Professor Ayensu explains for the various state lists in the USA. Some agreed standards are needed and he proposes a new and comprehensive set of criteria for the United States which would enable the essential synthesis to be made from the differing state lists and the priorities to be set. On an international level, the most widely used criteria are the 'Red Data Book categories' of IUCN, which are a relatively subjective measure of the degree of threat to individual species and so are more widely applicable than the more fixed criteria. (The full definitions and explanatory notes are in Appendix 3. To avoid confusion over the use of words like endangered and vulnerable, we show them in normal print when used in the dictionary sense, in single quotes when defined by the author – e.g. 'endangered' – and with a capital initial when used according to the IUCN definitions – e.g. Endangered.)

It is remarkable that the British Government report in 1947 cited by Professor West recommended population studies to be undertaken on rare plants yet until recently there have been very few examples of such studies. As T. C. E. Wells shows, even for a group like orchids, of interest to the layman and of prime importance to conservation, little has been written until now on their demography and population ecology. His paper, too, provides a link with the autecological section, which demonstrates the techniques available to be as diverse as the number of experimenters; all relate to what the conservationist needs to know. For example H. J. Harvey and T. C. Meredith used a wind tunnel to study seed dispersal. Equally fascinating are the phenogrammes of E. J. Moll and A. A. Gubb, which show the annual cycle of *Staavia dodii* from the Cape of Good Hope. C. Boucher's study of another South African species, the famous Marsh Rose Protea (*Orothamnus zeyheri*), has enabled successful conservation measures to be taken, increasing the population many-fold.

Professor Pigott's work on *Tilia platyphyllos*, whose habitat and ecology he describes in detail, shows some of the problems to be faced. Planting makes it difficult to work out natural distributions, and the tree may live for 1000 years so population studies are barely practicable! L. Ward demonstrates very elegantly how a species, in her case English Juniper, retrenches into its heartland as pressures mount. J. Greig-Smith and G. R. Sagar show the value of comparative studies of rarity by studying species that are only locally rare, partly because disruptive experimentation is permitted on wild populations and partly because comparisons can be made with other sites.

Anatomy too has a role as H. E. K. Hartmann explains for two sympatric genera of Mesembryanthemaceae in south-west Africa. They adapt quite differently to their arid environment and a comparative study of their anatomy enables conclusions to be drawn that show the different conservation strategies needed in each case. Plant/animal relationships also come up; Dr Ward explains the relationship between the size of a juniper population and the diversity of its dependent invertebrate fauna. The relevance of the exciting study of co-evolution to conservation, however, must wait for a later meeting.

Many of the ecological papers touch on re-introductions. S. D. Prince and A. D. R. Hare, for example, use ordination techniques to predict whether certain sites would be good places to introduce their two rare and declining composites. The practical problems of re-introduction and translocation are illustrated by B. Brookes' cautionary tale of *Schoenus ferrugineus*: here is a plant virtually exterminated from its only British locality by collectors and then totally submerged by a hydroelectric scheme in the 1940s. It was translocated to a nearby site, but this was washed away in the first year. Many other introductions were made in the neighbourhood, but the records were woefully inadequate and Mr Brookes' work involved a detective study in locating these sites. Documentation is essential! But re-introductions can succeed, as D. M. Parker's short account of the re-introduction of *Saxifraga cespitosa* to a site in Wales shows well. B. H. Green looks at the policy aspects of re-introductions and of the related problem, damage to native ecosystems by introduced species. He reviews the effect of introductions to Britain and shows how the British flora, untypically, has been exceptionally resistant to introduced plants. This is emphasized by D. S. Ranwell, who puts the case for encouraging introductions in Britain, at least to coastal sites. In most parts of the world, however, introductions are often very damaging. In South Africa, and on many islands, introduced species are wreaking havoc with native endemic flora and penetrating undisturbed vegetation as well as ruderal sites. This is a subject not covered here; as part of the UNEP Wider Caribbean Conservation Programme, IUCN is hoping to organize a meeting on the problems of introduced species in the Caribbean islands and we hope this will be one way of drawing attention to the problem.

Protecting the habitat of a rare species is usually the best way of ensuring its survival, but contact between phytosociological and taxonomic approaches to conservation has been very limited. In one of the major review papers of the book, A. Medwecka-Kornaś describes a methodology for evaluating both the floristic and phytosociological significance of a conservation site and shows how this was done for the Ojców National Park in Poland. It is a most impressive synthesis, which provides a good opening to the final section on establishing and managing reserves for threatened species. D. A. Wells and J. Fay describe the conservation programmes in the UK and the USA respectively, and evaluate success in protecting rare plant sites. L. Godicl looks at national parks in Yugoslavia and the rare species they protect. L. Morse explains the programme of the US Nature Conservancy, a private organization that must have protected more land than any other; their Natural Heritage Programs put into practice many of the principles in this book. But it is not always a big reserve that is needed: L. C. Frost provides a fascinating account of the $\frac{1}{4}$-acre Badgeworth Nature Reserve, the main site in Britain for *Ranunculus ophioglossifolius*. This too exemplifies the result of the conference in showing how biological studies enable a species to be managed successfully on a small and vulnerable site.

An evening session was held on the fate of lower plants, a subject rarely discussed at conservation meetings. The organizers hope that the extended record of the session (Chapter 11) provides an adequate summary of the state of knowledge on lower plant conservation and will stimulate a longer and broader discussion. Almost the first point to emerge was the need for more taxonomy. It was generally felt that information on individual rare species of lower plants, just as of vascular plants, provided the best argument with which to convince decision-makers of the need to create nature reserves. However, all speakers accepted that information on rare species of lower plants could be made available for only a few temperate countries at present. They emphasized that the priority must be to conserve good representatives of primary forest around the world and that this policy should protect the majority of lichens, mosses and liverworts.

Indeed, this dilemma arises for higher plants too, especially in regions where rain forest is the dominant vegetation. One of the most marked contrasts in the conference was the difference between the detailed and precise single-species studies done in countries like Britain and the lack of even a basic taxonomy in, for example, the Amazon. There are very few ecological studies of individual tropical species. The paper presented by M. D. Swaine and J. B. Hall on the unusual Ghanaian tree *Talbotiella* is an exception, but even here the key question of whether the tree is ectomycorrhizal or not is still to be answered.

N. Myers outlines the threats to the tropical rain forests of the world and explains the present basis on which conservation is being planned. P. S. Ashton concentrates on rarity in tropical forests and the biological principles behind identifying which areas to protect. He shows that this task must be based on a knowledge of the biology of the flora and of the patterns of endemism. He underlines the need for more studies into the breeding systems, ecological genetics and demography of tropical forest plants.

The diversity of some tropical ecosystems is well known and the threats to the flora well publicized. There was a great feeling at the meeting that efforts must be made to redress the imbalance in research and conservation activities between the tropics and some of the temperate countries. In view of the speed at which tropical vegetation, especially forest, is disappearing this must be the most urgent of priorities.

Hypotheses on plant biology must also be tested in the tropics. P. B. Tomlinson and P. H. Raven (1978, cited in Chapter 1 of this book) express it like this:

Any comparative study of plant form or structure is based on incomplete premises if it does not take into consideration the total range of natural variability in plants, i.e., including the enormous diversity of plant life in the tropics. Any physiological mechanism or ecological response has been analyzed insufficiently if it does not consider how these mechanisms or responses are mediated in tropical climates and especially in the non-seasonal climates of the lowland tropics. Any evolutionary idea has been incompletely scrutinized if it has not been tested against tropical examples. Any generalizations of plant population biology must apply to the frequently distinctive composition of tropical forests.

*   *   *   *

A successful conference depends on good organization and good support. I would like to record here, on behalf of the Organizing Committee, our thanks to the financial sponsors; we are most grateful to the Commonwealth Foundation, the

British Council, the Royal Society and the British Ecological Society, who paid
for a number of distinguished speakers from overseas to attend; to the Nature
Conservancy Council, who gave a grant to cover the costs of the Secretariat; and
to the University of Cambridge for their reception. I would like, too, to express
our thanks to Dr Hilary Birks, who is the most efficient and capable of conference
managers.

Thanks to good planning and to our financial sponsors, the conference ended
without debt and so the royalties from this book will be made available to support
studies on rare and endangered plants and to promote the conservation of these
plants. The Organizing Committee have decided that this money should be paid
into the '100% Fund' of the Fauna and Flora Preservation Society (ffPS), ear-
marked for projects along these lines, with emphasis on the tropical floras where
work was agreed to be urgently needed. The ffPS only recently took flora under
their wing, but have established over many years a reputation as trend-setters in
conservation. Their particular skill is the donation of small grants to stimulate a
wider conservation project or programme. Indeed, as the leading scientific society
concerned with plant and animal conservation world-wide, they may hope to
interest many readers in joining, attending their regular evening meetings in
London and receiving their journal *Oryx*. The address to write to is:

> The Fauna and Flora Preservation Society,
> c/o The Zoological Society of London,
> Regent's Park,
> London NW1 4RY.

This is a most pleasing conclusion to the meeting and we hope it will draw further
money and support for the kind of studies outlined in this book.

After the meeting there were successful excursions to two rare plant sites in the
fens. At Chippenham Fen a keen member discovered a plant in flower of
Pinguicula vulgaris, a species not seen there in recent years and thought to be
extinct in Cambridgeshire. It was raining at Wicken Fen but Dr H. J. Harvey,
Secretary of the National Trust Wicken Fen Committee, gave an impromptu
lecture on fen vegetation and included an account of studies on *Peucedanum
palustre*, host for the extinct Swallowtail larvae. The organizers are very grateful
to him and to Dr Meredith for producing a written account of their fascinating
work at short notice.

The conference ended in a most fitting way when at the final dinner Ö. Nilsson
presented S. Max Walters, Chairman of the conference Organizing Committee,
with the Silver Medal of Linnaeus from the Swedish Linnean Society, given in Dr
Nilsson's words,

> as a badge of merit to persons working within the field and spirit of Lin-
> naeus. In Max's case it is given as a sign of gratitude for his work in the con-
> servation of threatened plants, in particular for the practical conservation

work demonstrated in the Cambridge Botanic Garden and for his role as host to the conference.

On a personal note I would like to thank the many friends and colleagues who helped with this book, in particular Charlie Jarvis, Christine Leon and Sara Oldfield in the Kew Conservation Unit, David Field for his meticulous indexing, and the expert typists at Kew for their fast and accurate production, which has enabled us to get a book of this length smartly to press in under 4 months. It has been a pleasure as always to call on Max Walters for thought-provoking advice whenever needed. I am particularly grateful to Gren Lucas for his support. I hope the result may be as rewarding to others as it has been to me.

HUGH SYNGE

Priorities in rare species conservation for the 1980s

S. M. WALTERS *University Botanic Garden, Cambridge, England*

My starting-point is a question from the floor: why it was that the conservation of rare species is 'left to the taxonomist' rather than being a matter for the concern of biologists as a whole, and ecologists in particular. I would wish to remind the conference that, even if the Botanical Society itself is mainly a society of taxonomists (at least in the wide sense), the same could hardly be said of its fellow sponsoring Society, the Linnean Society of London. Even more pertinently we should recall the generous financial support afforded to this conference by the British Ecological Society to enable ecologists to attend and present their papers. Having said these things, it remains true that taxonomic botanists, and institutions such as Kew which are primarily taxonomic, have played and are playing a leading part in the movement for botanical conservation.

The success of the first Kew Conference (Simmons *et al.*, 1976) concerned with aspects of the role of botanic gardens in conservation stimulated a great deal of useful discussion, not least about the value of scientific evidence and experiment applied to conservation problems. The present conference springs from such discussions initiated by my colleague, Dr Franklyn Perring, who rightly saw the next step as an exchange of views between ecologists, taxonomists and conservationists on the aims and procedures for protecting rare species, and brought into existence in 1979 the Organizing Committee for this conference. The general shape of the programme was, in fact, that laid down in the early stages by Frank himself after preliminary talks; it is a tribute to the clarity of his vision that, broadly, the programme structure survived unchanged.

In biological science there is always the danger that we remain in our isolated specialisms and see the work of other groups as very separate and even irrelevant. This tendency is particularly clearly represented by the division between the taxonomists, often caricatured as having a weird obsession with Latin binomials, and the experimental scientists, who often seem a race apart. The particular dichotomy has a long history. Let me read you a short passage from the writings of a Professor of Botany in this University:

But still I must consider the claims of Botany are not sufficiently appreciated among us. There are persons of great mathematical and classical attainments who have very erroneous notions respecting the ultimate aim and object of this science. Many persons, both within and without the Universities, suppose its objects limited to fixing names to a vast number of plants, and to describing them and classing them under this or that particular 'system'. They are not aware that systematic Botany is now considered to be no more than a necessary stepping-stone to far more important departments of this science, which treat of questions of the utmost interest to the progress of human knowledge in certain other sciences which have been more generally admitted to be essential to the well-being of mankind.

We might well conclude that little has changed in the subject since Henslow wrote those words in 1846! His plea for a proper understanding of the role of systematic botany as 'a necessary stepping-stone' to more important developments of the science is as relevant today as it ever was.

The interaction between the descriptive (or observational) and the experimental science in a sense underlies the whole purpose of our deliberations, and I am sorry that, in one important respect, our early planned programme failed to materialize. It was our hope that Professor David Webb, of Trinity College, Dublin, would have been able to accept our invitation to give this closing paper, but this was unfortunately not possible. I can, however, at least quote the opening lines from Professor Webb's excellent address to the 'Corresponding Societies' of the British Association at its meeting in Dublin in 1957 under the title 'The vasculum and the microtome':

I have chosen for the title of my address today two instruments which are meant to be symbolic of two different approaches to the problems of biology. The vasculum stands for outdoor biology, field studies, natural history; the man who wears it is no doubt interested in many things besides taxonomy, but he is always in some measure concerned with taxonomy; and he is brought inevitably into fairly intimate contact with the complex diversity which characterizes any biological community. This is the field of the amateur as well as the professional. The microtome, on the other hand, stands for the analytical science of the laboratory, which, insulated from the complex flux of the community, pursues more recondite enquiries, often on a single plant or animal, or on a single part of a plant or animal; its studies belong to the realm of physiology or anatomy or cytology, but seldom taxonomy; and it is virtually the preserve of the professional today (Webb, 1957).

This is a delightfully-written paper, asking for more tolerance and co-operation from both sides; I strongly recommend it to you for enjoyment and instruction.

So much for history. How does this apply to our present concerns? I should like here to make three points. First, any field biologist in the tradition of Ray and Linnaeus is fascinated by variety, whilst on the contrary 'the man with the microtome', the analytical scientist, is seeking for the underlying principles to explain variety and bring order out of chaos. But these two people can be, and often are, combined into a single biological scientist: perhaps Charles Darwin is the most famous example. The paper given by Professor Harper on the meanings of rarity, and the papers on monitoring individual populations illustrate perfectly the dependence of each approach on the other. Without the detailed case-histories of individual species we could not devise general explanations and testable hypotheses; without any general theory we would be forced to an indefinitely prolonged *ad hoc* procedure of trial and error.

The second point is that, in a very important way, some ecologists are bridging the gap with increasing effect. The excellent paper by Professor Anna Medwecka-Kornaś points the way to a clear, practical assessment of plant communities and vegetation complexes in terms of their conservation importance – an essential step to bring the individual, taxonomically-based assessments of *species* into the ecologically-based assessments of *communities* for the purposes of nature conservation.

Thirdly, I must restate the basic role of taxonomy (which can include phyto-sociology as the taxonomy of vegetation) as providing a necessary basis for all further scientific or administrative activity. As all the speakers dealing with survey and assessment have shown, no comparable descriptions of potential nature reserves can be made available without at least a minimum of taxonomic (including distributional) information. This may be self-evident to all of us here, but it is worth remembering that it may not be at all self-evident to politicians and administrators who determine priorities for research funds, and that, particularly in tropical and subtropical floras, the absence of even a minimum floristic survey may well mean large-scale extinctions before we can even know of the threat.

This gloomy assessment brings me logically to face the question Professor Harper very reasonably asked: what does the conservationist want from the biological scientist? Again, three answers came to mind as the conference proceeded, and I will deal with them in order of complexity. Much of our deliberation has pointed to *answers to particular questions* as the first need of conservation which can be supplied by science. The preparation of indexes and Red Data Books as described by Professor Ayensu illustrates one very necessary activity which answers the question which species are actually threatened in which territory, and the monitoring of populations as described by Dr Margaret Bradshaw answers the further questions about the fate of rare species in their surviving habitats. It is here, of course, that the world view is so challenging and indeed so depressing; we are forced to the conclusion that large-scale extinctions are inevitable, especially in the most threatened vegetation types such as lowland tropical rain forest, and that the saving of remnants, both floristic and vegetational, may be the best we can do. Such urgent action, as exemplified by

Dr Norman Myers, is obviously important, and we have no alternative, given the size of the threats.

A second answer, less precise, might say that the practising conservationist needs *sympathetic support* from scientists. In terms of politics, this may be even more important than the provision of facts. The World Conservation Strategy of IUCN mentioned by Mr Lucas needs the enlightened support of *all* scientists, not just the minority. How to get this support is a difficult subject involving the general attitude of scientists to ethical problems which arise from the application of their scientific knowledge, and to pursue it would need a separate conference – although it is by no means clear that scientists would attend!

The third answer is that the conservation movement needs the occasional distinguished scientist who can, as it were, stand apart (or above), take a *balanced, overall assessment*, and then see where to innovate. The movement for botanical nature conservation in Britain had one such figure in the previous generation – Sir Arthur Tansley, who was neither a typical 'vasculum man', nor an experimentalist, yet largely created many of the organizations we now use – the British Ecological Society and the Nature Conservancy Council among them! How does science produce such a man of vision? There is clearly no formula, but I firmly believe (as Tansley himself did when he helped to form, for example, the International Phytogeographical Excursion (IPE)) that occasions such as our present international conference are of very great importance.

At this point my remaining theme is obvious. Are there topics which would abundantly repay further examination at similar future conferences? Several come readily to mind, but two in particular seem to combine both urgency and the possibility of practical value. The first is squarely in the court of the ecologists: how can we, in practice, define and select potential nature reserves or protected areas for those territories where the need and the opportunities are greatest? The second concerns our common responsibility for the urgently threatened tropical and subtropical floras: how do we best use the limited scientific expertise, most of which is in the developed countries, to cope with the grave and urgent threat to tropical floras and vegetation? This question must remain for all of us the one which demands our attention.

References

Simmons, J. B., Beyer, R. I., Brandham, P. E., Lucas, G. Ll. and Parry, V. T. H. (Eds.) (1976). *Conservation of Threatened Plants*, Plenum Press, New York and London.
Webb, D. A. (1957). 'The vasculum and the microtome' (Address to the British Association, Dublin meeting), *The Advancement of Science*, **55**, 183–90.

Section 1
Survey and Assessment of Rare and Threatened Species

The Biological Aspects of Rare Plant Conservation
Edited by Hugh Synge

1
The assessment and conservation of threatened plants around the world

GREN LUCAS AND HUGH SYNGE *The Herbarium, Royal Botanic Gardens, Kew, England*

Summary

Rapid and continuing population growth and increasing poverty in many countries will put more pressure on vegetation and species in the future. A brief review from the literature is made of the estimated decline in those habitats where plant losses are most likely. These predicted losses underline the need for data on threatened plants and 'centres of endemism' now, despite the large imbalance in research effort between tropical and temperate floras. In this context the programme of the IUCN Threatened Plants Committee is presented.

Introduction

To predict the future is always a dangerous occupation, particularly for the scientist. Yet it is not hard to see that in 20 years time many parts of the world will be far poorer for biologists like ourselves if the present destruction of vegetation continues. This is not a selfish viewpoint but the sad reality. Many countries will have lost all their primary rain forest, others the very ground cover of their drylands. Tragically most of the plant species lost will be in those regions where we know least about the flora. Where success was possible and governments did declare reserves and national parks in time, species may continue to be lost from these 'protected' areas owing to their growing isolation, as might be expected from the theory of island biogeography.

First we want to show how the conservation movement is failing to halt the major threats to natural habitats and how this in turn affects not just botanists but every decision-maker, politician, businessman, and inhabitant of our world.

This is not a slur on the world's conservation bodies; they have grown rapidly but the threats have grown even more rapidly. Twenty years ago who would have predicted that the major rain forests of the world, once symbol of remote places, would be in danger of total degradation and that many areas might not survive the twentieth century?

Before showing how the conservation movement is developing in the face of these threats, we would like to summarize some of the evidence which shows the scale of the threats and their effects on vegetation around the world. Although this phenomenon is apparent to any traveller, it is essential we have the evidence to support our concern. During 1980, several major reports were published, which when considered together give a global view of what is threatening diverse habitats on earth. For the first time we have the essential overviews that we need. The picture is sketchy and uncertain and many areas on the ecological map are still blank, but it is a start.

Neil Armstrong's vision of the earth from the moon as a small green haven in the emptiness of space – 'a tiny spaceship fuelled by solar power thanks to the chlorophyll-bearing members of the plant kingdom' in David Bellamy's words (1979) – proved a great stimulus to global thinking. In recent years many minds have been moving in the same direction.

One such mind was that of ex-President Jimmy Carter who in 1977 told his Council on Environmental Quality, in co-operation with other government agencies, 'to make a one-year study of the probable changes in the world's population, natural resources, and environment through the end of the century'. He continued, 'This study will serve as the foundation of our longer-term planning'. The report was published as *Global 2000*. First examined is population, and the message is stark: 'Rapid growth in world population will hardly have altered by 2000'. The most recent figures in the report show world population at 6.18 billion in the year 2000 (vol. 1, p. 12), an increase of over 50 per cent from the total of 4.09 billion in 1975, and this prediction *assumes* a big drop in fertility levels, especially in developing countries. In fact the assumptions about the success or failure of family planning programmes do not greatly change the population predicted for the year 2000, because of the built-in momentum for further growth from the great increase over the last generation (but do of course radically alter the growth predicted after 2000). World population will still be rising by more people each day in 2000 than now. Also, 'ninety per cent of this growth will occur in the poorest countries'. So here is the most potent factor increasing the threat on natural systems, and one which conservationists cannot ignore.

Global 2000 predicts that the gap between rich and poor nations will widen. Gross National Product (GNP) will rise almost everywhere, but because of population increase, per capita GNP may not increase at all in many countries. The report predicts that Bangladesh, for example, will increase its per capita GNP by a trifling 8 per cent over the period 1975 to 2000, from the present unbelievable figure of US$111 per annum.

On agriculture, *Global 2000* predicts a 90 per cent increase in food production from 1970 to 2000, assuming no deterioration in climate. Much of the increase will occur in developed nations and, against the trend for many decades, real prices will increase dramatically. This is because of the greatly increased costs of the petroleum and petrochemicals needed to secure this increase. Accordingly many countries will be no better off than they are today. The study predicts that per capita consumption will hardly improve at all in most south Asian countries and will actually decline in Africa south of the Sahara. The World Bank estimates that the number of malnourished people in 'less developed countries' could rise from 400–600 million in the mid 1970s to a terrifying 1.3 billion in 2000 (quoted in *Global 2000*, vol. 1, p. 17, vol. 2, ch. 13).

From its very different starting point, the Brandt report comes to similar conclusions: 'There is a real danger that in the year 2000 a large part of the world's population will be living in poverty'. Almost certainly there will be more hungry people then than now, and they will be compelled to cut down essential shelter trees and overgraze rangelands to survive from day to day, so destroying those very resources which if not over-exploited could free them from poverty. The desperation of short-term survival prevents there being a prosperous future.

The value of the *Global 2000* study is that the predictions have been compared to some extent and evaluated together. For example it is the combination of population estimates and food estimates that makes the per capita predictions look so gloomy. Similarly the authors have taken into account loss of forests, trends in energy prices, and availability of water. But this important achievement in the study is also its biggest drawback, because it implies a vicious circle from which we cannot escape. Yet it is important to remember that the study depicts conditions that will develop if policy does not change rather than what is most likely to happen. For example the estimate that Mexico City will contain 31.6 million people by 2000 (vol. 1, p. 12, vol. 2, Table 13-9) is unlikely to come true because it may prove impossible to provide food and water for a city of that size (see Ehrlich *et al.*, 1977).

More important it does not allow for the way in which pressure of events can turn policies around very quickly and in which creative thinking can find solutions to apparent impasses. Indeed the Brandt report is an attempt to stimulate the first and a means of achieving the second.

Another aspect not taken into account is the way science could help: biotechnology, for example, is now advancing at a quickening pace; if plants can be made to grow with less maintenance and reduced needs, such as less nitrogen fertilizer, or be made easier to harvest, and if more efficient methods are found to control pests or create herbicides, then the energy inputs for the increased agricultural production could be considerably less than predicted in the study and this will have a beneficial effect on food prices.

One hopes that the experience of those countries where conservation and land use are succeeding will also counter some of the trends identified in *Global 2000*. For example, in Costa Rica, a small country of 49 900 sq. km that is exceptionally rich in plants and animals, there has been great pressure to remove forests for cattle ranching to serve the US demand for 'fast foods'. Yet, under President Daniel Oduber's leadership, Costa Rica has recently established a Natural Resources Institute to undertake ecological studies and develop land-use plans;

more exciting still Costa Rica has created a network of national parks that, according to Norman Myers,

> contains more units, and covers a greater proportion of national territory, than is the case in any other Latin American country. Thirteen units total 1260 sq. km, an area that is scheduled to expand several times over ... Together with Forest Reserves, either established or proposed, this will bring the total of protected areas in Costa Rica to 37 per cent of national territory (Myers, 1979).

This is a shining record that no developed nation can dream of matching! It is also important to realize this does not inhibit sustained development and improvement for the whole population.

Examples like Costa Rica are no cause for complacency – just the opposite because they show success is possible. Indeed, some problems that appear daunting at global level look less formidable when tackled at a local or national level, even if in the context of a world-wide shift in attitudes and policies. Global thinking may change the political climate and stimulate creative ideas, but most of the problems we are discussing can only be solved at the village or community level. So the central problem remains and we should now look at the implications for the plant kingdom.

The threats to plant life

The environment in which most species losses are likely in our lifetimes is the tropical rain forest. The US National Academy of Sciences has produced a report entitled *Conversion of Tropical Moist Forests* (Myers, 1980), which is the most comprehensive guide to loss of rain forest. The decline in the three countries with most rain forest – Brazil, Zaïre and Indonesia – is among the most difficult to estimate and there are no numerical data for Zaïre at present. Sensibly therefore, the author hesitates to give an overall figure for annual forest loss and emphasizes a country-by-country approach. This analysis makes gloomy reading; part of the summary reads:

> Virtually all lowland forest of the Philippines and peninsular Malaysia seem likely to become logged over by 1990 at the latest, possibly much earlier. Much the same applies to most parts of West Africa. Little could remain of Central America's moist forests within another 10 years, probably less. Almost all of Indonesia's lowland forests have been scheduled for timber exploitation by the year 2000, and at least half by 1990. Extensive areas of Amazonia in Colombia and Peru could be claimed for cattle ranching and various forms of cultivator settlement by the end of the century; and something similar is true for much of the eastern sector of Brazil's Amazonia.

From the information available, it appears that only the rain forest in Central Africa and Western Amazonia is likely to survive the year 2000 unscathed. Prance (1979) quotes an estimate from Dr Warwick Kerr, Director of the National Amazon Research Institute in Manaus, that 'at least 25 per cent of the Amazon rain forest has been destroyed'. It is not the percentage in itself that is so alarming, but the speed at which it has happened and the very small and short-term economic gain to the Brazilian people. At least the destruction of Europe's forests enabled her to create an industrial base, and so provide unprecedented material benefits for her peoples.

The tragedy of the moist tropical forests is that without their forest cover they tend to be unproductive. When the forest cover is removed, erosion can be rapid and few nutrients left (see for example Jordan and Medina, 1978). The science of agroforestry – growing crops among the trees on a sustainable basis – is only in its infancy. Furthermore, even moderate and selective logging changes the species composition of some parts of the forest and so can lead to species extinctions.

For tropical forests as a whole, the *Global 2000* study estimates a 40 per cent decline in forest cover by 2000 in Latin America, Africa, Asia and Oceania (vol. 1, p. 23). More encouraging, however, is the prediction of a rapid and continuing increase in the price of tropical timber. This may encourage nations to conserve their forests in much the same way that oil price rises meant the OPEC countries now find their best investment is to keep their oil underground rather than sell it and invest the money elsewhere.

Turning to drylands, the United Nations Conference on Desertification in 1977 provides an overview of the present situation. Again, the predictions for arid zone floras are grim. The map produced at the conference showed 'regions already in the grip of desertification or at high to very high risk cover 20 million sq. km – an area twice the size of Canada' (UN, 1978; quoted in IUCN, 1980). The map, reprinted in the *World Conservation Strategy* (IUCN, 1980), shows many centres of plant endemism to be within the areas at risk: the Horn of Africa for small succulent *Euphorbia* species, the Anatolian plateau of central Turkey, and west southern Africa for Crassulaceae.

The endemic floras in Mediterranean-type climates are also in danger. Probably under most threat is the fynbos, the heath and protea vegetation of the Cape of South Africa, and often called the Cape Floristic Kingdom. It is probably the richest flora in the world with 1300 species per 10 000 sq. km. Today it has been reduced to an area of about 1.8 million hectares (the area of the Kruger National Park), mostly in patches and narrow corridors and much of what remains is threatened by alien plants. Although it covers less than 1 per cent of southern Africa, the fynbos contain 65 per cent of the region's threatened plants – 1244 species out of a present total of 1915 (Hall *et al.*, 1980; A. V. Hall, pers. comm.). So here again the threats to species are intense and increasing.

Perhaps the highest *percentage* losses are likely on islands. Already there are examples like Rodrigues where all but 2 of the 34 endemic angiosperms are

Extinct or Endangered. In St Helena the flora was devastated before 1805–10, when the island was first botanized properly, so we will never know how many species were lost; today 10 species are Extinct and 15 Endangered out of the 30 known endemics. In both these cases grazing by introduced animals, principally goats, was to blame. Later on the goats were followed by introduced plants, which could establish themselves in the disturbed ground created by the animals, and now present an even more intractable problem. The threats to island floras and the numbers of endangered species are relatively well documented (see Lucas and Synge, 1978; Lucas, 1979a; Melville, 1979). These examples may refer to islands where most species were lost in previous centuries, but the devastation continues on a grand scale elsewhere. Two areas of extreme species losses are Hawaii and Madagascar: Fosberg and Herbst (1975) list 1186 species, subspecies and varieties as 'extinct', 'endangered', 'rare' or 'local' in Hawaii, out of a known flora of about 2200 species. In Madagascar, home of about 10 000 angiosperm species, over 80 per cent of which are endemic, the great majority of the natural vegetation has been destroyed and most if not all that remains is under severe threat (Rauh, 1979).

In northern Europe, too, the picture is bleak; for Britain the Nature Conservancy Council estimate that out of approximately 750 sites identified in the *Nature Conservation Review* (Ratcliffe, 1977) as of prime importance to conservation, 63 are known to have been totally destroyed or seriously damaged since the survey was undertaken in 1969–70. An even more alarming indication of the continued loss of habitats is the decline of lowland raised bogs in Britain: a recent study by Dr Goode for the Council shows that in most counties only around 10 per cent of the area of bog in 1850 (estimated from maps) remains. In Lancashire it is just 1 per cent. The losses have been to agriculture, forestry and peat cutting (D. A. Goode, pers. comm.)

The World Conservation Strategy

Yet conservation of plants in their native habitats is essential to our daily lives. We all know the arguments about how natural vegetation cover on watersheds stops erosion, prevents irreparable flood damage and reduces siltation behind dams. We know about how new drugs and even new crops are being found from little-known and hitherto obscure plants, and about the shrinking genetic base of modern, industrial agriculture as crop varieties become less diverse and wild crop relatives decline steadily (see Mooney, ?1979). We know that all but a small proportion of the world's population rely on medicinal plants to maintain their health (see for example Ayensu, 1979) and how some peoples depend entirely on their native forests for all the necessities of life.

There are many, many arguments for conserving natural vegetation, yet the message is still not getting through to the right people. We may know the arguments ourselves, but are they being heeded? How do we as botanists convince the politicians and their advisors, the permanent officials in government and the governing bodies of development agencies? These are the people who make the final decisions which affect plants.

To reach these people and convince them of the case for conservation, the International Union for Conservation of Nature and Natural Resources (IUCN), with the advice, co-operation and financial support of the United Nations Environment Programme and the World Wildlife Fund, has prepared a *World Conservation Strategy* (IUCN, 1980). It was launched in a multitude of countries on 5 March 1980. Its objectives are ambitious but simple:

a. *To maintain essential ecological processes and life-support systems* (such as soil regeneration and protection, the recycling of nutrients, and the cleansing of waters), on which human survival and development depend;
b. *to preserve genetic diversity* (the range of genetic material found in the world's organisms), on which depend the functioning of many of the above processes and life-support systems, the breeding programmes necessary for the protection and improvement of cultivated plants, domesticated animals and microorganisms, as well as much scientific and medical advance. technical innovation, and the security of the many industries that use living resources;
c. *to ensure the sustainable utilization of species and ecosystems* (notably fish and other wildlife, forests and grazing lands), which support millions of rural communities as well as major industries.

The two-page 'Executive Summary' goes on to explain why achieving these objectives is urgent:

a. *the planet's capacity to support people is being irreversibly reduced in both developed and developing countries:*
   – thousands of millions of tonnes of soil are lost each year as a result of deforestation and poor land management;
   – at least 3,000 sq. km of prime farmland disappears every year under buildings and roads in developed countries alone;
b. *hundreds of millions of rural people in developing countries, including 500 million malnourished and 800 million destitute, are compelled to destroy the resources necessary to free them from starvation and poverty:*
   – in widening swaths around their villages the rural poor strip the land of trees and shrubs for fuel so that now many communities do not have enough wood to cook food or keep warm;
   – the rural poor are also obliged to burn every year 400 million tonnes of dung and crop residues badly needed to regenerate soils;
c. *the energy, financial and other costs of providing goods and services are growing:*
   – throughout the world, but especially in developing countries, siltation

cuts the lifetime of reservoirs supplying water and hydroelectricity, often by as much as half;
- floods devastate settlements and crops (in India the annual cost of floods ranges from $140 million to $750 million);

d. *the resource base of major industries is shrinking:*
- tropical forests are contracting so rapidly that by the end of this century the remaining area of unlogged productive forest will have been halved;
- the coastal support systems of many fisheries are being destroyed or polluted (in the USA the annual cost of the resulting losses is estimated at $86 million).

The Strategy goes on to describe the main obstacles to conservation. It outlines the mistaken belief that conservation concerns only a limited sector of government rather than being a process and a way of thinking that cuts across departmental boundaries. It describes the general failure to integrate conservation with development and shows how development projects are often unnecessarily destructive (see Curry-Lindahl, 1979; Sitwell, 1980). It explains the weaknesses in existing conservation agencies, in their mandates and resources. It highlights the need for more information, and so on. The Strategy itself shows how these obstacles can be overcome, e.g. by better law, more personnel, anticipatory environmental policies, more effective and widespread use of the conservation treaties, etc. It is an impressive document and all those concerned with conservation should read it; for that reason we will not quote any more of its proposals!

The need for information

To persuade anybody and to be of practical value, recommendations like those of the Strategy must be supported by facts. This is easy to say but very hard to carry out. We all realize this, but surely we must improve our communications, our method of approach, the way we 'sell' data to those who have the power to implement recommendations. I do not believe we are succeeding fast enough nor on a sufficiently global scale.

One great difficulty is the great imbalance between where the botanists live and where the plants grow. Most people in this conference are from Britain, a country with a flora of around 1500 native species and a mere handful of endemics (15 at the last count, excluding apomictic groups – C. Leon, pers. comm.). Yet there are probably at least 1500 amateur and professional botanists in Britain who can identify plants in the field and many thousands of books or papers on the flora. (Books on the British flora in the Kew Library, excluding journals, pamphlets and folio books, occupy approximately 30 m of shelving!) How easy it is for us in comparison with our colleagues in the American tropics, where individual countries contain tens of thousands of species, yet are rarely covered even by a check-list, and the botanists are few and often isolated from big herbaria. Again using the Kew Library example, the whole of South America is covered by approximately 10 m of shelf space.

Prance (1978) provides some very useful figures for the size of tropical floras. He estimates that 155 000 out of the 240 000 angiosperm species are tropical. Of these a staggering 90 000 are from tropical America (compared to 35 000 in tropical Asia and 30 000 in tropical Africa). It has been estimated that Colombia, for example, contains of the order of 45 000 or 50 000 species (Schultes, 1951; Prance, 1978). The figures for other plant groups are even more remarkable: Prance says that 11 000 out of 12 000 ferns are tropical and 9000 out of 12 000 mosses are tropical (Prance, 1978).

Clearly we must try to redress the balance and bring more of all our resources to bear on the taxonomy of tropical flora and at the same time develop conservation action plans. This has been said many times, for example in the stimulating series of papers on 'Perspectives in Tropical Botany' (*Ann. Miss. Bot. Gard.*, **64**(4), 1978) and in Hedberg (1979), but it cannot be repeated too often.

Recently the US National Academy of Sciences called for a four- to five-fold increase in 'the pool of taxonomists studying tropical organisms from its present level of about 1500 people world wide' to greatly accelerate the speed of biological inventory in the tropics (US National Academy of Sciences, 1980). They list the regions most in need of study and their report, *Research Priorities in Tropical Biology*, should be required reading for all organizations who sponsor the biological sciences whether or not they are governmental.

It is pleasing to see the renewed interest in compiling and completing the basic regional Floras of the tropics, and a new and parallel tendency for local or minifloras (e.g. Dodson and Gentry, 1978; Croat, 1978). This year, for example, the University of Mexico, the Missouri Botanical Garden and the British Museum (Natural History) in London have announced plans to write a *Flora Meso-Americana*, covering Panama to southern Mexico. Yet the basic Flora is only a beginning for species studies in fields such as co-evolution (see Janzen, 1978) and population biology, both of which will surely provide insights of fundamental value to plant conservation.

The heavy bias in this meeting to botanists from Europe and North America underlines the emphasis in financial support and institutions in these countries. By definition the developed world will have the expertise and money which the emerging nations do not. As problems increase in the coming years, our role must be expanded, not allowed to decline. The countries where most species will be lost are precisely those with the biggest problems of population, agriculture and development. As Peter Raven (1978) put it,

> The countries involved, which will mostly become preoccupied with life-and-death questions of food and energy, will be unlikely to be able to divert many of their precious financial reserves to the study of the forests and

other natural ecosystems, even though the sustained productivity of their lands ultimately depends on such knowledge [cf. Janzen, 1973]. It therefore will apparently be up to developed countries such as the United States to devote the necessary capital to gaining whatever ecological knowledge it might be possible to accumulate during these critical years. Only by doing so will it be possible to gain a measure of world stability for our successors in the twenty-first century.

Europe too must play its part in helping in this way. This is the message we must ensure the aid agencies, governments and private funding bodies receive. And these are the areas in which we must develop and concentrate our resources!

Or almost: we have gone a long way down the path of destruction in Europe and North America and many once-common species are now far more rare. The data indicate we do not have much further to go to remove maybe a further 10 per cent or so of those plants which give pleasure, are scientifically interesting or even have some minor economic role. It is not right and it is not even necessary that we should lose any more. As a result of previous destructive action, it is ironic that the rare and endangered species are now mostly confined to small sites unsuitable for agriculture and forestry, and so their conservation need not cause much economic hardship if any. Where conflicts do arise, most notably with draining of wetlands for agriculture, conservationists must establish clear priorities for sites that need protection and governments should accept that whatever the conflicts, the most important of these sites should be conserved as part of the national heritage.

In virtually every case, the best way to conserve a plant is to protect its habitat. But first we need to know which are the threatened species and where they still grow.

In the last 10 years, as the following chapters in this section of the book show, there has been a great deal of effort in assessing which species are under threat. Lists of threatened species for most temperate and some subtropical countries have been prepared or are underway. Appendix 2, which is a bibliography of Red Data Books and published threatened plant lists, shows what has been achieved in each country. These lists must now be related to habitats and localities on the ground, so it is clear which areas should be given protection. And finally we need to gather the biological knowledge necessary to ensure the successful conservation management of those species and the habitats of which they form a part.

We all know how sketchy our overall botanical knowledge is world wide – so many new species yet to be described, so many species only known from a short Latin description and a few herbarium specimens. But because of the threats to plants we cannot afford to wait. As we have tried to show, the natural world will be dramatically different in 20 years time. So lists must be compiled and areas be identified quickly, on the best available knowledge. We can always refine and update them later on.

In most developed, temperate countries, the taxonomy is relatively tidy and there are plenty of research workers. So here our lists can be formed rapidly and should quickly show which areas need to be conserved. Compiling the list is only the first step in a logical process towards ensuring these species survive.

In areas where the flora is little known, but where large areas and whole vegetation types are under threat, the concept of 'centres of endemism' or 'centres of diversity' may be more helpful than the threatened plant list. The first priority is obviously to protect as many large areas as possible – and fast. Botanical expertise may be best used in identifying areas of known species richness rather than in compiling species lists; a plant may not be known to have been threatened until after it has become extinct! Sadly many species losses are inevitable whatever happens. So we need to find these sites of greatest floristic diversity and use information on the species in them to convince politicians of the importance of conserving them. Preferably, this work should be done within each country by local botanists, in co-operation with and supported by institutions in the 'developed' nations, UN agencies, etc., both with training programmes and with personnel.

The Threatened Plants Committee of IUCN

IUCN's Survival Service Commission set up the Threatened Plants Committee (TPC) in 1974 to provide a focus for information on threatened plants and to ensure that appropriate botanical data reached the decision-makers. In many regions of the world there are now active national programmes to identify and conserve threatened species, most notably in North America (for the USA see Ayensu and Fay, Chapters 2 and 37), Australia (see Good and Lavarack, Chapter 5), New Zealand (see Given, Chapter 4), South Africa (Hall *et al.*, 1980), the USSR (see Beloussova and Denissova, Chapter 6, and Tikhomirov, Chapter 7), and in many individual European countries. In these cases, TPC helps in any way it can, but does not undertake the basic work of compiling the list. Wherever possible TPC tries to encourage countries to use the standard IUCN 'Red Data Book categories' as a measure of the degree of threat to individual species. (They are defined and explained in Appendix 3.) As the TPC must first concentrate on species threatened world-wide, TPC lists for these regions may complement national lists, since the latter usually contain all national rarities, whether or not threatened elsewhere. Indeed, the presence of both types of list establishes two levels of priority for conservation.

TPC started with Europe and here the pattern is beginning to emerge. The many national Red Data Books published or underway coincided with TPC's own effort, which resulted in the publication of a list of species rare and threatened on a European scale (IUCN Threatened Plant Committee, 1977). The list was commissioned by the Council of Europe, whose Council of Ministers passed a strong resolution on many aspects of plant conservation. The Council of Europe commendably did not stop there, but proceeded to build a legal treaty for conservation of European plants and animals in their native habitats. This is the Berne Convention, properly called the 'Convention on the Conservation of European Wildlife and Natural Habitats'. Nineteen nations have already signed, indicating they intend to pass appropriate legislation in their own parliaments to put the treaty into law. The TPC provided a list of 119 European species in most danger of extinction and this forms Appendix I of the agreement. Governments who ratify will have to protect these species from picking and uprooting, and more important will also have to protect the habitats of those species as well. The Council have designed complicated machinery to monitor success and gradually to strengthen the provisions of the treaty. So here botanical data supplied through TPC have been of particular value in stimulating conservation action.

Also, TPC have compiled a preliminary report for the European Economic Community (Leon, 1980); this lengthy report contains as much background information as possible on the habitats and localities of species Endangered in the EEC countries and provides an analysis of what action is needed for each. The Commission is rightly keen to highlight conservation measures and there are many practical initiatives which it is hoped they will take, such as supporting field studies to verify sites of Endangered species from the literature and from old records, and to study the autecology of those species with the aim of ensuring survival in the habitat.

These examples show the value of the data. Information from field workers who are concerned about the survival of their local flora is gathered by TPC and fed into a computer, where it is associated with a wide range of other information. Regional and country lists are produced as required by governments and agencies; these organizations make appropriate conservation recommendations, which in turn create the climate in which field conservation receives support and where those who are fighting to save their local floras stand a better chance of success. So, through TPC, the data go full circle, a relationship explored in more detail elsewhere (Lucas, 1979*b*).

We will be updating the list for a second edition later in 1981 – at present 2237 species are listed as Extinct, Endangered, Vulnerable, Rare or Indeterminate – and building up more information on the sites of each, so that IUCN can make detailed recommendations in each case. As part of a Council of Europe project we are also relating each species to a designated habitat type, and suspect that this will show the necessity for renewed efforts in wetland conservation. All these tasks are made possible by the generous support of the European Science Foundation, who have given us a 3-year grant for a TPC Research Assistant for Europe. Miss Christine Leon was appointed to this post in early 1980.

We have already said that no more plant species should become extinct in Europe (Lucas, 1980). Only lack of purpose will thwart this aim.

This progress is exciting, but Europe is the easiest region to cover. In other parts of the world, great difficulties of taxonomy and botanical exploration remain. Our activities in other regions continue to develop and are described below:

North Africa and the Middle East. A draft list is now available, compiled by TPC, but is very incomplete for many of the countries of the Middle East.

Tropical Africa. Early in 1980 TPC appointed Dr Charlie Jarvis as Research Assistant for Africa, following generous funding from IUCN, WWF and UNEP. The aim is to produce a draft list by 1982, building upon the initial work done through the Conservation Committee of the Association pour l'Etude Taxonomique et Floristique de la Flore de l'Afrique Tropicale (AETFAT). The flora has around 30 000 species (Brenan, 1979; Prance, 1978). Between 1953 and 1973, however, 7478 new species were described from Africa (including Madagascar), nearly one per day (Brenan, 1979). Many other names were shown to be synonyms, so the taxonomy is very active at present. In many parts of the region, though, field work is sadly not easy today and some parts are little explored (see Hepper, 1979). Moreover, the progress in completing the big regional Floras, such as the *Flora Zambesiaca* and the *Flora of Tropical East Africa*, is still tantalizingly slow; at present rates none of the three will be completed during this century.

As a result we are trying to identify the centres of endemism or diversity on the ground, following Brenan's survey (1979) of the continent as well as listing those species known to be threatened. The aim is to show which are the sites where conservation action can prevent most plant extinctions while taking into account the need for continued economic development.

Central and South America. Here a similar project to the African one is under way, though based at the Smithsonian Institution in Washington, DC, under the joint direction of Professor Edward S. Ayensu and the TPC. Miss Jane Lamlein has been appointed as the Research Assistant for the region, and the Central American flora is first to be covered. The work is described by Ayensu (1980):

> The desired results for Latin America include lists of Endangered and Vulnerable endemic plants for each country; the identity of centres of botanical endemism that should be protected in the form of national parks and reserves; an in-depth appraisal of the current threats to plant species in the region and where they are operating; and approximately 100 detailed Red Data Sheets for Latin American species by the end of 1981.

India. A project to list threatened plants is being developed between the Botanical Survey of India, the Smithsonian Institution and the US Department of the Interior.

The Caribbean. IUCN have recently become involved with the UNEP Plan for the Wider Caribbean and hope to contribute a *Species Atlas*, listing the threatened and endemic plants and animals, and showing where protection is needed. TPC is undertaking the plant list. An interesting development is the link in the project between the species approach to habitat conservation and the ecosystem approach, which is being carried out by IUCN's Commission on National Parks and Protected Areas; we hope that the Atlas will provide a joint synthesis from both approaches and show which are the most important conservation sites.

Programmes for south east Asia and the Pacific region will be started in 1981 and the work on the islands of the Indian Ocean and South Atlantic Ocean will also be boosted.

Conclusion

The TPC has received widespread and enthusiastic support from research and field workers all over the world and without this there would be no opportunity to develop rational conservation plans for plants. It gives us great pleasure to acknowledge this work here. As a result, within the next few years basic information on which plants are threatened will be available for most regions, and reports on centres on endemism for others.

But this is only the first step. We must make progress on relating these species to their habitats so that their conservation in the habitat can be built into development plans. We must find out which are already in national parks and reserves to make sure they are adequately protected there. We must make certain that appropriate legislation is created and enforced. We must also continue our efforts to ensure the survival of threatened plants in botanic gardens (a programme not considered here; see Lucas, 1979*b*; Synge, 1979; Synge and Townsend, 1979; Ashton, Chapter 13).

As the pressures on vegetation mount in the coming years, the preparatory data-gathering undertaken now will be of crucial importance for long-term conservation action. In many cases action is already too late but we can try to prevent these escalating threats from destroying all we stand for if we co-ordinate our data now and ensure it is integrated into the development plans for the twenty-first century. We cannot stand back   we must act now!

References

Ayensu, E. S. (1979). 'Plants for medicinal uses with special reference to arid zones', in *Arid Land Plant Resources* (Eds. J. R. Goodin and D. K. Northington), pp. 117–78, International Center for Arid and Semi-Arid Land Studies, Lubbock, Texas.

Ayensu, E. S. (1980). 'The TPC–SI Latin American Programme', *Threatened Plants Committee Newsletter*, **6**, 2–3, Kew, England.

Bellamy, D. (1979). 'The rôle of the media in conservation', in *Survival or Extinction* (Eds. H. Synge and H. Townsend), pp. 175–7, Bentham–Moxon Trust, Kew, England.

Bramwell, D. (Ed.) (1979). *Plants and Islands*, Academic Press, London.

Brenan, J. P. M. (1979). 'Some aspects of the phytogeography of tropical Africa', *Ann. Missouri Bot. Gard.*, **65**(2), 437–78.

Croat, T. B. (1978). *Flora of Barro Colorado Island*, Stanford University Press.

Curry-Lindahl, K. (1979). *Development Assistance with Responsibility: Environment and Development in Developing Countries*, Swedish Government.
Dodson, C. H. and Gentry, A. H. (1978). 'Flora of the Rio Palenque Science Center, Los Rios Province, Ecuador', *Selbyana*, **4**.
Ehrlich, P. R., Ehrlich, A. H. and Holdren, J. P. (1977). *Ecoscience: population, resources, environment*, Freeman, San Francisco.
Fosberg, F. R. and Herbst, D. (1975). 'Rare and endangered species of Hawaiian vascular plants', *Allertonia*, **1**(1).
Hall, A. V., de Winter, M., de Winter, B. and van Oosterhout, S. A. M. (1980). *Threatened plants of Southern Africa*, South African National Scientific Programmes Report No. 45.
Hedberg, I. (Ed.) (1979). *Systematic Botany, Plant Utilization and Biosphere Conservation*, Almqvist and Wiksell, Stockholm.
Hepper, F. N. (1979). 'The present stage of botanical exploration – Africa', in *Systematic Botany, Plant Utilization and Biosphere Conservation* (Ed. I. Hedberg), pp. 41–6, Almqvist and Wiksell, Stockholm.
Heywood, V. H. (1979). 'The future of island floras', in *Plants and Islands* (Ed. D. Bramwell), pp. 431–41, Academic Press, London.
Independent Commission on International Development Issues (1980). *North–South: A Programme for Survival* ('The Brandt Report'), Pan, London.
IUCN (1980). *World Conservation Strategy*, IUCN–UNEP–WWF, Gland, Switzerland.
IUCN Threatened Plants Committee (1977). *List of Rare, Threatened and Endemic Plants in Europe*, Nature and Environment Series No. 14, Council of Europe, Strasbourg.
Janzen, D. H. (1973). 'Tropical agroecosystems', *Science*, **182**, 1212–19.
Janzen, D. H. (1978). 'Promising directions of study in tropical animal–plant interactions', *Ann. Missouri Bot. Gard.*, **64**(4), 706–36.
Jordan, C. F. and Medina, E. (1978). 'Ecosystem research in the tropics', *Ann. Missouri Bot. Gard.*, **64**(4), 737–45.
Leon, C. (1980). 'Endangered plants' in *A Draft Community List of Threatened Species of Wild Flora and Vertebrate Fauna*, Vol. I. Prepared for the Environment and Consumer Protection Service of the Commission of the European Communities, by the Nature Conservancy Council of Great Britain, November 1980.
Lucas, G. (1979*a*). 'The Threatened Plants Committee of IUCN and island floras', in *Plants and Islands* (Ed. D. Bramwell), pp. 423–30, Academic Press, London.
Lucas, G. (1979*b*). 'Organizations and contacts for conservation throughout the world', in *Survival or Extinction* (Eds. H. Synge and H. Townsend), pp. 15–23, Bentham–Moxon Trust, Kew, England.
Lucas, G. Ll. (1980). 'We can do it', *Naturopa*, **34/35**, 21, Council of Europe, Strasbourg, France.
Lucas, G. Ll. and Synge, A. H. M. (1977). 'The IUCN Threatened Plants Committee and its work throughout the world', *Environ. Conserv.*, **4**(3), 179–87.
Lucas, G. and Synge, H. (1978). *The IUCN Plant Red Data Book*, IUCN, Morges, Switzerland.
Melville, R. (1979). 'Endangered island floras', in *Plants and Islands* (Ed. D. Bramwell), pp. 361–77, Academic Press, London.
Mooney, P. R. (?1979). *Seeds of the Earth: A Private or Public Resource?*, Inter Pares, Ottawa, for Canadian Council for International Co-operation and the International Coalition for Development Action (London).
Myers, N. (1979). *The Sinking Ark*, Pergamon, Oxford.
Myers, N. (1980). *Conversion of Tropical Moist Forests*, US National Academy of Sciences, Washington, DC.

Prance, G. T. (1978). 'Floristic inventory of the tropics: where do we stand?', *Ann. Missouri Bot. Gard.*, **64**(4), 659–84.

Prance, G. T. (1979). 'Exploitation and conservation in Brazil', in *Systematic Botany, Plant Utilization and Biosphere Conservation* (Ed. I. Hedberg), pp. 146–9, Almqvist and Wiksell, Stockholm.

Ratcliffe, D. (Ed.) (1977). *A Nature Conservation Review*, 2 vols, Cambridge University Press.

Rauh, W. (1979). 'Problems of biological conservation in Madagascar', in *Plants and Islands* (Ed. D. Bramwell), pp. 405–21, Academic Press, London.

Raven, P. H. (1978). 'Perspectives in tropical botany: Concluding remarks', *Ann. Missouri Bot. Gard.*, **64**(4), 746–8.

Schultes, R. E. (1951). 'La riqueza de la flora Colombiana', *Revista Acad. Colomb. Ci. Exact.*, **8**, 230–42.

Sitwell, N. (1980). 'The deadly handshake', *Now!*, October 24, 1980, pp. 58–66.

Synge, A. H. M. (1979). 'Botanic gardens and island plant conservation', in *Plants and Islands* (Ed. D. Bramwell), pp. 379–90, Academic Press, London.

Synge, H. and Townsend, H. (Eds.) (1979). *Survival or Extinction*, Bentham–Moxon Trust, Kew, England.

Tomlinson, P. B. and Raven, P. H. (1978). 'Perspectives in tropical botany: Introduction', *Ann. Missouri Bot. Gard.*, **64**(4), 657–8.

UN (1978). *United Nations Conference on Desertification: Round-up, Plan of Action and Resolutions*, United Nations, New York.

UN Conference on Desertification (1977). *Desertification: An Overview*, A/CONF, 74/1.

US Council on Environmental Quality and US Department of State (1980). *The Global 2000 Report to the President: Entering the Twenty-First Century*, 3 vols. (Study Director: G. O. Barney), US Government Printing Office, Washington, DC.

US National Academy of Sciences (1980). *Research Priorities in Tropical Biology*, Washington, DC.

The Biological Aspects of Rare Plant Conservation
Edited by Hugh Synge, published by John Wiley & Sons Ltd.
© 1981 Smithsonian Institution

2
Assessment of threatened plant species in the United States

EDWARD S. AYENSU *Office of Biological Conservation, Smithsonian Institution, Washington, DC*

Summary

The criteria used by various state and regional committees and government agencies to assess the status of 'endangered' and 'threatened' plant species in the United States vary to a considerable extent. A comparison of the criteria developed by the Smithsonian Institution, selected state agencies, and the federal government is presented, and the desirability of considering population biology studies and recent research into the phenomenon of rarity during the assessment procedure is emphasized.

It is suggested that criteria based on observations of population structure and stability, environmental factors affecting population size, reproductive strategies, and the role of natural succession should be more regularly utilized. Research undertaken in botanic gardens will yield data that is both important and relevant to these determinations.

Recommended National Assessment Criteria are included as a stimulus for the ultimate standardization of assessment procedures in the United States, as has similarly been attempted on a world basis by IUCN. (See Appendix 3 to this book.)

Introduction

There is a growing concern throughout the world about the uncontrolled exploitation and depletion of the earth's natural resources. This concern is becoming so critical because of the world-wide drive toward highly technological societies which have to depend upon natural resources for energy and all the other complex requirements needed to sustain mankind today. To understand the environmental problems facing the world would require all sorts of sectoral assessments at the national, regional and international levels.

In his presentation at the first Kew Conservation Conference, Raven (1976) noted that inventories of plants need to be undertaken before rational consideration can be given to the concept of preservation. A major step toward achieving such a goal is the systematic assessment of species that are thought to be threatened with extinction.

This chapter presents examples of the different assessment methodologies currently being pursued by various groups within the United States. During the preparation of this paper I consulted freely all the published and unpublished state reviews, and held discussions with a number of colleagues who have given considerable thought to the subject. I am most grateful particularly to my colleagues Dr Robert A. DeFilipps who assisted me in formulating this contribution, and Dr Peter H. Raven and Dr William E. Rice for reviewing the manuscript and offering useful comments.

For purposes of summarizing the status of botanical exploration in North America, Shetler (1979) noted that after having been through the main thrust of the descriptive (or exploratory), floristic–phytogeographic, systematic, and biosystematic phases, we are now in the ecological–environmental phase. This phase has been precipitated by the modern environmental movement, which is requiring a whole new cycle of exploration and research on endangered plant species, in association with the requirements of the Endangered Species Act of 1973 passed by the United States Congress, 'critical habitat' determination by the federal government, environmental impact statements on federal actions as required by the National Environmental Policy Act (NEPA), and state laws and municipal ordinances such as for zoning purposes.

The need for an up-to-date inventory of natural vegetation in the United States is at a critical point, at a time when we are losing much of the habitat that is required to sustain vulnerable species (Ayensu, 1979). A recent study by Klopatek *et al.* (1979) indicated that of the 106 vegetation types recognized by Kuchler predominating in the conterminous United States, 23 have each been reduced by over 50 per cent by man-induced land uses (Figure 1). For example, pine–cypress forest in California and sand pine scrub forest in Florida have declined from a potential 53 000 and 241 000 hectares to 23 000 and 37 000 hectares, respectively. Klopatek's study of the vegetation of the United States was done on a county-by-county basis, and clearly indicates the need for critical assessments before it is too late.

The extinction potential of a species is related to the degree of biological vulnerability and degree of threat (MacBryde, 1979), and it is the techniques and criteria being used in the United States to recognize which species are endangered or threatened that I shall survey in this chapter.

The assessment of threatened species in the United States varies according to individual, state, regional and national requirements. With approximately 10 per cent of the native flowering plants of the continental United States, and 50 per cent of the Hawaiian flora, in need of critical field study and protection on the official list of 'endangered' and 'threatened' species, it can only be hoped that the assessment process at various levels will advance at a pace faster than that of local extirpation of populations and political constraints of obvious appeal to the pork-barrel constituency.

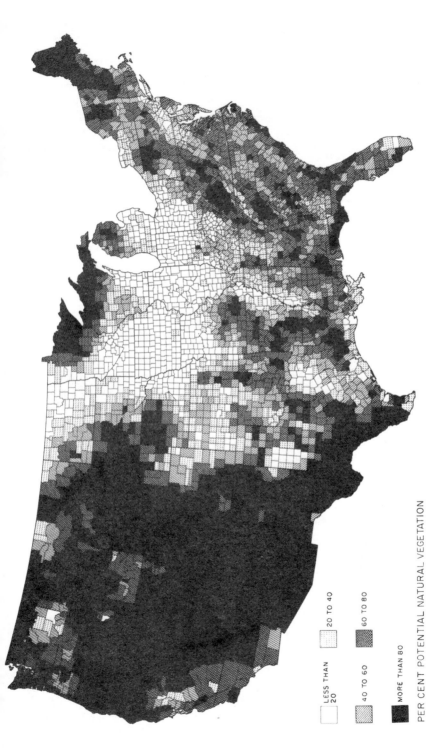

PER CENT POTENTIAL NATURAL VEGETATION

LESS THAN 20   20 TO 40

40 TO 60   60 TO 80

MORE THAN 80

Figure 1   Percentage of area potentially capable of supporting natural vegetation (assuming that present land-use changes, such as to agriculture, will remain) for counties of the conterminous United States (from Klopatek *et al.*, 1979). (Reproduced from *Environmental Conservation* by permission of the Foundation for Environmental Conservation)

Smithsonian Institution assessments

The exercise of assessing the status of the native fern, gymnosperm and angiosperm species of the United States, including the State of Hawaii, was undertaken by the Smithsonian Institution in response to a Congressional request to the Secretary of the Institution in the Endangered Species Act of 1973 (Ayensu, 1978, 1980; Ayensu and DeFilipps, 1981). At the time of the act the vulnerability of the United States flora as a whole was unknown. Our work in co-operation with botanists around the country and specialists from Canada and the United Kingdom resulted in a *Report on Endangered and Threatened Plant Species of the United States* (Smithsonian Institution, 1975), upon which the Department of the Interior has proceeded with the official listing process. The recommended lists of species have since been revised and updated, including a list for Puerto Rico and the Virgin Islands, and issued in a book entitled *Endangered and Threatened Plants of the United States* (Ayensu and DeFilipps, 1978).

The original (1975) lists were prepared by reviewing the best available published Floras of regions, states, and localities in the United States. Species with a very limited distribution or a rare status were listed and all available data were compiled. These and additional species were reviewed in the latest available monographs and revisions of families, genera and species groups. Collections were checked in herbaria, and taxonomic specialists were consulted. The lists were then compared with available state lists of rare and endangered plants. For species endemic to a single state, the rarity status given in the state lists proved to be valuable; for the more wide-ranging species, however, the local designations of abundance in the state often had only limited value for the national lists.

In my capacity as the then director of the Endangered Species Program, I submitted the preliminary lists to a Workshop held in September 1974. The participants, reflecting a broad spectrum of eminent botanists from various institutions, organizations, herbaria and arboreta, evaluated and improved the preliminary lists based on their specialist knowledge. The participants also helped in the preparation of recommendations for conserving plant species.

After a number of species had been referred back to specialists for verification, the revised list was circulated a second time for final evaluation to the Workshop participants, other specialists, and to compilers of some state lists. The Report was subsequently published by the US Government Printing Office.

Publication of the 1975 Report precipitated the arrival of a wealth of additional information at the Smithsonian, resulting in significant revision, updating and further documentation of the lists. When research and mapping of species uncovered questions regarding their taxonomy, distribution, or rarity, the recognized authorities on the taxa were consulted. New contacts were made with interested botanists as well as state rare plant committees throughout the country. Information continued to come from the original contributors following further studies.

The influx of newly published and unpublished data, and expert opinion, has substantially augmented the assessment of the status of our 'endangered', 'threatened', 'exploited', and 'extinct' flora. A few species, such as the Furbish lousewort, *Pedicularis furbishiae* S. Watson (Scrophulariaceae), and the Virginia round-leaf birch, *Betula uber* (Ashe) Fernald (Betulaceae), that were thought to be extinct have since been rediscovered, some formerly thought to be rare have been found to be more abundant or even taxonomically untenable, and a number of previously overlooked species were brought to our attention. The revised lists were published in 1978, and included a thoroughly expanded text and bibliography.

During the preparation of both publications, we were acutely aware of the problem presented by the use of *rarity* as a criterion. Plant taxa that are known from the type locality only were almost automatically given the status of 'endangered'.

The question of rarity will always present itself in considerations of status. A rare plant species is one that has a small population in its range. It may be found in a restricted geographic region or it may occur sparsely over a wider area. When a rare species, subspecies, or variety appears on a list as 'endangered', 'threatened', or 'possibly extinct', it becomes particularly subject to two critical questions:

1. Has the taxon been correctly categorized as a natural entity? Perhaps it is a taxonomically untenable segregate of a more common or widespread species; it may be a rarely produced hybrid, polyploid, aberrant, or mutant; it could be an unusual phenotype owing to some unusual edaphic condition or environmental stress.
2. Is the 'extinct' species truly extinct? Perhaps it actually does occur in small numbers or is more common or widespread but has not been observed or collected because, (a) it is small or inconspicuous, (b) it blooms rarely, briefly, or at unusual times, germinates infrequently or has long dormant periods, or (c) it occurs only in difficult or inaccessible terrain or habitats rarely visited by collectors.

We will return to a consideration of rarity later in the discussion.

State committee and regional assessment criteria

Virtually every state has by now produced a list of endangered, threatened and rare plants, with a varying complexity of data among the lists, and sometimes in conjunction with state laws protecting specific endangered plants (Appendix V). There is only space here to mention a few of these, and the variation in their criteria for determining 'endangered' status.

For Wisconsin, Read (1976) suggested that native plants with three or fewer stations known to exist in the state should automatically be included in the category of 'endangered'. In the 1976 publication the categories were advisory only and did not carry legislative force. Specifically, the definitions are:

> *Threatened.* Rare native species which are known from more than three stations in the state, but of very limited distribution in Wisconsin so as to cause concern of future endangerment.
> *Endangered.* Native plants with three or fewer stations known to exist in the state. Some with more than three stations are included where it is believed that a substantial number of the stations are destroyed or actively threatened. Species are included in this category even if the only station is protected, as in the case of plants on state scientific areas (Read, 1976).

In the list for Oregon (Siddall *et al.*, 1979), all species known from only one population in the state were considered to be 'endangered', as well as species known from very few localities that are highly sought after by collectors or are being subjected to active threat (Figure 2).

In the Florida list, Ward (1979) observed that the circumstances which cause the distribution and frequency of a particular plant are as numerous as the species themselves. Furthermore, the student of a particular group will frequently view the protection needs of its less common members much more tenderly than will a botanist with a more general background.

GROUP 1 - Range circumscribed, species endemic to a given area.

    1a Very local endemic, from one site or very small area.

    1b Regional endemic, limited to one region of botanical interest.

GROUP 2 - Range wide, rare, threatened or endangered throughout range.

    2a Thinly scattered over wide range, often singly or in small groups, rarely collected.

    2b Known from a few widely disjunct populations.

GROUP 3 - Rare, threatened or endangered in state , but more abundant elsewhere, disjunct and peripheral in state. Of state concern only.

GROUP 4 - Unusual, such as primitive diploid populations in otherwise polyploid species.

Figure 2   Oregon criteria groupings (from Siddall *et al.*, 1979)

Botanists are familiar with such terms as 'abundant', 'common', 'frequent', 'occasional', 'infrequent', and 'rare', but this terminology tends to carry with it the implication that the status is itself constant in time. Certainly every field botanist is familiar with the changes in frequency that accompany the successional replacement of one vegetation type by another, and the changes associated with environmental modification caused by man. Yet, as Ward notes, the usual terminology is not useful for conveying information on the decrease in numbers of a species with the passage of time, and the terms 'endangered' and 'threatened' should seek to accommodate these changes in frequency.

The species on the Florida state list are divided into several categories, which include the following.

Endangered. Species in imminent danger of extinction or extirpation and whose survival is unlikely if the causal factors presently at work continue operating. These species are those whose numbers have been reduced to such a critically low level or whose habitat has been drastically reduced or degraded that immediate action is required to prevent their loss.

Threatened. Species believed likely to move into the 'endangered' category in the near future if the causal factors now at work continue operating. Included are species in which most or all populations are decreasing because of overexploitation, massive depletion of habitat, or other environmental disturbance; species whose populations have been heavily depleted by adverse factors and the ultimate security of which is not yet assured; and species with populations which may still be abundant but are under threat from serious adverse factors throughout their range in the state.

Rare. Species with small populations in the state which, though not presently 'endangered' or 'threatened' as defined above, are potentially at risk. Included are species that may be localized within a restricted geographical region or habitat or thinly scattered over a more extensive range. They may be insular or otherwise isolated species or relicts with wide distribution. They may also be forms that are seldom recorded and which may be commoner than supposed, although there is reasonably good evidence that their numbers are low (Ward, 1979).

In essence, the 'endangered' species is one whose extinction or extirpation is imminent; the 'threatened' species is one whose numbers are declining but not yet to the point where it becomes 'endangered'; the 'rare' species is one whose numbers are very few but are not known to be declining. (This classification is almost identical to the IUCN one – see Appendix 3 to this book – but with the term 'threatened' substituted for Vulnerable.)

In the North Carolina report, Cooper *et al.* (1977) noted that the concept of rarity, as a criterion for listing 'endangered' or 'threatened' species, is difficult to define precisely since it involves two functions or variables: first, the overall distribution; and second, the relative density or frequency of individual plants within that distribution. This is compounded by the fact that the limits of both variables are entirely subjective. It is therefore particularly difficult to categorize species that have both a broad distribution and a high density, but whose conservation may none the less be a matter of concern.

There are also plant species in North Carolina that may be at the periphery of their range, or may be long-range disjuncts or endemics. They are considered as either 'endangered' or 'threatened' by the very fact that they are rare. Peripheral species may be fairly common in areas either north, west, or south of North Carolina, but rare at the extreme limit of their distribution in the state. These native, peripheral species are believed to represent an integral part of the state's flora and probably a significant element of the total genetic diversity of the species; the state considers itself to be the 'keeper' of this important segment of their entire range. Their elimination is felt to represent a considerable loss to the gene pool, and also a great loss to the natural history of North Carolina. An example is the palmetto palm, *Sabal palmetto* (Walter) Loddiges, which although common farther south is a rare and unique element in the forests of Smith Island and the southern coast.

The California Native Plant Society (Smith *et al.*, 1980) has adopted a system known as the R–E–V–D code (pronounced rev-dee) to score the status of Californian species. The code is based on four major components or concepts. First, *rarity* is the amount of the plant, both in terms of manner and extent of distribution. Second is *endangerment*, the concept of a plant being threatened with extinction or extirpation for whatever reason. Third is *vigor*, a concept involving the dynamics of the plant in terms of numbers of individuals or populations. The fourth concept is *general distribution*; a plant is termed endemic if restricted to California, and for plants not endemic to California, the coding indicates whether or not it is rare outside California.

Each component is divided into three classes or degrees, ranging from 1 – least cause for concern, to 3 – of highly critical concern. For example 'Vigor' (V) is divided into: 1 – stable or increasing, 2 – declining, 3 – approaching extinction or extirpation. When a plant is endemic to California, this does not automatically indicate highly critical concern. The full code is shown in Figure 3.

The very large number of rare plants in California was an important factor in the decision to develop the comprehensive scoring system. The list of Californian plants was divided after scoring into a main list of 645 plants of highest priority and several lists of 683 plants of lower priority. To be included in the main list, a plant had to have at least one score of 2 or 3 in the R–E–V portion of the R–E–V–D rating. All others for which R is 1 (including some with incomplete data) are on the secondary list.

In a series of publications on endangered species in the various New England states produced in co-operation with the US Fish and Wildlife Service (see Appendix V), the criteria developed by the New England Botanical Club were

---

RARITY R

1. Rare, of limited distribution, but distributed widely enough that potential for extinction or extirpation is apparently low.

2. Confined to several, or one extended, population.

3. Occurs in such small numbers that it is seldom reported, or in one or very few highly restricted populations.

P. E. Presumed extinct

ENDANGERMENT E

1. Not endangered.

2. Endangered in part.

3. Totally endangered.

VIGOR V

1. Stable or increasing.

2. Declining.

3. Approaching extinction or extirpation.

DISTRIBUTION D

1. Not rare outside California.

2. Rare outside California.

3. Endemic to California.

Figure 3   California R–E–V–D code of criteria (from Smith *et al.*, 1980)

used. The criteria are arranged approximately in order of biological significance; those used for Massachusetts (Coddington and Field, 1978) are shown in Figure 4. The most important question about a rare species in the New England state lists is whether its numbers are declining or are likely to decline. Next is the size of its range both in the state and in the region, the pattern of its occurrence and number of stations known for the species, followed by data as to whether it is a peripheral species. This hierarchy, plus the total number of criteria listed for each species, allows some estimate of how critical the status of a given species is relative to that of other species.

Let us now turn to a consideration of the Nevada Test Site (Rhoads and Williams, 1977; Rhoads *et al.*, 1978). In the course of studying the plants on this 1350 square mile nuclear testing site in southern Nevada, the R–E–V–D code used in California was employed, in combination with factors accounting for a

DCLN	Declining numbers in recent years.
VULN	Vulnerable to depletion from collection and or habitat destruction.
ENMA	Endemic to Massachusetts.
ENNE	Endemic to New England.
RSTR	Restricted range. Total range equal or less than size of New England, not necessarily endemic to New England.
DSJCT	Disjunct distribution in New England. Populations reproductively isolated or separated by at least 50 miles.
SNES	Single New England station.
SMAS	Single Massachusetts station.
LC RE	Both local and rare.
RARE	Usually occurring as one or few individuals per population.
LCAL	Local, occurring in few places in state, though populations may be large.
FEW	Five or fewer vouchered stations in state.
SLR, NLR, WLR, ELR	A population at the southern, northern, western, or eastern limit of its range.

Figure 4   Massachusetts criteria in order of biological significance (from Coddington and Field, 1978)

species' tolerance to disturbance and the peculiar variability in numbers of desert plant populations (Figure 5). This variability, which depends on precipitation and a complex range of other environmental factors, constitutes a major difficulty in assessing some aspects of the status of most, if not all, the species populations studied at the Test Site.

An example of the highly variable productivity of vegetation from year to year on deserts is given by the annual *Phacelia parishii* A. Gray (Hydrophyllaceae), which was initially collected in 1941 and was not found again until 1976. No specimens were seen in 1977 in the same area, but in 1978, when rainfall was high during the spring months, the plants were abundant. Thus it is likely that observation over a number of years will have to be considered before any conclusions can be reached about *long-term population trends* for some of the Test Site species, since rarity in any one particular year could not be considered unequivocal evidence for a dwindling population.

For the factor of *Vigor*, which denotes the dynamics of plant populations, the Nevada Test Site survey included the following categories which, due to the hazards of evaluating population stability of desert annuals, refer to the species for 1 year only: 1 – common, 2 – scattered, 3 – occasional, 4 – rare. An additional category added is *Tolerance*, which covers the tolerance a species may have for disturbance and modification of its habitat, or alternatively an ability to colonize new habitats created by disturbance. The divisions of this category are: 1 – very tolerant, common on disturbed sites, 2 – occasional on disturbed sites but primarily found on undisturbed sites, and 3 – never found on disturbances.

The stability or instability of the preferred habitat, i.e. the amount of suitable habitat that is changing from either natural causes or human intervention, thus acquires an importance as far as the vulnerability of the species and its ability to recolonize disturbed habitats are concerned. Natural factors (such as predation by herbivores, disease, fires, natural erosion) or other factors that can be recognized as threats to the populations are also taken into consideration.

The Tonopah Test Site, situated due northwest of the Nevada Test Site, was surveyed using essentially similar criteria by Rhoads *et al.* (1979), who included as an additional criterion the *aspect* of individual plants, i.e. plants inconspicuous, versus plants showy and attractive to collectors; several cacti on the site require the latter category. Here is a criterion that is tailor-made to fit the characteristics or vulnerability of a particular plant group, in this case cacti.

For the state of Texas (Johnston, 1974), the species are ranked on a scale of frequency ranging from abundant to extinct. Range considerations are denoted by the seven major phytogeographic regions or vegetation areas of Texas (such as Edwards Plateau, Trans-Pecos, etc.), and by the number of counties in each region in which a species occurs (Figure 6). The species lists are presented

---

1. Geographical extent of the species on site.

2. Existence or nonexistence of other populations off-site.

3. Density of individuals within populations.

4. Population trends over time, expanding or shrinking in areal extent or density of individuals.

5. Stability of preferred habitat, and amount of suitable habitat changing due to natural or human factors.

6. Human activities threatening the populations or species habitats.

7. Natural factors – herbivores, disease, fire, erosion – threatening the populations.

Figure 5 Nevada Test Site criteria (from Rhoads and Williams, 1977)

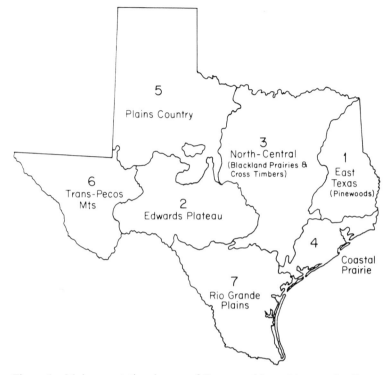

Figure 6   Major vegetational areas of Texas used in ranking species (from Johnston, 1974)

A	Occurs widely in North America or worldwide.
B	Distributed broadly but regionally in North America and extending into Texas.
C	Distributed widely in Texas.
D	Distributed over several vegetational areas.
E	Occurs in two vegetational areas.
F	Occurs in one vegetational area.
G	Limited to 4 to 8 counties in one vegetational area.
H	Limited to 1 to 3 counties in one vegetational area.
I	Known from one or a few populations.

Figure 7   Scale of Texas distribution criteria (from Johnston, 1974)

separately for each of the different vegetation areas, a variation of style due to the enormity of the state and the great variation of vegetation within its boundaries. State-wide frequency of a species is based on a scale from 1 to 7, ranging from abundance to extinction, and only the highest ranking numbers are included on the list, namely: 5 – scarce, endangered in Texas; 6 – very rare, acutely endangered in Texas; 7 – presumed extinct, with no records since 1930 from Texas.

The extent of the total known distribution is indicated by various letter-symbols, which are shown in Figure 7.

Assessment criteria of the US Federal Government

The Endangered Species Act of 1973 (Section 3) defines the term 'endangered species' to mean any species which is in danger of extinction throughout all or a significant portion of its range. The term 'threatened species' means any species which is likely to become an 'endangered species' within the foreseeable future throughout all or a significant portion of its range. Section 4(a) of the Act lists five factors, by any of which the Secretary of the Interior may officially determine that a plant or animal is 'endangered' or 'threatened':

1. the present or threatened destruction, modification, or curtailment of its habitat or range;
2. utilization for commercial, sporting, scientific, or educational purposes at levels that detrimentally affect it;
3. disease or predation;
4. absence of regulatory mechanisms adequate to prevent the decline of a species or degradation of its habitat; or
5. other natural or manmade factors affecting its continued existence.

With regard to Factor 4, Rhoads *et al.* (1979) explained that, essentially, if a species is protected by internal policy decisions or by other efforts to insure the species survival (such as protection by the federal agency administering the land on which it occurs), it may not be as endangered as other species not so protected. It may be noted here that Jenkins (1975) has surmised the likelihood that an estimated two-thirds of the recommended 'endangered' plants of the United States may occur on federal lands (e.g. Department of the Interior, Defense, Bureau of Land Management – National Forests, National Parks and Wildlife Refuges).

The Endangered Species Act of 1973, including the Amendments of 10 November 1978, now states that the 'critical habitat' (to the maximum extent prudent) is to be specified at the time of proposal of the status of a species; formerly it could be designated afterwards. Incidentally, except in special circumstances, 'critical habitat' shall not include the entire geographical area which can be occupied by the species. Another new proviso is that, in the determination of 'critical habitat', the economic impact of specifying any particular area as 'critical habitat' shall be considered.

A further modification to the act requires of any federal agency that a biological assessment to identify any proposed or listed 'endangered' or 'threatened' species likely to be affected by construction activities should be undertaken and completed within 180 days after initiation, before any contract for construction is entered into.

The act also provides for emergency listing for plants, equal land acquisition for plants, and cooperative agreements with the states for conservation of 'endangered' plants.

Clearly, the Endangered Species Act now calls for more intensive and extensive field surveys and assessments than were previously expected. In this connection, let us review the parameters to be studied by reference to the definition of 'critical habitat'.

Notices published in the *Federal Register* of 22 April and 16 May 1975, which describe the concept of 'critical habitat', indicate that for any given 'endangered' or 'threatened' species, habitat is considered 'critical' if the destruction, disturbance, modification, or subjection to human activity of any constituent element of the habitat might be expected to result in a reduction in the numbers or distribution of that species, or in a restriction of the potential and reasonable expansion or recovery of that species. Among the vital needs which are relevant in determining 'critical habitat' for a given species are space for normal growth of the species and sites for reproduction.

The term 'habitat' in this context means the spatial environment in which a species lives and covers all elements of that environment including (but not limited to) land and water area, physical structure and topography, flora, fauna, climate, human activity, and the quality and chemical content of soil, water, and air. Incidentally, if publication of 'critical habitat' maps in the *Federal Register* would make an over-collected species more vulnerable, the Department of the Interior may determine it is not prudent to publish the 'critical habitat'.

Under the revised definition of 27 February 1980, 'critical habitat' includes:

1. the specific areas within the geographical area occupied by a species, at the time it is listed in accordance with the act, on which are found those physical or biological features, (a) essential to the conservation of the species, and (b) which may require special management considerations or protection;
2. specific areas outside the geographical area occupied by a species at the time it is listed upon a determination by the Director of the US Fish and Wildlife Service that such areas are essential for the conservation of the species.

Requirements to be considered in determining 'critical habitat' include:

1. space for individual and population growth and for normal behavior;
2. food, water, air, light, minerals, or other nutritional or physiological requirements;
3. cover or shelter;
4. sites for breeding, reproduction, rearing of offspring, germination, or seed dispersal;
5. habitats that are protécted from disturbance or are representative of the historic geographical and ecological distributions of listed species.

In order to categorize the sets of data to make federal assessments conform to expectations, outlines for detailed status reports and field surveys of population status have been developed (Henifin *et al.*, 1981a; Henifin *et al.*, 1981b). Portions of these comprehensive outlines relating to population biology of the species are included as Appendices I and II to this chapter.

Another federal activity where detailed assessments are undertaken is the recovery program, the central goal of which is to restore protected species to a point where their existence is no longer endangered. The northern wild monkshood, *Aconitum noveboracense* A. Gray, which was listed officially as 'threatened' on 26 April 1978, became the first listed plant to be named as the sole subject of a Service recovery plan (Anonymous, 1979). This species occurs mostly on a few cliff habitats in the unglaciated portion of southeastern Wisconsin. Little is known about the properties and ecology of this rare species, and state investigators will inspect and classify habitat, identify threats to the species, and interview landowners, scientists, and State endangered species officials.

In March 1980, a second plant recovery team was appointed (Anonymous, 1980) for the Tennessee purple coneflower, *Echinacea tennesseensis* (Beadle) Small (Compositae).

Assessment by priority numbers and holistic environmental approaches

In the field of conservation, it is unanimously agreed that decisions on the preservation of rare, endangered and threatened species should be based on biologically sound information. But what is the most important kind of information? Massey and Whitson (1977) have observed that the key is 'species biology', a holistic approach to the understanding of individuals, populations and population systems using evidence from many different fields or disciplines. It involves an understanding of the structure, function and position of organisms within a time reference.

A general model seems necessary to relate and develop information systems and to establish priorities as well as to pose basic high-priority questions. In the Massey and Whitson model for collecting information on species biology, data are divided into four basic fields: reproduction, dispersion, establishment and maintenance. They propose two subsystems based on priority; these are shown in Figure 8.

For the section Reproductive System (Subsystem 1, No. 1), they provide a preliminary list of questions that species biologists address for each of the four types of data and this is shown in Figure 9. These questions should be answered for each site selected for study and summarized for each species prior to decision-making.

Specific characters and selected character states for the high priority Subsystem 1 are given in Appendix III to this chapter.

The following points show the relevance of selected characters from reproductive evidence to decisions on species preservation in general, and for selection of specific populations or sites for preservation in particular:

1. The maintenance of maximum variability with greatest potential for flexibility can best be accomplished by giving protection priority to sexually reproducing populations.
2. The type of breeding system is often a critical factor in determining the size of an area to be protected. To preserve the greatest genetic variability, outcrossing species with specific pollen vectors generally will require larger areas than autogamous species or outcrossers with promiscuous pollination.
3. An analysis of pollination systems may indicate that species other than the one being studied also serve as major food sources, nesting sites, etc., for the pollinator of a rare, endangered or threatened species. Preservation of one species is therefore contingent upon preservation of another species.
4. In a series of populations, those with high reproductive capacity, potential or

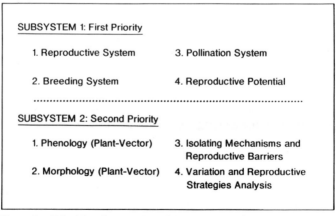

Figure 8   Priorities for species biology studies (from Massey and Whitson, 1977)

REPRODUCTION	DISPERSION	ESTABLISHMENT	MAINTENANCE
OCCURRING?	ARE PROPAGULES PRESENT?	NEW INDIVIDUALS PRESENT?	IS RANGE OF AGE & MATURATION CLASSES PRESENT?
WHAT TYPES?	WHAT TYPES?	ORIGINS OF NEW INDIVIDUALS?	ORIGINS OF CLASSES?
WHAT BREEDING SYSTEMS?	WHAT DISPERSAL SYSTEMS?	WHAT ESTABLISHMENT PROCESSES?	% OF EACH CLASS IN THE POPULATION?
WHAT POLLINATION SYSTEMS?	WHAT DISPERSAL UNITS OR AGENTS?	WHERE IS ESTABLISHMENT OCCURRING?	SPATIAL RELATIONS OF DIFFERENT AGE-MATURATION CLASSES?
WHAT IS REPRODUCTIVE CAPACITY OR STATUS OF POPULATION?	DISPERSAL EFFECTIVENESS OF POPULATION?	ESTABLISHMENT EFFECTIVENESS OF NEW INDIVIDUALS BASED ON THEIR ORIGIN?	SURVIVABILITY OF INDI-VIDUALS PROGRESSING INTO NEXT AGE CLASS?

Figure 9   Question matrix for Subsystem 1 of priorities in species biology studies (from Massey and Whitson, 1977)

actual, are better candidates for preservation than ones with low reproductive capacity.

5. In cases where reproduction is low, species biology studies may identify causes which may be corrected to some extent by management.

Botanic gardens have an important role to play in species biology research (Ayensu, 1976; Raven, 1976), of which 'one aim is to map out the ecological "envelope" within which survival and regeneration is possible' (Heslop-Harrison, 1976). Aspects of reproduction biology that can be studied in cultivation include flowering in relation to age, season, and local variation in weather; effects of photoperiod, light intensity, temperature, and thermoperiod on flowering; and flower characteristics including dichogamy and whether the species is monoecious or dioecious.

The species-biology approach has been discussed by the authors on several other occasions (Massey and Whitson, 1980; Whitson and Massey, 1981) and provides sound reasoning for the necessity of population biology status reports proposed by Henifin *et al.* (1981*a*, 1981*b*). Particularly valuable contributions on the use of population biology studies for rare plant conservation are given by Davy and Jefferies (Chapter 18) and by Williams (Chapter 19).

The role of an endangered species in its ecosystem is gradually being appreciated more fully, and being taken into account in determinations of which natural areas are to be either preserved or affected adversely by human activity. In the preparation of Environmental Impact Statements the degree to which a proposed action may adversely affect an 'endangered' or 'threatened' species or its 'critical habitat' must now be evaluated (Council on Environmental Quality, 1978). Endangered species as an element of ecological diversity are studied by The Nature Conservancy (Jenkins, 1978) in deciding which areas to acquire for future protection, as well as in State Heritage Programs undertaken to preserve ecologically significant land in cooperation with the Conservancy (Sanders, 1978).

Endangered species are also a factor in designating Research Natural Areas, of which there are approximately 389, comprising about 4.4 million acres in 46 states and 1 territory (Federal Committee on Ecological Reserves, 1977). The Research Natural Area designation is used by the federal land agencies to establish areas on which natural features and processes are preserved with minimal human intervention for research and educational purposes. This designation differs from others such as wilderness sanctuary, refuge, or preserve, which have broader use-management objectives.

Each area is administered by one of eight cooperating agencies: Forest Service in the Department of Agriculture; Bureau of Indian Affairs, Bureau of Land Management, Fish and Wildlife Service and National Park Service in the Department of the Interior; Air Force in the Department of Defense; Energy Research and Development Administration; and the Tennessee Valley Authority.

A massive inventory of the elements of natural diversity of the United States is being undertaken by the Heritage Conservation and Recreation Service (HCRS) of the US Department of the Interior, in conjunction with the National Heritage Policy Act (HCRS, 1979). The ecological classification system proposed to be utilized by the HCRS for the inventory is basically one developed by Dr Albert Radford (1981), which, while very complicated, allows for seeing an endangered species in the context and matrix of the multitude of ecological and plant community permutations that exist in the United States. As the system is very complex, only parts are reproduced here as Appendix IV to this chapter (Radford, 1978).

Natural diversity is assumed to be the foundation of our natural heritage. The elaboration of our natural heritage requires a holistic, comprehensive classification of the natural features in our environment for the basic inventory and conservation of species, communities and habitats. Radford's system includes distinctive entries for various hierarchical levels in each of the following major themes: (1) Biotic, (2) Climatic, (3) Pedologic, (4) Geologic, (5) Hydrologic, (6) Topographic, and (7) Physiographic.

The Radford Classification System is based upon the following assumptions:

1. Each species is selectively and uniquely adapted to a habitat.
2. *Species diversity is related to habitat diversity within an area.*
3. Habitat diversity is related to the diversity of climate, geology, soils, hydrology, and topography within an area.
4. Species assemblages are recurring combinations under similar habitat conditions within an area at a given time.
5. Species assemblages are the result of interaction of species and habitat diversity in an area through time.

Recent studies of the phenomenon of rarity

David Du Mond (1973) presented a standard list of guidelines for decision-making in the selection of endangered species. He noted that a rare species can be:

1. A species found out of its expected geographical context, e.g. a short- or long-range disjunction.
2. A species particularly subject to extinction or severe reduction in total population size by those of *man's activities* which have already caused a significant reduction in its numbers, e.g. American ginseng, *Panax quinquefolius* L.
3. A species found only in a *very specific habitat* of limited occurrence.
4. A species thought to be a relict of a no-longer extant vegetation association, e.g. glacial relict.
5. A species which is an indicator of a *unique extant vegetation association*, e.g. on granite outcrops.

6. A species which is recognized as an example of a *wide disjunction pattern*, e.g. *Shortia galacifolia* Torrey & A. Gray.
7. A species which has its natural *distribution limits* within the area in question, e.g. for North Carolina, *Sabal palmetto* terminates its northward range in North Carolina and is found there on only one or two coastal islands.
8. A species which is known to be introduced and has become naturalized on a *very small scale*, e.g. the Japanese climbing fern *Lygodium japonicum* (Thunberg) Swartz in North Carolina.
9. A species that does *not* consistently occur as *a member of* any particular natural *plant community*, but is none the less rare in the study area, e.g., the columbo *Swertia caroliniensis* (Walter) Kuntze in North Carolina.

Also, Du Mond favors the preservation of *unique* species that are rare, such as the Venus flytrap, *Dionaea muscipula* Ellis, which is unique in habit (folding-trap leaves), habitat (pocosins and bog-margins), and ecological niche (carnivorous). Endangered species would, in this scheme, be those to which any of the nine above guidelines of rarity apply, and which are found in habitats that are about to be altered directly or indirectly by man's activities.

A series of papers presented at the Symposium on Rare and Endangered Plant Species in New England, held in May 1979 at Harvard University and published as the January 1980 issue of *Rhodora*, yielded some stimulating and rather new concepts of rarity, which may have implications as to which species, or subspecies, should be preserved as far as the conservation of relevant gene pools is concerned. They bring up philosophical considerations such as which (sub-) populations or infraspecific elements of a species should be conserved. (At present, however, under the Endangered Species Act, only *entire species* of plants, rather than selected populations of them, may be listed.) Also, the concepts may lend credence to some current opinions that entire *habitats* should be preserved in order to preserve the species that occur in them, as we shall see in the case of Stebbins' comments below.

Some of the points raised reflect on the manager's concerns, such as the question: Is 'natural' extinction permissible? Bratton and White (1980), who work in the Great Smoky Mountains National Park in Tennessee, noted that preserves are 'islands' that lose and gain species from the viewpoint of plant succession. Should populations of rare species such as sundew (*Drosera*) in bogs be allowed to be 'shrubbed-in' or 'succeeded-in' and thus lost? Crow and Storks (1980) reported that in New Hampshire the showy lady's slipper orchid (*Cypripedium reginae*), which was growing in a bog area known as the 'Bottomless Pit' from 1889 to 1891, has undergone natural extirpation due to the bog being 'shrubbed-in' in the process of succession. Species competition due to natural succession, we recall, was also recognized as a cause of endangering plants by the compilers of the North Carolina state list. The effects of disturbance suppression on disturbance-dependent species has been reviewed by White (1979, cf. p. 282) and should be considered also.

William Drury (1980; see also Drury, 1974) noted that an operational definition of a rare species might include the criterion that its numbers are divided into widely separated, small subpopulations so that interbreeding among subpopulations is seriously reduced or eliminated, or, in extreme cases, the species is restricted to a single population. Drury stated that it has usually been assumed that a rare species is not successful and that it suffers from reduction of a genetic variability and lack of aggressiveness, or suffers from depauperization of habitat. Some recent studies of 'masked' genetic polymorphism based on enzyme electrophoresis, however, suggest that some small populations and some inbreeding populations retain a large amount of heterozygosity, such as in *Drosophila* and Horseshoe crabs (*Limulus*).

Because each subpopulation may thus tend to have a somewhat different genetic composition, one would expect that the number of subpopulations is more important for the persistence of a species than the total population size. Because isolation of an inbreeding population may encourage specialization and 'conservatism', it may be, he concludes, that the first steps in rehabilitation of a relict population is to discourage this isolation by encouraging the species to break up into a number of more or less independent subpopulations, and then by breeding and release of progeny into the wild encourage interchange among the populations. Drury readily admits, however, that this idea is contradictory to traditional protectionist policy.

Primack (1980), in connection with his studies on variability in *Plantago*, has also suggested that additional studies are required on genetic variability both within and among populations of rare species and closely related common species to determine if rare species are, in fact, less variable (more genetically depleted) than common species. Stebbins (1980) appears to reinforce this concept by noting that the California Big Tree, *Sequoiadendron giganteum* (Lindley) J. Buchholz, is not genetically depleted as was previously thought, but indeed has been found to consist of approximately 25 morphologically recognizable variants, as grown in Great Britain from seed probably collected in the wild.

Professor Ledyard Stebbins (1980) basically rejected his previous (1942) observations that rare species are characterized by genetic depletion, and now has synthesized a theory that combines elements of climatic, edaphic and gene pool factors, and borrows from his 1976 'ecological islands' hypothesis; it is known as the 'population–environment hypothesis of ecological rarity' or the 'gene pool–niche interaction theory'. This hypothesis contends that there are small land areas having particular characteristics of geology and soils; these areas stand out as ecological islands from the surrounding region and should be preserved as habitats of rare species. The endemic species occurring on these 'islands' are rare as a result of close, highly specific, genetic adaptation (including seed dispersal mechanisms) that confines them to a demanding and restrictive habitat; they are isolated with respect to their ability to colonize neighboring areas. Examples include many of the serpentine soil areas in California. Species having a rich gene pool may not be able to produce variants that are extremely adapted enough to overcome the barriers of the niche conditions and escape to colonize the surrounding areas outside the 'ecological islands'.

Let us briefly illustrate this theory further. There are some common plants in California that grow on all serpentine areas. Pine Hill east of Sacramento, however, is an 'ecological island' of basalt surrounded by serpentine. This basaltic habitat probably causes a restriction of the movement of the species occurring there, rather than the genetics of the species alone causing the restriction to the locality.

Discussion and conclusion

Finally, I would like to present some viewpoints on the whole question of assessment techniques and criteria. It is obvious that a great variety of ways and means to approach the determination of 'endangered' and 'threatened' plants are in operation in the United States at local, state and federal levels.

Since the survival of highly vulnerable plant species is at stake, perhaps we may not wish to fault too strongly any particular sets of criteria which have been accepted as satisfactory at various political levels to prove that a species is endangered. Prominent plant taxonomists and ecologists in each state have designed techniques applicable for their own requirements that will get the job done. Clearly, however, the various criteria and categories set up by different people are not very comparable or compatible in many cases, and a certain amount of amalgamation and standardization, in my judgement, is mandatory for collecting data. The future monitoring of populations would very likely be made easier if such was the case.

In the United States we would benefit by coming to a resolution point so that when speaking in terms of defining 'rare', 'endangered' and 'threatened' species we would all be speaking in the same context.

A glance at the assessment criteria of various states and regions shows certain points of variance being featured, and others omitted, according to discerned characteristics of the species or the ecological niches present in their habitats. Let us briefly note some of this variation in schemes as a recapitulation.

Some features of state assessments

1. Wisconsin: Three or fewer stations in the state means automatically that the species is 'endangered', even if on protected sites.
2. Oregon: Species known from only one population in the state are automatically 'endangered'.
3. North Carolina: Peripheral species are stressed as significant elements of genetic diversity in a species.
4. California: R–E–V–D code includes Vigor of populations (stable, increasing, declining).

5. Massachusetts: Vigor is most important, followed by vulnerability to collection and habitat destruction. The degree of endemism, size of range and pattern of occurrence are also considered.
6. Florida: Status involves conveying information as to the decrease in numbers of a species with passage of time.
7. Nevada Test Site: Tolerance to disturbance and special variability in numbers of desert plant populations are included.
8. Tonopah Test Site (Nevada): Aspect of the plants, i.e. attractive to collectors versus inconspicuous.
9. Texas: Species are arranged by phytogeographic regions.

It seems reasonable to assume that from these various criteria, a uniform set of assessment criteria could be developed for the United States that would involve elements common to all species or aspects of their habitats in all parts of the country. Computer technology (Crovello, 1977) may be called to the forefront to aid in dissemination of the data from national and regional data banks. We should remind ourselves, however, that many qualitative, and ultimately subjective, determinations from thorough field studies will be needed, and these may not lend themselves easily to computerization. The human element will, necessarily, have to play a discretionary role in assessment, as always.

I would like to recommend the following as overall National Assessment Criteria (NAC) for study in determining status of species.

Recommended National Assessment Criteria

1. Similarity of appearance to closely related species that may occur in the same area.
2. Vigor of populations, whether stable, increasing or declining.
3. Extent to which variability in numbers of individuals may be due to particular environmental factors that affect long-term population trends, e.g. desert annuals in many parts of western United States.
4. Frequency and density of populations.
5. Species biology, including reproduction, breeding systems, pollinators, dispersion, establishment of new individuals, maintenance of age and maturation classes.
6. Species in the area which may be highly competitive to the species under study.
7. Aspect of the species: attractive to collectors, both casual and commercial, versus inconspicuous.
8. Location of marginal or disjunct range of the populations.
9. Tolerance of the species to disturbance; ability to colonize disturbed land.
10. Natural factors such as herbivore predation, disease, fire, affecting the species.

11. Stability or instability of the preferred habitat, as to the amount of suitable habitat being changed due to natural or human causes.
12. Impact of natural succession of plant communities, particularly if frequency of a short-term successional species is involved.
13. Habitat or genetic characteristics earmarking a possible or potential occurrence on an 'ecological island' requiring conservation of more habitat than is usual.
14. Human threats, especially notice of construction activities if species occurs on federal land.
15. Accessibility of localities both protected and unprotected to the public, e.g. public parks versus restricted military zones.
16. Accessibility of plants to humans at the site, e.g. steep cliff-faces versus flat prairie sites.
17. Recommendations for 'critical habitat' designation, including that of pollinators and dispersal agents in the habitat.
18. Ownership of the habitat, including existing regulations or federal agency policy decisions already in effect.
19. Discernible economic impact deriving from conservation of the species in a proposed development area.
20. Importance for possible chemical screening for medicines, drugs, pharmaceuticals; potential for propagation in botanic gardens or legal nursery trade to alleviate stress to natural populations.

These criteria are not arranged in order of priority, but are rather a series of factors which should be taken into consideration in assessments.

Various authors have advocated systems for ranking species and/or their role in designating natural areas, by means of the weighting of priority factors, for example Adamus and Clough (1978, Maine), Gehlbach (1975, Texas), Rabe and Savage (1979, Idaho), and Sparrowe and Wight (1975, US Endangered Species Program). A numerical weighting of the value of the recommended criteria should be the next step for investigation, to determine the feasibility of applying a ranking system to help in drawing conclusions as to the status of a species.

Worldwide, IUCN uses standardized categories and definitions to assess the status of rare and threatened plant and animal species in their wild habitats. These are called the IUCN 'Red Data Book categories' and are defined below:

> *Extinct (Ex).* Used only for species which are no longer known to exist in the wild after *repeated* searches of the type localities *and other known or likely places.*
>
> *Endangered (E).* Taxa in danger of extinction and whose survival is unlikely if the causal factors continue operating. Included are taxa whose numbers have been reduced to a critical level or whose habitats have been so

drastically reduced that they are deemed to be in immediate danger of extinction.

Vulnerable (V). Taxa believed likely to move into the Endangered category in the near future if the causal factors continue operating. Included are taxa of which most or all the populations are *decreasing* because of over-exploitation, extensive destruction of habitat or other environmental disturbance; taxa with populations that have been seriously *depleted* and whose ultimate security is not yet assured; and taxa with populations that are still abundant but are *under threat* from serious adverse factors throughout their range.

Rare (R). Taxa with small world populations that are not at present Endangered or Vulnerable, but are at risk. These taxa are usually localized within restricted geographical areas or habitats or are thinly scattered over a more extensive range.

Indeterminate (I). Taxa *known* to be Extinct, Endangered, Vulnerable or Rare but where there is not enough information to say which of the four categories is appropriate.

An elaboration of these definitions by the IUCN Threatened Plants Committee, including examples of species that fit them, forms Appendix 3 to this book and is available as a booklet from the TPC. The category of 'threatened' used in the United States is most closely approximated by the Vulnerable category of IUCN. While it would be a difficult exercise to amend the definitions of 'endangered' and 'threatened' in the US Endangered Species Act, we believe that the various states could aim for a more consistently defined usage of these terms.

I hope that the National Assessment Criteria proposed here will be given an early hearing, so that in the very near future we may move forward to standardization for the United States as a whole, in a manner similar to the uniform criteria of IUCN for assessing the world's endangered flora.

References

Adamus, P. R. and Clough, G. C. (1978). 'Evaluating species for protection in natural areas', *Biol. Conserv.*, **13**(3), 165–78.

Anonymous (1979). 'First plant recovery plan', *Endangered Species Technical Bulletin*, **4**(12), 3.

Anonymous (1980). 'Service names two recovery teams', *Endangered Species Technical Bulletin*, **5**(4), 7.

Ayensu, E. S. (1976). 'International co-operation among conservation-orientated botanical gardens and institutions', in *Conservation of Threatened Plants* (Eds. J. B. Simmons, R. I. Beyer, P. E. Brandham, G.Ll. Lucas and V. T. H. Parry), pp. 259–69.

Ayensu, E. S. (1978). 'The U.S. Red Data Book', *Garden*, **2**(5), 2–3.

Ayensu, E. S. (1979). 'Keeping the wildnerness', in *The American Land*, pp. 108–17, Smithsonian Exposition Books, Washington, DC.

Ayensu, E. S. (1980). 'Evaluating impacts on endangered and threatened flora', in *Biological Evaluation of Environmental Impacts*, pp. 129–32, Council on Environmental Quality, Biological Services Program, US Department of the Interior, Washington, DC.

Ayensu, E. S. and DeFilipps, R. A. (1978). *Endangered and Threatened Plants of the United States*, Smithsonian Institution and World Wildlife Fund – US, Washington, DC.

Ayensu, E. S. and DeFilipps, R. A. (1980). 'Smithsonian endangered flora computerized information', in *Geographical Data Organization for Rare Plant Conservation* (Eds. L. E. Morse and M. S. Henifin), The New York Botanical Garden (in press).

Ayensu, E. S. and DeFilipps, R. A. (1981). 'Smithsonian Institution endangered flora computerized information', in *Rare Plant Conservation: Geographical Data Organization* (Eds. L. E. Morse and M. S. Henifin), pp. 111–122, The New York Botanical Garden.

Bratton, S. P. and White, P. S. (1980). 'Rare plant management – after preservation what?', *Rhodora*, **82**(829), 49–75.

Coddington, J. and Field, K. G. (1978). *Rare and Endangered Vascular Plant Species in Massachusetts*, US Fish and Wildlife Service, Newton Corner, Massachusetts.

Cooper, J. E. *et al.* (Eds.) (1977). *Endangered and Threatened Plants and Animals of North Carolina*, North Carolina State Museum of Natural History, Raleigh.

Council on Environmental Quality (1978). 'National Environmental Policy Act: implementation of procedural provisions; final regulations', *Federal Register*, **43**(230), 55997, 56006. 29 November.

Crovello, T. J. (1977). 'Computers as an aid to solving endangered species problems', in *Extinction Is Forever* (Eds. G. T. Prance and T. S. Elias), pp. 337–46, The New York Botanical Garden.

Crow, G. E. and Storks, I. M. (1980). 'Rare and endangered plants of New Hampshire: a phytogeographic viewpoint', *Rhodora*, **82**(829), 173–89.

Drury, W. H. (1974). 'Rare species', *Biol. Conserv.*, **6**(3), 162–9.

Drury, W. H. (1980). 'Rare species of plants', *Rhodora*, **82**(829), 3–48.

Du Mond, D. M. (1973). 'A guide for the selection of rare, unique and endangered plants', *Castanea*, **38**(4), 387–95.

Federal Committee on Ecological Reserves (1977). *A Directory of Research Natural Areas on Federal Lands of the United States of America*, Forest Service, US Department of Agriculture, Washington, DC.

Gehlbach, F. R. (1975). 'Investigation, evaluation, and priority ranking of natural areas', *Biol. Conserv.*, **8**(2), 79–88.

Henifin, M. S., Morse, L. E., Griffith, S., and Hohn, J. E. (1981*a*). 'Planning field work on rare or endangered plant populations', in *Rare Plant Conservation: Geographical Data Organization* (Eds. L. E. Morse and M. S. Henifin), pp. 309–312, The New York Botanical Garden.

Henifin, M. S., Morse, L. E., Reveal, J. L., MacBryde, B. and Lawyer, J. I. (1981*b*). 'Guidelines for the preparation of status reports on rare or endangered species', in *Rare Plant Conservation: Geographical Data Organization* (Eds. L. E. Morse and M. S. Henifin), pp. 261–282, The New York Botanical Garden.

Heritage Conservation and Recreation Service (1979). *The National Heritage Policy Act*, US Department of the Interior, HCRS, Washington, DC.

Heslop-Harrison, J. (1976). 'Reproductive physiology', in *Conservation of Threatened Plants* (Eds. J. B. Simmons, R. I. Beyer, P. E. Brandham, G. Ll. Lucas and V. T. H. Parry), pp. 199–205, Plenum, New York and London.

Jenkins, R. E. (1975). 'Endangered plant species: a soluble ecological problem', *The Nature Conservancy News*, **25**(4), 20–1.

Jenkins, R. E. (1978). 'Heritage classification: the elements of ecological diversity', *The Nature Conservancy News*, **25**(1), 24–5, 30.

Johnston, M. C. (1974). *Rare and Endangered Plants Native to Texas*, Rare Plant Study Center, University of Texas, Austin.

Klopatek, J. M., Olson, R. J., Emerson, C. J., and Joness, J. L. (1979). 'Land-use conflicts with natural vegetation in the United States', *Envir. Conserv.*, **6**(3), 191–9.

MacBryde, B. (1979). 'Plant conservation in North America: developing structure', in *Systematic Botany, Plant Utilization and Biosphere Conservation* (Ed. I. Hedberg), pp. 105–9, Almqvist and Wiksell International, Stockholm.

Massey, J. R. and Whitson, P. D. (1977). 'Species biology: definition, direction, data and decisions', in *Conference on Endangered Plants in the Southeast*, USDA Forest Service Gen. Tech. Rep. SE-11, pp. 88–94, Southeastern Forest Experiment Station, Asheville, North Carolina.

Massey, J. R. and Whitson, P. D. (1980). 'Species biology, the key to plant preservation', *Rhodora*, **82**(829), 97–103.

Primack, R. B. (1980). 'Phenotypic variation of rare and widespread species of *Plantago*', *Rhodora*, **82**(829), 87–95.

Rabe, F. W. and Savage, N. L. (1979). 'A methodology for the selection of aquatic natural areas', *Biol. Conserv.*, **15**(4), 291–300.

Radford, A. E. (1978). *Ecological Classification in the National Heritage Program*, unpublished first working draft manuscript, University of North Carolina, Chapel

Radford, A. E. (1981). 'Introduction to a system for ecological diversity classification', in *Rare Plant Conservation: Geographical Data Organization* (Eds. L. E. Morse and M. S. Henifin), pp. 199–205, The New York Botanical Garden. Botanical Garden (in press).

Raven, P. H. (1976). 'Ethics and attitudes', in *Conservation of Threatened Plants* (Eds. J. B. Simmons, R. I. Beyer, P. E. Brandham, G. Ll. Lucas and V. T. H. Parry), pp. 155–79, Plenum, New York and London.

Read, R. H. (1976). *Endangered and Threatened Vascular Plants in Wisconsin*, Scientific Areas Preservation Council Technical Bulletin 92, Department of Natural Resources, Madison.

Rhoads, W. A., Cochrane, S. A., and Williams, M. P. (1978). *Status of Endangered and Threatened Plant Species on Nevada Test Site – A Survey. Part II: Threatened Species*, Santa Barbara Operations, EG & G Inc., Goleta, California.

Rhoads. W. A., Cochrane, S. A., and Williams, M. P. (1979). *Status of Endangered and Threatened Plant Species on Tonopah Test Range – A Survey*, Santa Barbara Operations, EG & G Inc., Goleta, California.

Rhoads, W. A. and Williams, M. P. (1977). *Status of Endangered and Threatened Plant Species on Nevada Test Site – A Survey. Part I: Endangered Species*, Santa Barbara Operations, EG & G Inc., Goleta, California.

Sanders, R. (1978). 'The state natural heritage programs: a partnership to preserve natural diversity', *The Nature Conservancy News*, **28**(1), 13–19.

Shetler, S. G. (1979). 'North America', in *Systematic Botany, Plant Utilization and Biosphere Conservation* (Ed. I. Hedberg), pp. 47–54. Almqvist and Wiksell International, Stockholm.

Siddall, J. L., Chambers, K. L., and Wagner, D. H. (1979). *Rare, Threatened and Endangered Vascular Plants in Oregon – An Interim Report*, Natural Areas Preserves Advisory Committee, Salem.

Smith, J. P., Jr., Cole, R. J., Sawyer, J. O., Jr., and Powell, W. R. (Eds.) (1980). *Inventory of Rare and Endangered Vascular Plants of California*, Ed. 2, California Native Plant Society Special Publication No. 1, CNPS, Berkeley.

Smithsonian Institution (1975). *Report on Endangered and Threatened Plant Species of the United States*, Government Printing Office, Washington, DC.

Sparrowe, R. D. and Wight, H. M. (1975). 'Setting priorities for the endangered species program', *Transactions of North American Wildlife and Natural Resource Conference*, pp. 142–56.

Stebbins, G. L. (1942). 'The genetic approach to problems of rare and endemic species', *Madroño*, 6, 240–58.

Stebbins, G. L. (1980). 'Rarity of plant species: a synthetic viewpoint', *Rhodora*, 82(829), 77–86.

Ward, D. B. (Ed.) (1979). *Rare and Endangered Biota of Florida, Volume 5: Plants*, University Presses of Florida, Gainesville.

White, P. S. (1979). 'Pattern, process and natural disturbance in vegetation', *The Botanical Review*, 45(3), 229–99.

Whitson, P. D. and Massey, J. R. (1981). 'Information systems for use in studying the population status of threatened and endangered plants', in *Rare Plant Conservation: Geographical Data Organization* (Eds. L. E. Morse and M. S. Henifin), pp. 217–236, The New York Botanical Garden.

Appendix I. Population biology criteria (Henifin *et al.*, 1981*a*)

Population biology information to be recorded each time a population is visited

1. Number of individuals in each population and area population covers.
2. Size/age classes present (define terms used) and number (or percentage) of individuals in each class.
3. Phenology – estimate of percentage for each population in vegetative, flowering, fruiting, or senescent stages.
4. Number of seedlings observed.
5. Observations relating to survivorship and nature of mortality at each life stage (predation on seedlings, competition, etc.).
6. Evidence of herbivores, predators, diseases, and/or pests.
7. Evidence of disturbance by exotic plants, animals, microbes.
8. Human impacts observed or suspected (trampling, damage by vehicles, wild flower collecting, etc.).
9. Other threatening factors and their severity (land development, grazing, etc.). Give both existing and potential threats.
10. Assessment of the vigor and status of individuals and the population.

Also, general information recorded earlier should be reviewed and revised as necessary on each site visit.

Other useful population biology information that may be recorded each time population is visited

1. Types of reproduction noted (seeds, vegetative, etc.).
2. Pollinators (wind, water, insect, etc.). Distinguish between those visiting plant and other suspected pollinators.

3. Observations on seed dispersal (general mechanisms, dispersal patterns, amount of seed, germination requirements).
4. Seedling ecology (morphology, microhabitat, localized conditions restricting establishment).
5. Other species of this genus at or near site, and hybrids observed, if any.
6. Evidence of symbiosis or parasitic relationships.
7. Response of taxon to disturbance.

Appendix II. Population biology and ecology categories for status reports (Henifin *et al.*, 1981*b*)

Population biology of taxon

Summary of information on various populations, referenced to specific status reports on each population, when available. See Whitson and Massey (1981) for a more complete treatment of species biology. Harper's *Population Biology of Plants* presents additional material that may be helpful.

A. General summary of population biology of the taxon.

B. Demography

1. Number and geographical spacing of known populations (estimated if necessary), with estimate of currently known number of individuals per population, if available. Define age (or size) classes used and describe census method(s) used to determine area and numbers; see Mueller-Dombois and Ellenberg's text for a description of various censusing techniques. Mention also any pertinent historical observations, such as past estimates of abundance.
2. General demographic details of each population, including:
   (a) Area of the population(s)
   (b) Number, and age (or size) classes of individuals
   (c) Density (number of individuals per unit area)
   (d) Presence of dispersed seeds
   (e) Evidence of reproduction (seedlings, etc.)
   (f) Evidence of population expansion or decline such as review of historical accounts or consideration of demographic observations.

C. Phenology

1. Patterns and observed times of budding, leafing, flowering (anthesis), fruiting, seed or fruit dispersal, senescence, germination, etc.

2. Relation of phenological phenomena to climatic and microclimatic events such as exposure, drought, late frosts, and precipitation patterns.

D. Reproductive biology

1. Types of repdroduction, relationship to age of plant, and evaluation of relative importance of each type to maintenance of population
   (a) Outbreeding (dioecy, protandry, heteromorphy, self-incompatibility, etc.)
   (b) Inbreeding (cleistogamy, autogamy, etc.)
   (c) Cloning (nature, rate, and extent)
   (d) Other asexual reproduction and/or dispersal (rhizomes, tubers, layering, agamospermy, etc.).
2. Pollination
   (a) Pollination mechanism(s) (mechanical, insect, wind, water, etc.)
   (b) Specific *known* insect (or other) pollinators, or other known agents (e.g. wind or rain), if applicable; state nature of evidence for each
   (c) Additional insect visitors or other possible or suspected pollination agents
   (d) Vulnerability of pollinators (or other pollination mechanisms) to pesticides, pollution, land-use changes, succession, exotic animals or plants, etc.
3. Seed dispersal
   (a) General mechanisms (wind, water, animal, etc.)
   (b) Specific agents
   (c) Vulnerability of dispersal agents or mechanisms to disturbance and/or habitat modification
   (d) Patterns of propagule dispersal (distance, frequency of distribution in a particular area, etc.) (Note some propagules may be dispersed to areas in which they cannot grow.)
4. Seed biology (indicate whether observations based on natural or laboratory conditions)
   (a) Amount and variation in annual seed production
   (b) Seed viability and longevity – percentage of seeds germinating after specific time intervals
   (c) Dormancy requirements, if any known
   (d) Germination requirements, such as scarification, cold temperatures, soil type, moisture, and light
   (e) Percent germination under various conditions.
5. Seedling ecology. Include important ecological and microhabitat factors, such as light, moisture, nutrient requirements, and soil disturbance.
6. Survival and nature of mortality of plants at each life stage, e.g. seedling

mortality due to predation or due to intraspecific competition, or mortality from shading of mature plants by canopy growth.

7. Overall assessment of taxon's reproductive success.

Population ecology of species

Summary of information on various populations, referenced to specific population status reports, if available.

A. General summary of population ecology of the taxon.

B. Positive and neutral interactions with mature plants, pollen, seeds, seedlings, and juveniles of this taxon. Include plants or animals with which this species is obligatorily or facultatively associated.

C. Negative interactions with mature plants, pollen, seeds, seedlings, and juveniles of this taxon

 1. Herbivores, predators, pests, parasites, and diseases (native or exotic) affecting this taxon
 2. Evidence of competition for light, water, pollinators, or other requirements
 (a) Intraspecific
 (b) Interspecific
 3. Toxic and allelopathic interaction(s) with other organisms.

D. Hybridization; specify the nature of evidence
 1. Naturally occurring
 2. Artificially induced
 3. Potential for spontaneous occurrence in cultivation.

E. Other factors of population ecology.

Appendix III. Character classes, characters and character states for pollination-reproductive biology studies (Massey and Whitson, 1977)

Subsystem 1

A. Reproductive system

 1. Amphimixis
 2. Apomixis
 3. Combination.

B. Breeding system (fertilization type based on origin of the pollen)

1. Autogamy
2. Allogamy
   (a) Xenogamy
   (b) Geitonogamy
3. Combination (allautogamy).

C. Pollination system

1. Type of pollination based on agent
   (a) Anemophily
   (b) Melittophily
   (c) Etc.
2. Pathway
   (a) Chasmantheric
   (b) Cleistantheric.
3. Visitor–plant relationship
   (a) Polytropic
   (b) Oligotropic
   (c) Monotropic
   (d) Dystropic
   (e) Allotropic (allophilic)
   (f) Hemitropic (hemiphilic)
   (g) Eutropic (euphilic)
   (h) Other.
4. Vector(s)
   (a) Family
   (b) Scientific name
   (c) Vector sex.

D. Reproductive Potential

1. Sex
   (a) Flower
   (b) Inflorescence
   (c) Plant
   (d) Population.
2. Pollen
   (a) No. pollen grains/anther
   (b) No. anthers/flower
   (c) No. flowers/inflorescence
   (d) No. inflorescences/plant

(e) No. pollen grains/plant
(f) No. pollen viability – germination.
3. Seed
  (a) No. ovules/fruit
  (b) No. fruits/flower
  (c) No. possible fruits/plant
  (d) No. seed set/fruit.
4. Pollen/ovule ratio.
5. Seed germination
  (a) Percentage (specify conditions)
  (b) Phenology (specify conditions).
6. Reproductive potential through time (plant duration, i.e. length of generation).

Appendix IV. Natural areas and diversity classification system
(A. E. Radford, 1980)

HIERARCHICAL ELEMENT SUMMARY FOR DIVERSITY COMPONENTS, I. BIOLOGY

I. A. BIOTIC SYSTEM

1. Forb system
2. Grass system
3. Shrub system
4. Needleleaf forest system
5. Broadleaf forest system
6. Algal system
7. Moss system
8. Lichen system
9. Fungal system
10. Unvegetated system
11. Cave system
12. Plankton system
13. Nekton system
14. Neuston system
15. Periphyton system
16. Coral system
17. Mollusc system
18. Echinoderm system
19. Infauna system

I. AA. BIOTIC SUBSYSTEM

Sizes (S)
Trees
S1. Dwarf trees, less than 2 m
S2. Small trees, 2–5 m
S3. Large trees, 5–50 m
S4. Giant trees, more than 50 m

Shrubs
S5. Very low dwarf shrubs, less than 3 cm
S6. Low dwarf shrubs, 3–10 cm
S7. Typical dwarf shrubs, 10–30 cm

S8. Tall dwarf shrubs, 30–100 cm   S10. Tall shrubs, 2–5 m
S9. Normal shrubs, 1–2 m   S11. Giant shrubs, more than 5 m

Herbs
S12. Very small herbs, less than 3 cm   S15. Tall herbs, 3–10 dm
S13. Small herbs, 3–10 cm   S16. Very tall herbs, 1–3 m
S14. Medium herbs, 1–30 cm   S17. Extremely tall herbs, more than 3 m

Growth form (habit) (H)

Trees
H1. Excurrent   H4. Tuft
H2. Deliquescent   H5. Tall succulent
H3. Bottle

Shrubs and herbs
H6. Bulbous   H11. Root-budding
H7. Caulescent   H12. Scapose
H8. Cespitose   H13. Stoloniferous
H9. Reptant   H14. Succulent
H10. Rhizomatous

Vines
H15. Root climbers   H17. Tendril climbers
H16. Spread climbers   H18. Winding climbers

Aquatics
H19. Free-floating thalloid   H26. Submergent scapose
H20. Free-floating leafy   H27. Submergent stoloniferous
H21. Free-floating stoloniferous   H28. Emergent caulescent
H22. Rooted-floating leaf   H29. Emergent cespitose
H23. Submergent caulescent   H30. Emergent rhizomatous
H24. Submergent cespitose   H31. Emergent scapose
H25. Submergent rhizomatous   H32. Emergent stoloniferous

Duration (D)

Annual herbs
D1. Rain green   D3. Summer green
D2. Spring green   D4. Winter green

Perennial herbs, shrubs, trees
D5. Deciduous   D7. Evergreen
D6. Rhizocarpic   D8. Suffruticose

Density (Z)

Z1. Closed – 50 per cent or more cover

Z2. Open – 25 per cent to 50 per cent cover

Z3. Sparse – less than 25 per cent cover

I. B. COMMUNITY COVER CLASS (SELECTED EXAMPLES)
1. Trout stream
2. Lily pond
3. Sphagnum bog
4. Cactus flat
5. Mangrove swamp
6. Oak savanna
7. Cordgrass marsh
8. Grama prairie
9. Oak chapparal
10. Sedge tundra
11. Coral reef
12. Clam bed
13. Catfish pond
14. Seagrass bed
15. Oak-hickory forest

I. BB. COMMUNITY CLASS (NOT INCLUDED)

I. C. COMMUNITY COVER TYPE (SELECTED EXAMPLES)
1. Saguaro
2. Ponderosa pine
3. Sea oats
4. Oyster
5. Large mouth Bass/Bluegill
6. Buffalo grass
7. Mesquite
8. Englemann Spruce/Douglas Fir
9. White spruce
10. Fucus

I. CC. COMMUNITY TYPE (SELECTED EXAMPLES)
1. Reed grass
2. Eel grass–widgeon grass
3. Chestnut oal/Low blueberry
4. Buckeye–basswood/Glade fern
5. Chestnus oak/Mountain laurel/ Galax
6. Water tupelo/Duckweed/ Coontail/Spanish moss
7. Beech/Beech
8. Carex brunnescens/Rumex acetosella
9. Angelica triquinata/Polytrichum
10. Buckeye/Blackberry/ Thoroughwort
11. Yellow birch/Mountain maple/ Mixed herbs
12. Fraser fir/Purple rhododendron
13. White pine/Mountain laurel
14. Sea oxeye/Small cord grass

Appendix V. State lists of endangered and threatened plant species of the United States

ALABAMA

Thomas, J. L. (1976). 'Plants' in *Endangered and Threatened Plants and Animals of Alabama* (Ed. H. Boschung), pp. 5–12, Bulletin Alabama Museum of Natural History, Number 2, University of Alabama.

ALASKA

Murray, D. F. (1980). *Threatened and Endangered Plants of Alaska*, US Department of Agriculture, Forest Service and US Department of the Interior, Bureau of Land Management.

ARIZONA

Anonymous (1973). *Rare and Endangered Plants of Arizona*.

ARKANSAS

Tucker, G. E. (1974). 'Threatened Native Plants of Arkansas', in *Arkansas Natural Areas Plan* (Arkansas Department of Planning), pp. 39–65, Little Rock.

CALIFORNIA

Smith, J. P., Jr., Cole, R. J., Sawyer, J. O., Jr. and Powell, W. R. (Eds.) (1980). *Inventory of Rare and Endangered Vascular Plants of California*, Ed. 2., California Native Plant Society Special Publication No. 1, CNPS, Berkeley.

COLORADO

Weber, W. A. and Johnston, B. C. (1976). *Natural History Inventory of Colorado 1. Vascular Plants, Lichens, and Bryophytes*, University of Colorado Museum, Boulder.

CONNECTICUT

Dowhan, J. J. and Craig, R. J. (1976). *Rare and Endangered Species of Connecticut and Their Habitats*, Report of Investigations, Number 6. State Geological and Natural History Survey of Connecticut, Hartford.

Mehrhoff, L. J. (1978). *Rare and Endangered Vascular Plant Species in Connecticut*, US Fish and Wildlife Service, Newton Corner, Mass.

DELAWARE

Tucker, A. O., Dill, N. H., Broome, C. R., Phillips, C. E. and Maciarello, M. J. (1979). *Rare and Endangered Vascular Plant Species in Delaware*, US Fish and Wildlife Service, Newton Corner, Mass.

FLORIDA

Ward, D. B. (Ed.) (1979). 'Volume 5: Plants', in *Rare and Endangered Biota of Florida* (Ed. P. C. H. Pritchard), University Presses of Florida, Gainesville.

GEORGIA

McCollum, J. L. and Ettman, D. R. (1977). *Georgia's Protected Plants*, Georgia Department of Natural Resources, Atlanta.

HAWAII
Fosberg, F. R. and Herbst, D. (1975). 'Rare and Endangered Species of Hawaiian Vascular Plants', *Allertonia*, **1**(1), 1–72.

IDAHO
Henderson, D. M., Johnson, F. D., Packard, P. and Steele, R. (1977). *Endangered and Threatened Plants of Idaho – A Summary of Current Knowledge*, College of Forestry, Wildlife and Range Sciences Bulletin 21, University of Idaho Forest, Wildlife and Range Experiment Station, Moscow, Idaho.

ILLINOIS
Paulson, G. A. and Schwegman, J. (1976). *Endangered, Vulnerable, Rare and Extirpated Vascular Plants in Illinois – Interim List of Species*, Illinois Nature Preserves Commission and Department of Conservation, Rockford and Springfield (unpublished manuscript).

INDIANA
Barnes, W. B. (1975). *Rare and Endangered Plants in Indiana*, Indiana Department of Natural Resources, Indianapolis (unpublished manuscript).

IOWA
Roosa, D. M. and Eilers, L. J. (1978). *Endangered and Threatened Iowa Vascular Plants*, State Preserves Advisory Board Special Report 5, State Conservation Commission, Des Moines.

KANSAS
McGregor, R. L. (1977). *Rare Native Vascular Plants of Kansas*, Technical Publications of the State Biological Survey of Kansas 5, Lawrence, Kansas.

KENTUCKY
Baskin, J. M. and Baskin, C. C. (1978). 'The Ecological Status of Six Rare Plants in Kentucky, with Reference to a Recent Publication on Endangered Species', *Trans. Kentucky Acad. Sci.*, **39**(3–4), 135–7.

LOUISIANA
Curry, M. G. (1976). *Rare Vascular Plants of Louisiana*, VTN Louisiana Inc., Metairie, Louisiana (unpublished manuscript).

MAINE
Eastman, L. M. (1978). *Rare and Endangered Vascular Plant Species in Maine*, US Fish and Wildlife Service, Newton Corner, Mass.

MARYLAND
Broome, C. R., Tucker, A. O., Reveal, J. L. and Dill, N. H. (1979). *Rare and Endangered Vascular Plant Species in Maryland*, US Fish and Wildlife Service, Newton Corner, Mass.

MASSACHUSETTS
Coddington, J. and Field, K. G. (1978). *Rare and Endangered Vascular Plant Species in Massachusetts*, US Fish and Wildlife Service, Newton Corner, Mass.

MICHIGAN

Wagner, W. H., Voss, E. G., Beaman, J. H., Bourdo, E. A., Case, F. W., Churchill, J. A. and Thompson, P. W. (1977). 'Endangered, Threatened, and Rare Vascular Plants in Michigan', *Michigan Botanist*, **16**, 99–110.

Beaman, J. H. (1977). 'Commentary on Endangered and Threatened Plants in Michigan', *Michigan Botanist*, **16**, 110–22.

MINNESOTA

Morley, T. (1972). *Rare or Endangered Plants of Minnesota*, Department of Botany, University of Minnesota, Minneapolis (unpublished manuscript).

MISSISSIPPI

Pullen, T. M. (1975). *Rare and Endangered Plant Species in Mississippi*, Department of Biology, University of Mississippi (unpublished manuscript).

MISSOURI

Nordstrom, G. R., Pflieger, W. L., Sadler, K. C. and Lewis, W. H. (1977). *Rare and Endangered Species of Missouri*, Missouri Department of Conservation and USDA Soil Conservation Service.

MONTANA

Gale, R. (1980). 'The Riddle of Existence – Montana's Rare Plants', *Montana Outdoors*, **11**(1), 14–16.

NEBRASKA

USDA Soil Conservation Service (1975). *Threatened and Endangered Species of Vascular Plants in Nebraska*, USDA Soil Conservation Service, Lincoln (unpublished manuscript).

NEVADA

Beatley, J. C. (1977). *Endangered Plant Species of the Nevada Test Site, Ash Meadows, and South Central Nevada; Threatened Species; Addendum*, Department of Biological Sciences, University of Cincinnati.

Rhoads, W. A., Cochrane, S. A. and Williams, M. P. (1978). *Status of Endangered and Threatened Plant Species on Nevada Test Site – A Survey, Part 2: Threatened Species*, Santa Barbara Operations, EG & G Inc., Goleta, California.

Rhoads, W. A. and Williams, M. P. (1977). *Status of Endangered and Threatened Plant Species on Nevada Test Site – A Survey, Part 1: Endangered Species*, Santa Barbara Operations, EG & G Inc., Goleta, California.

NEW HAMPSHIRE

Storks, I. M. and Crow, G. E. (1978). *Rare and Endangered Vascular Plant Species in New Hampshire*, US Fish and Wildlife Service, Newton Corner, Mass.

NEW JERSEY

Fairbrothers, D. E. and Hough, M. Y. (1973). *Rare or Endangered Vascular Plants of New Jersey*, Science Notes 14, New Jersey State Museum, Trenton.

NEW MEXICO
Pierce, P. (1975). *Endangered and Threatened Cacti of New Mexico*, Albuquerque (unpublished manuscript).
NEW YORK
Mitchell, R. S., Sheviak, C. J. and Dean, J. K. (1980). *Rare and Endangered Vascular Plant Species in New York State*, US Fish and Wildlife Service, Newton Corner, Mass.
NORTH CAROLINA
Cooper, J. E., Robinson, S. S. and Funderburg, J. B. (Eds.) (1977). *Endangered and Threatened Plants and Animals of North Carolina*, North Carolina State Museum of Natural History, Raleigh.
NORTH DAKOTA
USDA Soil Conservation Service (1972). *Rare and Endangered Plant Species in North Dakota*, USDA Soil Conservation Service, Bismarck (unpublished manuscript).
OHIO
Stuckey, R. L. and Roberts, M. L. (1977). 'Rare and Endangered Aquatic Vascular Plants of Ohio: An Annotated List of the Imperiled Species', *Sida*, 7(1), 24–41.
OKLAHOMA
Zanoni, T. A., Gentry, J. L., Tyrl, R. J. and Risser, P. G. (1979). *Endangered and Threatened Plants of Oklahoma*, Department of Botany and Microbiology, University of Oklahoma, Norman.
OREGON
Siddall, J. L., Chambers, K. L. and Wagner, D. H. (1979). *Rare, Threatened and Endangered Vascular Plants in Oregon – An Interim Report*, Natural Area Preserves Advisory Committee, Salem.
PENNSYLVANIA
Wiegman, P. G. (1979). *Rare and Endangered Vascular Plant Species in Pennsylvania*, US Fish and Wildlife Service, Newton Corner, Mass.
RHODE ISLAND
Church, G. L. and Champlin, R. L. (1978). *Rare and Endangered Vascular Plant Species in Rhode Island*, US Fish and Wildlife Service, Newton Corner, Mass.
SOUTH CAROLINA
Forsythe, D. M. and Ezell, W. B., Jr. (Eds.) (1979). *Proceedings of the First South Carolina Endangered Species Symposium*, Nongame-Endangered Species Section, South Carolina Wildlife and Marine Resources Department and The Citadel, Charleston.
SOUTH DAKOTA
Schumacher, C. M. (1979). *Status of Endangered and Threatened Plants in South Dakota*, Technical Notes, Environment, 9, USDA Soil Conservation Service, Huron.

TENNESSEE
Committee for Tennessee Rare Plants (1978). 'The Rare Vascular Plants of Tennessee', *J. Tennessee Acad. Sci.*, **53**(4), 128–33.

TEXAS
Johnston, M. C. (1974). *Rare and Endangered Plants Native to Texas*, Rare Plant Study Center, University of Texas, Austin.

UTAH
Welsh, S. L. (1978). 'Endangered and Threatened Plants of Utah: A Reevaluation', *The Great Basin Naturalist*, **38**(1), 1–18.

Welsh, S. L. (1979). *Illustrated Manual of Proposed Endangered and Threatened Plants of Utah*, Denver Federal Center, US Fish and Wildlife Service, Denver, Colorado.

Welsh, S. L., Atwood, N. E. and Reveal, J. L. (1975). 'Endangered, Threatened, Extinct, Endemic, and Rare or Restricted Utah Vascular Plants', *The Great Basin Naturalist*, **35**(4), 327–76.

VERMONT
Countryman, W. D. (1978). *Rare and Endangered Vascular Plant Species in Vermont*, US Fish and Wildlife Service, Newton Corner, Mass.

VIRGINIA
Porter, D. M. (1979). *Rare and Endangered Vascular Plant Species in Virginia*, US Fish and Wildlife Service, Newton Corner, Mass.

Porter, D. M. (1979). 'Vascular plants', in *Endangered and Threatened Plants and Animals of Virginia* (Ed. D. W. Linzey), pp. 31–122, Virginia Polytechnic Institute and State University, Blacksburg.

WASHINGTON
Denton, M., Goldman, B., Hitchcock, C. L., Kruckeberg, A. R. and Mueller, M. (1977). *A Working List of Rare, Endangered, or Threatened Vascular Plant Taxa for Washington*, Department of Botany, University of Washington, Seattle (unpublished manuscript).

WEST VIRGINIA
Fortney, R. H., Clarkson, R. H., Harvey, C. N. and Kartesz, J. (1978). *Rare and Endangered Species of West Virginia: A Preliminary Report, Volume 1: Vascular Plants*, West Virginia Department of Natural Resources, Charleston.

WISCONSIN
Read, R. H. (1976). *Endangered and Threatened Vascular Plants in Wisconsin*, Scientific Areas Prevention Council Technical Bulletin 92, Department of Natural Resources, Madison.

WYOMING
Dorn, R. D. (1977). 'Rare and endangered species', in *Manual of the Vascular Plants of Wyoming*, Vol. 2, pp. 1394–1400, Harland, New York and London.

The Biological Aspects of Rare Plant Conservation
Edited by Hugh Synge
© 1981 John Wiley & Sons Ltd.

3
Techniques and constraints in survey and conservation of threatened plants and habitats in India

S. K. JAIN AND A. R. K. SASTRY *Botanical Survey of India, Howrah*

Summary

Correct taxonomic concepts are necessary for a proper survey of threatened plants. Examples are given of species actually rare, but reported as abundant due to wrong indentifications. Absence of collections for several decades indicates rarity or even extinction. Monitoring of populations adds to our knowledge on the survival or the danger of extinction, but has several limitations.

The varied and rich flora of a vast country like India places severe constraints on conservationists. The existence of only a few herbaria having pre-1900 collections poses limitations in assessing the status of habitats or areas of past distribution of threatened plants. Economic dependence and legal rights of the forest-dwellers on the forest products and exploitation even by botanists for laboratory materials are also significant constraints.

Sanctuaries for vulnerable plants have been possible only for a few species of *Rhododendron*, *Primula* and *Nepenthes*. Certain forest areas considered as unique ecosystems have been provisionally selected for study and consideration as Biosphere Reserves. The ecosystem of some such areas is under study. An assessment of the impact of development projects on ecosystems is now accepted as an integral part of planning. Also, supporting research such as taxonomic revisions, floristic studies in unexplored areas and *ex-situ* conservation, is being intensified.

In order to analyse this subject, it is useful to cover separately threatened plants and threatened habitats in terms of the four key words: techniques, constraints, survey and conservation.

Threatened plants

Techniques and constraints in survey

It is essential to have a proper understanding of the various terms employed in the study of threatened plants such as 'endangered', 'threatened', 'rare' and 'possibly extinct'. Until some years ago these terms have not been used in biological literature with enough precision. There is, however, a somewhat better consensus of interpretation now. This is necessary for proper emphasis and perspective in studies of threatened plants and for the successful understanding and application of the Convention on International Trade in Endangered Species of Wild Fauna and Flora (CITES).

An analysis of literature records, as in Floras, and of herbarium material, together with studying plants in gardens and in the wild, gives useful clues to the status of species. For example, a study in the orchid genus *Coelogyne* suggested the possible extinction of three species, *C. albo-lutea* Rolfe, *C. assamica* Linden & Reichb. and *C. treutleri* Hook.f. (Das and Jain, 1980).

A proper taxonomic evaluation of all complex groups is also essential. *Arthraxon lanceolatus* (Roxb.) Hochst. is a very rare grass confined to a small region in peninsular India. But confusion of its identity with *A. prionodes* (Steud.) Dandy led to reports of its abundant occurrence all over the country. *Arthraxon microphyllus* (Trin.) Hochst. is confined to the eastern Himalayas, but confusion of its identity with *A. lancifolius* (Trin.) Hochst. led to reports of its wide occurrence. This study (Jain, 1971, 1972) also led to the discovery of new, endemic and rare taxa in the genus, as exemplified by *A. deccanensis* Jain and *A. junnarensis* Jain & Hemadri.

Data from specialists in certain groups or on certain regions are also a very collections of *Manisuris divergens* (Hack.) Kuntz. from the western Ghats of India confirmed the rarity of the species (Jain, 1967). Analyses of collections in the herbarium and absence of any recent collections, say within the last 50 years, can indicate the present status of the species. For example, three species of *Ophiorrhiza* and three species of *Impatiens* in peninsular India have not been recollected and may be represented by their type specimens only (Henry, Vivekananthan and Nair, 1978).

Data from specialists in certain groups or on certain regions is also a very useful source for evaluating the status of species. The cases from *Coelogyne* and *Arthraxon* discussed above and the work of Vivekananthan (1980), who enumerated rare taxa of Idukki district in Kerala, are good examples.

Populations of certain selected plants have to be constantly monitored. Methodologies for this are not yet specific, each scientist trying to evolve his own, depending on the size and number of populations, vulnerability of habitat and other factors. The botanists of the Botanical Survey of India at Shillong have been keeping a watch on populations of *Nepenthes khasiana* Hook.f., the endemic and only pitcher plant of the country, and found that its populations were shrinking and needed protection. Its type locality has since been declared as a sanctuary. It was heartening to note that these populations have now responded to conservation measures.

C. D. K. Cook (1980*a* and 1980*b*) of the Zürich Botanical Garden, Switzerland, has been monitoring the status of certain endemic wetland species in south India. He first visited some areas in Kerala and Tamil Nadu in 1970 and revisited the areas in 1973 and in 1979. His field observations revealed that some endemic species like *Aponogeton appendiculatus* van Bruggen, *Rotala macrandra* Koehne, *R. malampuzhensis* R. V. Nair ex C. D. K. Cook, *R. verticillatus* L., *Nymphoides macrospermum* Vasudevan, *Cryptocoryne retrospiralis* (Roxb.) Kunth and *C. spiralis* (Retz.) Wydler, which were hitherto considered rare, were in fact relatively common and not immediately vulnerable although, according to Cook, much of the landscape and habitats of these species in Kerala and Tamil Nadu have been rapidly changing during this period. Of these species, *Rotala verticillatus* was once considered by him to be extinct. On the other hand, this monitoring also revealed that, (a) *Wiesneria triandra* (Dalz.) Micheli had only a single population of about 30 plants near Parappanangadi, Kerala, and (b) *Limnopoa meeboldii* (Fischer) Hubb. had a single population of a few hundred plants in an aquatic habitat of an area of about 100 m by 300 m, near Chottanikkara, about 14 km southeast of Ernakulam in Kerala. These are to be considered vulnerable. *Cryptocoryne cognata* Schott (recorded from the Nilgiris) and *C. consorbrina* Schott could not be found and may have become extinct due to the destruction of their habitats. *Hubbardia heptaneuron* Bor, a species already presumed extinct and listed in *The IUCN Plant Red Data Book*, is not to be found now in its type locality at Gersoppa Falls or other waterfalls in the Western Ghats.

The magnitude of the survey needed poses a considerable problem in India due to vastness of the country and the very varied and rich natural flora–vascular plants alone total about 15 000 species. The Botanical Survey of India is presently the chief agency involved in this activity, but interest is now evident among botanists in other institutions.

Very few revisionary studies on Indian genera have been done. Out of about 2800 genera of vascular plants, not even a hundred have been subjected to taxonomic revisions. Furthermore, herbarium sheets, particularly the old ones, lack data on the frequency of occurrence. Almost none of the sheets of pre-1900 collections have any mention of frequency or rarity. Only recently was the necessity of close and continuous observation on natural populations realized.

Monitoring of populations over long periods is nearly impossible as most of the populations remain exposed even to unnatural hazards. A hill-slope in the eastern Himalayas had been under observation for some years for its rich population of *Paphiopedilum fairrieanum* (Lindl.) Pfitz. (Rao and Hajra, 1977), till the story ended with the whole slope being cleared for development. By 1974, only a few plants survived with the associate species, *Bergenia ligulata* (Wall.) Engl., under the shelter of a rock.

Very few old herbaria and gardens exist in India, a country of over 3 million sq. km. Only four herbaria, namely the Central National Herbarium, Calcutta (CAL), the herbarium of the Forest Research Institute, Dehra Dun (DD), the herbarium of Botanical Survey of India, Coimbatore (MH) and the Blatter Herbarium at St Xavier's College, Bombay (BLAT), can claim to have any noteworthy collections from before 1900. This makes reconstructing the historical background of species distributions very difficult.

Techniques and constraints in conservation

Sanctuaries for individual species or groups of threatened species, whenever it is possible to establish them, are the best means of conservation. It has been possible to establish sanctuaries for *Nepenthes* in the Khasi Hills and for rhododendrons and primulas in Sikkim.

About a dozen areas in the country which are considered unique ecosystems and rich in threatened plant species are presently under study as prospective areas for being declared as Biosphere Reserves under the Unesco 'Man and the Biosphere' programme.

Another approach is by controls on trade in threatened species. India is a signatory to the Convention on International Trade in Endangered Species of Wild Fauna and Flora (CITES). Due to the efforts of the Indian National Committee, two rare orchids, *Vanda coerulea* Griff. and *Renanthera imschootiana* Rolfe, are now on Appendix I. Fortunately, certain restrictions on collections of plants and plant products from wild populations and their export have been in force in India even before the ratification of the Convention.

Establishment of 'germ-plasm banks' is also important. Considerable literature has been generated recently on the role of botanic gardens in conservation, chiefly due to the efforts of botanists of the Royal Botanic Gardens, Kew, and the University Botanic Garden, Cambridge (see Synge and Townsend, 1979). The activities of botanic gardens in India have been reviewed by Jain (1979). A start has been made in the experimental gardens of the Botanical Survey of India. For example, several species of *Rhododendron, Anoectochilus, Paphiopedilum, Dendrobium, Cymbidium, Coelogyne, Arundina* and other orchids are being grown in the Experimental Garden and Orchidarium at Shillong; *Nepenthes, Psilotum nudum* (L.) Beauv. and *Platycerium wallichii* Hook. are cultivated in the Botanic Garden at Howrah. The National Bureau of Plant Genetic Resources, New Delhi, and the National Botanical Research Institute, Lucknow, are also building germ-plasm collections of selected groups, particularly of the economically more useful genera. Thompson (1975) has reviewed the limitations of botanic gardens and other collections of living plants for conservation of germ-plasm.

Very little effort on conservation through seed banks has been possible so far in India. Thompson (1974, 1979) has reviewed the prospects of seed banks as a means of conservation. Olsen and Arnklit (1979) have written on how to set up a small seed bank.

The merits and prospects of re-introduction into the wild have been described by Jain and Kataki (1977). Professor Walter Lewis mentioned to the senior author (S. K. Jain) some advantages of wild-simulated populations on the basis of his experience with Ginseng in the USA. No organized large-scale effort in this area is being made to the knowledge of the authors. But it is proposed to put back some of the rare orchids from the cultivated populations of our orchidaria into suitable natural habitats.

Detailed data on biology and autecology of rare species are very important for monitoring populations, for successful re-introduction and for assessing causes of natural extinction (Cook, 1976; Lucas and Synge, 1978). Autecological work has been done on many species in India by Misra and his students at Varanasi, Saugar, Rajkot, Ujjain, Gorakhpur, Shillong, Indore, etc. We have not yet been able to analyse whether any of these studies cover threatened species.

The primary constraint, not only perhaps in our country but also elsewhere, and even among some botanists, is lack of concern and awareness about the threats to our floras (Heslop-Harrison, 1972; Prance, 1977; Raven, 1977; US National Research Council, 1980). Jain and Sastry (1978, 1980) have stressed this point in relation to the threatened flora of India.

The very large number of taxa, many seemingly of no practical value at present, is another serious constraint, rendering conservation management unwieldy and uneconomic. A related problem is lack of trained manpower; the subject of conservation requires an interdisciplinary approach, including fields such as taxonomy, phytogeography, autecology, population biology and physiology. Few people with knowledge of all these subjects are available and studies often tend to become narrow and partial.

Furthermore, the economic dependence of forest dwellers or traders on certain rare species inhibits control on their over-exploitation. For example, collections from the wild of *Coptis, Podophyllum, Rauvolfia* and many orchids bring easy income to local collectors or traders, and some of them try to thwart efforts on conservation.

The forest dwellers and certain tribal communities in India enjoy special rights to use the forests; these too sometimes result in depletion of rare taxa. Also, fancy for specimens or souvenirs of botanical curiosities such as all carnivorous plants, *Gnetum* and *Psilotum*, contributes to over-exploitation, even by botanists.

The actual methods of conservation *in situ* (that is, other than in the gardens and seed banks) under varying conditions are not well-defined. On a long-term basis, they also need heavy investments. Yet the destruction of habitats rich in endemic and threatened plants for inescapable development activities is unavoidable to a great extent. The case of the Lady's Slipper orchid, *Paphiopedilum fairrieanum*, discussed above, serves as a good example of this.

Threatened habitats

A simple and convincing definition of a threatened habitat seems to be one in which representative samples are not available elsewhere and whose annihilation can result in loss of that type of ecosystem.

Techniques and constraints in survey

For each area botanical exploration is necessary to gather data on the frequency of constituent species, in particular the rare plants. Work along these lines has been initiated in some areas such as Silent Valley in Kerala, Similipal in Orissa and Kanchendzunga in Sikkim.

Multidisciplinary studies on the ecosystem are also required. One such study is being initiated in Western Ghats at Idukki in Kerala.

To monitor changes, base-line or bench-mark data are necessary. Work has been initiated in some areas such as Kaziranga in Assam and Idukki and Silent Valley in Kerala.

It is valuable to have liaison with various agencies concerned with planning and development activities at national and state level for advance information on any significant deforestation, road-cutting, etc. This policy has now been adopted by the government and impact assessment is obligatory.

As with threatened species, the constraints are again a lack of data – few old base-lines are available for assessing the changes that have already occurred or for monitoring the evolution of the ecosystem; the magnitude of the task bearing in mind the vast size of India, the many types of habitat and the lack of resources of all kinds; and lack of techniques – simple methods for quick surveys to assess ecological impacts have not yet been developed and at present too many models are needed to depict the various parameters of an ecosystem.

Techniques and constraints in conservation

Establishment of biosphere reserves and in some areas conservation units of lower status such as national parks and sanctuaries seems to be the only solution. Though no biosphere reserves have so far been established, numerous national parks and wild life sanctuaries exist in India.

There is also an interesting category of forest areas in India called the 'Sacred Groves'. These are usually densely wooded areas protected from all biotic interferences simply due to religious faith and belief that any damage to the ecosystem may bring wrath from supernatural powers. Gadgil and Vartak (1975) and Hajra (1975) have written on the role of Sacred Groves in conservation and described some such groves.

The constraints include a lack of awareness and apathy, a point discussed earlier, and the legal rights of forest dwellers and others to exploit the forests. Furthermore many threatened habitats are on private property; for example, in the State of Meghalaya in Eastern India, about 90 per cent of the forested land is in private ownership. Laws on conservation are not yet perfect. The detailed laws required for satisfactory implementation of conservation of wild life, or punishment to those who violate, are still in the process of being made.

Generally it is the forest departments who are asked to undertake various conservation measures, in addition to other programmes in their hands. They are usually fully occupied with silvicultural operations, economic plantations and general forestry administration. Conservation of threatened habitats or particular species does not always receive priority with them. There is therefore a need for a unified agency.

Since the adverse impacts are not readily seen and cannot be converted convincingly into economic terms, there is apathy and even opposition to conservation measures from several quarters. For example, considerable literature has recently been generated with regard to the development project on Silent Valley, trying to challenge or contradict all scientific data put forth in support of conservation of that unique ecosystem. Immediate gains tend to take precedence over long-term considerations. Costs of management of forest reserves are also exorbitant in contrast to seemingly no economic returns.

Conclusion

The problems of conserving threatened plants and habitats in India are numerous. Recently, however, there has been much more awareness of the problem among official and non-official agencies, and research in many supporting areas such as taxonomic revisions, floristic accounts and impact assessments has been intensified.

Acknowledgements

The authors are grateful to the Department of Science and Technology, Government of India, for permitting participation in the conference, and to the Commonwealth Foundation for supporting the travel of the senior author to Cambridge.

References

Cook, C. D. K. (1976). 'Autecology', in *Conservation of Threatened Plants* (Eds. J. B. Simmons, R. I. Beyer, P. E. Brandham, G. Ll. Lucas and V. T. H. Parry), pp. 207–10, Plenum Press, New York and London.

Cook, C. D. K. (1980*a*). Personal communication.

Cook, C. D. K. (1980*b*). 'The status of some Indian endemic plants', *Threatened Plants Committee Newsletter*, **6**, 17–18, Kew, England.

Das, S. and Jain, S. K. (1980). 'Orchidaceae: *Coelogyne*' in *Fasc. Fl. India*, **5**, 1–33.

Gadgil, M. and Vartak, V. D. (1975). 'Sacred groves of India – a plea for continuing conservation', *J. Bombay Nat. Hist. Soc.*, **72**, 314–20.

Hajra, P. K. (1975). *Law–Lyngdoh (Sacred Grove) Mawphlang – Visitor's Guide*, Government Press, Shillong.

Henry, A. N., Vivekananthan, K. and Nair, N. C. (1978). 'Rare and threatened flowering plants of south India', *J. Bombay Nat. Hist. Soc.*, **75**, 684–97.

Heslop-Harrison, J. (1972). 'The Plant-Kingdom: An exhaustible resource?', *Trans. Bot. Soc. Edinburgh*, **42**, 1–15.

Jain, S. K. (1967). 'Notes on Indian grasses – VIII. *Manisuris divergens* (Hack.) Kuntze collected after thirteen decades', *Bull. Bot. Surv. India*, **9**, 293–4.

Jain, S. K. (1971). 'A note on *Arthraxon microphyllus* (Trin.) Hochst. (Poaceae)', *Indian For.*, **97**, 220–2.

Jain, S. K. (1972). 'The genus *Arthraxon* P. Beauv. (Poaceae) in India', *J. Indian Bot. Soc.*, **51**, 165–83.

Jain, S. K. (1979). 'India: Botanic gardens and threatened plants – A report', in *Survival or Extinction* (Eds. H. Synge and H. Townsend), pp. 113–16, Bentham–Moxon Trust, Kew.

Jain, S. K. and Kataki, S. K. (1977). 'Orchid culture with afforestation programme', *Indian Farming*, **26**, 99–101.

Jain, S. K. and Sastry, A. R. K. (1978). 'Plant resources of the Himalayas', in *Proc. Nat. Seminar on Resources, Development and Environment in the Himalayan Region*, pp. 98–107, Department of Science and Technology, New Delhi.

Jain, S. K. and Sastry, A. R. K. (1980). *Threatened Plants of India – A State-of-the-Art Report*, Botanical Survey of India, Howrah.

Lucas, G. and Synge, H. (1978). *The IUCN Plant Red Data Book*, Morges, Switzerland.

Olsen, O. and Arnklit, F. (1979). 'Setting up a practical small seed bank', in *Survival or Extinction* (Eds. H. Synge and H. Townsend), pp. 185–8, Bentham–Moxon Trust, Kew.

Prance, G. T. (1977). 'Floristic inventory of the tropics: where do we stand?', *Ann. Missouri Bot. Gard.*, **64**, 659–84.

Rao, A. S. and Hajra, P. K. (1977). '*Paphiopedilum fairieanum* (Lindl.) Pfitz. – Habitat, descriptive and cultural notes', *Indian For.*, **103**, 29–32.

Raven, P. H. (1977). 'Perspectives in tropical botany: Concluding remarks', *Ann. Missouri Bot. Gard.*, **64**, 746–8.

Synge, H. and Townsend, H. (Eds.) (1979). *Survival or Extinction*, Bentham–Moxon Trust, Kew.

Thompson, P. A. (1974). 'The use of seed-banks for conservation of populations of species and ecotypes', *Biol. Conserv.*, **6**, 15–19.

Thompson, P. A. (1975). 'Should botanic gardens save rare plants?', *New Scientist*, 636–8.

Thompson, P. A. (1979). 'Preservation of plant resources in gene banks within botanic gardens', in *Survival or Extinction* (Eds. H. Synge and H. Townsend), pp. 179–84, Bentham–Moxon Trust, Kew.

US National Research Council (1980). *Research Priorities in Tropical Biology*, National Academy of Sciences, Washington, DC.

Vivekananthan, K. (in press). 'Floristic studies in Idukki district, Kerala', *Bull. Bot. Surv. India*.

The Biological Aspects of Rare Plant Conservation
Edited by Hugh Synge, published by John Wiley & Sons Ltd.

4
Threatened plants of New Zealand: Documentation in a series of islands

DAVID R. GIVEN *Botany Division, DSIR, Christchurch*

Summary

New Zealand is a continental island with a high level of species endemism, a considerable waif element and great habitat diversity. The vulnerability of the flora and degree of vegetational change in historic times requires flexible but comprehensive documentation. Seven criteria are suggested for documentation to be most useful and the three systems used in New Zealand are briefly described. The problems of categories of rarity are discussed, including recognition of 'local' taxa. Priorities for conservation are suggested: preservation of maximum genetic diversity with prior attention to endemic higher taxa, consideration of regions or habitats undergoing rapid change, and documentation of taxa found in regions of high endemism.

Introduction

New Zealand is an archipelago consisting of three main islands (North Island, South Island and Stewart Island) with a combined area of about 275 000 sq. km and numerous off-shore and outlying islands. The main groups of satellite islands are the Kermadecs, Chathams and the scattered subantarctic islands (Figure 1). The New Zealand region stretches from about 29°S to 55°S, which in European terms is from about the Canary Islands to Denmark. A great diversity of climates is found in the region, ranging from subtropical on the Kermadecs to windy, cool, moist conditions on Campbell and Macquarie Islands in the far south. Geology is also highly varied with some parts of the main islands and the subantarctic islands being relatively old (pre-Cretaceous) but other islands such as the Kermadec group being of recent volcanic origin.

Along with some other islands such as Japan, New Caledonia and Fiji, New Zealand can be classed as a continental island harbouring not only waif biotic elements derived by long-distance dispersal, but also older elements presumably dating from times when New Zealand was connected or nearly connected with larger land masses (Carlquist, 1974). It is about 80 million years since New Zealand separated from southern continental Gondwanaland (Fleming, 1979) and

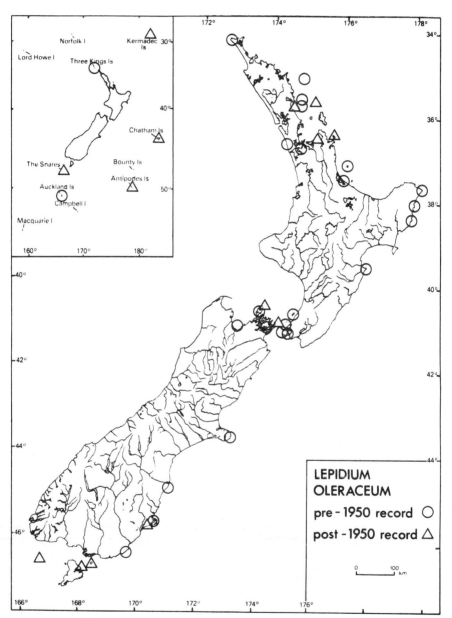

Figure 1   Distribution of *Lepidium oleraceum* (Cruciferae)

there has been ample opportunity for the immigration of a waif biota and its subsequent evolution in New Zealand. Within the islands making up the New Zealand botanical region there has been secondary dispersal with the evolution of distinct but related taxa on various island groups such as the Three Kings, Kermadec and Chatham Islands.

At the species level endemism is high in the New Zealand region; for higher plants it is about 81 per cent (Godley, 1975). Approximately 40 genera are endemic but no families are confined to the region although five have limited distribution elsewhere (E. J. Godley, pers. comm.). The level of endemism is particularly high on some outlying island groups where distinctive genera such as *Myosotidium* (Boraginaceae), *Elingamita* (Myrsinaceae) and *Pleurophyllum* (Compositae) occur. The New Zealand endemics clearly belong to both the older continental element and the younger waif element of the flora.

Even within the main islands of New Zealand there are insular characteristics. The alpine regions, for example, are discontinuous and separated by low passes and deep valleys which are effective barriers to dispersal. Sharp climatic gradients and topographical and geological discontinuities have resulted in considerable diversity of habitat over short distances. With the exception of forest, few homogeneous vegetation types extended continuously for more than a few tens of kilometres in primeval New Zealand. Insular features on the New Zealand mainland are probably similar to those described by Carlquist (1974) for 'nearly insular' freshwater lakes and equatorial highlands, and by Culver (1970) for caves.

Islands are notoriously vulnerable to the influence of man, both directly and indirectly through animal and plant introductions. The flora of New Zealand has evolved in the absence of grazing mammals and of man. Polynesians probably reached the country from the Pacific Islands to the north about 900 AD (McCulloch and Trotter, 1974). These early colonizers introduced a number of subtropical plants, and are estimated to have reduced the extent of forest cover to about 53 per cent of the land area (Wendelken, 1976). European occupation has reduced it to approximately 23 per cent, and has drastically depleted other vegetation types such as scrublands, wetlands and coastal communities. Feral mammals such as goats, chamois, European red deer and Australian brush-tailed opossums have modified a vegetation which previously was grazed only by grasshoppers and birds (e.g. Greenwood and Atkinson, 1977). The number of naturalized higher plants is probably about equal to the indigenous flora and in many lowland regions the indigenous flora and vegetation is an insignificant part of the landscape. Many species have declined since settlement. For example, the endemic crucifer *Lepidium oleraceum* was common enough to be used as an antiscorbutic by James Cook in 1769 but is now only known from a scattering of very small populations on off-shore and outlying islands (Figure 1).

The generally insular nature of the flora is reflected in the occurrence of numerous very locally distributed species both on off-shore and outlying islands, and on the mainland. These include, however, both 'continental' relicts and species and genera which have a waif origin. Two rare species, *Epilobium gunnianum* (Raven and Raven, 1976) and the orchid *Cryptostylis subulata* may only have reached New Zealand in the last few decades (Graham, 1976).

The nature of the threatened portion of New Zealand's flora affects its conservation in three ways. First, the wide range of types of 'rarity' demands flexibility whether at the level of documentation or in management. Secondly, the vegetation is adjusting itself to change so that even within the space of a few years geographic range and abundance of taxa can change significantly. Thirdly, the insularity and diversity of New Zealand means that there is a need to document and conserve at the local as well as the national level. None of these features is unique to New Zealand although they are probably a particular feature of islands in general at the present time.

Criteria for documentation

An integrated approach to threatened species conservation should have six aspects: documentation of individual taxa, provision of effective and appropriate legislation, reservation of selected wild populations in their natural habitat, garden cultivation, research into the biological parameters of the plants, and education of both the general public and botanists. Although all aspects are important, the effectiveness of the last five is largely determined by the thoroughness and accuracy of the first aspect – that is, documentation.

Taxa and their distributions should be clearly identified

Documentation systems should use names familiar to users or found in standard Floras and accessible literature. Many users of a documentation system are unschooled in the finer points of nomenclature and there is a strong case for the use of common names alongside latin binomials. Similarly, the general geographic range of each entity should be stated unambiguously without giving precise locality details.

Circumscription should be clearly indicated

When we talk about threatened plants we usually mean vascular plants only and most lists, registers and data books limit their scope to these. It is not always obvious if a whole flora has been screened or if only a selection is included, and whether only endemic species are being considered (e.g. Harley and Leigh, 1979) or all indigenous species including those found elsewhere (e.g. Argus and White, 1977; Perring and Farrell, 1977). *The IUCN Plant Red Data Book* (Lucas and Synge, 1978) deals with only a selection of the world's threatened plants (250 out of an estimated 20 000–25 000 species). Although the title page of the volume clearly states this, users tend to cite the contents as if it were comprehensive and all-inclusive.

Another aspect is the area covered; it needs to be made clear whether the plants are rare only within a certain area or throughout their whole range.

Data should be in a standard, directly comparable form

Merely asking for vague suggestions for a 'protected plant list' is an ineffectual method of approach likely to result in a motley collection of colourful large-flowered alpine and coastal plants, selections of conspicuous forest trees, species which are regional and national emblems, and a residue reflecting the parochial interests and personal idiosyncrasies of contributors. Terminology and categories need to be rigorously defined so that they are applied without ambiguity to all the species being covered.

It is useful to adopt a standard format for all entries to allow quick location of relevant information, and to show where data are missing.

Data should be accurate, comprehensive and up-to-date

Suspect or unsubstantiated information should be deleted or there should be clear indication of its nature and source. The date when specimens were collected can be of critical importance. For example indiscriminate citing of all records of *Lepidium oleraceum* without regard to their date gives an erroneous impression of its abundance as shown by Figure 1.

Data particularly relevant to management should be emphasized

Those with a responsibility for land management or implementing conservation programmes cannot be expected to spend a great deal of time searching through a mass of information to find what is relevant to their needs. Details such as general locality, habitat, and threats (both past and future) must be easily discerned. It is particularly useful to indicate if taxa are in cultivation or in a formal reserve.

Information must be effectively disseminated

Documentation is not an end in itself but provides background material for the conservation of species. It is one thing to accumulate information but quite another to disseminate it to those who will make best use of it. Agencies involved in land management and conservation programmes should be made aware of documentation schemes and of the species found in areas under their control.

TAXON: PITTOSPORUM DALLII Cheeseman Manual N.Z. Flora 1906, 1134.

1

Family: PITTOSPORACEAE   **Compiled by:** DRG   **Date:** 1977

DISTRIBUTION

Endemic to New Zealand Botanical Region ☑   **If not, indicate overseas range:**

Current Distribution in New Zealand Botanical Region: South Island: Boulder Lake, Snows River, Slate River, Cobb Ridge and head of Takaka River

Past Distribution in New Zealand Botanical Region: Probably similar

Type Locality: Specimen Creek, Nelson

FOLLOWING COMMENTS APPLY ONLY TO AREA IN REPORT

Report Applies to Whole Area of Current Distribution ☑

If not, indicate:

Herbarium: Snows River, Potts, 1947 (CHR); Snows River, Hay, 1951 (CHR); Snows River, Gibbs, 1914 (CHR); Cobb Valley: various collections at CHR - Holloway, 1975, Marshall, 1955, Pettersen, 1951, Moore, 1964, Pettersen, 1952, Lord, 1962, Wardle, 1960, Given, 1966, Brockie, 1965, Butcher, 1970, Talbot, 1971, Druce, 1974; Boulder Lake to Anatoki River, Soper, 1951, (CHR); Near Boulder Lake, Gibbs, 1912 (WELT); Snows Valley, Gibbs, 1913 (WELT); "Mountains near Collingwood", Dall (AK - type); Boulder Lake, Gibbs, 1912 (AK).

Other Records: J.Bartlett, pers.comm. - Magnesite Mine. Patterson & Patterson (1956) refer to a specimen in WELT labelled as Pelorus Sound, and to verbal reports from near Korere - not further substantiated.

Collection Dates 1850 60 70 80 90 1900 10 20 30 40 50 60 70 80 90
|⌐......|........|........|........|..X...|.X......|........|........|.X|.X..X.|.XXXX|XXX...|.......|

POPULATIONS

No. of Known Populations: Several   **Average Size:** No more than a dozen trees.

Location of Largest: Probably greatest numbers are on the Cobb Ridge east of the hydro lake; young plants occur along the road here.

ECOLOGY Rocky forested creeks, among large granite boulders, on forest margins and in beech forest 600-1000 m altitude. It appears to favour open habitats in the early stages of growth and Patterson & Patterson (1956) note its appearance along the road to the Cobb dam where it grows on clay bulldozed banks.

PROPAGATION AND CULTIVATION

Reproduction in Wild: none ☐   rare ☐   adequate ☑   abundant ☐   no data ☐

Artificial Propagation: easy ☐   moderate ☑   difficult ☐   no data ☐

Cultivation: scientific ☑   botanic garden ☑   private garden ☑   commercial ☐

A few plants are in cultivation, e.g. DSIR, Lincoln, Cawthron Institute, Nelson.

REFERENCES:
Patterson & Patterson, 1956
Moore & Adams, 1949

NOTES:
Patterson & Patterson give a detailed account of its occurrence as known in the early 1950's. This is an attractive tree noted as being sweetly scented in flower.

Figure 2   Data sheet for *Threatened Plants of New Zealand*

DISTURBANCE OF TAXON

Past Disturbance (left column):

Disturbance of forest in connection with early mining activity probably affected the populations near Boulder Lake. The Cobb ridge plants were disturbed during road formation in the 1950's.

Future Disturbance (right column):

Animal damage has not been documented although there seems to be a paucity of seedlings at many sites. Loss of individuals could continue in the Cobb area unless appropriate steps are taken (see below). The activities of predators in the form of over-enthusiastic plant collectors are an ever present risk for a species notorious for its rarity. Disturbance by mining in the upper Takaka Valley is a ~~ever present~~ possibility.

		farming/grazing
		forestry/harvesting
		burning
✓	✓	road construction
		building
		industry
		hydro development
		flooding/irrigation
		draining/reclamation
✓	✓	mining/quarrying
		recreational devt.
		noxious animals
		habitat pollution
	✓	indiscriminate coll.
		(other):

RESERVES

L. & S. Flora and Fauna ☐	Nat. Park Spec. Area ☐	NZFS Scientific Reserve ☐
L. & S. Scientific ☐	NZFS Research Area ☐	NZFS Flora & Fauna ☐
L. & S. Scenic ☐	Nat. Park Wilderness ☐	NZFS Wilderness/Sc. Area ☐
National Park General ☐	NZFS State Forest ☐	NZFS Forest Park ☑

Other reserve type (specify):

Comments: Much of north-west Nelson (the Tasman Mountains) is now included in Forest Park; known populations of this species are assured of some degree of protection.

CONSERVATION MEASURES

Taken Already: The plant is in limited cultivation. It may be grown from seed and this could be encouraged. The areas where it grows naturally enjoy limited reserve status.

Recommended (indicate in column):

The populations at Snows River and Slate River could be best preserved in their present state by discouraging development of the area. Those at Cobb ridge are more at risk - the area has been developed for mining and the main access road to the Cobb hydro dam passes through the area where the Pittosporum is probably most abundant. Recording of the position of individuals and sites of maximum regeneration would provide information useful to engineers and others should road alignments be carried out or buildings, etc., erected.

monitoring	✓
reservation	
stricter reservation	✓
animal control	
harvesting controls	
propagation	
cultivation	✓
planting into wild	
legislative controls	

CONSERVATION STATUS SUMMARY

Endangered Number

☐	0	Presumed extinct in wild
☑	I	Endangered
☐	2	Rare
☐	3	Depleted
☐	4	Local

Taxon in cultivation ⊘

Taxonomic relationships uncertain ◯

Threat Number

0	I	②	3	4	Distribution
0	①	2	3	4	Accessibility
0	I	2	3	④	Attractiveness
⓪	I	2	3	4	Abundance change
0	I	②	3	4	Reservation
0	①	2	3	4	Site threat

Geographic range uncertain ◯

Present Conservation Measures:

non-existent ◯   minimal ◯   adequate ⊘   good ◯   excellent ◯

Mechanisms must exist for updating and revision

Information on species at risk quickly becomes out of date. The documentation of species at risk records a constantly changing situation and there will be frequent need to review existing data and to disseminate new or modified material.

Documentation systems in New Zealand

Two lists of threatened plants for the New Zealand botanical region have been published (Given, 1976, 1979) and a further list is in preparation. The first list was a preliminary one including not only entities known to be at risk, but also those suspected of being in this category. The second list is more critical and includes the IUCN 'Red Data Book categories' for each species – see Appendix 3 to this book. These lists are a basis for the systematic compilation of reports on plants at risk and include a loose-leaf register and Red Data Book entries. Lists have not been prepared for lower plants.

A continuing scheme started in 1976 is a register of taxa called *Threatened Plants of New Zealand*. This is a series of two-page reports for each species (Figure 2) arranged in a loose-leaf binder which allows new reports to be inserted in whatever order is convenient. The register applies to all indigenous higher plants whether or not endemic to New Zealand and includes infraspecific taxa. About 50 per cent of the species listed in Given (1979) have been covered so far, and the scheme is described in more detail there and in Given (1976).

The loose-leaf register reports do not include detailed descriptions of the sites where species at risk occur, but give generalized descriptions of the areas concerned. This is to prevent locality information being used indiscriminately and possibly leading to unwarranted disturbance of the plants. At present, requests for detailed site information are treated individually by reference to the original records.

A red data book has been proposed for animals and plants of New Zealand to be published late in 1981. It will include only endemic taxa, and infraspecific taxa will not be dealt with unless they are of particular interest (e.g. *Ranunculus crithmifolius* ssp. *paucifolius*). For the most part, only taxa in the IUCN 'Red Data Book categories' of Extinct, Endangered and Vulnerable are likely to be considered. The general format will approximate that of *The IUCN Plant Red Data Book* of Lucas and Synge (1978). This will make information on about 40 per cent of the more threatened species available to a wider, international audience, although as a bound volume it will become progressively out-of-date following publication. Fourteen plants endemic to the New Zealand region are included in Lucas and Synge (1978) which, as mentioned above, is a world-wide selection of threatened taxa.

The problem of categories

Some of the most vexing problems in documenting threatened plants arise from differences of opinion over what taxa should be included and to what categories they should be assigned. As Du Mond (1973) points out, the term 'rare' (used in a general sense and not as a strict category) is elusive and has no concrete meaning. He suggested that a 'rare plant species is one that is not usually found within its total range by those who have occasion and ability to recognize it'. Alongside this Du Mond suggests nine guidelines to be used in the selection of 'rare' species of vascular plants. His approach is a useful one for, regardless of whether we agree or disagree with his criteria, it is an attempt to grapple with the diversity of types of rarity.

There is probably substantial agreement on a core group of plants at risk in New Zealand as elsewhere. *Tecomanthe speciosa* (Bignoniaceae) is known in the wild from a single plant on the Three Kings Islands and is undeniably endangered. The Castle Hill Buttercup (*Ranunculus crithmifolius* ssp. *paucifolius*), *Baumea complanata*, and *Gunnera hamiltonii* are known only from single populations of a few hundred individuals or less and are, in most people's eyes, endangered. Plants endemic to small islands often come into this category of species existing as single populations. At the next level up, where there are several populations but the total number of plants is comparable to a single population, there is often substantial agreement. For example, *Celmisia adamsii* var. *adamsii* of the Coromandel Peninsula, North Island, is known from several localities but the number of plants in the wild is probably only 200–300.

A more difficult situation is reached when there are many very small or declining populations, the plant exists as scattered individuals or it is common over a very restricted area. New Zealand examples are *Fuchsia procumbens* of the northern North Island coast, *Myrsine coxii* of the Chatham Islands and *Davallia tasmanii* of the Three Kings Islands. In some respects a species like *Myrsine coxii* is under greater threat than the Castle Hill Buttercup because each isolated individual or group of plants is exceedingly vulnerable to depletion or even elimination. A particular problem is posed by those species which appear to be relatively widespread but which are believed in at least some areas to be disappearing or declining in numbers. An example in New Zealand is *Desmoschoenus spiralis* (Cyperaceae). The shrinking of its geographic range is comparable to that of *Lepidium oleraceum*, discussed earlier, but the species is more difficult to assess because there are few figures or accurate observations available from which to assess the rate or degree of depletion in absolute terms.

I do not think that the solution lies in adopting a geographically based cut-off point as was done for the *British Red Data Book* (Perring and Farrell, 1977), where the species included are 'native and probably native species which were recorded in 15 or fewer 10 kilometre squares from 1930 onwards'. In New Zealand this would exclude some taxa that were widespread but whose populations were very low. Du Mond's approach seems to me to be more promising: that terms are not defined formally but that clear guidelines be used to indicate the *kinds* of taxa which may be regarded as at risk and the levels of threat to which they can be assigned. Although the New Zealand documentation system began with its own set of definitions (Given, 1976), I have increasingly used the IUCN 'Red Data Book categories'. An additional category in New Zealand is 'local' for taxa which do not strictly qualify for any of the IUCN categories but which are sufficiently infrequent or in small enough numbers that their presence at particular sites is worth noting. Some of these such as *Coprosma intertexta* (Rubiaceae) occur in habitats which are suffering from attrition; monitoring them now should allow more effective conservation when and if they become species at risk in the future.

Determining priorities for conservation

One of the chief purposes of a documentation scheme for species at risk should be to indicate which species are in most urgent need of protection, whether from restricted geographic distribution, small population size, vulnerability or deterioration of habitat, poor reproductive capacity, exploitation by man, decline due to competition with other plants or predation by animals.

One way of determining which taxa should receive first order conservation is to assume that New Zealand has an international obligation to preserve examples of genetic diversity throughout its whole flora. First priority should be given to preserving those taxa which are confined to the region and which differ most from taxa found in other parts of the world. In practice it means ensuring that endemic families and genera are conserved before endemic species belonging to genera with overseas representatives. No families of higher plants are endemic to the New Zealand region, but Godley (1975) lists 39 endemic genera to which can be added *Toronia* (formerly *Persoonia toru*), *Knightia* (two New Caledonian species now removed from the genus) and *Trilepidea* (= *Elytranthe adamsti*). The fern genus *Anarthropteris* is probably also endemic. Table 1 lists the wholly or partly threatened endemic genera, which amount to over 25 per cent of the total outlined above. Surprisingly, most of these genera are threatened to a high degree, some acutely so. *Elingamita*, for example, is known only from a few trees on the Three Kings Islands; less than 300 individuals of *Chordospartium* may exist in the wild. *Loxoma* is an interesting example of a taxon at risk; its only near relative is *Loxomopsis* which consists of several very rare central American species. Collectively they constitute the fern family Loxomaceae, the sole member of the order Loxomales (Pichi Sermolli, 1977). Of the genera in Table 1, *Chordospartium*, *Desmoschoenus* and *Sporadanthus* are not in adequate reserves,

Table 1　Endemic genera of New Zealand which are wholly or partly at risk

Genus	Family	No. of species	Degree of threat
Chordospartium	Leguminosae	1	Endangered*
Dactylanthus	Balanophoraceae	1	Vulnerable
Desmoschoenus	Cyperaceae	1	Vulnerable
Elingamita	Myrsinaceae	1	Endangered
Loxoma	Loxomaceae	1	Rare
Myosotidium	Boraginaceae	1	Vulnerable
Notospartium	Leguminosae	3	1 Endangered, 2 Vulnerable
Simplicia	Gramineae	2	1 Vulnerable, 1 Rare
Stilbocarpa	Araliaceae	3	1 Endangered, 1 Vulnerable
Sporadanthus	Restionaceae	1	Vulnerable
Teucridium	Verbenaceae	1	Rare
Trilepidea	Loranthaceae	1	Extinct

*IUCN 'Red Data Book categories' after Lucas and Synge (1978) and outlined in Appendix 3

and most are not widely cultivated. *Dactylanthus* is threatened by use for ornamental purposes as the 'wood rose'.

Another approach is to consider those regions and habitats where rapid environmental changes are taking place. Such an example is North Auckland at the northern end of North Island, which is increasingly exposed to use by New Zealand's largest centre of population (Auckland) and is regarded as having considerable potential for agriculture, forestry, tourism and mining (Northland Regional Development Council, 1978). Within its boundaries are more than 60 taxa at risk, about one third of which are endemic to the region. Much of the remaining areas of more or less natural vegetation in Auckland may be threatened in the near future, making conservation of representative examples of vegetation and individual species a matter of urgency. A second example is provided by wetlands. Although it is difficult to estimate their pre-European extent, the degree of depletion can be suggested from two North Island areas, North Auckland and Bay of Plenty. In the former, only 0.8 per cent of the land area is expected to remain as wetland by the end of this century, and in the latter less than 1 per cent of former wetlands survive today (Thompson, 1979). Although the number of species at risk is not as high as in some other vegetation types, the extent of depletion and destruction of habitat has resulted in a high proportion of species being classed as Endangered or Vulnerable. The value of considering regions or geographically restricted habitats is that it allows an 'insular' approach, considering particularly threatened areas or communities as islands within a more stable sea of other regions and communities. It allows for the possibility of including several threatened species within a single reserve, and a consideration of networks of reserves to preserve a series of populations.

A third approach, which only becomes practicable when a significant proportion of plants have been documented and mapped, is to look for areas of
endemism, or geographical concentrations of species at risk. These are likely to
mark areas of unusual habitat, sites which are markedly isolated or where there
has been particularly severe habitat depletion. It may be assumed that such sites
are functionally 'islands' differing greatly from the more uniform biological sea
around them. In New Zealand, the northernmost part of the North Island at
North Cape has several endemics over an area of only a few square kilometres.
North Cape is an isolated block of laterite soils on serpentine, and has at various
times in the past been isolated as a sea-surrounded island. Banks Peninsula on the
east coast of the South Island is another centre of endemism, as are the Eyre
Mountains in the southern South Island. The Castle Hill basin in inland eastern
South Island is a locality where not only do local endemics occur on isolated
Tertiary limestones surrounded by greywacke mountains, but also populations
survive of depleted species now largely eliminated from other localities.

It is sometimes suggested that a 'triage' strategy is appropriate for setting
priorities for conservation of species at risk. (By 'triage' we mean a way of deciding which threatened species to conserve actively and which to leave to their fate.)
Where a flora is poorly known, or extinction is likely for some species because of
the rate of depletion, this may be so. However, in New Zealand, with the possible
exception of some lower plant groups, other means of determining priorities for
conservation seem more appropriate.

In New Zealand, documentation is only one aspect of the general conservation
of threatened plants, which in turn is one part of the overall conservation of the
New Zealand biota. Our obligations are international for as Sherwin Carlquist
wrote in 1974:

> The faunas and floras of oceanic islands possess many distinctive
> characteristics that have long attracted attention. Interest in these lands as
> 'evolutionary laboratories' crystallised during the Darwin–Wallace era and
> has not yet diminished.

References

Allan, H. H. (1961). *Flora of New Zealand 1*, Government Printer, Wellington.
Argus, G. W. and White, D. J. (1977). 'The rare vascular plants of Ontario', *Syllogeus*, **14**.
Carlquist, S. (1974). *Island Biology*, Columbia, New York.
Culver, D. C. (1970). 'Analysis of simple cave communities: I. Caves as islands',
    Evolution, **24**, 463–74.
Du Mond, D. M. (1973). 'A guide for the selection of rare, unique and endangered plants',
    Castanea, **38**, 387–95.
Fleming, C. A. (1979). *The Geological History of New Zealand and its Life*, Auckland
    University/Oxford University.
Given, D. R. (1976). 'A register of rare and endangered indigenous plants in New
    Zealand', *N.Z. Jl Bot.*, **14**, 135–49.

Given, D. R. (1979). 'Threatened plants in New Zealand', in *A Vanishing Heritage: the problem of endangered species and their habitats* (Nature Conservation Council), pp. 22–45, New Zealand Nature Conservation Council, Wellington.

Godley, E. J. (1975). 'Flora and vegetation', in *Biogeography and Ecology in New Zealand* (Ed. G. Kuschel), pp. 177–229, Junk, The Hague.

Graham, D. K. F. (1976). 'An Australian orchid, *Cryptostylis subulata* (Labill.) Reichb.f., in northern New Zealand', *N.Z. Jl Bot.*, **14**, 275–7.

Greenwood, R. M. and Atkinson, I. A. E. (1977). 'Evolution of the divaricating plants in New Zealand in relation to moa browsing', *N.Z. Ecol. Soc. Proc.*, **24**, 21–33.

Hartley, W. and Leigh, J. (1979). *Plants at Risk in Australia*, Australian National Parks and Wildlife Service Occ. Paper 3.

Lucas, G. and Synge, H. (1978). *The IUCN Plant Red Data Book*, IUCN, Morges, Switzerland.

McCullough, B. and Trotter, M. (1974). 'The first twenty years. Radiocarbon dates for South Island moa-hunter sites, 1955–74', Pre-print from *N.Z. Archaeol. Assoc. Newsletter*, **18**(1).

Moore, L. B. and Edgar, E. (1970). *Flora of New Zealand 2*, Government Printer, Wellington.

Northland Regional Development Council (1978). *Northland Regional Development Resources Survey*, Whangarei.

Perring, F. H. and Farrell, L. (1977). *British Red Data Books: 1. Vascular Plants*, Society for the Promotion of Nature Conservation, Lincoln.

Pichi Sermolli, R. E. G. (1977). 'Tentamen Pteridophytorum genera in taxonomicum ordinem redigendi', *Webbia*, **31**, 313–512.

Raven, P. H. and Raven, T. E. (1976). 'The Genus *Epilobium* (Onagraceae) in Australasia: A systematic and evolutionary study', *New Zealand Department of Scientific and Industrial Research Bull.*, **216**

Thompson, K. (1979). 'The status of New Zealand's wetlands and peatlands: A question of conflicting interests', in *A Vanishing Heritage: the problem of endangered species and their habitats* (Nature Conservation Council), pp. 65–89, New Zealand Nature Conservation Council, Wellington.

Wendelken, W. J. (1976). 'Forestry', in *New Zealand Atlas* (Ed. I. Wards), pp. 98–103, Government Printer, Wellington.

Note

Plant names in this paper follow Allan (1961) and Moore and Edgar (1970); species described since that time are referenced in the text.

The Biological Aspects of Rare Plant Conservation
Edited by Hugh Synge
© 1981 John Wiley & Sons Ltd.

5
The status of Australian plants at risk

R. B. GOOD *National Parks and Wildlife Service of New South Wales, c/o CSIRO, Canberra, ACT*
and
P. S. LAVARACK *Queensland National Parks and Wildlife Service, c/o Animal Research Institute, Yeeroongpilly, Brisbane, Queensland*

Summary

The high percentage of endemics in the Australian flora makes its conservation an urgent priority. The various lists of plants at risk are assessed and the criteria for species inclusion explained. Data from the latest list are analysed to show where concentrations of threatened species occur. The threat of the cut-flower trade is considered and the conservation value of existing legislation reviewed. Some conservation successes are highlighted and a set of objectives for the future is outlined.

Introduction

Australia, as an island continent long separated from any other continent, has evolved a unique flora, so there is an international responsibility to ensure all species are effectively conserved.

Within the Australian flora two elements have evolved, one centred in the western and one in the eastern half of the continent. Geographical isolation of the eastern and western floras, as with continental isolation, has resulted in many restricted endemics, particularly in the south-west provinces. Eighty per cent of the flora is endemic to the Australian continent.

Australia is a country where agriculture is extensive; land development for farming continues, but new markets for other primary products such as minerals and timber have caused an increasing rate of destruction of natural vegetation during the last decade. Forests cover only 7 per cent of the continent, a very small area, and the recent widespread modification of native forests and continued habitat destruction have resulted in many plant species coming to the verge of extinction.

Small-scale commercial exploitation of native plants for cut flowers has also put pressure on several species for many years, but the recent and increasing appreciation of our flora as a national heritage has led to an extensive, local, interstate and export trade in a much wider range of native wild flowers. Until recently this trade has included many endangered and some rare species and has further threatened their existence. The local and interstate trade also includes many species for use in landscaping, in which a very lucrative market has developed, making the illegal acquisition and sale of several species a 'worthwhile risk', particularly where demand exceeds the supply of stock legally taken from the wild or propagated in nurseries.

The need for some control over the sale of native plants was recognized by the states as early as 1930, but the control of export sales was limited until 1976, when Australia ratified the Convention on International Trade in Endangered Species of Wild Fauna and Flora (CITES). To meet the obligations of this convention, an Endangered Flora Working Group was established to study and recommend plants for listing on the convention appendices. During these studies a list of 'rare', 'endangered' and 'vulnerable' species for each state and for the continent as a whole was prepared. The latter list is now encompassed in *Australian Plants at Risk* (Hartley and Leigh, 1979). The list serves as a basis for the study of all aspects of rare-plant conservation.

Plants at risk

Due to the wide and varied interpretation of the terms 'rare', 'endangered' and 'threatened' by the working-group members and by botanists from herbaria and universities, Hartley and Leigh have produced an hierarchical classification for the distribution and conservation status of listed species. This system defines the status of threatened species in Australia more accurately than other systems. This classification provides a set of codes to show the degree of risk to listed species, as follows:

Distribution category (numerical code)

1. Species known only from the type collection or type locality. Further study usually needed to ascertain present distribution and taxonomic status.
2. Restricted endemics whose known populations are limited in range (e.g. normally less than 100 km in maximum range).
3. Rare species occurring only in small populations, but over a wider area; often restricted to specific habitats (e.g. sandstone areas, high mountain peaks).
4. Species of geographical importance, especially those with a disjunct distribution in Australia and overseas and listed only if the Australian populations are localized or sparse.
5. Species not fitting closely into the above categories, but considered to be at risk. This includes some once common species which, though still widely distributed, have suffered marked depletions in overall population size.

Conservation status (alphabetical code)

X. Species believed to be extinct. Not collected in recent years.
E. 'Endangered'. Species in serious risk of disappearing from the wild state within one or two decades if present land use and other causal factors continue to operate.
V. 'Vulnerable'. Species not presently 'endangered' but at risk over a longer period or if land use patterns are introduced which would be deleterious to the species.
N. Other species listed under 1–5 which are not known to occur in national parks and other declared reserves.
C. Species listed under 1–5 which are not currently 'endangered' or 'vulnerable', and which are known to occur in national parks and other declared reserves.

These codes are being refined at present by Leigh and Hartley.

Early studies on endangered flora were reported by Specht *et al.* (1974). This report listed species considered to be threatened in individual states and those not afforded protection in reserves. At the time the report was compiled very few detailed regional flora surveys were available, and many rare and endangered species were not listed due to lack of information. Similarly, many species were listed although their actual status had not been fully assessed. The taxonomy of many species of rare plants was incomplete and these species were also not considered. There were many inconsistencies between the lists for individual states, with some species being listed as 'rare', 'endangered' or 'depleted' in one state, but often being very common in another state.

Following review of additional data and of information available from herbaria and other institutions, 963 species were deleted from the 3027 listed by Specht. After studies of the individual state floras and comparing occurrences across state borders, the Specht list was reduced by a further 1167 species (W. Hartley, pers. comm.). However, detailed species studies by members of the Endangered Flora Working Group resulted in 1156 species being added to the list because of their distribution and conservation status. Today 2053 species are listed as at risk, under the binary classification system outlined above. The list is only provisional but does provide a basis for more detailed species studies and hence for continual revision of the list itself. The 2053 species are approximately 8–10 per cent of the total number of indigenous species in Australia described so far. The percentage for each state varies greatly.

Furthermore in Western Australia 20–30 per cent of the flora remains undescribed, so the eventual number of species listed could be as much as 40 per cent of the total state flora. Due to its geographical isolation from the eastern half of the continent, Western Australia has a unique and diverse flora. Many genera and species have a closer affinity with South African plants than with the flora in the rest of Australia. Hence a very high percentage of the species are endemic to

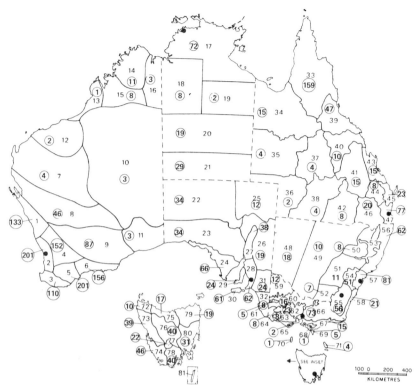

Figure 1   Regional subdivisions within Australia, with the number of species from the national list encircled. (Reproduced by permission of Australian National Parks and Wildlife Service)

the state and many are restricted to the south-west provinces (Regions 2–6 in Figure 1). Much of the flora of Western Australia remains to be described and probably many arid land species have never been collected. Nevertheless, as Table 1 shows, the species already listed for the state constitute approximately 45 per cent of all the plants listed as at risk in Australia. The percentages for the eastern states are much lower.

Table 1   Number of families, genera and species listed for states

	New South Wales	Western Australia	Victoria	Northern Territory	Queensland	South Australia	Tasmania
Families	64	62	39	45	68	52	45
Genera	160	233	83	85	187	119	85
Species	305	936	136	108	311	249	138
Percentage at species level	14.9	45.6	6.6	5.3	15.1	12.1	6.7

141 families, 596 genera and 2053 species are now represented on the Australian list

Queensland has much of the subtropical and tropical rain forest of Australia and many of the species listed at risk for the state grow in rain forest. The occurrence of rare species of the Indo–Malaysian rain forest account for the many disjunct species in the Cape York region of Queensland (region 33 in Figure 1).

Table 2 shows that 1027 (50.0 per cent) of the listed species are restricted endemics and 728 (35.5 per cent) are rare species occurring in small populations with specific habitat requirements, although often widely distributed. The full extent of species to be included in the latter category has still to be ascertained as many species habitats have not been determined. It is very difficult to find where many species still occur and to ascertain their local distribution. For example two orchids, *Rhizanthella gardneri* R. S. Rogers and *Cryptanthemis slateri* Rupp, are underground species and have only been seen in several very disjunct locations. *Rhizanthella gardneri* is a Western Australian endemic of which very few collections have been made in the last 100 years. *Cryptanthemis slateri* occurs in the eastern states, but its full range and status can only be determined by accidental discoveries, in the same way as the localities known at present have been found.

Analysis of the conservation codes shows that 221 species are considered as 'endangered', 30 per cent of these again being Western Australian species, which emphasizes the floristic diversity and importance of the south-west provinces. In turn 544 species (26.5 per cent) are 'vulnerable', and only 561 species (27.3 per cent) are adequately conserved in conservation reserves in viable populations. Only 6–8 per cent of these are adequately conserved throughout their full geographical range, and effective conservation cannot be ensured until this is achieved.

Table 3 lists the number of listed species in each family. Myrtaceae, Proteaceae, Orchidaceae, Fabaceae and Mimosaceae have the greatest numbers of species listed at risk. These families are also very large families in the Australian flora. The genera having the greatest number of listed species are *Eucalyptus* (119),

Table 2   Statistical table of conservation categories

Conservation code	Distribution code						
	1	2	3	4	5	Total	%
X	7	2	0	0	0	9	0.4
E	17	147	52	5	0	221	10.8
V	6	286	187	51	14	544	26.5
n	14	297	294	38	9	652	25.8
C	6	295	195	36	29	561	27.3
Total	116*	1027	728	130	52	2053*	
%	5.6	50.0	35.5	6.3	2.5		

*These totals include 66 species in Distribution category 1 without a conservation code at present; their status is being assessed

Table 3   Species occurrences within families containing five or more listed species

Myrtaceae	249	Xanthorrhoeaceae	16
Proteaceae	193	Brassicaceae (= Cruciferae)	15
Orchidaceae	154	Sapindaceae	15
Fabaceae (= Leguminosae:		Frankeniaceae	15
Papilionoïdeae	126	Haemodoraceae	14
Mimosaceae (= Leguminosae:		Scrophulariaceae	14
Mimosoïdeae	109	Droseraceae	11
Asteraceae (= Compositae)	97	Ranunculaceae	11
Epacridaceae	84	Thymelaeaceae	11
Rutaceae	67	Amaranthaceae	10
Poaceae (= Gramineae)	58	Restionaceae	10
Cyperaceae	49	Lycopodiaceae	9
Goodeniaceae	49	Boraginaceae	8
Rhamnaceae	47	Caryophyllaceae	8
Lamiaceae (= Labiatae)	37	Loganiaceae	8
Liliaceae	37	Rubiaceae	8
Sterculiaceae	33	Centrolepidaceae	7
Apiaceae (= Umbelliferae)	32	Aizoaceae	6
Chenopodiaceae	28	Arecaceae (= Palmae)	6
Dilleniaceae	27	Zamiaceae	6
Haloragidaceae	21	Asclepiadaceae	5
Myoporaceae	18	Convolvulaceae	5
Tremandraceae	18	Eriocaulaceae	5
Hymenophyllaceae	17	Thelypteridaceae	5
Solanaceae	17		

Acacia (107), *Grevillea* (60), *Leucopogon* (38), *Pultenea* (32), *Hibbertia* (26), *Stylidium* and *Caladenia* (25). The family Orchidaceae has a large number of species listed (27 per cent of the family), but only the genus *Caladenia* has many species of the genus listed. The Orchidaceae listings occur in most of the genera.

Table 4 provides guidance for conservation planning in New South Wales by showing the numbers of listed species in each regional subdivision of the state. For example 256 of the 305 listed species (83.9 per cent) occur in regions 53–58, but these are the regions where the major conservation reserves already exist. These regions also contain the greatest number of listed species not known to occur in any conservation reserve, and also the greatest number of species in the conserved categories. This would suggest that additional reserves are still required in regions 53–58, particularly in 57 where the majority of species in the 'E' categories exist. In contrast only 49 of the 305 species (16.0 per cent) are listed for the semi-arid and arid regions; this reflects a state of adequate conservation, even though the arid regions cover a large area of New South Wales.

Cape York in Queensland is an example of a region where flora conservation is achieving some success. Figure 1 shows that Cape York (region 33) has 159 species listed as 'at risk'. The only other regions with a similar or greater number

Table 4   Conservation status and distribution of plants at risk in New South Wales

| | Regions | | | | | | | | | | | |
	48	49	50	51	52	53	54	55	56	57	58	Total
1	1						1		1	1		4
1n	1											1
2E			3			2	1	4	2	8	2	22
2V	1	1		3		3	6	5	11	7	2	39
2C			1	2		2	7	12	1	16		41
2n			1				1	1		1	4	8
3E	1					1	1	1	8	5		17
3V	7	3		3	4	5	11	4	18	7	5	67
3C			3			6	11	16	13	17		66
3n	6	1		1			3	1	5	1		18
4V	1			1			3			1	1	7
4C							1	3	1			5
4n									1			1
5V		1		2			2		1	2		8
5n					1							1
	18	6	8	10	7	19	48	47	62	66	14	305

of listed species are in the south west of Western Australia. If species listed as 'endangered' or 'vulnerable' only are considered, Cape York is second with 84 species to region 2 (near Perth, Western Australia) with 90. Thus Cape York appears to be one of the key areas in Australia for the conservation of plants at risk. Acknowledging this, many national parks have been established in Cape York in the last 5 years. The area reserved for conservation has increased from 125 000 hectares in 1974 to 1 570 000 in 1980, an increase of over 12 times. Unfortunately the flora of these new reserves is little known and so it is not yet possible to draw definite conclusions about the conservation status of the plants listed as 'endangered' and 'vulnerable' at this stage, but obviously the overall situation for rare-plant conservation in Cape York has improved markedly.

The Cape York Peninsula is a region of generally poor soils and inhospitable climate, and there are relatively few land-use conflicts, so planning for effective rare-plant conservation is still possible. In most other regions, however, many other conflicts exist and the conservation of viable populations of species at risk is much more difficult.

There are also many locally rare species that do not appear on the national list of plants at risk. For example, Willis (1978) lists 507 species as rare in Victoria, but only 84 occur on the national list. This then suggests that if conservation reserves are established on the basis of the Australian national list many locally rare species may be lost from individual states, but not from the Australian flora as a whole. The national list of plants at risk does highlight the species which are under greatest threat on a continental basis, and these will become the priority for conservation in each state.

Exploited plants at risk

While many species have been recognized as being 'vulnerable' and some face extinction, commercial exploitation of many native species, including many of those listed, continues. This exploitation is for both the local trade and for export, and continues in contradiction of the call for adequate conservation. Of the 68 species on the list which are commercially exploited, 13 are 'endangered', all these being Western Australian species from the south-west provinces. A further 43 species on the list are exploited, but at present are adequately conserved in other areas and in conservation reserves distant from the sites of exploitation. These 43 species will only be adequately conserved if management of the reserves is focused upon the plants at risk and not for conservation *per se*, as is the usual objective in national parks and reserves.

Many other species are exploited, e.g. *Telopea speciosissima* (Sm.) R.Br. for the local and export trade, but do not qualify for the national list at present since nursery-grown stock supplies the market. The tree ferns (families Cyatheaceae and Dicksoniaceae), however, are very popular landscaping plants and supply is entirely from wild populations. The tree ferns are not on the national list but have been placed on Appendix II of CITES. The listings were by other signatories but were supported by Australia, as giving some protection against the current land-scaping fashion and the possible extension of the potential export market, although it should be remembered that CITES only controls and monitors the *international* movement of species on the Appendices. Continued illegal exploita-tion of wild populations will eventually lead to their inclusion on the national list of plants at risk.

Other species may be added in future, particularly those from Western Australia, where the floristic richness and diversity provides a potential for a major industry in wild-flower sales. Today the export trade earns up to A\$1 million annually, but the industry is only in its infancy. Any increase in harvesting pressure for fresh-cut flowers, dried wild flowers, live plants and seed must inevitably have a pronounced effect on wild populations, unless it is adequately assessed and controlled.

Appendix II of CITES includes all tree ferns, cycads and orchids, and currently provides some control over the export of 990 species, 184 genera and 16 Australian plant families. Of these species 373 were in groups proposed by Australia and now covered by the Convention; the majority of them (178) are orchids, and this reflects the world-wide problem of identifying wild orchid species in trade and controlling the market.

Protected plant lists

All states within Australia have legislation for the protection of flora within their territories. Protected plant lists have been compiled to meet legislative needs, but species have been added to these lists so far without any real cognizance being given to flora conservation strategies within individual states or between states. Very few 'rare', 'endangered' or 'vulnerable' species are included on these protected plant lists, and in New South Wales, for example, only 12 such species out of a total of 305 for the state are included. The protected plant list covers 128 species, the majority of which were listed because of their potential as cut flowers. Half of the species on the protected plant list are orchids (65 species) from 17 genera, acknowledging the problems in controlling the collecting of wild orchids.

Furthermore the current 'protected plant lists' do not really provide protection, but only provide some means of monitoring and controlling the number of individuals taken. Even under the existing legislation there is scope for considerable exploitation. As shown above, Region 57 in New South Wales contains the greatest number of 'endangered' category species and the greatest number of exploited species, but during the year 1979–80 licences were issued under the Native Flora Act for taking some 400 000 live plants of species listed on the current protected plant list. Over half of these (224 525) were from rain forest species and this exploitation pressure is extending to all regions where rain forest occurs.

Currently an Australian protected plant list is being compiled by P. S. Lavarack, incorporating 'rare', 'endangered' and 'vulnerable' species, as well as other common but exploited species. The acceptance by individual states of this list, even where many species do not occur in a particular state, will control the sale between states of species which presently are rare and protected in only part of their range.

Current status of Australian flora

Only 4–5 per cent of the total Australian flora is at direct risk at this time and only nine species are considered to be 'extinct'. This contrasts with continental USA which has approximately the same total number of plant species, but where over 100 species are extinct (Elias, 1976). On endangered flora Australia is at a point that the USA reached in the 1800s, and so is in a good position to ensure that further species extinctions do not occur. Even so, all native species must be considered to be at some risk with the continuing destruction of native plant communities and with the gross modification of habitats of remaining species. The future conservation and preservation of flora at risk will only be assured when a number of objectives are satisfied:

1. The completion of detailed regional flora surveys to identify areas for reservation, specifically for species at risk. Approximately 2.5 per cent of Australia is now reserved as national parks and equivalent conservation reserves but only one or two parks have been proclaimed solely for the conservation and protection of a rare plant species.
2. The acquisition of viable samples of plant communities in which species at risk are adequately conserved, throughout their full geographical range.
3. The effective management of conservation reserves to ensure preservation of species at risk.
4. The control of the modification of rare plant habitats and the implementation of control on further land development for primary production and urban spread, particularly in areas where rare plants occur.
5. The propagation of rare and endangered species by botanic gardens, universities and government agencies so they may be re-established in areas where they were known to occur before.
6. The implementation of uniform flora legislation by states to enable enforcement of controls on exploitation and trade within and between states.
7. The provision of education programmes to provide a public appreciation of the Australian flora and the need for its conservation and preservation in its natural environment.

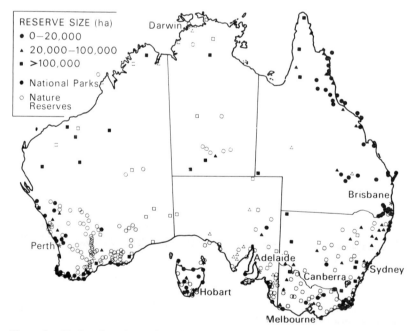

Figure 2   National parks and equivalent reserves in Australia. (Reproduced by permission of Australian National Parks and Wildlife Service)

If these objectives can be met in the near future, the status of plants at risk in Australia should eventually improve with the increase in number, area and distribution of conservation reserves throughout the full geographical range of species at risk.

Acknowledgements

The assistance of Dr J. Leigh and other members of the Working Group on Endangered Flora is acknowledged. This paper has been prepared and presented on behalf of all members of the working group.

References

Elias, T. S. (1977). 'An overview' in *Extinction Is Forever* (Eds. G. T. Prance and T. S. Elias), pp. 13–16, New York Botanical Garden, Bronx, New York.

Good, R. B. (1975), 'Endangered flora', *Parks and Wildlife*, 2(2), 28–36.

Good, R. B. (1979), 'Current Australian work on endangered flora', in *A Vanishing Heritage: The Problem of Endangered Species and their Habitat*, Nat. Conserv. Council, New Zealand.

Hartley, W. and Leigh, J. (1979). *Australian Plants at Risk*, Australian National Parks and Wildlife Service Occasional Paper No. 3, Canberra.

Leigh, J. and Boden, R. (1979). *Australian Flora in the Endangered Species Convention – CITES*, Special Publication 3, Australian National Parks and Wildlife Service.

Specht, R. L., Roe, E. M., and Boughton, V. H. (Eds.) (1974). 'Conservation of major plant communities in Australia and Papua New Guinea', *Aust. J. Bot.*, Suppl. Ser., 7.

Willis, J. H. (1978). '507 species of indigenous Victorian plants, which are variously rare, very localized and/or endangered', Unpubl. report prepared for the Forests Commission of Victoria.

The Biological Aspects of Rare Plant Conservation
Edited by Hugh Synge
© 1981 John Wiley & Sons Ltd.

6
The USSR Red Data Book and its compilation

L. BELOUSSOVA AND L. DENISSOVA *All-Union Research Institute of Nature Conservation and Reserves, Znamenskoye-Sadki, Moscow Region*

Summary

About 10 per cent of the USSR flora – about 2000 species – seem to be 'rare' and 'endangered', and so require protection. These plants tend to be narrow endemics, species on the edge of their range and species whose populations are small in number. Range size, number, existing conditions and vitality are taken into account while identifying the species which need protection.

The *Red Data Book of USSR* was published in 1978 and is an official reference book; it contains 444 species and subspecies of rare and endangered vascular plants. The book is compiled by the All-Union Research Institute of Nature Conservation and Reserves, who promote the conservation of rare and endangered species in the Union Republics and in the various botanical regions. Preservation of natural habitats within protected areas such as strict nature reserves, partially protected natural areas and national parks is the most effective means of plant conservation. Partial protection takes place in botanic gardens. Investigations into species biology and ecology are carried out to develop recommendations on how species can best be protected.

The concept of a 'rare' species

The USSR flora includes more than 20 000 species of higher plants, over 2000 of which are considered 'rare' and 'endangered' in some regions of the Soviet Union, representing 10 per cent of the total flora.

Those plants which have a narrow range and a small population within the USSR are regarded as 'rare'. This group includes a great number of narrowly endemic relict species which have survived in some parts of their former, more extensive range, either because parts of their habitat have stayed the same over geological time or because they have adapted to new conditions; in most cases their ranges are isolated or disjunctive.

Abies gracilis Kom., which grows only on the Kamchatka Peninsula, in the valley of the Semlyachik River which falls into the Kronotskiy Bay, is an example of a 'rare' species. It covers an area of 22 hectares.

The important centres of relict vegetation in the USSR are the Carpathians and the southern shore of the Crimea, the west and east Transcaucasus Region, western Kopet-Dag, Tian-Shan, the Pamir mountain ranges and Primorskiy. The Tertiary relicts, which are characterized by high ecological conservatism, are concentrated in these areas. That is why any kind of human activity, either direct such as felling and uprooting, or indirect such as alteration of their habitat, may result in species vanishing rapidly.

Endemics with a narrow range can also be evaluated as 'rare' species; the endemism of some plants is caused by recent formation. For example, an endemic of the Crimea, *Pinus brutia* Ten. ssp. *stankewiczii* (Sukacz.) Nahal, is restricted within the narrow limits of the area from Ayia Cape to Sudak.

A rich and diverse species composition, as well as a high level of endemism, are characteristics of some regions of the Soviet Union. The southern flora of our country, especially in the mountains, is the richest and most interesting of all. In the mountains of Middle Asia, 60 genera are endemic, in Kazakhstan 7, in the Caucasus 12, and in the Far East only 4.

Plants with narrow ranges in the USSR whose main range is outside the Soviet Union are also ranked as 'rare'. An example is *Rhamnus tinctoria* Waldst. & Kit., which occurs in the northern part of Moldavia on rocky slopes and in light forests; its main range is in Central and Western Europe. In the flora of the south Crimea and western part of the Transcaucasus, *Arbutus andrachne* L. is 'rare', but is common and widespread in the Mediterranean.

Species with a relatively wide distribution within the Soviet Union are considered 'rare' if they occur rarely or sporadically. An example is the aquatic plant *Marsilea quadrifolia* L., which has a wide range in the European part of the USSR, the Caucasus and Middle Asia, but occurs very rarely everywhere.

Apart from these plants which are 'rare' because of their biology and origin, species whose numbers and distributions have decreased due to exploitation are also ranked as 'rare'. For example, in historical times vast areas of steppes have been ploughed up and steppe species tend to survive only on the field margins, in non-ploughed ravines and in protected areas. There are many 'rare' plants of the steppe zone in the genera *Stipa*, *Tulipa* and *Crambe*. In the Kolkhida lowlands, as a result of drainage, *Osmunda regalis* L. nearly vanished; previously it had occurred in Imeretinskaya Bay near Adler on the Black Sea and in the Kobuletskiye marshes in Ajaria.

Not all rare species need urgent protection, however. We consider 'rare' only those species under heavy pressure from man.

The compilation of the Red Data Book

The specialists of the All-Union Research Institute of Nature Conservation and Reserves have carried out a magnitude of investigations to identify the 'rare' and 'endangered' species of the USSR fauna and flora. In 1974 the Board of the USSR Ministry of Agriculture established the book of 'rare' and 'endangered' animal and plant species of the USSR – the USSR Red Data Book – and approved the statute for it.

While preparing the preliminary lists for the Red Data Book, we used the literature and our own field observations, following the criteria described above. At the next stage a wide discussion of the lists by Soviet specialists took place. As a result of the discussion we received amendments and additional proposals concerning rare species from the different regions.

The final lists were presented to the Main Administration for Nature Conservation, Nature Reserves, Forestry and Game Management, USSR Ministry of Agriculture; they were then co-ordinated with the Council of Ministers of the Union Republics and were adopted by the USSR Ministry of Agriculture. So far 444 plant species have been inserted in the USSR Red Data Book. Of course this figure is not final.

In accordance with the statute for the USSR Red Data Book the entry on each plant in the book contains information along the following lines:

1. Name (genus, species, family)
2. Status (degree of rarity)
3. Distribution
4. Habitats – their present state
5. Population
6. Reproduction
7. Causes of decline
8. Cultivation
9. Conservation measures taken
10. Conservation measures proposed
11. References

A drawing of a species and a map of its range are also given.

The book covers plants in the categories of 'rare' and 'endangered'. The future existence of these species will excite apprehension if necessary measures for their conservation are not undertaken.

We consider as 'endangered' *Stelleropsis caucasica* Pobed., an endemic of the central Caucasus, known only in four localities, with a total population of no more than 500 individuals. Natural regeneration of the species is almost absent. *Ilex hyrcana* Pojark. is typical of hyrcan Tertiary forests, preserved in Talysh and Nagornyj Karabach; the total area of its sites does not exceed 40 hectares. This plant is extremely rare. *Sanguisorba magnifica* I. Schischk. & Kom. is a narrow endemic, and grows only in Primorskiy, the Chandalaz range, in the valley of the Partizanskaya River. *Mandragora turcomanica* Mizgir., an endemic of the western Kopet-Dag, is ranked as 'rare'; in the wild there are some thousands of individuals, most of which are mature plants. Regeneration is poor and the number has decreased due to uprooting for medicinal purposes.

In the USSR *Albizzia julibrissin* Durazz grows only in the hyrcan forest on the border with Iran. The number of populations and its range decreased due to felling, grazing and agricultural development. Today the localities for *A. julibrissin* do not exceed 50 hectares.

Botrychium simplex L. in the Soviet Union occurs on the north-eastern border of its range and has declined because of land-reclamation.

Apart from the categories 'rare' and 'endangered', we use the other categories identified by the International Union for Conservation of Nature and Natural Resources (IUCN), as in *The IUCN Plant Red Data Book* (Lucas and Synge, 1978). In addition, the categories 'probably extinct' and 'decreasing' are given in the *Red Data Book of USSR*.

Conservation of rare species at regional level

The All-Union Research Institute of Nature Conservation and Reserves has now considered the proposals received during the discussion of the first edition of the lists. The total number of the proposals is more than 5000 taxa. Not all of them require nationwide protection; a considerable number only require protection at the regional level as they are common in other parts of the USSR. The Red Data Books of the Union Republics are established for conservation at this level. The Moldavian and Ukrainian Red Data Books have been issued, Red Data Books for the Baltic Republics, Azerbaijan, Kazakhstan, Turkmenia and others have been prepared. In addition regional lists of 'rare' and 'endangered' plant species of large regions such as Siberia and the Far East are being compiled, as well as of some administrative units such as autonomous republics. About 500 species have been listed for the 'Central Non-black Soil Zone' of the USSR, over 600 for the Far East, 200 for Siberia, 195 for Estonia, 109 for Latvia, 254 for Lithuania, 340 for Georgia and 440 for Turkmenia. Appropriate legislation has been passed in some of the republics.

The scientific workers of the All-Union Research Institute of Nature Conservation and Reserves are working out and perfecting the criteria to estimate the rarity of a species and the use of these categories to determine the degree of threat. At present a system of indices has been worked out and is applied in the work. Regional rare plant conservation schemes are discussed in more detail by Tikhomirov (Chapter 7).

Criteria for the identification of rare species

While assessing rare species of the USSR flora which require protection, we took into account the following characteristics:

1. The size of the range and number of populations:
    1.1 A narrow endemic, which occurs in small quantity in restricted and very specific habitats. According to quantitative characteristics it is possible to identify several groups:
    (a) 'unique' – the only plant or the only population with rare individuals up to 3;
    (b) 'the rarest' – one or a few populations with rare individuals totalling up to 20;
    (c) 'exceptionally rare' – several populations with dozens of individuals in each of them totalling up to 100 individuals;
    (d) 'very rare' – up to ten populations with the total number of individuals no more than 1000.
    1.2 A species with a sufficiently wide range within which it occurs rarely and sporadically:
    (a) 'sufficiently rare' – dozens of populations, dispersed unevenly, containing the same number of individuals, totalling up to 20 000 individuals;
    (b) 'rare' – up to 100 populations distributed evenly with the total number no more than 100 000 individuals.
2. Habitat conditions:
    2.1 The conditions have deteriorated in part of the range.
    2.2 The conditions have deteriorated within the entire range.
3. Vitality of a species:
    3.1 'a prosperous species' – normal development and renewal.
    3.2 'an oppressed species' – poor renewal, in some cases incomplete cycle of development.
    3.3 'a vanishing species' – renewal is absent.

A species is identified as 'endangered' if it falls into groups 1.1 (a) or (b), 2.2 and 3.2 or 3.3.

This work helps to prepare the lists of 'rare' and 'endangered' plant species requiring nationwide conservation. At present the second edition of the *Red Data Book of USSR* is being prepared. This book is a working document and the lists of the species requiring protection will change in the course of time.

Measures on plant conservation

We believe that the most effective measures of conservation for any species of the USSR flora are habitat protection in strict nature reserves (zapovedniks), nature reserves with partial protection (zakazniks) and national parks.

Nature reserves (state zapovedniks) are strictly protected areas withdrawn from economic use forever. They protect endemics and species that are nationally or regionally rare. There are now 120 such nature reserves in the USSR. Some species do not extend out of the reserves: *Abies gracilis* Kom. only grows in the Kronotsky State Nature Reserve, *Pinus brutia* Ten. ssp. *eldarica* (Medw.) Nahal in the Turianchaisky State Nature Reserve and *Erica tetralix* L. in Grini State Nature Reserve.

In state nature reserves research is undertaken on the ecology of rare species, in particular on their population structure; this makes it possible to understand their reproductive potential, age groups, biometric characteristics of growth and hence the vitality of the population.

As in any strict nature reserve the entire ecosystem is conserved but protecting the ecosystem does not always promote the survival of individual species. Succession results in changes of floristic composition, which may cause a rare species to disappear. For example, ceasing to mow or graze steppe areas causes bush and scrub to appear and eventually predominate. A management regime is necessary for the preservation of a rare species.

Partially protected natural areas (zakazniks) are another form of rare plant protection. These are natural areas with limited and controlled economic use, which does not damage the natural features. Rare plants are protected in special nature reserves with partial protection. Their total number is about 1000.

The Laspi Natural Area in the Crimea protects 11 orchid species, *Pinus brutia* Ten. ssp. *stankewiczii* (Sukacz.) Nahal, *Juniperus excelsa* Bieb. and other rare plants. In a partially protected nature reserve in Kazakhstan, situated by the River Charyn, Tertiary relicts such as *Berberis iliensis* M. Pop., *Fraxinus sogdiana* Bunge and *Elaeagnus iliensis* Musheg. survive.

Natural and national parks are a comparatively new form of nature conservation in our country. These areas are usually sub-divided into several zones of different protective regimes and uses. The sites where rare species grow are strictly protected. The Lithuanian National Park protects 75 species 'rare' in the republic, of which *Lobelia dortmanna* L. and *Cypripedium calceolus* L. are included in the USSR Red Data Book.

Botanic gardens are of great importance for rare plant conservation. They carry out work on studying and cultivating rare species. Living collections of 'rare' and 'endangered' species are created. An account of the work of USSR botanic gardens in rare plant conservation is given by Gogina (1979). In the collection of the Main Botanical Gardens of the USSR Academy of Sciences there are more than 200 'rare' and 'endangered' species of the USSR flora, including many arboreal-shrubby species included in the Red Data Book. The establishment of a seed bank of rare and endangered species of the USSR flora is also being discussed.

Regional botanic gardens should preserve regional floras. The Botanical Garden of Voronesh conserves about a half of the rare species of the 'Central Black-soil Region'. The living exposition of rare plants of the Central Siberian Botanical Gardens exhibits 250 relict species, 50 endemics and 24 'endangered' plants of Siberia.

Botanic gardens, however, can maintain only a few individuals of each species and so conserve only a small part of the gene pool. Species are also important as components of their ecosystems. That is why conservation of populations in nature, both in the centre and on the borders of their range, is a preferable policy.

All this work will help to prevent many species from vanishing, restore their resources and preserve the gene pool of the USSR flora for future generations.

Bibliography

Anon (1979). *List of Rare and Disappearing Species of the Flora of Armenia*, Akad. Nauk Arm SSR, Botanicheskii Institut, Erevan (in Armenian).

Borodin, A. M. *et al.* (Eds.) (1978). *Red Data Book of USSR*, Lesnaya Promyshlennost, Moscow (in Russian).

Chopik, V. I. (1978). *Rare and Threatened Plant Species of the Ukraine*, Kiev (in Russian).

Gogina, E. E. (1979). 'USSR: The policies of botanic gardens and their activities in the conservation of threatened plants', in *Survival or Extinction* (Eds. H. Synge and H. Townsend), pp. 141–7, Bentham–Moxon Trust, Kew, England.

Kononov, V. N. and Shabanova, G. A. (1978). *The Rare and Endangered Plants of Moldavia*, Moldavskoe Obshchestvo Okhrany Prirody, Kishinev (in Russian).

Lucas, G. and Synge, H. (1978). *The IUCN Plant Red Data Book*, IUCN, Morges, Switzerland.

Malyshev, L. I. and Peshkova, G. A. (1979). *They Stand in Need of Conservation – Rare and Endangered Plants of Central Siberia*, Akad. Nauk SSSR, Sibirskoe Otdelenie, Novosibirsk (in Russian.)

The Biological Aspects of Rare Plant Conservation
Edited by Hugh Synge

7
Regional rare plant conservation schemes in the USSR

V. N. TIKHOMIROV *Botanical Garden, Moscow State University*

Summary

With the intensity of threats to the USSR flora, there is a valuable role for regional rare plant conservation schemes in addition to nationwide activities. The first step is to identify which species are under threat and which areas need protection. Alongside the national Red Data Book, some state Red Data Books have been compiled. Work in the Moscow region is described as an example of a local flora conservation scheme; as a result many recommendations were made concerning conservation, some reserves have already been declared and species given legal protection.

The need for conservation of the floristic gene pool has been appreciated in the last 20 years not only by scientists but also by broad sections of the USSR population. The intensity of the human influence on nature and the rate of vegetational destruction have been very evident and cannot fail to cause grave concern. So it is quite natural that alongside the initiatives put forward by central governmental bodies and central botanical and nature conservation agencies, efforts are being made and projects for overall nature conservation, specifically of flora, are being elaborated in a number of union and autonomous republics, administrative territories and regions of the USSR.

Local undertakings are usually initiated either by research centres, or higher education institutions (as a rule by biology departments of universities), or by local branches of Republic Societies for Nature Conservation.

The work has several stages, of which the first one proves to be the most complicated. It involves identifying the species to be safeguarded in this or that territory, drawing up a register of them and substantiating the need for conservation. The arguments should be convincing not only for botanists, but also for civil servants as well as for industrial, agricultural and other officials.

No doubt the practical organization of protection for individual species should ideally be based on a detailed study of their biological characteristics, as scientific groundwork for conservation projects. Under conditions in the USSR, however, the stupendous task of studying profoundly the biology of all species requiring conservation cannot have a short-term solution. The vast territory of the USSR, the richness of its flora numbering about 21 000 species, the inadequate floristic data for areas far away and difficult of access, and even for densely populated central areas with well-developed industry, farming and forestry, make it expedient to find a different approach to flora conservation. In practice it is better first to ensure basic safeguards for manifestly rare and threatened species and only then to provide a detailed study of their biological, ecological and coenotic characteristics with the aim of correcting conservation techniques and regimes. The identification of objects requiring conservation both on a nationwide scale and in individual areas and regions remains a top priority present-day task of Soviet botanists. Substantial progress in this field is evident.

Thus, alongside the *Red Data Book of USSR* (1978), state Red Data Books have been compiled in many union republics. In some republics the editions were large enough for the books to be available to the average reader (Kazakhstan, the Ukraine). In other republics such as Latvia and Lithuania the State Red Data Book exists only as several copies to be used by specialists and republic officials responsible for economic development and fulfilment of nature preservation undertakings. The second way seems more suitable in principle. The appearance of exact data on rare and disappearing species in the press, and much more so the publicity given to Red Data Book plants on television and in films, often poses additional threats to plants requiring protection. Nevertheless, the first way is overwhelmingly predominant in the USSR at present.

Recent years have been characterized by a growing concern for flora and vegetation conservation in individual administrative regions of the largest union republic – the Russian Soviet Federative Socialist Republic. The lists of plants in need of protection have been compiled and in some cases published for many regions, for example the Bryansk, Murman, Ryazan, Yaroslavl, Ivanovo, Vladimir, Saratov, Leningrad, Tomsk, Gorky, Kuibishev regions, for the Stavropol territory and the Karelian Autonomous Soviet Socialist Republic.

Such registers usually include not only individual species, but also some landscapes; areas of natural vegetation, unique for, or typical of, the given zone; individual natural landmarks (islands of forest, chalk and limestone outcrops, ravines, swamps, water basins, etc.); old gardens and parks. These registers, being essentially the botanists' scientific recommendations, serve as a basis for special ordinances passed by local authorities to regulate the use of wild plants (in particular prohibiting their sale), to give complete protection to certain species and to establish a system of protected areas.

Local flora conservation is most often effected through botanical reserves; individual plants are given protection as natural monuments. In the areas thus protected economic and recreational activities are limited to the degree necessary to prevent the decline of the plants concerned. The immediate responsibility for this generally lies with the land-user.

As a good example of regional efforts in flora and vegetation conservation one can cite the interesting and challenging work carried out by Moscow botanists. The work was assigned and partly financed by the Institute for Master Development Plans of the Moscow region. This important and complicated research was done by the Botanical Garden of Moscow University (the chief executor and organizer), the Main Botanical Garden of the USSR Academy of Sciences, the Central Laboratory for Nature Conservation of the USSR Ministry of Agriculture (now the All-Union Scientific Research Institute of Nature Conservation and Reserves of the same ministry), the Laboratory of Silviculture of the USSR Academy of Sciences, the Chair of Higher Plants of Moscow University, the Prioksko–Terrasniy State Reserve, and other agencies. In the course of two field seasons the territory of the region (about 47 000 sq. km) was covered with a network of elaborately planned routes to find areas of natural vegetation for immediate protection and to be withdrawn from economic utilization. Concurrently the data on numerous species regarded as rare and in danger of extinction in the region were made more precise with respect to their distribution, ecological adaptation and quantity. As a result a register of plant sites requiring preservation in the Moscow region was compiled and submitted to the Institute of Master Development Plans. The register describes 99 sites which are to be declared reserves or natural monuments.

As a rule, these areas, being of a certain landscape interest, also contain concentrations of rare and disappearing plants. The list of species requiring protection in the Moscow region was itself made more precise while compiling the register. In addition, it has been recommended to distinguish vast areas in the region which are to be spared industrial utilization and town construction and to be preserved in a state suitable for further establishment of national parks, in whose territory the local areas included in the register will exist as nature reserves.

There are reasons to hope that the botanists' recommendations will be carried out. Now 27 reserves and natural monuments have been set up in the Moscow region under the decisions of the Regional Executive Council of the Soviet of People's Deputies, 14 of them primarily to safeguard botanical objects. Likewise over 50 plant species whose populations are speedily dwindling are under special protection in the Moscow region and in Moscow's Green Belt. These are mainly ornamental plants, such as *Hepatica nobilis* Miller, *Anemone nemorosa* L., *Pulsatilla patens* (L.) Miller, *Platanthera bifolia* (L.) L. C. Rich., *Nymphaea candida* C. Presl, *Campanula persicifolia* L., *C. latifolia* L. and *Jovibarba sobilifera* (Sims) Opiz. It is prohibited to gather these plants. The sale of wild plants in Moscow is permitted only through the state trading network.

In the adjacent Ryazan region a network of areas protected by regional authorities as botanical, zoological, geological or complex reserves or natural monuments has also been established thanks to the efforts of the botanists and zoologists from the Ryazan Pedagogical Institute, the Oka State Reserve and the Botanical Garden of Moscow University. A number of animal species and vascular plants are also being given special protection.

Similar instances are numerous and important as they reflect the overall trend of the work. It is well understood that in every region priority protection is given to species included in the *Red Data Book of USSR*. It is in this way that the overall state strategy of flora conservation is put into effect.

Unfortunately, similar work has not been fulfilled in all administrative regions of the USSR, which is mainly accounted for by shortages of the taxonomists and phytocoenologists who could efficiently tackle it. However, the necessity for such work is evident and an organizational framework is certain to be found.

The Red Data Books drawn up for vast regions have become a valuable addition to the research done in the republics, administrative territories and regions. Namely, the compilation of the *Red Data Book of Siberian Flora* is now over; it was preceded by a well-written popular science book about Central Siberian plants – *Must Be Safeguarded* by L. I. Malyshev and G. A. Peshkova. The *Red Data Book of the Soviet Far East Flora* is now at the printer. The year 1980 will see a second edition of the academical inventory *Red Book: Native Plant Species to be Protected in the USSR*, edited by Academician A. L. Takhtajan. Such registers are not legislative, juridical acts. However, they reflect an opinion based on the special research of large bodies of experienced botanists; they make it possible to define more exactly the present condition of the flora and greatly facilitate the compilation of state Red Data Books.

Of paramount importance in protecting the floristic gene pool are state reserves. They number more than 130 in the Soviet Union, but their distribution is far from even and their total area still accounts for only a fraction of 1 per cent of the country's territory. In some reserves, especially those set up in recent years, the floristic survey is not yet completed, and some reserves do not have botanists on their staff. So today it is impossible to give the total number of plant species protected in USSR reserves, i.e. to state which part of the flora is under this optimum form of protection. In this connection of paramount importance becomes the compilation of the register on *Flora of the USSR Reserves* from the data available, as well as intensified floristic efforts in such reserves; they fall behind the present-day requirements in this respect.

References

Borodin, A. M. *et al.* (Eds.) (1978). *Red Data Book of USSR*, Lesnaya Promyshlennost, Moscow (in Russian).

Takhtajan, A. (1975). *Red Book: Native Plant Species to be Protected in the USSR*, Leningrad (in Russian).

References for regional Red Data Books from the USSR are listed in the preceding chapter by L. Beloussova and L. Denissova. See also Appendix 2 (pp. 520–1 and 529).

The Biological Aspects of Rare Plant Conservation
Edited by Hugh Synge
© 1981 John Wiley & Sons Ltd.

8
Project Linnaeus:
Assessing Swedish plants threatened with extinction

ÖRJAN NILSSON *Botanical Garden, University of Uppsala*

Summary

Saving threatened plants in Sweden has been the aim of Project Linnaeus for the last 5 years. The work is in three phases: field inventory, analysis (and publication) of the results, and action to help conserve those species. About 180 species were found to be threatened; of these 28 are Extinct (since 1850), 34 Endangered (mostly one or two sites each), 57 Vulnerable and 50 Rare, but this last figure is incomplete. A further group of 'care-demanding' species has been included in the work.

The distributions and habitats of the threatened species are analysed. There are few threatened endemic taxa; most of the threatened species occur in the south of Sweden. Many are plants of open grassland, lowland pasture or similar habitats, followed by wetland and aquatic habitats. Plans to conserve these plants are briefly presented and the results achieved so far are discussed.

The aim of Project Linnaeus is simple – to ensure the conservation of as much of the Swedish flora as possible. First to be covered are the vascular plants, since they are the only plant group in which it is possible at present to assess whether or not species have been reduced in number. The project falls into three stages:

1. A thorough field inventory to find out which species are threatened;
2. An analysis of the field results and publication of a report on each threatened species (Nilsson and Gustafsson, 1976–80);
3. Action to initiate conservation work in close co-operation with the relevant authorities, monitoring of the results, helping to build a broadly-based understanding of the need for conservation, and finally scientific studies of the threatened plants themselves.

The first two steps are almost finished now and we have started on the third. A project like this can never be regarded as fulfilled, however, as long as the threats to the flora remain.

The field work was done during the last 5 years by about 250 botanists, mainly amateur and usually on a voluntary basis (Gustafsson, 1976). Some have been responsible for the inventory of those parts of the country which they know well; others have worked over the whole country. Some species only known from one or two sites in Sweden have been easily studied, whereas others with more extensive distributions have needed a plan of action. An example from the first category is *Lathyrus sphaericus* Retz., only known to survive in two localities. The Black Vanilla Orchid, *Nigritella nigra* (L.) Rchb.f., represents the opposite situation; the inventory on it was made by many people forming a particular action group. This small orchid had been known from several hundreds of places, with its centre in the province of Jämtland, and often it had occurred in large numbers, yet in 1975 a total of 2500 specimens was recorded for the whole of Sweden. This is a disastrous reduction in the millions of individuals which existed only 50 years ago (Björkbäck *et al.*, 1976). *Nigritella nigra* is also an example of those plants which fluctuate greatly in number from one season to another and thus require repeated monitoring to find out their population sizes. *Viola uliginosa* Bess., which has two centres of distribution, was studied by about 20 different botanists during 4 years (Gustafsson, 1978), but in contrast the inventory of *Cinna latifolia* (Trevir.) Griseb., with a similarly large distribution, was done by one person in a single season.

During the first phase of our project only comparatively rare species were covered, because they needed priority attention. It is now evident, however, that several more common species are also decreasing. These reductions are more serious indicators of adverse trends than the decline of rare species. A reduction in the occurrence of a common species is often very difficult to discover because of the lack of reliable background material with which to compare the present situation. Examples of previously rather common species which now are becoming rarer are *Anthemis arvensis* L., *Brassica campestris* L. and *Antennaria dioica* (L.) Gaertn. – all species that people know well. One such species, although a not very common one, *Polygala comosa* Schkuhr, has been investigated by the project as a pilot study; in 1960 it was known from 30 different localities in a parish north of Uppsala. During a very thorough inventory in 1978 it was rediscovered in only ten of these localities, but it was also found in 39 new sites. This investigation indicates a reduction in its formerly known localities, but it also shows that the knowledge is incomplete. The investigation demonstrates that a comparison between present and previous knowledge indicates changes in the occurrence of a species – while all the new finds must be added to indicate the current status of a species (Lindberg, 1980).

About 190 species have been considered and surveyed in this project and studied in the field. About 10 of these were, however, soon found not to be threatened and consequently were excluded. A few species of critical genera or of doubtful origin have also been excluded. A preliminary analysis of the remaining threatened species (about 10 per cent of the flora) gives the following results. The species are grouped into the IUCN 'Red Data Book categories', which are a measure of the degree of threat.

Twenty-eight species are Extinct or considered extinct as regenerating populations. Only those species which have disappeared since 1850 have been covered. That year was chosen because several local Floras which give reliable background information were written at the time; also considerable changes started then in Sweden as a result of agricultural reforms and industrialization. Probably the most serious of the agricultural reforms was the splitting of the villages.

Half the Extinct species were only known from a single locality before they were lost. About eight were weeds, and among these one whole group, the weeds of flax-fields, disappeared entirely a few years after the Second World War. One species, *Cyperus fuscus* L., has an interesting history: it increased suddenly during the last three decades of the 19th century as a result of the extensive drainage of lakes and swamps, which created a suitable habitat. Now, however, the drained land has become fields and suitable natural habitats are lacking (Lindberg, 1977). In 1976 Project Linnaeus declared *Orobanche purpurea* Jacq. to be Extinct; this probably stimulated the botanists on Öland and in 1978 the plant was rediscovered in two places. Now it is regarded as Endangered.

Thirty-four species are classified as Endangered. This group is somewhat heterogeneous regarding the size of remaining populations and the pressure of the threats. On the one hand only two trees of *Tilia platyphyllos* Scop. are left (see Pigott, Chapter 25) and about eight individuals of *Ceterach officinarum* DC., but on the other hand there are about 400 specimens of *Viola alba* Bess. in at least four different localities. All, however, are endangered by urbanization; the population of *Viola alba* is estimated to have been halved since 1950. *Genista germanica* L. is known from two places; in one there are only two individuals left and in the other about 100. In both places the species has steadily decreased mainly because of ineffective management of the 'nature reserves' in which it grows. Nineteen species of this group are now known only from one or two places. Only three of the Endangered species have occurred in several localities and more than two different provinces; examples are *Lycopodium tristachyum* Pursh and *Botrychium simplex* E. Hitchc. Two species, *Agrostemma githago* L. and *Bromus secalinus* L., are weeds of mainly winter-rye fields. They have decreased very rapidly in the last four decades and are now extremely rare with only a few localities known in the large Baltic Islands.

The Vulnerable species are 57 in number. The majority, 40 species, have been known from many localities and often from several provinces. In this respect the group differs from the previous ones. Examples are *Potamogeton rutilus* Wolfg. and *Leucorchis albida* (L.) E. Meyer, which are both known from seven provinces. Not only has the number of recent localities been reduced but the populations at individual sites have declined. *Nigritella nigra* is a good example of a Vulnerable species. From the conservation point of view this is a difficult group, because most of the species need protection in several places. Only a few are effectively protected at present. *Stipa pennata* L. is one of these; it has increased considerably in its three localities in the last 15 years as a result of successful management. In about 1950 it survived a critical point when there was only a single specimen left in two of the localities. Now it can soon be transferred to the Rare category. The case of *Stipa* is of theoretical interest because it perhaps can give us some information on what happens when a species passes the stage of very small, isolated populations.

A rather recent member of our flora is *Iris spuria* L., which invaded the Scanian south-west coast around 1950, originating from Denmark. Now it is Endangered in Denmark and severely threatened in Scania by urbanization.

The group of Rare plants contains about 50 species, but the group is not complete because several of the Rare species were not included in the project as threatened species at the beginning. The Rare category includes species with distributions as different as that of *Potentilla hyparctica* Malte, known only from two mountain tops, and *Vicia dumetorum* L. with several localities in the southern provinces.

The Rare species may have small, spot populations or wide, but very thinly distributed, ones. None of the species is under immediate threat – thus they were not given a high priority in the inventory work. As Project Linnaeus continues the group of Rare plants will be increased; about 25 species should be added. During the project three new native species have been discovered in Sweden – *Gentiana purpurea* L., *Athyrium crenatum* (Sommerf.) Rupr. and *Allium strictum* Schrad. The first two are Rare and only known from a single locality each, but *Allium strictum* has been found in several places on the island of Öland.

A fourth group of species has been included in the activities of the project. The group may be called the 'care-demanding' species; it covers taxa that have specific requirements and need special attention. Most of the species have a divided distribution in Sweden and in one of these areas they may be threatened. This group is particularly important in Sweden where the conservation authorities usually work on a provincial basis. A few examples: *Pedicularis sceptrum-carolinum* L. is common in the alpine area of north Sweden; however, it also occurs as a relict in south Sweden, now only in a few sites where it is Endangered. *Carex bicolor* All. has a bicentric distribution in the Swedish mountain range; in the northern part the species is Rare but in the south it is only known from a single spot of half a square metre where it is Endangered. *Gymnadenia odoratissima* (L.) Rich. is not very rare on the island of Gotland but is Endangered on the Swedish mainland.

The endemic taxa of the Swedish flora are few and mostly concentrated in four areas – the mountain range along the Norwegian border, the Bothnian Gulf coast, the two large islands of the Baltic, and various ultrabasic mountains. At the start of the project much attention was paid to these taxa, but most of them were found to be not threatened. *Helianthemum oelandicum* (L.) DC. ssp. *oelandicum*, an endemic to the island of Öland, is fairly common and still covers large areas of the island. *Sorbus teodori* Liljefors is in contrast very rare; at present there are only about 300 trees and bushes known in a very restricted area in the island of Fårö north of Gotland. *Taraxacum crocodes* Dt. of the *Palustria* group is a Scandinavian endemic now extinct in Finland and threatened in Sweden. Here, however, it must be admitted that our knowledge on the present status of the species in some of the apomictic genera, particularly *Taraxacum* and *Hieracium*, is still only fragmentary. In our work with the endemic taxa we have interpreted them often from a Fennoscandian basis (Nilsson, 1979); *Alisma wahlenbergii* (Holmb.) Juz. is Rare in Finland but Endangered in Sweden; *Papaver laestadianum* (Nordh.) Nordh. is Rare in both Norway and Sweden.

Much attention has been paid to the status of plants in neighbouring countries, which we now know well. In a difficult economic climate it is better to conserve the rare *Astragalus arenarius* L., which in the Nordic countries only occurs in Sweden, rather than *Primula elatior* (L.) Hill, which is also Rare in Sweden but rather common in Denmark.

The regional distribution of the threatened species in Sweden is of much interest, particularly with regard to future conservation work. There is a very marked concentration of threatened species in the southern fifth of the country. No less than 98 threatened species occur or have occurred in Scania, the southernmost province of Sweden. This figure might be compared to 13 in the northern mountains. Twenty-one of the 28 Extinct species occurred in Scania and 21 of the Endangered species have or have had localities there. In contrast there is at present only one Endangered species in the mountains, no Extinct species and only a few Vulnerable species. The Endangered alpine is *Platanthera oligantha* Turcz., which is now threatened by highway construction very near to its localities in the National Park of Abisko.

These regional differences have several explanations, three of which are important:

1. The Scanian flora is the most species-rich in Sweden;
2. In this area many species are at the northern limit of their European distribution and they are therefore perhaps more susceptible;
3. The pressure on the flora from different human activities is by far the heaviest in this part of the country. There are only comparatively small areas left for natural vegetation.

An analysis of the habitats of threatened species has indicated that more than a quarter of the species occur in open grassland, lowland pastures or similar habitats kept open by grazing or mowing. The next largest group, almost as large, comprises the wetland and aquatic species. Far-reaching changes in forestry practice have taken place in Sweden during recent decades but the number of threatened species from forest habitats is not yet very high, although the number has been increasing recently, especially among the ferns. Only a few alpine plants are Endangered or Vulnerable but several are Rare. A large group of threatened species are the weeds, several of which are Extinct, Endangered or Vulnerable. Both the weeds of the flax and the winter-rye fields are characterized by a high degree of specialization.

Agricultural practice has altered much and these changes are probably the main factors behind the threats to most Swedish species. It is seldom easy, however, to explain the way in which plants disappear – on the contrary this process is usually extremely complex (see Sukopp and Trautmann, Chapter 9). Plants of open grasslands and meadows are threatened by drainage, reforestation, overgrowth by trees or tall herbs when grazing and mowing stops or decreases, or by the use of artificial fertilizers. Also the type of grazing itself has changed: new breeds of cows are used, a new starting time for grazing is introduced, etc. All these factors together change the environment entirely. To conserve open grasslands and their species, which once depended on agricultural practices which are no longer profitable, is at present a difficult problem. And it is not only difficult but also very expensive. Several experiments have been done with very different results and now an evaluation is badly needed. In recent years co-operation between the nature conservation bodies and those concerned with land-scape and culture has begun, and I think this will be most beneficial. On the island of Gotland there is a practical experiment to conserve as nature reserves some rye-fields with their weeds together with an old type of rye.

Only a few Swedish species are threatened from natural causes; one example is *Ceterach officinarum* DC., now threatened by competition from *Asplenium trichomanes* L.; another is *Betonica officinalis* L., which now exists only as a self-sterile clone.

In this context it is impossible to give a full account of the conservation work in Sweden directed to saving plant species. However, I want to say a few words about how Project Linnaeus has been involved; the reason is that achieving effective conservation measures is more important than all our lists, which must be seen as just a help and stimulus to action, providing advice on what must be done.

Project Linnaeus has been consulted as an expert consultative body on matters relating to the creation of nature reserves and proposals for official protective measures. Several species and habitats have been given an acceptable level of conservation as a direct result of initiatives from the project. One example is that the only certain locality of *Alisma wahlenbergii* was included in a nearby nature reserve since its locality was being damaged by bathing. The project was also recently consulted on a somewhat different problem – what type of grass seeds should be used on the roadsides of a highway in the Abisko National Park to avoid gene-erosion.

Public information to increase knowledge of the current status of threatened species is of the utmost importance and of extreme urgency. The aim must be to create a broadly-based understanding of their situation and the measures which must be taken to save them. In doing this the project has tried to voice its message in different media.

To elucidate the conservation work in Sweden I want finally to give a brief commentary on legislation and other conservation measures. The legislation gives the following main types of protection:

1. National monuments or parks. As a rule these comprise more or less undisturbed, natural areas with a minimum of management.
2. Nature reserves, which are smaller and generally intended for conserving one or more particular objects, e.g. a rare plant. The establishment of a reserve is usually followed by a management plan. The purpose of the plan is to conserve the site in such a way that the rare plant or animal can be guaranteed survival. We regard these reserves as the best method to conserve plants. The cost of land and of continuous management, however, has increased considerably in recent years; therefore the guarantee is now sometimes a bit hollow. There are at present about 950 reserves in Sweden and their management costs about 150 million Swedish Crowns a year. About 50 of the threatened plants grow in nature reserves. In the long term the frequent isolation of the reserves must be cause for concern. This often means that previous gene exchange between different populations has been cut off. Sometimes the reserves are not established until the population of a species is very small.
3. Special regulations prohibiting the removal of a plant or causing damage to it. This protection is only operative within a provincial jurisdiction. About 130 taxa are protected in this way in Sweden. This type of conservation has a limited effect in conservation, particularly for plants threatened by environmental changes. There are now plans to revise this part of the law and Project Linnaeus is actively involved. Its greatest value is the fact that people know what it means.

A gene-bank for all the Nordic countries is now being established. In the first place it will concentrate on agricultural plants. However, an attempt to conserve some of the very rare weeds is being made.

In Swedish botanic gardens several of the threatened plants are grown but only on a small scale and without co-ordination. The gardens play an important role in telling the public about threatened plants. In the Uppsala Botanical Garden we have also experimented on growing different types of threatened plants to find methods by which they can be propagated and held using routine horticultural techniques.

The Department of Nature Conservation has recently started a research project on the conservation of habitats and species; some threatened plants are represented in the project. One part concentrates on two *Gentianella* species and the future management of the nature reserves in which they grow. Another covers the biology and ecology of six threatened species in Scania. The finance for this project is very limited, so priority has been given to grazed land in south Sweden and its management, because this habitat is rapidly disappearing or changing and effective conservation is badly needed for both the animal and plant species it contains.

The future of Project Linnaeus is at present somewhat uncertain. The Swedish flora urgently needs a watchman – the project has shown that – and therefore I am optimistic. I am also optimistic because of a floristic revival movement that is developing strongly in our country and this will give us good support.

References

Björkbäck, F. C. *et al.* (1976). 'Något om brunkullans (*Nigritella nigra*) utbredning och ekologi i Sverige. Exempel på ADB-anpassad katalogisering och registrering', *Fauna och Flora*, 1976, 49–60.
Gustafsson, L.-Å. (1976). 'Projekt Linné samlar landets botanister till kraftinsats', *Fauna och Flora*, 1976, 189–201.
Gustafsson, L.-Å. (1978). 'Sumpviolen *Viola uliginosa* – hotad våtmarksväxt', *Fauna och Flora*, 1978, 241–50.
Lindberg, P. (1977). 'Dvärgagen (*Cyperus fuscus*) i Sverige', *Svensk Bot. Tidskr.*, **71**, 69–77.
Lindberg, P. S. (1980). 'Toppjungfrulin, *Polygala comosa*, en växt på tillbakagång', *Svensk Bot. Tidskr.*, **74**, 213–19.
Nilsson, Ö. (1979). 'Threatened Plants in the Nordic Countries', in *Systematic Botany, Plant Utilization and Biosphere Conservation* (Ed. I. Hedberg), pp. 72–5, Almqvist and Wiksell, Stockholm.
Nilsson, Ö. and Gustafsson, L.-Å. (1976–80). 'Projekt Linné rapporterar', *Svensk Bot. Tidskr.*, 1976–80. (An index of threatened species will be published in 1981.)
Wahlberg, S. (1979). 'God Created, Linnaeus arranged: Project Linnaeus, an effort to save that good work for the future', in *Survival or Extinction* (Eds. H. Synge and H. Townsend), pp. 25–30, Bentham–Moxon Trust, Kew, England.

The Biological Aspects of Rare Plant Conservation
Edited by Hugh Synge
© 1981 John Wiley & Sons Ltd.

9

Causes of the decline of threatened plants in the Federal Republic of Germany

HERBERT SUKOPP *Institute of Ecology, Technical University of Berlin*
and
WERNER TRAUTMANN *Federal Research Centre for Nature Conservation and Landscape Ecology, Bonn*

Summary

Threats to plants may be divided into the actual causes (ecofactors) which make species decline and the causal agents or land-use systems ultimately responsible. An analysis of threats to 581 rare and threatened plants in West Germany is presented. Twenty causes or ecofactors are identified; of these the most species are threatened by habitat elimination, especially removal of the ecotones between two land-use systems, followed by drainage. Out of 11 causal agents identified, agriculture affects the most species. It is suggested that an analysis of threats in other central European countries would show similar results.

Effective measures for the protection of threatened species require a thorough understanding of the causes of threat. In central Europe threats can be traced almost without exception to the activities of man, and are only rarely of natural origin. We may distinguish between the actual causes or ecofactors affecting the decline of plant species, and the causal agents or land-use systems ultimately responsible for these impacts. For example, different forms of land utilization may be the source of the same actual cause of threat. Herbicides kill plant species in fields (the causal agent is agriculture), in forests (forestry), in water (water management, fish farming), along roads (traffic management) and so on.

It has been estimated that about 31 per cent of the 2667 native and naturalized vascular plant species in the Federal Republic of Germany are either extinct or threatened with extinction. The species listed in the Red Data Book fall into different categories, according to the degree to which they are threatened:

> 58 species are 'extinct or presumed extinct'
> 161 species are 'endangered'
> 388 species are 'vulnerable' and
> 215 species are 'potentially threatened',
> total 822 species

For all of these species, except those in the 'potentially threatened' group, we have attempted to indicate the specific causes of threat and the causal agents (Sukopp *et al.*, 1978). Exact data on the population decline and causes of decline, however, are available for only a few species. Therefore, this paper could only be based on the evaluation of single observations. The result is an assessment, an approximation, as is the classification of species into certain categories of degree of threat.

We have been able to discover particular threats in the case of 581 species; corresponding information on 26 other species in the Red Data Book is still lacking. Many species are endangered through the effects of more than one factor. A combination of several causes will, of course, lead to an increase in the degree to which a species is endangered.

In order to classify the numerous causes of threat we have compiled a list of 20 actual causes or ecofactors affecting the decline of species in West Germany and another list specifying 11 causal agents ultimately responsible for these impacts, in the sense of land users or types of industry. The classification scheme of the lists have proved to be appropriate for German conditions as shown by the examination of other lists.

The designation of the threatening pressures on the 581 species compiled in the Red Data Book to different factors and land-use systems leads to the results shown in Figures 1 and 2. The elimination of transition areas between two land-use systems (ecotones), and of special sites is the most important cause of threat to species. More intensive use of land, especially in farming areas, results in the disappearance of terraces in fields and vineyards, dry walls, slopes, ponds in rural areas, broad verges of forests and roads, unproductive areas and so-called wastelands, whereas boundaries between the single land-use systems will sharpen.

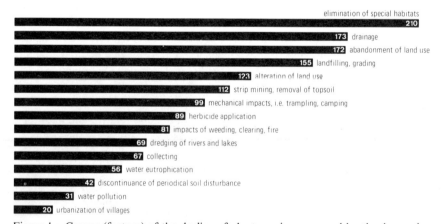

elimination of special habitats
210
173 drainage
172 abandonment of land use
155 landfilling, grading
123 alteration of land use
112 strip mining, removal of topsoil
99 mechanical impacts, i.e. trampling, camping
89 herbicide application
81 impacts of weeding, clearing, fire
69 dredging of rivers and lakes
67 collecting
56 water eutrophication
42 discontinuance of periodical soil disturbance
31 water pollution
20 urbanization of villages

Figure 1   Causes (factors) of the decline of plant species, arranged by the decreasing number of threatened species involved. (Due to multiple listing of species endangered by different factors the sum of species in the diagram is greater than the total number of individual species)

Almost all plant formations are affected by this, in particular dry grasslands (83 species), wet meadows (41), and ruderal sites (34).

Drainage is the second commonest cause of species decline. Wetland plants are most affected, especially those in moorlands (mires), swamps, waters (rivers and lakes), and wet woodland.

Important changes in floristic composition may occur when land is abandoned. This is especially noticeable on land used as sheep pastures, as meadows, or as rough grazing, where low-intensity farming enables many rare or threatened species to survive. Alterations in agricultural land-use almost certainly mean a change from extensive to intensive farming systems with the result that in general, species richness and diversity decline.

The devastation of sites by landfill projects and deposition and grading of soil, which often occurs in connection with the construction of housing, industrial plants and roads, has similar consequences to excavation, strip mining and removal of topsoil, especially for rare species in rough grassland, moorland and wet meadows.

Direct impacts on plant stands are less responsible for the threat to species than indirect influences such as changes in and devastation of sites. The most important factors of direct impact are trampling, camping, boating, application of herbicides, removal of aquatic vegetation, land clearing, fire and, finally, the collection of attractive species. Other factors which affect plant species include the regulation, management, eutrophication and pollution of water; discontinued periodical soil disturbance; urbanization of villages; and several factors of less importance, such as soil eutrophication, introduction of exotic plants, air and soil pollution, construction of artificial waters, and discontinued cultivation of certain field crops.

Agriculture is by far the most important threat to and cause of decline in species. In West Germany 397 species are estimated to be threatened by agriculture including land consolidation and improvement. Tourism in the broad sense, including recreational activities such as water sports, winter sports, riding,

Figure 2   Causal agents (land-use systems) responsible for the decline of plant species

camping, and the indirect effects of cable railways, ski lifts, look-out points, and similar facilities, ranks in second place among the causal agents (112 species).

Other causal agents include mining of raw materials (especially gravel extraction) (106 species), urban-industrial land-use (99), water management (92), forestry and hunting (84) as well as waste and sewage disposal (67). All the remaining agents are of lesser importance.

It is not surprising that agriculture ranks first among the primary causes of the threat to plant species, since more than 50 per cent of the territory of the Federal Republic of Germany is intensively farmed. A return to less intensive land-use systems is improbable. A great deal can still be done to reduce the threat to species in rural areas, however, in particular with regard to land consolidation and improvement. Attention should be focused on the need to maintain at least some agriculturally unproductive areas, transition areas and special sites, while at the same time examining the development and use of farming practices that would be both highly productive and economic yet favourable to wild plants.

In conclusion we would stress that the results obtained from this study do not apply only to West Germany. We believe that similar threats to wild plant species exist in most European countries (Nature Conservancy Council, 1977; IUCN Threatened Plants Committee, 1977; Delvosalle *et al.*, 1969). The similarity of the extent and causes of the threat to plant species in many countries requires the development of a standardized catalogue of measures which will be effective in preventing the extermination and in controlling the decline of our plant species.

References

Delvosalle, L., Demaret, F., Lambinon, J., and Lawalrée, A. (1969). 'Plantes rares, disparues ou menacées de disparition en Belgique: l'appauvrissement de la flore indigène', *Service des Réserves Naturelles domaniales et de la Conservation de la Nature*, 4.

IUCN Threatened Plants Committee (1977). *List of Rare, Threatened and Endemic Plants in Europe*, Nature and Environment Series No. 14, Council of Europe, Strasbourg.

Nature Conservancy Council (1977). *Nature Conservation and Agriculture: Appraisal and Proposals*, NCC, London.

Sukopp, H., Trautmann, W., and Korneck, D. (1978). 'Auswertung der Roten Liste gefährdeter Farn- und Blütenpflanzen in der Bundesrepublik Deutschland für den Arten- und Biotopschutz', *Schriftenreihe für Vegetationskunde*, **12**, Bonn-Bad Godesberg.

The Biological Aspects of Rare Plant Conservation
Edited by Hugh Synge
© 1981 John Wiley & Sons Ltd.

10
Surveying rare plants in Eastern England

G. CROMPTON *University Botanic Garden, Cambridge*

Summary

Since 1974 the Nature Conservancy Council has financed a project to survey rare plants in ten counties of Eastern England, based at the University Botanic Garden, Cambridge. This paper covers the gathering of locality data and the survey of field sites which forms part of the project. Examples of the data prepared are given and their confidential nature discussed. These detailed surveys, county by county, provide a basis for conserving rare species in their native habitats, for assessing the threats to their survival and indicate the frequency of distributional change. They also demonstrate the urgent need for detailed monitoring of populations in the wild on a regular and continual basis.

To conserve rare plants, it is clearly essential to know where they grow, and for each site to have an estimate of their abundance or rarity from year to year. This information enables effective advice to be given to those planning land-use changes and also allows land owners to be notified of the precise location of these species on their land. This last point is particularly important for those 21 species which in Britain are protected from picking and uprooting by the Conservation of Wild Creatures and Wild Plants Act, 1975. Monitoring of rare species is important to ensure that any reduction in population numbers from known and alterable causes is remedied whenever possible. It is also important to be aware of trends, particularly downward, of those species just outside the 'rare' category.

In 1974 the Nature Conservancy Council, the British Government's official agency for nature conservation (see Wells, Chapter 40), financed a project with the Cambridge University Botanic Garden:

1. To study the problems of gathering data on past and present distribution and population numbers of rare plants in Eastern England.
2. To collect seed and propagules for use in educational displays, research purposes and as a source of re-introduction if this is thought desirable.

The first part of the contract is my responsibility and forms the subject of this paper. The second part, also based at the University Botanic Garden, is now mainly the responsibility of the Conservation Propagator, in charge of the Conservation Section. Seed is collected for the Kew Seed Bank at Wakehurst, and a documented collection of rare species is kept in cultivation for research and educational displays. Research into genetic-related problems would still require the use of wild material, but the availability of garden origin seed or plants for all other research projects should reduce collection from the wild. A guide to the rare plants in the garden has been published (Donald, 1980).

The two parts of this project are thus closely integrated. This leads to close co-operation between the Propagator and myself, and enables best use to be made of field surveys in collecting and cultivating wild plants, and conversely providing valuable reference material for field work.

The establishment of this project signified a major shift in emphasis, from recording only the presence or absence of species in 10 km grid squares, as in the *Atlas of the British Flora* (Perring and Walters, 1962, 1976) to a recognition of the need to record the exact location of rare species and evaluate conservation measures for their survival. This change in emphasis arose largely through the work of IUCN and resulted in the publication of the *British Red Data Book* (Perring and Farrell, 1977), and the revision of criteria for the selection of Sites of Special Scientific Interest as designated by the Nature Conservancy Council to take into account nationally rare species.

The area covered by the project, Eastern England, extends from Lincolnshire to the Thames and from Nottinghamshire to the North Sea – for a map see Walters (1979). It covers the ten counties of Essex, Hertfordshire, Suffolk, Norfolk, Cambridgeshire (with Huntingdonshire), Bedfordshire, Northamptonshire, Lincolnshire, Leicestershire (with Rutland) and Nottinghamshire, following the county boundaries defined after local government re-organization in 1974. The county boundaries are similar, but not identical, to those of the botanical 'Vice Counties' defined by Watson over 100 years ago and used for botanical recording in Britain ever since; the major exception is Lincolnshire, which formerly extended to the Humber, but lost its northern part to Humberside in 1974.

The species selected for the survey are vascular plants rare on a national scale, following the 'Lists of rare species not to be collected or picked by members' (published in Richards, 1972) and a list of nationally rare species issued in 1973 by F. H. Perring, then Director of the Biological Records Centre. As work proceeded on the *British Red Data Book*, the standard adopted in that work was used, i.e. 'all native or probably native species which were recorded in 15 or fewer 10 km squares from 1930 onwards' (Perring and Farrell, 1977). The list has continued to be updated as new records are made or sites destroyed; the present list, covering about 100 species in Eastern England, of which 32 are now known to be extinct in the region, is given in Crompton (1978). In those counties where few nationally rare species occur, however, a small number of regionally or locally rare species are also included in the work.

The aim of the project is to locate the past and present sites for these listed species, county by county, and to record the biological data for each site in which any of the species still survive. To do this all plant records for the region are inspected at the main national herbaria of the British Museum (Natural History) (BM) in London, the Royal Botanic Gardens at Kew (K) and the Botany School Herbarium in Cambridge (CGE). These are augmented by records from local County Museums, Biological Records Centres, County Floras, and the conservation files of the Nature Conservancy Council and of the County Naturalists' Trusts. The help from the official County Recorders designated by the Botanical Society of the British Isles and of other local botanists has been of immeasurable value.

These records are sorted as far as possible into sites and form the basis for the Site Histories, as well as for field work. Figure 1 shows the Site History for extinct sites of *Veronica spicata* L. It illustrates one of the problems in identifying sites: the area known in the 18th century as Culford Heath was near the River Lark, and about $2\frac{1}{2}$ miles south of the railway cutting at 'Culford Heath' 100 years later.

During the field work coloured flags mounted on steel surveyors' pins are used to mark either individual plants or, if there are large numbers of plants, to mark the boundary of the population. In some cases fibron tapes are laid out in a rectangle around the edge of a population to obtain greater accuracy in mapping individual plants. Colour photographs are taken to show not only the habitat but to record the exact site in relation to the surrounding landmarks, and to illustrate the distribution of individual plants. Taking colour photographs of the site marked with flags considerably reduces the time needed to map and describe it. (Where the plants are hidden by tall vegetation, as in a reed bed, flags are mounted on canes or held by an assistant.)

A Population Form is completed for each site; this gives details of the locality, including a section of the $2\frac{1}{2}$ inch:1 mile Ordnance Survey map, a sketch map of the population, numbers of plants, associated species, conservation status and ownership.

One county is surveyed each year and the report of the year's work is deposited at the regional office of the Nature Conservancy Council. The report is in loose-leaf folders, in which each site for a rare species is given a code number. Information on each species is summarized for quick reference in a County Schedule, as shown in Figure 2; the example used is the Perennial Flax, *Linum perenne* L. ssp. *anglicum* (Miller) Ockendon. It is one of the most famous rarities of the Cambridgeshire chalk country, and is chosen to illustrate the project because it is a species still just outside the 'rare' category, but with a declining trend which needs to be monitored.

The folders contain a set of $2\frac{1}{2}$ inch:1 mile Ordnance Survey maps showing the site boundaries. The rest of the folders contain the Site Histories, Population Forms and prints of the colour photographs. Although this annual report represents the formal completion of a county survey, it is more the first stage in

Site No.	SPECIES	*Veronica spicata*		Status	
	SITE	Miscellaneous: Extinct or unconfirmed Parish			
	HABITAT				V.C. 26

	Date	*History of Site*

Culford   ca. 52/82—70—

(1.6.1773	*Veronica scutellata* on Culford Heath not far from the Mill, in a moist place.	
3.6.1773	*Genista pilosa* . . . just within Culford Park Pales, between the two Keepers Houses.	
	Sir John Cullum, annot. *Hudson* pp. 5, 272–3.)	
11.11.–	*Veronica spicata* . . . I have gathered it in great beauty, on the dryest and barrenest Part of Culford Heath so late as 11 Nov. Sir John Cullum, annot. Hudson p. 3	WSRO
– 1805	Culford Heath Sir T. G. Cullum *Bot. Guide*	

ca. 52/85—74—

5.8.1869	Ingham and Wordwell J. D. Gray, Hb F. J. Hanbury	BM
–.8.1878	Culford Heath J. D. Gray, Hb F. J. Hanbury	BM
26.8.1878	On a farm field track leading from chalk cutting to Wordwell, Culford Heath. Rev. J. D. Gray	K LIV
(1878	Root per near Bury. Rev. Gray comm. A. Bennett	BM)
	(see Cavenham)	
26.8.1879	Culford Heath J. D. Gray comm. E. F. Linton	BM
8.1879	+ On the left side of the field track leading from Seven Hills signal box towards Wordwell. 300 yards from belt of trees at the bottom of the dip. J. D. Gray	
	+ This station is I fear now lost. J.D.G.	CGE
8.1879	sandy lane, Culford Heath Rev. J. D. Gray in Hb Hind	IPS
n.d.	'Mr Arthur Bennett . . . adds; – I cultivated *V. spicata* from Culford Heath, Suffolk, for several years. It kept to the dwarf state, as found wild, never assuming the luxouriant condition of the West of England *V. hybrida.'*	
	W. G. Clarke TNNNS *11* : 544	
1888	Culford Heath A. Bennett	LIV
(15.7.1915	origin Culford Heath E.F. Linton, cult. Ledbury,	
	Hb S. H. Bickham	CGE
	'' '' '' '' '' '' '' ''	
	Writing from memory I led Mr Bickham to suppose that this plant of *V. spicata* came from Culford Heath, whence the Rev. J. D. Gray sent me specimens long ago. I find however that the plant I have in cultivation and sent Mr Bickham a root of, was given me by Mr F. J. Hanbury who gathered it in August 1890 & on his label wrote 'Cambs' witholding any more precise locality.	
	E. F. Linton BM)	

Euston

20.7.1912	Mr W. H. Burrell and I found a new Suffolk locality between Euston and Rushford where there were some hundreds of plants in an area 80 x 15 yards, . . . at Euston among bracken, heather and sand sedge, the two latter species being of poor growth and outliers from the main association to the westward. W. G. Clarke, TNNNS *11* : 543	
– 1889	*Herringswell* Green Lane Rev. F. Tearle } Fl. Hind and	
	Thetford Heath Hb Mrs French } TNNNS *11* : 543	

Figure 1   The Site History for extinct sites of *Veronica spicata*

Rare species site no.	Grid ref.	Parish	Name of Site	NNR NHI CTR RSV	Species name and status	Habitat	Owner
C.9	TL 45 482555 484558	Cambridge	Cherry Hinton	SSSI	*Linum perenne* subsp. *anglicum*, in chalk pits both sides of Limekiln Rd since 1830.	Steep chalk banks	Caravan Club; Portland Cement Co.
C.17	TL 55 523515	Babraham	Babraham Road	RSV	*Linum perenne* subsp. *anglicum*, a small colony growing with *Thalictrum minus*.	Chalk grassland	CCC
C.19	TL 45 494544	Fulbourn/ Stapleford	Roman Road	SSSI	*Linum perenne* subsp. *anglicum*, long established colony on both sides of the road.	Chalk grassland	CCC
C.20	TL 45 49–53– 48–53– 49–54– 48–54–	Gt Shelford and Stapleford	Gog Magog Golf Club		*Linum perenne* subsp. *anglicum*, the largest surviving colony of this endemic British subspecies. Plentiful in all semi-roughs cut once or twice a year.	Chalk grassland	Gog Magog Golf Club
C.21	TL 45 487528	Stapleford	Stapleford Pit	CTR	*Linum perenne* subsp. *anglicum*, a few plants on the floor of the pit.	Chalk grassland	Parish Council
C.31	TL 55 511538	Fulbourn	Babraham Road		*Linum perenne* subsp. *anglicum*, not seen since the verge was cleared and levelled about 1972.	Chalk grassland	CCC
C.32	TL 54 508454	Hinxton/(Gt Chesterford, Essex)	A 11	RSV	*Linum perenne* subsp. *anglicum*, a large spreading colony known here for over 100 years.	Chalk grassland	CCC
C.55	TL 54 512466	Gt Abington	A 11		*Linum perenne* subsp. *anglicum*, discovered in 1975, colonizing new verge and chalk bank.	Chalk grassland	CCC

Figure 2   A County Schedule, showing the summary of sites for *Linum perenne* subsp. *anglicum*

building up a body of information on the behaviour and status of these rare plants – information which may be vital to their continued survival. Additions and corrections have already been made in the form of appendices to the surveys of Cambridgeshire, Norfolk and Suffolk. Records and information continue to be sought even after a county has been 'completed'.

This project is dependent to a large degree on receiving information in confidence. The completed survey is only presented to the Nature Conservancy Council, for when planning applications are referred to them, it is the Conservancy who must know whether a site for a rare species is involved. A confidential copy of the County Schedule (as in Figure 2) is given to the BSBI County Recorder; normally the only other person to be informed of the precise locality of a confidential record is the land owner.

Many nationally rare species are of little interest to botanical photographers or gardeners; other species are so locally abundant within a very restricted area that there is little danger to their survival except from the wholesale loss of their habitats. But for those species which are now reduced to only a few localities, or whose survival depends on an untrampled habitat, safeguarding their localities has become of vital concern. In Eastern England sites for rare plants are being destroyed at an alarming rate. Some botanists have felt in the past that the best protection for the site of a rare plant has been to keep its location a secret, but unfortunately this has often resulted in the destruction of a site, because neither the conservation bodies nor the County Planners knew of its existence. Before the publication of the *British Red Data Book*, sites had also been lost unnecessarily because recorders had not realized in time the importance of their finds. The confidentiality of records accepted in this project is an attempt to avoid this problem.

The remarkable co-operation and goodwill by all concerned in helping with this project has continued the long and outstanding British tradition of amateur and professional botanists working together, and has ensured the successful results achieved so far. The British climate is not so reliable, however! Quite apart from the weather providing less than ideal conditions for field work (e.g. snow in April while searching for *Muscari atlanticum* Boiss. & Reuter), it has made it difficult to plan the best time to carry out a survey of a particular species. In 1980, for example, *Herminium monorchis* (L.) R. Br. and *Melampyrum arvense* L. flowered 2–3 weeks earlier than usual.

One of the results of the work is that for rare species, presence or absence and population size at a given site vary much more than has been appreciated in the past. If *Orobanche purpurea* Jacq. had been surveyed in Norfolk in 1977, when there were only five plants at its main known site, and only two other sites were supposedly extant, its status would have been thought to be very precarious. In 1978, however, this species had a good year; there were 53 flowering spikes at its main site and seven other localities were recorded. *Gnaphalium luteoalbum* L. had not been seen on the north Norfolk coast for 5 years while Norfolk was being surveyed, but in 1978 it re-appeared and 155 plants were counted at its old station. Since then the boundary of the population has extended for some distance, although the numbers of plants are less than before. There are many similar examples of rapid fluctuations in populations or of species long thought to be extinct appearing again to our surprise and delight.

In other cases a species may appear at first sight to be rare because only a few sites, well-known to everyone, are visited, and it is not until all the information is assembled and a thorough search made that the present distribution can be assessed accurately. The county surveying itself has provided a most welcome stimulus for botanists to look for species and has led to the re-finding of old sites and the discovery of new ones.

Since the time of published records some species have always been rare. For example only 25 identifiable sites have been recorded for *Scleranthus perennis* L. ssp. *prostratus* P. D. Sell since Ray's time, and at no time have there been records for more than six sites in any 1 year. Even in the 1950s, at a time when botanists were particularly active and before the modern agricultural revolution, only six sites were known. This British endemic is a species of short-lived habitats such as fallows, field edges and tracks, and its reduction to only two sites is not surprising. What is surprising is the great length of time (100–200 years) over which it has been found, albeit intermittently, at some of its stations.

In some cases analysis of the information shows when and how a species may have arrived in Britain. For example, it is possible that *Muscari atlanticum* was introduced with seed from Europe over a period of about 70 years. It is likely that the margins and hedgerows of the fields where it now survives were those sites into which it was originally introduced. In some sites it survived for only a few years after introduction and has never been found in them again.

The maps of past and present distributions often show not only a decline in numbers of sites but a retreat into the heartland of the species' former geographical range, as shown for Juniper by Ward (Chapter 26). Under more favourable conditions, whether climatic or agricultural, such species were present in what are now marginal habitats. This point is particularly well illustrated by mapping the sites for all the nationally rare Breckland species; not only does this help delimit those species confined to Breckland, but it enables a floristic boundary of Breckland to be defined, one which is, incidentally, significantly different from the Breckland boundary drawn by the ecologist Farrow (1916) and by the geographers Mosby (1938) and Schober (1937), who based their boundary on land-use.

Although a great deal of information has been collected about nationally rare species, very much more is needed. There are still large gaps in the historical record and this includes any period from last year to 350 years ago. But the most important need at present is for accurate and systematic monitoring of rare species by regular visits to the sites, and accurate recording of the size, performance and location of the populations. It is pleasing to report that, partly as a result of this work in Eastern England, the Nature Conservancy Council have financed a project organized on similar lines to cover Northeast England, based at Newcastle University.

Those people who have volunteered to undertake the monitoring of rare species have found the task surprisingly interesting. Their work has made an important contribution to knowledge; it is this knowledge which is so necessary to the survival of our rare species.

References

Crompton, G. (1975). 'Rare species recording in East Anglia', *BSBI News*, No. 11, 6–7, Bot. Soc. Brit. Isles.

Crompton, G. (1976, 1977). 'The Eastern England Rare Plant Project', *BSBI News*, No. 14, 6–8 and No. 17, 5–6, Bot. Soc. Brit. Isles.

Crompton, G. (1978). 'Eastern England Rare Plant Survey' (and) 'Nationally rare species in Eastern England', *BSBI News*, No. 20, 5–6, Bot. Soc. Brit. Isles.

Donald, D. (1980). *Guide to the British Conservation Display Area in the University Botanic Garden*, University Botanic Garden, Cambridge.

Farrow, E. P. (1916). 'On the ecology of the vegetation of Breckland I. General description of Breckland and its vegetation', *J. Ecol.*, **3**, 211–28.

Mosby, J. E. G. (1938). *The Land of Britain. The Report of the Land Utilisation Survey of Britain. Part 70. Norfolk* (Ed. L. Dudley Stamp).

Perring, F. H. and Farrell, L. (1977). *British Red Data Books: 1. Vascular Plants*, Society for the Promotion of Nature Conservation, Lincoln.

Perring, F. H. and Walters, S. M. (Eds.) (1962, 2nd ed. 1976). *Atlas of the British Flora*, EP Publishing, Wakefield, for Bot. Soc. Brit. Isles.

Richards, A. J. (1972). 'The code of conduct: a list of rare plants', *Watsonia*, **9**, 67–72.

Schober, H. (1937). *Das Breckland*. PhD Thesis, University of Breslau.

Walters, S. M. (1979). 'The Eastern England Rare Plant Project in the University Botanic Garden, Cambridge', in *Survival or Extinction* (Eds. H. Synge and H. Townsend), pp. 37–46, Bentham–Moxon Trust, Kew, England.

The Biological Aspects of Rare Plant Conservation
Edited by Hugh Synge
© 1981 John Wiley & Sons Ltd.

11
The conservation of lower plants: Report from a panel discussion

The fate of lower plants and the threats to their survival are rarely if ever discussed at conservation meetings and despite the formation of a TPC Lichen Group and several other exciting initiatives in Sweden (described below), very little has been achieved in cryptogam conservation. The organizers of this conference felt that a general discussion led by an expert panel would be the best way to open up this subject and to decide what should be done. They were delighted to welcome Mr P. James of the British Museum (Natural History), Mr H. Powell (Scottish Marine Biological Association), Dr D. A. Ratcliffe (Nature Conservancy Council) and Professor P. W. Richards as the panel. Mr D. M. Henderson, Regius Keeper of the Royal Botanic Garden, Edinburgh, acted as Chairman and instigator. The term 'lower plant' or 'cryptogam', as used here, covers algae, lichens, mosses and liverworts but not ferns, fungi or bacteria. The Editor is most grateful to Vilma McAdam for her kind help in recording this fast-moving discussion so efficiently and to the speakers and Dr Mark Seaward for their help in preparing this written version.

The state of knowledge

D. M. Henderson: Angiosperms are only a small part of the plant kingdom yet have been the focus for nearly all efforts in plant conservation. Some cryptogams may be included in some national parks, but this has mainly happened by chance. The first question to ask is what do we know about the rarity and endangerment of the various lower groups.

P. James: For lichens the degree of knowledge is very patchy, despite the fact that lichens are more permanent than many other organisms. In the northern hemisphere, there has been a critical evaluation of species taxonomy and distribution and some discussion of rarity, based on the accounts in Floras and Checklists. Many macrolichens appear to have very limited distributions. Information is almost totally lacking for tropical regions. The most important habitat is probably primary woodland, and its conservation, especially in the tropics, is of especial importance.

H. Powell: Turning to marine algae, the British flora contains some 900 species of seaweeds and about a third of these are ranked as rare, in the sense that experts would not be able to locate them in a single season. Many British species are rare because they are near their northern or southern limits; for example, one species of *Codium* recorded from the south coast of Britain has not been found this century, but is present in France. There is probably more known about algae from Western Europe, North America and Australia than elsewhere in the world.

P. W. Richards: As far as knowledge of rare and endangered species is concerned, the situation for bryophytes is similar to that for lichens, but overall the distribution of bryophytes is probably somewhat better known than that of lichens. The British Isles is perhaps the best known area in the world. Recording on a vice-county basis has been carried on for many years by the British Bryological Society (formerly the Moss Exchange Club); the first Census Catalogue of hepatics was published in 1905, and of mosses in 1907; new editions of both are in preparation. A provisional atlas showing the distribution of 105 species of bryophytes on a kilometric grid system (Smith, 1978*b*) has been published, together with a new Moss Flora (Smith, 1978*a*). Large parts of Europe are almost equally well known and an atlas of the distribution of European mosses is under consideration. The distribution of bryophytes in the USA is relatively well known, also in parts of Canada and in Japan.

K nowledge of both the taxonomy and the distribution of tropical bryophytes is very inadequate. Taxonomic revisions of genera are necessary before it will be possible to give reliable information about tropical bryophyte distributions. Many tropical species have a wide distribution. Taxonomic work in recent decades has shown that many bryophyte species in tropical Africa are the same as tropical American species and many supposed endemics have proved to be conspecific with widespread species. In the past it was often assumed that almost any bryophyte brought back from a tropical country must be a new species. There are undoubtedly rare and endemic species in some parts of the tropics, e.g. in Hawaii.

G. M. Fearn (UK): What progress has been made in the mapping of cryptogams, at least in Britain, along the lines of the atlas for ferns and flowering plants based on 10 km grid squares (Perring and Walters, 1962, 1976)?

D. M. Henderson: As we have heard there is at present a provisional atlas for 105 British bryophytes (Smith, 1978*b*). There is a continuing programme to map lichen species in the British Isles, the information being stored at the Computer Centre of the University of Bradford. A number of the resulting maps have been published in *The Lichenologist* over the last 10 years; these show the particular impact of man in many areas and many species are chosen to highlight land-use changes in particular. In press is an atlas of over 170 lichen maps for the British Isles; the emphasis is on species with interesting distributions (M. R. D. Seaward, pers. comm.). Furthermore, the British Phytological Society has a scheme for mapping seaweeds under the direction of Trevor Norton at Glasgow University.

D. M. John (British Museum (Natural History)): The Characeae is the only group of algae whose distribution in the British Isles is being mapped by the Biological Records Centre at Monks Wood Experimental Station, in collaboration with the Botany Department, British Museum (Natural History). In the field this group of aquatic macrophytes can be recognized without too much difficulty due to its unique morphology, and there are standard works on the British representatives by Groves and Bullock-Webster (1920, 1924) and Allen (1950) while they are dealt with by Wood and Imahori (1964, 1965) on a world-wide basis. Many British taxa have not been reported in recent years or else on only few occasions; this may reflect a general lack of interest in the group following the death of Allen coupled with the destruction of suitable habitats (see Moore, 1979). The taxa and distributions of most other groups of freshwater algae are insufficiently known to consider incorporating them into a mapping scheme, or to critically evaluate them for a conservation programme.

The need for Red Data Books?

D. M. Henderson: Should we then be compiling Red Data Books on cryptogams? Lists of threatened cryptogams have been prepared for FRG (bryophytes by G. Philippi and lichens by V. Wirth, in Blab *et al.*, 1978) and for Sweden (see below) and papers have been published on individual threatened species, e.g. the lichen *Erioderma pedicellatum* in North America by Maass (1980), and the exploitation of *Cladonia stellaris* in Finland by Kauppi (1979), as well as on general lichen conservation in Britain (Gilbert, 1975, 1979, 1980).

P. James: It is the ecosystems and habitats of cryptogams that should be conserved. Very often rare cryptogams grow together. A Red Data Book would however be useful for species threatened by over-collecting or for the more prominent species, but would not be practical for the species that are more difficult to identify.

P. W. Richards: A Red Data Book could, and probably should, be prepared for the bryophytes of Britain, Europe, North America and Japan, but a world-wide Red Data Book would not be possible.

G. Ll. Lucas (Kew): I very much support this because we badly need species data, especially on endemics, though clearly the taxonomy has to be sound and well worked following what Paul Richards said earlier on the taxonomy of many 'endemics'. The arguments for conserving a particular site are greatly strengthened if one can say there are so many species which grow nowhere else in the world. It does not greatly matter to the politician whether these plants are angiosperms, bryophytes or lichens. It is the high number of endemics that catches his eye. We in the IUCN Threatened Plants Committee (TPC) spend a great deal of time making lists of threatened and endemic plants and welcome data from all sources. It has, however, proved very difficult so far to get any data on rarity in lower plants as the information is simply not available and the species tend to be more widespread and less endemic than in higher plant groups. However TPC recently set up a lichen committee under the chairmanship of Dr M. R. D. Seaward at Bradford University and I am hopeful that this will provide a focus for data and a lead for similar action with other groups. He is at present collecting the results of the questionnaire on rare and endangered lichen species and sites, and reports a good, albeit patchy, response. As I said, we would welcome and could use data from all cryptogamic botanists.

S. K. Jain (India): As Mr Lucas has said, the very first step or stage of the problem is to know what is rare. We first of all need to study, survey and list rare and threatened cryptogams. Unless we know what species are rare and where they occur, how can we protect them? The case of Silent Valley in southern India shows this well: in order to support the case for protecting that rich humid tropical forest, data were available only for animals and phanerogams and a few ferns. There were no data to suggest that any rare or endemic bryophytes or lichens also grew there and needed to be saved. The Botanical Survey of India commissioned a team of botanists to make a quick assessment of the cryptogams in Silent Valley and so species from all groups were used to support the conservation case. The basic data on rarity and distribution of threatened species is as essential for cryptogams as for vascular plants. Floristic lists on these groups must indicate endemism, rarity, preferred habitats, etc. The question whether they should be conserved individually or in habitats comes only next.

D. A. Ratcliffe: In logic it is right to apply the Red Data Book concept for all organisms. In practice it is just not possible because of the inadequacy of knowledge.

The need for more taxonomists

D. R. Given (New Zealand): Perhaps the greatest need is for more taxonomists in the field. There is only one lichenologist in New Zealand and every large collection seems to yield new species (see Galloway, 1979, for details and bibliography). The same is true in Australia; we neither know the taxa nor their distributions. We are on the horns of a dilemma for we cannot select lichen sites to be conserved on the basis of vegetation studies, as for much of the world, including New Zealand, the ecologists do not yet have an acceptable classification of communities. Also rare species data is by far the best way to convince decision-makers and administrators of the need to conserve individual sites and to answer the question 'You have got one reserve, why do you need another?' The fact that one or more species may be found nowhere else except in the site proposed for conservation cannot be contradicted by any administrator and is always of interest to the public at large.

D. A. Ratcliffe: The data too need to be accurate and reliable. The forces opposing conservation will quickly find out if the species are suspect or open to debate and use this as a means of obscuring the real issue. The story of Upper Teesdale (see Bradshaw, Chapter 20) illustrates a slightly different aspect of this problem very well – the scientific case for conserving the site was attacked by hired biologists who questioned the validity of the arguments on phytogeographical value of the botanical assemblage.

A. C. Jermy (British Museum (Natural History)): I accept Dr Given's point that planners can accept that we as botanists may want to conserve a site of a unique species, but if that species is found on a second site the first becomes doubly vulnerable, and yet it may be the more important site to conserve. Somehow we must get planners to accept the unique ecosystem concept, thereby overcoming Dr Ratcliffe's point about the rare arctic-alpines in Teesdale. One way we might do this is to show species richness and diversity, i.e. numbers of species, genera and families. This was used effectively to impress politicians in Sarawak when the Royal Geographical Society's survey of Gunung Mulu National Park estimated 8000 species of plants and up to 20 000 animals as a result of sampling by specialist taxonomists. Obviously only a small percentage of many groups were identified to species but the lists made were impressive enough to substantiate the claim. In temperate sites it may be the invertebrates that will be impressive, e.g. over 400 species of beetle on Lopham Fen Nature Reserve, Suffolk, but on others, e.g. Glendrum Wood National Nature Reserve, Argyll, it may be cryptogams; in the latter c. 350 lichens and 250 bryophytes have been recorded.

F. H. Brightman (British Museum (Natural History)): As has been said, the basic problem is that there are not enough taxonomists who can make exhaustive lists of all the species in different habitats. Therefore, I suggest, their task should be to help general botanists in the field to be able to recognize cryptogamic communities. Red Data Books of species threatened on a world scale are a matter for the distant future, but perhaps Red Data Books of communities might be a possibility.

V. Williams (Cardiff): In the Welsh universities, there has been a trend towards the biochemical and physiological aspects of plant science. The possibilities of an undergraduate learning angiosperm taxonomy, let alone bryophyte taxonomy, are minimal and we cannot therefore train the 'good general botanist' Mr Brightman says we so urgently need.

G. M. Fearn (UK): One consequence of this is that there is great demand for places on extramural courses on taxonomy.

D. M. Henderson: The University tutor faces a dilemma. He may desperately want to encourage students to become taxonomists but he has to warn them that jobs are very scarce.

J. G. Tracey (Australia): There is not one new job in Queensland for a taxonomist. Maybe, to ease this desperate situation, conservation agencies should consider direct funding of tropical taxonomy as well as using their influence with governments to provide more jobs in this field.

G. Powell (Scotland): Individual taxonomists know too little about the full range of species within any community. In trying to establish reserves in Britain, could the Nature Conservancy Council co-ordinate research studies by phycologists, bryologists and lichenologists so as to put a better case forward to Government?

D. A. Ratcliffe: The NCC always tries to marshall as much evidence and scientific support as possible for its reserve proposals. One problem is the decreasing availability of funds for basic ecological research, and another is that ecology and field biology have lost caste within the scientific 'Establishment', and now have less support than formerly in places where the main decisions on the distribution of money for research are made.

A. C. Jermy (British Museum (Natural History)): It greatly helps if the few herbarium botanists can get out into the field and become exposed to conservation realities and feel the sense of urgency involved. At the same time they should do all they can to encourage local people to study and conserve their floras.

G. Ll. Lucas (Kew): We should go further and train local people on expeditions overseas. This is an integral part of Kew's expeditions programme and was, for example, a conspicuous part of the Royal Geographical Society's expedition to Gunung Mulu National Park in Sarawak that Mr Jermy has described. We must sadly accept that there is no prospect of many more jobs in taxonomy in the near or middle future. It seems to be impossible to get the importance of taxonomy across to governments, virtually anywhere. Yet taxonomists are crucial to the conservation effort and as Dr Jain said earlier species data is the first step towards saving the right habitats as well as providing a boost to conservation action.

A. C. Jermy (British Museum (Natural History)): We could ask ourselves here as to whether we are putting our research priorities in the right order. Should we, in fact, push for more funds to get whatever taxonomic expertise and manpower is available, including graduate students, into those habitats that are under threat, rather than elaborate on what are often academic studies into the taxonomy and biology of British and European plants?

Conserving the habitats

D. M. Henderson: The rate of loss of primary habitats is so fast, however, that we must go for reserves of key areas now, justifying them with what data we can but without waiting for the basic taxonomy to be completed. Even in Britain we clearly do not have the knowledge or the manpower to compile cryptogamic Red Data Books with any degree of completeness at the moment. The fact that we cannot save lower plants through cultivation in botanic gardens also places great emphasis on the need to conserve their habitats.

D. A. Ratcliffe: To answer the question of whether Red Data Books should be prepared, at least for Britain, it is valid to ask how far present conservation policies succeed in conserving cryptogams. By relying on choosing a full range of vegetation types for protection, one automatically covers a range of cryptogamic communities and the species within them. The Nature Conservation Review (Ratcliffe, 1977), the analysis by the NCC of the most important sites for biological conservation in Britain, attempts to take account of bryophytes and lichens (if not algae and fungi), especially where they are conspicuous elements in the ecosystem. Britain does have some communities dominated by bryophytes and lichens, especially in the north and west. I am less confident, however, that all the British species would be included through this approach and this becomes more unlikely as rarity increases except where we do know and have selected particular sites for their rich assemblage of rare species, such as some of the western oakwoods. I am nevertheless fairly sure that the number of species of bryophyte and lichen not represented on at least one key site (grade 1 and 2) in Britain will be very small.

P. W. Richards: Conserving the habitat is probably in general the best policy for bryophytes, but habitats need to be conserved which are not important for higher plants, as bryophytes are small and often grow on specialized substrata, e.g. old trees, walls, tombstones, cowpats. Wetlands are a habitat very important for bryophytes but much less so for lichens; the only moss species which have certainly become extinct in Britain in the last 100 years are *Helodium lanatum* and *Paludella squarrosa*, both wetland (fen) species. Threats to bryophytes often arise from causes other than destruction of the habitat, e.g. atmospheric pollution (responsible for the disappearance of many *Orthotrichum* species and other epiphytes over a large part of Great Britain) and collecting; one species, the moss *Cyclodictyon laetevirens*, became extinct in its only English locality, Mousehole Cave in Cornwall, about 50 years ago owing to over-collecting. The locality was very small and would have been very difficult to protect effectively.

D.A. Ratcliffe: Artificial man-made habitats such as graveyards, walls and hedges are also the most difficult to protect by the nature reserve approach. One cannot rely on their survival without some protective measures, but these often have to depend on individuals, and individuals tend to be impermanent. We have had only limited success in effecting improvements in more pervasive kinds of environmental degradation, such as atmospheric and other pollution. Here, it is the ability to influence the other resource users, especially industry, and access through the corridors of bureaucracy is an important element in the process.

F.H. Brightman: The English churchyard is probably unique in that it contains exposed stones of all types of chemistry and age. In urban areas they are almost the only places in which lichens may be found. Certainly it is worthwhile trying to conserve them. It is also worthwhile trying to save isolated trees in parkland because of the big assemblage of lichen species that grows on them. But in both these habitats the lichen flora is only a relict one, and conservation will only be possible in the short term. In the long term the most important types of habitat to consider are natural exposures of rock, and primaeval forest and ancient woodland. The British Lichen Society has collected much information on the best sites in Britain and classified them into ones of international, national and regional importance. We hope that as a next step other countries will do likewise, especially for sites of international importance, and communicate this information to the TPC Lichen Group. (*Note:* Mr Brightman is Secretary of the British Lichen Society Conservation Committee.)

P.W. Richards: I would guess that over 90 per cent of tropical bryophytes are forest species, so the survival of many tropical bryophytes must depend on forest conservation. The montane forests, as opposed to the lowland rain forests, are the richest in bryophytes, though the latter are much richer in angiosperm species. It is fortunate that for several reasons the tropical montane forests are less endangered at present, and somewhat easier to conserve, than lowland rain forests.

P. James: The same applies to lichens. Mist forests in the tropics are especially rich. But the tall trees of lowland forest may well contain more lichens than is generally thought because the best sites are in the tree canopy. Trees felled for road-making in south-east Asia have been found to contain many lichens in their tops.

D. R. Given (New Zealand): May I make a plea for habitats other than forests, in particular for ecosystems in which lower plants are the dominant species? In geothermal sites, for example, the warmest rocks are dominated by bryophytes, but very few papers have been published on them.

A. C. Jermy (British Museum (Natural History)): As many people have pointed out we must orientate our conservation strategy for tropical rain forests towards ecosystems rather than species. In other words we must identify habitats rich in both cryptogams and angiosperms.

The arguments for conservation

D. M. Henderson: Moving into the political sphere, how can we justify the conservation of cryptogams beyond the argument that they are of interest to scientists and are part of the natural heritage?

P. James: Primarily because cryptogams are a *vital brick* in the ecosystem and part of the mosaic of life. For example, lichens break up the monotony of the urban landscape, although following the Clean Air Acts in Britain, only the more common and more widespread species have recolonized urban sites (Seaward, 1979). There are also many examples where mosses and lichens provide a home for insects. Their survival has implications for the whole balance of nature. Lichens in Scandinavia provide the valuable food source for reindeer, and have also proved valuable indicators for measuring radioactive fall-out.

G. Ll. Lucas (Kew): In the First World War, *Sphagnum* was used for dressing wounds. I do not advocate this today, but because of energy shortages in the future, we will have to re-assess our use of natural products and find substitutes for the numerous materials we use today based on oil as a chemical feedstock and source of energy. Lichens have been traditionally used as dyes (see Bolton, 1960). The moss *Hypnum cupressiforme* has been used to measure differences in heavy-metal concentrations in the environment resulting from heavy industry (Rühling and Tyler, 1969). Lichens have also been used for this purpose and an extensive literature exists on the subject (e.g. Ferry *et al.*, 1973).

P. W. Richards: It is of course impossible to say that any bryophyte will never be useful to man but apart from minor uses in the past such as the use of sphagnum for absorbent bandages, and the commercial use of mosses for making wreaths, we must accept that no bryophytes are at present useful. The position may change when the phytochemistry of bryophytes is better known. The fact that many mosses are remarkably resistant to decay suggests that they should be investigated for possible antibiotic substances. The value of bryophytes, apart from aesthetic, is in the part they play in various ecosystems, e.g. peat formation in mires, as epiphytes in some tropical forests.

D. A. Ratcliffe: It is tempting to overstretch the utilitarian argument to the point of ridiculousness where it becomes an easy target to be attacked by those who oppose conservation and can be easily demolished. It is the common, widespread species that tend to be the ones of economic value and these will survive anyway. Nevertheless, the case for conserving species because of their potential value to mankind has been well stated in the World Conservation Strategy (IUCN, 1980), and we should all memorize some of the most convincing examples, because they can make telling points in debate on the merits of nature conservation.

The Swedish experience

Swedish speaker: There is much concern in Sweden over the native flora (see Nilsson, Chapter 8, and Wahlberg, 1979). One activity has been to identify which species are threatened by forestry; so far 90 bryophytes, 70 lichens and 50 fungi have been identified as rare or disappearing. We are now putting together information on their distribution, ecology and tolerance to forestry measures. Many species have been found in only 3 or 4 to 10 localities in the whole of Sweden, although their habitat appears to be very common in the country. Almost none were found to be in reserves and the authorities have only recently become interested in cryptogams. We expect to get several more reserves soon. This means that we need data on individual species, and cannot conserve rare lower plants effectively by a set of reserves selected on purely vegetational characteristics.

We are also working on a set of rules to be used in forestry to preserve the rich and diversified flora. We want to teach the forest officers how to minimize harmful effects on the flora and fauna. Many of these are quite simple; for example, one can leave small patches of dead trees in the forest and this does not cost anything.

S. Bråkenhielm (Sweden): Sweden is carrying out an inventory of 'virgin' forests aimed at preparing a list of the best areas for protection to the regional authorities who are responsible for nature reserves. The outcome is intended to be a network of natural, undisturbed forests through the country representing all important forest types. Some of the sites will be big but most will be small. One of the criteria adopted in the selection and ranking is the presence of endangered natural-forest-demanding species, either animal or plant, phanerogam or cryptogam. The emphasis placed on cryptogams in selecting these areas depends on the degree of endangerment of species concerned. As soon as we are convinced that a species is really endangered, we put great weight on it. *Usnea longissima* is the flagship of our effort!

I can also announce the forthcoming publication in the Växtekologiska studies from the Department of Ecological Botany, Uppsala (Växtbryologiska Institution) that will contain the results of many years' work by Åke Sjodin, Librarian at Uppsala, in assembling distribution maps of bryophytes and lichens from various publications all over the world.

G. Ll. Lucas (Kew): We have heard about exploitation of lichens for wreaths: Kauppi (1979) estimates that 2397 metric tonnes of *Cladonia stellaris*, worth nearly £1.6 million, was exported from Finland, Norway and Sweden in 1975 alone, for use in wreaths, floral decorations and architect's models. It is of considerable local economic value.

Nature conservation in Sweden is the most sophisticated in the world. Its example should be followed by all developed countries. Yet the work described by our Swedish colleagues is highly specialized. The lowland and upland tropical rain forests are the areas where most species occur and here the devastation rolls on (see Myers and Ashton, Chapters 12 and 13). We need to remember this.

Summary and conclusions

D. A. Ratcliffe: I am left at the end of this session, as indeed at the end of the whole conference, with a clear feeling that there are two dimensions to the conservation problem. First there are the small and well-known countries such as Britain where, despite the need for more survey work especially in certain groups, our taxonomic basis for operation is largely complete and gives a solid framework. We can pinpoint the gaps in knowledge and prescribe fairly specifically what conservation measures need to be taken. By contrast, there are tropical regions where species are being destroyed before they can be described and the whole taxonomic base is much more on shifting sands. Here, any attempt to identify especially important areas for lower plants must be largely a matter of inspired guesswork based on extremely fragmentary knowledge. The potential for loss of cryptogam species in the humid tropics must be enormous, yet the opportunity for adopting specific measures for conservation of these plants must be minimal, and they will mostly have to take their chance of being represented in such reserves, etc., as may be chosen largely for vascular flora or fauna.

In Britain it is clear that deliberate collecting by specialists is one of the most serious threats to the survival of many rare bryophytes and lichens, yet this is a problem which it would be absurd to mention in many parts of the world.

D. M. Henderson: The discussion investigated a problem which seems not to have been looked at previously by the various cryptogamic interests together. Some fairly clear conclusions have emerged from our discussion:

1. The Threatened Plants Committee welcomes data on all rarities including cryptogams.
2. There is general agreement that in view of the sketchy knowledge of the

cryptogams much conservation of them must proceed by conservation of good vegetational areas.

3. There is a desperate need to conserve primary forests and especially upland forests in the humid tropics.

4. It is difficult to produce a substantial case for conserving cryptogams other than as part of the general balance of nature. Nevertheless, a list of rare cryptogams is often useful in supporting the need for conserving any specific area.

5. The sketchy knowledge of cryptogams especially in the tropics emphasizes the great need for more taxonomists to work on these groups.

6. There was some suggestion that the cryptogamic societies could with some merit hold a joint meeting, perhaps under the aegis of the Linnean Society, to discuss the conservation of cryptogams further.

References

Allen, G. O. (1950). *British Stoneworts (Charophyta)*, Haslemere Natural History Society, Surrey (printed by Buncle, Arbroath, Scotland).

Anon (1980). 'TPC Lichen Group now underway', *Threatened Plants Committee Newsletter*, No. 5, 14, Kew, England.

Blab, J., Nowak, E., Trautmann, W., and Sukopp, H. (1978). *Rote Liste der gefährdeten Tiere und Pflanzen in der Bundesrepublik Deutschland*, Naturschutz, aktuell nr. 1.

Bolton, E. M. (1960). *Lichens for Vegetable Dyeing*, Studio Vista, London.

Ferry, B. W., Baddeley, M. S., and Hawksworth, D. L. (Eds.) (1973). *Air Pollution and Lichens*, Athlone Press, London.

Galloway, D. J. (1979). 'Biogeographical elements in the New Zealand lichen flora', in *Plants and Islands* (Ed. D. Bramwell), pp. 201–24, Academic Press, London.

Gilbert, O. L. (1975). *Wildlife Conservation and Lichens*, Devon Trust for Nature Conservation, Exeter.

Gilbert, O. L. (1979). 'Lichen Conservation in Britain', in *Lichen Ecology* (Ed. M. R. D. Seaward), pp. 415–36, Academic Press, London.

Gilbert, O. L. (1980). 'Effect of land-use on terricolous lichens', *Lichenologist*, **12**, 117–24.

Groves, J. and Bullock-Webster, G. R. (1920). *The British Charophyta I. Nitelleae*, Ray Society, London.

Groves, J. and Bullock-Webster, G. R. (1924). *The British Charophyta II. Chareae*, Ray Society, London.

IUCN (1980). *World Conservation Strategy*, IUCN–UNEP–WWF, Gland, Switzerland.

Kauppi, M. (1979). 'The exploitation of *Cladonia stellaris* in Finland', *Lichenologist*, **11**, 85–9.

Maass, W. S. G. (1980). '*Erioderma pedicellatum* in North America: A case study of a rare and endangered lichen', *Proc. Nova Scotian Inst. Sci.*, **30**, 69–87.

Moore, J. A. (1979). 'The current status of the Characeae (Stoneworts) in the British Isles', *Watsonia*, **12**, 297–309.

Nash, T. H. and Dibben, M. J. (1979). 'On the ethics of group lichen collecting', *Int. Lichenological Newsletter*, **12**(1), 1–3.

Perring, F. H. and Walters, S. M. (1962, 2nd ed. 1976). *Atlas of the British Flora*, EP Publishing, Wakefield, for Bot. Soc. Brit. Isles.

Ratcliffe, D. (Ed.) (1977). *A Nature Conservation Review*, Cambridge University Press, 2 vols.

Richardson, D. H. S. (1975). *The Vanishing Lichens*, David and Charles, Newton Abbott.

Rühling, Å. and Tyler, G. (1969). 'Ecology of heavy metals: A regional and historical study', *Bot. Notiser*, **122**, 248–59.

Seaward, M. R. D. (1979). 'Lower plants and the urban landscape', *Urban Ecology*, **4**, 217–25.

Smith, A. J. E. (1978*a*). *The Moss Flora of Britain and Ireland*, Cambridge University Press.

Smith, A. J. E. (Ed.) (1978*b*). *Provisional Atlas of the Bryophytes of the British Isles*, Biological Records Centre, Monks Wood.

Wahlberg, S. (1979). 'God created, Linnaeus arranged: Project Linnaeus, an effort to save that good work for the future', in *Survival or Extinction* (Eds. H. Synge and H. Townsend), pp. 25–30, Bentham–Moxon Trust, Kew, England.

Wood, R. D. and Imahori, K. (1964). *A Revision of the Characeae, 2. Iconograph*, J. Cramer, Weinheim.

Wood, R. D. and Imahori, K. (1965). *A Revision of the Characeae, 1. Monograph*, J. Cramer, Weinheim.

Note

As mentioned by Mr Lucas the TPC Lichen Group, created through the good offices of the International Association for Lichenology, is actively seeking data on rare and endangered lichen species and sites. If there is any way you the reader can help, please write to:

Dr Mark Seaward
Postgraduate School of Studies in Environmental Science,
University of Bradford,
Bradford,
West Yorkshire BD7 1DP,
England.

Section 2
Tropical Forests – The
Conservation Priority

The Biological Aspects of Rare Plant Conservation
Edited by Hugh Synge
© 1981 John Wiley & Sons Ltd.

12
Conservation needs and opportunities in Tropical Moist Forests

NORMAN MYERS *Consultant in Conservation and Development, and Senior Associate of the World Wildlife Fund – US, Nairobi*

Summary

Tropical Moist Forests rank among the most complex and diverse biomes on earth. Harbouring some 40–50 per cent of the planetary spectrum of species, they offer biotic resources that could, through sustainable utilization, serve society's needs into the foreseeable future. Yet the biome is being depleted more rapidly than any other on earth. If present exploitation patterns persist – and they are likely to accelerate – extensive sectors of the biome will be grossly disrupted, if not destroyed outright, by the end of the century, and the remainder has poor prospects of surviving, except in impoverished form, beyond another few decades.

Ecological and biogeographical theory suggests that between 10 and 20 per cent of the biome needs to be protected to ensure the survival of the majority of species and a representative sample of ecosystems. This situation represents a major challenge to conservationists. Just as the needs are great, so are the opportunities. Much of the biome is little disturbed as yet, and there is still time – albeit very little time – for conservationists to design comprehensive but realistic strategies to safeguard a representative range of ecosystems and the species they contain in the face of progressive pressures to misuse and over-use these forests.

Introduction

There are many conservation needs and opportunities in many parts of the world. There is scarcely a biome where they are more pervasive and pressing than in Tropical Moist Forests.

These forests are, ecologically speaking, among the most complex and diverse of ecosystems, matched or possibly surpassed only by coral reefs. Biotically they are among the richest areas on earth: as defined in Myers (1980), they encompass only 7 per cent of the earth's land surface, but harbour some 40–50 per cent of the planet's 5–10 million species, of all kinds, and some 100 000 of the planet's 250 000 higher plant species (Myers, 1980). Despite the fact that they represent a biological treasure-house beyond compare, they are less protected in national parks and reserves than any other biome. So far a mere 2 per cent or so of

141

Tropical Moist Forests have been set aside under protected status, and many of these areas amount to little more than 'paper parks' with few substantial safeguards on the ground.

At the same time, Tropical Moist Forests are less known to science than any other biome. Of their myriad species, the great majority have yet to be documented beyond a preliminary account of their location, morphology, and a few other rudimentary details. With regard to their ecological workings, we have hardly started on preliminary investigations of their basic physiobiotic relationships, community dynamics and energy flows. We now know more about part of the moon than we do about many tracts of Tropical Moist Forests. A striking example of this strange imbalance occurred in 1972, when a new rain forest tribe, the Tasaday, was discovered in the Philippines, separated from the outside world by a mere 25 km of forest and apparently isolated since Neolithic times.

Conservation needs are exceptionally urgent. Tropical Moist Forests are being disrupted and depleted more rapidly than virtually any other biome. If present trends in land-use and patterns of exploitation persist (and they are likely to accelerate), large sectors of the biome are likely to become markedly modified, if not fundamentally transformed, during the foreseeable future – the next 3–5 decades. According to many recent reports (Myers, 1979 and 1980; Persson, 1974, 1975 and 1977; Sommer, 1976; Unesco/UNEP/FAO, 1978), many of these forests may be reduced to degraded remnants by the end of the century, if they are not eliminated altogether. This will represent a biological débâcle to surpass all others that have occurred since life first emerged 3.6 billion years ago. Not only will it bring to an end many of the greatest concentrations of species and many of the most diverse ecosystems on earth, but it will precipitate a basic shift in some of the earth's most dynamic evolutionary processes. On a planetary timescale, it will all have happened in a twinkling of a geological eye.

The loss of potential benefits

These patterns of depletion will also mean the irreversible loss of unique natural resources that have the potential to offer many useful benefits to society, now and forever. Species, especially of plants, from Tropical Moist Forests have already made many thousands of contributions to modern agriculture, to medicine and to industry. Examples include vincristine, a drug that now gives a child with leukemia an 80 per cent chance of recovery (as compared with only 20 per cent in 1960) (Lewis and Elvin-Lewis, 1977); anti-cancer drugs, and compounds that help cure or prevent heart disorders and other major diseases (Altschul, 1977; Morton, 1977; Myers, 1978 and 1979; Schultes, 1976; Wagner and Wolff, 1977). The World Health Organization is currently searching for a way to manufacture a safer and more effective contraceptive pill; they believe that their best prospects lie with anti-fertility compounds from plants in Tropical Moist Forests. A host of new foods are available from these forests (Myers, 1978 and 1979; National

Academy of Sciences, 1975 and 1980), while many improved varieties of existing crops are only found there; for example a perennial species of maize has recently been discovered in Mexico (Hahn, 1980), with prospects for revolutionizing maize growing by eliminating the need to plough and replant. A number of tropical tree species produce many different oils, opening up the possibility of 'growing gasoline' in the form of petroleum plantations (Calvin, 1978). So far a mere 1 per cent of species from Tropical Moist Forests have been intensively screened for their potential useful benefits to society; it seems a statistical certainty that these forests harbour vast reservoirs of genetic material that could serve pragmatic purposes of humankind. From this standpoint alone, Tropical Moist Forests can be considered to rank among society's most valuable raw materials with which to confront the unknown challenges of the future. Yet these forests and their stock of species are being depleted more rapidly than some of the earth's most precious minerals.

The many benefits such forests have brought emphasize that their impending loss would be a significant economic setback to society, in both the developing and developed worlds. The decline of Tropical Moist Forests is of concern not only to researchers into abstruse biology and other forms of science that may seem esoteric at first sight, but should be an interest of priority to political leaders, economists, planners, development practitioners – to all charged with ensuring the survival and prosperity of an exceptionally valuable part of the earth.

An urgent priority is therefore to set aside as many protected areas as possible, to preserve their ecosystems in a form that is inviolate. At the same time there is a critical need to ensure that the remaining tracts of Tropical Moist Forests are exploited in ways that do not amount to misuse and over-use, but represent sustainable forms of utilization that will enable the many products and services of the forest to be available to humankind into the indefinite future.

So great, however, is the pressure to deplete if not destroy Tropical Moist Forests that it is appropriate to spell out some of the reasons for conservation. By showing the goods and services that become available through protected areas, such arguments can serve as a 'preservation rationale' to balance against incentives to exploit forests for conventional products such as timber. So it can be argued that setting aside unique and representative samples of Tropical Moist Forests would:

1. allow evolutionary processes to continue;
2. safeguard the role of the moist forests in regulating the biosphere, especially in maintaining climatic stability – local, regional and maybe even global;
3. provide a stock of plants and animals for pure and applied research;
4. provide undisturbed ecosystems for benchmark monitoring in comparison with which land-use strategies to use the forest can be evaluated;
5. conserve gene pools of plants and animals for their future use to man, and for maintaining ecosystem stability;

6. safeguard watersheds to prevent flooding and soil erosion and to maintain water supplies;
7. provide wildlands for recreation, for enjoyment and for education;
8. provide local income and foreign exchange through tourism.

The pattern of depletion

While present estimates of depletion rates should be considered as no more than preliminary and approximate at this stage, it is now believed that as much as 200 000–250 000 sq. km of primary Tropical Moist Forests are undergoing significant disruption, if not permanent elimination, each year (Myers, 1979 and 1980). This means, in theory, that the entire biome of some 9 million sq. km will disappear within only 37 years.

Of course the rate of depletion is likely to accelerate in many areas, and in hardly any areas is it likely to decline. It is facile, however, to suppose that the future prospect for tropical forests will amount to a straight extrapolation of the past. Already depletion patterns greatly differ from one region to another. Certain areas of forest are being depleted at rates fast enough to bring them to an end within less than one decade, whereas other areas could well remain little changed by the end of the century. Clearly this differentiated pattern is critical to conservation planning.

Virtually all lowland forests of the Philippines and peninsular Malaysia seem likely to become logged over by 1990 at the latest, possibly a good deal earlier. Much the same applies to most parts of West Africa. Little could remain of the moist forests of Central America within another 10 years, probably less. Almost all of the lowland forests in Indonesia have been scheduled for timber exploitation by the year 2000, and at least half by 1990. Extensive areas of Amazonia in Colombia and Peru could be claimed for cattle ranching and various forms of cultivator settlement by the end of the century; and similar claims may affect much of the eastern sector of Amazonia in Brazil.

In contrast, in Central Africa, i.e. Gabon, Congo and Zaïre, human density is low and mineral resources are abundant. This reduces the countries' incentive to liquidate 'forest capital' in order to fund economic development; hence they could well retain large expanses of little-disturbed forest by the end of the century. Similarly, the western portion of Amazonia in Brazil, because of its remoteness and perhumid climate – the heavy year-round rainfall makes any sort of conventional agriculture extremely difficult – may undergo only moderate change.

In summary, the overall outcome is likely to be extremely 'patchy', ranging from marginal disruption in some areas to outright elimination in others. A detailed analysis of the situation in each country is set out in Myers (1980), a report prepared for the US National Academy of Sciences. In the future the situation is likely to become even more differentiated than at present, in two important respects, (a) both between and within the three main regions, and (b) within several individual countries.

Exceptionally endangered areas

Certain parts of the biome feature unusually rich forest ecosystems. These include localities with centres of species diversity and high levels of endemism. In a number of instances, these exceptionally rich forest tracts are experiencing very rapid conversion. Thus they merit priority attention for conservation.

The following areas could be considered for urgent treatment, on the grounds that they offer both great scientific interest and they are under unusually severe threat. The list is short in order to include only those areas where the degree of urgency is acute. The list should not be considered as exhaustive; and the order of items does not imply any kind of 'merit ranking'.

1. Peninsular Malaysia – Lowland rain forest, especially localities along the northwestern and eastern coasts.
2. Ecuador – Pacific coast rain forest.
3. Middle America – Three rain forest blocks.
4. Madagascar – Eastern rain forests in which endemism for some groups of organisms reaches 75 per cent.
5. East Africa – Relict montane forests.
6. The Philippines – Lowland rain forests.
7. Indonesia – Lowland rain forests in Sumatra and Kalimantan.
8. Three areas of Brazil – Lowland rain forests in Amazonia where reputed centres of biotic diversity overlap with areas designated by the government as 'growth poles' for economic development.
9. Ecuador and Peru – Rain forests in the westernmost part of Amazonia, including the presumed Napo centre of species diversity.
10. Island groups of Melanesia, especially New Caledonia.
11. Sri Lanka – Rain forest remnants.
12. The Ivory Coast – Southwestern lowland forests, comprising part of a postulated Pleistocene refuge.
13. Brazil – Relict strip of Atlantic coast forest, already degraded virtually throughout its length.

Which sectors to safeguard

The scientific community faces the challenge of advising on which fragments of Tropical Moist Forest should be safeguarded, while watching the rest be swiftly swept away as a result of misuse and over-use. So a key question arises: which sectors of the biome shall scientists recommend for preservation in primary form?

This agonizing question is all the more difficult to answer because for most of the biome we have only vague ideas on what should constitute 'representative networks of preserves'. What, for example, do we mean by 'characteristic formations' in each of the three main regions? How do we define these formations, how numerous are they, what is their distribution? So preliminary is our inventory of the biome that we are far from having covered all the main forest types, possibly leaving significant formations still unidentified.

True, in some areas, recent research has provided a basic framework of vegetation types. In Amazonia, it is now thought that there are at least 8 main phytogeographical zones, or 'plant regions', that have their characteristic floral communities, and hence their distinctive faunal communities too (Prance, 1977 and in press). In Southeast Asia, a number of forest types have been identified and defined, though a biogeographical account of their location and extent is still very far from complete (Whitmore, 1975). In tropical Africa, with its main surviving tract of rain forest confined to the Zaïre Basin, ideas of where the boundaries lie between different forest formations and biogeographic zones are only rudimentary.

Centres of diversity and Pleistocene refugia

Conversely, the crucial question of 'which areas should scientists recommend for preservation?' can be partially answered through some recent documentation of 'centres of diversity'. Certain patches of Tropical Moist Forests feature exceptional concentrations of species, many of them endemics; and these areas may coincide with the so-called Pleistocene refugia that survived during times of greatest climatic dryness and greatest contraction of the forests during the late Pleistocene (MacArthur and Wilson, 1967; Myers, 1979; Prance, in press). According to the 'forest refugia' theory, the forests of Amazonia and of tropical Africa underwent a series of climatic fluctuations during the late Pleistocene; sometimes the regions were as wet as they are now, while at other times rainfall was much less, causing extensive sectors of the forest to disappear for a period. (Southeast Asia, by contrast, does not appear to have undergone such profound changes, since its archipelago, lying in a maritime rather than a continental setting, proved less prone to desiccation.) The cycle of advance and retreat of lowland rain forests in Amazonia and tropical Africa probably occurred at least twice during the late Pleistocene, and perhaps four times. During the drying-out phases, forest species were confined to a number of isolated patches of damp climate, or 'refuges', from which surviving species could later recolonize the expanding spread of forest when wetter times returned.

If the 'forest refugia' theory is correct – certain scientists believe the supposed refugia are artefacts of localized research – these areas may harbour a richer diversity of species than virtually any other areas of the biome. If these areas hold concentrations of species, with high levels of endemism, they clearly deserve priority for preservation. When we 'lock away' one of these localities as a national park or a reserve, we derive a better return per dollar investment than would probably be the case for much larger areas elsewhere.

Several centres of diversity, however, do not now seem to coincide so closely as was formerly thought with the presumed Pleistocene refugia. So scientists should not assume that if the refugia are set aside as parks and reserves, a representative set of unique rain forest ecosystems, with their associated stock of species, will be safe. In any case, there is a further constraint: if we preserve 10–20 per cent of the entire biome, whereupon the remainder becomes subject to exploitation that grossly degrades the predominant vegetation cover, climatic repercussions may arise that will critically affect the protected areas; this is discussed in more detail below.

The Theory of Island Biogeography

This leads to a further difficult question: how large do protected areas need to be, and how can they be strategically sited, in order to conserve as many of the species stocks as possible? Fortunately there are now some insights into this question, stemming from the Theory of Island Biogeography (MacArthur and Wilson, 1967).

Under the influence of natural processes, wildland habitats tend to become fragmented, resulting in a patchwork of ecological enclaves which behave in a similar way to islands. The process has been grossly compounded by man's activities, which reduce the size of ecological fragments and cause them to become increasingly isolated from each other. In these relict habitats, the theory postulates that the larger the area and the less it is isolated, the greater the number of species it can contain 'at equilibrium'. (Diamond, 1975; Terborgh, 1974; Simberloff and Abele, 1976).

This has critical implications for planning protected areas. When a national park is set aside, it is virtually certain to become an island of intact 'nature' in a sea of man-dominated, and hence alien, environments; and the species living there will decline from the number supported by the area when it was part of a 'continent', to the number it can support as an island. The total number of species will steadily fall until it reaches a new equilibrium. The key questions are: how great will the decline be, and are some species more susceptible to elimination than others? This leads to two practical considerations: what can we do to amend the process, and how can we make the conservation of species and habitats in protected areas as efficient as possible?

It is possible to estimate the likely losses in 'park islands' by looking at what has happened when geographical islands have appeared under natural circumstances, generally when a continental area has become submerged and has left behind a series of islands. Island archipelagos of the New Guinea Shelf, the Caribbean, and the Adriatic, and off the coast of California, reveal that the highest extinction rates have occurred on small islands with rare species – a finding that is dismal news for parks and reserves unless they exceed a critical minimum size. True, the investigations of Lack (1976) in the West Indies have suggested that larger islands, by virtue of their greater variety of habitats, are ecologically richer, and may thus tend to support more bird species than smaller islands. Furthermore, the work of Simberloff and Abele (1976) in Florida indicates that for certain categories of species, notably insects, spiders and other arthropods, relatively small islands can maintain their species stock. But the findings of island biogeography generally suggest that if 90 per cent of an original habitat becomes grossly disrupted, and the remaining 10 per cent is protected, we can expect to save no more than about half of the species in that particular area. Soon after the protected area is established, 'equilibriation' (the extinction process) will occur more rapidly than later on. Conversely, if the size of a protected area can be increased 10 times, the number of species with prospect of long-term survival may well be doubled. As a rough rule of thumb, arithmetic loss of space appears to lead to geometric decline in the value of the remaining space.

Now that biogeographers and ecologists can make rough estimates of extinction rates for the most vulnerable categories of species, notably mammals and birds, they can determine what minimal sizes are required to keep extinction rates 'reasonably low'. For example, Terborgh (1974) proposes that, if the aim is to keep the extinction rates of a community of bird species at less than 1 per cent per century, then we need to think in terms of a protected area of at least 2500 sq km. Most parks and reserves in Tropical Moist Forests are smaller than this not unduly large area.

The example of Amazonia

Now let us see how the combined theories of Pleistocene Refugia and Island Biogeography apply to conservation in Amazonia. Since the region is reputed to contain at least 1 million species (Prance, 1977 and in press), it will need an extensive network of protected areas to safeguard a representative array of ecosystems. According to the calculations of island biogeography, preserving 1 per cent of Amazonia's forest might correspond, very roughly, to saving 25 per cent of its species; and 10 per cent should correspond to saving 80 per cent. So 20 per cent, chosen extremely carefully for habitat coverage, might reasonably ensure that virtually the entire spectrum of species in Amazonia are safeguarded.

Approaching the challenge of Amazonia conservation from the standpoint of the related Theory of Pleistocene Refugia, recent research suggests that Amazonia features some 16 centres of species diversity, all of which deserve priority conservation (Prance, 1977 and in press). In addition, as we have already seen, there are eight phytogeographical zones in Amazonia, zones that likewise require urgent protection through a representative system of parks and reserves.

Translating these research findings into conservation programmes works out roughly as follows, according to the work of Wetterberg *et al.* (1976). Suppose that each of the eight phytogeographical subdivisions merits 3 protected areas, each measuring 2590 sq km. Then this would amount to 62 160 sq. km. A number of small parks and reserves would also be required, in order to protect centres of diversity, species of restricted range, unique micro-habitats and exceptional localities such as turtle and bird-nesting areas. Three such additional areas in each sub-division, measuring 1000 sq. km each, would amount to 24 000 sq. km. Each protected area would need a buffer zone around its perimeter, to hold off artificial disturbances from outside; if each such strip were 10 km wide, the total area involved would be 98 460 sq. km. All this makes for an overall total of just under 185 000 sq. km, or an area almost four-fifths the size of Great Britain or the entire state of Nebraska or South Dakota.

The Brazilian Government has accepted this strategy in principle, which represents a fine advance for conservation as compared with past practice. To date, Brazil has established only two major parks in the region, the Amazonas National Park of approximately 10 000 sq. km and the Rio Negro National Park of 22 000 sq. km. Regrettably these two giant parks contain only one of the Pleistocene refugia, and only fragments of the vegetation formations that are now designated as priorities for conservation.

Large as the total proposed area may appear to be, it amounts to only 3 per cent of Brazil's sector of Amazonia. There could lie a crucial limitation for the conservation strategy. Although the plan takes account of the Theory of Pleistocene Refugia, it does not seem to take much heed of the Theory of Island Biogeography. And it is hard to see how, for purposes of park planning, the one theory is much use without the other. As indicated earlier, conservationists may need to think in terms of preserving 20 per cent of Amazonia in order to safeguard the region's stock of species. Furthermore, Brazil's strategy postulates no criteria for 'minimum critical size' of each of the areas in question, half of which amount to around 1000 sq. km; according to the Theory of Island Biogeography, any protected area in Tropical Moist Forests that is less than 2500 sq. km could turn out to be too small for its purpose.

Worse still, although Brazil's conservation planners can do little about this, four of the presumed Pleistocene refugia fall entirely within those parts of the Amazon Basin that Brazil has designated as growth poles for intensive development through cattle ranching and small-holder cultivation, while major parts of other high-priority conservation foci overlap with development areas. If any one of these refuges were to be eliminated, a large number of species would probably go with it. Fortunately, Brazil's new President Joao Baptista Figueriedo, speaking of future development for Amazonia, has stressed the need for 'preservation of ecological equilibrium', to which protected areas of forest are 'indispensable'. How far the new President will be able to implement these principles remains very much an open question. His proposals for a new development strategy for Amazonia, which appeared promising in spirit in late 1979, appear to have encountered strong opposition in early 1980 from commercial interests, and many of the hopeful signs of a new future for Amazonia may well turn out to be unfounded.

What is happening in other parts of Amazonia? Peru has established two national parks in Amazonia, the 15 000 sq. km Manu Park and the 14 000 sq. km Pacaya-Samiria Park. Venezuela has expanded its Canaima Park to 30 000 sq. km, and has declared another four new national parks. Surinam, although a small country, has set an exceptional example in placing a large part of its forest under protected status. Colombia, with a huge zone of relatively undisturbed Amazon forest, states that it is planning several new parks. Major advances as these initiatives are, they are far from enough for a forest tract of over 5 million sq. km in the entire Amazon Basin.

Besides the fact that only limited areas of Tropical Moist Forests have been set aside so far, there is a further worry which could be critical. According to a number of Brazilian scientists, there could be little purpose in setting aside as much as 20 per cent of Amazonia's rain forests if the remaining 80 per cent were to be 'developed out of existence', because of hydrological and climatic repercussions arising from widespread deforestation. According to recent research by Molion (1977) and Salati *et al.* (1978), the Amazon rain forest recycles a vast amount of moisture within its system; in fact, less than half of the region's rainfall drains away through rivers into the sea, the rest being returned to the atmosphere from trees and other plants through evapotranspiration. In other words, the region derives much of its moisture from within its own boundaries. When a substantial sector of the rain forest is eliminated, evapotranspiration could be critically reduced. In turn, this could mean a steadily desiccating environment.

In these circumstances, it could be a risky strategy for conservationists to confine their efforts to supposed Pleistocene refugia and other concentrations of species, in conjunction with a planning framework derived from the Theory of Island Biogeography. No matter how carefully a network of protected areas might be designed, they could eventually dry out if the remainder of the forest were steadily destroyed, leaving mere remnants of the uniquely rich biotas they were intended to protect.

Conservation areas and multiple use

Fortunately, protection of primary forest tracts can be combined with other types of forest utilization. A patch of forest set aside for protecting species serves several other purposes, for example tourism, safeguarding watersheds, regulating local climate. Certain of these roles may appear to conflict with the strict 'no exploitation' philosophy of parks and reserves, but in actual operation there need be no significant conflict. The International Union for Conservation of Nature and Natural Resources (IUCN) recognizes at least ten types of conservation areas, ranging from Strict Nature Reserves to Multiple-Use Management Areas, each type being based on the objectives for which the area is to be managed.

So conservationists must not be too purist in their commitment to the pristine concept of national parks and reserves. Rather they might look at the idea of 'conservation zones' that protect other resources besides 'wildland amenities'. For example, there seems to be no practical reason why a patch of forest should not be subject to selective exploitation, e.g. through gathering of wild foods (honey, rodents, etc), or felling a few types of quality timbers (e.g. rosewood), or removing germplasm for agriculture, at the same time that they offer 'virgin nature' for visitors.

It is in this direction that the best prospect for long-term protection of Tropical Moist Forest tracts in relatively undisturbed form may lie. Indeed, there could even be a danger that for tropical forests the high prestige concept of national parks may be given excessive emphasis, leaving other forms of protection that are equally important in neglect. There is a major advantage in having a number of conservation land-use categories in the biome: each nation can design a system of protected areas that meets its own needs, including responsibility for protection of irreplaceable resources and contributing to local development on a sustainable basis.

Conclusion

As we have seen, Tropical Moist Forests at present are included in all too few protected areas. Worse still, many of these protected areas are faring badly in the face of economic pressures to put them to apparently more useful purposes.

In Southeast Asia, and specially in the lowland forest, parks and reserves now come under many kinds of attack. In Sumatra, two parks have been violated by logging operations, a nature reserve has been given out for timber concessions, a sawmill has been built on the edge of the Gunung Leuser Reserve, and forests supposedly protected as hydrological reserves are being exploited for various purposes. In East Kalimantan, one third of the 2000 sq. km Kutai Reserve has been taken for logging. In Malaysia, the 5000 sq. km Taman Negara Park is subject to threat by logging interests that eye the US$1.8 billion worth of timber within its borders; and something similar applies to the 2000 sq. km Endau Rompin Park. In many protected areas of the Philippines, there is much hunting and intensive collecting of firewood, while shifting cultivators seem to operate with impunity, and certain localities even include townships; the 73 000 hectare Mount Apo National Park in Mindanao, southern Philippines, contains many endemic species, plus a concentration of the extremely endangered monkey-eating eagle (now renamed the Philippines Eagle), yet the park may well be reduced to 13 790 hectares, the rest being given over to logging and settlement. Many other instances could be cited to indicate how protected areas often fail to withstand economic pressures. This process seems likely to become critical for conservation of Tropical Moist Forests in the years ahead, unless protection policies and practices can integrate these areas better with economic development.

At the same time, it is heartening to hear that several countries have recently set aside an impressive array of parks and reserves – impressive that is, compared with before, but barely significant compared with what is required. Peru hopes to protect almost 55 000 sq. km of its 650 000 sq. km of rain forests by 1980; several areas are to be established after the pattern of the Manu National Park, which covers the drainage of an entire tributary river system. Indonesia plans to expand its parks and reserves from 36 000 to 100 000 sq. km by 1983. Zaïre has proposals to increase its network from 78 130 to 350 000 sq. km, or 15 per cent of the country, by 1980; regrettably Zaïre seems to be falling behind this ambitious schedule, but the bulk of its forests continue to be little disturbed.

If the 'big three' countries with Tropical Moist Forests – Brazil, Zaïre and Indonesia – succeed in these plans, their protected areas will amount altogether to 625 000 sq. km or an area almost the size of Spain and Portugal put together, or Texas, representing well over 7 per cent of the entire biome. This will be highly encouraging, even if far short of the minimum 10–20 per cent postulated by the Theory of Island Biogeography. After all, to ask a country to set aside one tenth of its national territory is equivalent to asking the United States to set aside an area twice the size of California.

References

Altschul, S. von R. (1977). 'Exploring the herbarium', *Scientific American*, **236**(5), 96–104.

Calvin, M. (1978). 'Green factories', *Chemical and Engineering News*, **56**, 30–6.

Diamond, J. M. (1975). 'The island dilemma: Lessons of modern biogeographic studies for the design of natural reserves', *Biol. Conserv.*, 7, 129–46.

Hahn, C. (1980). 'The amazing Mexican maize story', *Threatened Plants Committee Newsletter*, No. 6, 3–5.

Lack, D. (1976). *Island Biology*, Studies in Ecology Vol. 3, Blackwell, Oxford.

Lewis, W. H. and Elvin-Lewis, M. P. F. (1977). *Medical Botany*, Wiley, New York.

MacArthur, R. H. and Wilson, E. O. (1967). *The Theory of Island Biogeography*, Princeton Univ. Press, Princeton, New Jersey.

Molion, L. C. B. (1977). *A Climatonic Study of the Energy and Moisture Fluxes of the Amazonas Basin with Considerations of Deforestation Effects*, Instituto de Pesquisas, São Paulo, Brazil.

Morton, J. F. (1977). *Major Medicinal Plants*, Charles C. Thomas, Springfield, Illinois.

Myers, N. (1978). *What Use is Wildlife?*, Earthscan Briefing Document No. 11, Earthscan, London.

Myers, N. (1979). *The Sinking Ark*, Pergamon, Oxford.

Myers, N. (1980). *Conversion of Tropical Moist Forests*, National Academy of Sciences, Washington, DC.

National Academy of Sciences (1975). *Underexploited Tropical Plants with Promising Economic Value*, National Academy of Sciences, Washington, DC.

National Academy of Sciences (1980). *Research Priorities in Tropical Biology*, National Academy of Sciences, Washington, DC.

Persson, R. (1974). 'World forest resources: Review of the world's forest resources in the early 1970s', *Research Notes* No. 17, Department of Forest Survey, Royal College of Forestry, Stockholm, Sweden.

Persson, R. (1975). 'Forest resources of Africa, Part I: Country descriptions', *Research Notes* No. 18, Department of Forest Survey, Royal College of Forestry, Stockholm, Sweden.

Persson, R. (1977). 'Forest resources of Africa, Part II: Regional analysis', *Research Notes* No. 22, Department of Forest Survey, Royal College of Forestry, Stockholm, Sweden.

Prance, G. T. (1977). 'The phytogeographic subdivisions of Amazonia and their influence on the selection of biological reserves', in *Extinction is Forever* (Eds. G. T. Prance and T. S. Elias), pp. 195–213, New York Botanical Garden, Bronx, New York.

Prance, G. T. (Ed.) (in press). *Proceedings of Symposium on the Biological Model for Diversification in Tropical Lowland Forests*, Columbia University Press, New York.

Salati, E. *et al.* (1978). *Recycling of Water in the Amazon Basin: An Isotopic Study*, Division of Environmental Science, Centre of Nuclear Energy and Agriculture, Piracicaba, Brazil.

Schultes, R. E. (1976). *Hallucinogenic Plants*, Golden Press, Racine, Wisconsin.

Simberloff, D. S. and Abele, L. G. (1976). 'Island biogeography theory and conservation practice', *Science*, **191**, 285–6.

Sommer, A. (1976). 'Attempt at an assessment of the world's tropical moist forests', *Unasylva*, **28**(112, 113), 5–25.

Terborgh, J. W. (1974). 'Preservation of natural diversity: The problem of extinction-prone species, *BioScience*, **24**, 715–22.

Unesco/UNEP/FAO (1978). *Tropical Forest Ecosystems: A State-of-knowledge Report*, Natural Resources Research 14, Unesco, Paris.

Wagner, H. and Wolff, P. (1977). *New Natural Products and Plant Drugs*, Springer Verlag, New York.

Wetterberg, G. A., Padua, G., deCastro, C. S., and Carvalho de Vaseoncellos, J. M. (1976). *An Analysis of Nature Conservation Priorities in the Amazon*, UNDP/FAO/IBDF/BRA 545, Tech. Ser. No. 8, Instituto Brasileiro de Desenvolvimento Florestal, Brasilia.

Whitmore, T. C. (1975). *Tropical Rain Forests of the Far East*, Clarendon Press, Oxford.

Note

The term Tropical Moist Forests is used in this chapter following the definition in Myers (1980). This reads:

> Evergreen or partly evergreen forests, in areas receiving not less than 100 mm of precipitation in any month for two out of three years, with mean annual temperature of $24+$ °C and essentially frost-free; in these forests some trees may be deciduous; the forests usually occur at altitudes below 1,300 m (though often in Amazonia up to 1,800 m and generally in south-east Asia up to only 750 m); and in mature examples of these forests, there are several more or less distinctive strata.

Discussion

C. O. Tamm (Uppsala): While I certainly support all what Dr Myers has said, I should like to emphasize that realistic attempts to preserve natural resources must pay much more attention to the socioeconomic problems than has so far been the case. Unique human cultures are destroyed or irreparably damaged when the forests disappear. The forests have provided raw material of various kinds, employment, and environmental benefits in addition to food from wild plants and animals as well as from small temporary fields. When natural forests are replaced by fields, pastures, forest plantations, or, as too often happens, waste land, the revenues go to quite different people than those suffering from the losses. There seems to be much to gain by improving the management of some of the land already damaged in order to provide wood for construction, cellulose and fuel as well as labour opportunities.

It might even be possible to join forces, at least for certain purposes, with some of the agencies now exploiting tropical forests. A first step would of course be, as Dr Myers advocated, to let the market prices include costs for recompensating the exploited countries and peoples for some of the environmental damage.

The Biological Aspects of Rare Plant Conservation
Edited by Hugh Synge
© 1981 John Wiley & Sons Ltd.

13
Techniques for the identification and conservation of threatened species in tropical forests

P. S. ASHTON *Arnold Arboretum, Harvard University*

Summary

The term 'rarity' defies definition in tropical forests. Though most plant species grow there in exceptionally low population densities and are self-incompatible, some pollen vectors range remarkably widely and adventive embryony is apparently frequent. Though seed dispersal is often restricted and conditions for seedling establishment specialized, populations probably do not fluctuate greatly in numbers over time. Nevertheless, these dispersal and establishment characteristics explain why rain forest is effectively a non-renewable resource following medium or large-scale conversion, and the low densities and patchiness of species populations indicates that fragmentation of the forests into isolated reserves is certain to lead to some extinction. It is still feasible, but now urgent, for continuing monitoring of tropical deforestation to be undertaken, and threatened habitats and regions exceptionally rich in endangered species to be identified. On this basis, an integrated system of inviolate reserves can yet be created and, simultaneously, genotypes of otherwise inevitably doomed taxa rescued for cultivation in botanic gardens. Meanwhile, more research is required into the propagation, reproduction, ecological genetics and demography of tropical forest plants.

Though the spread of the deserts has been attracting increasing concern, and deforestation is rapidly proceeding throughout the tropics, it is the climax lowland and mountain evergreen rain forests of the perhumid tropics that have the least developed capacity for self-repair. The trees as a rule have seeds which lack dormancy; conditions for germination and establishment are often specialized, and fruit dispersal is frequently poor (e.g. Gómez-Pompa *et al.*, 1972). The herbaceous ground flora and the epiphytes are dependent on the habitat that the trees provide. These forests are without doubt richer in angiosperm species than any other vegetation. (Throughout this chapter I will use the term richness to refer solely to intrinsic, vegetational richness.) The rate of conversion – and this almost always means permanent destruction – is now so rapid that, according to the conservative estimates of Myers (1980), there will remain only isolated fragments at the end of this century except perhaps in some eastern Andean foothills, and in the seasonal forests of the Congo where the flora is comparatively poor. His report moreover fails to emphasize that in the everwet lowlands below 500 m, where species richness is heavily concentrated, this state of affairs has already been reached except in inner Borneo and in some parts of South America. Our knowledge of species distributions in the tropics is meanwhile so generalized that it is frequently impossible to identify which species are endangered. Under such circumstances, serious consideration of appropriate techniques for the identification and conservation of the plethora of rare species confined to tropical rain forests might appear academic; but is the picture so bleak?

I wish here to explain my conviction that carefully planned and executed surveys, combined with further research into the propagation, and the size of breeding populations of tropical plants, can yet give us a sound biological basis for the greatly enhanced conservation program that is so desperately needed in the humid tropics. First priority, it is obvious, must be given to the conservation of sites, rather than individual species.

White (1968, 1976) and Gómez-Pompa's and van Steenis' colleagues have provided excellent examples of the usefulness of distribution maps in which individual locations are indicated, for the identification of regions and sites of high conservation priority. Their maps also confirm the patchiness of our knowledge of plant distributions in the tropics, and thus aid in establishing priorities for future exploration. Certainly, African forests are better known than South American. Tropical Asia is patchily explored; the relatively intensive collecting of Sri Lanka, India, peninsular Malaysia and Java contrasts with the situation in West New Guinea, Moluccas, south and west Borneo and parts of Indo-Burma. It is not a coincidence that knowledge is greatest where the forests are most depleted, for in these regions past civilizations, European colonization, and contemporary over-population were and still are concentrated.

In spite of that, regions of high species richness, and of high endemism, are being identified in all the major tropical forest areas by this approach. The highest species richness is associated with high and evenly distributed rainfall. The reasons for this are not yet understood except in the obvious case of the epiphyte flora; two correlates worthy of detailed study are the general lack of prevailing winds and the frequency of sporadic and supra-annual flowering in this climate. Though there is variation in species richness and endemism in the lowlands which is likely to be related to the degree of climatic change experienced during the Pleistocene, it also seems unnecessary to assume that floras rich in tree species, including those with high species endemism, predate the Pliocene *in situ*.

Thus, in the American tropics the outstandingly rich lowland forests are concentrated in perhumid regions of the South American continent; those of the Choco in north-west Colombia and the eastern equatorial foothills of the Andes, only now being explored intensively, may even come to vie in richness with some Far Eastern forests (A. H. Gentry, pers. comm.). For both plants and animals, islands of high species endemism in the Guyanas and in the Amazonian hylea to some degree coincide; it is supposed by many that they represent Pleistocene refugia (e.g. Vanzolini, 1973; Prance, 1973; Haffer, 1978), though they may also delineate regions of equable rainfall.

A similar pattern prevails in Africa, where the high species richness of the Cameroun forests coincides with the most extensive wet aseasonal lowland area on the continent. Pleistocene climatic changes are generally acknowledged to have been more drastic and extensive in Africa than elsewhere so that, though opportunities for migration routes were good, the flora is now rather poor as well as uniform. The notable exception is eastern and montane Madagascar which, capturing the moist easterlies off the Indian Ocean, is extraordinarily rich in endemic genera as well as species and may represent a refuge for many taxa now extinct on the continent.

In Asia, the high species richness of the New Guinea lowland forests (e.g. Paijmans, 1970), and those of Borneo (Ashton, 1964, 1977) and peninsular Malaysia (Poore, 1968; Whitmore, 1975; Ashton, 1978) is associated with currently perhumid climates; solid evidence for more seasonal rainfall distribution during the Pleistocene is so far lacking except where it should be anticipated, west of the peninsular mountains (R. Morley, pers. comm.).

Endemism, on the other hand, shows in part a distinctively different pattern, reflecting past opportunities for migration, and in the case of genera and higher taxa, of pre-Pleistocene isolation. Thus, the lowland tree flora of peninsular Malaysia is among the richest in the world yet endemism is surprisingly low. Species endemism is rather high in the Philippines, and very high in Sri Lanka where species richness of individual forest communities is low. This endemism would appear to have a post-Miocene origin; the Sri Lanka forests have apparently been unable to accumulate species through immigration since then, and their small area, perhaps throughout this period, may have led to attrition. The extraordinary generic endemism of New Caledonia clearly reflects a much longer period of isolation, currently considered to extend back to the early Tertiary (e.g. Raven, 1979).

The case of Madagascar emphasizes the very limited means of fruit dispersal of so many rain forest taxa. This is also demonstrated by the islands of Borneo and Celebes which are but 100 km apart, yet only two of the approximately 280 species of Dipterocarpaceae in Borneo occur also in Celebes; one of these is a riparian species which sometimes grows by brackish water (Ashton, in press). Similarly, in regions of broken relief or edaphic diversity, local endemism is frequently very marked. Sri Lanka provides an example of the former. There, in the minute everwet south-west region of about 150 × 150 km, over 800 endemic species of angiosperms occur; within it the low coastal, as well as the taller Sinharaja, central and Knuckles hills each bear a notable complement of endemics (Peeris, 1975). In north-west Borneo, the poorly consolidated sediments of the coastal hills bear characteristic soils, and a distinctive flora rich in disjunctly distributed taxa, vicariants and other endemics whose distribution can in part be explained by the opportunities for alternate migration and isolation that occurred during the Pleistocene (Ashton, 1972). By contrast, the limestone hills and ultrabasic exposures of western Malesia, also rich in endemics, have probably always been geographically fragmented. Though the tree flora now contains a minor element of widespread disjunct species which extend into the seasonal tropics where their ranges are more continuous, the endemics appear to have originated from the surrounding flora through ecotypic specialization. Such edaphically correlated endemism may be anticipated in South America too, where much is currently explained by Pleistocene refugia hypotheses (e.g. Prance, 1973; van der Hammen, 1979).

Studies in the Far East suggest that species richness of the primary forest flora follows a predictable pattern throughout a region sharing a common geological history. Richness varies considerably with soil fertility, but floras on soils of similar fertility are of similar richness even if the species they contain differ. Richness reaches its peak on deep well-watered soils of rather low fertility, and declines not only on exceedingly infertile, but more fertile soils as well, for reasons that are not understood (Ashton, 1964, 1977, 1978).

In summary we find that, though much of the present humid tropics is of recent origin and graced by a widespread and generalized, though usually rich flora, areas can be identified in most regions where the flora is exceptional in its richness; some of these are extremely rich in endemic taxa also, and their presence presumably reflects a greater climatic continuity there.

The extreme fragmentation of species distributions, which appears to be characteristic of areas of high endemism, poses a grave dilemma for conservation. It is further exacerbated by accidents of geography and human history: in Madagascar and Sri Lanka land shortages are already acute, while in Borneo the accessible coastal lowlands are those most rich in endemism. Furthermore, the distinctive and disjunct limestone and ultrabasic formations are rapidly being depleted by mining. It is obvious that much will go; it is also equally obvious that a conservation strategy is urgently needed which will take account of what little we do now know concerning rain forest biogeography. I am convinced that we must pursue dual priorities: designation of carefully selected reserves for *in situ* conservation, and rescue operations for selected taxa in areas when such reserves cannot, for one reason or another, be implemented.

Both approaches, but most particularly the first, require knowledge of the minimum size of stable populations. Of course, no single answer will be forthcoming. Relevant studies have to date been concentrated on species with comparatively high population densities; they constitute a small atypical minority of the rain forest flora (e.g. Richards, 1952). Biological studies are never easy under rain forest conditions; we must now challenge the brave to search out the typical species, which will occur in mean densities of 1 per 5 hectares or less, for study!

In spite of mean population densities that in general are extremely low, it seems that primary rain forest tree species are usually self-incompatible, and often dioecious (Ashton, 1969; Bawa, 1974; Bawa and Opler, 1975). Their populations may be genetically rather variable (Gan, 1976; Gan *et al.*, 1977), preliminary evidence suggesting high levels of local variation but rather low interpopulation variability throughout their range. These properties, however, must themselves vary according to the effectiveness of pollen and seed dispersal, and to the degree of habitat fragmentation, all of which exhibit wide variability within the tropical rain forest.

Clumping of sexually mature individuals is general in terrestrial rain forest plants, and is associated with tree species that have ineffective seed dispersal (Poore, 1968; Ashton, 1969; Chan, 1977). These clumps are themselves aggregated, and it seems likely that both clumps and aggregates concentrate and disperse over time, causing local oscillations in numbers at varying scales according to the life-form and species. Chan found that isolated individuals of the self-incompatible dipterocarp *Shorea leprosula* Miq. had exceptionally low fruit set. Whether oscillations occur in whole breeding populations is unknown, but they are unlikely in edaphically wide-ranging species.

There is, however, no obvious correlation between overall population density and pollen or seed dispersal efficiency, as the following Far Eastern examples testify: chiropterophily can provide an effective means of long-distance pollination. The nectarivorous megachiropteran bat *Eonycteris spelaea* Dobson will fly up to 50 km from its roost nightly, visiting individuals of one or a restricted number of tree species *en route* (Start, 1974). In peninsular Malaysia the four species of *Parkia* (Leguminosae–Mimosoideae) and eleven of *Durio* (Bombacaceae) appear to be exclusively pollinated by these mammals. Individuals of both genera tend to form isolated clumps in the forest, with mean population densities seldom exceeding 1 in 5 hectares (e.g. Whitmore, 1971) and often much less. The bats, however, preferentially feed on flowers of the genus *Sonneratia* (Sonneratiaceae), trees which grow gregariously in the mangrove. Dipterocarp trees of the genera *Hopea* and *Shorea* have been found to be pollinated exclusively by Thysanoptera, vectors which cannot normally be expected to fly far in the generally windless climate of the perhumid tropics (Chan, 1977; Appanah, 1979). Though these trees, too, form markedly clumped populations, few are gregarious and many have very low mean population densities.

Many dipterocarps, and a number of other rain forest tree species of both canopy and understorey, are now known to be at least facultatively apomictic through adventive embryony (e.g. Baker, 1960; Kaur *et al.*, 1978). Here again, however, species with high as well as low population densities, not surprisingly, have been found to exhibit this propensity. Their population variability suggests, nevertheless, that outcrossing does continue on a significant scale.

What then *is* a 'rare' species in a tropical rain forest? Clearly, there is no simple answer, and we currently know too little about the ecological genetics of species to prescribe the minimum size of populations, and hence the minimum areas which we may need for their conservation. Whitmore (1977) has estimated that a minimum population of 5000 interbreeding individuals of the wind-pollinated and generally gregarious rain forest conifer *Agathis* might be needed if genetic diversity is to be fully maintained, but one doubts whether breeding populations of this size, even in this genus, predominate in nature.

Certainly, guidelines for conservation of the tree species must also include safeguards for their pollen and fruit vectors. That may prove difficult, as in the case of *Eonycteris*, whose principal food source is being decimated by coastal development. In this case the inland tree species pollinated by the bat are dependent on it, but the bat is dependent on another. In another example, seeds of the genera *Xerospermum* and *Nephelium* of the Sapindaceae do not germinate unless the pericarp is removed; in nature this is effected by primates (Yap, 1976); extinction of the primates will lead to eventual extinction of the trees. Whereas leaf monkeys (*Presbytis*), however, do not swallow the seeds and thus do not disperse them far, gibbons do, ingesting a few at a time and moving on through the jungle some distance before defecating the seed which can still germinate (D. Chivers, pers. comm.). Clearly, the genecological effect of gibbon dispersal will be quite different from that of leaf monkeys; gibbons require larger territories for their own survival.

Many tropical tree species have specialized edaphic requirements (Ashton, 1964; Baillie, 1978), and persist in remarkably small breeding populations, sometimes perhaps of fewer than 100 individuals, which are separated by hundreds of kilometers in a widely disjunct distribution. Though one often finds species to be absent from islands of apparently suitable habitat (e.g. Whitmore, 1975, p. 185), I am often more struck by the overall predictability of those that are present. Clearly, these habitats must have been more widespread in the past, but are unlikely to have been so for at least 10 000 years. Yet many populations have survived since then. An analogous problem exists with epiphytes, many of which are confined to isolated locations with exceptionally high atmospheric humidity, and to ground herbs which so often occur in dense but isolated patches that may frequently have originated from a single plant: though such populations could probably have originated by long-distance dispersal, is occasional enrichment from nearby stock necessary, and how many such stands need to be conserved?

Unamenable as the problem is to investigation, it is likely that tropical forests always have been dynamic systems in which extinction as well as immigration and speciation has been a frequent event among small and low density populations. Theory would predict an inevitable attrition of 'rare' species when the extent of a forest is drastically reduced, however large the reserves that are set aside.

Administrators frequently ask what can be the minimum viable area of a conserved forest. The question is unfortunately unanswerable. We can say, however, from knowledge of the spatial distribution of tree populations, that even the commonest trees would be likely to experience extreme oscillations in numbers if confined to areas of less than 1 sq. km. In an earlier paper (Ashton, 1976), working on the assumption that a minimum viable size for a sexually mature population of outbreeders should be two hundred individuals, I calculated that reserves in species-rich Borneo should be at least 2000 hectares; this would be compatible with the needs of primates and other large fruit vectors. In many regions site variability requires that an area of at least this size should be represented in each habitat. In the case of species occupying small isolated habitats, such as mountain peaks, still larger areas of landscape would be required though many examples exist in nature of species, including trees, which are only known from single small populations on isolated peaks.

The very isolation of conserved forests in a sea of converted land will inevitably have profound effects which at present are little understood. Appanah (1979) found, for example, that even 1 km inside the now isolated 2000 hectare Pasoh research forest in peninsular Malaysia, meliponid bees, important pollinators previously thought to have very limited foraging ranges, were sometimes returning to their nests with 100 per cent oil palm pollen. In a more obvious way, hydrology will be affected, and there is some evidence that the rainfall pattern will change if the surface temperature of the adjacent converted land differs from that of the original forest.

Over a longer period, it is likely that even slight oscillations in regional climate will profoundly affect beleaguered natural forests. Examples exist in the relict sholas of southern India and the margins of some montane forests in Sri Lanka, where frost incidence appears to be increasing to the extent that it is penetrating the canopy and killing the tree regeneration which is susceptible to frost. Here the forest is reverting to cane brake or grassland.

Nevertheless, the best and only solution is implementation of a comprehensive network of inviolate reserves, each of ample size, representative of the diversity of habitats in a region as part of an integrated land use plan. The national parks of Costa Rica and Malaysia are shining examples of such an approach, and already attract researchers whose work will, in due course, provide biological foundations for conservation planning in tropical vegetation.

Even with the best planned parks systems massive extinction is inevitable in those regions of the humid tropics where local endemism is greatest. In particular, it is unrealistic to expect that areas of the most fertile lands will be conserved: the distinctive flora of these lands, once presumably widespread and now already largely annihilated as the loss of the ancestors of so many cultivated tropical forest trees attests, demands urgent action. The solution here, even though probably temporary and certainly inadequate, must be *ex situ* conservation. This has been discussed at length (Jong, 1979), but the biological basis for selection of genotypes for cultivation is yet to be established. On account of the extraordinary richness of tropical floras, and the prevalence of tree species lacking seed dormancy, orchards and seed banks must be rejected as impractical for general conservation purposes. The botanic gardens and arboreta of the tropics must play the main role, and major new investment in these languishing resources will be vital. Based on them, species inventories in forests currently undergoing conversion should be undertaken as a routine procedure. I know from personal experience that herbarium staff can – and should – screen incoming material immediately to identify the presence of species in immediate danger. Steps can then be taken to collect live material for cultivation, ensuring that several genotypes are grown, preferably from different provenances. At the Arnold Arboretum we cultivate 15 000 individuals of 6000 woody taxa. We calculate that we have spaces in our site of 100 hectares for 21 000 individuals representing 6500 taxa. This is approximately the extent of the Malaysian tree flora.

The unpredictable flowering, lack of seed dormancy, and poor suckering capacity of so many mature-phase rain forest trees pose major unsolved problems for propagation. Here is yet another field demanding higher priority in research: we will have to rely mostly on vegetative propagation as a means of introducing and maintaining species *ex situ*; from the little evidence presently available, there are many problems to be solved before simple standard procedures can be prescribed.

Our knowledge of those aspects of the biology of rain forest plants which relate to their conservation is embryonic. Meanwhile, the forests are disappearing at the rate of 100 000–200 000 sq. km per year (Myers, 1980). The planning and implementation of effective conservation programs are the responsibility of national governments, and are best advised by resident scientists. But scientists everywhere must share responsibility by sponsoring and collaborating in research that will underpin political decisions. This is urgently needed in the following areas:

1. Inventory. At the broadest level, we need global monitoring by satellite imagery, of tropical deforestation. This information should be used to establish priorities for plant exploration and inventory, concentrating on the regions known from ground surveys, or expected to be exceptionally rich in endangered species. The total enumeration of individual sample plots in representative communities is advocated; there are few areas of the world now where taxa of interest cannot be identified by this means, even if they cannot be named. For trees exceeding 10 cm diameter, samples of 1000 nearest neighbors have provided a useful indication of the degree of species richness, and of the species represented (Ashton, 1978). Felling areas can prove invaluable for sampling the epiphyte flora. To be sure, most material thus collected will be sterile, but this serves as a telling test of our motivation: identification of conservation priorities or collecting for our own research or for our institution!

2. Collection of live material of endangered species, particularly those of potential economic importance and those of outstanding biological interest, for cultivation in botanic gardens in their countries of origin and elsewhere.

3. We must greatly increase the level of research activity on tropical plants *in vivo*. On the one hand, methods of propagation have been little studied other than in the main crop plants. Many woody species remain difficult to propagate vegetatively, and difficult to transport as bare-rooted seedlings. Successful tissue culture appears yet further away. Seed storage is a major problem with rain forest plants too, and it seems unlikely that it will be possible to induce dormancy in many species.

On the other hand, we must greatly broaden our slender basis of knowledge on the biosystematics, breeding systems, population genetics and demography of tropical plants before we can safely make generalizations concerning the area and population size required for the long-term well-being of species, and of the ecosystems in which they occur.

In all these spheres, vital if we are to conserve a representative array of rain forest species, success will above all depend on a sensitive appreciation of the human element. International accords, formal recommendations at conferences and grand statements by prestigious people will achieve little. Success *must* depend on trustful collaboration between scientists resident in the tropics and colleagues from elsewhere who are sufficiently dedicated to commit themselves to a region, even a country where they can gradually build up working relationships to the level of activity that will be essential if research is to be established on a continuing basis. In this, the collaborative training of graduate students must play a central role.

In the difficult decades ahead the best protection of conserved areas will be an active community of field biologists. They will demonstrate that there is indeed a purpose behind the setting aside of inviolate conservation areas; they alone will have the motivation to watch the boundaries for the universal threat of illegal infringement.

References

Appanah, S. (1979). *The Ecology of Insect Pollination of Some Tropical Trees*, PhD thesis, University of Malaya.

Ashton, P. S. (1964). *Ecological Studies in the Mixed Dipterocarp Forests of Brunei State*, Oxford Forestry Memoirs, 25.

Ashton, P. S. (1969). 'Speciation among tropical forest trees: Some deductions in the light of recent evidence', *Biol. J. Linn. Soc.*, **1**, 155–96.

Ashton, P. S. (1972). 'The quaternary geomorphological history of western Malesia and lowland forest photogeography', in *Transactions of the Second Aberdeen–Hull Symposium on Malesian Ecology* (Eds. P. and M. Ashton), pp. 35–62.

Ashton, P. S. (1976). 'Factors affecting the development and conservation of tree genetic resources in South-east Asia', in *Tropical Trees: Variation, Breeding and Conservation* (Eds. J. Burley and B. T. Styles), Linnean Soc. Symp. Ser. 2, pp. 189–98. Academic Press, London.

Ashton, P. S. (1977). 'A contribution of rain forest research to evolutionary theory', *Ann. Missouri Bot. Gard.*, **64**, 694–705.

Ashton, P. S. (1978). 'Flora Malesiana precursores: Dipterocarpaceae', *Gard. Bull. Sing.*, **31**(1), 5–48.

Ashton, P. S. (in press). 'Dipterocarpaceae', in *Flora Malesiana* (Ed. C. G. G. J. van Steenis), Noordhoff, The Netherlands.

Baillie, I. H. (1978). *Studies of Site–Forest Relationships in the Mixed Dipterocarp Forest of Sarawak*, PhD thesis, University of Aberdeen.

Baker, H. G. (1960). 'Apomixis and polyembryony in *Pachira oleaginea* (Bombacaceae)', *Amer. J. Bot.*, **47**(4), 296–302.

Bawa, K. S. (1974). 'Breeding systems of tree species of a lowland tropical community', *Evolution*, **28**, 85–92.

Bawa, K. S. and Opler, P. A. (1975). 'Dioecism in tropical forest trees', *Evolution*, **29**, 167–79.

Chan, H. T. (1977). *Reproductive Biology of Some Malaysian Dipterocarps*, PhD thesis, University of Aberdeen.

Gan, Y.-Y. (née Yap) (1976). *Population and Phylogenetic Studies on Species of Malaysian Rainforest Trees*, PhD thesis, University of Aberdeen.

Gan, Y. Y., Robertson, F. W., Ashton, P. S., Soepadmo, E., and Lee, D. W. (1977). 'Genetic variation in wild populations of rain-forest trees', *Nature (Lond.)*, **269**, 5626, 323–5.

Gómez-Pompa, A., Vázquez-Yanes, G., and Guevara, S. (1972). 'The tropical rain forest: A nonrenewable resource', *Science*, **177**, 4051, 762–5.

Haffer, J. (1978). 'Distribution of Amazon forest birds', *Bonn Zool. Beitr.*, **29**, 38–78.

Hammen, T. van der (1974). 'The Pleistocene changes of vegetation and climate in tropical South America', *J. Biogeog.*, **1**, 3–26.

Jong, K. (Ed.) (1979). *Biological Aspects of Plant Genetic Resource Conservation in South-east Asia*, Transactions of the Fifth Aberdeen–Hull Symposium on Malesian Ecology, Scotland, 1977. Department of Geography, University of Hull Misc. Series 21.

Kaur, A., Ha, C. O., Jong, K., Sands, V. E., Chan, H. T., Soepadmo, E., and Ashton, P. S. (1978). 'Apomixis may be widespread among trees of the climax rain forest', *Nature (Lond.)*, **271**, 5644, 440–2.

Myers, N. (1980). *Conversion of Tropical Moist Forests*, US National Academy of Sciences, Washington, DC.

Paijmans, K. (1970). 'An analysis of four tropical rain forest sites in New Guinea', *J. Ecol.*, **58**, 77–101.

Peeris, C. V. S. (1975). *The Ecology of the Endemic Tree Species of Sri-Lanka in Relation to Their Conservation*, PhD thesis, University of Aberdeen.

Poore, M. E. D. (1968). 'Studies in Malaysian rain forest. I. The forest on the Triassic sediments in Jengka Forest Reserve', *J. Ecol.*, **56**, 143–96.

Prance, G. T. (1973). 'Phytogeographic support for the theory of Pleistocene forest refuges in the Amazon basin . . .', *Acta Amazonica*, **3**(3), 5–28.

Raven, P. H. (1979). 'Plate tectonics and southern hemisphere biogeography', in *Tropical Botany* (Eds. K. Larson and L. B. Holm-Nielsen), pp. 3–24, Academic Press, London.

Richards, P. W. (1952). *The Tropical Rain Forest*, Cambridge University Press.

Start, A. N. (1974). *The Feeding Biology in Relation to Food Sources of Nectarivorous Bats (Chiroptera: Megachiroptera) in Malaysia*, PhD thesis, University of Aberdeen.

Steenis, C. G. G. J. van (Ed.) (1948–). *Flora Malesiana*. Noordhoff, The Netherlands.

Vanzolini, P. E. (1973). 'Paleoclimates, relief and species multiplication in equatorial forests', in *Tropical Forest Ecosystems in Africa and South America: A Comparative Review* (Eds. B. J. Meggers et al.), pp. 255–7.

White, F. (1968). *Distributiones Plantarum Africanum*, 14, *Ebenaceae*, Jardin Botanique National de Belgique, Meise.

White, F. (1976). *Distributiones Plantarum Africanum*, 10, *Chrysobalanaceae*, Jardin Botanique National de Belgique, Meise.

Whitmore, T. C. (1971). 'Wild fruit trees and some trees of pharmacological potential in the rain forest of Ulu Kelantan', *Malay. Nat. J.*, **24**, 222–4.

Whitmore, T. C. (1975). *Tropical Rain Forests of the Far East*, Clarendon Press, Oxford.

Whitmore, T. C. (1977). *A First Look at Agathis*, Commonwealth Forestry Institute Tropical Forestry Papers 11.

Yap, S. K. (1976). *The Reproductive Biology of Some Understorey Fruit Tree Species in the Lowland Dipterocarp Forest of West Malaysia*, PhD thesis, University of Malaya.

The Biological Aspects of Rare Plant Conservation
Edited by Hugh Synge
© 1981 John Wiley & Sons Ltd.

14
Australia's rain forests: Where are the rare plants and how do we keep them?

J. G. TRACEY *Division of Forest Research, CSIRO, Atherton, Queensland*

Summary

Only about a quarter of Australia's rain forests survive intact, so the conservation of the remaining 20 000 sq. km is of great importance. The various types of rain forest in Australia are reviewed and their distribution and conservation status discussed. Some examples of rare species are given, arranged by the different forest types. The present emphasis is to classify the forest types rather than to study individual species and the flora is still poorly known. In the light of present threats, designating as wide a variety of forest types for protection as possible is the best way to save the maximum number of species. At the same time, forest management practices which ensure the continued existence of utilized, managed natural forest ecosystems as buffer zones surrounding strict natural reserves must be implemented.

Introduction

The total area of all types of rain forest in Australia when Europeans arrived in 1788 was approximately 80 000 sq. km; of this only approximately 20 000 sq. km remains today (Webb and Tracey, 1980). The clearing of rain forest in Australia is continuing mainly for agriculture and grazing or for forest plantations; lowland rain forest types are virtually extinct in the subtropics and only a few thousand hectares remain in the humid tropic region of north Queensland. All accessible upland rain forests outside national parks either have been logged or are due to be logged in the near future.

The definition of rain forest used here follows Webb (in press) and includes the structural subformations described previously by Webb (1959, 1968, 1978), e.g. complex mesophyll vine forests (tropical lowland rain forests), simple notophyll vine forests (evergreen upland rain forests), microphyll fern forests (temperate rain forests), deciduous vine thickets and semi-deciduous mesophyll vine forests (monsoon forests) and so on. Recent papers on Australian rain forests include Webb (in press), Webb and Tracey (1980), and Webb *et al.* (in press); an account of forest destruction in Australia is given in Webb (1966a), and more recently summed up in Routley and Routley (1973, 1980).

Australian rain forests today are restricted to a series of pockets extending along the east coast from Cape York (11°S) to Tasmania (42°S) and less continuously across northern Australia. These patches resemble an archipelago of refugia, a series of distinctive habitats that characterize a temporary end-point in climatic and geomorphological evolution. They share genera with rain forests elsewhere, but have many endemic species as well as some endemic genera and families, which include many primitive angiosperms. They are part of the wide range of habitats which were present on Gondwanaland, some of which are preserved in what eventually became the Australian landmass. This old relict flora has undergone much expansion and contraction since then; today most of the continent is dry and covered with sclerophyll vegetation dominated by *Eucalyptus* and *Acacia* (Martin, 1978).

Rain forest is a living system of plants and animals varying greatly within itself. It may be sharply different from adjacent vegetation, e.g. in Australia the sclerophylls. By its very nature its complex species composition does not easily fit into the usual criteria with regard to species occurrence, especially the definitions of rare and threatened species. To describe a plant as rare one presumes to know the structure and size of most populations of that species in the forest; this is usually not known even for big trees. Furthermore, more than 100 species from Australian rain forests are known to be undescribed. Data on the distribution and life history of most rain forest plants are minimal. The recent list of rare and threatened species in *Australian Plants at Risk* (Hartley and Leigh, 1979) virtually ignored rain forest species and they admit that 'information for large areas of tropical and arid Australia is very sketchy'.

The conservation status of rain forests published in the 'Specht Report' (Specht *et al.*, 1974) was based on structural classification and had insufficient data on which to base species preservation. Vegetation structure reflects comparable environments but not necessarily floristic similarity and our experience in Australia shows species composition changes within similar structural types. This is true for rain forests generally; for example Prance (1976) describes the forest on high (non-flooded) ground which covers 90 per cent of Amazonia as 'physiognomically uniform throughout the region but botanically very varied'.

No attempt has been made to analyse the conservation position of the Australian rain forests in relation to their flora. The New South Wales National Parks and Wildlife Service, however, have one forest botanist working on a project to assess the position in that state. When many rain forest types themselves are in danger of being lost through clearing, one might question the relevance of thinking in terms of individual species; preservation of the full range of habitat types would seem a much more rewarding approach.

The rain forest flora

Floristic analysis of Australian rain forests based on 561 sites and 1316 species of trees splits them into three distinct regions:

1. Cool–Wet forests; these are the temperate rain forests mostly dominated by *Nothofagus* and usually referred to as the Antarctic element in publications dealing with the Australian flora. Today they are restricted to Tasmania, Victoria and the uplands of New South Wales.
2. Hot–Wet forests; these are the tropical–subtropical forests mostly near the coast and on adjacent mountain ranges in Queensland, but occurring south of Sydney to about 36°S and with some representation in the wetter parts of the Northern Territory, e.g. the Arnhem Land escarpment.
3. Hot–Dry forests; these are the monsoon forests and other semi-deciduous and deciduous types which occur from the Kimberleys in north-western West Australia through sub-coastal Northern Territory, Queensland and northern New South Wales.

Forests of 2 and 3 comprise the so-called Indomalesian flora in Australia.

Ecological relationships of the forest types based on this analysis are given in Webb, Tracey and Williams (in press). Some perspective of the time scale involved in the evolution of this flora and its patterns of distribution today are discussed in Johnson and Briggs (1975), Martin (1978), Webb and Tracey (1980).

The Cool–Wet forests are often dominated by one or a few species of trees, e.g. *Atherosperma, Eucryphia, Nothofagus*, and they have many endemic species both inside the forests and in the surrounding vegetation, including the conifers *Athrotaxis, Diselma* and *Microstrobos*. Their floristic composition and ecological relationships are discussed in several publications, e.g. Gilbert (1959), Howard and Ashton (1973), Busby and Bridgewater (1977).

The Hot–Wet tropical and subtropical forests have complex species composition with widespread genera from many families including Apocynaceae, Cunoniaceae, Lauraceae, Meliaceae, Myrtaceae, Proteaceae, Rubiaceae, Rutaceae and Sterculiaceae. Certain families tend to dominate particular forests, e.g. Cunoniaceae, Lauraceae and Myrtaceae in upland and cooler forests, and Apocynaceae, Meliaceae, and Sterculiaceae in the lowland forests. The Australian tropics have more genera per family than the subtropics. Where genera are shared, the species are often different, notably in *Dysoxylum, Flindersia* and *Syzygium*. Species composition is ever varying as is species abundance, with dominance of fewer species at the environmental extremes, such as infertile soils or impeded drainage. Apart from the recent publications of Webb and Tracey (1980) and Webb, Tracey and Williams (in press), little has been published on the ecological relationships of the flora. Regional descriptions of Hot–Wet forest types based on a combination of structure and floristics including vegetation maps at 1:100 000 scale have been published for the humid tropic region of north Queensland (Tracey and Webb, 1975; Tracey, 1980) and for part of the Macpherson Ranges in subtropical southern Queensland (MacDonald and Whiteman, 1979). Forest classifications for specific purposes, such as logging operations or species preservation, which require knowledge of population structure of particular species, require much larger scales; for example the three types recognized on the map of north Queensland mentioned above were broken into 13 types from canopy features on low-level aerial photos (Hopkins and Graham, 1980). Clearly, if we take each individual species in turn and build upwards to forest types, the knowledge needed to preserve rain forests will probably never be available and certainly not in time to save the many kinds of rain forest being cleared so rapidly in the tropics of the world.

The Hot–Dry forests have fewer genera and species than the Hot–Wet forests and families Anacardiaceae, Bombacaceae, Celastraceae, Euphorbiaceae and Sapindaceae are prominent. These forests are often restricted to particular habitats such as limestone karsts, basaltic hill tops and granite outcrops. They are usually small in area, sometimes only a few hectares or less, and often have sharp boundaries resulting from frequent fires in the surrounding vegetation. In the sub-tropical inland region, however, some species usually found in these types are widespread as understorey in Brigalow forests of *Acacia harpophylla* F. Muell.; often different species of the closed forest genera such as *Geijera* and *Atalaya* are involved. In the tropics interspersion with *Eucalyptus* woodlands is widespread. Genera whose species are mostly in the closed communities have some species which are always part of the woodlands, e.g. *Siphonodon*, *Syzygium*, *Terminalia*. No work has been published on the floristic relationships of the Hot–Dry forests, but their presence is always mentioned as they are encountered in regional land-use surveys. A short report on the monsoon forests of the Northern Territory, which classified and discussed the relationships of the forests based on a floristic analysis of 45 sites by 318 tree species, drew attention to the fact that evergreen and semideciduous–deciduous types had different species composition (Webb and Tracey, 1979). Reports on Prince Regent Reserve (Miles and Burbidge, 1975), on Admiralty Gulf (Beard, 1976) and on Drysdale River National Park (Kabay and Burbidge, 1977) give some data on the forests and thickets of the Kimberleys in Western Australia but their lack of precise information on species composition underlines our ignorance of the flora there.

Where are the rare plants?

How do we answer such questions for the Australian rain forest flora when we do not even have a check list of species and when the only Flora of Queensland (Bailey, 1899–1905), the state which has a substantial part of the rain forest, was published so long ago that much of the information is now out of date? We must therefore rely on herbarium data scattered in different institutions often hundreds of kilometers apart. A stocktaking of data on herbarium collections would indicate some genuine rare plants, but would also be misleading through bias in collections. For example localities easy of access will have more information than other sites and plants with large showy flowers often are collected in preference to the more inconspicuous species.

The Australian Biological Resources Study (A.B.R.S.), a continuing study of the Australian flora and fauna in the Commonwealth Department of Science and the Environment, has recognized the need to build up information on Australian plants and has funded the computerization of data in some herbaria. Fortunately for those interested in rain forest species, the Queensland Herbarium data retrieval system is now in operation. This institution has the most comprehensive collections of rain forest plants in Australia.

Herbarium data should be supplemented with locality records and ecological notes from the inevitable species lists of botanists and ecologists, much of which is lost unless it happens to be published or used on the label of a voucher specimen lodged in an herbarium. The acceptance of A.B.R.S. of a uniform system of data input for each site, represented by a species list with information on latitude, longitude, altitude, soil parent material, etc., would soon build up a bank of knowledge about species. If published at intervals it would pinpoint inaccuracies and inadequate data, and should encourage both professional and amateur botanists to correct it – most of them like to add to the knowledge of plant distribution.

To illustrate the value of such data, an analysis was made of 561 sites, whose tree species lists added up to 1316 species; this allowed a floristic classification of Australian rain forests for the first time. This showed which species of trees occurred on one site, two sites, three sites and so on. The data were easily retrieved from the computer and are summarized in Table 1. Many species are very restricted in their distribution and hence are classed as 'rare plants' even though they may be common at the few sites on which they are recorded. From these, a few examples have been selected below for some of the major subformations of tropical rain forests to indicate the possibilities for their long-term survival under present pressures on rain forest in Australia.

1. Complex mesophyll vine forest – Tropical humid lowlands, north Queensland

Idiospermum australiense (Diels) S. T. Blake (Idiospermaceae) is the only member of a recently described endemic family (Blake, 1972). As far as we know it is a canopy tree with only two disjunct populations restricted to the alluvia and foothills of two streams, Harvey Creek and Noahs Creek in north Queensland. The Harvey Creek population has mostly been destroyed by clear felling the forest for growing sugar cane and cattle grazing but part survives inside Bellenden

Table 1   Tree species occurrence in Australian rain forests: 3116 species from 561 sites

Number of sites in which species occur	Number of species occurring in this number of sites	Percentage of total number of species	
1	173	13.1	23.1
2	131	10.0	30.7
3	100	7.6	35.6
4	64	4.9	41.1
5	73	5.5	45.3
6	56	4.2	48.5
7	42	3.2	51.2
8	36	2.7	53.3
9	27	2.1	56.0
10	35	2.7	

Ker National Park. A large part of the population between Noahs Creek and Daintree River has also been lost through clearing and the remainder was saved from a similar fate by the declaration of a national park. *Idiospermum* is a primitive angiosperm with large seeds (4–6 cm) distributed by gravity and capable of being swallowed by only one bird, the flightless Cassowary. Such species, which are specialized members of a specialized community, are easily destroyed by the activities of man.

Lindsayomyrtus brachyandrus (C. T. White) B. P. M. Hyland & Van Steenis (Myrtaceae) is another newly described genus (Hyland and Van Steenis, 1973) with a similar habitat to *Idiospermum*; it also occurs in the islands to the north of Australia. Its seeds are distributed by birds as the fruit is a fleshy drupe (2.5 cm) capable of being swallowed by many fruit-eating birds in this forest type. Its occurrence is very restricted, however.

Parrot Creek *'Eugenia'* (BRI. 174077) is undescribed and is probably a new genus of Myrtaceae. It has a capsular fruit and small wind-distributed seeds. It is known so far from only population on the foothills of Mt Finnegan towards the northern limit of the tropical humid region of north Queensland.

Neorites kevediana L. S. Smith (Proteaceae) is a primitive tree species in a family which has many endemic genera in the region, both on the lowlands and adjacent uplands (Johnson and Briggs, 1975). It has a restricted distribution mostly on the foothills in the Cedar Bay area between Cooktown and Daintree River. It has a wind-distributed seed approximately 1 cm long.

These are a few of the plants at risk but as the lowland rain forests themselves are vulnerable so their many species (see Appendix I in Tracey, 1980) will be lost unless reserves are declared for the remaining stands.

2. Simple notophyll vine forests and microphyll fern forests – Uplands in the humid tropical region, north Queensland

Many of the species in these forests would qualify as rare plants in the Hartley and Leigh 'Risk Coding', e.g. 'Restricted endemics whose known populations are limited in range (e.g. normally less than 100 km in maximum range)'. Examples include *Aceratium ferrugineum* C. T. White, *Dracophyllum sayeri* F. Muell., *Flindersia unifoliolata* T. Hartley, *Garcinia brassii* C. T. White, *G. mestonii* F. M. Bailey, *Podocarpus ladei* F. M. Bailey, and *Sphalmium racemosum* (C. T. White) Briggs, Hyland & Johnson.

3. Semideciduous mesophyll vine forests – Tropical monsoonal wet

Many species fit into Hartley and Leigh category 4: 'Species of geographical importance, especially those with a disjunct distribution in Australia and overseas and listed only if the Australian populations are localized or sparse'. Examples include *Caryota rumphiana* Mart., *Gulubia costata* Begg., *Maniltoa schefferi* K. Schum., *Nypa fruticans* Van Wurmb., *Pithecellobium arborescens* Kosterm., *Pternandra cyanea* (Blume) Triana, *Pterocarpus macrocarpus* Kuz, *Syzygium brandehorstii* Lauterb. and *Tetrameles nudiflora* R. Br.

In the Northern Territory, where these forest types are scattered in many small patches, *Cleistocalyx operculata* (Roxb.) Merr. & Perry and *Livistona benthamii* Baillon are restricted to swampy types and *Diospyros littorea* (R.Br.) Kosterm. to mangrove fringes. Many species, although found in most patches, show marked variation in population sizes between patches, e.g. *Dysoxylum oppositifolium* F. Muell. ex C.DC. and *Elaeocarpus arnhemicus* F. Muell.

4. Evergreen notophyll vine forests – Tropical monsoonal wet

These forests in Cape York Peninsula are characteristic of the well-watered swales and foredunes in the extensive sand areas between Cooktown and Cape Flattery, and between Olive River and Newcastle Bay in the extreme north of the peninsula. Endemic species are characteristic of these forests, which overlap with the sclerophyll communities, reduced to heaths in extreme sites. These species may be abundant but have a restricted range, e.g. *Eriostemon banksii* Cunn. ex Endl., *Eugenia banksii* S. Moore, *Melaleuca angustifolia* Gaertn., and *Xanthostemon youngii* C. T. White & Francis. Taller evergreen vine forests occur on siliceous parent materials inland especially near Mt Tozer (Hynes and Tracey, 1980). Although widespread species such as *Blepharocarya involucrigera* F. Muell. and

Grevillea pinnatifida F. M. Bailey are common, endemic species also occur and are often abundant locally; examples are *Acmena* sp. (Rocky River) BRI 145388 and *Flindersia brassii* T. Hartley. Several other undescribed species occur, underlining the need for further study 'to ascertain present distribution and taxonomic status' (Hartley and Leigh category 1).

Evergreen notophyll vine forests are found on the sandstone escarpments of Arnhem Land where they are dominated in the top layer by the endemic *Allosyncarpia ternata* S. T. Blake, which grows much taller in the gorges, where it is joined by other endemic trees such as two new species of *Syzygium* (to be published soon by B. P. H. Hyland) and on the drier fire-prone forest fringe by *Blepharocarya depauperata* R. L. Specht, *Eugenia bleeseri* O. Schwarz and *Metrosideros eucalyptoides* F. Muell.

Much of the forest flora in the soakage pockets at the base of the sandstone escarpment or in narrow creeks cut into sandy soils elsewhere, e.g. on Melville Island, shows marked disjunctions. Some species are found only in similar habitats hundreds of kilometers away. Examples include *Elaeocarpus grandis* F. Muell., *Euodia elleryana* F. Muell., *Hydriastele wendlandiana* (F. Muell.) H. Wendl. & Drude, *Ilex arnhemicus* (F. Muell.) Loes, *Kissodendron australianum* (F. Muell.) Seem, and *Ternstroemia cherryi* (F. M. Bailey) Merr. ex J. F. Bailey & C. T. White.

5. Deciduous vine thickets and interspread flora – Tropical monsoonal dry

The thickets are widespread but occur mostly in localized habitats, such as limestone karsts, stony basaltic hill tops, granitic rock outcrops, rock screes and crevices in sandstone areas (Webb and Tracey, 1980). The flora is not well known, but consists of both widespread species showing little variation, e.g. *Drypetes australasica* (Muell. Arg.) Pax & K. Hoffman, *Gyrocarpus americanus* Jacq. and *Strychnos lucida* R. Br., and of genera containing many species often with narrow ranges, e.g. *Croton, Diospyros* and *Terminalia.*

Interspersed flora now occurring as understorey in *Eucalyptus* woodlands includes species of *Albizia, Alstonia, Brachychiton, Buchanania, Planchonella, Siphonodon, Syzygium* and *Terminalia.* Little is known of their species distribution and ecological relationships but there are regional differences. For example many species from Northern Territory do not occur in north Queensland and vice versa.

Similar subdivisions within the rain forests of the subtropics and temperate regions reveal patterns of 'plants at risk' in many types. The flora is better known and numbers of species are lower but the pressure of development on particular areas often puts them in the 'vulnerable' category. Hartley and Leigh list *Cryptocarya foetida* R. T. Baker, *Diploglottis campbellii* Cheel, *Endiandra globosa* Maiden & Betch, and *E. hayesii* Kosterm.; all were previously in the notophyll vine forests of the lowlands of south Queensland and northern New South Wales, which are now almost totally cleared; they also list *Hernandia*

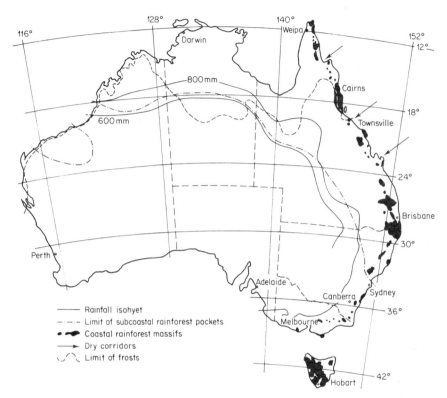

Figure 1   Distribution of rain forest vegetation in Australia. (From *Australian Vegetation*, edited by R. Groves; reproduced by permission of Cambridge University Press)

bivalvis Benth., a tree with restricted distribution in the Araucarian notophyll vine forests of south Queensland, *Planchonella eerwah* (F. M. Bailey) Van Royen and *Xanthostemon oppositifolius* F. M. Bailey, also in Araucarian notophyll vine forests but with emergent *Agathis robusta* (C. Moore ex F. Muell.) F. M. Bailey, a type all but extinct in south Queensland.

In the dry subcoastal subtropics the semi-evergreen vine thickets have a similar occurrence to the deciduous vine thickets of the tropics in having small isolated patches restricted to particular habitats. Often the most common species are restricted to a particular region and may be easily lost in land clearing for pasture development. Examples include *Albizia thozetiana* (F. Muell.) F. Muell. ex Benth., *Cadellia pentastylis* F. Muell. and *Macropteranthes leichhardtii* F. Muell. Amongst the interspersed species, *Flindersia maculosa* F. Muell. of the south and *F. dissosperma* Domin further north are of particular phytogeographic interest; this genus, which is mainly Australian but is also found throughout Papua New Guinea, Indonesia and New Caledonia, has different species in particular types of rain forests (Hartley, 1969).

The temperate rain forest endemics, e.g. *Athrotaxis laxifolia* Hook., *Eucryphia moorei* F. Muell., *Lomatia tasmanica* W. M. Curtis, *Orites milliganii* Meissner, often have restricted populations in specific habitats.

How do we keep the rare plants?

The concern shown for species preservation through such international agreements as the Convention on International Trade in Endangered Species of Wild Fauna and Flora (CITES), which aims to protect species threatened by trade, is commendable but the problem of rain forest conservation is not to be solved through this approach.

As indicated in Table 1 the plants of the rain forest mostly occur on very few sites which makes most of them 'plants at risk' under the Hartley and Leigh definition. To conserve them, the rain forests themselves need to be preserved. The emphasis in Australia on classifying rain forest and on relating the forest types to the environment rather than studying species individually has enabled us to identify habitats which include particular groups of species. In designing reserves with as much habitat variation as possible within each land system, some worthwhile reserves have been dedicated – the emphasis has been on preserving the natural plant communities. Outstanding recent examples are

1. the Kakadu National Park in the Northern Territory which covers parts of the Arnhem Land plateau, the deep gorges and escarpment and the out-wash plains with wetlands and woodlands through to the coast including most of the catchment of the south Alligator River;
2. the Jardine River system in the sand country near the top of the Cape York Peninsula, which has excellent examples of evergreen notophyll vine forests from swampy types through the mixed forests with sclerophylls to sclerophyll heath communities – see Lavarack and Stanton (1977).

Several other large reserves in the Cape York Peninsula were declared on the basis of surveys and recommendations by Stanton (1976). The methodology adopted and described by him in the RAKES report 1977 (Rapid Appraisal of Key and Endangered Sites) could well be applied in other tropical regions (Stanton and Morgan, 1977).

Many rain forest plants are already protected in some of Queensland's excellent national parks, which include a variety of rain forest types (Specht *et al.*, 1974). Examples include Lamington National Park in the subtropical uplands, Eungella Range in the central Queensland uplands, and Bellenden Ker and Daintree River in the north; these contain mostly foothill and upland forests but include some lowland types. The most urgent conservation need is in the wet lowland forests, specifically the few thousand hectares remaining between the Daintree River and

Cooktown. Proposals to declare a significant national park to include these lowland forests and the ranges to the west with Thornton Peak (1300 m) are before the legislators. Such a reserve would ensure the survival of hundreds of rare plants.

These more spectacular reserves must be supplemented by many more smaller ones which still have fragments of previously widespread forest types. Webb (1966*b*) recommended 20 specific habitats as reserves in the tropical humid lowlands of north Queensland; this led to the dedication of more than half as national parks, ensuring the survival of several types which otherwise would be fields of sugar cane by now. The practice of recommending specific habitat types for reserves is now accepted by the Queensland National Parks and Wildlife Service and several hundred proposals have been submitted, resulting in some worthwhile reserves. Progress is slow, however. Real problems arise in having Crown Land reserved, especially when state departments disagree amongst themselves on land-use priorities. Local government often object on the grounds that the land must be brought into production and so raise revenue from rates to provide goods and services. Opposition too is expressed in the strongest terms by often influential groups with vested interests such as the mining and timber industries. Final decisions rest with the state governments. The case for reservations therefore must be specific and include maps with the proposed boundaries. The reasons for the habitat protection must be convincing.

To do this we need to know more about the taxonomy of the plants and the ecology of the forests including the distribution patterns of the species and their population structures. Clearly this is an impossible task in the short term and priorities need to be set. The first steps are to classify the forest into its various habitat types, then to search for suitable land which has representation of these types, to design reserve boundaries and to submit recommendations to government. Often a change from a straight-line boundary to one which includes a complete catchment would ensure the survival of some forest types. On public lands such changes can be made by agreement between departments. Convincing the decision-makers and the public is a more difficult task!

To keep the rain forest plants, reserves are only part of the answer. Management of the logged forests is needed. The implementation of many of the management practices outlined in Roache (1979), including the establishment of 'strict nature reserves in secondary forest where logging operations are excluded', would be a practical solution to the preservation of many species. Other points made by Roache on preserving rain forests are worth repeating here:

The greatest contribution that the forestry profession can make to conservation in the tropics at the present time is to ensure that as large an area as possible of representative natural forest ecosystems is brought under management. The continued existence of utilized, managed natural forest ecosystems surrounding strict natural reserves and linking national parks and game reserves could be a major beneficial factor in conservation in the tropics.

That the forestry profession . . . expand very substantially its programmes of exploration, utilization and conservation of forest gene resources to include at least a portion of the vast array of tropical tree species which have value for purposes other than wood production. A major development in this direction would push forestry practice out of receding enclaves of forest reserves into large areas of partially logged land outside forest reserves . . . and integrate it with farming systems.

In Australia the needs of productive forestry should be met from this improved management and from the plantation forestry which can be applied on much of the cleared land that once carried most of the Australian rain forest. Implementation of these ideas seems unlikely in the short term and one can only hope that the view expressed by Roache is accepted: 'As far as forestry practice is concerned conservation must in the long run be viewed as an integral part of management and formally incorporated in the educational and training programmes of professional foresters and technicians', so that the portions of the World Conservation Strategy concerning tropical forests have some hope of success.

References

Bailey, F. M. (1899–1905). *The Queensland Flora*, Brisbane.

Beard, J. S. (1976). 'The monsoon forests of the Admirality Gulf, Western Australia', *Vegetatio*, **31**, 177–92.

Blake, S. T. (1972). '*Idiospermum* (Idiospermaceae), a new genus and family for *Calycanthus australiensis*', *Contrib. Queensland Herb.*, **12**.

Busby, J. R. and Bridgewater, P. B. (1977). 'Studies in Victorian vegetation, II: A floristic survey of the vegetation associated with *Nothofagus cunninghamii* (Hook.) Oerst. in Victoria and Tasmania', *Proc. R. Soc. Victoria*, **89**, 173–82.

Gilbert, J. M. (1959). 'Forest succession in the Florentine Valley, Tasmania', *Papers and Proc. Roy. Soc. Tasmania*, **93**, 129–51.

Hartley, T. G. (1969). 'A revision of the genus *Flindersia* (Rutaceae)', *J. Arn. Arbor.*, **50**(4), 481–526.

Hartley, W. and Leigh, J. (1979). *Australian Plants at Risk*, Australian National Parks and Wildlife Service Occasional Paper No. 3, Canberra.

Hopkins, M. S. and Graham, A. W. (1980). *Structural Typing of Tropical Rainforests Using Canopy Characteristics in Low Level Aerial Photographs*. Manuscript.

Howard, T. M. and Ashton, D. H. (1973). 'The distribution of *Nothofagus cunninghamii* rainforest', *Proc. Roy. Soc. Victoria*, **86**, 47–75.

Hyland, B. P. M. and Van Steenis, C. G. G. J. (1973). 'The generic identity of *Xanthostemon brachyandrus* C. T. White: *Lindsayomyrtus* novum genus (Myrtaceae)', *Blumea*, **21**, 189–92.

Hynes, R. A. and Tracey, J. G. (1980). 'Vegetation of the Iron Range area, Cape York Peninsula', in *Proc. Symp. R. Soc. Queensland*, Brisbane.

Johnson, L. A. S. and Briggs, B. G. (1975). 'On the Proteaceae – the evolution and classification of a southern family', *Bot. J. Linn. Soc.*, **70**, 83–182.

Kabay, E. D. and Burbidge, A. A. (Eds.) (1977). 'A biological survey of the Drysdale River National Park, North Kimberley, Western Australia', *Wildl. Res. Bull. West Aust.*, **6**, 1–133.

Lavarack, P. S. and Stanton, J. P. (1977). 'Vegetation of the Jardine River catchment and adjacent coastal areas', *Proc. Roy. Soc. Queensland*, **88**, 39–48.

MacDonald, W. J. F. and Whiteman, W. G. (1979). 'Explanatory booklet for Murwillumbah sheet', *Moreton Region Vegetation Map Series*, 58 pp., Queensland Dept. of Primary Industries, Brisbane.

Martin, H. A. (1978). 'Evolution of the Australian flora and vegetation through the Tertiary evidence from pollen', *Alcheringa*, **2**, 181–202.

Miles, J. M. and Burbidge, A. A. (Eds.) (1975). 'A biological survey of the Prince Regent River Reserve, North-west Kimberley, Western Australia'. *Wildl. Res. Bull. West Aust.*

Prance, G. T. (1976). 'The phytogeographic subdivisions of Amazonia and their influence on the selection of biological reserves', In *Extinction Is Forever* (Eds. G. T. Prance and T. S. Elias), New York Botanical Garden, Bronx, New York.

Roache, L. (1979). 'Forestry and the conservation of plants and animals in the tropics', *Forest Ecology and Management*, **2**, 103–22.

Routley, R. and Routley, V. (1973). *The Fight for the Forests*, Research School of Social Sciences Publication, Aust. Nat. University, Canberra.

Routley, R. and Routley, V. (1980). 'Destructive forestry in Melanesia and Australia', *The Ecologist*, **10**, 56–67, Cornwall, England.

Specht, R. L., Roe, E. M. and Boughton, V. H. (Eds.) (1974). Conservation of major plant communities in Australia and Papua New Guinea. *Aust. J. Bot.*, Suppl. Ser., 7.

Stanton, J. P. (1976). *National Parks for Cape York Peninsula*, Aust. Conservation Publication, Melbourne.

Stanton, J. P. and Morgan, M. G. (1977). *Rapid Appraisal of Key and Endangered Sites. Report No. 1. Queensland Case Study*. University of New England, N.S.W. School of Natural Resources.

Tracey, J. G. (1980). *The Vegetation of the Humid Tropical Region. North Queensland.* Manuscript.

Tracey, J. G. and Webb, L. J. (1975). *Vegetation of the Humid Tropical Region of North Queensland. 15 Maps at 1:100,000 Scale and Key.* CSIRO Long Pocket Laboratories, Indooroopilly, Queensland.

Webb, L. J. (1959). 'A physiognomic classification of Australian rain forests', *J. Ecol.*, **47**, 551–70.

Webb, L. J. (1966a). 'Rape of the forests', in *The Great Extermination* (Ed. J. K. Marshall), Heinemann.

Webb, L. J. (1966b). 'The identification and conservation of habitat-types in the wet tropical lowlands of North Queensland', *Proc. Roy. Soc. Queensland*, **78**(6), 59–86.

Webb, L. J. (1968). 'Environmental relationships of the structural types of Australian rain forest vegetation', *Ecology*, **49**, 296–311.

Webb, L. J. (1978). 'A general classification of Australian rainforests', *Australian Plants*, **9**, 349–63.

Webb, L. J. (in press). 'An ecological framework of Australian rainforests. I. Some recent perspectives', *Aust. J. Bot.*

Webb, L. J. and Tracey, J. G. (1979). *An Ecological Survey of the Monsoon Forests of the North Western Region of the Northern Territory*. Report to Australian National Parks and Wildlife Service, Canberra.

Webb, L. J. and Tracey, J. G. (1980). 'Australian rainforests: patterns and change', in *Ecological Biogeography of Australia*, 2nd Edn. (Ed. A. Keast), W. Junk, The Hague.

Webb, L. J., Tracey, J. G. and Williams, W. T. (in press). 'An ecological framework of Australian rainforests. II. Floristic classification', *Aust. J. Bot.*

The Biological Aspects of Rare Plant Conservation
Edited by Hugh Synge
© 1981 John Wiley & Sons Ltd.

15
The biology of Asiatic rattans in relation to the rattan trade and conservation

JOHN DRANSFIELD *The Herbarium, Royal Botanic Gardens, Kew, England*

Summary

Forest destruction and increasing demand for cane furniture have resulted in many rattans (Palmae: Lepidocaryoideae) becoming scarce or reduced to dangerously small populations. Features of their biology, in particular their growth form and flowering and fruiting behaviour as well as their growth rates, are discussed as a basis for development of cultivation and conservation strategies. Cultivation of elite species and control of exploitation of existing wild populations are seen as the only effective means of conservation.

Rattan plants are the source of rattan and cane for furniture manufacture but many items of furniture marketed as rattan are made of bamboo, willow, reed (*Arundo donax* L.) or buri (petioles of the palm *Corypha utan* Lam). There is no doubt, however, that of these 'wicker' type products true rattan is the best quality and much preferred to any other. The product comes from the stems of spiny climbing palms belonging to the major group of scaly-fruited palms (Lepidocaryoideae) (Moore, 1973). I believe rattans to be one of the least protected groups of flowering plants, with many species being very severely threatened and becoming very rare, and although we know little of their biology I think it important they should receive attention in this conservation conference. Lepidocaryoid climbing palms are found in the Old World tropics; there are two other types of climbing palms found in the New World – spiny *Desmoncus* in the Cocosoid Major Group and *Chamaedorea elatior* Mart. in the Chamaedoreoid Major Group – but they do not have the same ethnobotanic significance as true rattans, even to forest-dwelling people. In Africa there are four rattan genera (three of them endemic) with about 25 species; they are rather insignificant in world trade, though I have heard of a local rattan industry in Senegambia (R. Kemp, pers. comm.). Asiatic and Malay Archipelago rattans comprise 11 genera and about 550 species; in the Far East they reach their greatest abundance in the perhumid areas of the Sunda Shelf (e.g. Malay Peninsula and Borneo), and throughout almost all Asiatic tropical rain forest types they are one of the most characteristic features. They extend from India and South China through to Queensland and Fiji and from sea-level up to 3000 m altitude in the mountains.

The table opposite will give indications of the diversity of rattans in southeast Asia, but it must be stressed that these are indications only, as we still know very little of the rattan floras of some areas such as Celebes and Moluccas.

Not only are geographical units such as Borneo extremely rich in rattan species, but individual forest areas carry an abundance of species with, for example, c. 20 species in one hectare of forest being by no means unusual.

Indigenous communities living near or in the forest have uses for almost all local species of rattans, the uses varying enormously from obvious ones such as cordage, binding and leaves for thatch and fruit through to medicine, tinder and toys. At the other end of the scale maybe only 20 or so species are regarded as elite commercial species. However, recent shortages of elite canes have resulted in the collection and use of species which until recently would have been regarded as useless. In view of their ethnobotanic significance, it may seem surprising that rattans are only very rarely intensively cultivated. It is not uncommon to see a few clumps of particularly good species such as *Calamus caesius* Bl., *C. minahassae* Warb. ex Becc., and *C. laevigatus* Mart. at the edges of villages, in village orchards or by longhouses, but such clumps probably only satisfy local demand for cordage. Until recently there seemed to be sufficient wild source rattan to satisfy commercial requirements in most places. Periodically there have been local shortages in the past – shortages sufficiently large to encourage forest research institutes to set up trial plots, the results of which have tended to be disappointing, largely because the shortages have been only temporary. Shortages of wild stocks now promise to be permanent, mostly due to forest destruction.

In central Kalimantan (Indonesia) two rattan species have been intensively cultivated on a large scale for over 100 years; the production from this cultivation has been sufficient to maintain whole villages at a relatively high standard of living, and has been partly responsible for Indonesia's domination of the supply end of the rattan trade. The value of world trade in rattan is considerably more than rattan's status as a minor forest product might lead one to expect; the end value of world trade in 1977 was over 1.2 billion U.S. dollars (Shane, 1977). Rattan is in fact the most important forest product after timber in southeast Asia. From a social point of view it is a most attractive forest product, tending to benefit local villagers much more directly than timber operations. Traditionally the exhausting and unpleasant task of rattan pulling is carried out during slack agricultural periods (such as after harvest and before sowing the rice crop) and is also greatly influenced by the current price of rubber; when rubber prices have slumped, rattan pulling has become a more attractive source of income.

With the preoccupation of the producing countries with the overwhelmingly lucrative timber industry, rattans have been much neglected until recently. Any forest statutes relating to rattan extraction have tended to be disregarded or treated lightly; often there just is not the manpower sufficient to deal with the

Table 1   Examples of rattan-rich areas (many species are found outside these sample areas)

	Total species in genus	Malay Peninsula	Borneo	Sumatra	Java	Thailand and Indochina	Philippines	New Guinea	Celebes
Calamus	370	62	c. 80	c40	15	c. 40	c. 40	? 50	21
Daemonorops	115	22	c. 45	c. 20	5	c. 10	c. 13	1	6
Korthalsia	29	9	13	9	2	3	5	1	1
Plectocomia	16	3	3	2	2	5	2	—	—
Ceratolobus	6	2	3	3	2	—	—	—	—
Plectocomiopsis	5	3	4	2	—	1	—	—	—
Myrialepis	2	1	—	1	—	2	—	—	—
Pogonotium	2	1	2	—	—	—	—	—	—
Retispatha	1	—	1	—	—	—	—	—	—
Calospatha	1	1	—	—	—	—	—	—	—
Bejaudia	1	—	—	—	—	1	—	—	—

excessive rate of timber exploitation, let alone control rattan exploitation. It has become the tacitly agreed right of local people to collect rattan and, in some areas, there is a statutory right to collect. Rarely, forest areas are marked off into rattan pulling concessions, but even in such instances the royalty payable has scarcely increased over the past 50 years even though the value of the product has soared, and there is normally no control of the intensity of extraction. In the setting up of national parks, the right to collect rattan has frequently been an integral part of the conservation statutes; this means that rattan is frequently collected within park boundaries. As rattan becomes scarce in exploitation forest, villagers turn to nature reserves for their own supply and, illegally, as suppliers to commerce. Even scientific expeditions to national parks will cut rattan for binding and constructing camps. The result is that rattans are almost nowhere strictly protected.

Of course, it is very difficult to assess the conservation status of any particular species of rattan, but in one instance, *Ceratolobus glaucescens* Bl., an elegant and biologically very interesting species from West Java, which is as yet unaccountably rare, the only known extant population has become reduced to critically low levels with about 30 clumps confined to the Sukawayana Nature Reserve on the south coast. It might be thought that its presence in a nature reserve would be some guarantee of its survival, but this particular reserve is a reserve in name only. Unless we have missed populations elsewhere on the coast of Java, the survival of this species is likely only in cultivation in botanic gardens. The widescale clearance of forest in the lowlands of the floristically richest rattan areas such as in Johore will almost certainly cause extinction of species in a group of plants where the rate of local endemism is high.

As rattans are ethnobotanically so significant, however, and can be managed as a renewable resource, it should be possible to make a case for their conservation right down to the grass roots of rural society (indeed some communities living near forest already have land-use systems which take account of rattans). There seem to me to be two main avenues of attack on the problem of rattan conservation: (a) the control of exploitation of wild stocks, and (b) the cultivation of elite species to relieve pressure on wild stocks and to boost production. This is where biological studies are of extreme importance; I discuss below some aspects of rattan biology in relation to the rattan trade and conservation.

Growth forms of rattans

Although rattans are defined as spiny climbing palms, some species of rattan genera are in fact acaulescent, and one species, *Calamus arborescens* Griff., is tree-like as its epithet suggests. Much of the diversity of form depends on the branching behaviour. In most species, branching is confined to basal suckering; only species of the genus *Korthalsia* consistently branch in the canopy; aerial branching accounts for their being difficult to harvest, and for the uneven condition of their canes so that they are not yet of much economic importance. Some species do not branch even at the base, and, like a coconut or oil palm, consist of one solitary stem.

It is most unfortunate that some of the elite canes originate from single-stemmed species. The consequences are obvious: no regeneration takes place from the cut stump, and unless cutting occurs after the plant has fruited, there will be no chance for regeneration from seed. In one species, *Calamus manan* Miq., perhaps the best of all large diameter canes (manau cane), lack of control of exploitation has resulted in population destruction; the price for manau is now so high that, as long as a cane length 3 m long is obtainable, any plant is cut, be it a juvenile 6 m long or a mature 80 m or longer (incidentally the longest rattan on record is a cane of *C. manan* 556 feet (169 m) in length (Burkill, 1935)). At the other extreme clustering is profuse and dense clumps of aerial stems are rapidly produced; in Sabah I recently observed a clump of *C. caesius* approximately 10 years old with over 100 aerial stems.

The type of clumping, whether open or close, is of some silvicultural importance, as competition between aerial stems may decrease the potential yield. Fine examples are provided by the two most important cultivated species, *C. caesius* and *C. trachycoleus* Becc. (Dransfield, 1977); these two species are closely related and have a similar growth pattern. Horizontal axes in the clump metamorphose to become erect aerial stems and, at the point of change, produce two branches which become horizontal axes, they in turn becoming erect and branching at the point of change and so on. In *C. caesius* the horizontal axes are short rhizomes, the clump thus becoming very dense and many of the lateral shoots do not develop because of competition. In *C. trachycoleus* horizontal axes are developed as long stolons, the clump thus becoming very open, the plant itself being vigorously invasive; there is little competition between aerial stems and the plant more nearly reaches its potential for an exponential increase in the number of aerial stems. The great advantages of this growth form difference make *C. trachycoleus* an ideal silvicultural subject; commercial scale plantations of this species are being established in Sabah at the moment, but seed supply is unfortunately very restricted. It is hoped that in Sabah at any rate, plantations of small-diameter class rattans such as *C. caesius* and *C. trachycoleus* will come into bearing just when wild stocks will be most scarce and threatened.

Flowering and fruiting behaviour

There are two main methods of flowering in rattans – hapaxanthy and pleonanthy. In hapaxanthic flowering inflorescences are produced in the axils of the uppermost leaves, the stem apex aborts, and the stem dies after flowering, though is usually replaced by basal suckers. In pleonanthic flowering inflorescences are produced throughout the adult life. The hapaxanthic flowering process is associated with the building up of food reserves in the stem pith; the stem tends to have a soft pith, is much prone to insect and fungal attack if harvested, and is difficult to bend. Until recently I classed such rattans as being useless; certainly they do not produce elite canes, but their canes are nevertheless now being used in accessories such as coat hangers and bric-a-brac. (It appears now that no species can be classed as useless – a worrying fact for the rattan conservationist.) In pleonanthic species, the stem is usually of a much more even texture.

All Asiatic rattans apart from the genus *Korthalsia* are dioecious (*Korthalsia* has hermaphrodite flowers). Little is known of flowering behaviour or of pollination, other than chance observations of insect visitors. We do now have information, however, on the number of fruits produced by individual stems of a few species. The range is enormous, varying from the rare *Pogonotium divaricatum* J. Dransf. with 1–2 fruits per inflorescence and *Calamus gonospermus* Becc. with 5 fruits (personal observation in Sarawak) to 5045 fruits on one stem in *C. manan* (Manokaran, 1979); the figures quoted by Manokaran were based on samples collected from individual stems sold at Kepong for growing and probably represent the products of more than one infructescence. Seedlings of many species may be recognized and, for example, *C. manan* may be abundant in the understorey, yet mature individuals are rare. A demographic study of *C. manan* in the wild would obviously be of great value in the preparation of management plans for 'manau cane' extraction and for setting up plantations.

Growth rates

Data on growth rates are available for only a very few species. *Calamus caesius* in a trial plantation in Selangor grew at a maximum rate of 4 m per year (estimated by Dransfield and Manokaran); *C. trachycoleus* is reported to grow at about 5 m per year in cultivation in central Kalimantan. *Calamus manan* appears to have very precise light requirements for maximum growth rates; Dransfield and Manokaran (Dransfield, 1979) have estimated maximum rates of 3 m per year in an abandoned trial plot in Selangor, though some individuals in the same plot had not produced any aerial growth during the 12 years since the plot was established, and in another plot, Manokaran (1977) recorded a maximum rate of 1.2 m per year. In the instance of *C. manan*, fickle rates of growth are coupled with single-stemmed habit (see above), a potential leaf spread of 16 m, 10 m of which carries photosynthetic tissue, and, presumably, great weight and potential damage to support trees. These problems associated with *C. manan* (which is indisputably the best large cane of all) suggest that it will be a difficult silvicultural subject, requiring replanting after harvest. An alternative approach would be to establish 'rotan manau' on an enrichment planting basis in forest which is not to be exploited for timber. Although this has never been attempted, it does hold out very attractive possibilities.

Protection forest – that is for example the forest on steep slopes surrounding watersheds for drinking water supplies – should not be exploited for timber;

politically protection forest is often unacceptable as it does not produce immediate revenue, though preventing negative revenue, and pressures build up for its illegal exploitation. As rattan extraction does almost no damage to forest structure, rattans such as *C. manan*, planted within protection forest, may provide a source of revenue helping to conserve the forest and indeed the species. As even a few aspects of the biology of *C. manan* become known, it has become apparent that for intensive plantations an alternative species should be tried, i.e. the selection of a multiple rather than single-stemmed rattan for silvicultural purposes. Very rarely multiple-stemmed forms of *C. manan* itself have been observed, and M. Shane (pers. comm.) reported the presence of apparently consistently multiple-stemmed *C. manan* in south Kalimantan; however, recent observations by Mustafa bin Abd. Rahman (pers. comm.) have shed doubt on this. It would seem more promising to select completely different species.

Unfortunately rattan species inventories are still so incomplete that such selection can be only partial. Good quality canes classed as 'tohiti', slightly smaller in diameter than average 'manau', are being extracted on a very intensive scale in Celebes; there are several large-diameter class rattans in Celebes such as *C. macrosphaerion* Becc. and *C. zollingeri* Becc. but the name usually quoted as the equivalent for 'tohiti' (*C. inops* Becc. ex Heyne) was published without description (Heyne, 1922) and can be seen not to be the correct name for the commercial species, if the specimens annotated by Beccari are examined. In fact we do not know the identity of this important cane and furthermore about one-third of the Celebesian rattans are probably undescribed and diminishing rapidly. In Sabah one species, *C. subinermis* H. Wendl. ex Becc. ('rotan batu'), seems to hold much promise as a multiple-stemmed large-diameter class rattan, but the biological studies necessary as a basis for the control of exploitation and its silviculture have not yet been undertaken.

Conservation of rattans

From the foregoing it will be obvious that the conservation of rattans presents peculiar problems, yet, because of their great ethnobotanic significance, it may be relatively easy to put across the need for their conservation to local people. Recently the governments of Indonesia, Thailand, Philippines, West Malaysia and Sabah have introduced measures to control the export of rattan, largely to protect local processing and manufacturing industries, but also tending to some extent to control extraction. Either a complete ban on the export of unprocessed cane has been introduced or else the royalty on unprocessed cane has been increased to the extent that it is uneconomic to export cane before it has been processed. Unfortunately these measures, though very necessary for the improvement of local rattan industries, have caused some hardship as indigenous people have lost the traditional outlets for their rattan (Hepburn, pers. comm.); well-organized processors are now extending their area of cane buying so that such hardships may only be temporary. Rattan demand still far outstrips supply, however, and it will be only by strict control by forest departments that rattan stocks will be conserved as a renewable resource.

In order to secure seed supplies it will be necessary to set aside some accessible stands of elite species as seed orchards. It has however proved difficult to maintain seed stands; no rattan seems safe from rattan collectors. There is also the need for setting up living collections of wide ranges of rattan species in forest arboreta or botanic gardens; they are awkward plants to maintain in neat botanic gardens and require constant attention. The best way to maintain a living rattan collection is in a strict nature reserve, but I have already mentioned the problems associated with cutting by local people.

Conclusion

Rattans are a much-threatened group of tropical plants and their conservation is very closely linked with their ethnobotanic significance. There is no doubt that stricter control of the exploitation of wild stocks is essential, but given the problems of policing forest, this will not be the final remedy. Cultivation of elite species is seen as the only long-term method of conservation; this in turn may have promising side effects in forest ecosystem conservation. What little we know of the biology of rattans has given valuable hints on what species should be selected for cultivation and how silvicultural trials should be set up, but there is an urgent need for detailed demographic studies of such species.

References

Burkill, I. H. (1935). *A Dictionary of the Economic Products of the Malay Peninsula*, 2 Vols., Crown Agents, London. (Reprinted with amendments, 1966, Governments of Malaysia and Singapore.)

Dransfield, J. (1977). '*Calamus caesius* and *Calamus trachycoleus* compared', *Gardens' Bull.*, Singapore, **30**, 75–8.

Dransfield, J. (1979). *A Manual of the Rattans of the Malay Peninsula*, Malaysian Forest Records, No. 29, Forest Department, Malaysia.

Heyne, K. (1922). *De nuttige planten van Nederlandsch-Indië*, Batavia, Ruygrok.

Manokaran, N. (1977). 'Survival and growth of the economically important rattan, *Calamus manan*, in Ulu Langat', *Malaysian For.*, **40**, 192–6.

Manokaran, N. (1979). 'A note on the number of fruits produced by four species of rattans', *Malaysian For.*, **42**, 46–9.

Moore, H. E., Jr. (1973). 'The major groups of palms and their distribution', *Gentes Herb.*, **11**(2), 27–141.

Shane, M. (1977). 'The economics of a Sabah rattan industry', in *A Sabah Rattan Industry*, Markiras Corporation Sdn Bhd, Kuala Lumpur (mimeo).

Section 3
Understanding Rarity and Monitoring Rare Plant Populations

The Biological Aspects of Rare Plant Conservation
Edited by Hugh Synge
© 1981 John Wiley & Sons Ltd.

16
The meanings of rarity

JOHN L. HARPER *School of Plant Biology, University College of North Wales, Bangor, Gwynedd, UK*

Summary

Rare is a word to which different people ascribe different meanings, depending on the scale of their work and experience. As a concept rarity is a phenomenon in time as well as in space, and examples are given of species which have become more rare and of species which have become more common in the course of time. The rate of change of a population is discussed as a variable and types of population fluctuation analysed. As a phenomenon in space, the rarity of a species can be related to the sites it can inhabit; the rarity or abundance of the species then depends on the size of these habitable sites, their number, their carrying capacity, the time over which a site remains habitable, the dispersal ability of the plant, and the effect of predators and pathogens. Emphasis is placed on the vital role of pathogens; more information is particularly needed on the effect of viruses on natural plant populations. The impact of polyphagous and monophagous predators is discussed as causes of both rarity and extinction; in most cases only polyphagous or generalist predators cause plant extinctions. The concept of a habitable site highlights the distinction between conserving diversity and conserving species: some general opinions of how to conserve diversity are presented, but it is not possible to generalize about how to conserve individual species. Conservationists should, however, remember that population biologists can sometimes control the abundance of a species and if desirable make some rare species more common.

Introduction

Rare: (extracts from definitions in *The Shorter Oxford English Dictionary*)

1. Having the constituent particles not closely packed together.
2. (a) Having the component parts widely set; of open construction; in open order.
   (b) Thinly attended or populated.
3. Placed or stationed at wide intervals; standing or keeping wide apart.
4. Few in number and widely separated from each other (in space or time); forming a small or scattered class.
5. Of a kind, class or description seldom found, met with, or occurring; unusual, uncommon, exceptional.

6. Unusual in respect of some good quality; remarkably good or fine. *colloq.* Splendid, excellent, fine.

All natural environments have a grain or patchiness; any observer is limited in the observations that he makes or the generalizations that he draws by the range of the environment whose grain he samples. Nowhere is this more apparent than in the way in which the word 'rare' is used by students of natural vegetation. Rarity has a quite different meaning to the internationally travelled biologist from that of a taxonomist concerned with the flora of his own country, his vice-county, his 10-km square or an intensively studied quadrat. This conference includes speakers who sample the grain of natural vegetation at all of these different scales. Discussions will soon be at cross-purposes if it is not clearly recognized that our concepts of what is rare will depend on the scale of our individual experience and on the range or narrowness of our special interests. For many field observers intense nationalism, patriotism or parochialism affects judgements about rarity: a species may be rare in Sweden but common in Norway, and be of no concern to conservationists on one side of a national boundary but of much concern on the other. Floras are usually written as if it is political boundaries that are of interest, whether they are those of a parish, a county, a state or a continent. Much of the concept of rarity expressed in Floras therefore derives from the grain of the political environment that is sampled. Without question there is a national pride that comes from the discovery of a new species within a state and some emotional sense of loss when a species disappears from a political region – though the gains and losses measured this way may have little more scientific interest than the losses of aircraft suffered by nations at war across similar boundaries.

When biologists become interested in rarity it is almost inevitably the rarity of *species* that is their concern. This is a very narrowly defined unit for recording biological change. The species is a taxanomic unit but differences in breeding systems between species have the effect that some contain a rich diversity of biologies while others (including taxonomists' toys) may be uniform and monotonous. The Red Data Book of rare and endangered species of the British Isles (Perring and Farrell, 1977) lists 13 species of *Sorbus*. If there had been in Britain as many experts on other apomictic groups (*Hieracium, Alchemilla, Rubus*) as there have been in Scandinavia, we might find species of these genera also figuring prominently in the Red Data Book. Of course, what we do not find included in the list of rarities are those highly specialized forms that apparently develop so easily under local selection pressure within outbreeding species. Forms of *Agrostis tenuis* that can grow on copper mines, zinc mines, lead mines or nickel mines are present in Britain but very rare and highly localized. They will not appear in any list of rarities because taxonomists group these as parts of a single taxonomic species. If a flora becomes impoverished, the change in the number of taxonomic species present need be no accurate reflection of the extent to which biological diversity has been lost.

The definitions quoted at the start of this chapter include a reference (no. 4) to

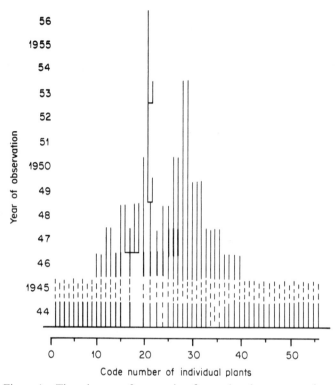

Figure 1   The change of a species from abundance to rarity. Changes in a population of *Centaurea jacea* within a quadrat $\frac{1}{4}$ sq. m in a hay meadow near Stockholm, Sweden. Shoots were mapped and counted annually from 1944 to 1956. I = Flowering; I = vegetative; ⊔⊓ = clonal multiplication; ¦ = no record. (From Tamm, 1956)

rarity as a phenomenon in space *or* time. Both spatial and temporal rarity can be recognized at any level of grain at which the environment is sampled. The beautiful and detailed repeated records made by C. O. Tamm in quadrats in Swedish meadows and forests include one $\frac{1}{4}$ sq. m quadrat within which *Centaurea jacea* is seen changing from abundant to rare (Figure 1); in other local sites within the sampled areas the same species was changing from rare to abundant. The time component and the spatial component of abundance need to be distinguished if we are to try to describe and understand rarity and ultimately bring the pace of extinction under our control.

Rarity as a phenomenon in time

We can recognize four extreme trends in the behaviour of plant populations (see Figure 2). We can first recognize species that have long been common and remain

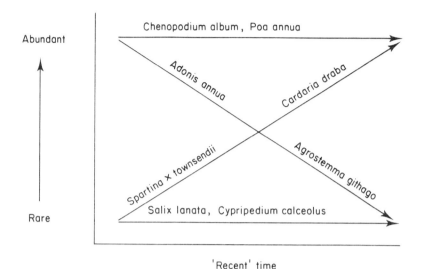

Figure 2   Frequency changes within a flora, with examples from the flora of
Britain

common. We need a time scale against which to measure change. If we consider
only this century, common species that have remained common in the British Isles
would include, for example, *Plantago lanceolata* and *Lolium perenne*. There are
other species that have been rare throughout this century and remain so, for
example *Salix lanata*. We can also recognize species that were rare or absent and
have now become very common (*Senecio cambrensis*, *Spartina* × *townsendii*,
Cardaria draba) and others that have been common and have become rare: this
last category includes a number of the annual cornfield weeds *Agrostemma
githago*, *Adonis annua*, *Centaurea cyanus* and one striking example among trees,
the English elm. We do not have measures of the numbers of individuals from
which to plot real graphs to show the rates of change. Ideally, any population
biologist would want to know the parameters to put into the simple equation

$$N_{t+1} \qquad = \qquad N_t \qquad + \qquad fN_t$$
(population at time $t + 1$)   (population at time t)   (rate of change × population at time t)

We do not have the values for such an equation except for a few special cases and
then only in part. Lacey (1957) analysed the rate of change in the number of vice-
counties in which *Galinsoga parviflora* and *G. ciliata* had been recorded. Both
species showed exponential increases but at markedly different rates. Such
calculations could usefully be made for other species though they need careful
interpretation. The number of vice-counties (like the number of '10-km squares')
in which a species is present is a measure of its distribution *not* of its abundance.

There is no necessary relationship between the size of a population (N_t) and its rate of change (f). Examples quoted above include cases in which populations that were rare have expanded extremely fast and species with abundant populations that have collapsed to a state of rarity. There may be some relationship between the size of the population and the chance of extinction by random events but it is not clear that even this relationship is at all simple and each case may depend upon the specific biological properties of the kind of organism being considered. Long-term trends of the sort that are vaguely indicated by the lines in Figure 2 cannot be supported with real data except in the few cases where very local patches in vegetation have been sampled intensively; the conclusions may then relate only to the changes within that tiny study patch.

Long-term trends may conceal quite spectacular changes in abundance within a patchwork of vegetation. Figure 3 illustrates extreme types of population fluctuation that appear to be represented among species of the British flora. Such fluctuations need not represent synchronized changes across populations of the same species in different parts of the country and may often be highly local and characteristic of a local patch in the environmental grain. Figure 3a illustrates population fluctuations of species that spend most of their time as repeated generations recovering from the last disaster. Such a form will be rare if the disaster was recent *or* if the rate of recovery from the disaster was slow. Many weedy species of cultivated land in rotational horticulture or agriculture must represent population dynamics of this sort. Populations of, for example, *Poa annua* or *Senecio vulgaris*, will usually be at levels that represent stages in recovery from the last cultivation or other weed control practise. They are the classic r species of MacArthur and Wilson (1976). These cases may also represent the population dynamics of the colonizers of blow outs in dune systems where the local rarity or abundance of a species may depend on the time elapsed since the last blow out. Similarly, the sand dune annual, *Vulpia fasciculata*, appears to be increasing its populations on both the east and west coasts of Britain and to have changed from being a rare species to being common. In this case we may be witnessing population explosion following the cessation (due to myxomatosis) of severe rabbit grazing. In this case the relative abundance of the species also reflects its very slow rate of natural increase, governed by the small number of seeds produced per plant (Watkinson and Harper, 1978; see also Watkinson, Chapter 21).

Figure 3b and c are idealized curves of population change for a type of organism in which most generations are in environments limited by resource supplies, 'bumping up against the limits of the environment's carrying capacity'. This carrying capacity may be high (Figure 3b) or low (Figure 3c) and the two curves in this diagram might represent these two extremes. In such a case, rarity or abundance is determined not by rates of population growth, nor by the frequency of disasters, but by the carrying capacity of the habitat. For some species, e.g. *Salix lanata*, which is restricted to rare types of habitat (highly inaccessible

194

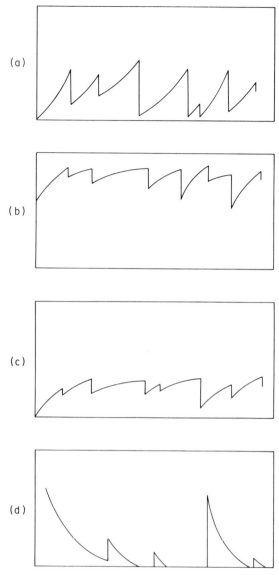

Figure 3   Idealized diagrams of the dynamics of plant populations. (a) Dynamics dominated by phases of population growth after recurrent disasters or episodes of colonization (r-species), (b) dynamics within a habitable site dominated by limitations on environmental carrying capacity. Carrying capacity high – species abundant (K-species), (c) as (b) but carrying capacity low – species rare (K-species), (d) dynamics within a habitable site dominated by population decay after more or less sudden episodes of colonization or recruitment from the seed bank in the soil

rock ledges), the occupied habitats may be filled to near carrying capacity but be few and far between.

Figure 3d illustrates the population dynamics of species that spend most of their generations in decline after sudden bursts of new establishment. This would seem to be the case for many monocarpic perennials such as *Digitalis purpurea* and species of *Verbascum*. In such cases, dense populations may be recruited from the buried seed bank after some environmental disturbance. Subsequently, the established plants flower and die with some individuals lingering, small and depauperate, within the community until they reach flowering size and die. Such plants may leave a buried seed population within the soil until the environment is disturbed again (e.g. a tree falls or a woodland is felled) and a new sudden flush of seedling recruits appears.

Populations of most species probably represent mixes of the dynamics illustrated in Figure 3 with local variations in frequency determined by, (a) the frequency of disasters, (b) the potential for recovery which is reflected in the reproductive capacity of the plants, (c) the longevity of the seed bank, and (d) the rate at which the carrying capacity of the environment itself changes. New recruitment by dispersal from other areas may, of course, also influence local dynamics and this is considered in the context of spatial rarity in the next section.

Rarity as a phenomenon in space

It is convenient, at least in theory, to regard an area of land (whether the surface of the earth or a quadrat 1 cm square) as composed of a mosaic of habitable sites (Gadgil, 1971). A habitable site is a patch of the mosaic that provides the conditions and resources needed by individuals of particlar plant species or populations to become established, complete their growth cycle and leave potential descendants. Clearly, habitable sites may be species-specific, habitable for some species and not for others. In a sense the concept of habitable site defines a spatial element in the 'abstractly inhabited hyper-volume' that is the fundamental niche of a species (Hutchinson, 1965). In some ways the concept of habitable site approaches the concept of niche used by Grinnell (1917) which has a strictly spatial context. For many species, perhaps most, the habitable sites that are available greatly exceed the number that are actually inhabited by a particular species, population or form. The rarity or abundance of a species depends on an interaction between characteristics of the habitable sites and characteristics of the species themselves.

Size of habitable sites

Clearly, a species may be rare because its habitable sites are small. This may limit the population size of, for example, an annual such as *Iberis amara*, which colonizes (*inter alia*) the bare patches scratched by rabbits in short grassland.

Such patches provide small local sites suitable for establishment and growth of this plant.

Number of habitable sites

A rare species may be very abundant locally (i.e. its habitable sites are large) but there are few of them. The distribution of *Fritillaria meleagris* in Britain reflects these two attributes. *Fritillaria* meadows often contain very large numbers of plants at high density. The meadows are often extensive but there are few of them. The effects of the size and number of habitable sites on the abundance of a species are also nicely shown in the distribution of *Ranunculus* species in permanent grassland (Harper, 1953; Harper, 1977). Three species of *Ranunculus, R. acris, R. bulbosus* and *R. repens*, occupy different positions on the contours of the ridge and furrow system. In many fields all three species are present: *R. bulbosus* is common on the ridge and rare in the furrow, *R. repens* is common in the furrow and rare on the ridge, and *R. acris* occupies an intermediate position on the sides being rare both on the ridge and in the furrow. The relative abundance of the three buttercup species in a field is then a function of the size and the number of the ridges and furrows. The relative frequency of the habitable sites is peculiar to each of these species and so their rarity or abundance differs from field to field depending on the position of the water table, which is a major determinant of the frequency of the types of habitable site peculiar to each of the three species.

The carrying capacity of habitable sites

A site within which individuals of a particular species or form can complete their growth cycle may sustain different numbers of different species depending on the length of life and the size of individual plants. The carrying capacity of a site represents the limits on the numbers and/or biomass of individuals that it may support. A species may appear abundant in a community because its individuals are of large biomass or because, although they have small biomass, they are present in very large numbers. This distinction is important; for example *Pteridium aquilinum* may appear abundant in a community by virtue of its large biomass but be rare in the same community in respect of the number of genetic individuals present. *Pteridium aquilinum* is quoted by Coquillat (1951) as one of the five most abundant plants on the face of the earth but in most places it is abundant by virtue of the enormous vegetative extent and biomass of a few rare genetic individuals.

The carrying capacity of a habitat or of a habitable site is reflected in stands of single species, not by some upper asymptote of numbers (which appears to be the case for many animals), but by an asymptotic condition that is represented by the *combination* of numbers and individual size that can be sustained on any particular site. The relationship between the changing number of individual plants and their size as a population develops, represents one of the great generalities of plant ecology – the 3/2 thinning law. Crowded stands of a large number of species (trees, shrubs, herbs, mosses) all conform to one limiting relationship in which, as the average weight per plant increases by three orders of magnitude so the number of survivors falls by two orders of magnitude. The asymptotic limiting condition (the carrying capacity of a site) is then described by a line of slope –3/2 on the graph relating log mean plant weight to log number of survivors. Within narrow limits both the slope and position of the thinning line are the same for all species studied (Gorham, 1979). When pairs of species are grown together they also conform as a whole to the –3/2 thinning law but resources are shared between the two species and one may make most of the growth while the other suffers most of the thinning (Bazzaz and Harper, 1976; Malmberg and Smith, in press). This seems to be the way in which competitive exclusion occurs between different potential occupants of a habitable site as its carrying capacity is shared between individuals of the different species in a struggle for existence. This distinguishes between a fundamental and a realized carrying capacity, paralleling a distinction between a fundamental and a realized niche (Hutchinson, 1965). For many rare species it may be that habitable sites exist and that their carrying capacity is high, but that the species are prevented from filling a habitable site by other species

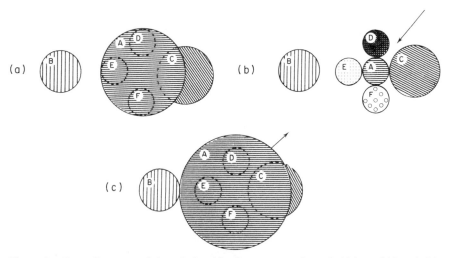

Figure 4   Venn diagrams of the relationships between species cohabiting within a habitable site showing partitioning of or exclusion from the realized carrying capacity. (a) Growth of species A excludes species D, E and F from habitable site and reduces the numbers (and/or biomass) of species C. Species B is unaffected by the presence or absence of A, (b) the numbers (and/or biomass) of species A is reduced – by predators, pathogens or other cause. Species D, E and F may now persist and occupy part of the habitable site – species C increases, (c) the numbers (and/or biomass) of species A is increased by reduction of damage by predators or pathogens compared to the condition in Figure 4a. Species D, E and F remain excluded, species C is reduced to rarity. Further increase in species A would begin to reduce the density of species B. (Adapted from Harper, 1977)

which are in some way more successful in pre-empting resources. This situation is modelled as Venn diagrams in Figure 4.

The time for which a site remains habitable

Natural succession and cycles in vegetation demonstrate that sites may remain habitable for strictly limited periods. Figure 1 illustrates a habitable site that became increasingly uninhabitable during the period of observation (i.e. a site in which the realizable carrying capacity for that species was continually declining). A species may be rare because only for very short periods do its habitable sites remain habitable. A species may be rare because its propagules fail to reach the habitable sites in the limited time available or are quickly excluded as the site is taken over by others.

Dispersal to habitable sites

There may be abundant sites suitable for the establishment and completion of the growth cycle of particular species or forms, yet propagules may fail to reach these sites because of weaknesses in the dispersal pattern of the species. An extreme example is the absence of *Eucalyptus* species from California but their very rapid spread after introduction, which implies that habitable sites for *Eucalyptus* were present in California but remained uninhabited because of the dispersal barrier between Australia and California. On a quite different scale it is not unreasonable to suppose that habitable sites are present within Britain in a particular vice-county or 10-km square, suitable for occupation by many of the species listed in *The Red Data Book* but that seed dispersal fails to reach them. Organisms with different dispersal capabilities sense or search the environment on quite different scales. The propagules of *Tussilago farfara* spread regularly and repeatedly in high numbers from established sites across 8–10 km of the Dutch polders (Bakker, 1960). In contrast, the large cannon-ball-like seeds of species of *Mora* in the tropical forest fall mainly beneath the parent tree and the species are said by Beard (1946) still to be expanding their range from the times at which the species originally evolved! The most realistic measure of the distance of habitable sites from each other is in terms of the dispersal powers of the propagules of the species concerned; this has more biological meaning than the anthropocentric measures of miles, kilometres or centimetres. Thus, habitable sites a mile apart may be readily reached by the seeds of an orchid or of *Tussilago farfara*, but be well outside the dispersal range of *Ranunculus ophioglossifolius*.

The rarity of a species may therefore be some function of the size and number of habitable sites, their carrying capacity, the time for which they remain habitable and the probability of their being discovered by dispersed propagules. If we seriously attempt to modify the degree of rarity or abundance of a species we might attack the problem at any one of these points (see postscript). We might deliberately increase the size of the habitable site occupied by *Ranunculus ophioglossifolius* by extending an area in which cattle trampled muddy soil (see Frost, Chapter 41). Alternatively, we might increase the number of places in which such conditions are found. We might increase the realizable carrying capacity of a site by reducing the density of competitors. We might extend the time for which sites remained habitable by slowing down natural cycles, delaying the processes of succession or deliberately restarting them elsewhere. We might deliberately increase the efficiency of dispersal by transporting seed of the species to habitable sites which it fails to reach by natural dispersal. In that way we might also reduce the fraction of seed that is wasted by falling 'on stony ground' (uninhabitable sites).

This essentially theoretical consideration of the causes and nature of rarity leaves a lot of questions unanswered and, in many cases, is still far from representing an operational guide that would enable one precisely to define the causes of rarity and abundance in any particular case. Nevertheless, it provides a framework on which hypotheses about present distributions might be based, and from which practical and operational techniques of description could be developed. It may also serve as a rough indicator or guide to the types of change that are required within vegetation if controlled changes in species abundance are to be attempted.

Predators and pathogens

A habitable site may be colonized and have a sufficient carrying capacity for a species to persist within it, but a predator (or pathogen) may exclude it. Evidence of the role of pathogens is sparse although two of the best documented cases of a decline of a species from abundance to rarity (chestnut blight in North America and Dutch elm disease in Britain) have clear pathogenic causes. Perhaps one of the most worrying areas of ignorance concerns the possible role of viruses in the decline in vigour of a species. We are abysmally short of information about the extent of virus infection that occurs in natural populations of plants. Yet, evidence from agriculture is that virus epidemics spread rapidly and quickly become chronic in established pasture systems. It may be that some of the rarities in the British flora have this status because they have accumulated a galaxy of virus infections and suffer from the consequent reductions in vigour. This is an area urgently in need of study because the opportunity does arise through meristem culture for plants to be freed of virus infection and restored to their intrinsic state of vigour.

Most of the evidence that particular animals can be responsible for the level of rarity or abundance of a plant species comes from experiments on and deliberate practice of biological control. The relevance of this to plant ecology is discussed in Harper (1977). Different sorts of predators have quite different effects on vegetation and it is important not to generalize too widely. A crude classification separates specific monophagous predators from generalists. Most of the experience in biological control of plants comes from the use of monophagous predators, usually insects, against weeds, e.g. *Cactoblastis* against *Opuntia* species and *Chrysolina* against *Hypericum* species. When biological control is successful, the density of the plant that is preyed upon is often spectacularly reduced and both predator and prey eventually settle down to a more or less equilibrial level at which the prey plants are at such a distance from each other that they are not often encountered within the search range of the predator. Thus, the degree of rarity of the plant concerned becomes some function of, (a) the search range of the predator, and (b) the dispersal range of the propagules of the prey. Both (a) and (b) are species-specific properties not easily generalized. Indeed, both the ranges of search and dispersal are more properly measured in terms of biological distance appropriate to the organisms concerned than in terms of the miles or centimetres of the anthropocentric biologist. A plant that is rarely encountered in the lifetime of a slow-moving slug or snail may be met many times in an hour by a rapidly moving butterfly or a wide ranging ruminant. This re-emphasizes the point made at the beginning of this paper that rarity is in the eye of the beholder. A plant that appears rare to a predator may appear common to a field naturalist and vice versa.

In the literature of biological control there appear to be no cases in which the introduction of a specialized predator has resulted in the extinction of the prey plant. Indeed, it is a feature of effective biological control that this should not happen. Ideally, the predator and its plant prey remain in an equilibrium at which the density of the plant prey is maintained low, i.e. rarity is ensured, not extinction. It is probably a general rule for the interaction between a monophagous predator and its prey that the prey are not brought to extinction. The only specialist predator likely to bring his prey to extinction is the human collector whose search for the prey increases in intensity as it becomes rarer!

In contrast to the monophagous predators, polyphagous predators may easily lead to the extinction of some prey species (see Williams, Chapter 19, for example). Polyphagous predators, probably without exception, differentiate between the range of available prey, choosing to take some and being forced to accept others only when the preferred food becomes hard to find. A preferred food species may then be driven to rarity and eventually extinction because the predator can always fall back on the less preferred food as the prey becomes rarer but continue to take any of the rare prey as they appear. Thus, from a species-rich habitat a polyphagous predator may progressively drive out one food species after another in order of their acceptability until what is left are only those plant species that are lowest in the acceptability rating. The situation is, however, potentially very complex; the effect of a polyphagous predator on vegetation will be determined in part by whether the most dominant species are highly acceptable to it or unacceptable. If the dominant species are highly acceptable then the effect of polyphagous predators may be to increase species diversity by allowing some rare species to enter and spread in a community, see Figure 4 (Harper, 1977). If the dominant species are themselves unacceptable, however, the presence of poly-phagous predators may simply be to drive the plant community towards yet more monotonous domination by the unacceptable components.

Conservation of rarities or conservation of diversity

Conservation policy may be directed to two quite distinct ends and these must not be confused. Policies of conservation may be directed to the maintenance of species diversity. To this end the biogeographic models of MacArthur and Wilson (1967) were developed by Diamond and May (1976) in an attempt to optimize con-servation policy. Most plant communities represent islands in space and in time and it is argued that optimal reserve areas for the conservation of diversity are those that maximize invasion and minimize emigration and loss: to this end reserves should be as large as possible and have the minimal circumference.

Higgs and Usher (1980), however, suggest conditions in which diversity may be better maintained by many smaller areas than by one large one. Much of the development of this theory has depended on observations made on bird and insect faunas, i.e. for organisms that are not only mobile but have some choice of the areas which they colonize and settle. It is not necessary that the same condi-tions are appropriate for organisms whose propagules are passively dispersed. Game (1980) suggests that for some species with passive propagules (such as plants) diversity may be best maintained in long linear reserves with maximal circumference because in such a situation diversity is better maintained by maximizing the trapping of new immigrants rather than by guarding against emigrants. These arguments, however, are all concerned with maintaining diversity. Conservationists may often be more concerned to guard a particular species against extinction rather than to conserve diversity *per se*. There is no reason to suppose that any conservation policy designed to maintain diversity will be appropriate for maintaining the presence of a particular, specified rare species. Indeed, the optimal shape, size and condition of a reserve appropriate for a particular rare species may, in every case, be biologically specific and peculiar to its life-cycle pattern, its mode of dispersal, its reaction to predators and all of those other peculiarities that distinguish the biology of individual species. Certainly, the rules for maintaining community diversity may be quite different from those appropriate for safeguarding particular species and these latter rules may be so species-specific as to defy generalization.

Postscript

During the course of this lecture I pointed out that the population biologist and experimental ecologist now have many of the techniques which make it possible to bring about controlled changes in the abundance of species. I asked members of the audience how many would wish to see rare species made more common – or, if rare species are 'splendid, excellent, fine' (see opening definition 6) whether they would wish to see more common species made rare. The audience clearly indicated that they wished to see no change (except to make a few noxious weeds less common). This would seem to indicate that by some remarkable chance the flora of 1980 is just right and that the conservationists' task is to maintain this condition!

References

Bakker, D. (1960). 'A comparative life-history study of *Cirsium arvense* (L.) Scop. and *Tussilago farfara* L., the most troublesome weeds in the newly reclaimed polders of the former Zuiderzee', in *The Biology of Weeds* (Ed. J. L. Harper), *1st Symposium of the British Ecological Society*, Vol. 1, pp. 205–22, Blackwell Scientific Publications, Oxford.

Bazzaz, F. A. and Harper, J. L. (1976). 'Relationship between plant weight and numbers in mixed populations of *Sinapis alba* (L.) Rabenh. and *Lepidium sativum* L.', *J. Appl. Ecol.*, **13**, 211–16.

Beard, J. S. (1946). 'The Mora forests of Trinidad, British West Indies', *J. Ecol.*, **33**, 173–92.

Clapham, A. R., Tutin, T. G., and Warburg, E. F. (1962). *Flora of the British Isles*, 2nd Ed., Cambridge University Press.

Coquillat, M. (1951). 'Sur les plantes les plus communes à la surface du globe', *Bull. Men. Soc. Linn. Lyon*, **20**, 165–70.

Diamond, J. M. and May, R. M. (1976). 'Island biogeography and the design of nature reserves', in May, R. M., *Theoretical Ecology: Principles and Applications*, Blackwell Scientific Publications, Oxford.

Gadgil, M. (1971). 'Dispersal: population consequences and evolution', *Ecology*, **52**, 253–61.

Game, M. (1980). 'Best shape for Nature Reserves', *Nature (Lond.)*, **287**, 630–1.

Gorham, E. (1979). 'Shoot height, weight and standing crop in relation to density of monospecific plant stands', *Nature (Lond.)*, **279**, 148–50.

Grinnell, J. (1917). 'Niche relationships of the California thrasher', *Auk*, **34**, 427–33.

Harper, J. L. (1953). 'Some aspects of the ecology of buttercups in permanent grassland', *Proc. Brit. Weed Control Conf.*, **1**, 256–63.

Harper, J. L. (1977). *Population Biology of Plants*, Academic Press, London and New York.

Higgs, A. J. and Usher, M. B. (1980). 'Should nature reserves be large or small?', *Nature (Lond.)*, **285**, 568–9.

Hutchinson, G. E. (1965). *The Ecological Theater and the Evolutionary Play*, Yale University Press, New Haven, Conn.

Lacey, W. L. (1957). 'A comparison of the spread of *Galinsoga parviflora* and *G. ciliata* in Britain', in *Progress in the Study of the British Flora* (Ed. J. E. Lousley), pp. 109–15, *B.S.B.I. Conference Reports*, Vol. 5, Arbroath.

MacArthur, R. H. and Wilson, E. O. (1967) *The Theory of Island Biogeography*, Princeton University Press, Princeton, New Jersey.

Malmberg, C. and Smith, H. (in press). 'The effect of thinning on plant weight and density in a mixed population of *Medicago sativa* L. and *Trifolium pratense* L.', *Oikos*.

Perring, F. H. and Farrell, L. (1977). *British Red Data Books: I. Vascular Plants*, Society for the Promotion of Nature Conservation, Lincoln.

Tamm, C. O. (1956). 'Further observations on the survival and flowering of some perennial herbs, I', *Oikos*, **7**, 273–92.
Watkinson, A. R. and Harper, J. L. (1978). 'The demography of a sand dune annual: *Vulpia fasciculata*. I. The natural regulation of populations', *J. Ecol.*, **66**, 15–33.

Note

Plant names in this chapter follow Clapham, Tutin and Warburg (1962) except for *Vulpia fasciculata* (Forssk.) Samp., previously known in Britain under the name *V. membranacea*.

The Biological Aspects of Rare Plant Conservation
Edited by Hugh Synge
© 1981 John Wiley & Sons Ltd.

17
Seven forms of rarity

DEBORAH RABINOWITZ *Division of Biological Sciences, University of
Michigan, Ann. Arbor, Michigan, USA*

Summary

There are many ways in which a species can become rare and this path has profound
evolutionary and ecological consequences. A theoretical framework of an eight-celled
table is proposed for the different types of rarity depending on range, habitat specificity
and local abundance. Seven forms of rarity are discussed with examples from the North
American flora, in particular that of the narrow endemic. Studies of the competitive
abilities of sparse and common prairie grasses provide insights into the biological nature of
rarity and show that competitive abilities are more critical to persistence than to the
regulation of abundance. Natural selection may operate to favor traits which offset the
disadvantages of local small population size. We reach conclusions that are both
unexpected and relevant to practical conservation philosophies.

Introduction

Perhaps the most common conclusion in this book is that there are many sorts of
rare species. This fact is probably because species become rare by several
pathways. If rarity has a variety of causes, then the evolutionary and ecological
consequences of rarity may be equally diverse.

For instance, a species may be rare because it is especially subject to a density-
dependent fungal pathogen, as it is the case with American Chestnut, *Castanea
dentata* (Marsh.) Borkh. (Nelson, 1955). Let us contrast this case with one of
rarity because of range contraction due to climatic change: *Pelliciera rhizophorae*
Tr. & Planch., a mangrove usually placed in a monotypic family, the Pellicie-
raceae, close to the Theaceae, is now restricted to the Pacific coast from Costa
Rica to Colombia, but occurred in Chiapas, southeast Mexico, in the Oligo-
miocene (Langenheim *et al.*, 1967). In the case of the chestnut, the fungus has
produced a major shift in life history, converting a large tree to a shrub. No such
radical morphological or demographic changes accompany the contraction of
range in *Pelliciera*. Its local densities remain high, and monospecific stands may
still occur, albeit over a smaller area. For *Pelliciera*, we expect that island
biogeographic or genetic consequences of drift will predominate; for *Castanea*,

the local consequences are ecological and epidemiologic. These two pathways to rarity show remarkably divergent responses. If we can dissect the varieties of rarity, our understanding of rare species may benefit from the provision of a basis for investigating causes and consequences of rarity.

Because authors are often concerned with consistent traits among special sorts of rare species (Griggs, 1940; Stebbins, 1942; Drury, 1974; Smith, 1976), the state of being rare seems rather monolithic from the literature. For instance, Griggs (1940) regards rare species, in his case geographic outliers of the Laurentian shield, as being competitively inferior. Drury (1974) views rare species as those where interbreeding among populations is severely restricted. A great amount of fascinating heterogeneity among rare species is unfortunately obscured by these generalities. In this paper I have two goals, first to construct a general scheme to characterize the varieties of rarity, and secondly, to show how natural selection operates on rare species (Rabinowitz, 1978; Rabinowitz and Rapp, in press).

This classification of rarity differs from the others in this book (see Ayensu Chapter 2), Good and Lavarack (Chapter 5) or Bratton and White (Chapter 39) for three fundamental reasons. First, the aim of drawing up a list of species is not imposed upon me, and so I need not employ the categories to fulfil a legal charge. Secondly, no specific taxa, geographical locality, or administrative units need be kept in mind. Thirdly, the endangered or threatened status of plants is not my central concern. These factors free me from the constraints of pragmatism, and this may contribute some clarity in exploring the biological consequences of rarity. Hopefully, the exercise will permit some new perspectives for people engaged in more practical concerns.

A classification of rare species

To construct flexible categories for rarities, I distinguish three aspects of the situation of a species: geographic range, habitat specificity, and local population size, all of which have been introduced by previous contributors. Most of us would agree that each of these attributes is related to rarity in some way. For instance, illustrating with plants from America, *Andropogon gerardi* Vitman has a huge range – Florida to southern Quebec, westward to northern Mexico and Saskatchewan – whereas *A. niveus* Swallen is restricted to central Florida, and thus is more rare. With respect to habitat specificity, *Solidago canadensis* L. seems quite 'plastic' about where it grows – in thickets, roadsides, forest edges, clearings, prairies, fallow fields, varying soil types, moisture regimes and successional states. *Solidago bartramiana* Fern occurs only on slaty ledges, and *S. sempervirens* L. grows only in brackish conditions of coastal dunes; these two latter species, due to their habitat restriction from whatever causes, are validly regarded as rarer than *S. canadensis*. With respect to the third trait, local population size, *Festuca scabrella* Torr. and *F. idahoensis* Elmer are co-dominants with

Agropyron spicatum (Pursh) Scribn. & Sm. in the Palouse prairies of western North America, and thus their local abundances are large even though this type of grassland is quite limited in geographic extent. In contrast *Festuca paradoxa* Desv. is never dominant or really very common, and because of this 'chronic' local sparsity, we would consider it rarer than the other fescues, despite its more extensive range.

If each of these attributes is dichotomized, a $2 \times 2 \times 2$ or eight-celled block emerges (Figure 1). Although creating the hazard of false reification – that is, converting an idea into an object – such a simple scheme can aid in focusing our thoughts, and this is my intention. The patina – a gloss or incrustation conferred by age – of monolithic rarity may have hindered our understanding of an exceedingly heterogeneous assemblage of organisms. Since the products of rarity are diverse, the causes of rarity and the genetic and population consequences of rarity are undoubtedly equally multiple.

A second caution with such a scheme is that it is a typology of results (by intention) and not a typology of mechanisms or causes (Gould, 1977). Results of similar appearance may mask divergent processes; for instance geographically restricted species may be relictual (Cain, 1940; Ricklefs and Cox, 1978) or incipient (Lewis, 1966). In the absence of the relevant studies, the classification of processes resulting in rarity is a distant goal.

Seven of the eight cells contain rare species in some sense of the word. Only the upper left cell, species with wide ranges, several habitats, and locally high abundances, do not merit the designation. *Chenopodium album* L. is an example: it is circumtropical, nearly circumtemperate, and can occur in dense or sparse stands in weedy and non-weedy situations (Kapoor and Partap, 1979).

Directly beneath is probably the most ignored category of inconspicuous and unspectacular plants, sparse species – those with large ranges, several habitats, but consistently low populations. Such species are familiar (and pedestrian) to most botanists and especially to entomologists. In North America, *Dianthus armeria* L. is a familiar example. One is never really surprised to see Deptford Pink, but one would be quite startled to see it occupy 80 per cent of the biomass in a large field. Sparse plants are those, which, when one wants to show the species to a visitor, one can never locate a specimen! To me, they are the most curious form of rarity because they seem not to have a 'favored' habitat. They almost never appear on lists of 'threatened' or 'endangered' species. Sparse species of prairie grasses in Missouri are the topic of our current studies on the mechanisms of persistence (Rabinowitz, 1978; Rabinowitz and Rapp, in press).

Two of these cells appear to have very few residents, namely species of narrow geographic range but broad habitat specificity. Is this *modus operandi* unfeasible for some evolutionary or ecological reason or do ecologists simply pay little attention to such species? If the former is true, it is of great interest to know why such species either do not arise or have large probabilities of extinction. For instance, demographic stochasticity, which is a process in small populations analagous to

GEOGRAPHIC RANGE	Large		Small	
HABITAT SPECIFICITY	Wide	Narrow	Wide	Narrow
LOCAL POPULATION SIZE				
Large, dominant somewhere	Locally abundant over a large range in several habitats	Locally abundant over a large range in a specific habitat	Locally abundant in several habitats but restricted geographically	Locally abundant in a specific habitat but restricted geographically
Small, non-dominant	Constantly sparse over a large range and in several habitats	Constantly sparse in a specific habitat but over a large range	Constantly sparse and geographically restricted in several habitats	Constantly sparse and geographically restricted in a specific habitat

Figure 1   A typology of rare species based on three characteristics: geographic range, habitat specificity, and local population size

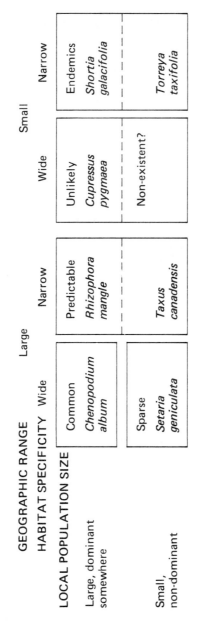

Figure 2   Summary and illustrations of species for the typology of rare species shown in Figure 1

genetic drift and which results in fluctuating population numbers, due to small sample phenomena (May, 1973; Mertz *et al.*, 1976), may cause local extinction. These deletions of populations may reduce the variety of habitats occupied and, in essence, convert a perhaps unstable species into one in the categories on the right in Figure 1, namely an endemic. Examples of such unusual species are *Cupressus pygmaea* (Lemmon) Sarg., a dwarf conifer found on coastal terraces of Mendocino County, California (Westman, 1975; Westman and Whittaker, 1975) and *Fuchsia procumbens* R. Cunn. ex. A. Cunn., a New Zealand plant (Given, Chapter 4), with small range but several habitats.

Species which have wide ranges but are associated with particular habitats are generally quite predictable in their occurrence (especially if you are a good systematist). If one is in a bog, on the strand, or on serpentine soils, one can generally find the plants peculiar to these places with relative confidence. In Caribbean Panama, on calm marine shorelines, for instance, one is very likely to find *Rhizophora mangle* L. and other mangroves, which are characteristically abundant where they occur. These species tend to be precarious as a result of habitat destruction. Mangrove swamps often are endangered because they are a habitat that many people find objectionable for a variety of reasons, usually that the trees are between them and the sea. In contrast to mangroves, which are nearly always locally common, Dr Given (Chapter 4) has given us the example of *Lepidium oleraceum* Forst.f., Cook's scurvygrass, once collected for vitamin C and now found on coastal rocks in several scattered sites around New Zealand but in locally very low densities.

Species with both narrow geographic range and narrow habitat specificity are the classic rarities in the sense of restricted endemics, often endangered or threatened. These rare endemic plants are often showy or newsworthy in some way. *Shortia galacifolia* T. & G., an attractive member of the Diapensiaceae, is endemic to several escarpment gorges of the Appalachian mountains and has endeared itself to the attentions of botanists for over a century (Gray, 1878; Ross, 1936; Davies, 1955, 1960; Rhoades 1966; and Vivian, 1967).

On an autecological level, such species receive a lot of attention. Terrell *et al.* (1978), for instance, have recently provided an excellent comparative study of the endemic aquatic *Zizania texana* Hitchc. and the widespread *Z. aquatica* L. *Zizania texana* lives on only 2.4 km of the upper San Marcos River in Texas in unusual alkaline conditions where water temperatures vary only 5°C annually, in contrast to the more varying conditions of *Z. aquatica* (see also Lucas and Synge, 1978).

The extreme of a restricted rare species is one that is known to have existed, but has been subsequently lost. The intuitive notion of a rare organism is one that is difficult to find, and the most endangered that a species can become is to be declared extinct! Lost species hold a particular fascination, rather like ships lost at sea. A fine example is *Betula uber* (Ashe) Fernald, Ashe's Birch or Virginia Round-leaf Birch, mentioned by Ayensu (Chapter 2), first collected in 1914 from

Smyth County, Virginia. The only other collection, near the first locality, was a single undated specimen rediscovered in 1973 (Mazzeo, 1974). After numerous searches, Johnson (1954) asserted:

> The only conclusion that seems warranted at this time from these several failures to rediscover this birch is that it probably no longer exists as an individual and very likely never did so in the form of a population. Ashe's birch has probably died or been destroyed in the process of urbanization of the community in which he found it 40 years ago. It is probable that this birch variety was founded solely on an aberrant individual and certainly does not appear to deserve further consideration as a species.

Sixty-one years after the original collection, the plant was rediscovered in 1975 by Douglas Ogle, who found the tree by employing an 'if I were a horse' strategy (Preston, 1976). Reasoning that when Ashe collected, the present paved roads did not exist, Ogle searched along traces of logging roads shown him by an elderly resident. The tree is extant in a population of 12 mature trees, some of which were reproductive, one sapling, and 21 seedlings (Ogle and Mazzeo, 1976). *Betula uber* is so rare that it was lost for over 60 years and is an example of the tenacity of botanists, who continued to hunt for living representatives for over half a century, against all reasonable likelihood of its continued existence. Its rediscovery was reported in *The New Yorker* magazine (Kinkead, 1976).

This eight-celled scheme does not include the category of 'pseudo-rare' organisms about which, perhaps, the most sound data exist and which tells us the most about the biological processes occurring in small populations. Species on the margins as opposed to the central portions of their ranges have been an active aspect of evolutionary studies (Stebbins, 1974), especially for *Drosophila* (Lewontin, 1974). In plants, for example, marginal and central populations of *Paeonia californica* Nutt. ex. T. & G. (Stebbins and Ellerton, 1939; Walters, 1942; Grant, 1956, 1975) and more recently of *Hordeum jubatum* L. (Schumaker and Babble, 1980) were compared to assess the relative effects of reproductive isolation, genetic drift, and selection on genetic structure. Ecophysiological and reproductive studies on marginal populations shed light on mechanisms determining or controlling range as shown, for example, by Pigott's studies on *Tilia platyphyllos* Scop. in Britain (Chapter 25). These studies on marginal rarity have the major advantage that they have an automatic control. Monitoring rare species (for instance, Bradshaw's long term assessments of the Teesdale rarities) tells us a lot about the characteristics of these taxa. However, in the absence of comparative data for related common taxa, essentially control species, we cannot judge whether the traits of rare plants are unique to them or are some random sample of plant traits in general and unrelated to the rare state.

Perhaps the least information is available on the fine scale causes of changes in abundance within what seems on casual view to be a homogeneous and appropriate site. Changes of orders of magnitude in population sizes occur on the scale of meters without striking underlying heterogeneity, and this garden-variety variance in density is very puzzling. Greig-Smith and Sagar (Chapter 32) investigated the causes of local rarity in *Carlina vulgaris* L. in a dune site where the plant was locally common very close by. Excluding both the absence of disturbance to produce new sites for establishment and also nutrient deficiencies of the substrate, they found that augmentation by sowing fruits increased local populations and that the likely source of propagule depletion was mammal predation on seeds.

Competitive abilities of sparse species

One aspect of our study of sparse prairie grasses in Missouri is illustrative of the difficulties in dissecting causes versus consequences of rarity. In order to examine the common assumption that rare species are inferior competitors (McNaughton and Wolf, 1970; Schlesinger 1978; Grime, 1979), we established de Wit competition experiments from seed in the glasshouse from May to September (see Harper, 1977, for a general explanation of de Wit plots and Rabinowitz in review for experimental details and a more thorough analysis of the data).

We find the paradoxical result that the sparse species are very nearly uniformly superior competitors to the common grasses. This result is seen in the bottom four graphs (Figure 3) which show the average total yield of a sparse grass on the left of each diagram and the average total yield of a common grass on the right. For the sparse grasses, yield falls above that expected on the basis of the monocultural yield (the dashed line descending to the right). In contrast, for the common grasses, the yields fall below expectation (dashed lines descending to the left). Thus, the convex curves of yield demonstrate the superior competitive abilities of the sparse species.

As a consequence of the superior competitive abilities, however, individuals of the sparse species grow largest when planted in low proportion with a common grass in high proportion (Figure 4). Presumably, this results because the presence of the common grass is more like empty space to a sparse individual than is the presence of other sparse individuals. The two top diagrams (Figure 4) show the dry weight of an individual of a sparse species versus its proportion in a mixture. The identity of the competing species is shown beside each line. For instance, in the upper left diagram, individuals of the sparse species *Festuca paradoxa* are largest when planted as 10 per cent in a mixture with the common grass *Andropogon gerardi* planted as 90 per cent. Individuals of *Sphenopholis obtusata* (upper right diagram) also grow largest when planted in low proportion with either of the common grasses. Contrariwise, the individuals of the common species grow largest when in monoculture or in the presence of other common species (Figure 4, the bottom two diagrams). Thus, an initially paradoxical result is reinterpreted into the Panglossian ('the best of all possible worlds') result (Gould

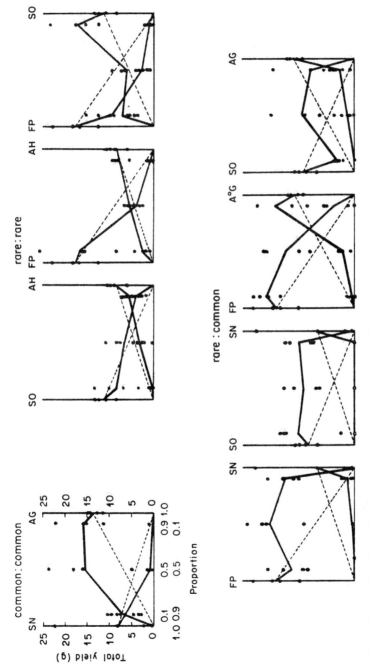

Figure 3   De Wit plots of the total yield from pairwise competition experiments with rare and common species of prairie grasses. Symbols: for common grasses, SN = *Sorghastrum nutans* (L.) Nash, AG = *Andropogon gerardi* Vitman; for sparse grasses, SO = *Sphenopholis obtusata* (Michx.) Scribn., AH = *Agrostis hiemalis* (Walt.) B.S.P., and FP = *Festuca paradoxa* Desv.

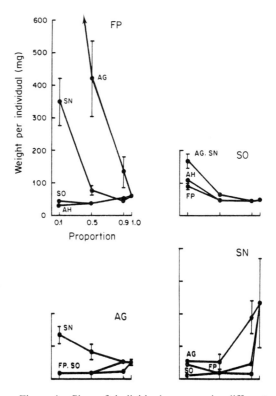

Figure 4   Size of individuals grown in different proportion and with different competitors for rare and common species of prairie grasses. The symbols are the same as for Figure 3. Sparse species are in the top row, common species in the bottom row

and Lewontin, 1979) – that sparse species grow best when sparse, and common species grow best when common.

Natural selection and sparse species

Natural selection cannot, clearly, select for rarity, and it is impossible for rarity to be an adaptive strategy. An individual may be at an advantage because it is rare, for instance, if its herbivores or pathogens cannot find it. Rausher (1980) provides an interesting example for the locally rare *Aristolochia serpentaria* L. and its herbivore *Battus philenor*. As a consequence of the advantage, the individual will reproduce more, become locally more common, and therefore automatically loses the advantage. Thus it is quixotic to say that an organism is adapted to be rare.

But one can assert that an organism may be adapted to the condition or situation of being rare. If an organism is rare for whatever reason (for instance, the fungal pathogen *Endothia parasitica* which infects chestnuts), there are additional disadvantages customarily associated with small population size, for instance being a long way from potential mates. Natural selection can act to favor traits which offset the disadvantages of small local population size, no matter what its cause, and thus render local extinction less likely.

The competitive abilities of the sparse species are best viewed in this light. Since the sparse grasses are competitively superior, the competitive abilities (at least in the short term) cannot be the cause of the sparsity. But given that the species are sparse, the trait that they grow best when surrounded by many individuals of common species is clearly advantageous and will function to render persistence more likely. The competitive abilities are best understood as having nothing to do with the regulation of population size but as a mechanism that offsets a major disadvantage of rarity.

Acknowledgments

I am pleased to acknowledge the assistance of Thora Ellen Thorhallsdottir and Christian Puff. This paper was written while I was a NATO Postdoctoral Fellow at the University College of North Wales, and the research was supported by a grant from the US National Science Foundation (DEB78-11179).

References

Cain, S. A. (1940). 'Some observations on the concept of species senescence', *Ecology*, **21**, 213–15.

Davies, P. A. (1955). 'Distribution and abundance of *Shortia galacifolia*', *Rhodora*, **57**, 189–201.

Davies, P. A. (1960). 'Pollination and seed production in *Shortia galacifolia*', *Castanea*, **25**, 89–96.

Drury, W. H. (1974). 'Rare species', *Biol. Conserv.*, **6**, 162–9.

Gould, S. J. (1977). *Ontogeny and Phylogeny*, Belknap, Cambridge, Mass.

Gould, S. J., and Lewontin, R. C. (1979). 'The spandrels of San Marco and the Panglossian paradigm: a critique of the adaptationist programme', in *The Evolution of Adaptation by Natural Selection* (Eds. J. Maynard Smith and R. Holliday), pp. 581–98, The Royal Society, London.

Grant, V. (1956). 'Chromosome repatterning and adaptation', *Adv. Genet.*, **8**, 89–107.

Grant, V. (1975). *Genetics of Flowering Plants*, Columbia University Press, New York.

Gray, A. (1878). '*Shortia galacifolia* re-discovered', *Amer. J. Sci.*, Ser. III, **16**, 483–5.

Griggs, R. F. (1940). 'The ecology of rare plants', *Bull. Torrey Bot. Club*, 67, 575–94.

Grime, J. P. (1979). *Plant Strategies and Vegetation Processes*, Wiley, Chichester.

Harper, J. L. (1977). *Population Biology of Plants*, Academic Press, London.

Johnson, A. G. (1954). '*Betula lenta* var. *uber* Ashe', *Rhodora*, **56**, 129–31.

Kapoor, P. and Partap, T. (1979). 'New approach to conserve fossil fuels by harnessing efficient energy-capturing systems: under-exploited food plants', *Man-Environment Systems*, **9**, 305–8.

216 *The biological aspects of rare plant conservation*

Kinkead, E. (1976). 'Our footloose correspondents: the search for *Betula uber*', *The New Yorker*, **51**, 58–69 (January 12).

Langenheim, J. H., Hackner, B. L., and Bartlett, A. (1967). 'Mangrove pollen at the depositional site of oligo-miocene amber from Chiapas, Mexico', *Bot. Mus. Leaflet, Harvard Univ.*, **21**, 289–324.

Lewis, H. (1966). 'Speciation in flowering plants', *Science*, **152**, 167–72.

Lewontin, R. C. (1974). *The Genetic Basis of Evolutionary Change*, Columbia University Press, New York.

Lucas, G. and Synge, H. (1978). *The IUCN Plant Red Data Book*, IUCN, Morges, Switzerland.

May, R. M. (1973). *Stability and Complexity in Model Ecosystems*, 2nd Ed., Princeton University, Princeton, New Jersey.

Mazzeo, P. M. (1974). '*Betula uber* – what is it and where is it?', *Castanea*, **39**, 273–8.

McNaughton, S. J. and Wolf, L. L. (1970). 'Dominance and the niche in ecological systems', *Science*, **167**, 131–9.

Mertz, D. B., Cawthon, D. A. and Park, T. (1976). 'An experimental analysis of competitive indeterminacy in *Tribolium*', *Proc. Nat. Acad. Sci.*, **73**, 1368–72.

Nelson, T. C. (1955). 'Chestnut replacement in the southern highlands', *Ecology*, **36**, 352–3.

Ogle, D. W. and Mazzeo, P. M. (1976). '*Betula uber*, the Virginia Round-leaf Birch, rediscovered in southwest Virginia', *Castanea*, **41**, 248–56.

Preston, D. J. (1976). 'The rediscovery of *Betula uber*', *Amer. For.*, **82**, 16–20.

Rabinowitz, D. (1978). 'Abundance and diaspore weight in rare and common prairie grasses', *Oecologia (Berlin)*, **37**, 213–19.

Rabinowitz, D. and Rapp, J. K. (in press), 'Dispersal abilities of sparse and common prairie grasses', *Amer. Jl Bot.*

Rausher, M. D. (1980). 'Host abundance, juvenile survival, and oviposition preference in *Battus philenor*', *Evolution*, **34**, 342–55.

Rhoades, M. H. (1966). 'Seed germination of *Shortia galacifolia* T. & G. under controlled conditions', *Rhodora*, **68**, 147–54.

Ricklefs, R. E. and Cox, G. W. (1978). 'Stage of taxon cycle, habitat distribution, and population density in the avifauna of the West Indies', *Amer. Nat.*, **112**, 875–95.

Ross, M. N. (1936). 'Seed reproduction of *Shortia galacifolia*', *J.N.Y. Bot. Garden*, **37**, 208–11.

Schlesinger, W. H. (1978). 'On the relative dominance of shrubs in Okefenokee Swamp', *Amer. Nat.*, **112**, 949–54.

Schumaker, K. M. and Babble, G. R. (1980). 'Patterns of allozymic similarity in ecologically central and marginal populations of *Hordeum jubatum* in Utah', *Evolution*, **34**, 110–16.

Smith, R. L. (1976). 'Ecological genesis of endangered species: the philosophy of preservation', *Ann. Rev. Ecol. Syst.*, **7**, 33–55.

Stebbins, G. L. (1942). 'The genetic approach to problems of rare and endemic species', *Madroño*, **6**, 241–58.

Stebbins, G. L. (1974). *Flowering Plants: Evolution Above the Species Level*, Harvard University Press, Cambridge, Mass. and Edward Arnold, London.

Stebbins, G. L. and Ellerton, S. (1939). 'Structural hybridity in *Paeonia californica* and *P. brownii*', *J. Genet.*, **38**, 1–36.

Terrell, E. E., Emery, W. H. P., and Beaty, H. E. (1978). 'Observations on *Zizania texana* (Texas wildrice), an endangered species', *Bull. Torrey Bot. Club*, **105**, 50–7.

Vivian, V. E. (1967). '*Shortia galacifolia*: its life history and microclimatic requirements', *Bull. Torrey Bot. Club*, **94**, 369–87.

Walters, J. L. (1942). 'Distribution of structural hybrids in *Paeonia californica*', *Amer. J. Bot.*, **29**, 270–5.

Westman, W. E. (1975). 'Edaphic climax pattern of the pygmy forest region of California', *Ecol. Monogr.*, **45**, 109–35.

Westman, W. E. and Whittaker, R. H. (1975). 'The pygmy forest region of northern California: studies on biomass and primary productivity', *J. Ecol.*, **63**, 493–520.

The Biological Aspects of Rare Plant Conservation
Edited by Hugh Synge
© 1981 John Wiley & Sons Ltd.

18
Approaches to the monitoring of rare plant populations

A . J . D A V Y *School of Biological Sciences, University of East Anglia, Norwich, England*
and
R . L . J E F F E R I E S *Department of Botany, University of Toronto, Canada*

Summary

The underlying reasons for monitoring populations of rare plants are briefly considered, as a prelude to a survey of a wide range of possible techniques. Approaches which are based on plant demography, genetics and resource allocation studies respectively are described and exemplified.

Long-term studies are illustrated with reference to the Breckland plots set up by Dr A. S. Watt in 1936 and which are still monitored; their value in assessing the influence of climate and biotic interactions is discussed in relation to cyclic changes associated with pattern and process. Complementary, intensive, demographic studies which analyse and display the internal workings of single-species populations are also illustrated mainly by work in the Breckland. The importance of subjecting monitored populations to experimental perturbations of environment which correspond with potential management techniques is considered.

The genetic approach recognizes that many plant species exist as a mosaic of genetically differentiated populations which have evolved in response to strong local selection pressures arising from environmental heterogeneity. Monitoring is aimed at characterizing and understanding this genetic variability.

Monitoring of resource allocation in different plant populations is shown to give an insight into the strategies adopted to meet environmental stringencies. Responses to scarcity of a resource (e.g. energy, nutrient elements or water) are especially important in plants at the limit of their range.

The conservation value of the various approaches suggests that integrated monitoring studies which contribute towards a complete understanding of the biology of rare species are most useful as a basis for conservation management. Even these will be of little help, however, where rarity is due to wholesale habitat destruction.

Introduction

What is the conservation value of monitoring populations of rare plants? A practical purpose for monitoring is to ascertain the status of particular populations or species. Inventories which establish the rarity of species, and whether or

not their populations are changing, are undoubtedly prerequisites for conservation. In itself, however, such monitoring usually does not provide the
scientific basis for a practical management policy. Successful management of a
rare plant population, whether that involves making it less rare or preventing its
extinction, implies the ability to manipulate the size and structure of that population. If monitoring is to contribute significantly to this ability it must be of a more
fundamental type, which yields a predictive understanding of population structure
and function.

Thus the potential approaches to population monitoring for conservation
purposes are essentially the same as those to plant population biology generally.
Solbrig (1980) has identified three principal approaches which differ in the major
variable studied, and this classification is adopted here with only slight modification: approaches based on demography, genetics and resource allocation studies
are considered. The main concern of this chapter is to survey and exemplify the
variety of approaches, so as to begin to assess their respective strengths, weaknesses and potential contributions towards constructing a predictive knowledge of
rare plant populations.

Demographic approaches

Monitoring which is based on numbers of individuals (or their parts) is perhaps
the most obviously relevant to problems of rarity. The same is true if some
measure which can be related to numbers, not necessarily in a simple fashion, is
employed (e.g. frequency or cover; Kershaw, 1973). A wide spectrum of methods,
varying in both resolution and time-scale, is possible; the one selected for a
particular study should be appropriate to the life-cycle and morphology of the
species in question as well as to the objectives of the study. In practice, it is rare
for the intensive studies to be of very great duration or for the long-term work to
be strictly demographic. Welcome exceptions to this are the studies of mainly
long-lived species of arid environments where it has proved feasible to produce
actuarial life tables of annual cohorts over very long periods (Williams, Chapter
19). However, for the relatively short-lived herbaceous species of mesic environments which have been the subject of most work, the long-term and intensive
studies have tended to serve somewhat different ends.

Long-term monitoring

This approach generally depends upon setting out permanent quadrats and then
mapping their vegetation at regular intervals over a period of several decades.
Recording is commonly carried out annually, at about the same time each year, in
order to exclude as far as possible variation arising from phenology and life-cycle;
alternatively the plots may be mapped two or three times a year, so as to take
some account of such variation.

A classic example of this approach is represented in the plots established in the Breckland of East Anglia by Dr A. S. Watt in 1936 and recorded by him until 1973 (Watt, 1962, 1971, 1981*a,b*). Subsequently we have continued to record the plots annually by the same method. The changes in total frequency, over a period of 44 years, of three species which have been the physiognomic dominant at one time or another in a plot protected from rabbit grazing are shown in Figure 1. The changes have been dramatic and the plots in 1980 are very unlike their original composition in 1936. *Festuca ovina* had a high initial frequency but declined rapidly between 1947 and 1956, and now maintains only about 25 per cent of its former frequency. *Hieracium pilosella* appeared in the plot for the first time in 1944, as seedlings, and then rose to dominance with a peak frequency in 1953; like the *Festuca*, it declined rapidly and has remained at a rather low frequency since 1964. *Thymus* appeared in 1959 and has increased in frequency to become overwhelmingly the dominant species in 1980. (*T. drucei* and *T. serpyllum* are present; the latter has recently qualified for the *British Red Data Book*, Perring and Farrell, 1977). Of course, many other species have been represented in the plot over this period.

Although the mechanisms underlying these changes are not entirely clear, they have changed systematically and radically during 44 years of isolation from the direct effects of human interference and fluctuations in rabbit grazing pressure. Presumably, only an active and continuing form of management would have had any chance of maintaining particular, constant populations. Moreover, the

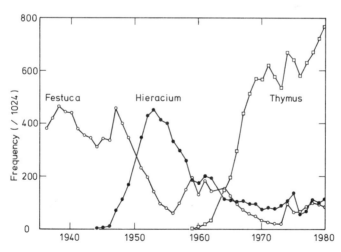

Figure 1   Changes in frequency (out of a possible 1024) of *Festuca ovina* (○), *Hieracium pilosella* (●) and *Thymus drucei* and *T. serpyllum* (□) in an exclosed plot on Grassland A of the Breckland between 1936 and 1980. Data up to 1973 by courtesy of Dr A. S. Watt. (Parts reproduced by permission of the British Ecological Society)

The biological aspects of rare plant conservation

(a)

```
44
45
46
47
48
49
50
51
52
53
54
55
56
57
58
59
60
61
62
63
64
65
66
67
68
69
70
71
72
73
74
75
76
77
78
79
80
```

(b)

```
59 ....................................................1..1........................................................................
60 ..............................1....................11122........................................................................
61 ..............................21...................12232311..1..................................................................
62 ..............................21................221221445311.1...................1.................1............................
64 ..1........................4432122........2..324457357547753444....1.............11..11.......................3..1111.2243442244
65 ..111...............3.22223111..12.111....2226443152678866434442121..............1..1111.............111.....1311243214356445654
66 ..112............31.44.2335522..3.1.2.12211156555788558888764586652....3........1211.................234......321267524647576676
67 ..221.1......1112342133676663311542121.2572187768888878888888888866852313.......1633.21231..1.....1..222.1..15654578777676577775
68 .1131211..22....5441357543331235532246785348888888787888888888886777663321......4762.2345141......1112.33112466565688887555588886
69 14151233..151354754324344635544331345587864586668877888866578887777777342212 1.11265444635344.211..211.2131.44767778877886565 6674
70 12346252212355278876635676613153265455777357848787778888755586887768785542 2....12632254555433323..2..3.231145443464755845243 6666
71 53361154233345368885742573553863446665874676777777887888668888888888757443 12.1.14531457554314411 1.212134332425454567668653568655
72 52454244312335468657643543754754465577557754558745784788888873777777656233 11.1.34641345666452231..22.11331324245465574885542475 4
73 51354644.1.32447876553446354434445766586747467666576776778864586684565532221...15451355454423..3..211.232134233564555675436315 34
74 4558287631.5258888867555646565353766787888788888788888888888877678878876642 1....55344356754322221.1.123254444355646755354664567 3
75 7576385551146666786853555574421427475788868878888888888888876888888877776553 2...33423233566341.23..1.2121232325477676564234665656
76 556846655223444657765325436531231776778887888888768888658645788888876865521 1....4431.234543443222....1223122225686653255565332364
77 45545544324746656756533246644142468888768888866887888888887888888888888874112 11.33731335547125244 11.1343.2231256555561545245655355
78 336854541465666335662132467632345666787888888788888868888887888888888886476112 2155654235664332313222532.54332576466678565355 55578
79 23767656448688735775232.37852433278688888887888878868888886686688888888888862115443353131874333212565645466623676588878873476 44577
80 2485676555678883375644336885322.377888878888888888888888888888888888888888877522336633347865523.2556466455642367787868886574 63676
```

Figure 2 Changes in frequency (out of a possible eight) for 128 contiguous rows of the exclosed plot on grassland A of the Breckland. (a) *Hieracium pilosella* (1944–80); (b) *Thymus* spp. (1959–80); *T. drucei* and *T. serpyllum*). Data up to 1973 by courtesy of Dr A. S. Watt. (Parts reproduced by permission of the British Ecological Society)

strengths of the approach are apparent. Populations may be affected by extrinsic factors, particularly climatic ones, and such records are sufficiently long-term to be correlated readily with climatic changes and episodes. In Breckland, the occurrence of spring droughts and the severity of winter frosts are of especial interest (Watt, 1981*b*). By virtue of its excellent representation of spatial relationships through time, the approach also gives an insight into possible interactions between populations of different species. For instance, the relative distributions of *Hieracium pilosella* and *Thymus* spp. are better characterized if the scores for each of the 128 contiguous rows of the quadrat are examined (Figure 2). *Hieracium* may be seen to spread from a single point to the whole length of the quadrat in only 6 years. In decline its solid cover fragments into local patches, which vary in size and drift laterally somewhat, but which nevertheless can be traced right through to the present day. Comparison with the *Thymus* record reveals that the initial points of establishment of *Thymus* were in the gaps then only recently vacated by the *Hieracium*. Similarly, the last areas to be colonized by *Thymus* are those occupied by the larger patches of *Hieracium*. Watt (1981*b*) has provided detailed interpretations in terms of climatic change, interactions between species and the changing vigour of even-aged populations.

This kind of information should eventually help resolve one vitally important issue: the extent to which the changes observed are cyclic and hence due to 'pattern and process' (Watt, 1947) which is intrinsic to the vegetation (but perhaps extrinsic to single species populations). If they are substantially cyclic, the only requirements for the conservation of a rare species would be the preservation of a suitable area, preferably large enough to accommodate any spatial pattern, and patience. Conversely, if long-term, directional changes are taking place, as is likely for some populations of rare plants, this strategy would be disastrous.

Perhaps the major deficiency of the long-term approach as exemplified here is that it reveals nothing of the internal processes of populations; one is monitoring their net result without knowing precisely how it was arrived at. Also, by monitoring at the same time each year, only one stage in the life-cycle (in annuals) or one phenological stage (in perennials) is considered. We certainly give the winter annuals short shrift in the Breckland plots. Both of these difficulties may be overcome by more intensive studies of single species populations.

Intensive monitoring

Here the objective is usually to monitor individual plants, or even their component modules (Harper, 1977). This requires that recruitment (seedling establishment, clonal growth and immigration), losses (mortality and emigration), reproductive success and dispersal strategy be recorded. Thus critical autecological information on life-history, phenology, population flux, survivorship and the causes of mortality is obtained; if a suitable range of population densities is studied, then density-dependent processes may be identified and the mechanisms of population regulation discovered (Sarukhán and Harper, 1973; Watkinson and Harper,

1978). The majority of herbaceous plants, in temperate habitats at least, must be mapped very frequently (perhaps every 2–3 weeks) in order to achieve this resolution, so it is not surprising that these studies are rarely sustained for more than a few years.

The recent study of *Hieracium pilosella* in Breckland by G. F. Bishop makes an interesting comparison with the approach of Watt. Details of the background and methods are given by Bishop *et al.* (1978). The population flux over $4\frac{1}{2}$ years of individual rosettes in a grazed population is shown in Figure 3. In this site the net population size varied rather little during the study, but the turnover of rosettes was considerable as may be seen from the cumulative losses and gains. Very few seedlings became established and none succeeded in reproducing. Consequently most of the recruits were daughter rosettes produced vegetatively at the end of stolons. There was a marked seasonality in recruitment and mortality, episodes of both in July and August tending to be followed by long periods of relative stability. This occurs because stolon production is tightly coupled to flowering

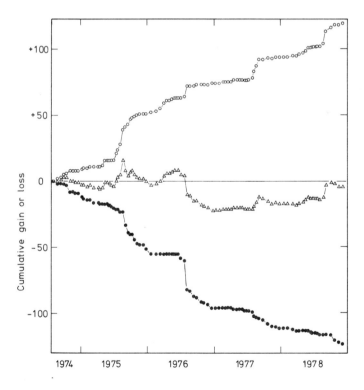

Figure 3   Changes in population size of an initial population of 59 rosettes of *Hieracium pilosella* in grazed Breckland grass heath, 1974–8. Cumulative gains (○); cumulative losses (●); cumulative net gain or loss (△). Data from Bishop (1980). (Parts reproduced by permission of the British Ecological Society)

and the rosettes are monocarpic. Thus, flowering is accompanied by the production of daughter rosettes, typically two, and is followed shortly by the death of the parent rosette. The greater mortality in the dry summers of 1975 and 1976 contrasts with that in 1974, 1977 and 1978. Moreover it was found that the effects of drought were more severe in the grazed plots than in exclosed ones, indicating that the rabbits became more destructive to *H. pilosella* when water was scarce. It is possible to predict, therefore, when major changes to the population are likely to take place; similar predictions for rare species ought to be of direct, practical value in their conservation.

Successive depletion curves for the same population reveal further features (Figure 4). Overall, depletion is linear (on a logarithmic scale) indicating an approximately constant risk of death from year to year; superimposed upon this is the annual pattern of mortality which is especially obvious in 1975 and 1976. The annual mortality peak also has the effect tending to aggregate the curves, which start regularly at 6-week intervals, into four annual nests. This depletion represents a half-life of 1.4 years, whereas that of the exclosed population was 2.2 years. It is probably of significance for conservation that the half-life of a not especially palatable species can be increased by 57 per cent by excluding rabbits.

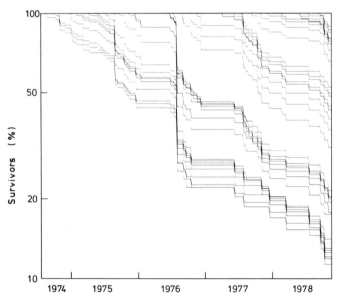

Figure 4   Logarithmic depletion curves for a *Hieracium pilosella* population of grazed Breckland grass heath. The data are expressed as percentage of the initial population for each curve. Curves start at 6-week intervals from July 1974 to December 1978. Data from Bishop (1980)

Implicit in the examples described has been the idea that it is more informative to experiment on populations, by examining their responses to environmental perturbations, than simply to monitor them. In fact, the perturbing influence frequently corresponds with a potential management procedure, e.g. grazing, nutrient addition, irrigation, drainage, burning, etc. Grazing has been dealt with, but a striking variety of responses may be evoked by nutrient perturbation.

Additions of nitrogen and phosphorus to salt marsh sediments for 5 years did not affect the numbers of individuals of the various species significantly; but it did greatly stimulate flowering and seed production in *Halimione portulacoides* and *Limonium vulgare* (Jefferies and Perkins, 1977). A similar experiment in the Breckland resulted in the extinction of *Hieracium pilosella* from nutrient-treated plots within about 4 years (Figure 5), chiefly because its rosette habit was susceptible to shading from the accumulated litter and biomass resulting from the stimulated growth of grasses. Jeffrey (1971) found that the Red Data Book species *Kobresia simpliciuscula* was similarly susceptible to phosphorus addition in Upper Teesdale. Clearly, the dangers of perturbation experiments must be weighed against the likely benefits for populations of rare plants.

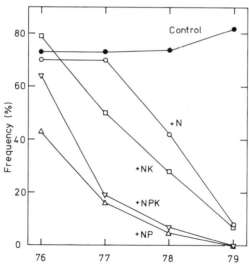

Figure 5   Effects of nutrient addition on the frequency (%) of *Hieracium pilosella* in exclosed Breckland grass heath 1976–9. Control (●); plus Nitrogen (○); plus Nitrogen and Potassium (□); plus Nitrogen and Phosphorus (△); plus Nitrogen, Phosphorus and Potassium (▽). Nutrient addition began in October 1975. Frequency was determined in June each year. Quantities of salts applied were as in Willis (1963)

The demographic approach leaves certain important problems unaddressed and prominent among these are genetic issues. Indeed, more often than not, the genetic structure of a population is necessarily obscured by the confounding of ramets of different genetic individuals (genets) because the genets cannot be identified.

Genetic approaches

It is increasingly appreciated that Linnean species are often genetically differentiated into very local populations which have evolved in response to heterogeneity of the environment. Given the strong selection pressures which appear to be operating, this differentiation can be maintained over extremely short distances despite the gene flow associated with pollen and seed dispersal. Hence plant populations are dynamic in a genetic sense as well as in a numerical sense, and a demographer's population may include a host of smaller, genetically distinct populations. It can be argued that monitoring this genetic variation is as fundamental to understanding population structure and that it has practical implications for conservation as trenchant as those of the numerical approach. Solbrig (1980) has pointed out the necessity for also studying the mode of inheritance of phenotypic characteristics, but this is beyond the scope of monitoring. Local populations may be genetically distinct with respect to almost any aspect of their population biology, physiology and morphology which confers a selective advantage.

A striking example of small-scale heterogeneity is provided by salt marshes of north Norfolk, where the complex patterns of tidal inundation in space and time give rise to an environmental mosaic; the environment at any point is highly predictable from year to year and this constitutes a cyclic form of stability which permits differentiation. Populations of *Salicornia europaea* agg. show different phenologies and growth patterns in different parts of the marsh. Plants of high marsh areas, which become hypersaline and nitrogen-deficient in early summer when the tide fails to cover them, show very slow growth at this time. They grow much faster in late summer, however, when the tides again cover the marsh. This trait cannot be modified by irrigating the marsh with seawater and adding nitrogen to the sediments during the critical hypersaline period; i.e. it has become genetically fixed. In contrast, low marsh plants, which receive regular inundation, grow quite rapidly throughout the season (Jefferies *et al.*, 1979, 1981).

Furthermore, these *Salicornia* populations are annual with discrete generations; they exist between November and March only as enormous seed-banks in the marsh sediment, but practically no seed is carried over to the following summer (Figure 6). Yet on the south shore of the Hudson Bay, Canada, where the environment is harsh and unpredictable and *S. europaea* is at the limit of its range, a more persistent seed-bank has evolved, with a density of up to 15 000 per sq. m before seed is shed in the autumn. The behaviour of *Salicornia* illustrates the importance of monitoring all the phases of the life-cycle and phenology of a species rather than just the more obvious vegetatively active stages.

The general principles involved in conserving genetic variability have been reviewed succinctly by Berry (1971, 1974). One of his conclusions was that intra-population variation is large and resistant to loss. Nevertheless in the case of rare plants, whose populations are frequently small and disjunct, there is a danger of losing the variation associated with whole populations. Their variation is rather poorly understood; it seems likely that they can ill afford to lose any of it if they are to survive in the long term.

Resource allocation approaches

This approach is based on studies of the capture, transformation and use of resources. The resource in question may be energy, which has the major advantage of providing a common currency to assess costs and benefits (Solbrig, 1980), or it may be an important material such as water, a nutrient element or metabolite. At any stage of development resources may be allocated to growth, maintenance or reproduction and this allocation is readily amenable to monitoring

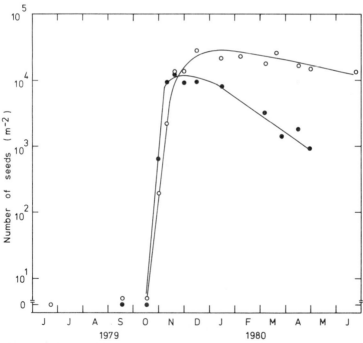

Figure 6 The seed-bank (number of seeds per sq. m) of *Salicornia europaea* agg. in the low marsh at Stiffkey, Norfolk from June 1979 to July 1980. Readily germinatable seeds (O) on 10 cm sq. turves in 20 °C day/12 °C night regime; residual ungerminated seeds (●) extracted by flotation in saturated K_2CO_3 solution

by analysis of the various plant organs. The major focus of interest is on those resources which are scarce either generally or episodically, and which thus present the need for compromises in their allocation. The total of such compromises in a population represents an allocative strategy for evolutionary fitness in its particular environment. Consequently monitoring the allocation of scarce resources yields an insight into the mechanisms by which populations cope with the stresses and vagaries of their environments; alternatively it can provide crucial explanations of their failure to survive, which for rare species might easily constitute the basis for remedial action.

Again, an illustration of the approach may be found in the salt marsh environment. Plants of high marsh populations of the long-lived perennial *Triglochin maritima* tend to be slow growing and to tolerate hypersalinity and water-stress well. Low marsh plants grow faster and are less tolerant. The two populations were found to distribute their dry weight (and therefore energy) to various organs in a similar fashion, but their distribution of nitrogen was considerably different (Jefferies, 1980). High marsh plants allocated a much higher proportion of their nitrogen to soluble forms and especially to proline, a compatible osmotic substrate which is associated with the maintenance of adequately low water potentials in the tissues. Thus there has been a trade-off between soluble and structural nitrogen, or put another way between survival and growth, to meet the environmental stringencies of the high marsh. As in the case of *Salicornia*, these differences are genetically fixed and cannot be modified by watering and nitrogen fertilization experiments.

The approach is probably of greatest value in investigating species close to the limits of their geographical distribution or in otherwise marginal habitats, as is not infrequently the case with rare plants. If energetic or nutrient allocative considerations suggest that a particular population is unable to accommodate adequately the local environmental extremes, it is probably wiser to concentrate conservation effort in less marginal areas.

Conclusion

A wide diversity of approaches to the monitoring of plant populations has been reviewed. Most of the illustrations relate to relatively common species, but we believe that similar methods could with benefit be applied to rare species in all cases. Naturally it would not be possible or even desirable to apply all of these approaches to all populations. The methods employed would depend on the species and the specific conservation problem that had to be resolved. Neither is the presentation of this variety of approaches intended to detract from the idea that rarity is essentially a demographic problem; rather, it is meant to display the ways in which genetic and physiological information can provide insight into many of the mechanisms underlying demographic change. Moreover, in investigating rare species it would seem prudent to consider the possibility of interactions with populations of other species that are not necessarily rare; populations of species with significant niche-overlap, grazers, parasites and pathogens are all potentially powerful, external influences on single-species populations.

Perring and Farrell (1977) have called attention to the pressing need for knowledge of the biology of each rare species. Integrated approaches to population monitoring, using all of the available evidence, show much promise in helping to unravel the complexities of rare plant populations and meet this need. But however nearly complete our understanding of the biology becomes, it will be of little avail for conservation if the primary cause of rarity is wholesale habitat destruction.

Acknowledgements

We are very grateful to Dr A. S. Watt FRS and Dr G. F. Bishop for allowing us the use of unpublished data.

References

Berry, R. J. (1971). 'Conservation aspects of the genetical constitution of populations', in *The Scientific Management of Animal and Plant Communities for Conservation* (Eds. E. Duffey and A. S. Watt), pp. 177–206, Blackwell Scientific Publications, Oxford.

Berry, R. J. (1974). 'Conserving genetical variety', in *Conservation in Practice* (Eds. A. Warren and F. B. Goldsmith), pp. 99–115, Wiley, London.

Bishop, G. F. (1980). *The Population Biology of* Hieracium pilosella *L. in a Breck Grassland*, Ph.D. thesis, University of East Anglia.

Bishop, G. F., Davy, A. J., and Jefferies, R. L. (1978). 'Demography of *Hieracium pilosella* in a Breck grassland', *J. Ecol.*, **66**, 615–29.

Clapham, A. R., Tutin, T. G., and Warburg, E. F. (1962). *Flora of the British Isles*, 2nd Ed., Cambridge University Press, London.

Harper, J. L. (1977). *Population Biology of Plants*, Academic Press, London.

Jefferies, R. L. (1980). 'The role of organic solutes in osmoregulation in halophytic higher plants', in *Genetic Engineering of Osmoregulation: Impact on Plant Productivity for Food, Chemicals and Energy* (Eds. A. Hollaender, D. W. Rains and R. C. Valentine), Plenum Press, New York.

Jefferies, R. L., Davy, A. J., and Rudmik, T. (1981). 'Population biology of the salt marsh annual *Salicornia europaea* agg.', *J. Ecol.*, **69**, 17–31. A. J. Davy), pp. 243–68, Blackwell Scientific Publications, Oxford.

Jefferies, R. L., Davy, A. J., and Rudmik, T. (in press). 'Population biology of the saltmarsh annual *Salicornia europaea* agg.', *J. Ecol.*, **69**.

Jefferies, R. L. and Perkins, N. (1977). 'The effects on the vegetation of the additions of inorganic nutrients to salt marsh soils at Stiffkey, Norfolk', *J. Ecol.*, **65**, 867–82.

Jeffrey, D. W. (1971). 'The experimental alteration of a *Kobresia*-rich sward in Upper Teesdale', in *The Scientific Management of Animal and Plant Communities for Conservation* (Eds. E. Duffey and A. S. Watt), pp. 79–89, Blackwell Scientific Publications, Oxford.

Kershaw, K. A. (1973). *Quantitative and Dynamic Plant Ecology*, 2nd Ed., Edward Arnold, London.

Perring. F. H. and Farrell, L. (1977). *British Red Data Books: 1 Vascular Plants*, Society for the Promotion of Nature Conservation, Lincoln.

Sarukhán. J. and Harper, J. L. (1973). 'Studies on plant demography: *Ranunculus repens* L., *R. bulbosus* L. and *R. acris* L.: I. Population flux and survivorship', *J. Ecol.*, **61**, 675–716.

Solbrig, O. T. (1980). 'Demography and natural selection', in *Demography and Evolution in Plant Populations* (Ed. O. T. Solbrig), pp. 1–20, Blackwell Scientific Publications, Oxford.

Watkinson, A. R. and Harper, J. L. (1978). 'The demography of a sand dune annual: *Vulpia fasciculata*: I. The natural regulation of populations', *J. Ecol.*, **66**, 15–33.

Watt, A. S. (1947). 'Pattern and process in the plant community', *J. Ecol.*, **35**, 1–22.

Watt, A. S. (1962). 'The effect of excluding rabbits from grassland A (xerobrometum) in Breckland, 1936–60', *J. Ecol.*, **50**, 181–98.

Watt, A. S. (1971). 'Factors controlling the floristic composition of some plant communities in Breckland', in *The Scientific Management of Animal and Plant Communities for Conservation* (Eds. E. Duffey and A. S. Watt), pp. 137–52, Blackwell Scientific Publications, Oxford.

Watt, A. S. (1981*a*). 'A comparison of grazed and ungrazed Grassland A in East Anglian Breckland', *J. Ecol.*, **69**, 499–508.

Watt, A. S. (1981*b*). 'Further observations on effects of excluding rabbits from Grassland A in East Anglian Breckland: the pattern of change and factors affecting it (1936–73)', *J. Ecol.*, **69**, 509–36.

Willis, A. J. (1963). 'Braunton Burrows: the effects on the vegetation of the addition of mineral nutrients to the dune soils', *J. Ecol.*, **51**, 353–74.

Note

Plant names in this chapter follow Clapham, Tutin and Warburg (1962).

The Biological Aspects of Rare Plant Conservation
Edited by Hugh Synge
© 1981 John Wiley & Sons Ltd.

19
Monitoring changes in populations of desert plants

O. B. WILLIAMS *CSIRO Division of Land Use Research, Institute of Earth Resources, Canberra, Australia*

Summary

Recently there has been increased interest in demography of desert plants. This chapter reviews studies on monitoring desert plant populations and surveys their findings, using mainly examples from arid lands in Australia. The problem of how to choose the best species to monitor is discussed and the techniques for recording change in populations described. These techniques are principally assessing the time-course of individual plants in permanent quadrats, fixed-point landscape photography and studies of age structure or population change or species range. Results from such experiments allow some conclusions to be made about what makes desert plants rare; attention is drawn to the selectivity of grazing animals and the episodic nature of seedling recruitment in desert conditions. Seedling mortality and the effect of competition and erratic rainfall are discussed.

One of the consequences of the development of the theory of vegetational climax has been to guide the observer's mind forwards. Vegetation is interpreted as a stage on the way to something. It might be more healthy and scientifically more sound to look more often backwards and search for the explanation of the present in the past, to explain systems in relation to their history rather than their 'goal'. J. L. Harper (1977)

Introduction

The monitoring of desert plant populations is a sign of growing concern about declining populations of plants that are of direct value as food for herbivores or of indirect value for erosion control; other plant species may be considered as undesirable weeds and here it is their increase which causes concern. Sustained research is fuelled by curiosity, and occasionally the vegetation and climate permit the experimenter to succeed. Few studies have been unqualified successes even though the field techniques are simple and there is an unsatisfied market for the output. This chapter aims to draw attention to the methodology behind recent contributions and to current ideas concerning experiments involving populations of desert plants in arid communities in Australia and, to a lesser extent, in the western rangelands of the United States; it complements the previous chapter of Davy and Jefferies whose survey of monitoring techniques relates to mesic environments. Australian literature on the impact of the herbivore on plant populations in arid Australian rangelands has already been reviewed (Williams, 1977).

The contemporary interest in the demography of desert plants is gratifying. For example, the information from permanent quadrats established in 1915 at the Jornada Experimental Range in south-central New Mexico to monitor changes in populations was not treated demographically until the preliminary studies of Wright and Van Dyne (1976). The studies by R. Roe on *Bassia birchii* from 1938 to 1946, given limited exposure by Everist *et al.* (1976), are only now being treated in terms of life-table compilation; this information appears sufficiently robust to withstand the type of statistical treatment meted out to the data base behind Williams and Roe (1975) in order to contribute to the questions raised by Harper (1977, pp. 596, 598) and West *et al.* (1979).

Choice of species

Species monitored have been desirable and undesirable bunch or tussock grasses, shrubs and small trees (Hall *et al.*, 1964; Norton, 1978; Michalk and Herbert, 1978; Davies and Walsh, 1979). Stoloniferous and rhizomatous plants pose an additional set of problems in interpreting what is an individual. Studies on species with contrasting behaviour, such as *Danthonia caespitosa* and *Chloris acicularis* at Deniliquin, New South Wales (Williams, 1970), or *Astrebla* sp. and *Dichanthium sericeum* in south-west Queensland (Williams and Roe, 1975) have more than a parochial value. Population studies based on one or several species along a cline could be important; the choice of *Chloris acicularis* by Michalk and Herbert (1978) and its different performance under grazing and exclosure at Trangie, New South Wales, some 300 km north of the Deniliquin site, alert us to the value of such a choice as well as indicating that even under similar treatments the demography of a species need not be constant over its range.

Although there is little excuse for a 'blind' choice of species to monitor in view of published papers and the demographer's compendium (Harper, 1977), and there is agreement that declining populations, rarities and weed species are candidates, there is still a substantial unpredictable element in species performance. *Dichanthium sericeum* in the *Astrebla* grassland (Williams and Roe, 1975) was not expected to perform as it did; the 'fluctuating climax' (Blake, 1938) between *Dichanthium* and *Astrebla* species, described by Holland and Moore (1962) in both historical and contemporary terms, is more properly a population explosion by *Dichanthium*, which obscures but does not diminish the resident *Astrebla* population (Groves and Williams, in press).

In some situations where grassland is degraded, another hazard in the choice of species stems from the absence of the restraining hand of a long-lived dominant species on possibly four or more short-lived perennials, which can almost singly dominate the landscape for upwards of 3 years; there seems to be no ordered sequence (i.e. succession) in these circumstances.

Techniques for recording change

Most techniques used in recording changes in populations of desert plants are variants of: (a) the time-course of individual plants in permanent quadrats (Shreve, 1929; Osborn *et al.*, 1935; Carneggie *et al.*, 1971); (b) fixed-point landscape photography (Correll and Lange, 1966; Pond, 1971); and (c) surveys in which the age structure or population changes of a species (Crisp and Lange, 1976) or range of a species (Barker, 1979; Lay, 1979) are estimated.

Charting (mapping) individual plants in permanent quadrats is tedious and time-consuming fieldwork, but it is the method behind most of the successful (i.e. published) studies. Only rarely can photography as described by Wells (1971) be used; constraints include resolution sufficient to permit species identification, seedling occurrence and identification, and obscuring of small plants by shrubs or tall grasses. Photographic techniques require a substantial additional field input. Large-scale aerial photography (1:650) can be used in conjunction with the charting of transects or with photo points in open desert vegetation (Carneggie *et al.*, 1971). In arid vegetation charting can be made a little easier by counting recruits, if they are numerous, at monthly or two-monthly intervals until the survivors reach a reasonable number; the advent of copying machines enables the first charts to be copied after redrawing in the laboratory and the copies (together with notes and questions to the operator) used as the base chart at the next sampling. Maintenance of interest in the project is assisted by using the life-table format and entering the data promptly.

Fixed-point photography is usually an effective adjunct to plot studies as exemplified for the Santa Rita Experiment Range in Arizona by Glendening (1952), Martin and Reynolds (1973) and for the Koonamore Vegetation Reserve 1926–62 by Hall *et al.* (1964). Even without plots it has been shown that sets of photographs can be used to indicate the dynamic nature of vegetational change over time. Correll and Lange (1966) used a 23-year time interval to assess the disintegration time for a newly dead *Acacia sowdenii* tree as 100 years; they found its life-span exceeded 250 years. Crisp (1978) used photopoint series with transparent overlays to complement information on the shrub *Maireana sedifolia* and the tree *Acacia aneura* in infrequently charted quadrats. Young and Evans (1974) were able to use growth rings to establish age classes in their quadrats and then construct height-age indices.

Survey techniques rely on the surveyor's access to reliable age class information and the ability to determine the age of individual plants in the landscape. Age-size relationships for *Acacia burkittii* and *A. aneura* were developed by Crisp and

Lange (1976) and by Crisp (1978) from long-term quadrat studies and then applied more widely. A series of Australian studies based on the 'piosphere' concept (Lange, 1969) has used relative age-size relationships for shrubs (Barker, 1979; Barker and Lange, 1969, 1970), but such an approach has risks when applied to grasses.

Demographic studies are not easy to perform and they have to be endured for many years. Therefore the objectives need to be clear and the vegetation should be chosen as being capable of giving expression to the treatments which are proposed. Vegetation and soil mosaics should be defined and permanent quadrats placed accordingly. The numbers of quadrats quoted in some studies appear to be low and statistical analyses are lacking. In Australia the absence of published population data for a number of important perennial shrubs is known to be due to the omission of the numbers of deaths and recruits. Further, instead of placing exclosures and associated permanent quadrats on slightly or moderately degraded sites where some recovery of vegetation is possible, many studies concentrated on grossly degraded and eroded sites.

The treatments of most interest in Australian and United States arid lands are: 'grazing' and 'released from grazing for x years'; drought (Williams, 1974; Wright and Van Dyne, 1976; Norton, 1978; West et al., 1979); and burnt and 'protected from burning for x years' (Young and Evans, 1978). Although Davies and Walsh (1979), in their study of the regeneration of shrubs over a 10-year period under commercial pastoralism with sheep, did not have a 'released from grazing' treatment, they were able to discern trends in the nine variously stocked paddocks ranging from 6.9 to 13.7 hectares per sheep. Some species previously considered unacceptable to sheep regenerated faster in quadrats subjected to higher stocking rates than in other quadrats where stocking rates were lower; the reverse held for several shrub species eaten by sheep.

The 'piosphere' approach (Lange, 1969) is a procedure designed to assess the response by vegetation to grazing pressure within a large paddock at one time, taking advantage of the usual one watering point and the decreasing intensity of grazing as distance from it increases. Recent studies of this kind include those by Graetz (1978) and Fatchen and Lange (1979). Repeated sampling could give a time-specific life-table, but the definition of grazing pressure would present difficulties.

Plant rarity in arid lands

A measure of the extent to which sheep explore large paddocks has been given by Lange and Willcocks (1980) using a lucerne pellet as a simulated seedling in a paddock of 4050 hectares containing 900 Merino sheep. The rapid removal of this 'seedling' throughout the paddock showed that a domestic herbivore has the capability to rapidly eliminate scattered populations of small scarce plants, which are an insignificant fraction of the material on offer and make up an equally insignificant component of their diet. Such extreme dietary pressures play an important role in making plants rare as is seen in the studies by Crisp and Lange (1976), Lange and Purdie (1976) and Fatchen (1978). The selective elimination of seedlings of various indigenous trees and shrubs since pastoralism began is even noted in paddocks that do not have a history of overstocking. Although the making of rare plants is in progress, it is not a universal phenomenon in arid lands; the impression is one of non-recruitment mainly in the southern half of the continent (predominantly cool season rainfall) and the endangered species are widespread geriatrics.

The episodic nature of recruitment is exemplified by *Acacia sowdenii*, which prior to the Lange and Willcocks study had main seedling inputs in the flood years of 1921 and 1946 'with minor episodes in between'. Williams and Roe (1975) estimate that there were about eight substantial recruitments of the dominant perennial grass *Astrebla* sp. in the period from 1900 to 1973 (now updated to 1980). The period between these substantial recruitments has been longer than the life-span of the longest-lived individual and the species presence is maintained by scattered individuals belonging to small cohorts produced during these long periods.

Grazing has been erroneously blamed for depleted grasslands on some of these occasions; for example, an area of vigorous *Astrebla* grassland removed from grazing in 1962 has experienced no recruitment and has seen a reduction in *Astrebla* density from the 400 per 100 sq. m in the period 1962–6 to 54 per 100 sq. m in 1978. In contrast, a nearby paddock, half of which was ploughed and variously cropped from 1958 to 1966, was found in 1973 to support *Astrebla* plants at a density of 4.32 ± 2.88 per sq. m, compared with only 1.67 ± 1.86 per sq. m on the unploughed portion; all of the paddock was open to sheep grazing. From these examples and others we can conclude that some species require the coincidence of bare ground and appropriate rain for recruitment.

Seedling mortality is known to be substantial and various reasons are given for this. Silcock (1977) determined the fate of over 2100 seedlings in a former *Acacia aneura* arid woodland and found that more than half of the emerging seedlings died within 14 days and only 7 per cent flowered. Tupper (pers. comm.) by-passed this seedling phase by transplanting seedlings of *Atriplex nummularia* into either cultivated ground (and watering until the plants established), or into non-cultivated ground without supplementary watering; he found at the 11-year stage that only 5 of 45 *A. nummularia* transplants in cultivated treatments had died, compared with 32 of 45 transplants into the non-cultivated ground; 29 of these 32 had died during the first summer.

Competition and its effect at the seedling phase is exemplified by information for *Nitraria billardieri* obtained by J. Noble (pers. comm.). Permanent quadrats were placed over a natural stand of *Nitraria* seedlings which were weeded once, several weeks after germination, or not at all. At 40 weeks after weeding the weeded plots had lost 20 per cent of their plants compared with 96 per cent in the non-weeded plots. At 220 weeks after this single weeding event the weeded plots had retained 24 per cent and the non-weeded plots only 2 per cent of the *Nitraria* seedlings – extinction dates for these cohorts were calculated at 2000 and 1984 respectively.

Both *Atriplex nummularia* and *Nitraria billardieri* are warm-season indigenous plants; although the agent of death in the first case was summer and in the second case was competition from *Medicago* spp., which are introduced mediterranean-type annual legumes, the explanation in both cases appears to be early depletion of soil moisture by cool-season annuals in a region of reliable cool-season rainfall and erratic summer rainfall.

In a final example of measures which can reverse the declining population trend in desert plants, Milthorpe (1978) reports that the long-lived *Maireana pyramidata* required a resident shrub population to aid soil stability and provide seed; other prerequisites were exclusion of domestic livestock and rabbits (*Oryctolagus cuniculus*), and rainfall to inititate and establish the cohorts.

In conclusion, the making of rarities has been ascribed to the high levels of dietary selection exercised by domestic herbivores even at low stocking rates, the depredations of rabbits, the low probability of appropriately timed rains and bare ground occurring together, competition in the seedling phase from naturalized annual species, and a resident population of the declining species which is too small to produce sufficient seed and to hold unstable soils in place so that recruitment can occur.

In terms of techniques for monitoring populations of desert plants, the following of individual plants through their life-span and constructing age-specific life tables for important species enables the status of the species to be determined. Studies of recruitment, whether regular or episodic, and the survivorship of cohorts enable calculations to be made of the age composition, and future trends to be assessed. Fixed-point photography is a valuable adjunct to detailed quadrat and plot investigations. Survey techniques are diagnostic and have their place, but are seldom used to monitor plant populations. Permanent quadrat studies and rapid survey techniques, however, have been successfully used together, in large measure overcoming the deficiencies of scale in the former and the lack of precision in the latter.

References

Barker, S. (1979). 'Shrub population dynamics under grazing – within paddock studies', in *Studies of the Australian Arid Zone IV. Chenopod Shrublands* (Eds. R. D. Graetz and K. M. W. Howes), pp. 83–106, Division of Land Resources Management, CSIRO, Australia.

Barker, S. and Lange, R. T. (1969). 'Effects of moderate sheep grazing on plant populations of a black oak–bluebush association', *Aust. J. Bot.*, **17**, 527–37.

Barker, S. and Lange, R. T. (1970). 'Population ecology of *Atriplex* under sheep stocking', in *The Biology of Atriplex* (Ed. R. Jones), pp. 105–20, Division of Plant Industry, CSIRO, Australia.

Blake, S. T. (1938). 'The plant communities of western Queensland and their relationships, with special reference to the grazing industry', *Proc. R. Soc. Queensland*, **49**, 156–204.

Carneggie, D. M., Wilcox, D. G., and Hacker, R. B. (1971). *The Use of Large Scale Aerial Photographs in the Evaluation of Western Australian Rangelands*, Dept. Agric. W. Aust. Tech. Bull. No. 10.

Correll, R. L. and Lange, R. T. (1966). 'Some aspects of the dynamics of vegetation in the Port Augusta–Iron Knob area, South Australia', *Trans. R. Soc. S. Aust.*, **90**, 41–3.

Crisp, M. D. (1978). 'Demography and survival under grazing of three Australian semi-desert shrubs', *Oikos*, **30**, 520–8.

Crisp, M. D. and Lange, R. T. (1976). 'Age structure, distribution and survival under grazing of the arid-zone shrub *Acacia burkittii*', *Oikos*, **27**, 86–92.

Davies, S. J. J. F. and Walsh, T. F. M. (1979). 'Observations on the regeneration of shrubs and woody forbs over a ten year period in grazed quadrats on Mileura station, Western Australia', *Aust. Rangel. J.*, **1**, 215–24.

Everist, S. L., Moore, R. M., and Strang, J. (1976). 'Galvanized Burr (*Bassia birchii*) in Australia', *Proc. R. Soc. Queensland*, **87**, 87–94.

Fatchen, T. J. (1978). 'Change in grazed *Atriplex vesicaria* and *Kochia astrotricha* (Chenopodiaceae) populations, 1929–1974', *Trans R. Soc. S. Aust.*, **102**, 39–42.

Fatchen, T. J. and Lange, R. T. (1979). 'Piosphere pattern and dynamics in a chenopod pasture grazed by cattle', in *Studies of the Australian Arid Zone IV. Chenopod Shrublands* (Eds. R. D. Graetz and K. M. W. Howes), pp. 160–9, Division of Land Resources Management, CSIRO, Australia.

Glendening, G. E. (1952). 'Some quantitative data on the increase of mesquite and cactus on a desert grassland range in southern Arizona', *Ecol*, **33**, 319–28.

Graetz, R. D. (1978). 'The influence of grazing by sheep on the structure of a saltbush (*Atriplex vesicaria* Hew. ex Benth.) population', *Aust. Rangel. J.*, **1**, 117–25.

Groves, R. H. and Williams, O. B. (in press). 'Natural grasslands', in *Australian Vegetation* (Ed. R. H. Groves), Cambridge University Press.

Hall, E. A. A., Specht, R. L., and Eardley, C. M. (1964). 'Regeneration of the vegetation on Koonamore Vegetation Reserve, 1926–1962', *Aust. J. Bot.*, **12**, 205–64.

Harper, J. L. (1977). *Population Biology of Plants*, Academic Press, London.

Holland, A. A. and Moore, C. W. E. (1962). *The Vegetation and Soils of the Bollon District in South-Western Queensland*, Plant Ind. Tech. Pap. No. 17, CSIRO, Australia.

Lange, R. L. (1969). 'The piosphere: sheep track and dung patterns', *J. Range. Manage.*, **22**, 396–400.

Lange, R. L., and Purdie, R. (1967). 'Western myall (*Acacia sowdenii*), its survival prospects and management needs', *Aust. Rangel. J.*, **1**, 64–9.

Lange, R. L., and Willcocks, M. C. (1980). 'Experiments on the capacity of present sheep flocks to extinguish some tree populations of the South Australian arid zone', *J. Arid Envmts*, **3**, 223–9.

Lay, B. (1979). 'Shrub population dynamics under grazing: a long term study', in *Studies of the Australian Arid Zone IV. Chenopod Shrublands* (Eds. R. D. Graetz and K. M. W. Howes), pp. 107–24, Division of Land Resources Management, CSIRO, Australia.

Martin, S. C. and Reynolds, H. G. (1973). 'The Santa Rita Experimental Range: Your facility for research on semidesert ecosystems', *Ariz. Acad. Sci.*, **8**, 56–67.

Michalk, D. L. and Herbert, P. K. (1978). 'The effects of grazing and season on the stability of *Chloris* spp. (windmill grasses) in natural pasture at Trangie, New South Wales', *Aust. Rangel. J.*, **1**, 106–11.

Milthorpe, P. L. (1978). 'Some factors affecting establishment and growth of black bluebush (*Maireana pyramidata* (Benth.) R. G. Wilson) in western New South Wales', in *Proc. 1st Int. Rangel. Congr.*, pp. 362–5.

Norton, B. E. (1978). 'The impact of sheep grazing on long-term successional trends in salt desert shrub vegetation of southwestern Utah', in *Proc. 1st Int. Rangel. Congr.*, pp. 610–13.

Osborn, T. G. B., Wood, J. G., and Paltridge, T. B. (1935). 'On the climate and vegetation of the Koonamore Vegetation Reserve to 1931', *Proc. Linn. Soc. N.S.W.*, **60**, 392–427.

Pond, F. W. (1971). *Chapparal 47 Years Later*, USDA Forest Service, Res. Paper RM-69, 11 p., Rocky Mts Forest Range Experimental Station, Fort Collins.

Shreve, F. (1929). 'Changes in desert vegetation', *Ecol.*, **10**, 364–73.

Silcock, R. G. (1977). 'A study of the fate of seedlings growing on sandy red earths in the Charleville district, Queensland', *Aust. J. Bot.*, **25**, 337–46.

Wells, K. F. (1971). 'Measuring vegetation changes on fixed quadrats by vertical ground stereophotography', *J. Range Manage.*, **24**, 233–6.

West, N. E., Rea, K. H., and Harniss, R. O. (1979). 'Plant demographic studies in sagebrush-grass communities of southeastern Idaho', *Ecol.*, **60**, 376–88.

Williams, O. B. (1970). 'Population dynamics of two perennial grasses in Australian semi-arid grassland', *J. Ecol.*, **58**, 869–75.

Williams, O. B. (1974). 'Vegetation improvement and grazing management', in *Studies of the Australian Arid Zone II. Animal Production* (Ed. A. D. Wilson), pp. 127–43, Division of Land Resources Management, CSIRO, Australia.

Williams, O. B. (1977). 'Reproductive wastage in rangeland plants, with particular reference to the role of herbivores', in *The Impact of Herbivores on Arid and Semi-arid Rangelands*, (Ed. K. M. W. Howes), pp. 227–48. Proc. 2nd US/Aust. Rangeland Panel, Aust. Rangeland Soc. Perth.

Williams, O. B. and Roe, R. (1975). 'Management of arid grasslands for sheep: Plant demography of six grasses in relation to climate and grazing', *Proc. Ecol. Soc. Aust.*, **9**, 142–56.

Wright, R. G. and Van Dyne, G. M. (1976). 'Environmental factors influencing semi desert grasslands perennial grass demography', *Southwestern Naturalist*, **21**, 259–74.

Young, J. A. and Evans, R. A. (1974). 'Population dynamics of green rabbit-brush in disturbed big sagebrush communities', *J. Range Manage.*, **27**, 127–32.

Young, J. A. and Evans, R. A. (1978). 'Population dynamics after wildfires in sagebrush grasslands', *J. Range Manage.*, **31**, 283–9.

The Biological Aspects of Rare Plant Conservation
Edited by Hugh Synge
© 1981 John Wiley & Sons Ltd.

20
Monitoring grassland plants in Upper Teesdale, England

MARGARET E. BRADSHAW *University of Durham, England*

Summary

In studying the population biology of a species there are great advantages in actuarial-type monitoring over annual population counts. Such a technique, which involves 'labelled' plants, has been used in monitoring the rare plants of Upper Teesdale, a British site of great botanical importance. Various methods to define the individual in terms of ramets and genets are explained and the detailed method of monitoring each 'labelled' individual plant using a portable grid frame described. The results of this work have shown that rare plant populations fluctuate considerably. Actuarial monitoring can pinpoint the exact stage in the life cycle where changes are initiated, knowledge which has valuable management implications for rare plant conservation.

Introduction

This chapter advocates the great advantages of monitoring the fate of individual plants within a population – called actuarial monitoring, following Harper (1977) – over an annual population count, and describes a technique for recording 'labelled' plant units which could be adapted and used in many types of vegetation. The work developed out of the need to monitor the rare plants in Upper Teesdale, one of the most important botanical sites in Britain.

Upper Teesdale is on the eastern slopes of the Pennines in north England, lat. 54° 40′ N, long. 2° 15′ W. Its flora is justly described as unique, because of the assemblage of rare species which include not only arctic elements, such as *Minuartia stricta*, arctic-alpines such as *Tofieldia pusilla* and northern elements, but also southern, continental species such as *Helianthemum canum* and well-known plants of the Central European mountains such as *Gentiana verna* (Godwin and Walters, 1967). Many of these species are national rarities, and some, such as the gentian, are among the 21 species protected by British laws from picking and uprooting (see Wells, Chapter 40).

Upper Teesdale holds a late glacial relict flora and vegetation, now largely obliterated from continental Europe. Here lies its great phytosociological and phytogeographic importance. Such vegetation was widespread in Britain and

241

northwest Europe some 10 000–12 000 years ago when conditions similar to Arctic tundra today prevailed.

A further reason for studying the site was that in 1965 the Tees Valley and Cleveland Water Board proposed to build a reservoir in the area to supply, primarily, Imperial Chemical Industries Ltd. (ICI). It immediately became imperative that the detailed distribution and frequency of these rare species should be known. Despite unprecedented efforts by the conservationists, Parliament granted permission for the reservoir. In the aftermath of this decision, ICI provided money for research in Upper Teesdale and some of the work described here was supported by that fund. Although most of the Teesdale rarities had been found there by 1805 (Clapham, 1978), the first description of the plant community was not published until 1956 (Pigott), so there was a great deal of work to be done.

The reason such a vegetation-type survived in Teesdale may be found in the combination of unstable base-rich soils and climate, which have prevented forest or bog becoming dominant (Godwin and Walters, 1967). Climatic data for Widdybank Fell (510 m) in Upper Teesdale over the 10-year period 1968–78 show an annual rainfall of 1487 mm and a mean daily temperature of 5.7°C, the monthly means varying from 0°C to 1.5°C between December and March, and reaching 10–12.3°C in June to August. Ground frosts can occur in every month and completely still days are rare, the average wind speed of the calmest month (August) being 4.3 m per sec.

The geological structure is mostly Lower Carboniferous with limestone, sandstone and shale bands. Mineralization is widespread and lead, zinc, fluorspar and barytes have been mined. A quartz-dolerite igneous intrusion has metamorphosed some rocks to give a saccharoidal limestone, sometimes called 'sugar limestone', and fine-grained porcellanite, a mudstone, both of which weather rapidly when exposed to the climate. Glacial deposits of various thicknesses cover much of the area. The typical widespread vegetation of the surrounding hills comprises blanket bog, wet heath and acid grasslands of the phytosociological classes *Oxycocco-Sphagnetea* and *Nardo-Callunetea*, and herb-rich meadows of the *Molinio-Arrhenatheretea* in the valley. Amongst these, and especially on Widdybank and Cronkley Fells of Upper Teesdale, are the dry to slightly moist limestone grasslands of the *Seslerio-Caricetum pulicaris* Association in the *Mesobromion erecti* Alliance and the wet flush and short-marsh calcareous communities of the *Pinguiculo–Caricetum dioicae* Association in the *Caricion davallianae* Alliance. These two Associations support most of the rare species. Some measure of protection is given to these species in the Upper Teesdale National Nature Reserve, a reserve established by the Nature Conservancy by agreements with the owners of the land, in 1963 to the south of the Tees and in 1969 to the north of the river and the reservoir.

These research projects in Upper Teesdale have produced information at three different levels:

1. Vegetation maps based on a phytosociological study of Widdybank Fell have been produced at the scale of 1:10 000 and 1:2500 (Bradshaw and Jones, 1976). These follow the technique of the Zürich–Montpellier School (Jones, 1973).

2. Distribution maps of some 25 rare species on the same Fell and adjacent to the reservoir have been recorded on maps (scale 1:2200) constructed from aerial photographs. Amateur botanists did most of this recording in 2- or 3-week periods per year and eventually covered 1.6 km × 0.4 km in 10 years. Similar work is being carried out in other parts of the National Nature Reserve.

3. From this work arose a more intensive study of the population dynamics and some aspects of the autecology of a small number of the rare species. At that time very little was known about the behaviour of the plants and their populations in the wild. Were they threatened if the sheep ate the *Primula farinosa* flowers or people dug up the *Gentiana verna* plants?

Defining the individual

Influenced by the work of Tamm (1948, 1956*a* and *b*) and the zoologists on population dynamics, I devised a method for the collection of actuarial data from samples of the populations of rare species on Widdybank and Cronkley Fells. The first problem was deciding what to record – defining the individual is not always straightforward. Some idea of the magnitude of the problem is provided by Harper (1978), a paper on clonal growth, and White's review of the plant as a metapopulation (White, 1979). I agree with White that the choice must be pragmatic, depending on the purpose of the study and the nature of the plant. Here the conservationist, like the agriculturalist, is a field worker and practitioner and is best guided by what can be counted as an individual in the field. Consequently the individuals in these studies represent several different units and sub-units, also termed modules (White, 1979; Harper, 1978). Each may be a genet (a plant derived from a seed) or a ramet, such as a separate shoot or rooted part of a clone; these are sub-units of a genet.

All the species are herbaceous perennials, winter-green in Teesdale, and include only one monocotyledon. Completely deciduous herbs without visible winter buds are very difficult to record (e.g. *Carex capillaris* – we tried!). Defining the individual in four of the species was straightforward: *Draba incana* and *Polygala amarella* each produce a basal rosette and occasionally several lateral rosettes, but the original plant which developed from the seed, the genet, is always clearly visible; therefore these records are of genets. In *Gentiana verna* and *Carex ericetorum*, the genets produce clones of shoots from underground stolons. In the gentian each shoot (a ramet) is a solitary rosette, as multiple rosettes are uncommon in the grazed communities. The shoots of the sedge are distinct and even where these are dense in the tussock state, which is rare and small in Teesdale, the individuals can be mapped. In both species the population records comprise ramets of different genets. At present there is no satisfactory field method of identifying the sub-units of each genet, but the development of sensitive techniques such as enzyme electrophoresis for identifying genets could become a powerful tool (Harper, 1978).

Initially, *Viola rupestris* presented a physically complicated problem, mainly because the short, woody, stem-stocks were hidden in the matrix of moss, lichen and plant bases. Although there is no vegetative propagation of separately rooted plants, there appeared to be some form of branching and production of new shoots. As the plant connections could not be determined without disturbing the substrate, each shoot, a rosette of three or four leaves, was recorded as an individual. It is now known that each genet usually divides into two shoots after about 3 years; additionally one or more lateral shoots may be formed, especially if the terminal shoot is damaged (eaten or killed by drought) and, surprisingly, stems apparently dead for up to 2 years can produce new shoots. Therefore, the individuals of *Viola rupestris* can be genets with a single shoot, pairs of shoots from the same genet, or one or more shoots from identified and unidentified genets; thus the records comprise genets and ramets. With the accumulated experience of monitoring the same sample population over several seasons, it has been possible to identify the relationships between the majority of the individuals. Most other parameters of the life-cycle and biology of each species have been monitored; these include seedlings, plants with flowers and fruits, number of flowers and fruits per plant and seeds per fruit.

The actuarial data are collected from a permanently marked, long, narrow plot. Monitoring has been done in spring, summer and autumn; in Teesdale these are May, July, and September to October. In order to obtain an adequate sample for the other parameters, records are made in a second, larger marked plot. This is monitored once or twice a year in the main flower and fruit production period each year. Here the individuals are counted but not identified.

A relatively simple method and fairly light portable grid frame has been devised to identify and repeatedly record the individual plants in the short grassland, suitable for the wet and windy conditions on the fells. Each plant is identified by its co-ordinates on the grid, which is placed above the plants on fixed sites year by year. The equipment and techniques are described in detail in the Appendix to this chapter; they could well be adapted to other areas with similar conditions. In Teesdale the terrain has a small-scale unevenness with hummocks up to 10 cm high and slopes of up to 10°. The grazed herb-rich community is only 1–15 cm in height from the basal matrix; the individual plant units or sub-units vary in size from seedlings 1 mm across to plants 0.5–3 cm across, but larger plants could be recorded by this method.

Accuracy at this stage is of the uttermost importance for it is on these data, collected in the field, that all calculations, analyses and conclusions will be based. 'Garbage in, garbage out' is not only applicable to computers. It should be appreciated that a high degree of stamina is needed to maintain integrity under the climatic conditions which may be experienced. Indeed it may be an advantage if the human element should be of the same geographical group as the plants; in Teesdale a physiological arctic-alpine by heredity or naturalization may be expected to perform most successfully.

Plant demography as an aid to rare plant conservation

The simplest and most frequently collected record is the annual count of the total or sample population. Such data for eight Teesdale species (ten populations) recorded over 8–12 years are shown in Figure 1. Immediately, it is clear that most populations have fluctuated considerably during the period; only the small population of *Primula farinosa* has remained almost stable. Although each increased in the first few years of observation and most decreased in the dry seasons 1975 and 1976, further generalization is impossible and each species must be considered separately. These graphs do emphasize, however, the need for long runs of records to determine the amplitude of the fluctuations to help the conservationist decide if the habitat management should be changed.

These fluctuations can be shown by the two populations of *Polygala amarella*. Both populations increased in 1969; then, that on Cronkley Fell decreased whilst the Widdybank Fell population remained stable for several years before falling in 1974; thereafter both populations began a more rapid decline to reach minimum levels before increasing again in 1977 and 1978 respectively. In this case, it was obvious that the reason for the decline on Cronkley Fell was due to the increase in grazing by rabbits (absent from Widdybank Fell), caused by a series of mild winters from 1970/71 which had allowed a large increase in their numbers. As the low total of 1976 comprised some 95 per cent of the known population of pink-flowered *Polygala amarella* in Teesdale, it was decided to exclude sheep and rabbit grazing from the site.

On Widdybank the recorded population became even smaller due directly to the droughts and indirectly to the consequential relatively higher grazing pressure which has continued until 1980. As this was only part of the whole population on the Fell, it was decided to sit tight and wait; already the population has begun to increase again.

It is open to question whether we interfered unnecessarily on Cronkley Fell in 1976, as a severe winter in 1978/79 almost eliminated the rabbit population in that area. We will never know whether sufficient plants would have survived the grazing pressure of 1976, 1977 and 1978 to provide the gene-pool for expansion in 1979. In a blue-flowered population, all known plants disappeared before protection from grazing allowed seedlings to re-establish the population, now of nine plants. In this case, obvious external factors were affecting the size of the populations and the records of the population totals were sufficient to provide the guideline of when to interfere. But such simple totals provide only a bare minimum of information; they cannot pinpoint the phase in the life-cycle

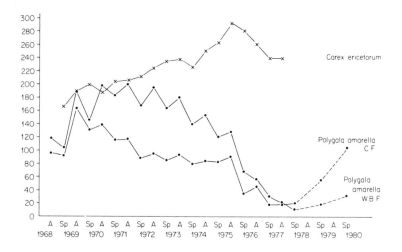

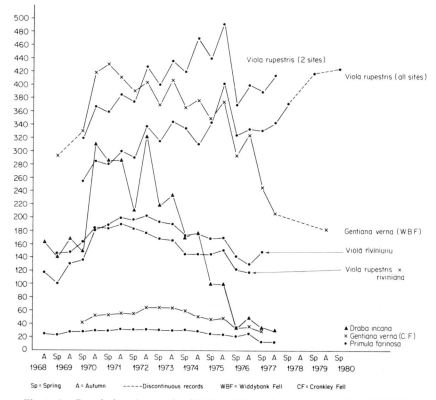

Sp = Spring   A = Autumn   -----Discontinuous records   WBF = Widdybank Fell   CF = Cronkley Fell

Figure 1   Population changes in eight Teesdale herbaceous perennials, 1968–80

where changes are initiated. They cannot tell whether the initial increase in *Gentiana verna* (Figure 1) was due to a very low mortality of the existing plants or a high recruitment of new ramets or both. Only actuarial-type monitoring of 'labelled' individuals will provide this more discriminating information.

For example, the initial increase shown in Figure 1 for *Gentiana verna* was due to a very high recruitment rate in 1970 of 0.8924 (9-year mean = 0.4398); also the totals of 1975 to 1977 mask higher than average mortality and recruitment rates, shown in Table 1. Similarly in *Viola rupestris* actuarial-type records show that the higher than average mortalities of 0.3364 in 1975/76 and 0.3990 in 1976/77 (9-year mean = 0.1854) were followed by a large increase in ramets in 1977, giving a recruitment rate of 0.6721 compared with the 8-year mean of 0.1546, whilst the recruitment rate of the seedlings remained much nearer to the mean of 0.1074. Obviously, these actuarial-type records can show when and where in the life cycle changes are initiated but even they do not provide the cause – the answer to the question why?

Table 1 *Gentiana verna*

| Mortality | 1975/76 | 0.5426: | 1976/77 | 0.6586: | 9-year mean = 0.3542 |
| Recruitment | 1976 | 0.7743: | 1977 | 0.7538: | 9-year mean = 0.4398 |

In this conference the primary aim of studies in species population dynamics is likely to be orientated towards the formulation of a habitat management policy for the survival of a particular rare species. The actuarial-type records provide almost infinitely more useful information than the all-too-simple and easy annual count of the total population or population sample (see also Bradshaw and Doody, 1978*a* and *b*).

The conservationist should not be deterred by the potential complexity of the herbaceous perennial, especially that with a clonal system. Field experience will dictate what plant unit or sub-unit should be recorded as the individual and this can be defined. Of greater importance is consistency in what is monitored and the compilation of information that is as full as possible on the relationship of one individual to another, e.g. in *Viola rupestris* (above) or ramets of a clone. Nor should the prospect of frequent monitoring deter; where time and manpower are genuinely scarce a start can be made by monitoring only the established plants, including seedlings and young ramets only at the end of their first growing season. Admittedly a minimum frequency will still have to be determined, like a minimal area in vegetation sampling, but this will be controlled by the rate of turnover of the established individuals and worked out by experience. In *Carex ericetorum* an annual record sufficed, though no recruits from seeds were ever found in five years; seedlings could have been and gone between monitoring times, but I do not think so. Obviously, long series of data are most desirable. Had the Teesdale studies only run for the usual research grant periods the conclusions on the behaviour of these species in the field would have been very different from those derived from the complete period, which was funded by several sponsors.

Clearly the roles of the conservationist and plant demographer need to coalesce, or at least a symbiosis should be established between these field and desk researchers. Field data should be collected in a form which facilitates the maximum utilization by the demographer, witness the use and re-use by Harper *et al.* of Tamm's excellent, meticulously collected and presented data (Tamm, 1948, 1956*a* and *b*, 1972*a* and *b*). Little can Professor Tamm have anticipated the value of his studies started in 1943. This is particularly important when the species is rare; site visits and disturbance should be kept to a minimum lest the second greatest threat to each rare plant should be an over-zealous plant demographer.

Acknowledgements

It is my pleasure to acknowledge the contributions of several Research Assistants, in particular J. P. Doody, R. B. Gibbons, P. R. Marren, J. Valentine, R. C. Fordham and J. Hilliam and students of the Department of Adult and Continuing Education and financial support from the Teesdale Trust (ICI), the Natural Environment Research Council and the Manpower Services Commission.

References

Bradshaw, M. E. and Doody, J. P. (1978*a*). 'Plant population studies and their relevance to nature conservation', *Biol. Conserv.*, **14**, 223–42.
Bradshaw, M. E. and Doody, J. P. (1978*b*) in *Upper Teesdale* (Ed. A. R. Clapham), pp. 48–63, Collins, London.
Bradshaw, M. E. and Jones, A. V. (1976). *Phytosociology in Upper Teesdale: Guide to the vegetation maps of Widdybank Fell.*
Clapham, A. R. (Ed.) (1978). *Upper Teesdale*, Collins, London.
Doody, J. P. (1975). *Studies in the Population Dynamics of Some Teesdale Plants.* Unpublished PhD thesis, University of Durham.
Fordham, R. C. (1979). *An analysis of the population dynamics of* Draba incana, Polygala amarella *and* Gentiana verna *in Upper Teesdale.* Unpublished MSc thesis, University of Durham.
Gibbons, R. B. (1978). *Further Studies in the Population Dynamics of some Teesdale Plants.* Unpublished PhD thesis, University of Durham.
Godwin, H. and Walters, S. M. (1967). 'The scientific importance of Upper Teesdale', *Proc. Bot. Soc. Brit. Is.*, **6**, 348–51.
Harper, J. L. (1977). *Population biology of plants*, Academic Press, London.
Harper, J. L. (1978). 'The demography of plants with clonal growth', in *Structure and functioning of plant populations* (Eds. A. H. J. Freysen and J. W. Waldendorp), pp. 27–48, North-Holland Pub. Co., Oxford.
Jones, A. V. (1973). *A Phytosociological Study of Widdybank Fell in Upper Teesdale.* Unpublished PhD thesis, University of Durham.
Pigott, C. D. (1956). 'The vegetation of Upper Teesdale in the north Pennines', *J. Ecol.*, **44**, 545–86.

Tamm, C. O. (1948). 'Observations on reproduction and survival of some perennial herbs', *Bot. Notiser*, 1948(3), 305–21.

Tamm, C. O. (1956a). 'Composition of vegetation in grazed and mown sections of a former hay-meadow', *Oikos*, **7**, 144–57.

Tamm, C. O. (1956b). 'Further observations on the survival and flowering of some perennial herbs, I', *Oikos*, **7**, 273–92.

Tamm, C. O. (1972a). 'Survival and flowering of some perennial herbs II. The behaviour of some orchids on permanent plots', *Oikos*, **23**, 23–8.

Tamm, C. O. (1972b). 'Survival and flowering of perennial herbs III. The behaviour of *Primula veris* on permanent plots', *Oikos*, **23**, 159–66.

Tutin, T. G. *et al.* (Eds.) (1964–80). *Flora Europaea*, 5 vols, Cambridge University Press.

White, J. (1979). 'The plant as a metapopulation', *Ann. Rev. Ecol. Syst.*, **10**, 109–45.

Note

Plant names in this chapter follow *Flora Europaea* (Tutin *et al.*, 1964–80).

Appendix: A technique for recording 'labelled' individuals

The position and size of each plot to be recorded was determined by the distribution and density of the particular species. The corners of the plots were marked with pegs sunk flush with the soil, thus providing no attraction to animals or humans. These were relocated from one or more easily found fixed objects by measuring a recorded distance along a compass bearing. Rock exposures and large heavy boulders are good reference points; small boulders, trees and bushes are not – each can move or disappear. If no natural object is available, a large marker can be buried flush with the ground, its top surface painted for easy recognition and its position identified by triangulation to more distant objects. Provided the distance from the reference point to the plot is less than 15 m and preferably under 10 m, one point has proved to be adequate, though a second would be insurance against accidental loss.

The positions of at least two corners of each plot should be recorded. The corner pegs are of nylon tube, about 1 cm diameter, stiffened with steel rods. Most are about 15 cm long, none are less than 10 cm; some had to be sunk into rock, bored with a star-drill and hammer. Surprisingly, 'temporary' pegs of bamboo cane about 1.5 cm diameter have survived for over 10 years. Often I place a small coloured stone over each peg for easy recognition.

The grid frame is 100 × 30 cm, a more practical width than a metre square (Figure 2.) If the central 25 cm only is worked, there is the dual advantage of avoiding the edge of the frame and having a sample area of 0.25 sq. m. The frame is of an aluminium alloy 1 × 0.25 inch, glued and rivetted at the corners and bored to take a coarse milled brass rod as a leg, with two milled nuts to use as levelling screws. When in position the legs fit into the tops of the pegs in the corners of the plots. The frame and legs need to be strong enough to prevent

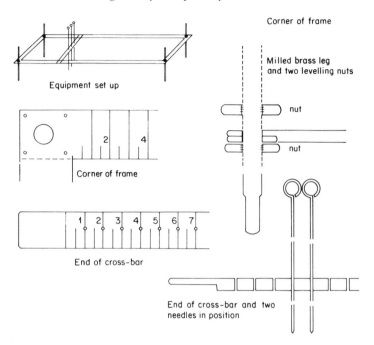

Figure 2   The grid frame for recording the 'labelled' plants

accidental bending. A loose cross-bar as long as the outer width of the frame, about 0.75 × 0.25 inches, has recessed ends so it will lie across the frame without slipping, though it can be additionally secured with a bull-dog clip. Both long and short sides of the frame and the cross-bar are inscribed and numbered at 1 cm intervals. On the cross-bar these are perforated to take needles made of 16 gauge stainless steel welding rods which have a blunt point at one end and a loop at the other. When several of these are positioned vertically through the cross-bar into the vegetation, a very accurate record of the position of each plant can be made. Obviously the length of the legs and the needles can be varied according to the height of the vegetation.

In Teesdale the plots varied in length from 50 cm to several metres. Where the plots are more than 2 m long it is helpful to stretch a string taut between each corner peg in order to keep the frame 'in line'. When a plot has been located and marked out with string, the first metre is thoroughly searched and the position of each plant is marked by lightly pushing a thin plastic 'cocktail stick' into the soil. This ensures that no plants are missed when making the written record. Next, with the frame accurately positioned over the corner pegs and using the cross-bar and needles, the co-ordinates of each plant, shoot and seedling can be determined and recorded.

A visual record of the position of each plant is made to scale on drafting film. Both the material and method are weatherproof. Working at a scale of 1 cm to 0.1 inch the details of 2 m can be recorded on a piece of hardboard about 35 × 25 cm; this is large enough to hold comfortably and not too large to be caught by the wind. A sheet of 1.0 and 0.1 inch scale graph paper was stuck on the board and covered with adhesive, transparent, waterproof film, and the corners strengthened with PVC insulating tape; both the PVC and the adhesive are waterproof. The drafting film is a polyester sheet, 0.002 mm thick with one matt and one smooth surface. Staedtler Mars Lumochrom leads can be sharpened to a fine point and are excellent on this film in wet and dry conditions. When wet the lead does not run but care must be taken not to smudge the surface of the film. Errors can be removed with some erasers. Leads of different colours can be used to make several records on one sheet. I use one sheet for each year and a different colour for each set of records, i.e. three to five. The first record of the next year is made on a new film laid over that of the previous year. For the accurate identification of each plant I find it helpful to have the previous record at hand as for a variety of causes plants do disappear.

The Biological Aspects of Rare Plant Conservation
Edited by Hugh Synge
© 1981 John Wiley & Sons Ltd.

21
The population ecology of winter annuals

A. R. WATKINSON *School of Biological Sciences, University of East Anglia, Norwich, England*

Summary

The factors governing the abundance of winter annuals in open but relatively predictable habitats are discussed with particular reference to mortality and reproduction. Survivorship curves for ten winter annuals are presented, illustrating how the pattern of mortality in annuals can vary from the extreme Deevey Type I to the extreme Deevey Type III. The shape of the survivorship curve for each species is related to the reproductive output of the plants and the habitats in which each species is found. Low fecundity and the presence of no or virtually no bank of dormant seed are features of all the species considered. The importance of understanding how density affects mortality and fecundity is stressed, and it is shown how the interaction between density-dependent and density-independent control of reproduction and survival can determine population size. The reasons for variations in population density, and the importance of predation and competition in determining community structure are also considered.

Introduction

In Great Britain some of the weeds of arable land are amongst the most severely threatened plants in the flora. Species of other man-made habitats such as roadsides and quarries are also under pressure, and in 1977 there were 35 species listed as Endangered or Vulnerable in lowland grassland and other natural open habitats (Perring and Farrell, 1977), many of them annuals.

Until recently almost all our knowledge of the population ecology of annual plants has come from species of agronomic interest with annual monocarpic or annual indeterminate life-cycles. This information has been well summarized by Harper (1977), Sagar and Mortimer (1976) and Snaydon (1980). Species that are rare or only locally abundant and that are restricted to non-agricultural ecosystems have received much less attention. There have recently been a number of intensive studies, however, on the monocarpic winter annuals of open but not uncertain habitats, both common and rare.

This chapter is concerned with a comparative analysis of the factors which are important in determining the abundance of some of these winter annuals. The approach is demographic and involves asking questions about the numbers of plants and seeds, and attempting to quantify the flux of numbers that occurs in natural populations. To this end it is essential not only to monitor the number of individuals in populations but also to establish the parameters of population behaviour such as birth rates and death rates, and so far as possible to discover the mechanisms that determine numbers and rates of change.

Patterns of mortality

Since the pioneering studies of Tamm (1956), Sagar (1959) and Sarukhán and Harper (1973) on perennial species, there have been a large number of studies in which the fate of individually marked plants and seeds has been followed in permanent quadrats. The patterns of mortality shown by such studies are best summarized in life tables (see Sharitz and McCormick, 1973; Leverich and Levin, 1979), but for comparative purposes the shape of the survivorship curve summarizes much of this information. General survivorship curves for populations of ten winter annuals from the time of seed maturation of flowering are presented in Figure 1. Some, however, are only approximate. Survivorship data for complete life-cycles have only been published for *Minuartia uniflora* (Walt.) Mattf. and *Sedum smallii* (Britt.) Ahles (Sharitz and McCormick, 1973), *Vulpia fasciculata* (Forskål) Samp. (Watkinson and Harper, 1978) and *Phlox drummondii* Hook. (Leverich and Levin, 1979). The approximate survivorship curves for the remaining species have been calculated from published data on counts of plants at different stages of the life-cycle and from data on seed production in the field.

The ten annuals show a great variety of survivorship curves ranging from the extreme Deevey Type I curve (Deevey, 1947) of *Vulpia fasciculata* to the Deevey Type III curve of *Spergula vernalis* Willd. It is clear from these curves that there is a general correlation between the number of seeds produced per plant and the shape of the survivorship curve.

Leverich and Levin (1979) have suggested that the survivorship curve for *Phlox drummondii* has two distinct phases which coincide with the major divisions of the plant's life-cycle; a linear Type II curve during the seed phase of the life-cycle and a Type I curve during the vegetative phase. Perhaps the same could be argued for the other annuals of semi-arid habitats on the rangelands of California (*Avena barbata* Brot., *A. fatua* L., *Bromus mollis* L., *B. rubens* L.) and the dunes of Great Britain (*Cerastium atrovirens* Bab., *Vulpia fasciculata*) and Poland (*Spergula vernalis*), although for some of the species the survivorship curve during the vegetative phase lies more between a Type I and a Type II. In contrast *Minuartia uniflora* and *Sedum smallii*, which are early successional species on granite outcrops (Sharitz and McCormick, 1973), show Type III survivorship curves during the vegetative phase of the life-cycle with heavy mortality during seedling establishment. The differences in survivorship during the vegetative phase of the life-cycle would thus appear to be related to the type of environment in which the plants are found.

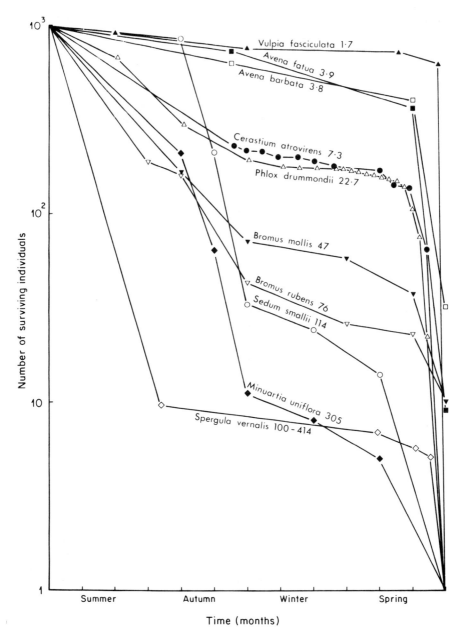

Figure 1   Survivorship curves for natural populations of ten winter annuals from seed production to maturity. Data on the average number of seeds produced per plant are also given. ▲ *Vulpia fasciculata* (from Watkinson and Harper, 1978); ■ *Avena fatua* and □ *A. barbata* (calculated from data of Marshall and Jain, 1967); ● *Cerastium atrovirens* (calculated from data of Mack, 1976); △ *Phlox drummondii* (from Leverich and Levin, 1979); ▼ *Bromus mollis* and ▽ *B. rubens* (calculated from data of Wu and Jain, 1979); ○ *Sedum smallii* and ◆ *Minuartia uniflora* (from Sharitz and McCormick, 1973); ◇ *Spergula vernalis* (calculated from data of Symonides, 1974a, b)

One characteristic of all the species in Figure 1, which is emphasized by the plotting of a survivorship curve, is that they have either no or virtually no bank of dormant seed in the soil. This contrasts markedly with the large seed banks generally associated with annual weeds (Harper, 1977) and is related to the fact that the species occupy habitats which are largely predictable (Watkinson, 1978). Populations of these annual plants are therefore unlikely to reappear at a later date if current populations are destroyed.

Reproduction

Salisbury (1942) gives the average seed output for a range of annual species from various habitats, and these values range from 39 to 176 000 seeds per plant. The seed outputs of five of the species reported here (Figure 1) fall below the lowest extremity of this range whilst the remaining five fall within the lowest part. Clearly the seed output of the species from predominantly open but not uncertain habitats is low in comparison with the more weedy species in which Salisbury was predominantly interested. Most of the species in Figure 1, however, are capable of attaining much higher fecundities when grown in cultivation. For example, *Vulpia fasciculata*, the plant with the lowest fecundity in the field, yields an average of 1208 seeds per plant when grown in an unheated glass-house with adequate water and nutrients.

The growth potential for a population of course depends not only on seed production but also on survivorship. On the fixed dunes at Aberffraw and Newborough Warren, each plant of *V. fasciculata* produced on average 1.7 seeds, 90 per cent of which germinated and 69 per cent of the seedlings survived to flowering (Watkinson and Harper, 1978). From these data it can be calculated that the ratio between the number of seeds produced in generation $t + 1$, N_{t+1}, and generation t, N_t, is 1.06, indicating that during the period of study the populations were just producing enough seeds to replace themselves. These figures were derived from populations at a variety of densities. At low population densities the average number of seeds produced per plant increased to a maximum of 3.2 and, assuming survivorship remained constant (see later), N_{t+1}/N_t increased to a maximum of 1.99. This value can be considered to be the net reproductive rate, R_0, for *V. fasciculata* on the fixed dunes before the population density starts affecting birth and death rates.

Knowing the multiplication rate per generation, R_0, it is also possible to calculate the maximum rate of population growth per individual, r, in the field as $r = (\ln R_0)/T$ (where T is the length of the generation time). *V. fasciculata* has a generation time of 365 days and consequently r has a value of 0.0015 per individual per day, a rate much lower than the maximal intrinsic rate of natural increase, r_{max}, measured under optimal environmental conditions. Leverich and Levin (1979) have suggested that the flowering performance by greenhouse plants may be used to obtain an estimate of r_{max} if survivorship is assumed to be unity. Using a value of 1208 seeds per plant for *V. fasciculata* gives a value of

r_{max} = 0.0194 which is higher than that for *Phlox drummondii* (r_{max} = 0.0102), which has a higher potential growth rate in the field (Leverich and Levin, 1979). The approximate values of r_{max} for *Bromus mollis* (0.021) and *B. rubens* (0.024) calculated from data in Wu and Jain (1979) are of the same order of magnitude as would be expected. Variations in fecundity alter r_{max} only slightly compared to changes in generation time. As might be expected the intrinsic rate of natural increase is generally not correlated with the rareness or commonness of species (Slobodkin, 1961).

The effect of plant to plant variation

Average fecundity and survivorship of individuals in a population are of course abstractions and obscure any plant to plant variation. The distribution of actual reproduction by individuals has been recorded for *Vulpia fasciculata* in the field (Figure 2) and for some of the other winter annuals (Jain, 1969; Leverich and Levin, 1979). These frequency distributions are typically skewed as in most plant populations (see discussion in Harper, 1977), the differences between individuals

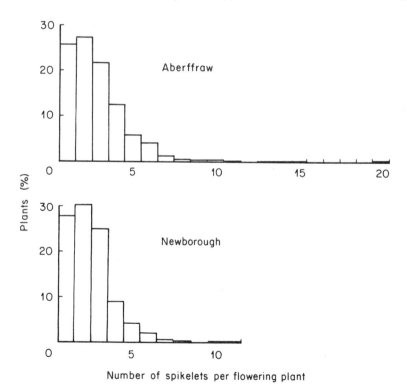

Figure 2 Frequency histograms of the number of spikelets per flowering plant in natural populations of *Vulpia fasciculata* at Aberffraw and Newborough Warren, North Wales (Watkinson, unpublished data)

resulting from variations in microhabitat, germination time, density, species associations and genetic variation.

In populations of *Phlox drummondii*, Leverich and Levin (1979) found that there was a strong correlation between early vigour and the realized fitness of individuals. Although early vigour had little effect on survivorship it had a very large effect on fecundity. Similarly, Newman (1964) working on the winter annual *Teesdalia nudicaulis* (L.) R. Br. on the East Anglian Breckland found that a delay in germination of 3 weeks caused a considerable decrease in the early vigour of individuals and a reduction in seed production by the order of 40 per cent.

Variations in demographic parameters in populations of *Vulpia fasciculata* are, however, more complex (Table 1) as there is selection both for and against early and late germinating plants, and when rabbit grazing occurs there is strong selection against tall individuals with a large number of spikelets. Early germination increases the number of spikelets produced per plant by increasing the length of

Table 1   Variations in demographic parameters in populations of *Vulpia fasciculata* at Aberffraw and Newborough Warren, North Wales

	Germination period							
	22 Aug. to 31 Aug.	1 Sept. to 6 Sept.	7 Sept. to 25 Sept.	26 Sept. to 11 Oct.	12 Oct. to 5 Nov.	6 Nov. to 8 Dec.	9 Dec. to 24 Jan.	25 Jan. to 27 Feb.

(a) The risk of death of seedlings germinating at different times in 1973/74 (Watkinson, unpublished data)

	22 Aug.–31 Aug.	1–6 Sept.	7–25 Sept.	26 Sept.–11 Oct.	12 Oct.–5 Nov.	6 Nov.–8 Dec.	9 Dec.–24 Jan.	25 Jan.–27 Feb.
Aberffraw	0.14	0.33	0.09	0.11	0.30	0.36	0.69	0.80
Newborough	0.09	0.29	0.12	0.10	0.23	0.35	0.45	—

	Germination period							
	22 Aug. to 31 Aug.	1 Sept. to 6 Sept.	7 Sept. to 25 Sept.	26 Sept. to 11 Oct.	12 Oct. to 5 Nov.	6 Nov. to 8 Dec.	9 Dec. to 24 Jan.	25 Jan. to 27 Feb.

(b) The number of spikelets produced by plants that germinated at different times in 1973/74 (Watkinson, unpublished data)

	22 Aug.–31 Aug.	1–6 Sept.	7–25 Sept.	26 Sept.–11 Oct.	12 Oct.–5 Nov.	6 Nov.–8 Dec.	9 Dec.–24 Jan.	25 Jan.–27 Feb.
Aberffraw	4.09	3.09	3.34	2.44	1.93	1.74	1.17	2.00
Newborough	3.47	2.51	3.14	2.64	1.88	1.50	1.48	—

	Number of spikelets per plant						
Plot	1	2	3	4	5	6	7

(c) The probability of a plant being eaten by a rabbit at flowering time in relation to the number of spikelets per plant (data from Newborough, from Watkinson, 1975)

	1	2	3	4	5	6	7
3	0.01	0.07	0.36	0.63	0.56	0.67	0.67
4	0.03	0.18	0.33	0.17	0.45	0.67	0.50
5	0	0.05	0.17	0.17	0.43	1.00	1.00
6	0.02	0.14	0.13	0.15	0.35	0.40	1.00

the autumn growing season, but this advantage is offset by the increased likelihood of mortality by desiccation due to fluctuations in the soil moisture level in late summer and the increased probability of the whole inflorescence of plants being grazed. Late germinating individuals produce few spikelets and often fail to establish as the primary root is slow in growing and fails to anchor the seedling against wind drag. Clearly data collected by genotype are needed before one can assess the impact of such selection on the genetic structure of subsequent generations. There certainly is genetic variation for both germination time and spikelet number in populations of *V. fasciculata* (Watkinson, 1975), but most differences in plant size and fecundity in the field probably reflect environmental factors (Gottlieb, 1977).

Not only is there variation between individuals in the number of seeds produced but also in the time of flowering; the period of flowering for most of the annuals studied was 6–8 weeks (Leverich and Levin, 1979; Newman, 1964; Pemadasa and Lovell, 1974*b*). The significance of age-specific fecundity schedules in natural populations is discussed in detail by Leverich and Levin for *Phlox drummondii*.

Population regulation

If one is to understand what determines the number of individuals in a population it is not sufficient just to record fecundity and survivorship. It is also necessary to find out how fecundity and survivorship vary with density, and to do this it is necessary to perturb natural populations to densities above and below the existing ones. Watkinson and Harper (1978) thinned existing field populations of *Vulpia fasciculata* at the seedling stage and added seed to other plots to provide an extremely wide range of densities. The results showed a marked negatively density-dependent relationship between reproductive output and density, but provided no evidence for density-dependent mortality. The mortality observed in the field is therefore density-independent. Density-dependent mortality due to self-thinning is most unlikely on the nutrient poor, fixed dunes as the plants are unable to attain the size or density at which self-thinning occurs (A. R. Watkinson, unpublished data).

Williamson (1972) has shown how an interaction between a density-independent death rate and a negatively density-dependent birth rate can regulate population density and how any changes in the birth or death rates, which are functions of the physical and biotic conditions, will produce corresponding changes in population size. Combining the field estimates of density-dependent control of reproduction with the measured density-independent mortality was sufficient to account for the observed range of densities of *V. fasciculata* on the fixed dunes at Aberffraw and Newborough Warren. Although this model of population regulation was developed over a relatively short period, it nevertheless provides a basis for understanding annual variations in population density as all the parameters of population growth will normally vary with the physical and biotic conditions in which the population finds itself each year. For example, variations in rabbit grazing, seed predation and spring drought may all effect survivorship, whilst late germination in dry autumns (see previous section) and spring drought may reduce fecundity (A. R. Watkinson, unpublished data).

Unfortunately the density response of none of the other winter annuals has been studied in the field. Marshall and Jain (1969) and Wu and Jain (1979), however, have explored the density response of *Avena* spp. and *Bromus* spp. in artificial populations under controlled environmental conditions. They have indicated the way in which population regulation in the field may occur through density-dependent control of fecundity and survivorship in *Bromus mollis* and *B. rubens*, whilst principally through density-dependent control of fecundity in *Avena barbata* and *A. fatua*.

Interactions between populations

So far the species have been considered as occurring in virtually an ecological vacuum. There has been no mention of interference between species and predation has only been mentioned in passing. In this section I should like briefly to consider what role competition and predation play in determining the abundance of winter annuals.

Predation

Significant seed predation occurs in the annual-type grasslands of California (Borchert and Jain, 1978; Marshall and Jain, 1970) and in populations of *Vulpia fasciculata* (Watkinson and Harper, 1978; Watkinson, 1978). In a study of four winter annuals Borchert and Jain found that plant numbers of *Avena fatua* and *Hordeum leporinum* Link were reduced by 62 and 30 per cent respectively as a result of selective seed predation by mice. *Hordeum leporinum, Lolium multiflorum* Lam. and *Bromus mollis* responded to the competitive release from *Avena fatua* by increases in plant size and reproductive output. Undoubtedly predation may vary from site to site (Gulmon, 1979; Marshall and Jain, 1970) and from year to year, but nevertheless it would appear likely that rodent seed predation might in many years play an important part in regulating populations of winter annuals either directly by influencing the plant numbers in relation to the carrying capacity or by changing the outcome of interspecific plant competition.

Similarly, selective grazing by rabbits and seed predation by invertebrates reduces population densities of *Vulpia fasciculata* (Watkinson and Harper, 1978). Indeed *V. fasciculata* was formerly quite rare and seems only to have reached its present relatively common state on some dune systems following the massive reduction in rabbit populations caused by myxomatosis. Mack and Harper (1977) have also suggested that grazing by rabbits might prevent *V. fasciculata* from filling its fundamental niche, thus leaving unoccupied niche space for other 'weaker' species (see later).

Competition

Two species competition experiments carried out under controlled environmental conditions in pots have demonstrated that populations of *Avena barbata* and *A. fatua* have the properties of self-regulating systems in which frequency dependent selection allows the stable cohabitation of the two species (Marshall and Jain,

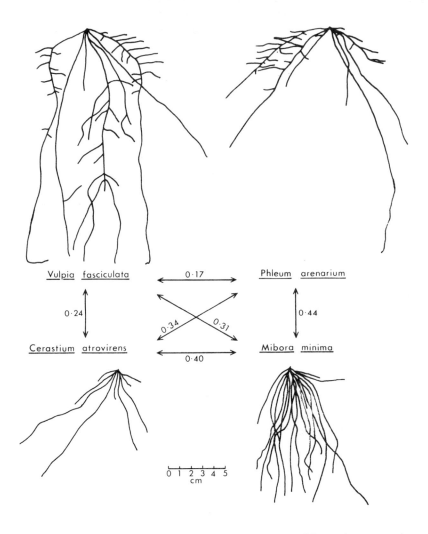

Figure 3   Representative diagrams of the root systems of four winter annuals grown in dune sand in glass-faced boxes in an unheated glasshouse. The figures refer to the proportional similarities (see Parrish and Bazzaz, 1976) of the four species in their use of underground space. (Jewell and Watkinson, unpublished data)

1969). Similarly mixtures of *Bromus mollis* and *B. rubens* are generally self-stabilizing, an initial high frequency of *B. mollis* giving *B. rubens* a selective advantage and vice versa (Wu and Jain, 1979). Gulmon (1979) on the other hand has suggested that persistence of *B. mollis* and *Lolium multiflorum* in mixtures with *Avena fatua* occurs because *A. fatua* is unable to reach sufficient densities at prevailing low levels of soil nitrogen to exclude the other two species. Field experimental evidence that competition may play a part in determining community structure in the grasslands of California comes from an experiment in which the contribution of *A. fatua* to community biomass was reduced by predation, while that of *Bromus mollis*, *Hordeum leporinum* and *Lolium multiflorum* increased as a result of competitive release (Borchert and Jain, 1978).

Greenhouse studies with plants grown in pots or shallow flats have also shown that although dune annuals are very small they interfere with each other's growth in a striking fashion (Mack and Harper, 1977; Pemadasa and Lovell, 1974*a*). These studies gave a precise ordering of the aggressiveness of species in the sequence *Vulpia fasciculata* > *Phleum arenarium* L. > *Mibora minima* (L.) Desv. $\geqslant$ *Cerastium atrovirens* Bab. > *Saxifraga tridactylites* L. Yet, *Vulpia fasciculata* does not dominate these communities to the exclusion of other species. Certainly grazing animals and seed predators may maintain diversity by determining the relative importance of different species (see earlier), but niche differentiation between the species will also promote diversity. The winter annuals differ in their optimal soil moisture requirements (Pemadasa, Greig-Smith and Lovell, 1974), flowering times and in their vertical exploitation of the soil system (Figure 3). Therefore experiments in which plants are grown under uniform conditions and in small pots will exaggerate the importance of competition in determining community structure. The direct method of removing neighbours from a plant and comparing its growth with a control remains by far the most satisfactory means of testing for interference in plant populations (Harper, 1977).

The importance of physical conditions in determining the outcome of competition is well illustrated by the study of Sharitz and McCormick (1973) on the pioneer species of granite outcrops. They found that the balance between *Minuartia uniflora* and *Sedum smallii* was a consequence of shifting competitive superiority as physical conditions, particularly soil moisture and depth, changed.

Concluding remarks

The abundance of a species depends upon the number and size of habitats which it can occupy and upon its population sizes within those areas. How many of the potential areas of habitat are occupied depends upon the dispersal strategy of the species in relation to the spatial and temporal heterogeneity of the environment, but the abundance of a species within an area of habitat depends upon the balance of births, deaths, immigrants and emigrants. Clearly the number of suitable habitats will have a major influence on whether the species is common or rare, and, therefore, the conservation of habitats is of prime importance in the conservation of species. However, as some species become threatened through habitat destruction, collecting and changes in arable farming it becomes increasingly important to understand how population size is determined in the remaining habitats. It is hoped that this comparative analysis of the population ecology of winter annuals has illustrated the type of demographic information which it is necessary to collect in order to understand how population size is determined in winter annuals of open but not uncertain habitats.

References

Borchert, M. I. and Jain, S. K. (1979). 'The effect of rodent seed predation on four species of California annual grasses', *Oecologia*, **33**, 101–13.

Deevey, E. S. (1947). 'Life tables for natural populations of animals', *Q. Rev. Biol.*, **22**, 283–314.

Gottlieb, L. D. (1977). 'Genotypic similarity of large and small individuals in a natural population of the annual plant *Stephanomeria exigua* ssp. *coronaria* (Compositae)', *J. Ecol.*, **65**, 127–34.

Gulmon, S. L. (1979) 'Competition and coexistence: Three annual grass species', *Am. Midl. Nat.*, **101**, 403–16.

Harper, J. L. (1977). *Population Biology of Plants*, Academic Press, London.

Jain, S. K. (1969). 'Comparative ecogenetics of two *Avena* species occurring in central California', *Evol. Biol.*, **3**, 73–118.

Leverich, W. L. and Levin, D. A. (1979). 'Age-specific survivorship and reproduction in *Phlox drummondii*', *Am. Nat.*, **113**, 881–903.

Mack, R. N. (1976). 'Survivorship of *Cerastium atrovirens* at Aberffraw, Anglesey', *J. Ecol.*, **64**, 309–12.

Mack, R. N. and Harper, J. L. (1977). 'Interference in dune annuals: spatial pattern and neighbourhood effects', *J. Ecol.*, **65**, 345–63.

Marshall, D. R. and Jain, S. K. (1967). 'Cohabitation and relative abundance of two species of wild oats', *Ecology*, **48**, 656–9.

Marshall, D. R. and Jain, S. K. (1969). 'Interference in pure and mixed populations of *Avena fatua* and *A. barbata*', *J. Ecol.*, **57**, 251–70.

Marshall, D. R. and Jain, S. K. (1970). 'Seed predation and dormancy in the population dynamics of *Avena fatua* and *A. barbata*', *Ecology*, **51**, 886–91.

Newman, E. I. (1964). 'Factors affecting the seed production of *Teesdalia nudicaulis*. I. Germination date', *J. Ecol.*, **52**, 391–404.

Parrish, J. A. D. and Bazzaz, F. A. (1967). 'Underground niche separation in successional plants', *Ecology*, **57**, 1281–8.

Pemadasa, M. A., Greig-Smith, P., and Lovell, P. H. (1974). 'A quantitative description of the distribution of annuals in the dune system at Aberffraw, Anglesey', *J. Ecol.*, **62**, 379–402.

Pemadasa, M. A. and Lovell, P. H. (1974*a*). 'Interference in populations of some dune annuals', *J. Ecol.*, **62**, 855–68.

Pemadasa, M. A. and Lovell, P. H. (1974*b*). 'Factors controlling the flowering time of some dune annuals', *J. Ecol.*, **62**, 869–80.

Perring, F. H. and Farrell, L. (1977). *British Red Data Books: 1. Vascular Plants*, Society for the Promotion of Nature Conservation, Lincoln.

Sagar, G. R. (1959). *The Biology of Some Sympatric Species of Grassland*. DPhil thesis, University of Oxford.

Sagar, G. R. and Mortimer, A. M. (1976). 'An approach to the study of the population dynamics of plants with special reference to weeds', *Ann. Appl. Biol.*, **1**, 1–47.

Salisbury, E. J. (1942). *The Reproductive Capacity of Plants*, Bell, London.

Sarukhán, J. and Harper, J. L. (1973). 'Studies on plant demography: *Ranunculus repens* L., *R. bulbosus* L. and *R. acris* L. I. Population flux and survivorship', *J. Ecol.*, **61**, 675–716.

Sharitz, R. R. and McCormick, J. F. (1973). 'Population dynamics of two competing annual plant species', *Ecology*, **54**, 723–40.

Slobodkin, L. B. (1961). *Growth and Regulation of Animal Populations*, Holt, Rinehart and Winston, New York.

Snaydon, R. W. (1980). 'Plant demography in agricultural systems', in *Demography and Evolution in Plant Populations* (Ed. O. T. Solbrig), pp. 131–60, Blackwell Scientific Publications, Oxford.

Symonides, E. (1974a). 'Populations of *Spergula vernalis* Willd. on dunes in the Torun Basin', *Ekol. pol.*, **22**, 379–416.

Symonides, E. (1974b). 'The phenology of *Spergula vernalis* Willd. in relation to microclimatic conditions', *Ekol. pol.*, **22**, 441–56.

Tamm, C. O. (1956). 'Further observations on the survival and flowering of some perennial herbs, I', *Oikos*, **7**, 273–92.

Watkinson, A. R. (1975). *The population biology of a dune annual*, Vulpia membranacea. PhD thesis, University of Wales.

Watkinson, A. R. (1978). 'The demography of a sand dune annual: *Vulpia fasciculata*. II. The dynamics of seed populations', *J. Ecol.*, **66**, 35–44.

Watkinson, A. R. and Harper, J. L. (1978). 'The demography of a sand dune annual: *Vulpia fasciculata*. I. The natural regulation of populations', *J. Ecol.*, **66**, 15–33.

Williamson, M. H. (1972). *The Analysis of Biological Populations*, Arnold, London.

Wu, K. K. and Jain, S. K. (1979). 'Population regulation in *Bromus rubens* and *B. mollis*: life cycle components and competition', *Oecologia*, **39**, 337–57.

The Biological Aspects of Rare Plant Conservation
Edited by Hugh Synge
Published 1981 by John Wiley & Sons Ltd.

22
Monitoring vegetation and rare plant populations in US national parks and preserves

PETER S. WHITE and SUSAN P. BRATTON *US National Park Service, Uplands Field Research Laboratory, Great Smoky Mountains National Park, Tennessee*

Summary

The lack of permanent reference points is perhaps the single most important hindrance to assessing change in species populations and natural systems. At Great Smoky Mountains National Park rare plant monitoring includes mapping of population locations, sampling of 0.1 hectare permanent plots, mapping of individuals from permanent reference points, and establishment of photo points. This monitoring is part of a continuing program to update baseline inventories, monitor changes and explore management alternatives.

Aspects of rare plant monitoring in the USA are discussed and a survey of monitoring in 33 US Biosphere Reserves is presented. Four levels of activity are outlined: (1) designation and listing of rare species and assessing priorities; (2) establishment of a record of locations from past data; (3) field verification of sites and exploration for new sites; and (4) establishment of a permanent record of populations, including permanent plot sampling and mapping of individuals. Much work is in progress and much remains to be done.

Introduction

Monitoring is essential to conservation goals: it allows detection and documentation of change. Thorough documentation of change is often necessary in legal action, in evaluating priorities for conservation resources, and for convincing natural area managers that a management change is needed. An important measure of the success of a nature preserve may be its ability to retain species and natural systems – this measure is furnished by baseline inventory and monitoring. The Unesco Biosphere Reserves program, implemented in the USA in 1974, includes directives for long-term data collection (US Department of State, 1979).

The opinions presented in this chapter are those of the authors and do not represent official US National Park Service policy.

Great Smoky Mountains National Park: A case history of preservation, change and monitoring

Great Smoky Mountains National Park, Tennessee and North Carolina, is the largest wilderness reserve in the Southern Appalachian Mountains. It extends over 209 000 hectares. It is administered by the US National Park Service and was one of the first Unesco Biosphere Reserves in the US. The diverse flora of 1600 vascular plants is associated with rugged topography over elevations from 225 to 2025 m, high annual precipitation which increases with elevation from 100 to 250 cm, and a continental warm temperate climate – 150–180 days per year are continuously above 0°C. Slopes are forested with a pattern of deciduous, broad-leaved and evergreen, coniferous vegetation (Whittaker, 1956). There is no climatic tree line, but treeless communities dominated by grasses and shrubs ('balds') occur. The region is rich in endemics and in northern plants at their southern range limit; about 10 per cent of the park's native vascular plants are on state or national rare species lists (Cooper *et al.*, 1977; Committee for Tennessee Rare Plants, 1978; Ayensu and DeFilipps, 1978; White, in press, *a*). The flora includes one strict endemic and four species nearly restricted to the park.

National park status was formalized in 1940. About 70 per cent of the land has been cleared, at one time or another, for logging or agriculture. Some uncut areas have histories of anthropogenic fire, livestock grazing, or selective cutting. The remaining land supports some of the most significant tracts of pristine forests in the eastern USA; trees reach 2 m dbh on mesic sites. Protecting remnant wilderness forest and rugged mountain scenery was foremost in the minds of conservationists advocating creation of the National Park; the biotic diversity was known, but protection of rare species was probably not a major consideration of those who fought for preservation. Indeed, national park status long antedates the current emphasis on endangered species.

The need for monitoring is well illustrated by the changes that have taken place during 40 years of protection at this park; these changes are described in Bratton and White (Chapter 39) and are caused both by people, such as visitor pressure and collecting of rarities, and by natural events such as windstorms. In essence ecological change occurs within preserves as well as outside their boundaries.

The evaluation of change is dependent upon the availability and quality of past data. The history of botanical research in the park can be divided into three periods: (1) an initial resource inventory directed by the Park Service, 1930–40; (2) a period when research was largely defined and conducted by academic institutions, though park naturalists recorded some information, 1940–70; and (3) the present period of research and monitoring, during which the Park Service is again taking a role in defining problems.

For rare species populations, the major data come from herbarium labels. During the 1930s, several thousand collections of vascular plants were made. The intensity of collecting varied within the park; the early work documented 75 per cent of the flora. Despite problems, the value of these collections is clear. Several species lists, unsubstantiated by voucher collections, survive from the 1930s; these cite species that are well out of range in the Great Smoky Mountains' flora but the reports cannot be evaluated.

As important as the collections are in documenting taxa, shortcomings are also evident; there is usually no information on population size, and location data is often vague. Most collections can only be mapped within 100 to 10 000 meters (White, in press, *b*), despite the fact that they are from a local herbarium devoted to floristics. Label data probably exhibit more precision than those at most herbaria, but problems with relocation contribute to uncertainty about species loss. *Linnaea borealis*, last seen in Tennessee in 1891, is known from 'Mountain woods, Servier County'; this describes an area of 40 000 hectares.

During the initial resource inventory in the 1930s, 1500 vegetation plots each of 0.08 hectare were established. These plots were not permanently marked, and data from individual plots were never analyzed, except as they contributed to a subjective forest typing and a vegetation map. A project has been recently initiated to analyze these data; they contain information on forest structure at the time of chestnut mortality.

During the phase of academic research, the first studies of grassy bald succession and chestnut replacement were conducted. Major research included R. H. Whittaker's studies of community pattern and production (Whittaker, 1956, 1966). Becking and Olson (1978) relocated some of Whittaker's plots and marked them for permanent reference.

Usefulness of the past data base is variable. The studies of grassy bald succession furnish our clearest example of the value of long-term, site-specific data. Maps from 1938 and 1944 of two grassy balds and photographs dating from the 1920s allowed Lindsay and Bratton (1980) to present an unambiguous view of succession in this habitat: Gregory Bald and Andrews Bald will be forested in the next 30 and 70 years, respectively, given present climatic conditions. The origin of the balds, however, continues to be unresolved due to lack of data from before 1920. The question of origin is relevant since the National Park Service is committed to management for pre-Columbian processes in wilderness areas.

In contrast to grassy bald succession, there is little information at site level on the loss of a major dominant, the chestnut, to give an indication of how it can be replaced. There are quantitative data from the 1930s vegetation survey and from a 1950s study (Woods and Shanks, 1959) but comparisons with present information lack detail on mechanisms of change and site variation in replacement. The 1930s survey did not contain adequate sampling of tree reproduction, and the 1950s study presented only summary tables.

No data from before 1970 exist on the impact of the European wild boar. Similarly, there are no past data on rare plant population decline in Cades Cove wetlands, though such decline has probably occurred because of extirpation of the beaver, 100 years of drainage manipulations, and use of floodplains for pasture and hay-making.

The changes evident in Great Smoky Mountains National Park and the lack of an unambiguous data base led to the present emphasis on monitoring and the establishment of the Uplands Field Research Laboratory. Monitoring has also been spurred on by the Unesco Biosphere Reserves Program (Herrmann and Bratton, 1977; Johnson and Bratton, 1978; Becking and Olson, 1978; US Department of State, 1979) and by endangered species legislation.

Some 300 permanent vegetation plots (50 × 20 m, 0.1 hectare) have been established within the last 3 years (Table 1); these will contribute (combined with aerial photography) to a new vegetation map for the park, but they have also been used to investigate problems of immediate concern to park managers (Bratton,

Table 1   An outline of monitoring at Great Smoky Mountains National Park

Vegetation monitoring – Permanently marked 0.1 hectare plots (50 × 20 m)
   Plot location: Mapped on USGS 7.5-min. quadrangles; field directions recorded from prominent landmarks with tape and compass.
   Permanent marking: Four steel rods, each a different color and bearing a different identifying tag; referenced to witness trees.
   Trees and saplings: All trees above 10 cm dbh mapped on plot; all woody stems 1–10 cm dbh recorded by 10 × 20 m subplots.
   Shrubs: Twenty-five individual 2 × 2 m quadrats sampled for cover and density (the latter in three diameter classes, 0–2, 2–6 and 6–10 mm at 5 cm above ground).
   Herbs: Twenty-five individual 1 × 1 m quadrats sampled for cover.
   Species list: A complete species tally is kept for each plot.
   Environment: Elevation, aspect, slope angle, measures of local topographic shape, slope position, kind of substrate.
   Disturbance: Indices of deer, wild boar, chestnut blight, flooding, windstorm, fire, logging, agricultural impacts.
   Miscellaneous: A convex mirror is used to superimpose 25 points on the canopy to measure canopy closure (in each 10 × 10 m plot).

Rare species monitoring
   Herbarium label data computerized.
   Field sightings (information also required on current herbarium labels): elevation, latitude, longitude, USGS map, watershed, location directions, habitat data, population size.
   Mapping of population locations.
   Assessing priorities among rare species based on listed status, geographic affinity, distribution of populations, number of populations, population size, population trends and threats.
   Permanent sampling: Mapping of individuals from reference points and in 0.1 hectare permanent plots.
   Photo points at mapped locations and in plots.

1981). Projects using the plots include investigation of wild boar impacts (for which exclosure plots have also been established), grassy bald succession, limestone vegetation patterns, impacts on historic zone management (Bratton *et al.*, in press), fire succession (Harmon, 1980), and gap phase regeneration. Recent studies of spruce fir forests (Becking and Olson, 1978; Hay *et al.*, 1978), heath balds (Becking and Olson, 1978), grassy balds (Lindsay and Bratton, 1980), and mesic hardwood forests (Becking and Olson, 1978), though based partially outside Uplands Laboratory, have all added permanently marked plots, as has the work of Golden and West (Darrel West, pers. comm.).

Herbarium labels and field sighting forms have been designed to maximize information recorded (White, in press, *a*). Photocopied sections of topographic maps, marked in the field, increase the precision of location data. UTM latitude and longitude can usually be recorded within a range of 10–100 m, and elevation within 10 m. Labels and sighting forms also require other information on location, habitat, vegetation and population size (Pyle *et al.*, 1979), information which is obvious in the field but soon lost if not recorded.

Rare plant monitoring, established within the last year, includes three levels of permanent records: (a) populations are mapped on topographic sheets and population size assessed; (b) permanent plots of 0.1 hectare are used for characterizing and monitoring habitats; and (c) individuals within populations are mapped from permanent reference points, and photo points are established. Except in the case of dramatic impacts, we envision resampling at 5–10 year intervals for rare populations and 10–20 year intervals for vegetation plots. Priorities in mapping of populations are established through a scale of seven weighted factors: 1 – listed status, 2 – geographic affinity, 3 – significance of park populations to distribution as a whole, 4 – number of locations, 5 – population size, 6 – population status, 7 – threats.

Monitoring schemes must be flexible. Species in the park vary widely in population size and distribution, in habitat, and in ecological strategy. No single series of categories predominate. Some species are known from many locations, but with very few individuals at each (e.g. the biennial *Adlumia fungosa*); others are abundant at a single location (e.g. *Prunus virginiana*). A few species are both rare and local (e.g. *Geum radiatum*). Some strict endemics are abundant in the park (e.g. *Cacalia rugelia*).

Some of the species are evidently weedy and prolific in reproduction and establishment (e.g. *Calamagrostis cainii*); other species are evidently conservative (e.g. *Geum radiatum*). The distribution of species relative to open habitats is notable: 32 per cent are characteristic of open habitats; 23 per cent are found in both open and forested communities; and 45 per cent are found in closed forest, though they may increase with small-scale canopy disturbance. Thus, just less than half of these species are found in virgin forests; monitoring must take into account both succession and mechanisms that maintain openness.

Aspects of rare plant monitoring in the USA

Much has been written on assessing which species of the US flora are in danger and monitoring rare plants (see in particular Ayensu, Chapter 2). Numerous projects are underway, involving a broad range of state and federal agencies, academic institutions, consulting firms and environmental groups. Much of the recent work is in progress or unpublished; some is in environmental impact statements and internal reports that are not widely circulated in the scientific community. At present there is little central focus. The National Heritage Program, a current proposal to be developed by the Heritage Conservation and Recreation Service (Department of the Interior), may eventually supply that focus (Merikangas, in press); if funded, that program will use the ecological inventory format developed by The Nature Conservancy for state Natural Heritage programs (S. Buttrick, pers. comm., see also Morse, Chapter 38). Guidelines for long-term ecological research in Biosphere Reserves have been developed (US Department of State, 1979) and may eventually serve as a national focus of biological monitoring efforts.

That work is in progress stems in part from the fact that federal legislation is so recent (1973). Moreover, plants are covered only secondarily by the Endangered Species Act and listing is still in progress as explained by Fay (Chapter 37); comparatively few plant species have been declared 'Endangered' or 'Threatened'. The Fish and Wildlife Service (Department of the Interior) was designated by the Endangered Species Act as the federal agency responsible for coordinating endangered species work. The *Endangered Species Technical Bulletin* of that agency is one of the few publications summarizing the status of lists, court cases, research and publications on endangered species. Nationally significant species are given the most attention, but local efforts have also been reported.

Programs to monitor rare plants in the US vary from informal (as when knowledgeable individuals keep watch on local populations) to formal (permanent plots and population mapping). Information recorded varies from presence/absence in a given locality to detailed demographic variables of growth, reproduction, and mortality. Four program levels can be described, progressing from less to more detail in monitoring: (1) assessment of which taxa are rare or threatened; (2) establishment of a permanent record of locations of rare taxa from herbarium surveys and published literature; (3) field verification of old sites and exploration to find new sites; and (4) creation of a permanent record of populations, including permanent plot establishment, mapping of individuals, establishment of photo points, and collection of demographic information. Some programs include aspects of all four kinds of work (e.g. that of the California Native Plant Society, in Powell, 1978); some have developed more or less along this sequence (e.g. our program at Great Smokies). The degree to which each level is expressed varies with constraints of time and money as well as the actual biological realities of rare species problems.

The Natural Heritage programs of The Nature Conservancy and state governments furnish the best example of establishment of a permanent record of baseline data on the distribution of rare taxa and are described by Morse (Chapter 38). These programs have been instituted in 20 states and in the 7 state areas of the Tennessee Valley Authority. Natural Heritage programs use a common format for ecological inventory and a system of mapping locations on standard topographic maps. This firmly establishes an easily accessed data base for environmental impact assessment and protection efforts. Heritage programs provide the best detailed information on the status of a species in a given state, and include species threatened at state level as well as at national level.

The next priority is to verify the sites on the ground through field work. This is being carried out by some Natural Heritage programs (e.g. see Lichvar and Stromberg, in press), but establishing ecological inventories of past data must come first and take precedence. Other examples of recent field projects include the work of Holland and Schramm (in press) in Death Valley, Thomas' study (in press) of population decline in *Sida hermaphrodita*, as well as numerous reports to Federal Agencies. Environmental groups like the California Native Plant Society (Powell, 1978) have developed extensive programs that span the four levels of work reviewed here. Conservationists in several other states have developed similar programs to assist the educational and research effort for rare plants.

Sampling plots and mapping populations are also under way in a few areas. Examples from Biosphere Reserves are cited in the next section; other examples include the work of S. L. Mehrhoff (pers. comm.) in which every known individual of the orchid *Isotria medeoloides* was mapped; Lowe (1977) on saguaro cactus; the permanent plot exclosures of Smith (1980); and the mapping of *Sequoiadendron giganteum* noted by Little (1975). Hastings and Turner (1965) showed clearly the value of photo points in assessing change in the Arizona desert. Easterly (1979) reported a resurvey of 154 rare taxa in oak openings in Ohio after 50 years of change. Ward (1977) reported a 20-year-decline in a population of *Gaultheria procumbens* in Indiana.

The Convention on International Trade in Endangered Species (CITES) of 1973 requires monitoring of export and import of listed species. This has inspired several monitoring programs, including one on *Panax quinquefolius* populations in North Carolina (R. Sutter, pers. comm.).

Monitoring in US preserves

To determine the amount and type of monitoring currently under way in US natural areas, the authors conducted a survey of the 33 US Biosphere Reserves (see descriptions in Risser and Cornelison, 1979). These preserves represent a wide variety of natural systems and are part of a worldwide network of natural areas designed, in part, to provide monitoring data (US Department of State, 1979).

The results of the survey are shown in Figure 1. Although 31 reserves have a checklist of vascular plants, 21 have an evaluation of whether nationally rare species are present, 18 have a list of state or locally rare species, and 4 have a published report on rare species. Thirteen reserves have some register of rare population locations, 11 have population estimates, 11 have an evaluation of threats, and 6 have population monitoring. By contrast, 25 reserves have permanent plot vegetation monitoring. Clearly, work is very much in progress; the Biosphere monitoring recommendations (US State Department, 1979) are still being implemented, and staff and funding problems for long-term data collection have not yet been fully resolved. Most US Biosphere Reserves are now progressing from inventory (level I of US State Department, 1979) and quantitative monitoring

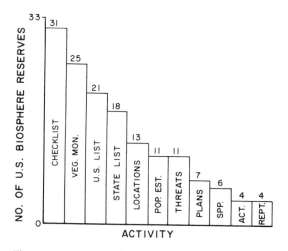

Figure 1   Results of a survey of monitoring activities in 33 US Biosphere Reserves. Work 'in progress' is tallied with completed work. Activity abbreviations are: checklist = vascular plant checklist; veg. mon. = vegetation monitoring program; US list = nationally rare species (an investigation reporting no known nationally rare species is counted as a 'list'); state list = list of state rare species; locations = mapped locations of rare species; pop. est. = estimate of population size for rare species; threats = assessments of threats to rare species; plans = management plans for rare species; spp. = monitoring of rare species populations; act. = active management for rare species; rept. = published report on rare species

(level II) to modeling and management (monitoring level III), a subject explored in Bratton and White (Chapter 39).

There is a difference in monitoring activity between reserves with a conservation mission and those with an experimental mission. All of the experimental reserves have permanent vegetation monitoring, but only half of these reserves have lists of nationally rare species. In contrast, only 66 per cent of conservation-oriented areas are engaged in vegetation monitoring, but 80 per cent have lists of nationally rare species. These differences may be due to differences in staff orientation, which is in part related to the economic objectives of some experimental areas (e.g. forest production research). Several experimental reserves had extensive schemes of permanent plots to gauge tree growth and recovery from disturbance; vegetation monitoring in conservation areas was frequently related to specific problems such as ungulate browse or visitor impacts.

Of the six reserves reporting some form of rare plant monitoring (four with a conservation mission, one with an experimental mission, and one with both kinds of mission), one was using non-quantitative annual observation (Virginia Coastal Reserve), four were using permanent plots and photo points (Everglades National Park, Channel Islands National Monument, H. J. Andrews Experimental Forest, and Great Smoky Mountains National Park), and one was using photo points exclusively (Olympic National Park). Loope (in press) reports work in the Everglades. Hawk *et al.* (1978) report on the detailed 1-hectare permanent plots used at H. J. Andrews Experimental Forest; in addition to population mapping and photo points, stream courses, boulders, and fallen logs are mapped.

A further study was undertaken of 43 national parks in the southeastern USA (see Bratton and White, Chapter 39). Most parks over 500 hectares in size, including historic areas, had had some work completed on a vascular plant collection or a checklist. Sixteen of twenty of these larger areas had a list of rare and endangered vascular plants completed or underway, based on the 1975 Smithsonian list or on state lists (see Ayensu, Chapter 2). Collections of non-vascular plants and records of endangered plant localities and population estimates are not available for most of these areas, though two of the largest parks, Great Smoky Mountains and Everglades, had published preliminary status reports on endangered plants. For areas less than 500 hectares, floristic information was scanty and few reported any rare species at all.

A discussion of monitoring issues

Biological monitoring, the periodic observation and quantitative analysis of the state of populations and natural systems, is essential (Jenkins and Bedford, 1973) – now is a time when both species and pristine habitats are being lost. Surviving natural areas are often marked by changes such as the loss of large predators, the invasion of exotic species, the spread of airborne pollutants, and direct visitor impacts. Most past data bases used to assess these changes, at least in our experience, allow only inference; measurements cannot be repeated. Assessments of change are needed for presentation to politicians, the general public and other scientists. Ironically, before these changes began there was no immediate need to establish baselines; now that species loss is occurring, we need that past data. Also ironic is the fact that much detail, if not actual plots, has been lost. There is now a need for certainty and site specificity.

Monitoring need not be passive; plots can be set up to test hypotheses (e.g. concerning climatic change, pollution effects, and exotic species invasions – Johnson and Bratton, 1978; Becking and Olson, 1978). Funding for science research in the USA has tended to be oriented around short-term questions involving 1–5 year periods of study. Our own monitoring was established only in conjunction with research on specific impacts and vegetation mapping. It is not clear whether monitoring could be funded where no acute problems have been recognized; it is also not clear if remeasurement of our plots will be considered part of resource management or of a science program. In the past National Science Foundation funding has also tended to work against long-term studies. The need for such studies, however, led to a trial program in the last year (Callahan, in press). This Long-Term Ecological Research (LTER) program will fund about five large-scale projects this year. The title (long-term *research*, not *monitoring*) underscores the role of hypothesis testing in organizing the studies. Monitoring data can also be used to build and validate models, useful in management programs (Johnson, in press); for rare plants, autecological information can be collected and used in management.

Permanent plot establishment is not the only sampling strategy. Large, independent, random samples can also document change. Several factors emphasize the need for establishing permanent reference points, however. Repeated measurement of the same plots can be used to compare change in different ecological situations. Because of the complicated nature of change in most forest stands, specific mechanisms of change can be explored on individual plots. Data unrecorded or unpublished by baseline studies can also be recovered.

For rare plant populations, large random samples would not suffice; we are often specifically interested in individual populations. For population changes, the only usual data base available is the information on herbarium labels, in the memories of collectors, or in the chance survival of photographs that can be used to assess change on specific sites.

The central issues in the establishment of a permanent plot data base are the assurance that plots can be relocated and that the measurements can be repeated. Challenges include the selection of data to be recorded (Becking and Olson, 1978; T.I.E., 1979; US Department of State, 1979), control of data quality, provision for archival storage of information (Herrmann and Bratton, 1977; Bratton, 1981) and planning for resampling. To a certain extent, data collected will depend on time and budget; data precision is usually an inverse function of cost. Archival systems must allow storage of raw data as well as summary publications. The system must allow periodic updating – this is the reason for putting on computer the checklist and herbarium data now under way in our program.

Monitoring is important both before and after legal protection of species and habitat. Before protection, monitoring supplies precision to the conservationist's predictions and allows critical situations to be identified. After legal protection, monitoring allows us to answer perhaps the most basic of all conservation questions: how effective are our national parks, wilderness areas, wildlife refuges and other conservation areas at preserving the ecosystems and species they contain? Nearly every preserve contains species rare enough to be vulnerable to loss (Hooper, 1971; Terborg, 1974). One of the most common and significant hindrances to answering this question, and in assessing current trends, is the lack of a data base or permanent reference point from which to judge change.

Acknowledgements

We would like to thank Mark E. Harmon, Jerry S. Olson, Jackie Merikangas, Larry Morse and Steven Buttrick for useful discussions of this subject. We would like to also acknowledge the support of Nicki Macfarland of Uplands Field Research Laboratory for help in preparing the manuscript. Finally, we thank Jay Blowers of the US Department of State for his encouragement to present this paper. Activities reported in this paper are part of the US Biosphere Reserves Program, jointly sponsored by the US Departments of State, Agriculture, and the Interior.

References

Ayensu, E. S. and DeFilipps, R. A. (1978). *Endangered and Threatened Plants of the United States*, Smithsonian Institution and World Wildlife Fund – US, Washington, DC.

Becking, R. W. and Olson, J. S. (1978). 'Remeasurement of permanent vegetation plots in the Great Smoky Mountains National Park, Tennessee, USA, and the implications of climatic change on vegetation', *Oak Ridge National Laboratories, Environ. Studies Div., Publ. No. 1111*, Oak Ridge, Tennessee, 94 pp.

Bratton, S. P. (1981). 'Information storage and population monitoring within Great Smoky Mountains National Park' in *Rare Plant Conservation: Geographical Data Organization* (Eds. L. E. Morse and M. S. Henifin), pp. 63–68, New York Botanical Garden.

Bratton, S. P., Mathews, R. C., Jr., and White, P. S. (in press). 'Agricultural area impacts within a natural area: Cades Cove, a case history', *Environ. Manage.*

Callahan, J. T. (in press). 'Initiating a program of long-term ecological research', in *Proceedings of the Second US–USSR Biosphere Reserve Symposium*, Everglades National Park, Homestead, Florida, March, 1980.

Committee for Tennessee Rare Plants (1978). 'Rare vascular plants of Tennessee', *J. Tenn. Acad. Sci.*, **53**, 128–33.

Cooper, J. E., Robinson, S. S., and Funderberg, J. B. (Eds.) (1977). *Endangered and Threatened Plants and Animals of North Carolina*, North Carolina State Museum of Natural History, Raleigh.

Easterly, N. W. (1979). 'Rare and infrequent plant species in the oak openings of north-western Ohio', *Ohio J. Sci.*, **79**, 51–58.

Fernald, M. L. (1950). *Gray's Manual of Botany*, 8th Ed., American Book Co., New York.

Franklin, J. F. (1977). 'The Biosphere Reserve Program in the United States', *Science*, **195**, 262–7.

Harmon, M. E. (1980). *The Influence of Fire and Site Factors on Vegetation Pattern and Process in the Western Great Smoky Mountains*, MSc thesis, University of Tennessee, Knoxville, 200 pp.

Hastings, J. R. and Turner, R. M. (1965). *The Changing Mile*, University of Arizona Press, Tucson, 317 pp.

Hawk, G. M., Franklin, J. F., McKee, W. A., and Brown, R. B. (1978). 'H. J. Andrews Experimental Forest reference stand system: establishment and use history. Coniferous Forest Biome', *US IBP Ecosystem Analysis Studies, Bull. No. 12*, 79 pp.

Hay, R. L., Eager, C. C., and Johnson, K. D. (1978). 'Fraser fir in the Great Smoky Mountains National Park: its demise by the balsam woolly aphid', *Rep. to the National Park Service, US Dep. of the Interior, Southeast Region, Atlanta, Georgia*, 125 pp.

Herrmann, R. and Bratton, S. P. (1977). 'Great Smoky Mountains National Park as a Biosphere Reserve: a research perspective', *US Dep. of the Interior, National Park Service, SE Regional Office, Research/Resources Manage. Rep. No. 23*, 38 pp.

Holland, J. S. and Schramm, D. R. (in press). 'Lake Mead and Death Valley rare plant studies', in *Proceedings of the 2nd Conference on Scientific Research in the National Parks*, November 1979.

Hooper, M. D. (1971). 'The size and surroundings of nature reserves', in *The Scientific Management of Animal and Plant Communities for Conservation* (Eds. E. Duffey and A. S. Watt), pp. 555–61, Blackwell Scientific Publications, Oxford.

Jenkins, R. E. and Bedford, W. B. (1973). 'The use of natural areas to establish environmental baselines', *Biol. Conserv.*, **5**, 168–74.

Johnson, W. C. (in press). 'Monitoring and modelling in tandem: a strategy to identify and predict successional change', in *Proceedings of the 2nd US–USSR Biosphere Reserves Symposium*, Everglades National Park, Homestead, Florida, March 1980.

Johnson, W. C. and Bratton, S. P. (1978). 'Biological monitoring in UNESCO Biosphere Reserves with special reference to the Great Smoky Mountains National Park', *Biol. Conserv.*, **13**, 105–15.

Johnson, W. C., Olson, J. S., and Reichle, D. E. (1979). 'Management of experimental reserves and their relation to conservation reserves: the reserve cluster', *Nat. Resour.*, **13**, 8–14.

Lawyer, J. I. (in press). 'Guide to U.S. State lists of rare and endangered plant taxa', *Mem. Torrey Bot. Club.*

Lichvar, R. and Stromberg, M. R. (in press). 'Wyoming Natural Heritage Program – inventory methodology for updating, defining, and mapping "rare" species', in *Proceedings of the 2nd Conference on Scientific Research in the National Parks*, San Francisco, California, 1971.

Lindsay, M. M. and Bratton, S. P. (1980). 'The rate of woody plant invasion on two grassy balds', *Castanea*, **45**, 75–87.

Little, E. L., Jr. (1975). 'Rare and local conifers in the United States', *US Dep. of Agriculture Forest Service, Conservation Res. Rep. 19*, 25 pp.

Loope, L. (in press). 'The flora of South Florida: how securely is it preserved in National Parks?', in *Proceedings of the 2nd Conference on Scientific Research in the National Parks*, San Francisco, California, November 1979.

MacBryde, B. (1979). 'Plant conservation in North America: developing structure', in *Systematic Botany, Plant Utilization and Biosphere Conservation* (Ed. I. Hedberg), pp. 105–9, Almqvist and Wiksell International, Stockholm.

McKitrick, J. A., Jordan, J. R., Jr., and Thurman, J. R. (n.d.). *TVA Regional Heritage Program: A Land-Use Planning Tool for Fish and Wildlife Resource Planners*, Tennessee Valley Authority, Division of Forestry, Fisheries, and Wildlife, Norris, Tennessee, 10 pp.

Merikangas, J. B. (in press). 'Endangered species and the National Heritage Program – HCRS', in *Proceedings of the 2nd Conference on Scientific Research in the National Parks*, San Francisco, California, November 1979.

Powell, W. R. (1978). 'The CNPS inventory – a progress report', *Fremontia*, 5, 28–9.

Pyle, C., White, P. S., and Bratton, S. P. (1979). 'Computerization of herbarium records at Great Smoky Mountains National Park', Rep. to the Great Smoky Mountains Natural History Association', *Int. Rep. Uplands Field Res. Laboratory*, Gatlinburg, Tennessee, 24 pp.

Risser, P. G. and Cornelison, K. D. (1979). 'Man and the Biosphere: US Information Synthesis Project, MAB-8, Biosphere Reserves', *Oklahoma Biol. Surv.*, Norman, Oklahoma, 109 pp.

Smith, C. W. (1980). 'Proposed native ecosystem restoration program for Halapé, Keuhou, and Apua Point, Hawaii Volcanoes National Park', *Cooperative National Park Studies Unit, Tech. Rep. 28, University of Hawaii*, Manoa, Honolulu, Hawaii, 35 pp.

Steenbergh, W. F. and Lowe, C. H. (1977). 'Ecology of the saguaro, II. Reproduction, germination, establishment, growth, and survival of the young plant', *US Dep. of the Interior, National Park Service Scientific Monogr. Series No. 8*, Government Printing Office, Washington, DC, 242 pp.

Terborg, J. (1974). 'Preservation of natural diversity. The problem of extinction prone species', *Biol. Sci.*, 24, 715–22.

Thomas, L. K., Jr. (in press). 'The decline and extinction of a rare plant species, Virginia Mallow (*Sida hemaphrodita* (L.) Rusby), on National Park Service areas', in *Proceedings of the 2nd Conference on Scientific Research in the National Parks*, San Francisco, California, November 1979.

T.I.E. (1979). *Long-term Ecological Research: Concept, Statement, and Measurement Needs*, National Science Foundation, Washington, DC, 27 pp.

US Department of State (1979). *Long-term Ecological Monitoring in Biosphere Reserves*, National Committee for Man and the Biosphere, Washington, DC, 31 pp.

Ward, D. B. (1977). '*Gaultheria procumbens* at Pine Hills, Indiana – Its measured decline, 1951–1971', *Proc. Indiana Acad. Sci.*, 86, 131–9.

White, P. S. (in press, *a*). 'Rare plant monitoring in Great Smoky Mountains National Park', in *Proceedings of the 2nd Conference on Scientific Research in the National Parks*, San Francisco, California, November 1979.

White, P. S. (in press, *b*). 'Herbarium computerization at Great Smoky Mountains National Park', *Proceedings of the 2nd Conference on Scientific Research in the National Parks*, San Francisco, California, November 1979.

Whittaker, R. H. (1956). 'Vegetation of the Great Smoky Mountains', *Ecol. Monogr.*, 26, 1–80.

Whittaker, R. H. (1966). 'Forest dimensions and production in the Great Smoky Mountains', *Ecology*, 47, 103–21.

Woods, F. W. and Shanks, R. E. (1959). 'Natural replacement of chestnut by other species in the Great Smoky Mountains National Park', *Ecology*, 40, 349–61.

Note

Plant names in this chapter follow Fernald (1950), except for *Geum radiatum* A. Gray, *Cacalia rugelia* (A. Gray) T. M. Barkley & Cronquist, *Calamagrostis cainii* Hitchc. and *Sequoiadendron giganteum* (Lindl.) Buchh.

Section 4
Ecological Studies of Rare Plants

The Biological Aspects of Rare Plant Conservation
Edited by Hugh Synge
© 1981 John Wiley & Sons Ltd.

23
Population ecology of terrestrial orchids

T. C. E. WELLS *Institute of Terrestrial Ecology, Monks Wood Experimental Station, Huntingdon, England*

Summary

Few population studies have been made on orchids, despite the fact that regular monitoring can be of great value in managing the habitats for the survival of individual species. The life cycle of a typical terrestrial orchid is described and the symbiotic relationship with the fungus explained. The annual cycle of growth is demonstrated for *Spiranthes spiralis* and *Aceras anthropophorum*. The results of monitoring populations of these species, together with *Herminium monorchis*, at two English sites are outlined and survivorship curves presented. This enables estimates to be made of the longevity of individual plants and an analysis to be undertaken of the age structure of the population. From these data various conclusions are drawn that are relevant to conservation management.

Introduction

Terrestrial orchids are among the most beautiful and biologically interesting of wild flowers native to the British Isles. Although numerically unimportant in terms of the total European flora – *Flora Europaea* (Tutin *et al.*, 1980) lists 115 species of orchid, of which about 50 are native to Britain – they nevertheless attract considerable attention from conservationists, especially when their habitats are threatened with destruction. They have a high emotional appeal, not only to the committed conservationist but also to the layman. It is not surprising, therefore, that the Orchidaceae has been a favourite family for collection and study and that there is a wealth of information on the distribution, morphology, variety of floral structures and pollination mechanisms of orchids in books and monographs such as Godfrey (1933), Summerhayes (1951), Camus and Camus (1921, 1929) and Vermeulen (1947). Studies on the population ecology and demography of orchids have been few, the most notable being the pioneer studies by Tamm (1948, 1972) on *Dactylorhiza sambucina, D. incarnata, Orchis mascula* and *Listera ovata* and the study by Wells (1967) of *Spiranthes spiralis*. Interest in fluctuations in orchid populations, and their general biology, has increased greatly over the past 10 years at various intensities of study, and the purpose of this chapter is to examine the information which can be gained from regular monitoring of orchid populations, using as examples data obtained from populations of *Spiranthes spiralis*,

Aceras anthropophorum and *Herminium monorchis* occurring in chalk grassland in Bedfordshire in the period 1966–80.

General biology

Like other higher plants, orchids begin life as a seed, but unlike most other higher plants, they require the presence of a fungus, usually a *Rhizoctonia*, before the seed will germinate. Although asymbiotic germination can be achieved in the laboratory with many species of terrestrial orchid (Stoutamire, 1974) it is generally agreed that in the field germination only occurs after the seed has been penetrated by fungal hyphae. Following germination, the juvenile orchid plant remains underground as a colourless mycorhizome, devoid of chlorophyll and totally dependent on the fungus for its nutrition. The time spent underground varies greatly from species to species (Table 1) but is always greater than 1 year and may be as long as 15 years. During this period, which is equivalent to the juvenile and young mature plant stage of many other herbaceous perennials, the mycorhizome is subject to the vicissitudes of the environment such as drought, water-logging, mechanical damage and predation. Very little is known about this important stage in the life-cycle of terrestrial orchids and this seems likely to remain an area of ignorance for a long time, because of the small size of the mycorhizomes and the difficulties in finding them in the soil.

In all orchids, the mycorhizome is replaced eventually by a root tuber or similar perennating organ, which is usually infected by the fungus, and after a period of time, which varies depending on the species, the first green leaf is produced and

Table 1 Time in years that elapses between germination and emergence of first green leaf and interval to inflorescence production for 11 selected terrestrial orchids (data from Summerhayes, 1951; Ziegenspeck, 1936)

	Year in which first leaf is usually produced	Period (years) in which first inflorescence is usually produced
Ophrys apifera	2	3–8
Dactylorhiza fuchsii	2	4–5
Orchis morio	2	4–5
Dactylorhiza incarnata	2	4–5
Orchis militaris	4	6–9
Orchis mascula	4	6–8
Anacamptis pyramidalis	4	7–8
Listera ovata	4	13–15
Cypripedium calceolus	4	c. 16
Spiranthes spiralis	11	13–15
Orchis ustulata	10–15	13–16

the plant becomes autotrophic. In *Spiranthes*, the mycorhizome apparently exists for 8 years before it is replaced by a root tuber (Summerhayes, 1951) and it is another 3 years before the first green leaf is found. These data should be treated with caution, however, as I have produced plants of *S. spiralis* with four green leaves and a tuber 5 mm long in asymbiotic culture within 18 months after sowing the seed. *Aceras* produces its first green leaf about 5 years after germination, but details of the growth of the mycorhizome are scanty.

Phenology

A generalized account of the annual cycle of events in *Spiranthes* and *Aceras*, based on monthly excavations of five plants over a 2-year period, is shown in Figures 1 and 2. Below ground, the mature *Spiranthes* plant in January consists of two mature tubers (occasionally only one) formed the previous year, the shrivelled remains of the tuber which produced last year's inflorescence, and small oval to pear-shaped protuberance(s) which will form the tuber which produces the inflorescence the following year. Above ground, the plant consists of 4–6(–8) small, oval-shaped leaves in a rosette, which remain green until about mid-June. The leaves then die and a new rosette is produced in September, at the same time as the inflorescence is produced. The plant has no roots, but the tubers are covered with a fungal mycelium which presumably serves to transfer nutrients and water from the soil to the plant. The tubers, but not the stems, are heavily infected with a *Rhizoctonia*.

Like most other members of the *Orchis* group, *Aceras* produces one new oval-shaped tuber each year (Figure 2). The new tuber appears in January as a small protuberance beneath the leaf sheaths, through which it bursts the next month, the yellow, meristematic tip contrasting with the whiteness of the tuber. Growth of the new tuber is rapid, and by June, when *Aceras* flowers, the new tuber is as large as the tuber which has produced the inflorescence. The old tuber dies quickly, as do the leaves which become yellowish by mid-May, and from early July to late September, the plant is totally below ground. Unlike *Spiranthes*, *Aceras* develops a number of large, white roots from the main stem axis above the tuber, and these are infected with the fungus. Like the tubers, these roots are replaced annually.

Both *Aceras* and *Spiranthes* are winter-green and have leaves throughout the winter, similar to many other temperate orchids, e.g. *Ophrys apifera*, *Himantoglossum hircinum*, *Orchis morio* and *O. militaris*, but whether they are able to photosynthesize effectively at low temperatures is not known – clearly the relative importance of the fungus within the plant during this period is also of importance and needs investigation. Not all temperate orchids have similar phenologies: *Herminium monorchis*, for example, produces its leaves in late May and these have generally withered by mid-October, the remainder of the year being spent underground. The importance of a knowledge of the phenology of

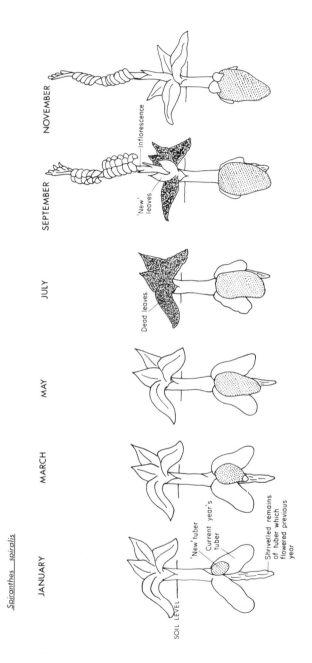

Figure 1   Generalized phenology of *Spiranthes spiralis*, showing formation of tubers and production of leaves and inflorescence

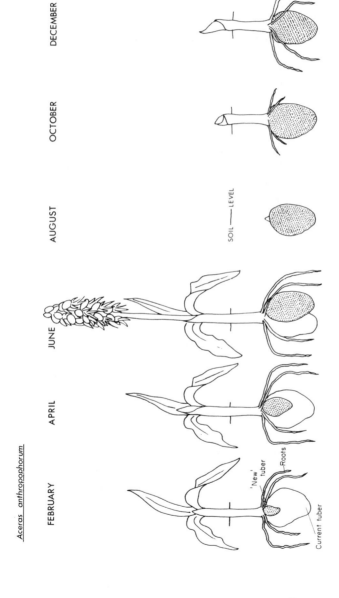

Figure 2   Generalized phenology of *Aceras anthropophorum*, illustrating tuber formation and annual production of leaves and inflorescence

terrestrial orchids before the grassland in which they grow can be effectively managed is obvious, but surprisingly, such basic information is often missing or inadequate.

Population dynamics

Populations of *Spiranthes spiralis* at Knocking Hoe National Nature Reserve and of *Aceras anthropophorum* and *Herminium monorchis* at Totternhoe Knolls Local Nature Reserve in Bedfordshire, England, have been studied since 1963 and 1966 respectively, using a method of recording which enables the position of individual plants in relation to permanent marker pegs to be plotted. The method is described in detail in Wells (1967). For each plant the following data were recorded: (a) state of plant – flowering or vegetative; (b) height of inflorescence above ground level; and (c) the number of flowers (except for *Herminium*). Using this method it is possible to return to the same plant in successive years (or at more frequent intervals if desired), thereby enabling the fate of individuals to be followed, which is essential if a full life-table analysis is made as an aid to understanding what is happening to a particular population.

Spiranthes spiralis (Figure 3)

The total population grew from 420 plants in 1963 to a maximum of 1050 in 1969, staying at between 870 and 950 plants until 1976 and falling to around 800 plants in 1979. Recruitment to the population has been uneven, with 383 new plants in 1966, but only three in 1978. Overall, there is a tendency for fewer new plants to be recruited since 1974.

Is it possible to relate differences in recruitment (and hence germination and establishment) to the management of the site? Accepting for the moment that the young *Spiranthes* plants take 11 years before the first leaf or first leaf and inflorescence is produced, then the large number of new plants recorded in 1966, 1967 and 1968 were probably produced from seed shed in 1955–7. At this time, the turf was short and heavily grazed by rabbits, and it can be speculated that the 'open' turf and lack of competition from coarse grasses (which increased post-1955 after myxomatosis) produced conditions suitable for seedling establishment. Since 1966, Knocking Hoe has been grazed lightly by cattle with intermittent rabbit grazing, but in general *Bromus erectus* increased until 1970, when a cutting regime was introduced. Interestingly, the period 1966–70 is similar to the years 1977–81, the first three of which have been poor years for new recruits to the population.

Mortalities, calculated as a percentage of the total population, remained fairly constant, varying from 15.3 per cent in 1969 to 3.9 per cent in 1973. The causes of death are many, but are difficult to quantify – physical destruction of the shallowly placed tuber by cattle hooves on steep slopes, destruction by beetle larvae which are specific to orchid tubers, and the competition of dense *Bromus* tussocks are probably of most importance.

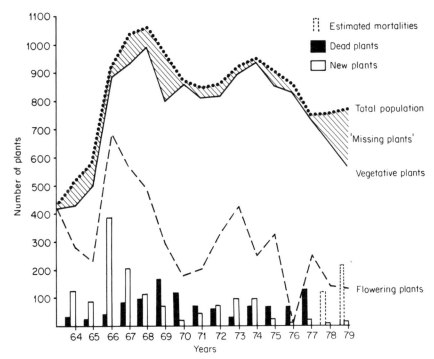

Figure 3   Population dynamics of *Spiranthes spiralis* at Knocking Hoe, Beds., 1963–79. 'Missing' plants are those with no above-ground organs, but are present as tubers and which reappear above ground in succeeding years

Aceras anthropophorum (Figure 4)

The total population remained relatively steady for the first 6 years (1966–71) at around 100–120 plants, but this was followed by a period of sustained growth which appears to be continuing, the population in 1980 exceeding 400 plants. New plants were recruited in all years, but numbers fluctuated widely from 116 in 1974 to less than 10 in 1969 and 1971. If one accepts that a plant takes about 5 years from germination to producing its first leaf or inflorescence, then the years of high recruitment (1972–4) may be correlated with some happening 5 years previously (1967–9). Extensive clearance of scrub, by the Bedfordshire and Huntingdonshire Naturalists' Trust, who manage the site, began in 1966 and has continued subsequently; it may be that habitat conditions were improved or created which favoured the germination and establishment of seedlings.

Mortalities, expressed as a proportion of the total population, varied from 3.6 per cent to 18.0 per cent but causes of death were not ascertained.

Herminium monorchis (Figure 5)

Unlike *Aceras* and *Spiranthes*, the Musk Orchid showed large fluctuations in the total population caused by high periodic inputs of 'new' plants, for example in

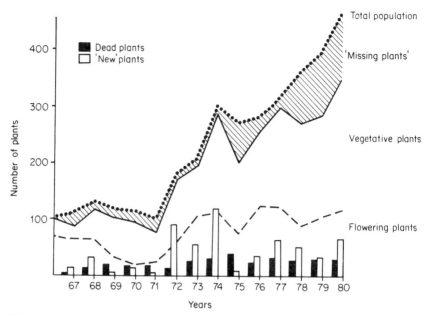

Figure 4   Population dynamics of *Aceras anthropophorum* at Totternhoe Knolls, Beds., 1966–80

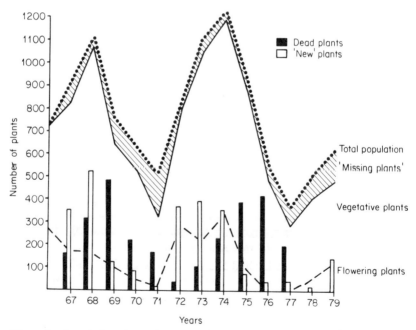

Figure 5   Population dynamics of *Herminium monorchis* at Totternhoe Knolls, Beds., 1966–79

1967, 1968, 1972, 1973 and 1974 followed by periods when mortalities were high, for example in 1969, 1975 and 1976. Because *Herminium* has an effective means of producing ramets at the end of stolons, which can extend for as much as 10–20 cm from the mother plant, it seems likely that many of the 'new' plants were produced in this way, but only extensive excavation (which would have been totally destructive) could prove this, and we have no way of telling whether the new plants were ramets or genets. It seems likely, however, that newly formed ramets would be unable to. obtain food from the larger 'mother plant' in an unfavourable year, and would die, thus contributing to a much larger turnover in the population than was observed in the other two species. (A ramet is the individual shoot or rooted plant of a clone and a genet an individual derived from a seed.)

Survivorship curves and longevity

Spiranthes spiralis (Figure 6)

Survivorship curves for nine cohorts (groups of plants in the same age-class) are shown in Figure 6. Although the slope of the lines differs for individual cohorts, suggesting that the chance of survival and hence longevity may vary depending on the year in which the cohort is formed, the outstanding feature of all of the survivorship curves is their linearity. The impression gained from these curves is that the death risk is constant in the population, which has experienced the vagaries of climate over a 16-year period (for the 1963 cohort), including the exceptional drought of 1976. There is no sign of good and bad years for survival. The calculated half-life for the nine cohorts varied from 4.6 to 9.2 years, but, perhaps of more significance, the calculated time for each cohort to decline to a single plant varied from 23 years for the small 1970 cohort of 18 plants to 67 years for the 1969 population of 75 plants. The mean expected life of all cohorts (i.e. longevity) which arose between 1963 and 1972 was 53 years.

Aceras anthropophorum (Figure 7)

Survivorship curves for six cohorts, for 1966, 1968, 1972, 1973 and 1974, are shown in Figure 7. Recruitment in other years was too small to allow meaningful survivorship curves to be drawn. Half-lives varied from 4.0 to 7.8 years. The survivorship curve for the 106 plants present in 1966 is remarkably linear, suggesting that the risk of death is constant throughout the life of the population. If the present trend continues, the 1966 population will be reduced to one plant by the year 2014. Although there appears to be a general linear decrease in plants with time in other cohorts, there are considerable variations in mortality, the 1968 cohort, for example, remaining constant from 1974 to 1976. There are similar episodes in the life of other cohorts when mortalities were either higher than or

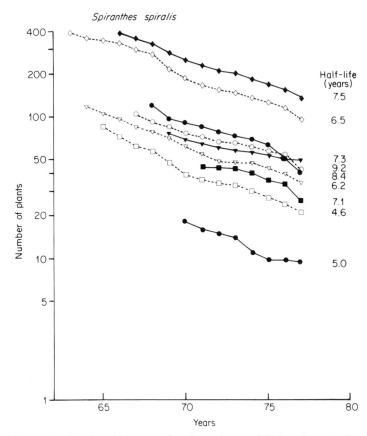

Figure 6   Survivorship curves for nine cohorts of *Spiranthes spiralis* which arose between 1963 and 1971

less than expected. Nevertheless, the general pattern is one which suggests a more or less constant risk of death and enables meaningful predictions to be made about the expected life-span of individual cohorts.

Age structure of population

A knowledge of the age structure of a population and the presentation of this information as a histogram is a useful way of summarizing the present state of a population. As an example, data from 377 *Aceras* plants, present in the 1979 population, are shown in Figure 8. It is immediately obvious that the population is not even-aged. About 40 per cent of the plants are in the 1–4 year age class, indicating that the population is recruiting sufficient new members to maintain the population. (This class is age above-ground and ignores the unknown time spent as a

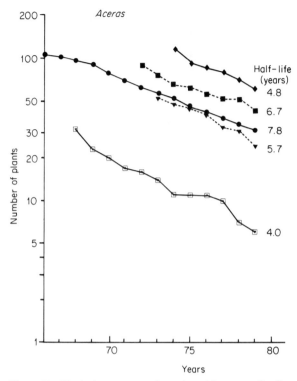

Figure 7   Depletion curve and survivorship curves for five
cohorts of *Aceras*, formed in 1966, 1968, 1972, 1973, and
1974

mycorhizome underground.) Furthermore, these data suggest that the current and recent management of the site has been beneficial for *Aceras* – if young plants had been absent it might have caused some concern to the managers and resulted in a change of management. The high recruitment to the population which occurred in 1974 is reflected in the 21 per cent of 6-year old plants present in the 1979 population. Similarly, the small numbers of plants in the 9–12 age classes is a result of low recruitment to these cohorts in the 1966–71 period, coupled with the effect of mortalities over a decade or more. Ten per cent of the population is more than 14 years old, confirming the predictions made from the survivorship curves concerning the longevity of *Aceras*.

Many orchids renew the vegetative body every year by producing new tubers, and as Harper (1977) so aptly states, 'spend their perennial life in a state of perpetual somatic youth'. This particular mode of life may therefore limit the value of a knowledge of the age structure of the population, for unlike animals, where age-specific fecundity schedules are used extensively for predicting the population dynamics of a species, in plants fecundity may only be loosely related to

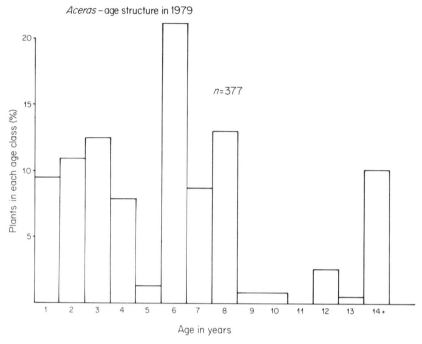

Figure 8   The age-structure of a population of 377 *Aceras* plants in 1979

age. This point may be illustrated by reference to *Aceras* (Figure 9), where those proportions of plants which flowered in two cohorts shows no obvious relationship with age, flowering being irregular and apparently unpredictable.

Flowering

The factors which control flowering in herbaceous perennials are highly complex and little understood, and orchids are no exception. The proportion of plants of *Aceras, Spiranthes* and *Herminium* which flowered in any year varied considerably (Figures 3–5) not only between years, but also between species (Table 2). Considering the whole population, *Aceras* is the most consistent species to flower, with a mean flowering of 41.1 per cent over a 14-year period, compared with 16.9 per cent for *Herminium* and 32.8 per cent for *Spiranthes* over the same period. A closer look at the behaviour of 38 plants of *Aceras* (Figure 10) present in the population for 14 years reveals a skewed frequency distribution with 25 plants (65 per cent) flowering for 5 years or less out of 14 years and only one plant flowering for 13 years out of a possible 14 years. A comparison of the habitats and micro-environment of these 38 plants in the field does not reveal any obvious site advantage and it seems likely from this preliminary examination that the propensity to flower may be governed by other factors, such as the activity of

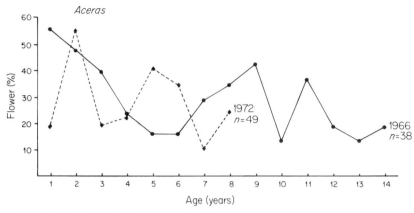

Figure 9   The relationship between flowering and age of plant in two cohorts of
Aceras, over a 14-year (1966 cohort) and 8-year (1972 cohort) period respectively

the fungal symbiont. It is clear from Figure 9 that the age of the plant has little
influence on whether the individuals flower or not, a result which agrees broadly
with the results obtained by Russian demographers, such as Uranov and Rabotnov, quoted in Harper (1977).

The relationship between flowering behaviour and meteorological data has been
examined using multiple regression and the detailed results will be published
elsewhere. In brief, a significant relationship was found between total rainfall in

Table 2   Annual percentage flowering, 1966–79, of populations of
Aceras and *Herminium* at Totternhoe, and of *Spiranthes* at Knocking
Hoe, Bedfordshire

Year	*Aceras*	*Herminium*	*Spiranthes*
1966	67.0	38.0	73.6
1967	72.7	12.8	57.0
1968	51.2	15.7	44.7
1969	31.2	16.2	33.0
1970	17.5	8.2	19.2
1971	30.9	7.1	22.9
1972	31.1	36.6	37.3
1973	52.9	19.4	42.3
1974	36.6	27.9	23.4
1975	33.0	10.6	34.8
1976	44.9	0.4	1.3
1977	38.1	0	30.8
1978	32.3	11.2	19.8
1979	35.6	32.1	20.7
Mean	41.1	16.9	32.8

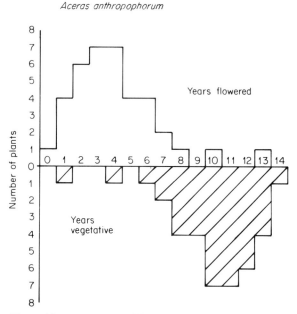

Aceras anthropophorum

Figure 10   Frequency of flowering in a population of 38
Aceras plants, recorded over a 14-year period

the period 1 April to 30 June and the percentage of plants which flowered
($r = +0.78$, $p = 0.05$) for *Spiranthes*, with earth temperature at 30 cm in the
period 1 January to 7 April also being positively correlated with flowering success
($r = 0.47$). In other words, a mild winter and a wet spring and early summer seem
to favour flowering. It is noteworthy that following the 1976 drought, only 1.3 per
cent of the *Spiranthes* population flowered (Table 2).

Summer rainfall also is of importance for *Herminium*. A significant relationship
($r = 0.87$, $p = 0.05$) was found between the percentage of plants which flowered
and the total rainfall in 1 June to 15 August period of the current year and also
with the rainfall from 16 August to 15 September of the previous year. It would
seem that stress conditions during the period of active growth (June–October)
adversely affect flowering performance, with a carry-over effect of the following
year, if conditions reoccur late in the year. It is noticeable that while only 0.4 per
cent of the population flowered in 1976, no plants flowered in 1977, although
vegetative plants were present and the population survived the 1976 drought.

Conclusions

1. The conservation of orchid populations requires an understanding of the
   dynamic aspects of the population; the most important aspects are recruitment
   (births), mortalities (deaths), survivorship, longevity and turn-over.

2. Careful monitoring of orchid populations on an annual basis, using a technique which enables the same individuals to be recorded and examined each year, will provide the basic facts about the population from which predictions can be made about its future structure.
3. Much more attention needs to be given to the phenological aspects of both the above and below ground parts of terrestrial orchids if we are to interpret their behaviour with respect to environmental factors, particularly different management regimes.
4. The role and importance of the mycorhizal associate of the orchid, particularly in the early stages, is still imperfectly understood, and special techniques will have to be developed before any progress can be made in this field.

Acknowledgements

I am indebted to the Nature Conservancy Council for permission to work at Knocking Hoe National Nature Reserve and to the Bedfordshire and Huntingdonshire Naturalists' Trust for permission at Totternhoe Knolls Local Nature Reserve; to Mrs Shirley Bell and various students who helped with field work on various occasions and to Miss Ruth Cox for data processing and analysis.

References

Camus, E. G. and Camus, A. (1921, 1929). *Iconographie des Orchidees d'Europe et du Bassin Mediterraneen*, Paris.
Godfrey, M. J. (1933). *Monograph and Iconograph of Native British Orchidaceae*, Cambridge University Press.
Harper, J. L. (1977). *Population Biology of Plants*, Academic Press, London.
Stoutamire, W. (1974). 'Terrestrial Orchid Seedlings', in *The Orchids* (Ed. C. L. Withner), pp. 101–28, Wiley, New York.
Summerhayes, V. S. (1951). *Wild Orchids of Britain*, Collins New Naturalist Series 19, London.
Tamm, C. O. (1948). 'Observations on reproduction and survival of some perennial herbs', *Bot. Notiser*, 1948(3), 305–21.
Tamm, C. O. (1972). 'Survival and flowering of some perennial herbs II. The behaviour of some orchids on permanent plots', *Oikos*, **23**, 23–38.
Tutin, T. G. *et al.* (Eds.) (1980). *Flora Europaea*, Vol. 5. Cambridge University Press.
Vermeulen, P. (1974). *Studies on Dactylorchids*, Schotanus and Jens, Utrecht.
Wells, T. C. E. (1967). 'Changes in a population of *Spiranthes spiralis* (L.) Chevall. at Knocking Hoe National Nature Reserve, Bedfordshire, 1962–65', *J. Ecol.*, **55**, 83–99.
Ziegenspeck, H. (1936). 'Orchideceae', in *Lebengeschichte des Blütenpflanzen Mitteleuropas* (O. Kirchner, E. Loew and C. Schroeter), Vol. 1, no. 4, Stuttgart.

Note

Plant names in this chapter follow *Flora Europaea* (Tutin *et al.*, 1980).

The Biological Aspects of Rare Plant Conservation
Edited by Hugh Synge
© 1981 John Wiley & Sons Ltd.

24
Ecology, distribution and taxonomy in Mesembryanthemaceae as a basis for conservation decisions

H. E. K. HARTMANN *Institut für Allgemeine Botanik, University of Hamburg, FRG.*

Summary

Two sympatric genera in Mesembryanthemaceae, *Argyroderma* and *Oophytum*, are selected to show different adaptations to the identical arid environmental conditions in south-western Africa. The leaf anatomy of both is described; in *Argyroderma* the leaves contain typically xeromorphic features but in *Oophytum* the leaf epidermis is thin. The significance of these differences is discussed in terms of the ecology and life cycle of the plants. It demonstrates the variety of life cycles in one locality and indicates future criteria for formulating how members of the Mesembryanthemaceae can best be conserved in their native habitats.

The conservation status of the Mesembryanthemaceae

Most members of the succulent family Mesembryanthemaceae are found in the drier parts of south-western Africa, in an area defined by Werger (1978) as the Namib and the Western Cape Domains. Here Mesembryanthemaceae dominate most associations, a status considered secondary in succession by Acocks (1953, 2nd Ed. 1975) and others, who suggest a strong re-introduction of grasses into the area, in order to re-establish the supposed primary status of vegetation – at the same time restoring the land's value as pasture.

Yet all genera with all their species are at present protected by South African Nature Conservation laws, and within the Karoo-Namib Region several nature reserves have been created (e.g. the Hester Malan Reserve near Springbok, the Darling Wild Flower Reserve and the Nortier Reserve near Lambertsbaai).

The basis for all conservation decisions, however, has been arbitrary because the taxonomy of the family is very poorly known. Consequently, the distribution and delimitation of taxa, and their respective ecological requirements, have only been studied in a few cases; the environmental pressures on different species can be analysed in even less species. In this connection it has to be mentioned that beside agricultural use of several taxa (vye-veld), all small-growing highly succulent species are much sought after by plant collectors for trade around the world.

Thus the situation, although promising at first view, turns out to be complex and ambivalent, and at the moment it is not certain whether endangered species or threatened sites can be protected successfully against destruction. It seems essential to increase investigations into the ecology and taxonomy of these plants, in order to understand the interactions between the plants and their environments more thoroughly, and to be able to suggest distinct steps for conservation in those cases where it is essential.

Different strategies in adaptation

Two sympatric genera, *Argyroderma* and *Oophytum*, are chosen to demonstrate two divergent strategies of adaptation to identical edaphic and climatic conditions. In both genera, species are known to occur in restricted numbers, and destruction of habitats through the creation of new roads and a new railway line has been severe. Both genera are much collected for plant growers, and as a result certain species are threatened by extinction.

Population studies were carried out during two extensive study periods in the field in 1969 and 1971; additional ontogenetic studies were undertaken in the greenhouse at Hamburg Botanic Garden from 1969 until 1977. The area was revisited in 1977.

The genera *Argyroderma* and *Oophytum* grow sympatrically in an area called Knersvlakte, about 300 km north of Cape Town, between the sea and the escarpment of the Bokkeveldberg, at elevations from sea-level to 300 m. The area is characterized by extensive and numerous quartz fields caused by decomposition of quartz bands where they reach the ground surface. Quartz pebbles of varying sizes cover shallow loamy-sandy ground, and these edaphic conditions seem to delimitate the distribution area of both genera. Since Marloth (1908) first described this close correlation, several suggestions have been made to explain the functional relations, but none have been satisfactory. Two features could be of major importance: plants of *Argyroderma* and *Oophytum* rarely grow mixed with shrubs in deeper soils, although in cultivation they do not require quartz; it seems that deep-rooting bushes cannot compete on shallow quartz fields. Furthermore, reflection from the quartz pebbles is high, raising the ambient air temperature in their immediate surroundings during daytime, but during the night the pebbles cool down considerably, so that condensation of water occurs in minute areas of higher water vapour underneath the stones. The effect allows the growth of algae, as can be seen when quartz stones are turned over, and the same source of moisture can be used by plants with root systems close to the surface, as they are in *Argyroderma* and *Oophytum*.

The climate is also identical for both genera: the annual expected rainfall can reach 250 mm; the values show an oscillation of about 20 years (Tyson, 1978) and the rainy season occurs in winter, mainly in May, June and July.

The genus *Argyroderma* (Hartmann, 1973, 1975, 1978) contains plants which produce one leaf pair per season; branching can take place. The plants grow sunken into the ground, e.g. *A. delaetii* Maass, or elevated above the surface, e.g. *A. sub-album* (N.E. Br.) N.E. Br.; this condition is genetically determined. In leaf anatomy, many typically xeromorphic characters are exhibited (Figure 1). In the

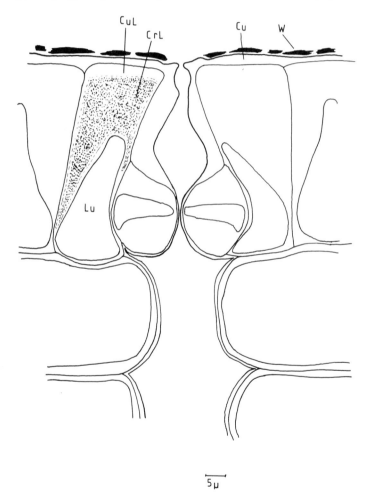

5 μ

Figure 1   Section through a leaf of *Argyroderma framesii* L. Bolus (Hartmann 1697 HBG!) exhibiting xeromorphic characters of the epidermis: sunken stomata, thick outer epidermal walls with incrustation of calcium oxalate crystals, outer cuticular layer and additional wax cover, cell lumen reduced. Crl = crystal layer, Cu = cuticle, Cul = cuticular layer, Lu = lumen, W = wax

thick outer epidermal wall (13–25 μm), three layers can be distinguished – an outer cutinized layer of about 2 μm, a central one containing calcium oxalate crystals, 10–20 μm in diameter, an inner cellulose stratum of 2–5 μm. In addition a cuticle of 1–3 μm covers the leaf surface, and on top of this a continuous verrucose wax layer 2–10 μm thick forms the outermost stratum. The stomata are positioned at the bases of the neighbouring cells, so that a chimney to the surface is formed.

The genus *Oophytum* (Ihlenfeldt, 1978) consists of highly branched plants forming clumps. The epidermis shows no xeromorphic characters (Figure 2): a thin outer epidermal wall is covered by a thin cuticle; both layers together do not exceed 8 μm in thickness and no wax cover has been found. Two types of cells can be distinguished in the epidermis – small 'normal' ones and large bladder cells; the latter probably play a role in photosynthesis, but their function is not yet

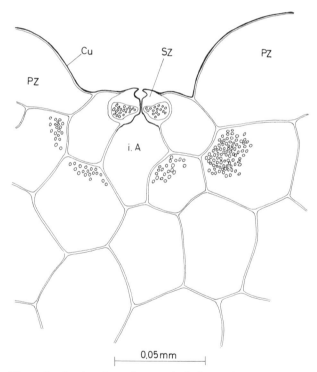

Figure 2   Section through an assimilating leaf of *Oophytum oviforme* (N.E.Br.) N.E.Br. (Hartmann 1357 HBG!) demonstrating mesomorphic characters: stomata not sunken, yet overarched by bladder cells (= idioblasts), outer epidermal walls thin. Cu = cuticle, i.A. = inner stomatic cavity, PZ = bladder cell (idioblast), SZ = guard cell. Drawing: courtesy Prof. Ihlenfeldt (Ihlenfeldt, 1978)

understood. The stomata are found level with the smaller epidermal cells, but they are over-arched by the bladder cells, thus reaching a position below the actual surface.

The differences in the anatomy of the epidermis of the two genera indicate fundamental divergencies between them, which become evident when the vegetation cycles are compared (Figure 3). In the genus *Argyroderma*, flowering of the earliest species starts before the rainy season begins, and during time of rain fruits and new leaves develop. Since water loss is extremely reduced by anatomical means, the leaves remain almost unchanged during the following dry season and only start withering when the leaf pair of the subsequent vegetation period is formed. At this time, the stored water supply is transferred to the newly developing leaves; thus water can be re-used over many years and individual plants can also survive elongated periods of drought. The only effect of lack of rain is a gradual reduction in the size of the subsequent leaf pairs, a feature that has been observed during the dry period from 1969 until 1974.

In the genus *Oophytum*, the development of leaves only starts after the first rains have come (Figure 3). Two pairs of leaves are formed, both identical in anatomy but slightly different in morphology and distinct in function: the first leaf pair serves as the photosynthetic organ during its entire lifetime, whereas the second fulfils this task during the rainy season only. With the beginning of the dry season, the second leaf pair withers and forms a papery sheath to protect the bud

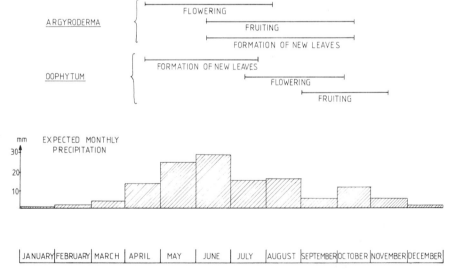

Figure 3   Differences in seasonal cycles of the genera *Argyroderma* and *Oophytum* in relation to expected annual rainfall in the distribution area. Rainfall data represent means from four stations near the area, over 4–12 years between 1969 and 1979 (after publications of the Weather Bureau, Pretoria)

which represents the immature stage of the following year's growth. Thus, by morphological means, a protection against desiccation is produced, and this dormant phase lasts until the rains start again – from September until April in most years.

Flowering only starts after both leaf pairs have been formed; fruiting takes place after the resting period has begun.

From the differences in vegetation cycles and in life cycles, it can be concluded that both genera show divergent oscillations in frequencies in single localities. In both genera, good rains will result in the production of numerous seedlings. In the genus *Oophytum*, however, the lifetime of the individual plants depends on regular rainfall during the subsequent seasons; in cases of prolonged drought, the plants will die, but will leave a seed-bank in the ground. Plants of the genus *Argyroderma*, on the other hand, can survive droughts as individuals, and it can be expected that populations remain more or less stable in one locality for long periods. Consequently, the distribution of *Argyroderma* populations will be constant on a long-term basis, whereas the sites of *Oophytum* populations can change depending on the frequency of rainfall. Frequency counts of populations will be needed to verify this hypothesis, but long-term changes must be taken into account when planning their conservation.

Conclusions for conservation

This example demonstrates the high degree of variety exposed by plants in one locality and indicates the abundance of genetic resources which enable plants to adapt to extremely arid environments. Similar studies of more taxa from the area would be required before decisions for conservation can be taken, and the following aspects must be considered:

1. Should those species of which only few populations are known be protected or would it be more effective to consider species with numerous populations and consequently larger genetic variability?
2. Would it be more useful to further evolution by protecting particular areas where well-adapted forms have been studied in order to allow natural associations to survive irrespective of the frequencies of individual taxa?
3. What is the succession in the endangered areas/species, and what means have to be taken to support the survival of certain units?
4. Seeing that long-term fluctuations occur, would it be advisable to suggest protection of certain units over defined periods?

There are many taxa of Mesembryanthemaceae, in which similar environmental pressures are suspected, but lack of information hinders further conclusions. It seems most urgent to provide additional investigations into the ecology and taxonomy of the family, in order to support means of nature conservation to protect these highly adapted plants of arid areas.

Acknowledgements

Field studies were made possible by grants from the Deutsche Forschungs-gemeinschaft (1969, 1971, and 1977) for which I should like to express my sincere thanks. My work in the field was supported by Curator Harry Hall, formerly of Kirstenbosch, and his wife Lisabel, who guided me in the region and gave leading examples of practical nature conservation. I owe much to both of them. Although I bear entire responsibility for the ideas expressed in this paper, I should like to mention that they could not have been developed without the numerous discussions which took place with colleagues working on the family Mesembryanthemaceae, and I should like to thank Dr B. Eller, Professor Dr H.-D. Ihlenfeldt and Professor Dr D. von Willert for their co-operation, criticism and assistance.

References

Acocks, J. P. H. (1953). 'Veld types of South Africa', *Mem. Bot. Surv. S. Afr.*, **28**, 1–192, (2nd Ed. 1975).

Hartmann, H. (1973). 'New combinations and a key for the genus *Argyroderma* N.E. Br. (Mesembryanthemaceae Fenzl)', *Nat. Cact. & Succ. J.*, **28**, 48–50.

Hartmann, H. (1975), '*Argyroderma*', in *Lexicon of Succulent Plants* (Ed. H. Jacobson), pp. 407–10, Blandford, London.

Hartmann, H. (1978) 'Monographie der Gattung *Argyroderma* N.E. Br. (Mesembryanthemaceae Fenzl)', *Mitt. Inst. Allg. Bot. Hamburg*, **15**, 121–235.

Ihlenfeldt, H.-D. (1978). 'Morphologie und Taxonomie der Gattung *Oophytum* N.E. Br. (Mesembryanthemaceae)', *Bot. Jahrb. Syst.*, **99**, 303–28.

Marloth, R. (1908). Das Kapland. *Wiss. Ergebn. Deutsch. Tiefsee-Exped. 'Waldivia', 1898–1899*, Bd. 2, T.3., Fischer, Jena.

Tyson, P. D. (1978) 'Rainfall changes over South Africa during the period of meteorological records', in *Biogeography and Ecology of Southern Africa* (Ed. M. J. A. Werger), pp. 53–69, Junk, The Hague.

Werger, M. J. A. (1978) 'Biogeographical division of Southern Africa' in *Biogeography and Ecology of Southern Africa* (Ed. M. J. A. Werger), pp. 145–70, Junk, The Hague.

The Biological Aspects of Rare Plant Conservation
Edited by Hugh Synge
© 1981 John Wiley & Sons Ltd.

25
The status, ecology and conservation of *Tilia platyphyllos* in Britain

C. D. PIGOTT *Department of Biological Sciences, University of Lancaster*

Summary

Tilia platyphyllos is a long-lived tree which is recorded in only a few localities in Britain, but is widespread in Europe. Its present status in Britain is assessed in comparison with that of *T. cordata*, its habitat and ecological requirements discussed and its history reviewed. It is concluded that at least some of the isolated populations in northern Europe are native and are fragments of the original vegetation, and so worthy of conservation.

Introduction

The conservation of rare trees presents a number of special problems related to their economic value, their size and their longevity. Vast areas of forest have been destroyed but trees have also been extensively planted, probably since prehistoric times, so that natural distributions have become obscured and geographic provenances mixed. Particular species, whose timber or fruit have not been highly valued, have decreased and some survive only in very small populations, sometimes even as single individuals. Such populations appear stable simply because the individuals live for several centuries. Indeed trees of the large-leaved lime, *Tilia platyphyllos*, may live for more than 1000 years.

Tilia platyphyllos is widely distributed in central and much of southern Europe, so that it is neither rare nor endangered as a native species in Europe as a whole (Figure 1). In contrast, the tree has a strong claim to be regarded as perhaps the rarest native species of northern Europe, being absent from northern Russia, the Baltic states, Finland and Norway, and occurring only in two localities in Bohus on the west coast of Sweden, where two trees occur on Öddö and two stems grow from a single root on Sydkoster (Lagerberg, 1948).

In the British Isles *T. platyphyllos*, and more especially its hybrid with *T. cordata* (*T. × vulgaris*), have been widely and frequently planted so the status of both are often uncertain but the species is nevertheless regarded as native in a few localities in England and Wales. It is the only forest tree considered for inclusion in the *British Red Data Book* but is, in fact, relegated to the appendix on the

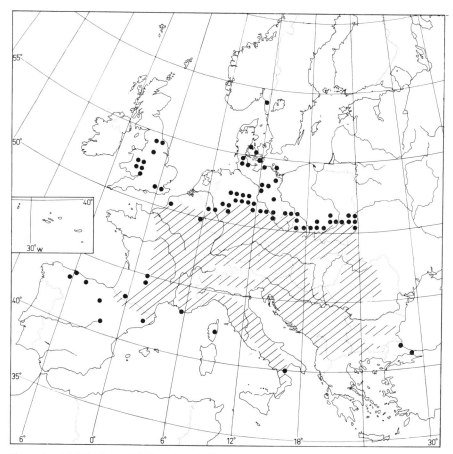

Figure 1   Distribution of *Tilia platyphyllos* in Europe, based partly on Meusel, Jäger, Rauschert and Weinert (1978) and on information provided by Professor J. Kornaś

grounds that it occurs in more than 15 of the 10-km squares of the National Grid (Perring and Farrell, 1977). Its classification in this respect therefore depends on the certainty with which it is possible to identify native populations that include at least some individuals which are genetically relatively pure examples of the species.

The present status of *Tilia platyphyllos* in Britain

Tilia platyphyllos and much more often its hybrid with *T. cordata* (*T.* × *vulgaris*) have been extensively planted in towns, parklands, hedgerows and, more rarely, woodlands throughout large parts of the British Isles. A few examples of *T. platyphyllos* that were planted before 1600 AD are still alive, such as the celebrated tree at Burghley near Stamford planted by Queen Elizabeth I. Other trees associated with Elizabethan houses, for example the one containing a small house at Pitchford in Shropshire (Figure 2), are also this species. The planting of the hybrid seems to have become fashionable after 1600 AD and several avenues of this tree are recorded or reputed to date from the first half of the seventeenth century (Hadfield, 1967).

Both *T. platyphyllos* and the hybrid frequently produce fertile seed, even in northern England where, in contrast, *T. cordata* is generally sterile (Pigott and Huntley, in press). Even though the northern limit of the natural distribution of *T. platyphyllos* lies so much further south than that of *T. cordata*, fertilization has been shown experimentally to be possible at significantly lower temperatures and, because of earlier flowering, there is a much higher probability that fertilized ovules will develop and ripen before autumn. Seedlings of *T. platyphyllos* are often plentiful in Britain and in a number of sites, saplings and young trees are also associated with parent trees showing that natural regeneration can occur.

Analysis of the variation in their progeny shows that trees which have predominantly the characters of *T. platyphyllos*, and in particular lack stellate hairs in the axils of veins on the abaxial surface of the leaf, breed true in vegetative characters, while those with supposedly hybrid characters show segregation and some saplings of the progeny closely resemble *T. platyphyllos*. Analysis of a

Figure 2   A small house in *Tilia platyphyllos* at Pitchford, Shropshire, demonstrates the age of individual trees; the tree probably dates from before 1580, and the tree house was recorded in a drawing of 1714. Photo C. D. Pigott

natural population of saplings surrounding two isolated trees of the hybrid in woodland of *Fagus sylvatica* and *Taxus baccata* at Headley in Surrey (O.S. National Grid Reference 15/185538) shows the same tendency for variation to range from individuals which resemble the parents to others with the characters of *Tilia platyphyllos*. There is thus the possibility that at least in this type of habitat selection favours survival of individuals with the genome of *T. platyphyllos* rather than that of *T. cordata*.

Arguments in favour of believing *T. platyphyllos* and possibly hybrids with *T. cordata* to be native in particular localities in Britain were presented in several local Floras at the turn of the last century. Purchas and Ley (1889) regarded both species as native in rocky woods in the Wye Valley and, in a letter quoted by Elwes and Henry (1906–13), Ley refers to *T. platyphyllos* being native in similar localities in Gloucestershire, Monmouth, Brecon, Radnor and Shropshire. Painter (1889), quoting Purchas, and Linton (1903) regarded the species and hybrids as native on cliffs or steep wooded slopes of limestone in Derbyshire, and Baker (1906) describes similar localities in Swaledale in Yorkshire. The essence of the argument for each site is simply that the trees are rooted on ledges or in fissures of rock 'where it is physically impossible that they were planted' and that they are associated with native species in 'aboriginal woodland'. This would be a strong argument if, like *T. cordata* in northern England, *T. platyphyllos* now regenerated rarely from seed but this is not the case, at least in England and Wales. Also the fruits are dispersed by wind and in this respect resembles *Acer pseudoplatanus*, with which it is often associated in continental Europe. Few would now claim that *A. pseudoplatanus* is native in Britain despite its occurrence on cliffs and rocky slopes. There is, however, other evidence that *Tilia platyphyllos* is native in some localities.

The history of *Tilia platyphyllos* **in Britain**

The history of *Tilia platyphyllos* has been described by Godwin (1975). Pollen of *T. platyphyllos* has been recorded in sufficient quantities in deposits of middle Flandrian age at several sites around the margins of the East Anglian fenland (Clark and Godwin, 1962; Godwin, 1968; Godwin and Vishnu-Mittre, 1975), from near Birmingham (Kelly and Osborne, 1964) and from Wales (Trotman, 1963), to show that the tree was present in Britain in prehistoric times. This is confirmed by the recovery of a flower (Clark and Godwin, 1962) and fruits (Kelly and Osborne, 1964) in deposits of middle Flandrian age. The tree seems to have spread into south-eastern England by about 5500 BC but remained generally less plentiful than *T. cordata*. The proportion of pollen of *T. platyphyllos* reached a maximum about 3000 BC, but subsequently decreased and ceases to be recorded after 2000–1500 BC in parts of East Anglia. Its decline seems likely to have been a consequence of destruction of forest and a failure to maintain itself in secondary woodlands.

The limits of the natural distribution of *T. platyphyllos* in the middle Flandrian forests are not known in detail because in many pollen diagrams its pollen has not been separated from that of *T. cordata*. Although it certainly extended across central England to Wales it is not known whether it spread as far north as *T. cordata*. All the sites where *T. platyphyllos* has been claimed as native lie within the area where the pollen of the genus is well represented.

The most convincing evidence that a particular population is native comes from Craig y Cilau near Brecon (32/1815). This is a high cliff of limestone; on narrow ledges and in fissures on its almost vertical face, there are not only several trees of *T. platyphyllos*, but also trees of four endemic apomictic species of *Sorbus, S. anglica, S. leptophylla, S. minima* and *S. porrigentiformis*. Immediately below the cliff is a raised bog from which a pollen diagram is available (Trotman, 1963). This shows a high proportion of *Tilia* pollen, including pollen of both species, during the period from approximately 4000 to 2000 BC, and then the occurrence of sparse grains up to the present surface.

There is therefore good evidence for believing *T. platyphyllos* to be native in this site and perhaps, by analogy, in other sites with this type of topography and associated vegetation, which often includes endemic species of *Sorbus*. Several localities in the Wye Valley are very similar but have no suitable deposits in close proximity which would allow their history to be established.

A site in Gloucestershire provides evidence of a different nature that *Tilia platyphyllos* is either native or long established. The name of the site is Lineover Wood, which in its earliest recorded form 'lind ofres', dates from c. 800 AD and means lime-tree bank (Smith, 1964). The wood occupies an exceptionally steep part of the escarpment of the Inferior Oolite (middle Jurassic) near Andoversford (32/9818) and several trees of *T. platyphyllos* and hybrids, some many stemmed and of very large basal diameter, grow rooted in outcrops of limestone. The field-layer contains *Convallaria majalis* and *Polygonatum odoratum*, both species which seem characteristic of ancient woodlands in the Cotswolds.

The evidence that some populations of *Tilia platyphyllos* in England and Wales are almost certainly native is consistent with the geographical distribution of the species in Europe (Figure 1). This is remarkably similar to the natural distribution of *Fagus sylvatica* (Jalas and Suominen, 1976) and indeed the two trees often grow together but mainly in those situations where the vigour of *F. sylvatica* is reduced by exposure, shallow soils and the consequent tendency for water and mineral nutrients to become deficient. *Tilia platyphyllos* is therefore almost always much less frequent than *Fagus sylvatica* but scattered throughout almost the entire range of the latter species.

Samples of leaves from the exposed parts of the crowns have been obtained from almost all the supposedly native populations in Britain; those from individual trees which seem to be relatively pure genotypes of *Tilia platyphyllos* all have the dense simple pubescence of ssp. *cordifolia*, which is also the native subspecies in north France and Germany. Many trees which, however, are certainly planted belong to this subspecies or to ssp. *platyphyllos*. Trees with glabrous leaves (ssp. *pseudorubra*), originating from south-east Europe, have very rarely been planted in Britain.

The ecology of *Tilia platyphyllos* in Britain

All the sites in Britain where *Tilia platyphyllos* has come to be regarded as native (Figure 3) are on cliffs or steep rocky slopes, or in woodlands in which these features are present, but this is not simply because the tree is judged to be native only in situations of this character. Unlike *T. cordata* there are in fact almost no occurrences of *T. platyphyllos* in the English lowlands in woodlands which are known to be ancient and which remain composed largely of native species.

Rugged topography is characteristic of hard rocks and the majority of native sites are on the harder limestones including the Carboniferous limestone in Wales,

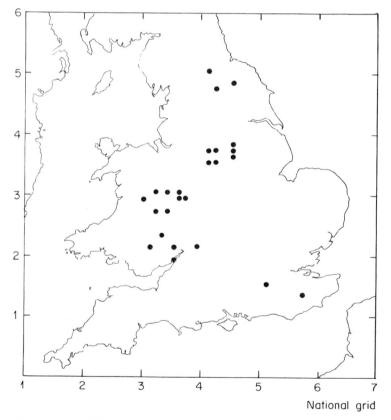

National grid

Figure 3   Localities in which *Tilia platyphyllos* is probably native in Britain

the Welsh borderland, Derbyshire and Yorkshire, and in small gorges ('grips') in the Permian magnesian limestone or dolomite of Derbyshire and Yorkshire (Jackson and Sheldon, 1949). At Pontesbury Hill in Shropshire *T. platyphyllos* grows on Precambrian (Uriconian) dolerite and basic volcanic tuffs. The basic and generally calcareous nature of the soils in all these sites is consistent with the ecological behaviour of *T. platyphyllos* throughout much of Europe and in this respect it is much more restricted than *T. cordata*.

The limestones of the neogenic part of England are generally softer and give rise to a gentler topography in which natural cliffs and outcrops are rare except along the coast. It is perhaps significant that Lineover Wood near Andoversford (p. 309) occupies one of the steepest parts of the escarpment of the Inferior Oolite, and similarly the small populations of *T. platyphyllos* and hybrids in east Yorkshire grow in woods on steep slopes or outcrops of Calcareous Grit or Kellaways Rock of the middle Jurassic.

The significance of the rarity of natural cliffs on the English chalk in relation to the distribution of plants has been discussed by Pigott and Walters (1953, 1954). One of the few sites which is exceptional is at Box Hill in Surrey (51/1751), where the river Mole not only undercuts the hill to create a very steep and unstable slope, but also has produced a number of crater-like swallow holes. Again it is surely significant that a few trees of *T. platyphyllos* grow at the foot of the cliff and on the rim of a swallow hole where there is an enormous tree with a basal girth of about 8 m (Figure 4). The earliest written record of the species in Britain probably refers to this site (Merrett, 1666–67). The associated vegetation consists of stunted trees of *Fagus sylvatica* and a dense scrub formed largely of *Buxus sempervirens*, *Taxus baccata* and *Sorbus aria*. *Tilia platyphyllos* occurs in similar communities on cliffs and screes of limestone in the Dordogne and the causses of the Cevennes. (Vanden Berghen, 1963.)

There are a few other localities in the English lowlands where *T. platyphyllos* may be native but they are of less exceptional character. Like *T. cordata*, large and probably very old trees occur on some ancient boundary banks, a situation described by the name 'lindover'. A possible explanation is that boundaries have been left undisturbed when the woodlands on the two sides were cleared or cleared and replanted, so that they retain trees derived from the original forest. Large trees of *T. platyphyllos* also occur in association with very old oaks in a few ancient parklands such as Moccas Park in Herefordshire (32/3442) and Sandringham Park in Norfolk (53/6828) but as the species was certainly being planted in the sixteenth century and can regenerate from seed, the status in such sites remains uncertain.

The great rarity of *Tilia platyphyllos* in ancient woodland in the English lowlands is in marked contrast to *T. cordata*, but is consistent with the ecological distinction between the two species. *T. cordata* is a more continental species, tolerant of cold winters and relatively low rainfall (600–800 mm per annum), and it is normally associated with *Quercus robur* or *Q. petraea* and

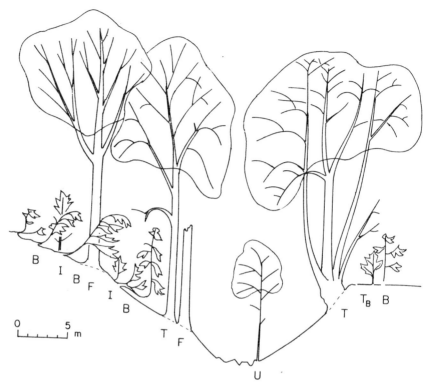

Figure 4   Transect of vegetation in a former sink-hole of the river Mole, Box Hill,
Surrey (T *Tilia platyphyllos*, F *Fraxinus excelsior*, Tb *Taxus baccata*, U *Ulmus
glabra*, I *Ilex aquifolium*, B *Buxus sempervirens*) (April 1980)

Carpinus betulus on well-drained sands, loams and even clays, sometimes, but by
no means always, over limestone. Many of the woodlands related to the early
pattern of English settlement and for which there is documentary evidence of
great antiquity occupy these heavier or infertile types of soil.

In contrast, *Tilia platyphyllos* is a tree of well-drained basic soils and especially
those which are calcareous in hilly regions of moderate rainfall (over 800 mm per
annum). In these respects it again resembles *Fagus sylvatica*, although that species
tolerates a much wider range of soils. It is in exactly these types of habitat that
Tilia platyphyllos survives in the north and west of England. For example, in
Derbyshire *T. platyphyllos* and hybrids grow on cliffs and steep slopes of limestone, while *T. cordata* usually occupies deeper soils of loam, sometimes on the
edge of the plateau from which, however, most of the forest has been destroyed
(Pigott, 1969, p. 503).

This clear correlation of the occurrence of *Tilia platyphyllos* with topography is
found throughout Europe and there is evidence it is only secondarily a consequence of such sites being unfavourable for agriculture. In regions which are still

largely covered by forest the tree still shows the same restriction implying that the primary cause is natural. In the Swiss Jura, for example, *T. platyphyllos* occurs almost exclusively on cliffs, outcrops and steep slopes of limestone and is absent from the dense forests of *Fagus sylvatica* and *Abies alba* on the deeper soils. There is ample evidence of regeneration in these situations as populations contain trees of all sizes (Figure 5) and they are clearly able to compete successfully with young trees of *Fagus sylvatica*, which are eventually of poor quality. In contrast, though seedlings of *Tilia platyphyllos* may be present in adjacent areas dominated by *Fagus sylvatica*, saplings and mature trees are absent.

The habitats in which *Tilia platyphyllos* can survive in forest are directly related to the topographical features of karst. Most of the National Park of Plitvice in Yugoslavia is still covered by dense forest of *Fagus sylvatica*, *Picea abies* and locally *Abies alba*. Very small populations of *Tilia platyphyllos* occur widely scattered, but always occupy one of three types of topographic feature. These are: (a) cliffs which may have a face no more than 2–3 m high and the blocks below them; (b) the rims of the circular crater-like vrtača ('dolines'), where *Picea abies* often occupies the bottom (Figure 6); and (c) the abrupt crests of the lower ridges (Figure 7). In all these situations the vigour and dominance of *Fagus*

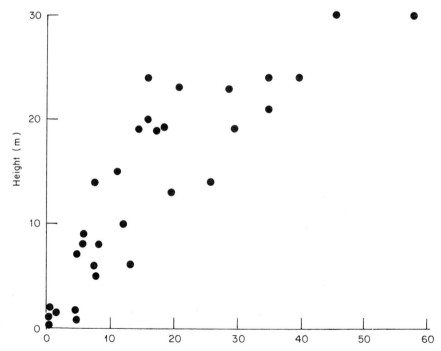

Figure 5   Relation between height and diameter at 1.3 m for saplings and trees of *Tilia platyphyllos* in an area 0.6 ha of the Forêt de l'Eter, above Cressier, Neuchâtel, Switzerland. The point at the origin represents 78 seedlings (July 1969)

Figure 6   Transect of vegetation on one side of a vrtača ('doline') in dense forest of *Fagus sylvatica* (F) at Karleušine plase near Uvalica, Plitvice (T *Tilia platyphyllos*, A *Acer pseudoplatanus*. P *Picea abies*, C *Corylus avellana*, R *Rhamnus alpinus* ssp. *fallax*) (July 1976)

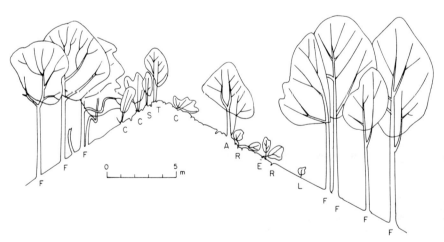

Figure 7   Transect of ridge of Veliki Turčić on Medvedak, Plitvice (T *Tilia platyphyllos*, F *Fagus sylvatica*, A *Acer obtusatum*, C *Corylus avellana*, S *Staphylea pinnata*, R *Rhamnus alpinus* spp. *fallax*, E. *Euonymus latifolius*, L *Lonicera alpigena*) (July 1976)

sylvatica is conspicuously reduced. Many of the trees of *Tilia platyphyllos* in Plitvice show breakage of their upper limbs by snow.

All these topographic features are almost absent from southern and eastern England and the types of woodland in which *T. platyphyllos* was probably native were those which occupied rendziniform soils along the steep escarpments of the chalk and Jurassic limestones. The tree still occurs in this type of habitat in northern France, both on the chalk and the Eocene (Lutetian) limestones in the Laonois. The historical evidence is consistent with this interpretation. From the assemblage of species associated with both fruits and pollen of *T. platyphyllos* at Shustoke (42/2290), Kelly and Osborne (1964) suggest that the tree grew in forest on well-drained neutral or calcareous soils on the hill sides which border the valley. The presence of the tree in East Anglia (Godwin, 1956, 2nd Ed. 1975), in a region of very subdued topography where hard limestones are absent, suggests that it occupied shallow soils on the chalk and chalky drift which fringe the fenlands.

The decline and eventual disappearance of *T. platyphyllos* in East Anglia was during the Bronze and Iron Ages, when archaeological evidence shows an exceptionally dense concentration of activity along the well-drained slopes and ridges of the chalk and oolites. It seems the relatively sparse forests on the light calcareous soils, the very habitat where *T. platyphyllos* would be expected to grow, were especially favoured and cleared at an early stage for both pasture and cultivation.

Conservation of *Tilia platyphyllos*

Evidence has been presented to demonstrate that some at least of the isolated populations of *Tilia platyphyllos* in northern Europe are native and are part of fragments of the original vegetation. This is their main scientific interest. Fortunately the very features which have allowed them to survive continue to make these particular sites of low value both for agriculture and forestry. Nevertheless destruction or serious modification of the surroundings by, for instance, afforestation destroys part of the evidence needed to understand their significance.

A more direct threat is the convenience such sites offer for quarrying. Craig y Cilau, possibly the most valuable site scientifically, has old quarries on its eastern part and a proposal to extend these was fortunately rejected. This type of exploitation is surely unacceptable in view of the limited number of sites, their small area and high scenic value.

It is important to emphasize that the sites support not only populations of a rare tree but fragments of a rare type of vegetation, in which other rare species occur such as, for example, the endemic species of *Sorbus*. Nor is the value restricted to plants. The swallow-hole at Box Hill, though so small, provides habitats for a remarkably rich fauna of invertebrates. Some, such as the molluscs *Acicula fusca* (Montagu) and *Clausilia rolphii* (Leach), are very local and of special biogeographical interest; others, such as the Isopod *Armadillidium pulchellum* (Zencker) and *A. pictum* (Brandt), are very rare, discontinuous in their distribution and possibly characteristic of karstic sites.

Finally there are the specific problems of conserving very small populations of long-lived trees. Some already survive precariously and could be lost by land-slips; some are heavily infected by decay. Tourism accelerates erosion and destroys young plants. It is by no means certain that the seedlings which do survive are not the products of pollination by planted trees, for at Box Hill *Tilia* × *vulgaris* has been planted within 100 m of the swallow-hole.

Acknowledgements

I thank Mr John Sankey and Mrs Dorothy Trotman for access to unpublished information on the fauna at Box Hill and the history of Craig y Cilau respectively, Professor Jean-Louis Richard, the Royal Society for a grant allowing me to work at Plitvice, and Dr Josip Movčan and Mr Franjo Salopek for their help and guidance in Plitvice.

References

Baker, J. G. (1906). *North Yorkshire*, Brown, London.
Clark, J. G. D. and Godwin, H. (1962). 'The Neolithic in the Cambridgeshire Fens', *Antiquity*, **36**, 10–23.
Elwes, H. J. and Henry, A. (1906–13). *The trees of Great Britain and Ireland*, Edinburgh.
Godwin, H. (1968). 'Studies on the post-glacial history of British vegetation. 15. Organic deposits of Old Buckenham Mere, Norfolk', *New Phytologist*, **67**, 95–107.
Godwin, H. (1956, 2nd Ed. 1975). *The History of the British Flora*, Cambridge University Press.
Godwin, H. and Vishnu-Mittre (1975). 'Studies of the post-glacial history of British vegetation. 16. Flandrian deposits of the fenland margin at Holme Fen and Whittlesey Mere, Hunts', *Phil. Trans. Roy. Soc. B*, **270**, 561–608.
Hadfield, M. (1967). *Landscape with trees*, Country Life, London.
Jackson, G. and Sheldon, J. (1949). 'The vegetation of magnesian limestone cliffs at Markland Grips near Sheffield', *J. Ecol.*, **37**, 38–50.
Jalas, J. and Suominen, J. (1976). *Atlas florae Europaeae 3. Salicaceae to Balanophoraceae*, Helsinki.
Kelly, M. and Osborne, P. J. (1964). 'Two faunas and floras from the alluvium at Shustoke, Warwickshire', *Proc. Linn. Soc.*, **176**, 37–65.
Lagerberg, T. (1948). *Vilda växter i Norden*, **3**, Stockholm.
Linton, W. R. (1903). *Flora of Derbyshire*, Bemrose, London.
Merrett, C. (1666, 1667). *Pinax rerum naturalium Britannicarum*, London.
Meusel, H., Jäger, E., Rauschert, S., and Weinert, E. (1978). *Vergleichende Chorologie der Zentraleuropäischen Flora*, Gustav Fischer, Jena.
Painter, W. H. (1889). *A contribution to the Flora of Derbyshire*, Bell, London.
Perring, F. H. and Farrell, L. (1977). *British Red Data Books: 1. Vascular plants*, Society for the Promotion of Nature Conservation, Lincoln.
Pigott, C. D. (1969). 'The status of *Tilia cordata* and *T. platyphyllos* on the Derbyshire limestone', *J. Ecol.*, **57**, 491–504.

Pigott, C. D. and Huntley, J. P. (in press). 'Factors controlling the distribution of *Tilia cordata* at the northern limit of its geographical range 3. Nature and causes of seed sterility', *New Phytologist*.

Pigott, C. D. and Walters, S. M. (1953). 'Is the box-tree a native of England?', in *The Changing Flora of Britain* (Ed. J. E. Lousley), pp. 184–7, Buncle, Arbroath.

Pigott, C. D. and Walters, S. M. (1954). 'On the interpretation of the discontinuous distributions shown by certain British species of open habitats', *J. Ecol.*, **42**, 95–116.

Purchas, W. H. and Ley, A. (1889). *A Flora of Herefordshire*, Jakeman and Carver, Hereford.

Smith, A. H. (1964). *The place-names of Gloucestershire*, Cambridge University Press.

Trotman, D. M. (1963). *Data for Late-glacial and Post-glacial History in South Wales*. Dissertation at the University of Wales (Swansea).

Tutin, T. G. *et al.* (Eds.) (1964–80). *Flora Europaea*, 5 vols, Cambridge University Press.

Vanden Berghen, C. (1963). 'Étude sur la végétation des Grands Causses du Massif Central de France', *Mém. Soc. Roy. Bot. Belg.*, 1.

Note

Plant names in this chapter follow *Flora Europaea* (Tutin *et al.*, 1964–80).

The Biological Aspects of Rare Plant Conservation
Edited by Hugh Synge
© 1981 John Wiley & Sons Ltd.

26
The demography, fauna and conservation of *Juniperus communis* in Britain

LENA K. WARD *Institute of Terrestrial Ecology, Monks Wood Experimental Station, Huntingdon, England*

Summary

Population sizes of all known juniper colonies in southern England are discussed, and their relationships to each other and to extinct sites described using a nearest neighbour analysis. An area where juniper is rare is contrasted to one where it is common.

The demography of representative populations shows that juniper colonization is often a transient event, and many colonies have restricted age classes. Examples of the role of grazing and burning are discussed; rabbit grazing is found to be having a deleterious effect on young stands in the south. In the absence of adequate regeneration, the ultimate life span of juniper of about 100 years in the south can be used to predict future losses of sites. Work on the arthropod fauna of juniper is summarized with reference to geographical distribution of the arthropods and to juniper site sizes. Measures needed for the conservation of juniper are discussed.

Introduction

Juniper, *Juniperus communis* L., is a locally common shrub in various areas of the British Isles, but there is concern that in parts of lowland Britain populations are declining, especially of subsp. *communis*. Juniper has become extinct on many sites in southern England (Ward, 1973), and colonies that at present have several hundred healthy bushes often have an unbalanced age structure with little or no regeneration. Relatively few sites have many young plants.

By studying the demography of juniper colonies we can try to understand some of the biological factors important in the continuing decline of this plant on sites which are already conserved for wildlife. Outside conserved areas the juniper survives precariously in the general agricultural landscape, its status there strongly related to land use, particularly grazing. The possible causes of loss in this general context were reviewed briefly in Ward (1973).

Population sizes and distribution

All known populations of juniper in southern England were surveyed from 1968 to 1973 (Ward, 1973). Surveys have also been made in northern England and results from them will be published shortly. These surveys have enabled comparisons between sites to be made and have given a baseline from which future changes in the juniper populations can be monitored.

Site size has much importance in conservation (Diamond and May, 1976). The sizes of all juniper colonies in southern England can be plotted from the survey data (Figure 1). The term 'colony' is related to conservation and in this context is defined as an area of juniper where no sharp topographical distinction in the age structure of the bushes can be detected; where the other vegetation is reasonably uniform; and where it is under the same ownership and management. Small colonies are abundant: 286 colonies had fewer than 100 bushes and indeed 142 had fewer than 10 bushes. Census of large colonies tends to be inaccurate (Ward, 1973), but certainly there are few really large colonies, only 18 with over 1000 bushes.

Distribution of colonies is not random. Juniper is almost restricted to the chalk and oolitic limestone soils, the few sites on heathlands being remnants of formerly more widespread juniper (Ward, 1973). In northern England, Scotland and in continental Europe, juniper is still common in some heathlands. In southern England juniper is common in some areas and rare in others: contrast for example the Berkshire Downs and the North Downs near the Medway Gap (Figures 2 and 3). Where juniper has been lost there appears to have been deleterious land-use changes earlier than in areas where the plant is still common. In particular sheep grazing seems to have been abandoned earlier. Where juniper is very common on Salisbury Plain the military use of sites has been compatible with the regeneration of the plant.

As juniper declines in numbers it seems to retreat towards centres of aggregation of the larger colonies, for example on the Berkshire Downs (Figure 3). The smaller living colonies tend to be at greater distances from the larger colonies, and the extinct sites are further away still. This is shown numerically using the pooled data for southern England and measuring the distance to the nearest living neighbour for a range of colony sizes and for sites which became extinct at different dates (Figure 4). The extinct sites have been divided into 50-year bands based on the date of the last known record. Data on extinct sites are of poorer quality. The results show that the larger sites are closer to their nearest neighbours than smaller sites are. The mean distance between present day sites is 1.91 km. Extinct sites are at greater distances, the mean distance to the nearest present-day site being 10.45 km. The earlier the date of extinction the more likely that the site is further away from present-day colonies. This confirms a long continued process of retrenchment. It is not surprising that the dispersal of seeds around a large site is successful and that there are usually near neighbours, but the data emphasize that there is little hope of colonization of suitably managed sites by high numbers of junipers if the local seed resources are inadequate. Miles and Kinnaird (1979) have also observed that the most effective dispersal of *Juniperus communis* is near to fruiting bushes.

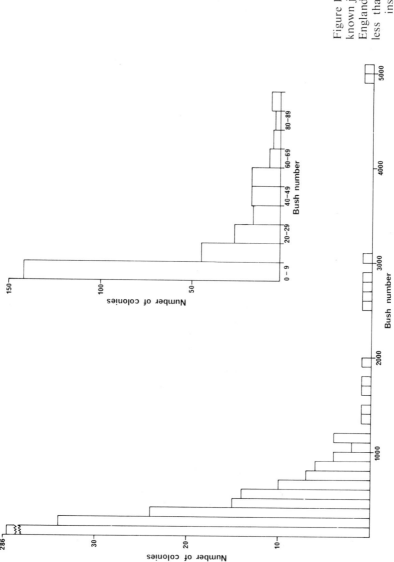

Figure 1 Population sizes of all known juniper colonies in southern England in 1973. (Colonies with less than 100 bushes are shown inset on a different scale)

× Extinct sites with last known date of record
2● Colonies with estimated numbers   ☐ Chalk

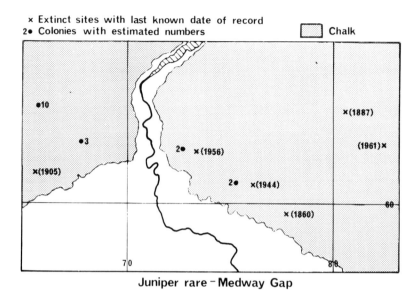

Juniper rare – Medway Gap

Figure 2   The Medway Gap area of Kent in 1973, an area where juniper is
rare (with 10 km grid lines) (Crown copyright reserved)

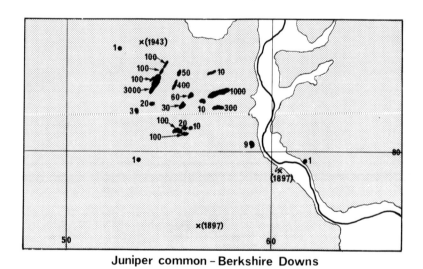

Juniper common – Berkshire Downs

Figure 3   The Berkshire Downs in 1973, an area where juniper is common
(with 10 km grid lines) (Crown copyright reserved)

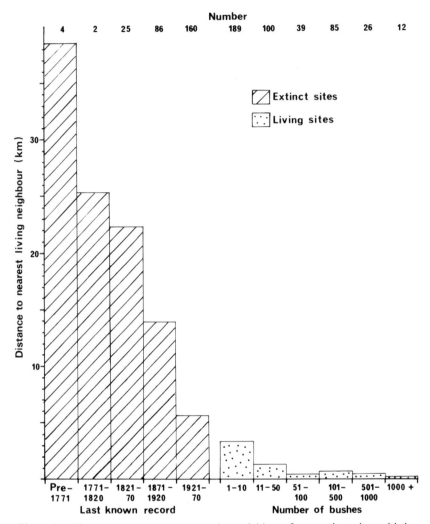

Figure 4 Distances to nearest present-day neighbour from extinct sites with last known record at different dates, and from present-day colonies of different sizes

Fauna of juniper

Plants have animals dependent on them, and this subject should not be neglected in conservation management. Generally, the objective should be to try to conserve the associated fauna, usually phytophagous insects and mites, perhaps with some specific predators and parasites, in a balance so that the plants are not severely damaged. Some damage must be tolerated. Introduced pests may cause the worst problems, e.g. juniper scale on *J. bermudiana* L. (Challinor and Wingate, 1971).

The total numbers of insect species associated with particular plant species is very variable, and seems to be related to the taxonomic position and biochemistry of the plant, its growth form and abundance. Rarer plants usually have fewer animals dependent on them, but such as do occur are likely to be particularly interesting and rare also.

The fauna of juniper has been studied in detail (Ward, 1977), and will be briefly described as an example of insect/plant relationships. A total of 35 insects and three mites has been recorded in the British Isles as specifically associated with *Juniperus* and a variable range of other Cupressaceae or Coniferae. Eight of them are introduced. Some species occur throughout the country wherever *J. communis* grows, and sometimes also where closely related Cupressaceae are cultivated, while other species are found in one region only. A particular microhabitat on juniper in different regions may be occupied by different species. Among Cecidomyiidae (Diptera) for example, *Schmidtiella gemmarum* Reub. galls buds in southern England, while *Oligotrophus juniperus* (L.) galls buds in northern England and Scotland; *O. panteli* Kief. appears to gall buds only on the northern *J. communis* ssp. *nana* Syme. Thus from the faunal standpoint juniper should be conserved in a range of areas.

The site size is important to the fauna of juniper in southern England (Ward and Lakhani, 1977). A site was defined as an area of juniper that was continuous. Multiple regression analysis related the total number of associated arthropods to various site variables. For data pooled from the North Downs and the Chilterns, the number of bushes explained 77 per cent of the variation in numbers of associated arthropods. Bush age, which was a crude measure of the continuity of the site in time, explained 5 per cent. Distance to the nearest 100-bush site, which was a measure of isolation, explained 4 per cent. Only the largest sites maintained most of the species. Recommended site sizes could not be given because there was so much variation, and three really rare species of the juniper fauna were poorly understood. A site with about 3000 bushes, however, had a probability of 0.5 of conserving all 15 of the commoner species of southern England while for a site with 300 bushes it was only 0.05. Those species feeding only on the berries of juniper are in the greatest danger of extinction because this microhabitat is more limited than the foliage. One of these species appears to have become extinct already: *Pitedia juniperina* (L.) (Hem. Pentatomidae) occurred on the North Downs in the last century, and its extinction may be related to the severe decline of juniper in that area. Probable losses of various other species were demonstrated locally at several sites by comparing the present fauna to the older records.

Juniper populations and age structure

The age structure of some typical populations of juniper has been determined by ring counts in ten studies (Figure 5). Examples have been included only where counts were from random samples, or all plants in a patch were taken. Because of

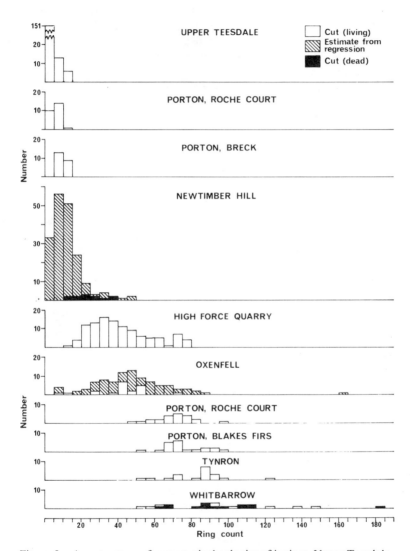

Figure 5   Age structure of some typical colonies of juniper. Upper Teesdale, Yorkshire (from Gilbert, 1980); Porton, Roche Court and Breck, Wiltshire, 1971; Newtimber Hill, Sussex (from data by Bristowe, 1974, pers. comm.); High Force Quarry, Yorkshire (from data by Bines, 1976, less accurate, as not all plants cut at the base, pers. comm.); Oxenfell, Cumbria, 1973; Porton, Roche Court and Blakes Firs, 1971; Tynron, Dumfries (from Kerr, 1968); Whitbarrow, Cumbria, 1977

the conservation value of juniper, only small samples can be taken of living bushes, and at Oxenfell and Newtimber Hill estimates of ages were made using regression of girth at the trunk base on ring count. Variability between sites is marked, and an individually calculated regression must be made for each site. Even this may be unsatisfactory where growth rates of individuals are very variable, as at Whitbarrow.

Many populations tend to have restricted age classes, although there often appears to be more spread in the older populations. The restriction of age classes points to historical events when colonization and subsequent establishment were favoured, and it is generally common in scrub stands (Ward, 1979). Populations with all ages are rarer, and are found where successful seed germination and establishment occurs frequently, for example where continual erosion provides area with bare soil on steep slopes and grazing is not intensive (Ward, 1973; Gilbert, 1980).

The youngest population was in Upper Teesdale (Figure 5), where Gilbert (1980) calculated that a 2-year-old seedling had about a 1 in 50 chance of surviving for 10 years. Death was mainly due to heavy grazing. This is typical of the problems caused where conditions for germination are satisfactory, but where establishment to maturity is very difficult. If overgrazing continues the colony will slowly be lost. This process is now occurring in various areas in Britain, and there are only remnant junipers left on some sites especially in northern England. Those plants that do survive to maturity are more frequent where grazing is locally reduced, as on steep rocky slopes or hummocks in boggy patches. Livingston (1972) found that stones in pastures helped in the survival of seedlings. If grazing is withdrawn or much reduced, juniper should establish well in these situations if sufficient seed-parents are still surviving. In chalk grassland the survival of juniper seedlings was better with a summer rather than a winter grazing regime (Fitter and Jennings, 1975).

The importance of catastrophic events for successful colonization by juniper is illustrated by the young populations on the Porton Ranges, where there was a sudden cessation of rabbit grazing because of myxomatosis in 1955. For a number of years after this event germination and establishment were successful, but eventually no more plants invaded. By 1971 no plants of under 3 years old were recorded. The reason for this failure of colonization is speculative, but probably the juniper could not germinate and grow in the denser wholly ungrazed vegetation that then developed. A similar flush of invasion and subsequent growth of bushes has been observed at Tynron Juniper Wood National Nature Reserve after a fire (Sykes, 1976). Abandonment of arable land may also produce the same effect.

Even after establishment the young junipers may still be at risk because of grazing. The populations at Porton have been severely damaged by rabbit grazing in the last few years. The 'Breck' population had 3 per cent dead bushes when first seen in 1971, while this had risen to 37 per cent by 1979 (counts of 100 bushes), and on Roche Court it rose from 0 to 22 per cent. The leggy juniper then remaining had little or no foliage still within reach of the rabbits, and any plant which had not grown above rabbit-grazing height of 45–60 cm appeared to have been killed by defoliation; ring-barking was also observed. At Bulford, most juniper comparable in age to that of Porton was still very healthy and ungrazed, but at the northern end of this large colony, some showed rabbit damage. All young stands must therefore be regarded as at risk if the number of rabbits increases, but the effect seems local and therefore potentially controllable.

The older populations at Porton (Figure 5) occur on areas described as pasture in the 1830s, and there are few bushes of under 50 years (Wells *et al.*, 1976). Thus although rabbit grazing ceased at the time of myxomatosis no regeneration occurred in the old stands. Only areas with no old juniper were colonized. The relative failure of young bushes to grow under old remains unexplained; Gilbert (1980) suggested that a specific replant disease could be involved. Old bushes at Porton are generally unhealthy. At Blakes Firs 25 per cent were dead in 1971, while this rose to 50 per cent in 1979. The number of healthy-looking seeds in the berries was also very low in these old bushes.

Whitbarrow on the carboniferous limestone is the oldest population studied (Figure 5). The data for dead bushes are included because although these plants may have died several years ago they do give a further indication of the age of the plants on the site. The ages ranged from 55 to 186 in ring counts. Again the bushes were dying; 42 per cent were dead and 25 per cent were unhealthy.

On these old unshaded stands the life span of juniper is thought to be a factor in the generally senescent appearance of living bushes and the death of others. Individuals do not necessarily die of old age *per se*, but of disease or disorder in which the outcome is influenced by their age, as for example basal rots or windblow. Exceptional individuals can live for long periods, and there are records in the literature of junipers of several hundred years of age. In England the maximum observed so far is 192 for Upper Teesdale (Gilbert, 1980), but in southern England the majority of the bushes appear to live to about 100 years. More details about the life span will be published elsewhere shortly. Generally the life span of populations has been little studied but it is obviously very important in the management of nature reserves, especially for species that do not reproduce vegetatively.

Discussion

Demographic studies of populations show that juniper colonization is often a transient event as conditions suitable for germination and establishment do not usually occur frequently. Most colonies in southern England have restricted age classes with few young plants among the older ones. New areas are colonized as opportunity allows, and die-out occurs in others with succession to woodland, or as the life span of juniper is reached. This life history makes juniper particularly vulnerable to loss as areas suitable for colonization are much less frequently created now than in the past. Even where there are many healthy colonies, as in the Lake District, the eventual outlook may still be bleak if the failure to produce young bushes is prolonged.

On nature reserves active management is needed to ensure continuity, though the knowledge needed to do this is only just beginning to accumulate. If a stand already has young bushes the need for management is less immediately urgent. The life of older bushes can be extended by clearing any vegetation shading out junipers, but ultimately the stand will decline as the juniper life span is reached. This is probably at about 100 years in southern England, but longer in the north. Large numbers of bushes need to be conserved on a site to maintain the associated fauna.

Regrettably no management techniques using natural colonization to produce young juniper stands have been put to practical test. I believe that it will be necessary to produce bare ground with reduced competition from other plants, probably by grazing, burning or disturbance. Areas to be managed for colonization are best sited adjacent to younger rather than older seed-parents. Older sites may have soil seed-banks as dormancy can sometimes be prolonged (Miles and Kinnaird, 1979), but these will deplete progressively as the numbers of local fruiting junipers decline also. In such places the apparently drastic step of burning the senescent juniper could prove the best way of stimulating colony regeneration. Artificial seeding holds some potential if site conditions are satisfactory, but has been little tried so far. Propagation from cuttings or growing from seed in nurseries is practicable if costly. Planting out onto roadsides and amenity sites has been successful, although there is some risk of loss through drought or vandalism. However produced, the young plants will need protection from heavy grazing, and rabbit numbers locally may have to be reduced for several years.

Acknowledgements

I thank the following colleagues and friends for help with this work – Heather Bristowe, Christine Brown, Heather Brundle, J. A. Grant, K. Lakhani, M. G. Morris and T. C. E. Wells.

References

Challinor, D. and Wingate, D. B. (1971). 'The struggle for survival of the Bermuda Cedar', *Biol. Conserv.*, **3**, 220–22.
Diamond, J. M. and May, R. M. (1976). 'Island biogeography and the design of natural reserves', in *Theoretical Ecology: Principles and Applications* (Ed. R. M. May), pp. 163–86, Blackwell Scientific Publications, Oxford.
Fitter, A. H. and Jennings, R. D. (1975). 'The effects of sheep grazing on the growth and survival of seedling junipers (*Juniperus communis* L.)', *J. Appl. Ecol.*, **12**, 637–42.
Gilbert, O. L. (1980). 'Juniper in Upper Teesdale', *J. Ecol.*, **68**, 1013–24.

Kerr, A. J. (1968). *Tynron Juniper Wood National Nature Reserve. Management and Research 1959–68*, Nature Conservancy Council, Edinburgh.

Livingston, R. B. (1972). 'Influence of birds, stones and soil on the establishment of pasture juniper, *Juniperus communis*, and red cedar, *J. virginiana* in New England pastures', *Ecology*, **53**, 1141–7.

Miles, K. and Kinnaird, J. W. (1979). 'The establishment and regeneration of Birch, Juniper and Scots Pine in the Scottish highlands', *Scot. For.*, **33**, 102–17.

Sykes, J. M. (1976). 'Regeneration of juniper. A summary of data collected at Tynron Juniper Wood NNR 1960–1974'. Institute of Terrestrial Ecology (NERC), Project 387, Report to the Nature Conservancy Council.

Ward, L. K. (1973). 'The conservation of Juniper I. Present status of Juniper in southern England', *J. Appl. Ecol.*, **10**, 165–88.

Ward, L. K. (1977). 'The conservation of Juniper: The associated fauna, with special reference to southern England', *J. Appl. Ecol.*, **14**, 81–120.

Ward, L. K. (1979). 'Scrub dynamics and management', in *Ecology and Design in Amenity Land Management* (Eds. S. E. Wright and G. P. Buckley), pp. 109–27, Wye College.

Ward, L. K. and Lakhani, K. H. (1977). 'The conservation of Juniper: The fauna of food-plant island sites in southern England', *J. Appl. Ecol.*, **14**, 121–35.

Wells, T. C. E., Sheail, J., Ball, D. F. and Ward, L. K. (1976). 'Ecological studies on the Porton Ranges: Relationships between vegetation, soils and land-use history', *J. Ecol.*, **64**, 589–626.

The Biological Aspects of Rare Plant Conservation
Edited by Hugh Synge
© 1981 John Wiley & Sons Ltd.

27
Aspects of the ecology of *Staavia dodii* in the South Western Cape of South Africa

E. J. MOLL *Botany Department, University of Cape Town*
and
A. A. GUBB *McGregor Museum, Kimberley, South Africa*

Summary

The obligate seed regenerating species *Staavia dodii* is one of the 1244 threatened plant species in the Cape Floral Kingdom. The 14 known populations of the species are confined to rocky, sandstone ridges in the Cape of Good Hope Nature Reserve and in the past have been subjected to pressures from flower-pickers and frequent bush fires. The species has a definite vegetative growth season in early spring to summer, it flowers from late spring to late winter, and the seeds are shed in spring. Germination is apparently stimulated by fire and seedling mortality in the first year is very high. The first flowers are produced some 5–8 years after fire with maximum flower production occurring on 12–16-year-old plants. Individuals over 20 years old have usually started to senesce, and about 30 years is apparently the maximum age the species can attain. As individuals age they produce fewer, progressively shorter shoots, hence fewer infloresences which contain fewer flowers and fewer seeds. The Cape of Good Hope Nature Reserve is subjected to a fire management programme which, if *S. dodii* is to be properly conserved, must aim at a fire frequency of 10 years or more.

Introduction

Staavia dodii Bolus is just one of the 1244 threatened plants in the Cape Floral Kingdom (Hall *et al.*, 1980). It belongs to the essentially Cape endemic family Bruniaceae (Goldblatt, 1978), a member of the Rosales. Ten species of *Staavia* are recognized (Dyer, 1975) and of these four are considered rare and endangered and one is already extinct. *Staavia dodii*, a slender, sympodially branched shrub up to 1.5 m (rarely 2 m) high, is an obligate seed-regenerating species after fire, and is presently confined to the Cape of Good Hope Nature Reserve (Figure 1). The extent of its former distribution is unknown. It is perhaps the most attractive member of the genus. The tightly packed flowers, which open spirally from the outside in a clockwise direction, are borne in terminal heads surrounded by oblong-acute, opaque, white bracts with a spread of 30–40 mm, giving it the

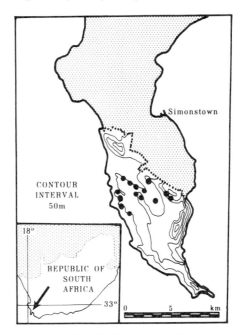

Figure 1   The 14 known populations of *Staavia dodii* in the Cape of Good Hope Nature Reserve

appearance of a composite (Figure 2). The simple, linear-elliptic, spirally arranged leaves tipped with minute black mucros are 8–12 mm long. The plants are relatively shallow-rooted (less than 1.5 m) with little or no tap-root, and the fine roots have a vesicular-arbuscular mycorrhiza association.

The reason for the apparent decline of the species is said to be due to flower-picking and frequent burning to provide new growth for large herbivores (both domestic, when the reserve was a farm and, since 1938, for the various non-indigenous and more recently indigenous ungulate species). Today frequent burning is the only real threat to *S. dodii*, and the reserve authorities are becoming increasingly aware of their responsibilities in conserving this and some 25 other endemic species occurring in the reserve (Taylor, 1969).

The climate of the reserve is of a typical mediterranean type (Figure 3). A feature of the *S. dodii* communities is that they occur on exposed, rocky, sandstone ridges (see Figure 2) subjected to the full blast of the prevailing southeast summer winds (which may gust up to 100 km per hr) and to the northwest winter winds. *S. dodii* occurs as scattered or clumped, usually even-aged individuals, in shallow, coarse-sandy, characteristically low nutrient soils common to the fynbos vegetation of the southwestern Cape mountains (Lambrechts, 1980). This fynbos vegetation (Taylor, 1978; Kruger, 1979) is a typical heathland (Specht, 1979).

Figure 2   A 12-year-old population of *Staavia dodii* in full flower. The other large shrubs in the photograph are mostly *Mimetes hartogii* and the surrounding tussocked, grass-like plants are members of the Restionaceae. The insets from left to right show: a 1-year-old seedling (fine scale in mm), a close-up of an inflorescence showing a wasp visiting an open flower, and the top portion of the stems of three *Staavia dodii* plants to indicate the degree and length of branching with age. Note that the 8-year-old plant (left) is unbranched and has flowered for the first time; the 12-year-old plant (centre) has produced six flowering stems in the current year; and the 25-year-old plant (right) has produced but one stem in the current year – the previous year's inflorescence stalk is arrowed

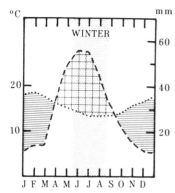

Figure 3 An ombrothermic climate-diagram indicating the typical mediterranean climate of the Cape of Good Hope Nature Reserve (Walter *et al.*, 1975). The wet, winter season is stippled

The aim of the present study of *S. dodii* was to investigate the biology and ecology of this rare species so that the reserve managers could be offered guidelines for the long-term conservation of the species. As fire is the important management tool it was apparent that the response of *S. dodii* to fire would be an important aspect of the study.

Shoot and flower growth, and population longevity

Phenogrammes for three different aged *Staavia dodii* populations (Figure 4) show that although new vegetative buds (dotted lines) are visible below the inflorescences from the beginning of winter (the wet season), growth does not really start until mid-winter. The younger plants start growing earlier but maximum growth for all plants, irrespective of their age, is in late spring to mid-summer. It is of note that in the period April 1979 to June 1980 while *S. dodii* plants were being carefully observed very little herbivory was recorded. The only damage recorded was in the 12-year-old community in spring when the larvae of an insect attacked the growing tips of some shoots which resulted in the depression in the growth curve shown (see Figure 4). These 12-year-old plants were all growing in a cluster between large sandstone boulders (17 individuals) and so presented a large target area for a herbivore (see Figure 2). None of the other plants in the population nor of the younger or older plants measured were eaten.

By the end of summer or early autumn (March) all vegetative growth had ceased and the terminal inflorescences, which began opening in mid-summer and which remained open until the middle to end of winter, were all fully developed. A close study of the phenogrammes shows that the 12-year-old *S. dodii* plants flower for longer than the younger and older plants, and that they produce more seeds.

Individual flowers open for a period of about 4 days and, from observations over a few years (mainly by Gubb, who was at one time employed as a Ranger in the reserve), the chief pollinating agents appear to be insects, a large variety of

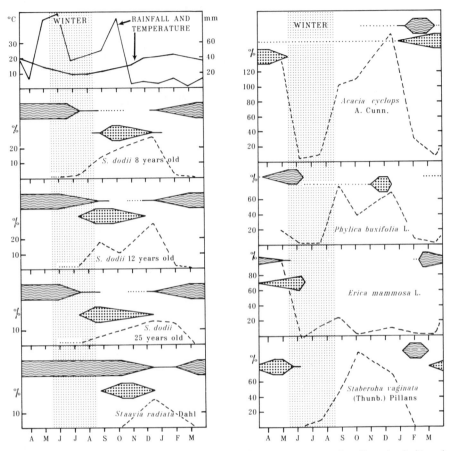

Figure 4 The net growth (of ten marked shoots) as a percentage for *Staavia dodii* and various other species (only five marked shoots of each) in the same community. The mean monthly rainfall and temperature recorded at adjacent climate stations (one for temperature and three for rainfall) for the period during which the plants were measured is given for comparison. The wet winter period is stippled. Flowering times (wavy lines) and periods when ripe seeds were present (large dots) are given for all species

which visit the flowers; they include beetles, ants, wasps (see Figure 2 inset) and bees, and perhaps even sunbirds. From pollination it takes some 6–10 weeks for the seed to develop. Towards the end of winter the carpel, which is now a brown husk, shears from the receptacle and is lifted above the surrounding mass of bracts. This leaves the dry, dehiscent fruit with the light brown, hard seed resting loosely on the inflorescence surface where the seed is free to be shaken off as the shrub is buffeted by wind. Some 8–15 seeds are produced per inflorescence and released mainly in spring.

Individual inflorescences may contain from 20–40 flowers, the former on old

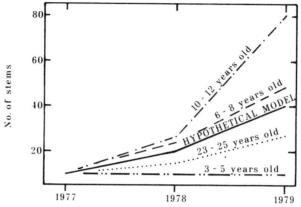

Figure 5 A diagrammatic representation of the degree of branching of *Staavia dodii* related to age. In 1979 3-year-old branches ($n = 10$) were removed from four populations (5-, 8-, 12- and 25-years-old), and from these branches the 2- and 1-year-old branches were removed and counted (see also Figure 2 inset). A hypothetical, dichotomously branching population has been given for comparison. The results show that the 5-year-old population which had not yet commenced flowering remains unbranched; that the 25-year-old population is senescing and producing only a few branches; that the 8-year-old population which has just begun to flower is beginning to branch rapidly; and that the 12-year-old population is producing many branches each year

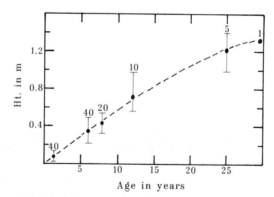

Figure 6 As *Staavia dodii* ages so it grows in height. The curve above is based on the mean height of a number of individuals in various populations (the sample size and range of heights measured is given for each population)

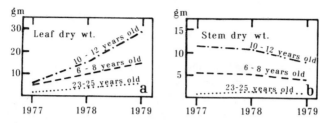

Figure 7   The leaf (a) and stem (b) dry weight from the twig
samples from different aged *Staavia dodii* populations (see also
Figure 5)

plants over 20 years old, and the latter on young and mature plants 8–16 years
old. The size of these inflorescences, excluding the surrounding bracts, varies from
6 to 10 mm in diameter respectively (see Figure 2 inset).

The first flowers are produced when the young plants are from 5 to 8 years old;
at this stage the plant consists of an erect, unbranched stem 0.2–0.5 m tall. From
then on new vegetative shoots are produced from the base of the inflorescence and

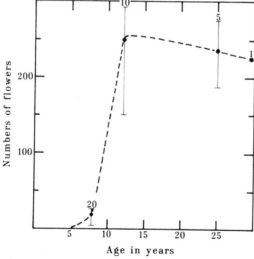

Figure 8   The numbers of inflorescences produced by *Staavia dodii* increase rapidly when the
plants are from 8–12-years old. From about
15–17-years old there is not only a gradual tailing-
off of inflorescence numbers per individual, but
there is also a decrease in the number of flowers
produced per inflorescence, so the seed production
potential of older individuals is greatly reduced.
The size of sample and range of inflorescence
numbers per individual in the various age classes is
indicated for each sample

the semi-dichotomously branching habit is assumed (Figure 5). Initially the vegetative growth is vigorous, but once plants are from 16 to 20 years old they begin to senesce and growth is drastically diminished (Figure 6 and see also Figure 2 inset). The biomass of new shoots is greatly reduced in old plants (Figure 7) as is the number of shoots produced from the base of each inflorescence (Figure 8). By the time bushes are about 25 years old they have begun to senesce and in some cases are already dead (one exceptionally old and large bush some 30 years old and nearly 1.3 m tall was discovered amongst large boulders where it had been protected from fire).

As the plants age they not only produce relatively fewer shoots and hence fewer flowers (Figure 8), but they also hold their leaves for a shorter period of time. Young plants up to 8 years old retain their leaves for 4 and even 5 years. By the time the bushes are mature (about 12 years old) leaves are retained for 3 years and are shed in their fourth summer. Old senescing bushes (over 20 years old) shed their leaves in the third summer. So there is a trend to hold leaves for a longer period in young, vigorously growing bushes.

Regeneration and establishment

Studies of soil-stored seed show that most seeds are found relatively close to the parent plant (Figure 9a), though some may apparently be washed further afield by surface run-off. Once a fire has been through a population, regeneration occurs freely with most seedlings distributed in a circle round the parent plant (Figure 9b), with only scattered individuals at greater distances. Seedling growth occurs some months after a fire (see Figure 2 inset) and appears to be related to soil moisture rather than season of burn. Most tiny seedlings have been found in autumn. Initially growth is slow, with first flowering occurring when the plants are

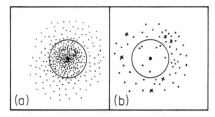

Figure 9   Diagrammatic representation of seeds in the soil under the canopy (circled) of a 10-year-old *Staavia dodii* individual (a). Following a burn the number and approximate position of seedlings beneath a burnt *Staavia dodii* individual (b) in May 1979 are indicated. By May 1980 only six seedlings (×) had survived

5–8 years old. Seedling mortality rate is apparently high. Of the 56 seedlings counted in May 1979, following a fire in March 1979, only six had survived in May 1980.

Observation of all the *Staavia dodii* communities over a number of years has shown that virtually no regeneration will take place unless the community is burnt. In all cases careful searching of unburnt communities has revealed only one or two young plants in each community. There are no unburnt, senescent *S. dodii* communities that are more than 30 years old, however, and it is not known for how long soil-stored seed remains viable. In fact all attempts to germinate seeds artificially have failed and it is not known how fire triggers germination. The seeds imbibe water readily but are quickly infected by a variety of fungi, the spores of which are almost certainly held by a sticky substance which coats the seeds.

Community phenology

A phytosociological classification of the plant communities of the Cape of Good Hope Nature Reserve (Taylor, 1969) indicated that *Staavia dodii* occurs in a recognizable community, the *Staavia dodii–Saltera sarocolla* community. *Acacia cyclops*, an Australian weed, is an aggressive invader of this community (particularly those nearer the coast), along with a great number of other communities not only in the reserve but in many parts of the Cape Floral Kingdom (Milton, 1980). In order to establish the phenological relationship of *Staavia dodii* to some of the more common associated species and that of *Acacia cyclops* in particular, a selection of species was also measured in 1979/80 (Figure 4). These studies showed that except for *Staavia radiata*, a vegetative resprouter after fire with a very similar phenogramme to *S. dodii*, and *Staberoha vaginata* (an aphyllous, evergreen hemicryptophyte belonging to the Restionaceae), that the growth of the selected associated species was not only more vigorous but almost more continuous throughout the year. *Erica mammosa* had a major growth flush in autumn, *Phylica buxifolia* grew mainly in spring and summer, and *Acacia cyclops* grew most vigorously in spring and summer, but also grew appreciably in autumn.

These species have quite different flowering and fruiting patterns compared to the two species of *Staavia*. Flowering in all cases is for a very much shorter period of time (summer to autumn). Fruits of *Acacia cyclops* mature in the following summer and autumn, and in this respect the species is unique amongst the Australian invasive *Acacia* spp. in the Cape Floral Kingdom (Milton, 1980). The fruits of *Phylica buxifolia* mature in early summer and this event is followed by the initiation of flower buds and a decline in vegetative growth. *Erica mammosa* grows, flowers and fruits almost simultaneously in autumn, and *Staberoha vaginata* flowers once the culms have ceased elongation and seeds are produced immediately and have fallen by early winter.

The phenological studies show that both species of *Staavia* have relatively short and distinct summer growth periods, and have flowers for most of the year, with a distinct seed release period in spring.

Management implications

As *Staavia dodii* is an obligate seed regenerating species after fire, and because fire has been shown to be a vital factor in stimulating mass regeneration, it is apparently essential that the species is burnt from time to time to ensure healthy populations. Since the first flowers are only produced from 5 to 8 years after fire, and as the plants take a number of years to produce more than just a few inflorescences per individual, it is assumed that it takes 10–16 years before a size-able seed-store is built up. As the individuals only begin to senesce when they are some 16–20 years or more old, it is apparent that the time interval between successive fires must be at least 10 years, preferably 15–20 years, if a vigorous and viable population is to be maintained. A further important research project that should be carried out in relation to the management of these populations is the determination of the length of time that soil-stored seed remains viable – this needs to be established before the population dynamics of *S. dodii* can be fully appreciated.

From the information gained in this study it is clear that a fire frequency of less than 10 years will have a detrimental effect on *S. dodii* as fire stimulates germination of soil-stored seed. Initially a fire régime based on less than a 10-year cycle would reduce the population size and once this reaches a critical low the population could succumb; there is some evidence to suggest that this point may already have been reached in 1 of the 14 populations. Since the fynbos vegetation of the reserve is fire-prone, management will have to ensure that adequate steps are taken to prevent wild fires sweeping through the *S. dodii* communities at too-frequent intervals. Fortunately there are 14 of these communities scattered over a fairly wide area (see Figure 1), and because the terrain is rugged with a great number of exposed rocks and boulders, it is to be expected that clean fires are the exception, unless there is a massive accumulation of fuel. Kruger (1980) has discussed the flammable nature of fynbos, which is extremely high because of the fuel characteristics and the dry, windy summer conditions, experienced in this mediterranean climatic region. In this respect fynbos is similar to all other mediterranean climate vegetation where fire is a significant factor of the environment (Mooney and Conrad, 1977).

The fynbos communities in the Cape of Good Hope Nature Reserve are capable of burning at any time of the year following a few days of dry weather. The most fire-prone season is summer, but fires in autumn and spring are also common (G. Wright, Warden of the Cape of Good Hope Nature Reserve, pers. comm. 1980). *Staavia dodii*, however, because it relies on soil-stored seed for survival, is not threatened by the time of year that a fire may destroy the community, but rather by the frequency of successive burns. It must not be forgotten that other species (and the reserve does contain another 24 known rare and endangered plant species) may be threatened not only by fire frequency but by fire season too, so more detailed autecological studies of other critical species are needed to enable a total management strategy to be devised.

These suggestions for the management of *S. dodii* must be seen holistically in the context of fynbos management and conservation in the Cape Floral Kingdom. It has been suggested that technological man has been responsible for a much increased fire frequency resulting in a general diminution of the size of the woody element in fynbos (Moll *et al.*, 1980), and that a fire cycle of at least 40 years is more natural. It is known that under conditions of prolonged intervals between fires, fuel build-up is such that fires may be devastating. Yet as long as such fires do not destroy species like *S. dodii*, they may benefit other species like *Leucospermum conocarpodendron* (L.) Buek and *Mimetes hartogii* R.Br., both large woody members (up to 2.5 m tall) of the Proteaceae, which are apparently not regenerating successfully under the present fire régime.

To conclude: a great deal more research is required into fire as an ecological factor in fynbos and the long-term conservation of *Staavia dodii* is not the only important consideration, but fynbos community conservation *per se* is the vital issue.

References

Dyer, R. A. (1975). *The Genera of Southern African Flowering Plants, 1: Dicotyledons*, Dept. Agric. Tech. Services, Pretoria.

Goldblatt, P. (1978). 'An analysis of the flora of southern Africa: its characteristics, relationships, and origins', *Ann. Missouri Bot. Gard.*, **65**, 369–436.

Hall, A. V., de Winter, M., de Winter, B., and van Oosterhout, S. A. M. (1980). *Threatened Plants of Southern Africa*, SA National Sci. Prog. Report.

Kruger, F. J. (1979). 'South African Heathlands', in *Heathlands and Related Shrublands of the World, A. Descriptive Studies* (Ed. R. L. Specht), pp. 19–80, Elsevier, Amsterdam.

Kruger, F. J. (1980). 'Fire', in *Fynbos Ecology: A Preliminary Synthesis* (Eds. J. Day, W. R. Siegfried, G. N. Louw, and M. L. Jarman), pp. 43–57, SA National Sci. Prog., Report 40.

Lambrechts, J. J. N. (1980). 'Geology, geomorphology and soils', in *Fynbos Ecology: A Preliminary Synthesis* (Eds. J. Day, W. R. Siegfried, G. N. Louw, and M. L. Jarman), pp. 16–26, SA National Sci. Prog., Report 40.

Milton, S. J. (1980). *Studies of Australian Acacias in the South Western Cape, South Africa*, unpublished MSc thesis, University of Cape Town.

Moll, E. J., McKenzie, B., and McLachlan, D. (1980). 'A possible explanation for the lack of trees in the fynbos, Cape Province, South Africa', *Biol. Conserv.*, **17**, 221–8.

Mooney, H. A. and Conrad, C. E. (Technical Coordinators) (1977). *Proceedings of the Symposium on the Environmental Consequences of Fire and Fuel Management in Mediterranean Ecosystems*, USDA Forest Service General Technical Report WO-3.

Specht, R. L. (1979). 'Heathlands and related shrublands of the world', in *Heathlands and Related Shrublands of the World, A. Descriptive Studies* (Ed. R. L. Specht), pp. 1–18, Elsevier, Amsterdam.

Taylor, H. C. (1969). *A Vegetation Survey of the Cape of Good Hope Nature Reserve,* unpublished MSc thesis, University of Cape Town.

Taylor, H. C. (1978). 'Capensis', in *Biogeography and Ecology of Southern Africa* (Ed. M. J. A. Werger), pp. 171–229, Junk, The Hague.

Walter, H., Harnickell, E., and Mueller-Dombois, D. (1975). *Climate Diagram Maps of the Individual Continents and the Ecological Climatic Regions of the Earth: Supplement to the Vegetation Monographs,* Springer, Berlin.

The Biological Aspects of Rare Plant Conservation
Edited by Hugh Synge
© 1981 John Wiley & Sons Ltd.

28
Autecological and population studies of *Orothamnus zeyheri* in the Cape of South Africa

C. BOUCHER *Botanical Research Institute, Stellenbosch, South Africa*

Summary

Orothamnus zeyheri, an attractive montane species from a few localities in South Africa, was critically endangered in 1968. Following the introduction of deliberate burning, the population has greatly increased in size. This paper reviews experimental studies on the autecology and population dynamics of the species. The age structure of the populations is discussed; the species shows cyclical fluctuations in population size depending on the interval between fires. Both hoeing and burning were found to stimulate regeneration from seed, but seedling mortality is high. The effect of picking is discussed. Further threats to the survival of the species, e.g. from pathogenic fungi, are outlined.

Introduction

Orothamnus zeyheri Pappe ex Hook. (Figure 1) is a monotypic genus of the Proteaceae. It is restricted to the Kogelberg State Forest in the southern end of the Hottentots Holland Mountains and to the Eddie Rubenstein Reserve in the Klein River Mountains of the south-western Cape Province of South Africa, in Mountain Fynbos vegetation.

This attractive montane species has excited the imagination of botanist and layman alike since the first specimen was purchased by Carl Zeyher from a flower picker at Cape Town. Carl Pappe subsequently described and illustrated it in the March 1848 edition of *Curtis's Botanical Magazine*. Its habitat preference for montane seepage areas and the rose-like appearance of its inflorescence led to its common name of Marsh Rose. As a cut-flower, *O. zeyheri* is esteemed because the inflorescence has exceptional lasting qualities of more than 1 month in a vase.

The terminal inflorescence of 22–27 flowers becomes lateral following shoot extension. The branches are dichotomous, becoming progressively shorter as the plant gets older with the inflorescences later being clustered at the ends of the branches. A maximum number of 23 hard-shelled nuts have been recorded in an inflorescence (Van der Merwe, 1977). The seed is dropped together with an attached parachute apparatus, within a month or two of flowering.

In 1968 the exact locations of three *Orothamnus* sites were pinpointed in the Kogelberg State Forest. These populations contained a total of ten plants. The

Figure 1   *Orothamnus zeyheri* Pappe ex Hook.

population in the Klein River Mountains near Hermanus consisted of 24 plants when it was devastated by an accidental fire in 1968. This latter colony was the subject of an intensive study by Van der Merwe (1977).

For many years, in response to the repeated agitation by botanists such as Levyns (1924), Pillans (1924) and Compton (1934), who condemned the destructive effects of fire on the Cape Flora, fire protection had been followed as a routine management policy. During the late 1960s the validity of this policy was questioned because good regeneration of the virtually extinct *Serruria florida* (Thunb.) Knight (Proteaceae) had occurred after an accidental fire in its natural habitat and because the only *Orothamnus* regeneration in recent times had occurred in fire belts or on footpaths.

The Department of Forestry consequently modified their fire protection policy during 1968. A series of controlled burns were experimentally undertaken in the mountains of the Kogelberg State Forest in an attempt to stimulate the regeneration of *Orothamnus* and of the more than 50 other endemic or near-endemic species occurring there. The first area to be burnt was some 1700 hectares in extent and included known *Orothamnus* localities.

The aims of this study of *Orothamnus*, which was started in 1968, are:

1. to collect incidental environmental data from the localities
2. to monitor its population dynamics
3. to measure its growth rates
4. to determine population juvenile periods
5. to record phenological information.

This study coincided with a survey of the vegetation of a surrounding 2400 hectare area (Boucher, 1977*a* and *b*, 1978). The inaccessible terrain, the danger of damaging plants and the habitat through trampling and the possible distribution of the pathogenic root-rot fungus *Phytophthora cinnamomi*, were factors limiting the scope of the study.

Results

Orothamnus zeyheri grows in the Winter Rainfall Region of South Africa yet the precipitation patterns in its habitat are extremely complex owing to the orographic effects of the mountains. Precipitation from the winter north-westerly winds (1000–12 000 mm per year) is complemented by over 500 mm of moisture being precipitated from the summer south-easterly clouds (Fuggle and Ashton, 1979; Van der Merwe, 1977; Weather Bureau, 1960). The weather is variable. Afternoon sea breezes alternate with strong south-easterly winds during the summer months, and occasional hot desiccating gusty winds occur especially during the cold, wet winter months. Snow falls are rare and of short duration. Winter mean temperatures are lower than in summer and are described in more detail, along with other weather conditions, in Boucher (1978).

Generally *Orothamnus* grows on cool steep (up to 45°) south-facing mountain slopes between 460 m and 850 m in altitude in very acid (pH = 4.00) peaty areas. The results of an analysis of soil from one locality are listed in Table 1.

On two occasions the area surrounding living plants of *Orothamnus* was cleared by hoeing, once in November and once in December. Fire was used on six occasions, twice in February and once in July, August, September and December. The fire in September was caused by lightning.

Both hoeing and burning resulted, in all instances, in regeneration of *Orothamnus* from seed, but fewer seedlings were found in areas burned during the wetter winter period (July and August) than those burned during the drier summer period. Little value, however, can be attributed to this observation because there

Table 1   Soil analysis results from a
locality of *Orothamnus zeyheri*

---

pH (in H_2O): 3.7
Resistance: 1080 ohms
Carbon percentage: 48.2%
Percentage weight loss at 600°C: 88.2%
Ca^{++} mc/100 gm (NH_4Ac): 6.32
Mg^{++} mc/100 gm (NH_4Ac): 9.71
Na^+ mc/100 gm (NH_4Ac): 2.20
K^+ mc/100 gm (NH_4Ac): 0.41
Exchangeable Al^{+++} mc/100 gm: 18.65

---

are no data about the size of the seed store in the soil at the different populations. The interval between the treatment application and the first appearance of seedlings varied between $3\frac{1}{2}$ months and $2\frac{1}{2}$ years.

The number of juvenile plant mortalities is high and, in one instance, a survival rate of only 10 per cent was recorded. The reasons for the high death rate are: (a) intra- and interspecific competition; (b) unsuitable local habitat conditions; (c) predator damage (i.e. rats, baboons and fungal attacks); (d) human trampling near the plants.

Branches of mature plants generally have bare stems with distal clusters of leaves. Picking an inflorescence, together with all the leaves, generally causes the branch to die or, in the case of an unbranched individual, it results in the death of the plant. Juvenile and young mature plants sometimes recover from flower picking because leaves are still present right down the stem. Trampling near plants leads to root damage and impeded soil water movement, as a result of compaction, which often leads to death of the plants. The pathogenic fungus *Phytophthora cinnamomi* has been isolated from dead plants in three distinct localities. An evaluation of this fungus and its threat to the Cape Flora has recently been discussed by Von Broembsen (1979). *Otomys saundersiae*, a bog rat, has been responsible for the destruction of more than half of the 180 plants in one colony. Raitt (in prep.) has determined that sodium accumulations in the leaves of *Orothamnus* can be double the quantity that causes leaf burn in some fruits. Possibly this indigenous rat utilizes the species not only for its food value, but also because it is a source of salt in this nutrient-poor heathland environment.

The growth rate of *Orothamnus* plants increases proportionately with age until flowering maturity is reached at an average age of 9 years (Figure 2) and at a height of about 1.08 m (Figure 3) for 50 per cent of the individuals in two populations in the Kogelberg State Forest. Plants in the Hermanus Reserve and those in cultivation mature at a younger age. The growth rate is slower in the higher montane and drier habitats. Rapid growth takes place during autumn and spring. Inflorescences have been observed during every month of the year with December and January having the least number of flowers.

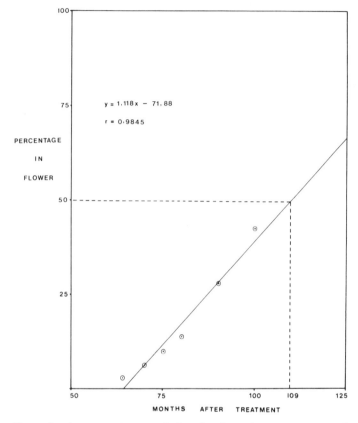

Figure 2   A regression analysis showing the percentage of *Orothamnus* individuals in flower in relation to time, in months, following burning or hoeing treatments

The species regenerates from seed after fires; its seed production and the seed store in the soil are important criteria determining the successful maintenance of population levels. Initially a single inflorescence is produced on each branch. This number increases from the fourth flowering year depending on the vigour of the plant. Approximately 15 mature nuts are produced in each inflorescence. Under normal circumstances a 12-year-old mature plant would have produced about 340 nuts which should be an adequate minimum number of seeds necessary to ensure the survival of the population although a longer interval would be preferable for a larger seed store to accumulate in the soil.

The regeneration of *Orothamnus* at a site where no plants had been seen for 19 years gives an indication of the longevity of its hard-shelled nuts. A considerable store of viable seed could therefore accumulate in a 15–24-year-old population, provided seed predation is not excessive.

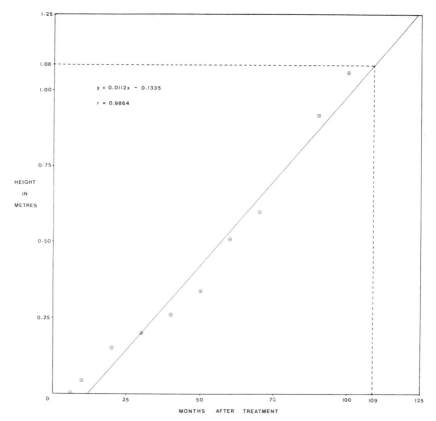

Figure 3   A regression analysis of the average height of 87 *Orothamnus* individuals
in relation to time, in months, following burning or hoeing treatments

The species regenerated well after a wild fire in 1945. For instance, one colony
was estimated to have some 450 seedlings in 1947. By 1968, this colony (Figure
4) had dwindled to nine plants. This suggests that the plants generally have a life-
span of less than 23 years. The colony was cleared of vegetation during 1970
(Figure 5) and it had reached a post-disturbance peak of some 800 plants by
1973. The daughter population (Figure 6) was therefore 75 per cent larger than
the parent population.

The present populations vary between 9 and 12 years in age. It is premature to
draw any conclusions about the optimum fire interval, but it appears as if a
minimum period of 15 years would be a reasonable approximation. Evidence
indicates, too, that the accompanying slow-maturing rare species, such as
Berzelia dregeana Colozza, *Mimetes argenteus* Knight and *Protea stokoei*
Phillips would also require a similar minimum inter-fire period.

There are seventeen known populations of *Orothamnus* in the Kogelberg State

Figure 4   The straggly moribund remains of an *Orothamnus* population some 20
years after a fire (photograph by E. G. H. Oliver)

Figure 5   The same area as in Figure 4 after clearing by hoeing and after the construction of a security fence around the remaining plants

Figure 6   This daughter population had 75 per cent more individuals than its parent at their maximum population levels

Forest. A total of 1956 plants was counted during maximum population levels. This is not a true reflection of the maximum number of plants which occurred in the area after the treatments, because some populations were only discovered after they had reached flowering maturity and deaths must have occurred during the juvenile period (Boucher and McCann, 1975). A count in January 1980 revealed that there were 1213 plants alive. This is a considerable improvement on the 10 plants known to exist in 1968 (Figure 7).

Fire is a more acceptable management tool than hoeing because it is cheaper, less disturbing to the substrate and is natural. By hoeing, the living plants are preserved but it could encourage the spread of *Phytophthora cinnamomi*.

Conclusions

Orthamnus zeyheri exhibits cyclical fluctuations in population sizes dependent on the length of the inter-fire interval. The longer the interval, the fewer the number of remaining plants. The species could survive a fire-free period of 34 years although a 15-year cycle would probably be optimal.

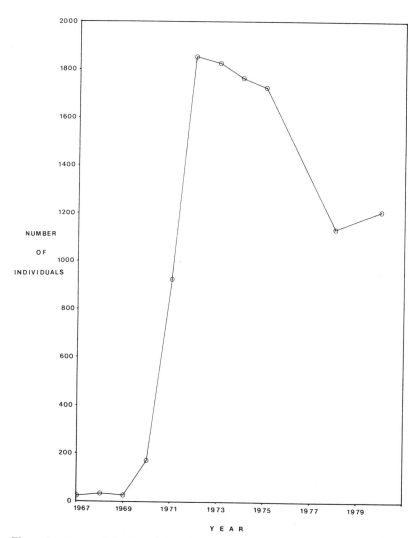

Figure 7   Curve of the fluctuations in numbers of *Orothamnus* individuals in the Kogelberg State Forest

The short-term danger to the survival of this montane species lies in too frequent fires, excessive trampling in populations and through an increase in *Phytophthora cinnamomi* infestations.

References

Boucher, C. (1977a). 'A provisional check list of flowering plants and ferns in the Cape Hangklip area', *J. S. Afr. Bot.*, **43**(1), 57–80.

Boucher, C. (1977*b*). 'Cape Hangklip area. I. The application of association-analysis, homogeneity functions and Braun–Blanquet techniques in the description of south-western Cape vegetation', *Bothalia*, **12**(2), 293–300.

Boucher, C. (1978). 'Cape Hangklip area. II. The vegetation', *Bothalia*, **12**(3), 455–97.

Boucher, C. and McCann, G. (1975). 'The *Orothamnus* saga', *Veld & Flora*, **61**(2), 2–5.

Compton, R. H. (1934). 'The results of veld burning', *The Education Gazette*, **33**, 644–55, Dept. Public Education, Cape of Good Hope.

Fuggle, R. F. and Ashton, E. R. (1979). 'Climate', in *Fynbos Ecology: A Preliminary Synthesis* (Eds. J. Day, W. R. Siegfried, G. N. Louw, and M. L. Jarman), pp. 7–15, S.A. National Sci. Prog., Report 40.

Levyns, M. R. (1924). 'Some observations on the effects of bush fires on the vegetation of the Cape Peninsula', *S. Afr. J. Sci.*, **21**, 346–7.

Pappe, C. (1848). '*Orothamnus Zeyheri*', *Curtis's Bot. Mag.*, **74**, t. 4357.

Pillans, N. S. (1924). 'Destruction of indigenous vegetation by burning on the Cape Peninsula', *S. Afr. J. Sci.*, **21**, 348–50.

Van der Merwe, P. (1977). 'Die morfologie en voortplanting van *Orothamnus zeyheri* (Proteaceae)', in *Cape Department of Nature and Environmental Conservation Research Report: Plants*, pp. 1–209.

Von Broembsen, S. (1979). '*Phytophthora cinnamomi* – a threat to the Western Cape flora?', *Veld & Flora*, **65**(2), 53–5.

Weather Bureau (1960). 'The weather bureau since Union and the weather climate of South Africa', in *Official Year Book*, **30**, Pretoria Weather Bureau.

The Biological Aspects of Rare Plant Conservation
Edited by Hugh Synge
© 1981 John Wiley & Sons Ltd.

29
The monospecific tropical forest of the Ghanaian endemic tree *Talbotiella gentii*

M. D. SWAINE *Department of Botany, University of Aberdeen, Scotland*
and
J. B. HALL *20 Fishergate, Ripon, North Yorkshire, England*

Summary

Talbotiella gentii is a small evergreen tree restricted to the drier parts of the forest zone of Ghana where it occurs as small, localized stands on rocky hills. Both canopy and understorey consist almost entirely of *Talbotiella*. Forests are known from other parts of tropical Africa which similarly exhibit unexplained dominance by one species of Caesalpiniaceous tree, though none seem to exclude competing species as completely as does *T. gentii*. The *Talbotiella* stands are endangered by forest clearing for charcoal making, and by plantation programmes. More effective conservation is needed to permit further investigation of their unique ecology.

Introduction

Tropical forest is notorious for its species-richness: it is not unusual to find several hundred tree species on one hectare. Great interest therefore attaches to those exceptional tropical forests dominated by one tree species, especially, as is the case with the *Talbotiella* forests, when they occur adjacent to more typical mixed forest under similar environmental conditions. *Talbotiella gentii* is not known outside Ghana; the genus *Talbotiella* includes two further species in eastern Nigeria and Cameroun.

Distribution and ecology

Talbotiella gentii is found only in a restricted part of the forest area of Ghana (Figure 1). It is confined to the driest forest types: Southern Marginal and Southeast Outlier (Hall and Swaine, 1976). Figure 1 shows some localities within the general area of the Dry Semi-deciduous type; in fact these sites are isolated patches of Southern Marginal forest-type on rocky hills where water retention is poor.

The tree is known only in hilly country where the soil is interrupted by rock

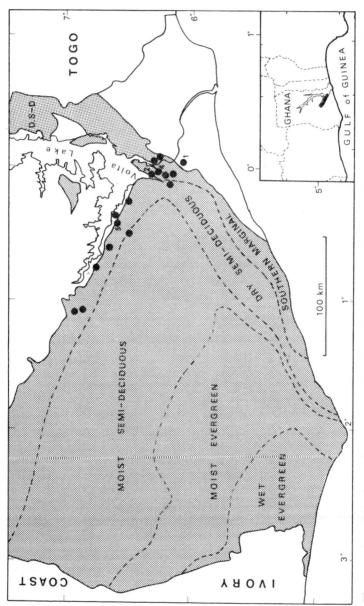

Figure 1 Localities for *Talbotiella gentii* in Ghana (●). 1 Krobo, 2 Yongwa Forest Reserve, 4 Sapawsu Forest Reserve, 5 Worobong, see Table 1. The forest zone is shown stippled, and is divided into the major forest types. (D.S–D = Dry Semi-deciduous)

Table 1   Environmental conditions at five *Talbotiella gentii* localities in Ghana

Sample number (see Figure 1)	Location	Geology	Total exchangeable bases (m-equiv. per 100 g)	Percent saturation	pH	Organic carbon (%)	Approx. annual precipitation (mm)
1	Krobo	Basic gneiss	22	96	6.6	2.9	750
2	Yongwa F.R.	Quartzites/Shales	12	100	6.6	1.6	1000
3	Yongwa F.R.	Quartzites/Shales	2	10	4.0	3.9	1000
4	Sapawsu F.R.	Quartzites/Shales	2	20	4.2	2.5	1000
5	Worobong	Sandstone	5	88	5.6	1.1	1250

outcrops. Its distribution spans several geological formations including Voltaian sandstones (Kwahu area), quartzites and shales of the Togo Series (Akwapim escarpment), and Dahomeyan basic gneiss (Krobo Mountain, Accra Plains).

Partly as a result of this diversity of parent material, and partly because of differences in rainfall, the soil conditions under *Talbotiella* forest are quite diverse (Table 1). Nutrient status varies from 2–22 milli-equivalents total exchangeable bases per 100 g dry soil – a range almost as great as that for the totality of Ghanaian forest soils. Similar variation in base saturation (10–100 per cent) accounts for the wide range of pH recorded, whilst organic carbon variation reflects wide differences in decomposition rates under different climates and at different elevations. It does not seem, therefore, that the distribution of *Talbotiella* is closely limited by environmental factors; the species is absent from many apparently suitable rocky hills.

Talbotiella usually occurs as monospecific patches of 1 or 2 hectares in a general matrix of mixed dry forest, though isolated individuals are occasionally seen, especially at the extremes of its range. The canopy is typically of uniform height (Figure 2a), in contrast to the surrounding mixed forest with its emergent crowns of such deciduous species as *Hildegardia barteri* and *Ceiba pentandra*. This smoothness of the canopy (very apparent in aerial photographs) presumably tends to reduce evapotranspiration, and could thus be adaptive under the prevailing conditions of low rainfall.

Floristic enumeration of 25 m × 25 m plots yielded lists exceeding 50 species in the surrounding mixed forest, but of only 20 species in the *Talbotiella* stands. Most species which do coexist with *Talbotiella* are sparse climbers or shrubs.

Talbotiella sets seed each year in the wet season (June–July), often profusely, and its seeds germinate freely under the canopy of the parents. Young trees may persist in shade for many years, though growth rate is better in gaps. The tree may also regenerate by basal sprouting from fallen adults. Regeneration is thus abundant and maintains a good stock in all size classes (Figure 2b).

Figure 3 shows the distribution of larger specimens of *Talbotiella* and other trees in part of a forest of South-east Outlier type on Krobo Mountain (Figure 1), an isolated inselberg surrounded by the short-grass savanna of the Accra Plains. Mixed forest gives way rather abruptly to *Talbotiella* forest, only the understorey tree *Drypetes parvifolia* being common to both. Seedlings of other species do occur, but do not seem to become established under *Talbotiella*. The lack of young trees of other canopy species and the abundant regeneration of *Talbotiella* argue convincingly against the possibility that the stand represents a seral stage.

Though none seem to exhibit diversity as low as that of the Ghanaian *Talbotiella* stands, forests dominated by a single Caesalpiniaceous tree species are known from many parts of tropical Africa. Letouzey (1968) lists the species concerned (see also Germain and Evrard, 1956, 1957; Gérard, 1960; Guillaumet, 1967; Nanson and Gennart, 1960; Voorhoeve, 1964). Convincing explanations are still lacking, however, both for the phenomenon of tropical single-species

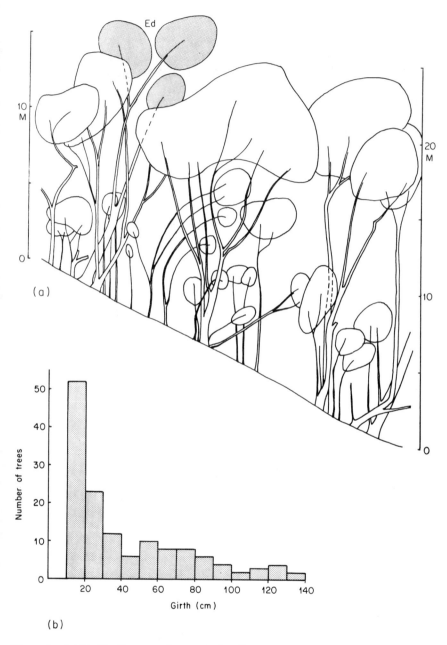

(a)

(b)

Figure 2   (a) Profile diagram of a stand of *Talbotiella* at Akosombo. The sample strip measured 5 × 30 m and all trees ≥3 m tall were recorded. Ed = *Elaeophorbia grandifolia*, all other trees are *Talbotiella*. (b) Girth class distribution of 140 trees of *Talbotiella* > 10 cm girth at breast height (1.3 m) on 0.1 ha at Akosombo

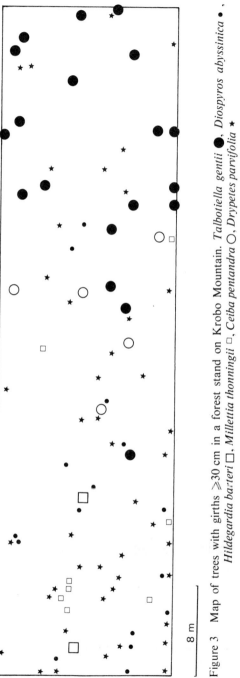

Figure 3   Map of trees with girths ⩾30 cm in a forest stand on Krobo Mountain. *Talbotiella gentii* ●, *Diospyros abyssinica* •, *Hildegardia barteri* □, *Millettia thonningii* ▫, *Ceiba pentandra* ○, *Drypetes parvifolia* ★

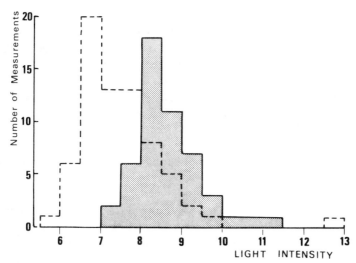

Figure 4   Light intensities (arbitrary units–photographic lightmeter) under *Talbotiella* forest (shaded), and forest without *Talbotiella* (open)

dominance, and for the disproportionate success of Caesalpiniaceae in achieving it. Connell (1978) proposes that diversity of a tropical forest diminishes if it is allowed to develop without disturbance. There is, however, no evidence that the *Talbotiella* stands are less disturbed than the surrounding forest. Adjacent to the Krobo Mountain stand, indeed, there is evidence of former human habitation from about a century ago.

Although the canopy of *Talbotiella* stands is fairly dense, the shade it casts is somewhat less than that of the surrounding forest (Figure 4), so that low light intensity on the forest floor cannot be adduced as the major cause for the failure of other species to become established.

The ectomycorrhizal condition, though very rare among tropical trees (Meyer, 1973), is known in five tropical African members of Caesalpiniaceae: *Afzelia africana* (Jenik and Mensah, 1967), *A. bella* (Redhead, 1968), *Brachystegia laurentii* (Fassi and Fontana, 1962), *Gilbertiodendron dewevrei* (Fassi, 1963), and *Julbernardia seretii* (Fassi and Fontana, 1961). The last three of these species typically form low diversity stands (Letouzey, 1968; Gérard, 1960).

We do not know if *Talbotiella* is ectomycorrhizal, or capable of symbiotic nitrogen fixation, nor whether its competitive success is due to some allelopathic effect. Its local dominance thus remains to be explained, and provides scope for interesting and significant work.

Conservation

Many of the known *Talbotiella* localities (and it is probable that more remain to be found in less accessible areas) are in forest reserves which were originally established as protection against the supposed advance of the savanna (Thompson, 1910). These reserves, poorly stocked with commercial timbers, are under increasing pressure for conversion to farmland or for the establishment of plantations of exotic trees such as teak (*Tectona grandis*).

The greatest concentration of *Talbotiella* stands is centred on the ridges around the gorge where the Volta River has cut its way through the Akwapim–Togo Hills at Akosombo, the location of the dam behind which the artificial Volta Lake has been impounded. *Talbotiella* favours the steeper, more broken scarps where roots and water can penetrate. On the dip slopes, where the rocks are bedded parallel to the land surface, soil is shallower and run-off greater, and the vegetation is savanna containing the rare cycad *Encephalartos barteri*. Many of the *Talbotiella* stands lie outside the forest reserves, at the mercy of farmers. Because its wood is dense, *Talbotiella* makes excellent charcoal, and is therefore cut preferentially to supply the expanding local market, and Accra. The most extensive *Talbotiella* forest in the district occupies the slopes of a hill (with *Encephalartos* savanna on its summit) overlooking the dam. Following recommendations made by the Department of Botany of the University of Ghana (Lawson, 1968), this hill was designated as Sapawsu Extension Forest Reserve, specifically to protect the *Talbotiella*. Recently, however, some of the reserve has been cut by farmers, and it is clear that the boundaries need better protection.

To conclude, *Talbotiella gentii* is a tree of great ecological interest, eminently worthy of conservation. It is well able to perpetuate itself in those forests where it occurs, but the forests themselves are in danger.

References

Connell, J. H. (1978). 'Diversity in tropical rain forests and coral reefs', *Science*, **199**, 1302–10.

Fassi, B. (1963). 'Die Verteilung der ektotrophen Mykorrhizen in der Streu und in der oberen Bodenschicht der *Gilbertiodendron dewevrei* (Caesalpiniaceae) – Walder im Kongo', in *Int. Mykorrhiza Symp., 1960*, pp. 297–302.

Fassi, B. and Fontana, A. (1961). 'Le micorrize ectotrofiche di *Julbernardia seretii*, Cesalpiniaceae del Congo', *Allionia*, **7**, 131–57.

Fassi, B. and Fontana, A. (1962). 'Micorrize ectotrofiche di *Brachystegia laurentii* e di alcune altre Cesalpiniaceae minori del Congo', *Allionia*, **8**, 121–31.

Gérard, P. (1960). 'Etude écologique de la forêt dense à *Gilbertiodendron dewevrei* dans la région de l'Uele', *Publ. Inst. Nat. Étude Agron. Congo (Sér. Sci.)*, **87**, 1–159.

Germain, R. and Evrard, C. (1956). Étude écologique et phytosociologique de la forêt à *Brachystegia laurentii*', *Publ. Inst. Nat. Étude Agron. Congo Belge (Sér. sci.)*, **67**, 1–105.

Germain, R. and Evrard, C. (1957). 'Caractères structurels du groupement à *Brachystegia laurentii* (D. Wild.) Louis ex Hoyle dans la région de Yangambi (1) (Congo Belge)', in *Huitième Congrès Int. de Bot., Paris 1954, Comptes rendus des séances et rapports et communications déposés lors du Congrès*, Sect. 7–8, 148–51.

Guillaumet, J.-L. (1967). *Recherches sur la Végétation et la Flore de la Région du Bas-Cavally (Cote d'Ivoire)*, ORSTOM, Paris.

Hall, J. B. and Swaine, M. D. (1976). 'Classification and ecology of closed-canopy forest in Ghana', *J. Ecol.*, **64**, 913–51.

Hutchinson, J. and Dalziel, J. M. (1954–72). *Flora of West Tropical Africa* (Revised by R. W. J. Keay and F. N. Hepper), Crown Agents, London.

Jeník, J. and Mensah, K. O. A. (1967). 'Root systems of tropical trees 1. Ectotrophic mycorrhizae of *Afzelia africana* Sm.', *Preslia*, **39**, 59–65.

Lawson, G. W. (1968). 'Ghana', in *Conservation of Vegetation* in *Africa South of the Sahara* (Eds. I. Hedberg and O. Hedberg), *Acta Phytogeogr. Suecica*, **54**, 81–6.

Letouzey, R. (1968). *Étude Phytogéographique du Cameroun*, Encycl. Biol. 69, Lechevalier, Paris.

Meyer, F. H. (1973). 'Distribution of Ectomycorrhizae in native and man-made forests', in *Ectomycorrhizae – Their Ecology and Physiology* (Eds. G. C. Marks and T. T. Kozlowski), Academic Press, London, pp. 79–105.

Nanson, A. and Gennart, M. (1960). 'Contribution à l'étude du climax et en particulier du pédoclimax en forêt équatoriale congolaise', *Bull. Inst. Agron. Gembloux*, **28**, 287–342.

Redhead, J. F. (1968). '*Inocybe* sp. associated with ectotrophic mycorrhiza on *Afzelia bella* in Nigeria', *Commonw. For. Rev.*, **47**, 63–5.

Thompson, H. N. (1910). 'Gold Coast: Report on forests', *Colon. Rep. Miscell.*, **66**, 1–238.

Voorhoeve, A. G. (1964). 'Some notes on the tropical rainforest of the Yoma-Gola National Forest near Bomi Hills, Liberia', *Commonw. For. Rev.*, **43**, 17–24.

Note

Plant names in this chapter follow the *Flora of West Tropical Africa* (Hutchinson and Dalziel, 1954–72).

30
Ecological studies of *Peucedanum palustre* and their implications for conservation management at Wicken Fen, Cambridgeshire

H. JOHN HARVEY *Department of Applied Biology, University of Cambridge*
and
T. C. MEREDITH *Department of Geography, McGill University, Montreal*

Summary

Peucedanum palustre is the food plant of the larvae of the Swallowtail butterfly (*Papilio machaon*). The Swallowtail became extinct at Wicken Fen, probably because of the low density and poor performance of *Peucedanum*, and re-introductions were not successful. Studies designed to find the limiting phase in the life cycle of *Peucedanum* are presented. Observations and experiments were made on seed production and dispersal, the size of the soil seed bank, germination and establishment, the fate of seedlings and the survival of established plants. The response of the species to grazing, competition, shading and flooding was also investigated. Conclusions are drawn about the factors limiting *Peucedanum* at Wicken Fen. Ways in which management may be modified to favour the species are discussed.

Introduction

Less than 0.1 per cent of the Peat Fens of Eastern England remain undrained. This drastic loss of habitat must have reduced the abundance in the region of all the plant and animal species of fenland and caused the extinction of the local populations of some, for example, *Senecio palustris*, the Fen Orchid (*Liparis loeselii*), the Large Copper butterfly (*Lycaena dispar*) and the Bittern (*Botaurus stellaris*). One of the last species to be lost from the Fens was the Swallowtail butterfly (*Papilio machaon*) which became extinct about 1952, when the last population at Wicken Fen, Cambridgeshire, died out (Smart, 1972; Dempster, 1976). Subsequent attempts at reintroduction failed (Dempster, 1976; Smart, 1977), leaving the Norfolk Broads population as the only one in Britain. The major conclusion of a study to discover possible causes for both the decline of the species at Wicken and the failure of re-introduction attempts was that both the abundance and performance of *Peucedanum palustre*, the sole food plant of the larvae of the Swallowtail in the United Kingdom, were inadequate to support a viable population (Dempster *et al.*, 1976).

The survival of the Wicken Fen population of the Swallowtail into the twentieth century was a consequence of the Fen being one of the few areas in the region to remain undrained. In the second half of the sixteenth century this undrained state was associated with part of the area being set aside as common land on which the traditional harvesting of peat, sedge (*Cladium mariscus*), litter (chiefly *Molinia caerulea* or *Calamagrostis canescens* and *C. epigejos*) and reed (*Phragmites australis*) could be continued (Evans, 1923), the remainder of what is now the Wicken Fen Nature Reserve being commercially managed for these same products. Two hundred years later, in the final years of the nineteenth century, the threat of drainage was countered by entomological collectors who purchased portions of the Fen as they came onto the market and handed them over to the National Trust (Evans, 1923). The National Trust has continued the traditional management regimes, particularly the cutting of *Cladium*-dominated communities at intervals of 3 or 4 years. The time of harvesting has not, however, been constant over the centuries. In the seventeenth century strict penalties were enforced against those who did not cut their sedge between 24 April and 24 June (Anon, 1656), but by the early twentieth century autumn or early winter harvesting was normal (Godwin and Tansley, 1929; Ennion, 1942). Sedge is currently cut in July, August or September.

The Swallowtail was one of the most obvious of the characteristic fenland species at Wicken Fen and its loss was a matter of some concern. Since the loss could be related to the abundance and performance of *Peucedanum palustre* any attempt at conservation demanded a better understanding of the biology of the food plant. A detailed study aimed at providing that understanding and at producing management recommendations for improving the number of plants and their growth was carried out between 1975 and 1978 (Meredith, 1976; Meredith, 1978). This chapter summarizes the general results of this study, the detailed results being prepared for publication elsewhere. The basic philosophy of the study was that some factor operating during the life cycle must regulate the number of individuals in a population and that a demographic approach should reveal the limiting phase or interphase (Sagar and Mortimer, 1976). Observations were therefore made on seed production and dispersal, the fate of seeds on the soil surface and in the soil, the size of the soil seed bank, germination and establishment, the fate of seedlings and the survival of established plants. The demographic study was carried out in three managed areas each at a different stage in the sedge cutting cycle, (areas cut in 1974 and 1977, 1975 and 1978 and 1976 and 1979), with a fourth unmanaged, but *Cladium*-dominated, area being studied for comparative purposes. Certain experiments were made in addition to the demographic study to investigate subsidiary problems.

The Species

Peucedanum palustre (L.) Moench is a semi-rosette hemicryptophyte belonging to the Umbelliferae. It is widely distributed in Europe up to about 1000 m, but is on the edge of its range in the United Kingdom and rarely occurs over 100 m altitude. In the United Kingdom it has been recorded in only 23 10-km squares since 1950, these mainly in south-east England (Perring and Walters, 1976), and is found almost exclusively in fens and marshes on peat and alluvium, especially on sites which are seasonally flooded (Clapham *et al.*, 1962). Association analysis of plant communities at Wicken showed a close association between *P. palustre* and *Cladium mariscus* and the absence of *Peucedanum palustre* from *Frangula alnus* scrub and areas cut every 1 or 2 years. The phenology of the species at Wicken Fen is summarized in Figure 1.

The species is frequently described as a biennial (Hegi, 1926; Clapham *et al.*, 1962), but generally behaves as a herbaceous perennial. Each rosette is monocarpic but the genet (the plant derived from a single seed) persists through the development of axillary buds on the basal stem to form one or more new shoots. Seedlings raised in a glasshouse can flower within 4 months of emergence and mature individuals overwintered in a glasshouse flower at the normal season. It therefore appears that vernalization is not a requirement for flowering, although long days may be. Plants may need to attain a certain minimum size before flowering occurs (Werner, 1975; Harper, 1977 and Chapter 16) for plants which flowered in an experimental garden, after 7 months in a glasshouse and 9 months outdoors, had significantly larger roots than plants which did not flower (4.55 ± 0.55 g cf. 2.15 ± 0.20 g, $n = 13$, $p < 0.001$). It may well be impossible for plants in the field to accumulate sufficient reserves in 1 year to meet this requirement.

Demography

Seed production

Plants in managed areas at Wicken characteristically have one flowering stem which produces about 4500 seeds. The mean density of plants in the study areas over the 3-year cutting cycle was just over one per sq. m, giving a potential seed input of about 5000 seeds per sq. m. The seed is large with mean seed weight generally falling in the range 0.20–0.35 mg.

Seed dispersal

The chief seed dispersal mechanism of *P. palustre* is open to doubt (Briquet, 1923; Hegi, 1926; Ridley, 1930). The presence of wings on the seed (mericarp) suggests

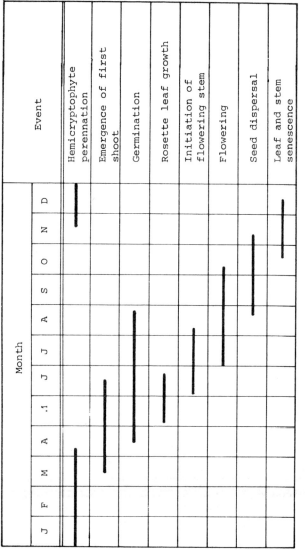

Figure 1   The phenology of *Peucedanum palustre* at Wicken Fen. The horizontal bars indicate the periods during which particular events occur. There is appreciable variation between areas and years

that wind dispersal is important while the existence of sponge-like tissue in the seed coat indicates that water dispersal may occur; both may of course be important. Seeds are not readily released from the umbel, being shed in still conditions only when the stem receives some shock.

The effectiveness of wind dispersal was tested in a wind tunnel. In one experiment umbels with ripe seed were exposed to winds of different speeds and the proportion of seed shed was calculated (Table 1). No seed was shed at 2.5 m per sec but the proportion shed rose sharply thereafter. A second experiment examined the distance over which seed released at a height of 50 cm was carried by winds of different speeds (Figure 2). At 2.5 m per sec the majority of the seed landed within 50 cm of the release point but at 7.5 m per sec almost 90 per cent of the seed travelled more than 250 cm.

For practical reasons the range of aerial dispersal in the field was tested only under still air conditions. Seed was displaced from eight selected umbels (mean height 152 cm) standing in a *Cladium* community (mean height of surface 86 cm) by gently tapping the stem. Seed was caught at the top of the *Cladium* community on double backed adhesive tape, 2.5 cm wide, mounted on wooden crosses with arms 1.7 m long and centred on the stems. The maximum movement of seed from the parent plant was 40 cm. The dispersal of seed in its passage through the sedge community was tested in a similar manner with the wooden cross at ground level and seed released by hand at the top of the vegetation. A lateral displacement of up to 30 cm was recorded.

Dispersal by water was also examined in both laboratory and field. Laboratory tests at 4°C revealed that more than 95 per cent of seed remained buoyant for at least 6 months. In a field study begun in January batches of marked seeds were placed on the surface of the water in both a sedge community, with 25 cm of standing water, and a litter community, with 15 cm of standing water. After 5 months soil cores of 10 cm diameter were taken at 5, 25, 50 and 100 cm north and west of the release points. The number of marked seeds was counted after recovery by observation and flotation and the extent of dispersal was calculated. In the litter community all the released seed were estimated to be within 1 m of the

Table 1 The mean proportion of seeds released from umbels at each of three wind speeds

Wind speed (m per sec)	Proportion of seeds released
2.5	0
5.0	44.2 ± 5.3
7.5	87.7 ± 2.8

$n = 5, p < 0.001$

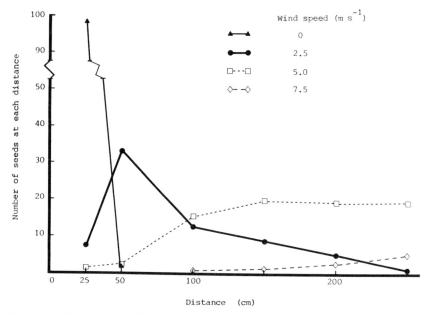

Figure 2   The influence of wind speed on the distance over which seeds were carried in a wind tunnel. Values are means of five replicates, 100 seeds released in each case

release site but only 62 per cent were within this distance in the sedge (Table 2). This difference was associated with the much less erect and more tangled nature of the litter vegetation.

These studies indicate that *P. palustre* has effective short-range dispersal mechanisms but that long-range dispersal may be limited.

Table 2   The estimated mean densities of seeds (number per 100 sq. cm) at four distances from release point in two community types after five months. (750 seeds released at each site, n = 4)

Distance from release point (cm)	Estimated density of seeds (number per 100 sq. cm)		Significance of difference
	Sedge	Litter	
0	97.1	354.7	$p < 0.001$
25	5.1	4.6	NS
50	1.3	0	NS
100	1.6	0	NS

Predation of seed on the soil surface

To measure seed losses to predators at the soil surface, plastic trays containing peat on which seed had been placed were sunk into the soil at Wicken and left from October to December, when the proportion of seeds remaining was determined. Half of the trays were placed in a *Cladium* community which had not been cut for 2 years and half in a similar community cut 2 months before. The population of small mammals in the uncut area was probably high and that in the recently cut area low (Flowerdew *et al.*, 1977); predation by birds was only likely in the recently cut area. In both areas trays were left unprotected or were covered by mesh screens with holes of 5.0, 1.3 or 0.1 cm. Up to 80 per cent of seed was lost from unprotected trays in the uncut area; losses in the cut area were much lower (Figure 3). Protection by 1.3 or 0.1 cm mesh considerably reduced predation.

Laboratory feeding trials with the four small rodents common on the Fen revealed that Bank Vole (*Clethrionomys glareolus*) and Harvest Mouse (*Micromys minutus*) would eat the seed of *Peucedanum palustre* but that Wood Mouse (*Apodemus sylvaticus*) and Field Vole (*Microtus agrestis*) would not. The seed remains from these trials resembled those found in the field. Clearly small mammals may remove considerable amounts of seed, as they also appear to do in the case of *Carlina vulgaris* (Greig-Smith and Sagar, Chapter 32). Predation by birds seems unlikely.

Fate of buried seed

The survival and germinability of batches of seed which had been introduced into the soil and left buried for different periods of time was examined. Seed was buried at two depths, 2 and 10 cm, in both a wet and a dry site in February. Replicate samples were collected at each site on eight occasions over the next 16 months. The majority of the seed was in a state of enforced dormancy but up to 20 per cent germinated, mainly from the shallower placement; only a little of the seed disappeared (Figure 4).

Natural seed bank

The size of the seed bank in the soil was assessed from the number of seedlings emerging from soil samples kept in a glasshouse together with a careful search of the samples at the end of the experiment. The technique was calibrated by recording the recovery of seeds added to a sample of peat without a natural population of *Peucedanum palustre*. Seed numbers ranged from 21 to 146 seeds per sq. m, one to two orders of magnitude greater than the population of established plants but only a small proportion of the potential seed input.

372   *The biological aspects of rare plant conservation*

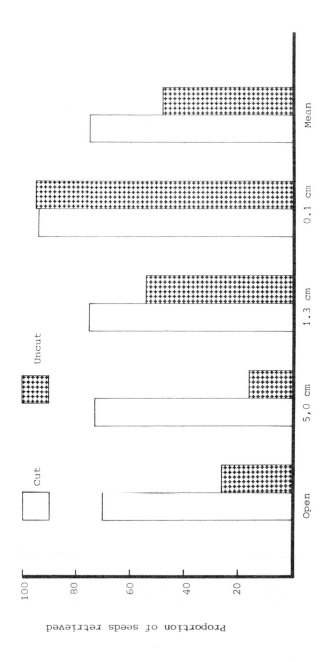

Figure 3   The influence of vegetation type and protection from predators on the proportion of seed recovered from trays after 2 months in the field (225 seeds per tray, $n = 4$)

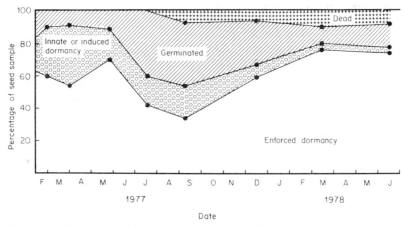

Figure 4   Changes with time in the size of the different fractions within buried samples of seed. Values are means for three replicates from each of three sites, seed recovery from 2 cm burial in the wet site being too low to include in the analysis. Each replicate initially consisted of 20 seeds

Seed germination

Laboratory tests revealed an innate dormancy in the shed seed; the period of this dormancy was reduced by vernalization and leaching. In the laboratory germination was stimulated by light and by fluctuating temperatures. In an attempt to discover the field conditions necessary for germination, batches of seed were introduced into three contrasting areas (recently cut *Cladium*, recently cleared scrub and uncut *Cladium*) in mid-April and their fate followed until mid-October. Seeds were either placed on the soil surface or on filter paper in petri dishes provided with a replenishable water supply; half the petri dishes were covered with Copenhagen funnels. All seeds were protected from predation by metal mesh screens. No germination occurred on the soil surface for 12 months. In the petri dishes germination was much higher in the cleared scrub and cut *Cladium* areas than in the uncut *Cladium* (30 per cent cf. 2 per cent). This difference was correlated to differences in the temperature and light regimes of the areas. Temperature fluctuations in the open communities were very similar to those shown in the laboratory to stimulate germination while the range was much less in the uncut area. In the cut areas light intensity was very close to incident (100 and 85 per cent) but in the uncut area it was very low (1 per cent of incident). These results indicate that, because of environmental limitations, only a few areas of Wicken Fen may be suitable for the germination of seed of *Peucedanum palustre*.

Seedling emergence and survival

Seedling numbers were regularly monitored for 2 years in small plots located in areas selected for their high density of seedlings (up to 300 per sq. m). Most seedlings had died by October, maximum survival being 5 per cent and average survival only 1 per cent. Observations suggested that many deaths were associated with grazing. To confirm this trays of peat, containing seed and covered with mesh with holes of 5.0, 1.3 or 0.1 cm or without mesh, were placed in the field in January. Seedling numbers were monitored monthly until June. The marked effect of protection (Table 3) suggests that grazing by small organisms, possibly slugs and snails, is very important.

Established plants

Trends in the population of established plants were followed in permanent quadrats and by a random point survey. Numbers were relatively stable over the study area as a whole but fluctuated at any one spot. These fluctuations appeared to be linked to the *Cladium* cutting cycle. Densities fell from 1.7 plants per sq. m in the year of cutting to 1.2 per sq. m in the following year and to 0.6 per sq. m in the next year. In the final year of the cycle numbers rose, as a result of recruitment from the seedling population, to once again reach 1.7 per sq. m. Cutting caused considerable mortality and losses were high in the year following cutting, perhaps as a result of increased exposure (see later); few deaths occurred in the final year of the cycle. In the cut areas the mean year-to-year survival rate for established plants was about 70 per cent, giving a half life of 2 years. Comparable values for Norfolk (Dempster *et al.*, 1976) and uncut areas of *Cladium* at Wicken (this study) were 6–7 and 7 years respectively.

Table 3   The mean number ($\pm$ S.E.) of seedlings found in trays protected by one of three sizes of mesh or left unprotected. Each tray contained 100 seeds at the start of the experiment (n = 4)

Mesh size (cm)	Maximum number of seedlings over period January–June (per tray)	Number of seedlings present at harvest in June (per tray)
No mesh	1.2 ± 1.5	0
5.0	1.2 ± 1.3	0.7 ± 0.7
1.3	8.2 ± 4.9	1.0 ± 0.7
0.1	75.2 ± 9.8	75.2 ± 9.8

Synthesis

The demographic study suggests that in areas of cut *Cladium* flushes of germination occur in the year following cutting and that the few survivors are recruited into the population of established plants 2 or 3 years later. This recruitment just balances the loss, through factors such as cutting, of flowering plants. Seed production is high but seed losses through predation may be considerable. Despite the heavy predation of seed the major limitation on population increase would appear to be the high mortality of seedlings.

Environmental effects

In addition to the demographic study experiments were made to examine the response of *Peucedanum palustre* to grazing, competition, shading and flooding regime.

The effect of grazing by single, third instar larvae of *Papilio machaon* was studied in both glasshouse and field. Grazing was concentrated on the upper part of the plants and most leaves here were removed, as were most flowers. A plant of *Peucedanum palustre* can survive this grazing pressure but seed production may be markedly reduced (number of seeds per plant in field 258 ± 110 cf. 912 ± 149, $n = 6, p < 0.05$).

To study competition effects 3-month-old seedlings were introduced into a range of sites in June and observed for 16 months. At each site all combinations of two treatments were imposed; seedlings were introduced either in a plant pot (to remove root competition) or into the soil, and the surrounding vegetation was either maintained at a height of 10 cm (no aerial competition) or allowed to develop normally. Survival was best in the uncut vegetation (83 per cent cf. 50 per cent, $p = 0.32$); protection from root competition also increased survival. The balance between water supply, likely to be lowest when root competition is

Table 4   The influence of aerial competition on the production of seed and the components of seed production (n = 24)

	Surrounding vegetation kept cut to 10 cm	Surrounding vegetation not cut	Significance of differences
Mean number of umbels per plant	11.3	4.7	$p < 0.001$
Mean number of rays per umbel	28.0	24.0	$p < 0.09$
Mean number of seeds per ray	18.2	13.0	$p < 0.001$
Calculated mean number of seeds per plant	5783	1463	$p < 0.001$

occurring, and water loss, highest in open areas, may explain this result. Much of the mortality took the form of plants failing to survive the winter, perhaps because water balance affected the ability of the plants to accumulate food reserves. Competition reduced seed production (Table 4).

Three levels of light intensity (5, 50 and 100 per cent of incident) and three levels of water supply (dry, flooded and intermediate) were combined in a factorial experiment to examine effects on growth (Meredith, 1976). Over 8 weeks, from seed, most growth was made at the 50 per cent level of light and under the intermediate moisture conditions. Flooding during this phase significantly reduced growth.

Implications for management

What conclusions may be drawn from this study for the conservation of *Peucedanum palustre* at Wicken Fen? In areas of cut *Cladium* where *Peucedanum palustre* already occurs the main problems are the short half life of established plants and the poor recruitment of seedlings. The heavy predation of seeds would appear to be of little significance.

Since harvesting appears to increase the mortality of established plants, both directly and indirectly, one solution might be to modify the cutting programme, either by altering the time of year at which cutting takes place or by changing the harvesting interval. Delaying cutting until late autumn or early winter, the pattern of early this century, would reduce direct mortality and allow the maturation and dispersal of seed. Predation of this seed should be low as small mammal populations would soon be depleted. Such a change might, however, affect other species, perhaps favouring *Phragmites australis* and increasing the susceptibility of *Cladium mariscus* to damage by frost. The effects of bringing cutting forward to its seventeenth century time of late spring to early summer is less easy to predict; germination rates should be high but no predictions can be made on the fate of seedlings or of established plants. If the sedge cutting cycle was extended to 4 years, which might aid *Cladium*, then the mean survival of *Peucedanum palustre* might be increased. It is unlikely that many new plants would be recruited to the population in this extra year. The benefits of changing the cutting cycle are therefore speculative.

If seedling mortality is the result of grazing by slugs and snails then it is not immediately clear how this can be reduced. Brindley (1925) noted that the populations of terrestrial slugs and snails were low at Wicken and suggested that they might increase as the drainage of surrounding areas reduced flooding on the Fen. No such increase has been documented but it does appear reasonable that it should have occurred and it would explain the apparent decline in *P. palustre* since the 1920s. Irrigation, to provide flooded conditions, might reduce mollusc populations, although terrestrial forms do appear to survive happily on the thick upper vegetation of sedge fields (O. Prŷs-Jones, pers. comm.) Irrigation might also improve the performance of *P. palustre*, for Dempster and Hall (1980 and pers. comm.) have noted a relationship between annual rainfall and plant numbers and between winter rainfall and flowering. Winter irrigation would be much preferable to irrigation during the growing season, because summer flooding might reduce growth and increase mortality while winter flooding would aid seed dispersal and the breaking of dormancy.

In areas where *P. palustre* is absent then it will be necessary, because of the limited dispersal range of the seed, to introduce the species. This introduction may be as seed (Godwin and Tansley, 1929) or as pot grown plants (Dempster *et al.*, 1976; Dempster and Hall, 1980). Some plants introduced into reed Swamp and litter communities may survive for some years (Dempster *et al.*, 1976 and personal observation) but introductions into areas without *Cladium* probably stand a low chance of success. Observations in the area of uncut *Cladium* suggest that in some situations introduced plants might survive for a long period. In areas of cut *Cladium* the introduction of seed, at the appropriate stage in the cutting cycle, should be an adequate means of establishment, although the use of pot-grown plants might remove the risk of a high mortality through grazing.

Areas occupied by litter communities are probably too dry, and cut too frequently, for *Peucedanum palustre* to survive, however introduced.

Postscript

This detailed study of the ecology of *Peucedanum palustre* has revealed something of the reasons for the present low density and poor performance of the species at Wicken Fen. It has also provided some pointers to the ways in which current management might be modified to favour the species. The effect of such modifications must, for the moment, be speculative and need to be confirmed by a series of field trials. The study does, however, demonstrate the potential value of demographic studies in the planning and execution of conservation management.

References

Anon (1656). *Wicken Court Book*, Cambridge University Library Doc. 3974.

Brindley, H. H. (1925). 'The Mollusca of Wicken Fen', in *The Natural History of Wicken Fen* (Ed. J. S. Gardiner), pp. 154–61, Bowes and Bowes, Cambridge.

Briquet, J. (1923). 'Carpologie comparée de l'*Archangelica officinalis* Hoffm. et du *Peucedanum palustre* (L.) Moench', *Candollea*, **1**, 501–20.

Clapham, A. R., Tutin, T. G., and Warburg, E. F. (1962). *Flora of the British Isles* (2nd Ed.), Cambridge University Press.

Dempster, J. P. (1976). 'The swallowtail butterfly at Wicken Fen', *Nature in Cambridgeshire*, **19**, 11–14.

Dempster, J. P. and Hall, M. L. (1980). 'An attempt at re-establishing the swallowtail butterfly at Wicken Fen', *Ecol. Entom.*, **5**, 327–34.

Dempster, J. P., King, M. L., and Lakhani, K. H. (1976). 'The status of the swallowtail butterfly in Britain', *Ecol. Entom.*, **1**, 71–84.

Ennion, E. A. R. (1942). *Adventurers Fen*, Herbert Jenkins, London.

Evans, A. H. (1923). 'The Fens of the Great Level, their drainage, and its effect on the flora and fauna', in *The Natural History of Wicken Fen* (Ed. J. S. Gardiner), pp. 3–49, Bowes and Bowes, Cambridge.

Flowerdew, J. R., Hall, S. J. G., and Brown, J. C. (1977). 'Small rodents, their habitats, and the effects of flooding at Wicken Fen, Cambridgeshire', *J. Zool., Lond.*, **182**, 323–42.

Godwin, H. and Tansley, A. G. (1929). 'The vegetation of Wicken Fen', in *The Natural History of Wicken Fen* (Ed J. S. Gardiner), pp. 385–446, Bowes and Bowes, Cambridge.

Harper, J. L. (1977). *Population Biology of Plants*, Academic Press, London.

Hegi, G. (1926). '*Peucedanum palustre*', *Illustrierte Flora von Mittel–Europa*, **5**(2), 1393–6, J. F. Lehmanns, Munich.

Meredith, T. C. (1976). 'The food plant of the swallowtail butterfly: experiments at Wicken Fen', *Discussion Papers in Conservation*, **12**, 1–49, University College, London.

Meredith, T. C. (1978). *The Ecology and Conservation of* Peucedanum palustre *at Wicken Fen*, PhD thesis, University of Cambridge.

Perring, F. H. and Walters, S. M. (Eds.) (1976). *Atlas of the British Flora*, 2nd Ed., E. P. Publishing, Wakefield.

Ridley, H. N. (1930). *The Dispersal of Plants throughout the World*, L. Reeve, Ashford, Kent.

Sagar, G. R. and Mortimer, A. M. (1976). 'The population dynamics of plants', *Appl. Biol.*, **1**, 1–47.

Smart, J. (1972). 'Butterflies and day-flying moths', *Guides to Wicken Fen*, **8**, 1–13, National Trust: Wicken Fen Local Committee.

Smart, J. (1977). 'Wicken Fen and the swallowtail butterfly', in *National Trust Yearbook*, pp. 45–51, National Trust, London.

Werner, P. A. (1975). 'Predictions of fate from rosette size in teasel (*Dipsacus fullonum* L.)', *Oecologia*, **20**, 197–201.

Note

Plant names in this chapter follow Clapham, Tutin and Warburg (1962), except for *Phragmites australis* (Cav.) Trin. ex. Steudel, otherwise known as *P. communis* Trin.

The Biological Aspects of Rare Plant Conservation
Edited by Hugh Synge
© 1981 John Wiley & Sons Ltd.

31
Lactuca saligna and *Pulicaria vulgaris* in Britain

S. D. PRINCE AND A. D. R. HARE *Department of Plant Biology and Microbiology, Queen Mary College, University of London*

Summary

Lactuca saligna and *Pulicaria vulgaris* are annuals which reach their climatic distribution limit in south-eastern Britain. They have never been common and recently there have been further declines in the populations of both species. Methods were selected to provide the basic ecological information needed to formulate management proposals within a short time. Vegetation analyses and population counts in the major British sites were used to describe the niches of both species and to document annual fluctuations in numbers. Mapped permanent quadrats and experimental manipulation of the cohabitant vegetation have raised hypotheses regarding the cause of their decline. Regeneration appears to be the critical stage in the life-cycle of both species, as may be expected in an annual. The cohabitant vegetation is primarily responsible for the exclusion of plants from neighbouring vegetation. Poaching by large animals provides open sites for regeneration and this is supplemented by seasonal flooding in *P. vulgaris* sites and by microclimatological effects on the vegetation in *L. saligna* sites. Conservation management should aim to maintain this habitat disturbance. Sites for re-introduction have been selected by means of an indicator scoring technique and experimental plantings of *L. saligna* have been successful in two such sites. Artificial re-introduction of *P. vulgaris* into sites in which it is now extinct may be acceptable since it amounts to reinstating the probable original means of dispersal.

Introduction

A large number of native annual species are becoming rare in Britain (Perring and Walters, 1962, 1976; Perring and Farrell, 1977). Many of these are inconspicuous and have been regarded as casuals with the result that their decline has not been noticed or documented to the same extent as that of more decorative, often perennial species.

The survival of annuals is often determined by the availability of open sites for regeneration. These sites are usually created by human activities or by animals or by physical processes which operate over a much larger area than that occupied by the species in question. This leads to conservation problems which are distinct from those encountered with many perennials. Unlike perennials simple protection of a colony of annuals from physical destruction is unlikely to preserve it unless the cycle of habitat disturbance can also be maintained – indeed the cause of a decline is often an unexpected and indirect consequence of changes in human activity. Failure of seedling establishment, vegetative growth or reproduction may also be implicated in the decline and ecological information is needed to assess which stages of the life-cycle and which factors are relevant.

The location of past and present sites in Britain of *Pulicaria vulgaris* and *Lactuca saligna*, two members of the Compositae, is shown in Figure 1. *Pulicaria vulgaris* was first recorded in 1570 at Barnards Green in Worcestershire (Pena and Lobel, 1570). There are intermittent records for this area until 1936, often mentioning occurrence of the plant in seasonally wet depressions in grazed common-land. This decline at a major site is repeated elsewhere. Turner and Dillwyn (1805) do not mention *P. vulgaris* in their guide to the less common British plants written in 1805, but Boswell Syme described it in *Sowerby's English Botany* (1866) as 'rather rare'. At the turn of the century it was found in 11 vice-counties but now occurs in only 4. In 1979 1 colony of less than 10 plants remained at Poulshot in Wiltshire, 1 colony of about 100 plants at Wood Street near Guildford in Surrey, 1 colony of about 200 plants near Bramshill in north Hampshire and at least 4 fragmented colonies of between 100 and 7000 plants in the New Forest, south Hampshire.

Lactuca saligna was first recorded in Britain by Ray (1660) in Cambridgeshire. In the mid-nineteenth century it was recorded from about nine vice-counties (Watson, 1873; Turner and Dillwyn, 1805), from five by the early twentieth century (Druce, 1928) and it is now found in only three. Its decline has not been so marked as that of *P. vulgaris*, but major losses have occurred on the shingle at Eastbourne and on the banks of the Bedford River in Huntingdonshire and Cambridgeshire. In 1979 a colony of between 20 and 30 plants remained at Rye on the

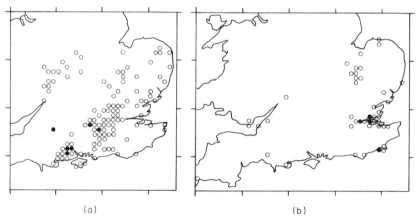

(a)   (b)

Figure 1   The distribution of, (a) *Pulicaria vulgaris*, and (b) *Lactuca saligna* in Britain. Reliable past records shown by open circles, present sites by closed circles. Data partly supplied by the Biological Records Centre, Monks Wood

Sussex coast, colonies of about 100 on sea walls at Cliffe in Kent and Purfleet in Essex and a colony of about 10 000 on old sea walls at Fobbing in Essex. The sites in Kent and Essex are currently threatened by reconstruction of the sea walls and by building development.

Both *P. vulgaris* and *L. saligna* occur elsewhere in the world and are relatively common in some countries (see Figure 2 for their European distributions), although the colonies of *P. vulgaris* in the New Forest may be the largest in Western Europe (F. Rose, pers. comm.) and the populations of *L. saligna* in Britain are physiologically distinct from those examined elsewhere (Prince, 1980). The centres of distribution of both species are in areas with higher summer temperatures than occur in Britain and the records for Britain itself are for the warmest parts of the country. There is no evidence for a marked association with any other localized habitat factors which could account for this distribution pattern and so it seems reasonable to conclude that the range of both species is primarily determined by the climate. Pigott (1970) gives the general arguments for this interpretation of the correlation of distribution limits and climate. In Britain the two species illustrate, therefore, the particular problems involved in conservation of species at the limits of their climatic ranges.

The rapid acquisition of autecological information for relatively unknown species which occur in small and widely separated populations presents practical problems worthy of study in themselves. In this work we have developed a

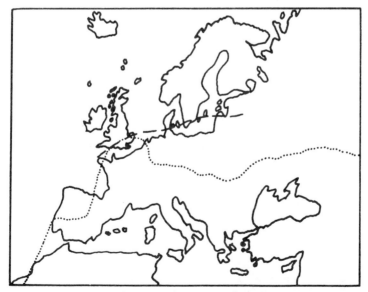

Figure 2   The northern distribution limits of *Lactuca saligna* (dotted line) and *Pulicaria vulgaris* (dashed line) in Europe. Data partly from Feráková (1977) and Hultén (1950)

strategy for the study of rare plants which may serve as a pattern for the initial study of other species.

Vegetation analysis

Ordination of floristic data is a powerful technique for the detection and display of phytosociological relationships. It has been used in this study to identify the characteristics of the niches occupied by *L. saligna* and *P. vulgaris*. Quadrats were placed in the major sites of both species and all the species present were listed together, in some analyses with a measure of their abundance. The ordination method known as reciprocal averaging (Hill, 1973) has been used since it generates simultaneous ordinations of species and quadrats – a characteristic which greatly facilitates interpretation of the ordination. Simpler techniques are available which can be calculated by hand (e.g. Bray and Curtis, 1957). The spatial arrangement of species and quadrats in the final ordination diagrams (Figure 3) represents the relationships of the individuals to each other: species which are plotted close together frequently occur in the same quadrats and probably are ecologically similar; quadrats plotted close together frequently contain the same species and their environments are probably similar. In this way disparate data are simplified and the likely characteristics of unknown individuals can be inferred from the properties of those individuals placed nearby in the ordination diagram.

The principal *L. saligna* site is at Fobbing and consists of a system of disused sea walls separated by rough grassland. The ordination (Figure 3a) shows how *L. saligna* occurs with annual and biennial species on the south-facing slopes of the sea walls and on other uneven ground. The species ordination for *P. vulgaris* at Brockenhurst (Figure 3b) shows it is also associated with annuals – in this case those occupying the mud exposed when the water level drops in seasonal pools.

The association detected by ordination between *L. saligna* and those species which occur with it – and any other characteristics of the sites which are associated with *L. saligna* – can be used as indicators of the suitability for *L. saligna* of sites which do not at present contain it. A list of species and site characteristics which distinguish the niche occupied by *L. saligna* has been derived with the help of an Indicator Species Analysis (Hill *et al.*, 1975). Each characteristic was given an indicator score (positive or negative) and the sum of the scores for each site was used to measure its suitability.

Population size

The longest continuous sequence of accurate counts of population size is for Cliffe where the *L. saligna* population has fluctuated between 48 and 303 plants over a 5-year period. Only a slightly greater decline than those which occurred in 1976 and 1978 could be sufficient to eliminate the plant. There is no information on the

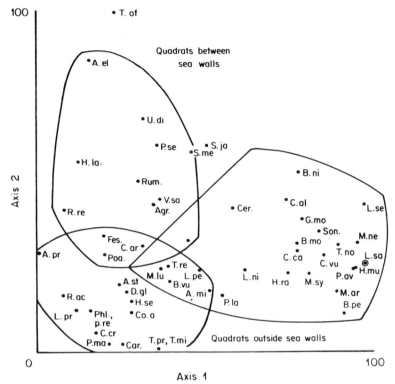

Figure 3(a) Ordination of the species recorded in 134 quadrats at Fobbing, Essex, in July 1978. On the same axes quadrats which occur on the sea walls and hummocks, in grassland between the sea walls and in improved grassland outside the sea walls fall in the three areas shown. Reciprocal averaging ordination (Hill, 1973). Abbreviations: A.el *Arrhenatherum elatius*; Agr. *Agropyron* spp.; A.mi *Achillea millefolium*; A.pr *Alopecurus pratensis*; A.st *Agrostis stolonifera*; B.mo *Bromus mollis*; B.ni *Brassica nigra*; B.pe *Bellis perennis*; B.vu *Beta vulgaris*; C.al *Chenopodium album*; Car. *Carex* spp.; C.ar *Cirsium arvense*; C.ca *Crepis capillaris*; C.cr *Cynosurus cristatus*; Cer. *Cerastium* spp.; Co.a *Convolvulus arvensis*; C.vu *Cirsium vulgare*; D.gl *Dactylis glomerata*; Fes. *Festuca* spp.; G.mo *Geranium molle*; H.la *Holcus lanatus*; H.mu *Hordeum murinum*; H.ra *Hypochoeris radicata*; H.se *Hordeum secalinum*; L.co *Lotus corniculatus*; L.ni *Lathyrus nissolia*; L.pe *Lolium perenne*; L.pr *Lathyrus pratensis*; L.sa *Lactuca saligna*; L.se *Lactuca serriola*; M.ar *Medicago arabica*; M.lu *Medicago lupulina*; M.ne *Malva neglecta*; M.sy *Malva sylvestris*; P.av *Polygonum aviculare* agg.; Phl. *Phleum* spp.; P.la *Plantago lanceolata*; P.ma *Plantago major*; Poa *Poa* spp.; P.re *Potentilla reptans*; P.se *Petroselinum segetum*; R.ac *Ranunculus acris*; R.re *Ranunculus repens*; Rum. *Rumex* spp.; S.ja *Senecio jacobaea*; S.me *Stellaria media*; Son. *Sonchus* spp.; T.mi *Tragopogon pratensis* spp. *minor*; T.no *Torilis nodosa*; T.of *Taraxacum officinale*; T.pr *Trifolium pratense*; T.re *Trifolium repens*; U.di *Urtica dioica*; V.sa *Vicia sativa*

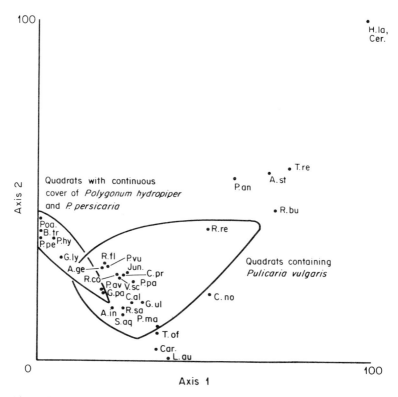

Figure 3(b)   Ordination of 26 contiguous quadrats in *Pulicaria vulgaris* site at Brockenhurst, August 1978. Locations of quadrats containing *Pulicaria vulgaris* and quadrats with continuous cover of *Polygonum hydropiper* and *P. persicaria* in the quadrat ordination on the same axes are also shown. Abbreviations: A.ge *Alopecurus geniculatus*; A.in *Apium inundatum*; A.st *Agrostis stolonifera*; B.tr *Bidens tripartita*; Cal. *Callitriche* spp.; Car. *Carex* spp.; Cer. *Cerastium* spp.; C.no *Chamaemelum nobile*; C.pr *Cardamine pratensis*; Gly *Glyceria* spp.; G.pa *Galium palustre*; G.ul *Gnaphalium uliginosum*; H.la *Holcus lanatus*; Jun. *Juncus* spp.; L.au *Leontodon autumnalis*; P.an *Potentilla anserina*; P.av *Polygonum aviculare* agg.; P.hy *Polygonum hydropiper*; P.ma *Plantago major*; Poa *Poa* spp.; P.pe *Polygonum persicaria*; P.po *Peplis portula*; P.vu *Pulicaria vulgaris*; R.co *Rumex conglomeratus*; R.bu *Ranunculus bulbosus*; R.fl *Ranunculus flammula*; R.re *Ranunculus repens*; R.sa *Ranunculus sardous*; S.aq *Senecio aquaticus*; T.of *Taraxacum officinale*; T.re *Trifolium repens*; V.sc *Veronica scutellata*

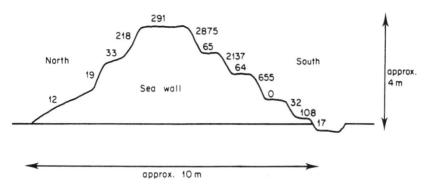

Figure 4   Number of *Lactuca saligna* plants on the north- and south-facing slopes
of a section of sea wall at Fobbing, Essex. High values occur on the inclines on the
south-facing slope and low values on the terraces and north-facing slope

longevity of *L. saligna* achenes in the soil although *L. serriola* achenes, which are
similar, are known to have a half-life of between 1.5 and 3 years (Marks, 1979). If
L. saligna achenes are equally short-lived then re-establishment from buried seeds
after an absence of even 1 year seems unlikely.

A survey of the distribution of *L. saligna* in different topographical subdivisions of the sea walls (Figure 4) showed that the plants were predominantly on
sloping ground on the south-faces and very few were on the terraces or the north-
facing slopes.

Demography

Permanent quadrats were established in all the major sites and the development of
mapped individuals recorded at regular intervals. In this way life-cycles have been
determined and compared between different parts of the sites. The vegetation in
other quadrats has been cleared to different extents in order to measure the effect
of the cohabitant vegetation.

The number of *L. saligna* plants at Fobbing reached a maximum in the winter
as a result of the major period of germination from November to January. Germination continued until May. Deaths were greatest in the seedling stage but continued until stem-extension in June when the population became stable until
normal senescence after fruiting in October. Germination in permanent quadrats
on the south-facing slopes of the sea wall was predominantly in the autumn,
whereas on the north-face and elsewhere the few seedlings which emerged did so
in the spring (Figure 5). Experiments in which the vegetation was removed from
plots suggests that delayed germination and low numbers is an indirect effect of
the change in microclimate with aspect on the cohabitant species and not directly
on *L. saligna* itself.

In *P. vulgaris* some germination occurs in open sites in the autumn but few of

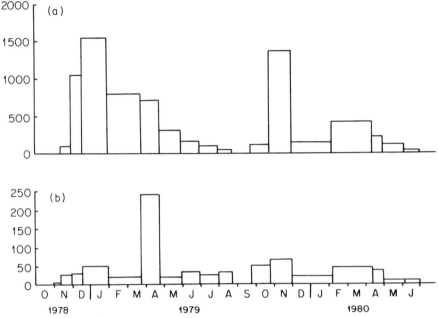

Figure 5   Germination of *Lactuca saligna* in permanent quadrats on, (a) south-facing slopes of sea wall, and (b) north-facing slopes and flat ground for the period between October 1978 and June 1980. The proportion of autumn germination to spring germination is considerably higher in south-facing sites

these plants survive winter flooding and poaching by animals. The majority of plants emerge in late spring following exposure of the mud. When vegetation was cleared in experimental plots in autumn as many as half the achenes which were sown germinated in November only to die during the winter. These results suggest that winter germination is normally suppressed by the cohabitant vegetation.

Discussion

Lactuca saligna and *Pulicaria vulgaris* are rare species in Britain and are in danger of extinction. The largest remaining colonies of *L. saligna* are all on sea walls in the Thames estuary and those of *P. vulgaris* are all in the New Forest. So long as conditions remain unchanged these major sites should continue to support their respective rare species, although none of the minor colonies are likely to persist without management of their habitats.

All the evidence suggests that the regeneration phase of the life-cycle is the most vulnerable and the single most important factor responsible for the exclusion of the two species from other vegetation. Open sites are created by cattle poaching on the sea walls where *L. saligna* grows; most of the plants are on the south-facing slopes, which have less vegetation cover than other parts of the site. It is not clear why *L. saligna* has declined in shingle sites where there is adequate bare ground, although there is evidence that rabbit grazing may be an important factor. In *P. vulgaris* sites there is an interaction of the seasonally high water table and disturbance of the ground by horses and vehicles. The most likely effect of this disturbance is to suppress perennial species and to create bare mud on which *P. vulgaris* can establish. In general, management of the remaining sites of both species should aim to maintain or reconstitute the type of disturbance typical of the existing colonies.

In Britain *L. saligna* has always been a predominantly maritime species and *P. vulgaris* has always been associated with common land on which domestic animals are kept. Both species only occur in south-eastern England. These associations are unexplained. Since there are so few British sites available for study it is unlikely that the causal relationship can be detected without a study of populations in continental Europe. Nevertheless these associations have been consistently remarked upon throughout the written history of the plants and, were any attempt to be made to re-introduce these species, it would be prudent to select sites in which similar conditions exist.

The indicator scoring procedure provides a rapid means of assessing the suitability of a site (albeit based on the conditions in the remaining sites) which could be used to select sites for re-introduction. For example, the banks of the Bedford River in Cambridgeshire, from which *L. saligna* was last recorded in 1951, were shown to have an indicator score as high as any site where *L. saligna* still survives. A trial of the technique was carried out at Fobbing and Cliffe where *L. saligna* plants were introduced into sea wall sites which had high indicator scores but no *L. saligna*. Two years later, 5 out of 20 of the new populations consisted of as many plants as were originally introduced or had increased in number.

For annuals such as *L. saligna* and *P. vulgaris* at their climatic distribution limits large fluctuations in population size from year to year are to be expected. When these fluctuations are coupled with a loss of populations from which seed can be re-introduced owing to changes in land use, as has happened in the cases of *L. saligna* and *P. vulgaris*, then the dynamic equilibrium between suitable sites with extinct populations and those populations which export seeds is upset and fairly rapid extinction in the whole region may follow. Under these circumstances deliberate re-introduction of the species may be justified and particularly so in the case of a species such as *P. vulgaris* in which the achenes are most likely to have been transported by animals and vehicles moving between agricultural settlements on unmetalled roads – a form of dispersal which cannot occur to the same extent with modern forms of transport.

Acknowledgements

We would like to thank Dr F. Perring and Miss L. Farrell for information and advice. A. D. R. Hare was supported by a Studentship from the National Environment Research Council.

References

Boswell Syme, J. T. (1866). *Sowerby's English Botany*, 3rd Ed., Vol. 5, *Compositae*, London.
Bray, R. J. and Curtis, J. T. (1957). 'An ordination of the upland forest communities of Southern Wisconsin', *Ecol. Monogr.*, **27**, 325–49.
Clapham, A. R., Tutin, T. G., and Warburg, E. F. (1962). *Flora of the British Isles*, 2nd Ed., Cambridge University Press.
Druce, G. C. (1928). *British Plant List*, Buncle, Arbroath.
Feráková, V. (1977). *The Genus* Lactuca *L. in Europe*, Univerzita Komenského, Bratislava.
Hill, M. O. (1973). 'Reciprocal averaging: an eigenvector method of ordination', *J. Ecol.*, **61**, 237–49.
Hill, M. O., Bunce, R. G. H., and Shaw, M. W. (1975). 'Indicator species analysis, a divisive polythetic method of classification, and its application to a survey of native pinewoods in Scotland', *J. Ecol.*, **63**, 597–613.
Hultén, E. (1950). *Atlas över Växternas Utbredning i Norden*, Stockholm.
Marks, M. K. (1979). *Aspects of the Physiological Ecology of the Wild Lettuce* (Lactuca serriola *L.*), PhD thesis, Queen Mary College, University of London.
Pena, P. and Lobel, M. (1570). *Stirpium Adversaria Nova*, London.
Perring, F. H. and Farrell, L. (1977). *British Red Data Books: 1. Vascular Plants*, Society for the Promotion of Nature Conservation, Lincoln.
Perring, F. H. and Walters, S. M. (Eds.) (1962, 2nd Ed. 1976). *Atlas of the British Flora*, E. P. Publishing, Wakefield, for B.S.B.I.
Pigott, C. D. (1970). 'The response of plants to climate and climatic change', in *The Flora of a Changing Britain* (Ed. F. Perring), pp. 32–44. B.S.B.I. Conference Reports, 11. Classey, Middx.
Prince, S. D. (1980). 'Ecophysiology of wild lettuce', *Proceedings Eucarpia Meeting on Leafy Vegetables* (Ed. J. W. Maxon-Smith and F. A. Langton), pp. 63–73, Glasshouse Crops Research Institute, Littlehampton.
Ray, J. (1660). *Catalogus Plantarum circa Cantabrigiam nascentium*, Cambridge.
Turner, D. and Dillwyn, L. W. (1805). *The Botanist's Guide through England and Wales*, Phillips and Fardon, London.
Watson, H. C. (1873). *Topographical Botany*, Thames Ditton.

Note

Plant names in this chapter follow Clapham, Tutin and Warburg (1962).

The Biological Aspects of Rare Plant Conservation
Edited by Hugh Synge

32
Biological causes of local rarity in *Carlina vulgaris*

JUNE GREIG-SMITH AND G. R. SAGAR *School of Plant Biology, University College of North Wales, Bangor*

Summary

Fruit production by *Carlina vulgaris* at Newborough Warren, Anglesey, was low. Its populations were not increased by removing neighbouring vegetation or by adding mineral nutrients, but were increased by sowing extra fruits. These increases in population size were often greater on plots where the plant was originally rarer.

Fruits of *C. vulgaris* were found to be destroyed by a small mammal. Predation was very heavy in the autumn, but less so in spring. In spring predation may have been less at sites where *C. vulgaris* was naturally rarer but in autumn the converse may have been the case. Plots from which mammals were excluded showed that populations of *C. vulgaris* may sometimes be regulated by predation rather than by edaphic or climatic factors or by interference from other plant species.

Introduction

The most sure and effective way of preserving a threatened plant species is to remove it from its habitat and to grow it in isolation from neighbours and protected from pests, pathogens and predators. The ability of gardeners to grow and multiply selected species is a perfect illustration of this phenomenon. It follows that the growth of a plant or a population of plants in its habitat is often subjected to constraints. If those constraints are relaxed, population size may increase; if they are severe, populations may decrease or a plant may grow and develop less well. This pragmatic argument identifies little more than Darwin's example of elephants or part of the Malthusian hypothesis (Darwin, 1859; Sagar, 1970). The causes of rarity are to be found by identifying the constraints on the potential rate at which the population size of the selected species can increase.

Our approaches have been of two kinds. The first has been analytical where demographic studies of selected populations potentially allow the identification of the stages in the life cycle when individuals die or fail to leave offspring. The second approach uses experimentation and involves deliberate interference by controlled treatments to relieve or reduce potential bottlenecks or regulating agents.

The price of the latter approach is a severe restriction on the choice of species because one is simply not allowed to make experiments with species that are really rare ('rare' in conservation terms) in their habitat on the sort of scale required. The solution to this dilemma, however, has a scientific bonus for in choosing a species which is in some places common and in others rare, effective comparisons of the two states become possible. Comparative ecology is often most rewarding (Harper *et al.*, 1961).

Carlina vulgaris, a composite, is a widely distributed facultative biennial. It has a stout tap root and produces a basal rosette of leaves. At the time of flowering the main axis elongates (5–60 cm) and bears 1–30 capitula each of which may contain from a few to approximately 300 fruits. Salisbury (1942) gives the mean number of capitula per plant as 4.4 and of fruits per capitulum as 154. The inner bracts of the capitulum spread out in dry air and close together in wet conditions (Salisbury, 1952). The fruits have a low achene weight/pappus weight ratio, a relatively short maximum dispersal distance but a relatively high terminal velocity in flight (Sheldon and Burrows, 1973). The species is a feature of short, more open downland and is also characteristic of more calcareous dune systems (Salisbury, 1942, 1952). In our study area the species can be found in communities where it is occasional to rare but close by in other communities it is frequent to common.

The sites

A full description of the Newborough dune system can be found in Ranwell (1959, 1960). The five study sites (AC, AR, BC, BR and D) were all in dune slacks. Sites AC and AR were at the drier end of the continuum, site BC intermediate and in site BR (which was close to BC) small patches were below the extreme winter-flooding level. Water, 2–4 cm deep, accumulated on site BR in the winter of 1977/78. Site D was at the drier end of the continuum. The pH of the areas was *c.* 8.5 and available nitrogen, phosphorus and potassium were scarcely measurable. All the sites contained plant species which are common: *Salix repens, Carex flacca, Lotus corniculatus, Leontodon taraxacoides* and *Poa pratensis*, together with *Viola canina, Thymus drucei, Festuca rubra, Senecio jacobaea* and *Ononis repens. Bellis perennis, Equisetum variegatum, Pyrola rotundifolia* ssp. *maritima, Hydrocotyle vulgaris* and *Mentha aquatica* were also present.

In site AC, *Carlina vulgaris* was frequent and in patches common, in AR rare, in BC occasional but common in patches, and in BR occasional to rare. In site D, *C. vulgaris* was frequent.

Demography

The approach was a straightforward one. Twenty-four permanent quadrats each 0.5 m × 0.5 m were mapped at intervals over a period of 2 years. At the beginning, the numbers of plants per plot ranged from 1 to 27 thus giving a fair range of

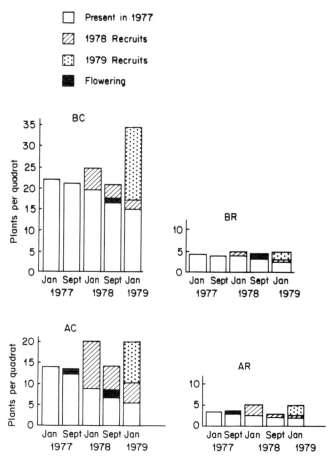

Figure 1   The populations of the common and rare plots of sites
A and B from June 1977 to June 1979

Table 1   Mortality   of   plants
and   seedlings   between   June
1978   and   June   1979.   Results
from   the   demographic   study.
Values are percentages

Site	Plants	Seedlings
BC	18	56
BR	21	50
AC	32	29
AR	20	0
BC+AC	26	31
BR+AR	30	33

mini-population densities. During each recording the arrival of new plants (as seedlings), flowering and survival were monitored at the level of the individual plant.

There was an apparent stability in populations seen over the 2 years of study. In particular the populations in the two common sites remained significantly higher than those in the two rare sites (Figure 1). Flowering was relatively uncommon over the 2 years of study and the percentage mortalities of plants and seedlings were similar for the combined common and combined rare sites (Table 1).

Experimental

This approach was much more extensive and to understand its rationale it is useful to refer to Figure 2. From this diagram it can readily be seen that the *only* potential for increase in population size of *Carlina vulgaris* lies in seed production or immigration of fruits but that every other phase of the life cycle has a probability of loss associated with it. Even seed production may of course be constrained by resources or agents.

The aim of the perturbation experiments was to remove or relieve potential constraints at what were believed to be the most critical phases. Only a few of the

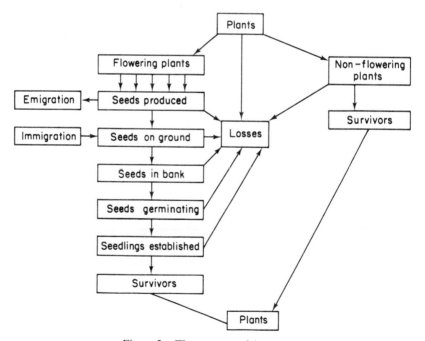

Figure 2   The strategy of the study

experiments can be reported here; but in effect the scientific process was being followed: a question was asked, a hypothesis created and then tested.

A seed is an evolutionary compromise. The price to the plant of mobility is twofold – an extremely nutritious food source for predators, pathogens and parasites, and a very precarious infancy before establishment. Among wild plants by far the greatest numerical losses occur between seed production and seedling establishment (Sagar and Mortimer, 1977). Only rarely are these losses recorded and even more rarely are the causes known. One of the main experiments was designed multifactorially around three hypotheses which identified seed supply, plant neighbours and substrate fertility as potential constraints on the size of populations of *C. vulgaris*.

Four sites were selected; in two of these *C. vulgaris* was common and in the other two rare. At each site 24 plots each 30 × 30 cm and separated by 15 cm wide paths were marked out and three replicates of eight treatments were imposed. All permutations of these treatments were made: a commercial fertilizer ('Vitax 4') was applied by hand three times during the study at a rate which gave 133 kg nitrogen, 199 kg phosphorus and 266 kg potassium per hectare (called N treatments); shoots and as far as possible roots of all plants except *C. vulgaris* were removed and regrowth periodically checked by hand (D treatments); and

Table 2   Emergence and survival in the experimental plots. Fruits sown in October 1976. Values are total numbers for three replicate plots

Treatment	Plants prior to treatment	Seedlings Spring 1977	Plants Sept. 1977	Plants March 1978
Site B *Carlina* common (BC)				
NIL	0	0	0	0
+D	2	4	2	1
+S	0	46	41	42
+N	2	2	2	0
+S+D	2	3	4	2
+N+D	1	0	0	0
+N+S	3	26	25	10
+N+S+D	1	5	2	2
Site B *Carlina* rare (BR)				
NIL	0	0	0	0
+D	0	0	0	0
+S	0	14	11	10
+N	0	0	0	0
+S+D	0	0	0	0
+N+D	0	0	0	0
+N+S	0	5	3	3
+N+S+D	0	0	0	0

+N, added minerals; +D, plants other than *Carlina* removed; +S, *Carlina* fruits sown.

Table 3   Emergence and survival in the experimental plots. Fruits sown in March 1978. Values are total numbers for three replicate plots

Treatment	Plants March 1978	Seedlings 1978	Plants Sept. 1978	Plants Sept. 1979
Site B *Carlina* common (BC)				
NIL	0	1	1	1
+D	1	0	1	2
+S	42	75	122	69
+N	0	9	8	0
+S+D	2	123	121	92
+N+D	0	0	0	2
+N+S	10	80	60	2
+N+S+D	2	101	99	48
Totals	57	389	412	216
Site B *Carlina* rare (BR)				
NIL	0	1	1	1
+D	0	0	0	0
+S	10	154	163	138
+N	0	0	0	0
+S+D	0	196	183	156
+N+D	0	0	0	0
+N+S	3	60	21	1
+N+S+D	0	171	155	155
Totals	13	582	523	451

+N, added minerals; +D, plants other than *Carlina* removed; +S, *Carlina* fruits sown.

fruits of *C. vulgaris* at a density equivalent to 3200 viable fruits per sq. m were sown (S treatments). In the first instance the treatments were made in October 1976, using for the S treatments fruits which were collected locally and not stored. Detailed assessments were made on sub-plots. The results of the treatments at two of the sites are presented in Table 2.

Out of an average of 213 fruits sown on each set of replicate sub-plots, the maximum mean recovery as seedlings was 46. Visits to the plots after sowing revealed signs of predation of fruits. These included discarded fruit walls from which the 'seed' had been removed.

With the small numbers of survivors it is not surprising that statistical analysis of these data was not very rewarding; but inspection shows a definite influence of sowing seeds (+S treatments) and allows a suggestion that removal of neighbours (+S+D and +N+S+D plots) may have reduced the chance of a sown fruit producing a seedling. It proved possible to introduce *C. vulgaris* into some plots from which it had been absent simply by adding fruits (+S and +N+S plots).

The level of predation recorded from this autumn sown experiment led us to repeat the experiment on the same plots on 29 March 1978. The re-sowing was preceded by repeating the removal of vegetation (except for *C. vulgaris*) and refertilization of the appropriate plots in early February and early March. The results of this experiment (Table 3) were somewhat different!

Immediately prior to sowing there were more than four times as many *C. vulgaris* plants on the common plots as there were on the rare ones; by September 1979 the corresponding numbers were 216 and 541 respectively (Table 3). The reversal of the relative population sizes was due to two interacting forces. More seedlings appeared in site BR (582) than in site BC (389) and survivorship of seedlings and plants was also greater in BR (75 per cent) than in BC (55 per cent). Only one of the three treatments had a major effect on population size; that was introducing fruits. The effect was nearly absolute in BR, only one individual, in the nil treatment, being recorded from all the unsown plots. From this evidence it does not seem unreasonable to suggest that in site BR, populations of *C. vulgaris* were low principally because of shortage of propagules. Certainly there do not appear to have been edaphic, microclimatic or competitive exclusions operating.

At both sites where nutrients had been added to +S plots the numbers of seedlings and survivorship were reduced below those of other +S plots. The poorer performance of *C. vulgaris* cannot have been due to the nutrient directly because the results for +N+S+D were not similarly affected. The plots which received the +N treatments, however, were transformed from a semi-open *Salix* associes to a vegetation dominated by *Holcus lanatus* and *Festuca rubra*. The additional vigour given to neighbouring plants of other species reduced the number of sites for seedling survival (Harper *et al.*, 1965).

One rather overwhelming conclusion must be reached from the results of this experiment. The frequency of safe sites for seedling establishment in site B far exceeded the natural supply of propagules. Such a conclusion merited further examination.

The production of fruits

In part to assess the maximum fruit production of plants of *Carlina vulgaris*, an experiment was made in the glasshouse from spring 1977 to late 1978. Seedlings of *C. vulgaris* were grown in acid-washed sand in 25 cm diameter pots and supplied with nitrogen, phosphorus and potassium in multifactorial combinations. The basic nutrition was a Long Ashton solution without these elements but nitrogen was added at 3, 9, 27, or 81 µg per cu cm, phosphorus at 1, 4, or 16 µg per cu cm and potassium at 1 or 16 µg per cu cm. The nutrients were supplied regularly and the pots were leached with deionized water at intervals. Many data were collected but only fruit production will be considered here (Figure 3).

In only four of the treatments (all associated with the lowest level of nitrogen) did any plants fail to set fruits. Mean values ranged from 33 to 292 fruits per plant (calculating from mean effect means), but the maximum from individual treatment

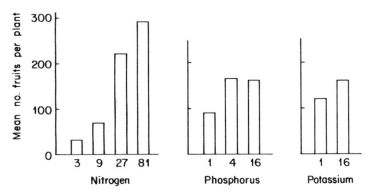

Figure 3   Fruit production by *Carlina vulgaris* in a glasshouse experiment. Values are means of main effect treatments

means was 484 fruits per plant from the pots which received the highest level of all
three nutrients.

From the demographic study it was discovered that flowering was a rare event.
In 1978 only 0.8 plants per quadrat flowered in the BC plots and 0.2 plants per
quadrat in the BR plots. Using the minimum values from Figure 3 this performance would have yielded 26.4 and 6.6 fruits per quadrat respectively.

In the summer of 1976 rabbits grazed young inflorescences, thus reducing the
potential for fruit production, but this activity was not repeated in subsequent
years.

The fates of fruits

There was little evidence from the field that maturing or mature fruits were predated or parasitized in the capitulum. In late 1979 fruits which had been collected
from the field became infested with a population of small orange larvae (not yet
identified) and by *Botrytis* sp. but these attacks may have arisen secondarily. The
larvae were most active around the point of attachment of the fruit to the
receptacle and damaged the base of some of the fruits.

The fruits of *Carlina vulgaris* are dispersed but probably only over short
distances (the capitula are borne c. 15 cm above ground level, the fruits are heavy,
the pappus is easily detached and closes when wet). The result is that emigration
or immigration by dispersal do not appear to be major events in the dynamics of
C. vulgaris populations and it can be fairly safely concluded that fruits produced
in a small area tend to be dispersed locally. To follow the fate of fruits on the
ground four studies were made.

In December 1977 12 plots were fixed on site A and 12 plots on site B. In each
plot 50 marked fruits of *C. vulgaris* were sown and in December, January,
February and March three plots at each site were removed from the field and

taken to the laboratory where visual searches and germination tests were made in attempts to recover the sown fruits. A synopsis of the results is given in Table 4.

These results must be treated with caution for the recovery of seeds is notoriously difficult. The low recoveries in December 1977 only 2 days after sowing could have been due either to technical failure or to rapid predation before the fruits had become hidden in the vegetation. Observations of the walls of some recovered fruits revealed attempts at predation.

Forty Petri dishes containing Newborough sand and fruits of *C. vulgaris* were wrapped in a double layer of muslin and planted, 20 at site B and 20 at site D in October 1977. They were recovered in March 1978 by which time 26.3 per cent of the seeds at site B and 32.1 per cent of the seeds at site D could not be germinated. Loss of germinability can have several causes including induced dormancy, loss of viability for physiological or cytological reasons or attack by pathogens. It is unreasonable to speculate about agents or agencies but useful to have a rough measure of losses due to agents other than macro-predators.

Macro-predators include birds and small mammals. Enclosures are a satisfactory preliminary way of investigating their role, despite criticisms of such techniques. A 2 × 3 plot grid was set up in site BC and one randomly selected plot of each pair was protected by enclosing it in a galvanized wire cage (0.64 cm mesh) 80 cm × 60 cm × 40 cm high and buried to a depth of 15 cm. One hundred marked fruits of *C. vulgaris* with pappus removed were sown in the central 10 × 10 cm of each plot on 7 March 1978. Emergence and survival were recorded in the plots up to the middle of June 1978. The numbers of seedlings found are given in Table 5 and the results show a clear difference between open and protected plots, together with one anomaly. A careful search of the protected plots revealed, in replicate 1, a hole in the ground which was identified as the entrance of a burrow of a small mammal. In the open plots between 80 and 90 per cent of the sown fruits failed to produce seedlings; in two of the replicates of protected plots less than 40 per cent failed. It seems a reasonable assumption that macro-predators played an important part in fruit-loss in *C. vulgaris*. The misfortune in

Table 4   The mean number of seeds recovered
(from 50 sown in December 1977)

	Site	
Recovery in	AC	BC
December 1977	33.7a*	22.0b
January 1978	27.0b	23.3b
February 1978	28.0b	32.3a
March 1978	18.7c	25.7b

*Where individual values in a column share a common letter, the values do not differ at $p = 0.05$.

Table 5   The numbers of seedlings found up to
14 June 1978 in open and protected plots. Fruits
(100 per plot) sown 7 March 1978

	Plots	
Replicate	Open	Protected
1	14	14*
2	10	65
3	17	63

*Entrance to burrow of small mammal found in plot
post hoc.

replicate 1 of the protected plots suggests that small mammals may be more important than birds. Accordingly, in December 1979 four woodmice (*Apodemus sylvaticus* L.) were caught in Longworth traps and supplied for 4 hours with a large quantity of imbibed fruits of *C. vulgaris*. The debris of totally and partially eaten fruits was entirely consistent with the debris found on the field plots at Newborough. Since the woodmice were not trapped at Newborough it is possible that some other species may be important there.

Discussion

Flowering, and hence fruit production at the Newborough sites, was comparatively rare; extra fruits sown at the normal time of dispersal were heavily predated. Exogenous fruits sown in the spring were less prone to predation and effective exclosures led to more than 60 per cent of spring-sown fruits producing emerged seedlings. It is suggested that shortage of propagules is the most severe constraint on population increase of *Carlina vulgaris* in both the BC and BR areas.

There have been a number of studies previously where attempts have been made to increase the size of species' populations by adding propagules. Often they have been associated with other perturbation treatments. Sagar and Harper (1961) showed that the size of populations of *Plantago lanceolata*, *P. media* and *P. major* was affected much more by the presence of other species than by seed supplies. Putwain *et al.* (1968) found that sowing fruits of *Rumex acetosella* had little effect on population size, recruitment being largely by vegetative reproduction. Foster (1964) increased populations of seedlings of *Bellis perennis* more markedly by management of neighbours than by seed input. Other authors have also suggested that neighbours control population sizes (Pemadasa *et al.*, 1974 for populations of dune annuals; Jeffrey and Pigott, 1973 for *Kobresia simpliciuscula*); indeed a large part of modern ecology is devoted to plant interference as the agency of population regulation (see for example Harper, 1977). The implications of studies of successful biological control seem to have been largely ignored by ecologists interested in plant distribution and abundance. Take a plant away from its predators and parasites and its population explodes (see for example *Hypericum perforatum*, Holloway, 1964); this must mean that for some plant species at least regulation is due to agents acting from above in the food chain. *Carlina vulgaris* in some of its sites at Newborough may be such an example.

Acknowledgements

We are grateful to the National Environment Research Council for the studentship which made this work possible, to the Nature Conservancy Council for permission to work at Newborough and to the technical staff of the School of Plant Biology and of Pen-y-Ffridd Research Station for support. We thank Deborah Rabinowitz for some pertinent comments.

References

Clapham, A. R., Tutin, T. G., and Warburg, E. F. (1962). *Flora of the British Isles*, 2nd Ed., Cambridge University Press.

Darwin, C. R. (1859). *The Origin of Species*, Murray, London.

Foster, J. (1964). *Studies on the Population Dynamics of the Daisy*, Bellis perennis, PhD thesis, University of Wales.

Harper, J. L. (1977). *Population Biology of Plants*, Academic Press, London.

Harper, J. L. with Clatworthy, J. N., McNaughton, I. H., and Sagar, G. R. (1961). 'The evolution and ecology of closely related species living in the same area', *Evolution*, **15**, 209–27.

Harper, J. L., Williams, J. T., and Sagar, G. R. (1965). 'The behaviour of seeds in soil. I. The heterogeneity of soil surfaces and its role in determining the establishment of plants from seed', *J. Ecol.*, **53**, 273–86.

Holloway, J. K. (1964). 'Projects in biological control of weeds', in *Biological Control of Insect Pests and Weeds* (Ed. P. DeBach), pp. 650–70, Chapman and Hall, London.

Jeffrey, D. W. and Pigott, C. D. (1973). 'The response of grasslands on sugar-limestone in Teesdale to application of phosphorus and nitrogen', *J. Ecol.*, **61**, 85–92.

Pemadasa, M. A. and Lovell, P. H. (1974). 'Factors affecting the distribution of some annuals in the dune system at Aberffraw, Anglesey', *J. Ecol.*, **62**, 403–16.

Putwain, P. D., Machin, D., and Harper, J. L. (1968). 'Studies in the dynamics of plant populations. II. Components and regulation of a natural population of *Rumex acetosella* L.', *J. Ecol.*, **56**, 421–31.

Ranwell, D. (1959). 'Newborough Warren, Anglesey. I. The dune system and dune slack habitat', *J. Ecol.*, **47**, 571–601.

Ranwell, D. (1960). 'Newborough Warren, Anglesey. II. Plant associes and succession cycles of the sand dune and dune slack vegetation', *J. Ecol.*, **48**, 117–41.

Sagar, G. R. (1970). 'Factors controlling the size of plant populations, in *Proceedings of the 10th British Weed Control Conference*, pp. 965–79.

Sagar, G. R. and Harper, J. L. (1961). 'Controlled interference with natural populations of *Plantago lanceolata, P. major* and *P. media*', *Weed Res.*, **1**, 163–76.

Sagar, G. R. and Mortimer, A. M. (1977). 'An approach to the study of the population dynamics of plants with special reference to weeds', *Appl. Biol.*, **1**, 1–47.

Salisbury, E. J. (1942). *The Reproductive Capacity of Plants*, Bell, London.

Salisbury, E. J. (1952). *Downs and Dunes*, Bell, London.

Sheldon, J. C. and Burrows, F. M. (1973). 'The dispersal effectiveness of the achene-pappus units of selected compositae in steady winds with convection', *New Phytol.*, **72**, 665–75.

Note

Plant names in this chapter follow Clapham, Tutin and Warburg (1962).

Discussion

D. M. Henderson (Edinburgh): The experiments on population dynamics seem to me to suffer from surprising major omissions. Seed viability and germination success are clearly affected by all sorts of physical and inter-plant competition, but no experiment ever seems to record that seed pathogens, especially seed-borne pathogens, are involved. From the evidence of commercial crops – one has only to think of *Helminthosporium* and *Fusarium* in cereals and *Ascochyta* in legumes – surely this important biological factor is being overlooked. Are seeds that die or fail to germinate just thrown out as 'mouldy' without the researcher realizing that a specific pathogen may be involved?

Section 5
Introductions and
Re-introductions

The Biological Aspects of Rare Plant Conservation
Edited by Hugh Synge
© 1981 John Wiley & Sons Ltd.

33
A policy on introductions to Britain

B. H. GREEN *Department of Environmental Studies and Countryside Planning, Wye College, University of London*

Summary

In 1978 a Working Party on Introductions was set up to review the issue of introductions to Britain and to advise on developing an introductions policy. The difficult issue of introductions to an island of impoverished flora like Britain is discussed and the conclusions of the Working Party's report presented. A series of arguments for and against introductions is given, with telling examples on both sides from the British flora. The fate of past introductions is analysed and the ecology of successful colonists described. On the basis of this evidence, some policy guidelines are established.

Introduction

The subject of introduced species is a vexed one among conservationists. Views tend to be polarized either for or against the introduction of species. But there are many different kinds of introductions, and some raise very different issues to others. In 1978 the UK Committee for International Nature Conservation, serviced by the Nature Conservancy Council, set up a working party to consider a policy on introductions in the UK. Its remit was to:

1. review the ecological factors and issues associated with the deliberate and accidental introduction of species;
2. advise on the principles and policies to be followed and to formulate guidelines to implement them.

  The Working Party on Introductions consulted widely amongst conservation, agriculture, forestry and fisheries organizations and individual views were solicited in journals. Many facts and opinions were received, covering a wide spectrum of views. The report of the Working Party, which was compiled in the light of these submissions and the views of its members, has now been published (Green, 1979). This chapter outlines some of its main points and the thinking behind them. Furthermore, since the report was concerned with all groups of

403

species and therefore could not go into any detail with any particular one, I have tried to elaborate on some of the particular issues relating to vascular plants.

Definitions

A number of terms have been used in different ways to describe different kinds of introductions. The Working Party adopted a terminology based on that used at the seminar on 'Re-introductions, techniques and ethics' organized by the Italian National Appeal of the World Wildlife Fund (Boitani, 1976):

Introduction

The deliberate or accidental release of animals or plants of a species or race into an area in which it has not occurred in historical times; or, a species or race so released.

Re-introduction

The deliberate or accidental release of a species or race into an area in which it was indigenous in historical times; or, a species or race so released.

Restocking

The deliberate or accidental release of a species or race into an area in which it is already present.

Naturalization

The establishment of self-regenerating populations of an introduced species or race in a free-living state in the wild.

Alien, exotic

An introduced species.

Translocation, relocation

Any kind of movement of a species by man.

The use of 'translocation' in this generic way to replace the looser use of 'introduction' raises the possibility of confusion with its use to describe introductions or re-introductions which do not cross political boundaries. These do indeed raise different issues to introductions or re-introductions from one country to another, but they are not ecologically different.

Reasons for translocations

There are not many examples of virtually cosmopolitan species like the barn owl, common reed (*Phragmites australis*) and bracken (*Pteridium aquilinum*). Most species appear not to have had the time, opportunity or capability to colonize all their potential habitat throughout the world.

Islands, or island habitats like rivers, lakes and mountain tops, are particularly difficult to colonize, their species complements reaching an equilibrium proportional to the size and isolation of the island. Extrapolation of the fossil record suggests that at least 67 per cent of the present flora of the British Isles was likely to have arrived by the time Britain was separated by the North Sea from the European mainland at the end of the Boreal period some 7000 years or more ago (Godwin, 1975). A glance at the European distribution maps of any group of species shows what an effective barrier to species migration even a small stretch of water like the English channel can be, surprisingly even to aerial species like birds or butterflies.

Had the British Isles not been cut off from the mainland so early in the period of recolonization of Northern Europe after the last glaciation, a number of species introduced by man might have been expected to have been a natural part of our flora and fauna, as indeed some were in previous interglacials. The little owl, sycamore (*Acer pseudoplatanus*), rhododendron (*Rhododendron ponticum*), and Norway Spruce (*Picea abies*) (so often reviled in forestry plantations) are examples.

Ireland has an even more impoverished flora and fauna than Great Britain. Its flora includes only some 70 per cent of that of all the British Isles, lacking for example common species like the limes (*Tilia cordata* and *T. platyphyllos*), beech (*Fagus sylvatica*), and hornbeam (*Carpinus betulus*). Its fauna lacks snakes (on account of St Patrick – or more likely the Irish Sea), frogs, the weasel, the mole and several other mammals and birds. The smaller offshore islands are even more impoverished.

Mainland Europe is itself rather poorer in species than other cool temperate parts of the world. Temperate deciduous forests in North America contain several score tree species but in northern Europe there are only a dozen or so. The barriers to southward migration which the predominantly east–west European, but not American, mountain ranges constituted in the glacial epoch are thought to have been the cause of the impoverishment of the European flora. Genera like *Magnolia* and the tulip trees (*Liriodendron*), which occurred in Europe in earlier periods and which will still grow here happily in gardens, are now confined to the Asian and North American deciduous woodland formations.

Considerable further impoverishment of our flora and fauna has come about in prehistoric and historic times through the activity of man. Habitat loss, particularly forest clearance and the drainage of wetlands, has led to the extinction of the bear, wolf, wild boar, stork, crane and numerous other species once native to these islands. It is estimated that of 20 species of flowering plants believed to have become extinct in this country since 1600, 11 have been lost through habitat change or destruction, mostly brought about by agriculture (Perring, 1970).

Direct persecution or collection have also contributed to the loss of many species and have been primarily responsible for the loss of many others, particularly birds of prey like the sea eagle, and attractive plants like the Lady's Slipper Orchid (*Cypripedium calceolus*).

With this background of an impoverished flora and fauna it is not surprising that attempts have long been made to introduce and re-introduce species to the British Isles. In 1860 a society was set up specifically to introduce species to Great Britain – The Society for the Acclimatisation of Animals, Birds, Fishes, Insects and Vegetables within the United Kingdom. Its objectives were mainly to naturalize species for food, something which had been successfully achieved with the rabbit and carp, which are likely to have first been introduced in Norman and Tudor times respectively. Earlier, the Romans were probably responsible for the successful introduction of the Sweet Chestnut (*Castanea sativa*) and the pheasant. Numerous species of trees and shrubs have subsequently been deliberately naturalized as forest crops or for ornament. Other species have followed the pheasant in being introduced as game; fallow deer and many freshwater fish species are examples. Plants like the Snowberry (*Symphoricarpos albus*) and *Gaultheria shallon* have been introduced as game cover. Finally some species like the little owl have, at least in part, been introduced to control pests. There are several classical examples of both spectacularly successful and disastrously unsuccessful attempts at biological control elsewhere in the world.

Only one vertebrate, the capercaillie, has been successfully re-introduced into the British Isles, but some like the blue hare have been re-introduced from one part of their range back to another. No species of any sporting or commercial value has been immune from restocking, often from overseas populations.

There are not many examples in the British Isles of species successfully naturalized for conservation reasons. But translocation is potentially one of the most useful tools available to conservation managers. It can:

1. Help restore the full ecosystem complement and functioning. It has been suggested for example that tree regeneration is poor in British woods because of the absence of the main predators or herbivore populations.
2. Lessen the risk of extinction of species by catastrophes in their native range. For example, the Parma wallaby population translocated to Kawau Island, New Zealand, is now the mainstay of the species.

3. Provide research data on factors controlling species distribution.
4. Help generate diversity, which is widely regarded as a desirable attribute on both aesthetic and scientific grounds.

Many species have been accidentally introduced or re-introduced into the British Isles. Most naturalized plants have become established either as escapes from cultivation or as contaminants of crop seed. Others are thought to have arrived in packing material; Canadian Fleabane (*Conyza canadensis*) is believed to have arrived as stuffing in a bird skin, and there is a whole spectrum of casuals associated with the use of wool shoddy as a fertilizer (Salisbury, 1961).

Problems resulting from translocations

Weeds and pests of agriculture and forestry. Some introduced species, like our own Perforate St John's Wort (*Hypericum perforatum*) in North America, and the American prickly pear cacti (*Opuntia* spp.) in Australia, have proved to be disastrous weeds. Wild Oat Grass (*Avena fatua*), having been with us so long as to be only dubiously an introduction under the present definition, causes comparable problems in the British Isles, but there are not many examples of introduced plants becoming pests that cause economic damage on a similar scale. But animal introductions like the rabbit, grey squirrel or coypu certainly have done so.

Carriers of disease. The translocation of species always involves the risk that the introduced species will carry disease or pests which may spread to native populations, or that native organisms will become a pest or disease of the introduced species. The latter has recently occurred with the exotic Lodgepole Pine (*Pinus contorta*), widely planted for forestry, which is now being devastated by the pine beauty moth previously in happy adjustment with our native Scots Pine (*P. sylvestris*).

Threats to native ecosystems. Natural and semi-natural ecosystems in Britain seem to have been remarkably resistant to competition from alien plants. *Oenothera* species have become widely naturalized in dunes, and *Epilobium adenocaulon* and *E. nerterioides, Impatiens* and *Mimulus* along stream sides, but not many alien species have become established in closed communities. Only perhaps rhododendron and sycamore in woods, *Elodea canadensis* in ponds and waterways, and, more recently, the Japanese Seaweed *Sargassum muticum* in coastal waters, have given rise to the concern that survival of native species and ecosystems might be in jeopardy. Much more concern has been expressed that alien animals like the grey squirrel and mink might threaten the native populations of the red squirrel and otter respectively. Whilst there seems to be little evidence of direct competition between alien and native species in these British examples, there is, none the less, no doubt that the loss of native species through competition or predation by aliens is a most important factor in the loss of species. It has been suggested that introductions account for some 19 per cent of bird and 23 per cent of mammal extinctions in the world since 1600 (Fisher, Simon and Vincent, 1969).

Translocated species can also change ecosystems by bringing about genetic changes in populations of indigenous species through hybridization. A new species of cordgrass, *Spartina anglica*, arose in Britain in this way from a natural cross between an accidentally introduced American species, *S. alterniflora*, and the native *S. maritima*. It can colonize lower down the shore than either parent, or any other vascular plant except *Zostera* species, and has converted thousands of acres of mudflat to salt marsh (see Ranwell, Chapter 34). Although selective pressures normally favour indigenous ecotypes, continuous introgression of alien genes might conceivably lead to loss of adaptation and weakening of native populations.

Also of concern to conservationists is the risk that the drain of individuals to provide a stock for translocating species can threaten the survival of the populations being exploited, and that resources used for translocations might be more profitably deployed in conserving endangered native species.

Evaluation

A policy on the translocation of species must inevitably consider both the benefits to be gained and the risks that species might be established which would cause enormous and expensive problems like some of the notorious examples already discussed. The benefits are usually obvious and often even quantifiable in monetary terms. The risks are not. The assessment of the likelihood of species becoming pests – that is injurious to man's interests – is thus a vital prerequisite to an introductions policy.

What constitutes man's interests is pivotal to any such assessment. An alien species like the rabbit, which might seem desirable to a conservationist as a means of maintaining herb-rich grassland, is very definitely a pest to the farmer. Although nature conservationists must be primarily concerned with the benefits and effects of translocated species on natural and semi-natural ecosystems, they cannot ignore their effects on agricultural and other land under crops, which constitutes by far the greater part of the countryside. Nor can they disregard species translocated for other than conservation purposes.

Some idea of the magnitude and seriousness of translocated species as pests is shown by those species which have been introduced or re-introduced to the British Isles. By far the greater majority have caused no problems whatever. Most have completely failed to establish themselves in the wild, or if they have done so have remained confined to limited areas. Of the few species which have become naturalized, few have become pests. And some of those that have reached pest proportions have settled back into lower, more stable populations after an initial explosive colonization. This has been the pattern followed by both *Spartina anglica* and *Elodea canadensis*, presumably as they have picked up predators and diseases checking their population growth, though Salisbury (1961) suggested that exhaustion of micronutrients might also be a factor with the latter.

Of some 32 000 flowering plants brought into this country, of which about 20 000 remain in cultivation, just over 600 species, or 2 per cent, are recorded by Clapham, Tutin and Warburg (1962) as established aliens. Of these about 30 species like *Lilium martagon* and *Foeniculum vulgare* are of dubious alien status because of uncertainty over their history, and a great many more, perhaps more than 350 species, are only dubiously naturalized, being transient casuals or maintaining only very small populations in one or two places. This leaves just over 200 species, or about 10 per cent of the flora, which are fairly widely naturalized aliens, though some are much commoner than others.

The likelihood of a species becoming a pest depends upon it becoming naturalized. Are there any common features among these 200 or so naturalized plants in the British Isles which would enable us to predict which kinds of species are likely to be able to successfully naturalize? Most of these successful colonists are from Europe (65 per cent), but 15 per cent are from North America, 12 per cent from Asia, 5 per cent from South America, 2 per cent from South Africa and 1 per cent from New Zealand. Some 70 per cent of these species are perennials. This is rather surprising for there is a tendency to think of successful alien colonists as fecund ruderal species, which are mostly annuals and biennials. The habitats recorded in the Flora confirm this proportion of ruderal species, about a third of the species being found in arable areas and waste places. Most of the perennial introductions, however, are species of open and seral communities. Some 9 per cent occur on rocks and walls, 14 per cent on verges and in hedgerows, 12 per cent on streamsides, 1 per cent in ponds and streams and 8 per cent mainly in coastal communities. Only 22 per cent of our widely introduced aliens seem to occur in closed, climax communities – 16 per cent in woods and 6 per cent in grasslands. Although therefore ruderals only account for perhaps a third of our well-established aliens, species of more open communities account for nearly 80 per cent of them. On this basis it would seem that ruderal and competitive species – R and C species in Grime's (1979) classification – are more likely to become successful colonists than stability (S) species of more permanent climax communities.

This is as would be expected, but there are still plenty of examples of successful alien colonists here and elsewhere in the world which are stability species of climax communities. Rose (1978) has considered the problem of predicting the fate of introductions in the light of recent ecological theory of niche, predation, competition, fecundity, life strategies, dispersal and island biogeography and concludes that generalizations are impossible, trial by experiment being the only reliable, but risky, means of assessment.

Policy

There can be no single policy to cover all kinds of translocation. Accidental introductions are a different case to deliberate introductions, and re-introductions are different again. Translocation within the country raises different issues to translocation into the country from abroad. Different groups of species like plants and birds and insects present different problems. The Working Party did, however, find some broad consensus of opinion and made a number of recommendations:

Accidental introductions. Escapes from cultivation and other more genuinely accidental introductions account for 54 per cent and 30 per cent respectively of the well-established aliens in our flora. Some of our worst alien animal pests like the rabbit, grey squirrel and mink have also been at least helped to become established by escapes. *It would seem axiomatic that accidental introductions are undesirable.*

Clearly it would be impossible, and undesirable, to try and prevent the massive trade in the introduction of species for agriculture, horticulture, medicine, pets and zoos. There is much existing legislation to prohibit import through restrictions on movement and powers to destroy certain species (see Green, 1979). *It needs to be reviewed for its effectiveness in controlling the establishment and spread of all alien species as well as the particular pest and disease organisms for which it is mainly designed.*

Introductions. Because of their dubious benefits, but many possible disadvantages to wildlife interests, and the difficulty in ensuring that an introduced species would not prove to be a pest, *deliberate introduction of alien species with the intent to naturalize them is seen as undesirable.*

It is accepted that farmers, foresters, fishery and other game managers and landscape architects may continue to want to introduce alien species into the countryside in ways by which they can interact freely with native species and perhaps become naturalized. *Conservation policy which presently encourages the use of native species for landscaping, game cover and ornamental purposes should be extended to a more positive presumption against exotics.* The Council of Europe's Convention on the Conservation of European Wildlife and Natural Habitats calls for its signatories 'to strictly control the introduction of non-native species'. This is accepted. *There should be powers whereby proposed introductions are carefully examined before implementation by a scientific authority.*

All species which are approved and released should be thoroughly monitored and recorded.

Reintroductions. The provision in the Council of Europe's Convention

to encourage the re-introduction of native species of wild flora and fauna when this would contribute to the conservation of an endangered species, provided that a study is first made in the light of the experiences of other Contracting Parties to establish that such re-introduction would be effective and acceptable

is accepted. Attempts to re-introduce species such as that currently being undertaken with sea eagles on the Isle of Rhum are important conservation measures provided:

1. there is a clear understanding why the species was lost: in general only those species lost through human agency and unlikely to recolonize naturally should be regarded as suitable candidates for re-introduction;
2. that there are suitable habitats of sufficient extent and isolation to which the species can be re-introduced;
3. that the individual plants or animals taken for re-introduction are of a taxon as close as possible to that of the native population;
4. that their loss does not prejudice the survival of the population from which they are taken.

Re-introductions of species into the country clearly presents similar problems to introductions and for this reason should also be considered by a scientific authority. Re-introductions within the country are less controversial and should be subject to a code of conduct along the lines of that already developed by the Royal Society for Nature Conservation.

Restocking. With the ever-increasing fragmentation of natural and semi-natural ecosystems by more intensive agriculture and forestry, there is no doubt that the natural loss of plants and animals from the remaining small island ecosystems and reserves will accelerate and the colonization of them from neighbouring areas decline. Restocking of species, re-introduction, and perhaps the local introduction of species may thus become essential in the future if the population levels of the rarer and less mobile species are to be maintained. We should perhaps now be more actively considering the restocking of species like the Lady's Slipper Orchid before re-introduction becomes necessary, and more sympathetically supporting and promoting the re-introduction of species to gravel pits, road verges and other new habitats to help buttress those populations still remaining on more natural situations.

References

Boitani, L. (1976). *Proceedings of the Seminar – Reintroductions: Techniques and Ethics*, World Wildlife Fund, Rome.
Clapham, A. R., Tutin, T. G., and Warburg, E. F. (1962). *Flora of the British Isles*, 2nd. Ed., Cambridge University Press.

Fisher, J., Simon, N., and Vincent, J. (1969). *The Red Book: Wildlife in Danger*, Collins, London.

Godwin, H. (1975). *The History of the British Flora*, 2nd. Ed., Cambridge University Press.

Green, B. H. (Ed.) (1979). *Wildlife Introductions to Great Britain*, Nature Conservancy Council, London.

Grime, J. P. (1979). *Plant Strategies and Vegetation Processes*, Wiley, Chichester.

Perring, F. (Ed.) (1970). *The Flora of a Changing Britain*. Classey, Hampton, Middx.

Rose, C. (1978). *Introduced Species and Conservation*, MSc thesis, University College, London.

Salisbury, E. (1961). *Weeds and Aliens*, Collins, London.

Tutin, T. G. *et al.* (Eds.) (1964–1980). *Flora Europaea*, 5 vols, Cambridge University Press.

Note

Plant names in this paper follow *Flora Europaea* (Tutin *et al.*, 1964–80).

Editor's note

Copies of the Working Party's report (Green, 1979) are available at £1.20 each (including postage) from the International Branch, Nature Conservancy Council, 20 Belgrave Square, London SW1X 8PY; cheques should be made out to the Nature Conservancy Council.

The Biological Aspects of Rare Plant Conservation
Edited by Hugh Synge
© 1981 John Wiley & Sons Ltd.

34
Introduced coastal plants and rare species in Britain

D. S. RANWELL *School of Biological Sciences, University of East Anglia, Norwich, England*

Summary

Examples of introduced coastal plants and their influences on rare species in salt marshes, arenohaline marshes, coast embankments, and coastal dunes are described. It is concluded that there is little evidence that introduced coastal species have had significant adverse effects on rare species populations in these habitats in Britain. Destruction of habitat by human activities has been responsible for losses of rare species on a far greater scale. There is a case for a more positive policy on introductions. Populations of rare species might be expanded and the potential geographical range of harmless aliens explored by carefully controlled transplant experiments.

Salt marshes

The advent of *Spartina anglica* in the past century in Britain has had profound biological consequences for many salt marshes in this country (Ranwell, 1972). I classify it as introduced on the grounds that it has foreign genes and has been widely propagated in many sites by man. The necessity of tolerating high salt concentrations and regular tidal inundation limits the number of higher plant species found on salt marshes. Very few rare species are found within the zone that *S. anglica* can occupy on salt marshes in this country; *S. maritima* is one of these.

This native salt marsh grass was probably in the Humber estuary in Bronze Age times (D. Cutler, *in litt.*), and in Devon within the last few decades. *S. maritima* is now limited in Great Britain to salt marsh sites in south-east England. Here, with one exception, it is found in small isolated populations at the edge of pans within the main salt-marsh sward. The exception is at Maplin Sands at the mouth of the Thames estuary where *S. maritima* thrives in a pioneer situation at the seaward limit of the salt marsh. *S. anglica* occurs within the marsh, but the two species appear rarely to be in direct competition with each other. It is difficult to get data for this site because salvoes of high explosive shells are shot over it daily by the army. However, at this site, silt accretion appears to be almost counterbalanced by downward isostatic adjustment of land and sea level, and the low net accretion seems to be more favourable for establishment of *S. maritima* than of *S. anglica*, at the extreme seaward limit of salt marsh growth. An experimentally introduced population of *S. alterniflora* (notified to the Botanical Society of the British Isles) has not increased signficantly at Maplin in the past 5 years. The *S. maritima* in Northern Europe is an almost sterile, dwarf form at its northern limit, and it was killed extensively by frost in Holland in 1963. In contrast, *S. maritima* forms vigorous growth nearly a metre high towards the centre of its range on the Huelva Delta in Spain. Indeed the two forms are so different it is surprising they are not classified as two different species.

The British population of *S. maritima* therefore seems to be a near-sterile, northern outlier of a species better adapted to a warmer climate; it is reduced in size and susceptible to frost. Yet, even with these disadvantages, environmental conditions at Maplin enable it to hold its own with *S. anglica*, though no doubt in some of our southern harbours *S. anglica* has invaded and replaced *S. maritima* populations locally.

S. anglica can replace *Zostera noltii* populations at the seaward edge of salt marshes and from examination of plant remains in salt marsh profiles there is plenty of evidence that it has done so, for example on the south coast (Bird and Ranwell, 1964). In contrast, the former landward limits of *Spartina anglica* marsh created by plantings made in 1929 at Bridgwater Bay, Somerset, now contain some of the greatest species diversity of any salt marsh in Britain. This is an indirect biological consequence of the creation of open spaces in mature *Spartina* marsh by the smothering effect of *Spartina* litter, and the establishment in them of many species from oligohaline zones up estuary brought into the tidal litter by littoral drift, and capable of tolerating reduced salinity at these highest levels of *Spartina* marsh. Rare species such as the Water Parsnip (*Sium latifolium*) have appeared in this habitat.

It is concluded that *S. anglica* cannot be held responsible for any significant reduction in populations of rare salt marsh species and that it has been responsible for paving the way for increased species diversity in the course of its own self-destruction at maturity, at least in the conditions at Bridgwater Bay.

Arenohaline marshes

Several of the rarer salt marsh species in this country such as the northern, low-growing Curved Sedge, *Carex maritima*, the prostrate and woody Sea Heath, *Frankenia laevis*, and the rosette Matted Sea Lavender, *Limonium bellidifolium*, are not strictly salt marsh species at all. They are all characteristics of a quite distinctive habitat that forms a zone between salt marsh and sand dune, and is neither the one nor the other. This Arenohaline marsh, as we might call it, is alternately affected by blown sand and infrequent, irregular, thin, interlayers of silt from occasional tidal overwash. This zone has not so far been invaded by any well-established introduced species, but it could be colonized by introduced shrubs such as *Tamarix* species, especially at a time when rabbit populations are depressed by myxomatosis, for *Tamarix* is very susceptible to rabbit grazing.

Tamarix is primarily a genus of much warmer climates than we have in this country (Baum, 1978). It is only likely to threaten rare species in Arenohaline marsh south of a line from the Bristol Channel to the Wash. *Tamarix* is also an Old World genus, however, and its introduction to North America in the early part of this century resulted in rapid spread over thousands of acres of marshland in southern states. It is a deep-rooted phreatophyte, transpiring large quantities of water in brackish areas and so causing an increase in soil salinity (Israelson and Hansen, 1962). So, both by shading and by increasing soil salinity, it probably had serious consequences for rare species in Arenohaline marsh in that part of the world, though I have been unable to find data to support this.

Coast embankments

As Elton (1958) has pointed out, in spite of the enormous interchange of plant material through accidental or deliberate introduction from one part of the world to another – for example nearly 200 000 named species and varieties of plants were officially introduced to the United States by 1940 – only a very small proportion of introduced plants actually establish. At the coast, two terrestrial coastal habitats particularly favour such establishment. These habitats are man-made coast embankments, and natural coastal dune systems. Significantly they are both associated with estuaries, and therefore with the ports and rail-heads which are the entry points for introduced species.

An unpublished study of coast embankments in the Harty Marshes, on the Isle of Sheppey in the Thames estuary, showed that a number of relatively rare species, such as the clover *Trifolium squamosum* and the grass *Puccinellia rupestris*, exterminated from natural transitions between salt marsh and lowland coastal grasslands by agricultural activities, find a refuge in these secondary embankment habitats. Their survival appears to depend far more on management activities related to sea defence than to any threat from introduced species, in spite of the high proportion of these that may be present. For example, a 2 km length of a 15-year-old coast embankment on the Ribble Estuary examined recently supported a very rich vascular plant flora of 166 species, of which no less than 22 per cent were alien species. In these exposed coastal situations the heights of taller growing aliens are effectively checked by strong salt-laden winds and they are less likely to replace the native flora. The native flora is thus enriched rather than diminished by the presence of introduced species at this site.

Coastal dunes

Over 1000 species of vascular plants occur on British dune systems, at least one third of our total flora. Unlike marshland, dune systems have great topographical diversity and a complex series of inter-related environmental gradients which provide many different sub-habitats for a great variety of species. While the mobile dune zone, like salt marsh, is a highly stressed habitat to which few species are adapted, open ground, at least in small amounts, is found in almost all parts of the system. It is this which especially favours the establishment of any species introduced by chance. Most of the introduced species, however, soon meet either ground occupied by native residents, or a topographical limit, and this checks their further advance, though they may persist for a very long period of time.

This seems to be the case with the low creeping herb *Acaena anserinifolia* introduced from New Zealand. In the Holy Island dunes, where it is now well established, it tends to occupy the bare ground of paths in *Ammophila* dune. A 3-year study recently completed by E. Culwick has produced no evidence of it actually replacing any rare species.

Very few introduced species have the power to suppress almost all other species and to range widely over varied topography. The dune shrub Sea Buckthorn, *Hippophae rhamnoides*, is one of these and there is no doubt that it has been responsible for the extermination of local populations of both phanerogam and cryptogam rare species within parts of particular dune systems, such as the Ainsdale National Nature Reserve in Lancashire. Even here, however, I have no evidence to show that it has been responsible for the extermination of *all* the populations of any particular rare species in the reserve. We must remember also that this reserve is only about one fifth of the area of the very large South Lancashire dune system as a whole. Moreover there is no comprehensive survey of the flora of the whole of this system, so we do not know the full range of rare species populations in this area.

The primary biological effect of *Hippophae* is to shade out all less tall species in its path; low-growing rare species like the orchid *Liparis loeselii* and the endemic *Primula scotica* would be especially vulnerable. But there is an important secondary effect. This shrub has root nodules with nitrogen-fixing bacteria and it therefore enriches the soil with nitrogen. As many authors have shown, dune soils are normally deficient in nitrogen and the dune flora is adapted to growth on such soils. At Gibraltar Point, Lincolnshire, the regrowth after the removal of mature *Hippophae* was a species-poor community of tall nitrophilous herbs such as *Urtica dioica* very different from the natural dune flora. So a secondary biological effect of *Hippophae* is to create a persistent, if not permanent, change in soil conditions which would prevent the re-establishment of many rare species adapted to the normal dune soil conditions.

For these reasons it has been considered expedient to exterminate *Hippophae* from certain dune nature reserves where it was originally introduced – at Braunton Burrows (Devon) and Whiteford Burrows (Glamorgan) for example.

As with *Spartina*, there is another side to be considered. In continental dunes, at Calais, long-established native *Hippophae* occurs together with a great variety of dune shrub species. There is a case therefore for allowing *Hippophae* to spread in certain dune systems where it has been long-established, and allow it to act as a nurse crop for the eventual development of these more diverse shrub communities. This is in fact the management policy at Gullane, East Lothian, where there is evidence that additional shrub species are able to establish as the canopy begins to open in mature *Hippophae*.

The introduction of conifers on a large scale to dune systems such as Culbin (Moray), Newborough (Anglesey) and Holkham (Norfolk) has had much more far-reaching consequences for rare species than any other type of introduction in coastal habitats, excepting of course the wholesale destruction of large areas of reclaimed pastureland by drainage, ploughing and introduction of cereal crops in south-east England and elsewhere.

In addition to shading out most of the dune flora, including populations of many rare species, large conifer plantations such as those at Tentsmuir, Fife, have materially lowered the water table both by transpiration and by the drainage activities associated with forestry management (Ovington, 1951). In most cases we have no measure of the losses of rare species, but Webster's records at Culbin suggest that several rare species (e.g. *Anagallis minima* and *Lepidotis inundata*) have been lost in the former Buckie Loch region in this way (Webster, 1968). It is very difficult to know when a species has been lost; for example two species believed extinct in Dorset (Ranwell, 1970) have re-appeared after 80 years.

There is again, however, a positive side to be considered. The conifer plantations themselves provide special conditions which favour a few rare species. These include the endemic *Epipactis dunensis* at Ainsdale, *Goodyera repens* at Golspie, Sutherland, and *Corallorhiza trifida*, *Moneses uniflora* and *Orthilia secunda* at Culbin (Moray), for example. Nor should we forget the newly created habitats for cryptogamic species, notably corticolous lichens and mosses that occur within these plantations.

Conclusions

I am keenly aware that most of the delegates at this conference are very much more knowledgeable than I am about the status of rare species in Britain. I am also aware of the reluctance of many botanists to endorse the deliberate introduction of species from one part of the country to another, let alone from abroad to this country, except perhaps under carefully controlled experimental conditions.

Several considerations, however, lead me to support the conclusion reached by Rose (1979) that a more positive policy on introductions might be appropriate at this time. Much evidence points to the conclusion that destruction of habitat at the coast and elsewhere by human activities has been responsible for losses of rare species on a far greater scale than any losses due to introduced species. The explosive spread of the few introduced species that have become problem plants is nearly always associated with large-scale disturbances of the environment carried out to meet expanding human population needs (Ranwell, 1967). Very little information seems to be available on the interaction of introduced species with rare species. Direct evidence of this is badly needed to ensure that management activities concerned with control of introduced species are soundly based.

The very few introduced species that *do* appear to have affected populations of rare species are tall-growing plants which can form mono-dominant stands and shade out nearly all species rare or otherwise which are lower growing. Such introduced species are habitat modifiers in just the same way as many taller mono-dominant native species like *Pinus sylvestris, Calluna vulgaris* or *Pteridium aquilinum*. At the coast, however, many taller-growing species are unable to attain their full heights because of wind and salt spray. Therefore, whether introduced or native, their threat to other species is minimal.

Most introduced plants that establish at least a toe-hold in Britain should be considered as welcome additions to our flora which was impoverished both by the last glaciation and by our subsequent severance from the continent, and they pose no significant threat to rare species.

Sir Arthur Tansley (1953) concluded: 'Though we cannot stop, or even check, the continuous introduction of fresh aliens (and I imagine that most botanists would not wish to if they could), we shall all agree, I think, in wanting to preserve as much of the native flora as we can'. I wonder if he might not agree that now, with the loss of so much diversity in the British landscape, there is a case for actively encouraging a positive policy on introductions. Such a policy would seek to expand populations of selected native rare species and to test out by transplant experiments the current potential range of these and even of selected aliens, considered by best botanical advice available to be innocuous, and indeed welcome newcomers to our flora.

I suggest that coastal dune systems might be the most appropriate habitats for this type of work because they are the home of both a great variety of rare species whether native or introduced, and have built-in safeguards to explosive population growth as a result of their topography, discontinuity, and climatic limits to growth.

References

Baum, B. R. (1978). *The genus* Tamarix, Israel Academy of Sciences and Humanities, Jerusalem.

Bird, E. C. F. and Ranwell, D. S. (1964). '*Spartina* salt marshes in Southern England IV. The physiography of Poole Harbour, Dorset', *J. Ecol.*, **52**, 355–66.

Elton, C. S. (1958). *The Ecology of Invasions by Animals and Plants*, Chapman and Hall, London.

Israelson, O. W. and Hansen, V. E. (1962). *Irrigation Principles and Practices*, 3rd Ed., New York.

Ovington, J. D. (1951). 'The afforestation of Tentsmuir Sands', *J. Ecol.*, **39**, 363–75.

Ranwell, D. S. (1967). 'Introduced aquatic, fresh-water and salt-marsh plants: case histories and ecological effects', in *Proceedings of the IUCN 10th Technical Meeting, Lucerne, 1966*, pp. 27–37, IUCN Pub. New Ser. No. 9.

Ranwell, D. S. (1970). 'Losses and gains in the wetland and coastal flora of Dorset', *Proc. Dorset Nat. Hist. and Arch. Soc.*, **91**, 134–46.

Ranwell, D. S. (1972). *Ecology of Salt Marshes and Sand Dunes*, Chapman and Hall, London.

Rose, C. I. (1979). *Nature Conservation and Species Introductions*, pp. 1–47. Discussion Papers in Conservation, University College, London.

Tansley, A. (1953). 'The conservation of British vegetation and species', in *The Changing Flora of Britain* (Ed. J. E. Lousley), Botanical Society of the British Isles, Oxford, pp. 188–96.

Tutin, T. G. *et al.* (Eds.) (1964–80). *Flora Europaea*, 5 vols, Cambridge University Press.

Webster, M. M. (1968). *A Check List of the Flora of the Culbin State Forest*, Webster, Dyke, Moray.

Note

Plant names in this paper follow *Flora Europaea* (Tutin *et al.*, 1964–80).

The Biological Aspects of Rare Plant Conservation
Edited by Hugh Synge
© 1981 John Wiley & Sons Ltd.

35
The discovery, extermination, translocation and eventual survival of *Schoenus ferrugineus* in Britain

BRIAN S. BROOKES *The Scottish Field Studies Association, Kindrogan Field Centre, Perthshire, Scotland.*

Summary

In 1884 the sedge *Schoenus ferrugineus* was discovered in Britain on the shore of Loch Tummel. In 1950 its site was submerged by a hydro-electric scheme, but only after numerous transplants had been made. The fate of these transplants today is analysed and the survival of the species in Britain assessed. From the experiences of the transplants in 1945–50, some questions are asked about translocation policy and about other issues of botanical practice and ethics highlighted by this remarkable species.

Introduction and discovery

Examples of translocations to save endangered species are rare and in most cases it is too early to know whether or not they have succeeded. The story of *Schoenus ferrugineus* is an example of a translocation, all the more remarkable because it happened 30 years ago. It is not just an unusual botanical tale, but an instance from which we can learn for the future. As habitats continue to be degraded and rare plant sites lost, translocation will of necessity become an increasingly important tool for conservation and a technique in which we cannot afford to fail. The story starts in the nineteenth century when the plant was first found in Britain.

The discovery of a new plant is always an exciting event and the first record for the Brown Bog Rush. *Schoenus ferrugineus* L., in Britain was published in three places by F. Buchanan White during 1885. Ridley in 1885 also described and illustrated the new find in the *Journal of Botany*; he wrote of its distribution

being entirely confined to Europe and by no means universally distributed even there. It is found, however, sparingly over 'the whole continent from Scandinavia to South Russia, excluding the extreme north and south, being apparently absent from the Spanish Peninsula, Italy and France, with the exception of the Jura.

He reported that it grew on open peaty moorland, often at high altitude.

It was, however, James Brebner, the first Rector of the Harris Academy in Dundee, who discovered the *Schoenus*. He found it on 15 July 1884 on the northern shore of Loch Tummel, Mid-Perth (vice-county 88) in central Scotland, a very different habitat from the continental localities. The existence of *Schoenus ferrugineus* in Britain seems always to have been precarious; it was after all a *rare* species, a plant at the edge of its geographical range. Brebner himself noted (*in litt.*, 1885) that the individuals were not very numerous and felt it was unwise to reveal the whereabouts of the colony. Nonetheless the plants soon had to contend not only with the ecological constraints of their habitat but with the plant collectors of the day.

By the end of the 1880s numerous botanists had visited the site and had collected the *Schoenus* for their private herbaria. Over the years, these many herbaria have been left to a few national institutions such as the Royal Botanic Garden, Edinburgh, and the British Museum (Natural History) in London. Ironically the *Schoenus* plants are together again, though as piles of sheets in herbarium cupboards. Here may be found, for example, 22 complete plants and 88 separate flowering stems collected on a single-day – 18 August 1888 – by one party.

Despite the rash of collecting, White (1892) asserted that the small population showed 'no falling off', but in 1900 'not a plant was to be seen' according to a saddened Brebner. A year later Barclay (1901a, 1901b) confirmed that only a few spikes remained.

Were the plants simply victims of the vasculum? A more likely explanation is that the decline was a natural setback caused by fluctuations in the water level of the loch. The plant occurred on that part of the shore between the summer and

Figure 1   *Schoenus ferrugineus.* (Drawn by Dr Hans Persson)

Figure 2   An impression of the Loch Tummel site. (Drawn from photographs by
Dr Hans Persson)

winter water-levels, so that it was normally inundated during the winter, but grew
and flowered when exposed during the summer. (The regular fluctuation in water-
level was probably important as it prevented competitor species which could not
survive inundation.) If the water level did not fall during one summer, the
Schoenus would be submerged all year and it might then disappear for a few years
until the shore was recolonized from plants higher up.

The population appears to have recovered, for by 1907 G. C. Druce included
the species in his list of specimens for exchange and the collecting continued. In a
trip on 19 July 1913, W. A. Shoolbred, E. S. Marshall and C. E. Salmon took 29
whole plants, which they completely uprooted, plus 142 separate flowering stems.
According to Marshall and Salmon (1915), the plants were abundant. Prominent
botanists continued to visit the site during the 1930s; J. E. Lousley and A. W.
Graveson, who visited the site in August 1932, found it was heavily grazed by
bullocks which they photographed standing on the *Schoenus* plants (pers.
comm.). A photograph in 1936 by R. M. Adam in the possession of the *Scots
Magazine* shows the tufts of *Schoenus* growing between large stones with much
Molinia caerulea (L.) Moench and young seedlings of *Fraxinus excelsior* L., on

an otherwise stony shore with little vegetation. Other botanists such as W. A. Sledge, E. C. Wallace and R. Mackechnie visited the site in these years and recorded some of the associated species. Evidence about the site is scanty and hard to come by today, but at least the plant was known to survive there.

Destruction and rescue

On Saturday, 10 February 1945 'The Times' announced that the North of Scotland Hydro-Electric Board planned to dam Loch Tummel and raise the water level 17 feet (5.1 m) to form the reservoir for a Power Station. Lousley (1946) reported the threat in the botanical literature and plans were made for transplanting some of the *Schoenus* population to a safe site.

In 1946 the Botanical Society of the British Isles made an excursion to study the *Schoenus* habitat on Loch Tummel (Campbell, 1948). They found the plant extending further along the shores of the loch than previously thought and discovered some individuals on the southern shore. They took soil samples and made plans for a series of transplants to save the *Schoenus*.

The plan was to move a large number of plants up the shore from the existing site, complete with the soil in which they grew, to the future level. A new site was designed by Miss M. Campbell and A. J. Wilmott and was prepared by the Hydro-Electric Board. This consisted of a rough stone wall enclosure of some 8 m by 3 m at the proposed new water level. In 1949 Miss Campbell appealed to members of the Botanical Society of the British Isles for help in transplanting the populations.

Early in 1950, at short notice, the level of the loch was raised. Just in time, H. Salzen (then H. Fairlie), from the newly formed Nature Conservancy, was sent in great haste to transplant tufts of *Schoenus* into the newly built site, helped by staff from the Hydro-Electric Board. Snow covered the ground and the operation was a hurried affair. She for one did not hold out much hope for the plants' survival (*in litt.*). The original site was submerged from 9 February until 25 July 1950 when the water level was reduced to its natural level again. On 26 July more plants were transferred to the higher site.

By October 1950 the loch reached its new level. The specially prepared site was completely submerged and during the following winter the retaining wall was destroyed by wave action. In a paper read to the Royal Physical Society in Edinburgh on 17 January 1955, J. Berry explained that sufficient allowance had not been made for 'the force of the wave action because of the increased and more exposed water surface and greater depth of the new Loch Tummel'. This finally destroyed *S. ferrugineus* at Loch Tummel and removed it from the British List.

Many other transplants had been made to other lochs, however, and large quantities were planted on the shore of Loch Rannoch and Loch Tay. There is a map made by Wilmott in 1947, now in the Botany Library of the British Museum (Natural History), that indicates some of the transplant sites. Wilmott himself

Figure 3   The Ben Vrackie site where Whellan transplanted *Schoenus ferrugineus* in 1945. (Drawn by Dr Hans Persson)

transplanted some further individuals to Loch Fincastle in 1949 and on 18 July 1949 D. M. McClintock and R. Graham took large clumps of *Schoenus* to the north shore of Loch Rannoch (McClintock, pers. comm.). In all some 14 transplants were made, involving hundreds of plants. Also plants were sent to the University Botanic Garden, Cambridge, and to the Royal Horticultural Society's Garden at Wisley in Surrey.

Only two plants survived. One was the plant sent to Cambridge, which was successfully propagated, and the other a plant taken by J. A. Whellan to Ben Vrackie in 1945. Ironically Whellan, who carefully recorded his transplant in the literature (Whellan, 1947), was criticized at the time, chiefly because he had moved the species to another vice-county on his own initiative.

Re-introduction

On 29 May 1975 I re-introduced 29 individuals from the Cambridge stock on to the north shore of Loch Tummel and nearby sites. The aim was to find sites ecologically similar to the original locality, but it proved very difficult to gather any useful information on this point. Associated species are mentioned in notebooks and correspondence; fragments of other plants, especially bryophytes, can be found on herbarium sheets of the *Schoenus*. Herbarium labels occasionally record associates and photographs provide additional information.

Two of the three re-introduction sites are on the present shore-line of Loch Tummel; the other, illustrated in Figure 4, is a calcareous flush on the slope above the loch. One loch-shore site is muddy and shaded – none of the transplants survived more than a year. The other is a cleared area of willow and alder scrub, heavily limed, in which most of the transplants have survived, although the site is now becoming very grassy. In the third site, some plants were protected from grazing by a small enclosure of wire-netting and these plants became smothered

Figure 4   One of the sites of the 1975 re-introduction. (Drawn by Dr Hans Persson)

with grass and survived for less than a year. One plant at this third site, unprotected from grazing, in an open stony area of the calcareous flush, has thrived and grown to a greater size in 5 years than the Ben Vrackie plant has grown in 35 years! Records of the 1975 re-introductions are held by the Nature Conservancy Council, Huntingdon.

The Loch Tummel locality is quite anomalous to localities outside Britain. Elsewhere *S. ferrugineus* is a plant of mires, especially calcareous mires. One herbarium label on a specimen of Üksip at Kew (1930) records the plant as common in limy swamps and a characteristic species of the *Schoenus ferrugineus–Pinguicula* association in Estonia.

Discussion

This study was inspired by a desire to put on record the events of the years 1945–50, so that any subsequent discovery of a colony of *Schoenus ferrugineus* could be correlated with the transplant record, so as to see whether it was a transplant or not. Secondly, it was thought desirable to attempt, 25 years later, to re-establish the progeny of 'rescued' material in the wild, if a site could be found. This raised questions about the nature of the original site in Britain as well as of continental sites and who transplanted it where. This paper is a summary of a lengthy file 'Schoenus ferrugineus *in Britain*' (Brookes, 1976) deposited at the Office of the Nature Conservancy Council in Edinburgh.

The achievement of the original aims has raised a number of fundamental questions, such as: To what extent does collecting endanger rare species? How much material of rare species is needed in herbaria? Which herbaria should they be in? Who should regulate this? How widely should the sites of rare species be known? Are steps being taken to ensure enough is known about the ecology of rare species before it is too late? When should rare species be rescued? When and where should re-introductions be attempted? Who decides? Certainly complete and clear records of transplants should be kept, a point made by Wilmott (*in litt.*, 1946), but where?

It took me a year of intensive correspondence, interviewing and research to find out where the transplants were made, gradually piecing together the fragments of evidence on events which happened only 30 years ago. Some transplants are only recorded on scraps of paper; in others the writing has faded away. Surely it should not be as difficult as this. Unless records are kept in some kind of co-ordinated system, they get lost, because people forget, change their names, change their addresses or die. Are we making it any easier today for botanists in 30 years time to know what we are doing?

Epilogue

There is a happy ending to this tale for in 1979 two large and extensive natural sites of *Schoenus ferrugineus* were found in Scotland (Smith, 1980a and b). The sites of these populations preclude the possibility that they are derived from the 1945–50 transplants.

The new localities are of the typical *Schoenus* habitat in Scandinavia and Eastern Europe – open peaty moorland. The Loch Tummel site is a very untypical site for *S. ferrugineus*. Herein too lies a botanical message: perhaps those who discovered the *Schoenus* in the 1880s and those who were concerned with its relocation in 1945–50 were too concerned with its local habitat; a study of its habitat on the continent could have paid great dividends.

Acknowledgements

Grateful thanks are due to all who have helped in the collection of data and to the Nature Conservancy Council who have generously given me a grant towards expenses.

References

Barclay, W. (1901a). In *Proc. Perth Soc. Nat. Sci.*, **3**, 73.
Barclay, W. (1901b). In 'Botanical notes and news', *Ann. Scot. Nat. Hist.*, **37**, 55.
Brebner, J. (1900). In 'Short Notes', *J. Bot.*, **38**, 87.
Brookes, B. S. (1976). Schoenus ferrugineus *in Britain*, Report in Nature Conservancy Council files, Edinburgh.
Campbell, M. S. (1948). In 'Excursions 1946', *Bot. Soc. and Exch. Club Brit. Isles Rep.*, **13**, 215–9.
Campbell, M. S. (1949). In 'Notice to members', *Bot. Soc. Brit. Isles Year Book*, 53.
Lousley, J. E. (1946). In 'Plant notes', *Bot. Soc. and Exch. Club Brit. Isles Rep.*, **12**, 690–1.
Marshall, E. S. and Salmon, C. E. (1915). In *30th Ann. Rep. Watson Bot. Exch. Club*, 2(10), 462.
Ridley, H. N. (1885). 'Two new British plants', *J. Bot.*, **23**, 289–90, t. 261.
Smith, R. A. H. (1980a). In *Bot. Soc. Brit. Isles Scottish Newsletter* 2.
Smith, R. A. H. (1980b). '*Schoenus ferrugineus* L. – two native localities in Perthshire', *Watsonia*, **13**, 128.
Whellan, J. A. (1947). 'Plant records', *Bot. Soc. and Exch. Club Brit. Isles Rep.*, **13**, 71.
White, F. B. (1885a). 'Opening address to meeting, November 12th 1885', *Proc. Perth. Soc. Nat. Sci.*, 220.
White, F. B. (1885b). '*Schoenus ferrugineus* L., a flowering plant new to Britain', *Scot. Nat.*, **7**, 130.
White, F. B. (1885c). In 'Short notes', *J. Bot.*, **23**, 219.
White, F. B. (1892). In *Proc. Perth. Soc. Nat. Sci.*, **1**, 160.

Section 6
Protected Areas for Plant Conservation

The Biological Aspects of Rare Plant Conservation
Edited by Hugh Synge

36
The floristic and phytosociological definition and description of conservation sites

ANNA MEDWECKA-KORNAŚ *Institute of Botany, Jagiellonian University, Krakow*

Summary

The definition and description of conservation sites should form the basis for their comparison and classification, and should assist in their proper management. The question of what kind of floristic and phytosociological information may be useful for this purpose is discussed. The floristic definition should consist of an inventory of plant taxa, their evaluation from a conservation point of view, information about the ecology of the species, and a synthetic characterization of the whole flora. The phytosociological definition, for which the working methods and concepts of the Central European school of Braun-Blanquet seem to be the most suitable, should comprise an inventory of plant associations, a description of their structure, composition, ecological and geographical features, and data on the local distributional patterns of the actual vegetation and of the potential natural vegetation. Taking into consideration all these features of the flora and vegetation simultaneously is rather difficult, but each element can be important in a particular situation. The task can be standardized through a check-sheet.

Introduction

With the destruction of natural environments on Earth, selected 'conservation sites' become more and more vital, and the need to build up and provide information about them more important to ensure their continued ecological well-being. This paper deals with the botanical aspects of the problem. In the description of conservation sites a number of scientists and organizations have been interested, e.g. IUCN, the Section 'Conservation Terrestrial' (CT) of the International Biological Programme (Nicholson, 1968) and the Unesco Programme 'Man and the Biosphere' (Castri and Loope, 1977). This topic is a very theoretical and broad one and I am indebted to the organizing committee of this conference for having encouraged me to discuss it, a task I would not have undertaken on my own initiative.

Let me start with some short remarks about the terms contained in the title. By the term 'conservation site' I mean all types of nature reserve, national park, zone of protected landscape, and so on. Classifications of these areas that take into account the nature of the site and the aims and means of conservation have been proposed, for example, by Bourdelle (1956), Symoens (1979) and Udvardy (1975), and a new system by IUCN's Commission on National Parks and Protected Areas has been published as the 1980 UN List.

In my opinion the floristic and phytosociological evaluation of a conservation site should consist of a description of the vegetational cover necessary for classification and comparison with other sites, and the ecological information needed to maintain the flora and plant communities in the state desired. In this chapter I should like to discuss the possible applications of floristic and phytosociological concepts and research methods for establishing this evaluation and description of a site. A check-sheet to bring together all the elements of the data has been designed, but will be mentioned only briefly, because there is a need to modify such a sheet depending on the situation. Under floristic description I will deal mainly with vascular plants.

I consider phytosociology to be the science that deals with plant communities and classifies them according to their floristic composition. Several approaches ('schools') may be distinguished (Whittaker, 1978). I shall follow the concepts of the Central European school of Braun-Blanquet (1964), which is broadly used in Poland and many other countries (Medwecka-Kornaś *et al.*, 1966). I realize very well that there is some controversy about these concepts, but there is much evidence that they may be applied with success for conservation purposes.

The floristic and phytosociological approaches are of course interrelated: information on the occurrence of particular plant species suggests the presence of plant associations they are connected with, and conversely, the data on plant associations always contain information about the species and the conditions of their existence.

I. Floristic description

This should comprise: (a) the inventory of plant species, (b) their evaluation from a conservation point of view, (c) an indication of ecological features; and possibly also (d) an assessment of the character of the flora as a whole. These are detailed below:

A. *Inventory of species and data about their occurrence*

1. A list of the more important (or preferably all) components of the local flora.
2. Information about the number of localities of particular species and their local distribution. The best documentation may be provided by dot maps.
3. Information about the size of populations and estimates of abundance of particular species, estimated according to any of the existing quantitative methods (e.g. by using the scale of abundance/dominance of Braun-Blanquet).

B. Evaluation of species according to various criteria

1. Taxonomic criteria: information about monotypic taxa, interesting hybrids, etc.
2. Historical and phytogeographical criteria: distinction of relicts from other species and of the different geographical elements in the flora, according to the total distribution of the taxa. Special attention should be paid to endemics, and the areas to which they are limited should be specified precisely.
3. Ecological criteria: distinction of particular life forms, e.g. epiphytes, succulents, carnivorous plants, and of species groups connected with especially interesting types of habitats, e.g. serpentine and gypsum rocks, saline soils.
4. Criteria relating to human influence: distinction between native species and introduced aliens (Kornaś, 1968), the presence of which can indicate environmental disturbance which may be caused, for example, by too heavy tourist pressure.
5. Degree of rarity and threat to particular species. These assessments are a high priority in the floristic description of conservation sites; they can be specified in terms of the total geographic range of a species or in terms of one country or of more limited regions in which the species occurs. The degree of rarity may be assessed according to a scale such as that proposed by Ayensu (Chapter 2) or that used for the Netherlands flora by Arnolds *et al.* (1976). For threatened species the 'Red Data Book categories' of IUCN (see Appendix 3 of this book), should be used; they distinguish Extinct (Ex), Endangered (E), Vulnerable (V), Rare (R) and Indeterminate (I) taxa. The placing of a species into these categories should be based if possible on *The IUCN Plant Red Data Book* (Lucas and Synge, 1978) and on international lists of threatened plants, such as that for Europe (IUCN Threatened Plants Committee, 1977) or on national Red Data Books such as Takhtajan (1975), Ayensu and DeFilipps (1978), Sukopp (1974), Perring and Farrell (1977).

C. Ecological information with a practical aim

1. A determination of the ecological requirements of the particular species and of the plant associations in which they occur, their coexistence with other plants and animals, dependence upon habitat conditions (soil and climate), and so on. The information should first of all concern those conditions and relationships which can easily be changed by natural succession or by human interference. Some ecological requirements of a plant species can be specified using numerical scales, as proposed by Ellenberg (1974) for Central Europe.
2. A determination of plant sensitivity to human impact, such as trampling, eutrophication, pollution of water, soil and air, which can arise on the conservation site itself or can reach this area from outside.

3. An estimate of the dynamic tendencies of the species. Information should be included here on whether the populations are relatively stable, decreasing in number, or expanding. This kind of data may be derived from observation of permanent plots or deduced from studies of the age-structure of populations, the production of diaspores and the survival rate of young individuals. The importance of an autecological approach in species conservation is emphasized by the many contributions on this theme in the book.

D. *An assessment of the character of the flora as a whole*

A complete list of the vascular plants (or any other systematic group) enables us to define synthetic features of the flora, e.g. its diversity (van der Maarel, 1971) from which sites can be graded according to floristic richness; in this context introduced aliens should be treated separately from native species. We may also compile full geographical spectra which show the proportions of particular geographical elements in the flora, or various ecological spectra dealing, for example, with the share of particular life forms according to the Raunkiaer system. The species list also forms a document which will permit future changes in the flora to be recognized. If sufficient data exist, it is possible to detect past changes (Michalik, 1974).

II. Phytosociological description

This part of the assessment of a conservation site consists chiefly in distinguishing plant community types. The use of plant associations as the basic units of classification of vegetation as defined by J. Braun-Blanquet (cf. Westhoff and van der Maarel, 1978) seems to be the most suitable system.

The aspects which could be taken into consideration for the phytosociological definition of a site are relatively numerous:

A. *Inventory of plant associations*

The plant associations should be distinguished after field records (relevés) have been taken for the site. They may also be identified without relevés in the regions where other sites have already been sufficiently studied or where a general conspectus of vegetational units has been compiled.

1. A list of plant associations. The list can contain only the more important units, such as the dominants, or it can be complete. If the latter is the case, the number of associations may be used as an 'index of vegetation diversity', but with more critical judgement than the figure for the number of species, because of the complex and more arbitrary character of phytosociological units.
2. A list of higher phytosociological units: alliances, orders and classes. These are

more widely distributed and better defined than the individual associations and therefore much more useful for a general assessment.
3. The cartographic approach. A phytosociological map of the actual vegetation is perhaps the best inventory of plant communities. Mapping is usually done on the large scale of $1:10\,000-1:20\,000$; this prevents overlooking any vegetation stands in the field with the exception of very small ones, and discloses the importance of individual associations and their distribution patterns.

B. Assessment of the floristic composition and structure of plant associations and their relative importance

1. The number of species in particular plant associations. This distinguishes floristically rich from relatively poor associations.
2. An analysis of floristic composition. Here attention may be paid to the role of characteristic and indicator species and species groups (Tüxen and Ellenberg, 1937). More essential for the aims of nature conservation is information on the groupings of species according to their ecological and geographical characters, as well as their position in the succession. The presence of rare and endangered species should be emphasized. This kind of information can point out the associations which particularly need protection.
3. A description of the vertical structure (stratification) of the plant associations. This feature indicates the organization of the vegetation stands and helps to show their role in the landscape.

C. Geographical description of plant associations as synecological entities

In addition to the distribution of individual species, we may also establish the geographical ranges of whole associations, and distinguish among them those which are widespread from those which are endemic. The latter are of particular interest to nature conservation. An analysis of this kind has been made in Poland recently by Matuszkiewicz (1980).

D. Estimate of the ecological requirements and relationships of plant associations

1. A description of habitats with which the particular plant associations are connected. The dependence of vegetation upon environmental factors should be investigated in the field. To some extent this may be inferred from comparison of the phytosociological maps with maps of other variables such as climate, soils and geology. Knowledge of the dependence of the plant associations upon the conditions of the site is often necessary for effective conservation. It also permits us to use the associations as indicators, for which they are much more reliable than individual species. The associations at specific sites may be

particularly interesting from the ecological point of view and may deserve special conservation treatment.

2. An estimate of animal influence, at least of grazing and browsing animals. Plant associations without visible animal impact or with only a moderate impact should be distinguished from those which depend on grazing, as do some xerothermic grasslands in Europe, and those which greatly deteriorate under excessive animal pressure, as has happened in some African national parks.

3. An estimate of the extent to which the plant associations depend upon human influence. It is important to distinguish between: natural plant associations existing spontaneously; semi-natural associations existing due to human activity, but composed of native plant species (as in the hay meadows of central Europe); and synanthropic ('artificial') associations with a high percentage of introduced aliens (as the associations of cultivated fields and ruderal places). Semi-natural and synanthropic types of communities are together called 'anthropogenic' or man-made associations. The presence, extent and type of anthropogenic associations indicate how far the natural vegetation of a given area has been altered (Sukopp, 1968; Faliński, 1966). It should be stressed that some man-made plant associations are very valuable and worthy of preservation as elements that increase the diversity of flora and vegetation and the beauty of the landscape (Duffey and Watt, 1971; Medwecka-Kornaś, 1977).

4. An estimate of the degree of stability of the plant associations and their position in the successional series. One has to distinguish among the plant associations: those of the pioneer stages, usually short lasting; the more advanced seral associations; and the relatively stable final stages – the climax associations. Information about the degree of stability of particular plant associations is of great importance for nature conservation. It indicates the types of vegetation which will quickly disappear as the succession progresses. To avoid this, processes that seem destructive such as erosion, floods and fire may have to be allowed in the protected areas. To maintain anthropogenic vegetation, some kind of direct human interference is usually necessary, either in the form of a traditional management such as grazing or mowing or of an ecologically equivalent treatment.

E. Recognition of phytosociological features of the landscapes and of geobotanical regional units

The distribution of plant associations usually shows distinct regularities; these patterns are especially clear on phytosociological maps and may be widely used to help characterize the landscape as integrated units (physiocoenoses – Wodziczko, 1950). The concepts of spatial complexes of plant associations, functionally coherent and connected with particular land forms, seem to be especially useful in this respect (see for example Medwecka-Kornaś and Kornaś, 1963). Usually a valley bottom, an adjacent southern slope, a northern slope and a plateau each have a different association complex. The enumeration of these complexes (called after their main natural associations) forms a concise set of information on the differentiation of the vegetation and landscape within a conservation site. When all associations of such a complex are seen in the field and when the extent of their stands within the site is estimated, we arrive at the so-called 'synassociations' or 'sigmassociations' recently distinguished by Tüxen (1973), Géhu (1974), Rivas-Martínez (1976) and others.

Attention can also be concentrated on geographic groups of plant associations which differ by region. This feature can be used in a comparison of the vegetation and landscape qualities of various conservation sites.

F. Assessment of the potential natural vegetation

By this term I mean the hypothetical vegetation that would establish itself on a given area in the habitat under conditions similar to the actual ones if all human interference ceased. The methods of recognizing and mapping such vegetation are well defined and fairly reliable (Tüxen, 1956). Maps of potential natural vegetation are very useful, especially for conservation purposes. They help to foresee the future successions which will take place when protection is secured, and to define the optimum shape of vegetation and landscape, which can then be the aim of management.

G. The biocenotic (ecosystem) approach

The phytosociological units of plant cover – the stands of associations – may be delimited relatively easily in the field. Therefore they can be successfully used as the basis for ecosystem studies. Examples of this approach are the Projects Solling (Ellenberg, 1971) and Ispina (Medwecka-Kornaś et al., 1974) of the IBP. Biocenotic investigations of conservation sites help to understand the principles of the dynamic equilibrium existing there.

On the following pages is a check-sheet for the Ojców National Park in Poland, to show how the various types of information referred to in this chapter may be standardized.

FLORISTIC AND PHYTOSOCIOLOGICAL DEFINITION OF CONSERVATION SITES

A. GENERAL INFORMATION

Name of the conservation site OJCÓW..NATIONAL.PARK..................

Category: national park ..✓... nature reserve ...... other ....

Exceptional interest of conservation flora and vegetation, landscape.........

Conservation: strict .13.%.. partial .87.%. (possibly percentage of area)

Site in the U.N. list: yes.✓..no....　　　Biosphere Reserve :yes....no.✓....

Location: country ..POLAND..........administrative region.Cracow. Province...

Latitude 50°.13'.. N/$ Longitude 19°.50'... E/∦ |...........................

Surface area .1570. ha.....Altitude maximum .470.m......minimum .286 m......

Type of the climate .temperate...............annual precip. ....ca. 700.mm

mean temp.: warmest month July....18.°C Coldest month February.....-2.°C

Main geological deposits Upper. Jurassic. limestones, loess, alluvial deposits....

Main types of the soil (No. 1,2,3) 1).rendzina soils; 2) brown forest soils;
3).warp..soils.; 4). podzolic. soils. on. deep. loess. on. the. plateau.,........

Landscape: sea coast .....lowlands.... highlands..✓..mountains....permanent

snow.....glaciers.....valleys..✓..ravines..✓.rivers....rivulets..✓.lakes.....

swamps.....peat-bogs.....rocks.✓...barren ground ......sand dunes..........

Most important plant formations mixed. and. deciduous. forests, xerothermic.....
brushwoods. and. grasslands, meadows..............................

Features of the fauna, more important species relatively. rich. fauna :.....
Coleoptera. 664. spp., lepidoptera. 617. spp., Aves. 126. spp., Mammalia. 45. spp,:..
roe-deer., badger., fox, wild boar. etc................

Human impact: not evident 20.%. limited.50%. strong.30.%.(percentage of area)

Management of ecosystems: needed.50%.not needed.50% (possibly percent.of area)

Major biological references A. Medwecka- Kornas, J. Kornas : Vegetation. map of the
Ojców. National. Park. Ochrona. Przyrody. 29. 17-87. 1963. S. Michalik; Vascular.
plants. of. the. Ojców National. Park., Studia. Naturae. 16: 7-171, 1978...........

Address of administration of conservation site Direction. of. the. Ojców.
National. Park., Zamkowa. Góra., 32-324. Ojców, POLAND

Name and address of Surveyor Anna. Medwecka- Kornas, Institute of Botany....
Jagiellonian. University, ul. Lubicz 46, 31-512 Kraków　　　Check Sheet completed 5 June 1980
POLAND

Conservation site:

B₁   FLORISTIC INFORMATION: particular taxa

Names of especially interesting taxa a)	(ecological) geographical character	degree of rarity (and endangerment)		No: of b) assoc.
		cons. site	wider area S.-Poland	
Aster amellus	pontic- pannonian	very rare	rare	7
Cerasus fruticosa	" "	very rare	rare	separate commn.
Cirsium pannonicum	" "	very rare	very rare	7
Inula ensifolia	" "	rare	rather rare	7
Stipa Joannis	" "	very rare	very rare	7,6
Potentilla alba	central- european	rather rare	rather rare	5
Aruncus silvester	central- europ., montane	rare	rather rare	4,14
Aconitum variegatum ssp. gracile	sudetic- carpathian, montane	extr. rare	rare	4
Dentaria glandulosa (= Cardamine glanduligera)	carpathian subendemic, montane	rather rare	rather rare	4,(3)
Aconitum moldavicum	as above	rather rare	rare	4
Betula oycoviensis	subendemic in Poland	rare	rare	2
		(Safeguarded in plantations)		

Species dominating in the important assoc.	life forms/taxonomic groups	local distribution	No. of assoc. b)
Pinus silvestris	coniferous tree	rocks, upland, partially planted	1,5 etc.
Fagus silvatica	deciduous tree	northern slopes etc.	2,14
Carpinus betulus	" "	slopes	4
Abies alba	coniferous tree	slopes, upland	1,2
Tilia cordata	deciduous tree	slopes	4
Acer pseudoplatanus	" "	slopes	4,2
Corylus avellana	deciduous shrub	slopes	5,4,2
Festuca pallens	tuft grass	limestone rocks	6
Brachypodium pinnatum	grass	slopes (rendzina)	7

Expanding aliens :

Impatiens parviflora	annual herb	in deciduous forest	4
Galinsoga parviflora	" "	gardens, cultivated fields	12 etc.
Bunias orientalis	" "	ruderal places	11

a) Species and subspecies. If essential also genera and families

b) Chief associations in which a species occurs; number according to the Sheet C₁

Conservation site:

B$_2$ F L O R I S T I C   I N F O R M A T I O N: synthetic features

Total number of vascular plant species 950/3500 ba.Presence or number in groups:

trees			Sedges and Grasses	Orchids	others-Monocot. and Dicot.
Gymnosp.	Monocot.	Dicot.			
...6.....	...—.....	...27.....	...124.....	...19.....	...774.........
Pterid.	Musci	Hepaticae	Macromycetes	Micromycetes	Lichenes
...34.....	...161.....	...73.....	...700.....	...417.....	...√.....

Life forms:	presence	spp. number		presence	spp. number and remarks
Trees	....√......	..22...	Epiphytes		
Shrubs	....√......	..61...	vascular ..	....—.....	
Dwarf shrubs......	....√......	...7...	others	....√.....	
Perennial herbs ..	....√......		Lianas	....√.....	...2.
Annuals and			Succulents...	....√.....	...3.
biennials......	....√.....		Aquatic plants	....√.....	..13.

Evaluation of the flora: [a)]   occurrence | spp.number | remarks

	occurrence	spp.number	remarks
Rare species	....√.....	ca. 100	
Endangered species.............	....√.....	ca. 50 ?	Orchids and others
Extinct (not found recently)...	....√.....	35	
Aliens , introduced............	....√.....	127	
Newcomers:			
settled in natural assoc.....	....√.....	14	
in synanthropic comm.	....√.....	23	
Endemics	....—.....		
Geographical elements:			
Pontic.- pannonian............	....√.....	ca. 150	"xerothermic" generally
Mountain (incl. Carpathian)....	....√.....	ca. 50	
Central - European...........	....√.....		
Euro-siberian...........	....√.....		

and some others

Kind of management necessary for maintenance of valuable species

control of succession (s. mu grasslands, meadows), preservation of ground water level (on valley bottoms), limitation of pollution.

---

a) If other groups than vascular plants will be considered enclose an additional Sheet.

Conservation site:

C₁ PHYTOSOCIOLOGICAL INFORMATION: particular plant associations

No. and names of associations: all...selected.V.	affiliation to alliances/orders	physiognomy ecological type	Soil No. a)	spatial role in: cons.site b)	wider c) area S-Poland	condition for maintenance d)
natural:						
1. Pino-Quercetum	Vaccinio-Piceetalia	mixed acidophilous forest	4	wide	not rare	protection
2. Dentario glandulosae-Fagetum	Fagetalia	beech forest	1,2	limited	not rare	"
3. Phyllitido-Aceretum	Fagetalia		1	very rare	very rare	"
4. Tilio-Carpinetum	Fagetalia	mixed deciduous forest	1,2	limited	not rare	"
5. Peucedano-Coryletum	Quercetalia pubes.	xerothermic brushwood	1	rare	rare	control of succession
6. Festucetum pallentis	Festucetalia valles.	epilitic grassland	1	rare	rare	protection
7. Origano-Brachypodietum	Festucetalia valles.	xerothermic natural grassland	1	rare	rare	control of
... inoctoxicetosum						...succession
semi-natural:						
8. Origano-Brachypodietum	Festucetalia	xerothermic grassland	1	rare	rare	control of
... agrimonietosum	valesiacae					succession-grazing
9. Arrhenatheretum elat.	Arrhenatheretalia	mowed meadow	2	rare	not rare	mowing-manuring
10. Cirsietum rivularis	Arrhenatheretalia	mowed, moist meadow	3	rare	not rare	mowing
synanthropic:						
11. Vicietum tetraspermae	Secali-Violetalia	cultivated fields	2	limited	not rare	—
12. Lamio-Veronicetum	Secali-Violetalia	cultivated fields	2	limited	not rare	—

a) After Sheet A;
b) Mark: dom.-dominant)50%; wid.-widespread 25-50%; lim.-limited 5-25%; r - rare, v.r.-very rare <5% of surface;
c) Mark rare - not rare, with additional information in which region-part of the country;
d) If maintenance not desirable mark: —

Conservation site:

C₂ P H Y T O S O C I O L O G I C A L   I N F O R M A T I O N : synthetic features of vegetation cover

Number of plant associations: natural .14.. semi-natural .6.. synanthropic .2.. together 22 and ca.10 fragmentary communum.

Association complexes – mutual relationship of primary and secondary associations a) :

Topographic location, soil b)	main primary (natural) associations	main secondary (man-made) associations semi-natural	main secondary (man-made) associations synanthropic	relatively stable association
Valley bottoms ... 2	Alno-Padion (fragm.) and Tilio-Carpinetum...	Caricetum, Arrhenatheretum...	Urticetum tetraspermae Lamio-Veronicetum...	
N-facing slope 1,2	×Dentario glandulosae-Fagetum...	—		
S.E.W-facing slope 1,2	Tilio-Carpinetum and ×Corylo-Peucedanetum...	Origano-Brachypodietum...	Urticetum tetraspermae Lamio-Veronicetum...	
Plateau ... 4	Pino-Quercetum...	Nardo-Callunetea fragm...	Urticetum tetraspermae Lamio-Veronicetum...	

Main series of primary succession (succession of natural communities) c)

Geomorphological land form Initial soil/substratum	pioneer or relatively less advanced association	intermediary association	relatively stable association
Valley bottoms ... 3	Alno-Padion (fragm.) →	Tilio-Carpinetum stachyetosum... →	Tilio-Carpinetum typic...
N-facing slope, limestone ... 1	×Festucetum pall. meckerelosum... → brushwood →	×Phyllitido-Aceretum... →	×Dentario gland.-Fagetum...
Other slope, limestone ... 1	×Festucetum pall. semperivetosum →	×Corylo-Peucedanetum...	Tilio-Carpinetum...
Plateau ... loess ...	?	?	Pino-Quercetum...

Recommendations:

Spatial proportion among associations in the landscape should be preserved .... changed ..√..

a) Mark by× the associations especially valuable for conservation and underline ass. which should be protected by active management; b) number according Sheet A; c) mark by arrows the direction of succession.

Concluding remarks

The steps proposed above for describing and evaluating a conservation site are numerous and not easy to undertake, especially all at the same time. Each of them, however, may be important in some particular situation.

In a check-sheet aiming at the standardization of the floristic and phytosociological definition of conservation sites, only some of these items should be selected. The preceding pages show an example of such a check-sheet, completed by myself for the Ojców National Park in Poland. The wider the geographical range of the inquiry, the shorter and simpler this sheet must be. When introducing a check-sheet it would be necessary to prepare instructions with symbols and numerical scales for expressing the features of vegetation and habitat in a way suitable for electronic data processing. Useful suggestions of this kind have already been published by Peterken (1967), Radford (1977) and others.

References

Arnolds, E. J. M., van der Meijden, R., *et al.* (1976). *Standaardlijst van de Nederlandse Flora*, Rijksherbarium, Leiden.

Ayensu, E. S. and DeFilipps, R. A. (1978). *Endangered and Threatened Plants of the United States*, Smithsonian Institution and the World Wildlife Fund, Inc., Washington, DC.

Bourdelle, M. (1956). 'Tableau de la nomenclature', in *Derniers refuges: Atlas commenté des Réserves Naturelle dans le monde* (Ed. M. Bourdelle), pp. 62–3, Elsevier, Brussels.

Braun-Blanquet, J. (1964). *Pflanzensoziologie: Grundzüge der Vegetationskunde*, 3rd Ed., Springer, Vienna.

Castri, Di F. and Loope, L. (1977). 'Réserves de la biosphère: théorie et pratique', *Nature et resources*, Bull. du MAB, Unesco, **13**(1), 2–8.

Duffey, E. and Watt, A. S. (Eds.) (1971). *The Scientific Management of Animal and Plant Communities for Conservation*, the 11th Symposium of the British Ecological Society, Blackwell Scientific Publications, Oxford.

Ellenberg, H. (Ed.) (1971). *Integrated Experimental Ecology*. Ecol. Stud. 2, Springer, Berlin.

Ellenberg, H. (1974). 'Zeigerwerte der Gefässpflanzen Mitteleuropas', *Scripta geobot.*, **9**, 1–97.

Faliński, J. B. (1966). 'La végétation antropogène de la Grande Fôret de Białowieża' (in Polish, with French summary), *Rozpr. Uniw. Warszawsk.*, **13**, 1–256.

Géhu, J. M. (1974). 'Sur l'emploi de la méthode phytosociologique sigmatiste dans l'analyse, la définition et cartographie des paysages', *C.R. Acad. Sci. Paris*, **279D**, 1167–70.

IUCN Commission on National Parks and Protected Areas (1980). *1980 United Nations List of National Parks and Equivalent Reserves*, IUCN, Gland, Switzerland.

IUCN Threatened Plants Committee (1977). *List of Rare, Threatened and Endemic Plants of Europe*, Nature & Environment Series No. 14, Council of Europe, Strasbourg, France.

Kornaś, J. (1968). 'A geographical–historical classification of synanthropic plants', *Mater. Zakładu Fitosocjol. Stosowanej Uniw. Warszawsk.*, **25**, 33–41.

Lucas, G. and Synge, H. (1978). *The IUCN Plant Red Data Book*, IUCN, Morges, Switzerland.

Maarel, E. van der (1971). 'Plant species diversity in relation to management', in *The Scientific Management of Animal and Plant Communities for Conservation* (Eds. E. Duffey and A. S. Watt), pp. 45–63, Blackwell Scientific Publications, Oxford.

Matuszkiewicz, W. (1980). 'Synopsis und geographische Analyse der Pflanzen-gesellschaften in Polen', *Mitt. florist.-soziol. Arbeitsgem.*, N.F. **22**, 19–50.

Medwecka-Kornaś, A. (1977). 'Ecological problems in the conservation of plant communities, with special reference to Central Europe', *Envir. Conserv.*, **4**(1), 27–33.

Medwecka-Kornaś, A. and Kornaś, J. (1963). 'Vegetation map of the Ojców National Park', *Ochr. Przyr.*, **29**, 17–87.

Medwecka-Kornaś, A., Kornaś, J., and Pawłowski, B. (1966). 'Survey of the most important plant associations in Poland', in *The Vegetation of Poland* (Ed. W. Szafer), pp. 294–534, Pergamon Press, Oxford.

Medwecka-Kornaś, A., Łomnicki, A., and Bandoła-Ciołczyk, E. (1974). 'Energy flow in the Oak-Hornbeam Forest (IBP Project 'Ispina')', *Bull. Acad. Polon. Sci., Sér. Sci. Biol.*, Cl. II, **22**(9), 563–7.

Michalik, S. (1974). 'The changes induced by man in the vegetation of the Ojców National Park since the beginning of XIXth Century to 1960', *Ochr. Przyr.*, **39**, 65–154.

Nicholson, E. M. (1968). *Handbook to the Conservation Section of the International Biological Programme*, IBP Handbook 5, Blackwell Scientific Publications, Oxford.

Perring, F. H. and Farrell, L. (1977). *British Red Data Books: 1. Vascular Plants*, Society for the Promotion of Nature Conservation, Lincoln.

Peterken, G. F. (1967). *Guide to the Check Sheet for IBP Areas*, IBP Handbook 4, Blackwell Scientific Publications, Oxford.

Radford, A. E. (1977). 'Natural area classification system: a standardization scheme', in *Proceedings of the Conference on Endangered Plants in the Southeast*, Asheville, North Carolina, pp. 95–104, USDA Forest Service General Technical Report SE-11.

Rivas-Martínez, S. (1976). 'Sinfitosociología, una nueva metodología para el estudio del paisaje vegetal', *Anales Inst. Bot. Cavanilles*, **33**, 179–88.

Sukopp, H. (1968). 'Der Einfluss des Menschen auf die Vegetation und zur Terminologie anthropogener Vegetationstypen', in *Pflanzensoziologie und Landschaftsökologie* (Ed. R. Tüxen), pp. 65–74, Junk, The Hague.

Sukopp, H. (1974). ' "Rote Liste" in der Bundesrepublik Deutschland gefahrdeten Arten von Farn und Blütenpflanzen' (1 Fassung), *Natur und Landschaft*, **49**(12), 315–22.

Symoens, J. J. (1979). 'Réserves naturelles, parcs nationaux, parcs naturelles: essai de mise au point', *Naturalistes Belges*, **60**(1), 2–43.

Takhtajan, A. (1975). *Red Book: Native Plant Species to be Protected in the USSR*, Izd. Nauka, Leningrad.

Tüxen, R. (1956). 'Die heutige potentielle natürliche Vegetation als Gegenstand der Vegetationskartierung', *Angew. Pflanzensoziol.*, **13**, Stolzenau/Weser.

Tüxen, R. (1973). 'Vorschlag zur Aufnahme von Gesellschaftskomplexen in potentiell natürlichen Vegetationsgebieten', *Acta Bot. Acad. Sci. Hung.*, **19**, 379–84.

Tüxen, R. and Ellenberg, H. (1937). 'Der Systematische und Ökologische Gruppenwert. Ein Beitrag zur Begriffsbildung und Methodik der Pflanzensoziologie', *Mitt. florist.-soziol. Arbeitsgem., Niedersachsen*, **3**, 171–84.

Udvardy, M. D. F. (1975). *A Classification of the Biogeographical Provinces of the World*, IUCN Occasional Paper 18, Morges, Switzerland.

Westhoff, V. and Maarel, E. van der (1978). 'The Braun-Blanquet approach', in *Classification of Plant Communities* (Ed. R. H. Whittaker), pp. 287–399, Junk, The Hague.

Whittaker, R. H. (Ed.) (1978). *Classification of Plant Communities*, Junk, The Hague.
Wodziczko, A. (1950). 'About the biology of landscape', *Przegląd geogr.*, **22**, 295–301, (in Polish).

The Biological Aspects of Rare Plant Conservation
Edited by Hugh Synge.
Published 1981 by John Wiley & Sons Ltd.

37
The Endangered Species Program and plant reserves in the United States

JOHN J. FAY *Office of Endangered Species, US Fish and Wildlife Service, Washington, DC*

Summary

The US Endangered Species Act of 1973 provides for the conservation of endangered species by preventing federal agencies from contributing to the decline of those species. Although it also prevents killing of endangered animals wherever they may occur, it does not prevent the destruction of listed plants on private land, unless there is federal involvement in the form of funding or permits, a situation that existed for the San Diego Mesa Mint, now successfully protected. The history of the Act is described and the situation explained whereby only 58 plants are so far listed under the Act as 'endangered' or 'threatened' out of a total of 1700 species proposed in 1975. The protection offered through 'Critical Habitat' designation is described and future plans outlined. The first US Fish and Wildlife preserve for 'endangered' plants – the Antioch Dunes in California – is also announced.

By way of introduction, I would like to sketch out the framework within which the US Endangered Species Program operates, because I suspect that it differs to a greater or lesser degree from programs of similar intent and purposes in other countries. Ours is a national program with fairly comprehensive interests and responsibilities in the area of endangered species. This means animals, including invertebrates, and plants. The expression 'and plants' is highly significant because, in a sense, plants were grafted onto a pre-existing endangered animal program, with some of the initial immunity and rejection problems that implies. This implantation took place in the form of the Endangered Species Act of 1973, a watershed in US conservation policy that put our Federal government on record as opposing species extinction in a very strong way. I think it is worthwhile to quote the Act in this regard: 'The purposes of this Act are to provide a means whereby the ecosystems upon which endangered species and threatened species depend may be conserved. . . .'

This principle of preservation of habitat and associated species is very important and, of course, is exactly what this conference is all about. The objectives of the program are advanced principally along two fronts – first, by the prohibition or restriction of trade in 'endangered' and 'threatened' species as defined by the Act, both domestically and internationally through the implementation of the Convention of International Trade in Endangered Species of Wild Fauna and Flora (CITES), which I will not cover here, and secondly through encouragement of conservation programs by Federal agencies and very strict constraints on activities of the Federal government that would tend to promote species' decline. In the case of animals, taking, that is killing, removing from the wild, harassing, etc., is also prohibited. Again, I think it is useful to quote the Endangered Species Act (Section 7[a] [2] and [5] *pro parte*):

> All Federal agencies shall, in consultation with and with the assistance of the Secretary, utilize their authorities in furtherance of the purposes of this Act by carrying out programs for the conservation of endangered species and threatened species ... each Federal agency shall ... insure that any action authorized, funded, or carried out by such agency is not likely to jeopardize the continued existence of any endangered species or threatened species or result in the destruction or adverse modification of habitat of such species which is determined ... to be critical.

Implementation of this provision rests in part on the requirement that all Federal agencies consult the US Fish and Wildlife Service of the Department of the Interior regarding their programs. The result of such a consultation is a biological opinion regarding the probable effects of a given action. We do not, however, have the authority, frequently ascribed to us, to 'stop government projects.' Rather, each agency is required to insure that its actions comply with the law. Practically speaking, most agencies do this by following our advice, though occasionally with some degree of reluctance.

This then is the framework within which our program has developed, but without a scientifically credible list of organisms protected under the Act, the frame is empty. As Dr Ayensu mentioned in Chapter 2, the preliminary assembly of such a list of plants was originally assigned to the Smithsonian Institution and published in 1975. The vicissitudes of government, however, require that formal addition of a species to the US list be a rather involved regulatory procedure, in which a proposal is made and in which public and governmental comment are invited before formal listing occurs. This can be a lengthy and involved process. Adding to the length and complexity of our task have been recent changes in the law (1978 amendments) that require consideration of the economic costs of conserving the species we intend to list. This, I think, is merely the reverse side of the rather stringent constraints on government activities possible as a result of a species' listing. Specifically, the examination of economic consequences is tied to the designation of what is called a 'Critical Habitat' for a listed species. The legal change that requires economic considerations also requires that, with certain limited exceptions, such a 'Critical Habitat' be designated at the time a species is listed. A 'Critical Habitat' is not, in the usual sense of the word, a preserve, but rather a device that grew out of the specification of the Endangered Species Act that Federal agencies should not destroy or adversely modify habitat considered critical to an 'endangered' or 'threatened' species. Such a designation advises agencies that an area so specified is one in which they should exercise caution, and concerning which they might be required to seek our advice.

The Fish and Wildlife Service used the Smithsonian report as the basis of a notice that it was reviewing the status of some 3000 species of plants for possible addition to the national list (US Fish and Wildlife Service, 1975). Later, about 1700 of these species were proposed for listing as Endangered (US Fish and Wildlife Service, 1976). Since that time, another change in the law (1978 amendments) required that any proposal be withdrawn unless formal listing were effected within 2 years. Even with the allowance in this amendment of 1 year's grace, this meant that the vast majority of the 1700 proposed species were withdrawn from that status in 1979. At present, 56 native and 2 foreign plant taxa are officially on the US list. Federal agencies, however, have generally taken some cognizance of the 3000 species still under review, which are essentially those contained in the Smithsonian report. We now recognize that the formal listing of all the species that should be added to the national list will be an enormously time-consuming task. Because our original review notice is out of date, however, we are currently consolidating all available information on the species we have previously been involved with, as well as those that have come to light since 1975; (this has included, in quite a few cases, funding state lists). In late 1980 we published an up-dated notice, with deletions and additions to the 1975 list as well as what were a considerable number of species listed in an 'uncertain' category, for which we have probable cause to believe they ought to be on our list, but for which we lack sufficient specific information to satisfy all the present procedural requirements for addition to that list. For the species in the 'uncertain' category we will pointedly seek new information to indicate whether they should be included or removed from further consideration. We intend to adjust these lists periodically, perhaps annually, but certainly more frequently than every 5 years.

The cooperation that we have received from other agencies has often been very encouraging with respect to undertaking management or research to conserve plants that we have not yet formally listed, but are considering for action. This is a purely voluntary policy, since there is no strict legal requirement to conserve such species.

Given this background concerning our law and list, what about preserves for plants? As a matter of fact, I was more than a bit nervous several months ago, when I was assigned that topic for this conference, but I can proudly announce that the National Wildlife Refuge System of the Fish and Wildlife Service now contains one preserve established in part to protect 'endangered' plants – Antioch Dunes in California, home of *Oenothera deltoides* ssp. *howellii* (the Antioch Dunes Evening-primrose) and *Erysimum capitatum* var. *angustatum* (the Contra

Costa Wallflower). In fact, this is not only the first unit of the National Wildlife Refuge System acquired with plants in mind, it is also the first such unit established to protect a unique endemic ecosystem, including an 'endangered' butterfly, Lange's Metalmark (*Apodemia mormo langei*), and several other insects that are candidates for our 'endangered' and 'threatened' list. This is not to imply that the Fish and Wildlife Service owns and administers the only preserve in the US harboring an endangered plant. A plethora of other public and private agencies are involved in similar activities directed at rare and endangered plants. The US Nature Conservancy, for example, has been very active both in identifying important areas of natural diversity and in arranging for their protection by easement or acquisition (see Morse, Chapter 38). The US Forest Service has developed a 'sensitive' plant list of its own, based in large part on our review list, has funded a series of status reports prepared by the California Native Plant Society and has, as a very small example, designated an area in the state of Florida as the *Harperocallis* Botanical Area to preserve *Harperocallis flava* – a monotypic genus in the Liliaceae that is known from a total area on the order of 1 hectare. Peter White and Susan Bratton in Chapters 22 and 39 outline some of the programs of the National Park Service within US national parks, particularly in the southern Appalachians, an area of notable plant endemism.

What I would like to discuss now, however, are not preserves in an ordinary sense, but the phantom preserves that are set up whenever species go on our list. These are preserves without boundaries, although in some cases they may be defined coincidently with a 'Critical Habitat'. They are definitely not inviolate in any ordinary sense, and they rarely belong to the Fish and Wildlife Service. They exist because, in effect, every listed species has a 'Do not jeopardize' sign hanging on it – a sign, however, perceivable only by Federal agencies. For practical purposes, then, every plant on our list is situated on a preserve in terms of the US Federal government. We cannot, however, prevent the destruction of listed plants on private land unless there is a very clear Federal involvement in the form of funding or permits. This, I am told, is part of the legacy of British Common Law that is ours as former colonies. The ownership of game, and therefore of 'endangered' animals, is assigned to the Crown, therefore to the Federal government, while plants – therefore 'endangered' plants – belong to the owner of the land on which they grow. Ergo, it is contrary to law to shoot a whooping crane, but not to destroy a population of *Pogogyne abramsii* (San Diego Mesa Mint), provided it grows on land that you own. In fact this species, endemic to San Diego County, California, is a good example of how our program can work. It was added to our 'endangered' list in 1978, and has been a source of interest and controversy since then. The Mesa Mint is found only in vernal pools, which are characteristic features of the Mediterranean climate of California. They are low, poorly-drained areas that fill with water during winter rains and then gradually dry out during summer drought. The uninformed generally refer to them as 'mud puddles'. They support a unique assemblage of endemic plants, mostly annuals that begin life as aquatics, but are growing under desert-like conditions by the time they set seed. The San Diego Mesa Mint may be locally abundant in those pools in which it grows, but is absolutely confined to these pools. San Diego, in turn, is one of the fastest-growing communities in the US. Over 90 per cent of San Diego's original vernal pools have now probably been destroyed.

Within days of the legal notice listing this plant, one private developer plowed up over 100 acres containing vernal pools with the species, and we had no way to stop that activity, no control of the situation. In the ensuing 2 years we, principally in the person of a botanist in our Sacramento Office, have been trying to work with all the parties involved to develop an acceptable plan for the species' conservation as well as the inevitable development. The crucial link in the process turned out to be the involvement of the US Army Corps of Engineers, who have not always seen things from the same perspective as we. It developed that the Corps, in addition to its widely-known jurisdiction over inland navigable waterways, has discretionary authority to permit or prohibit activities that would affect seasonal wetlands, including vernal pools. The Endangered Species Act, in turn requires Federal agencies to utilize their authorities in furtherance of the purposes of the Act, and the Corps of Engineers had this authority. In accordance with the law, the Corps informed local governments and private landowners that alteration of vernal pools containing the 'endangered' plant would require Federal permits and that these would not be granted unless acceptable provisions were made for conservation of the Mesa Mint, as determined by the Fish and Wildlife Service. Under these circumstances, negotiations have proceeded on a vernal pool preservation plan which is now nearly complete. Some vernal pools will be irretrievably lost, others will become preserves, others will be protected from development as enclaves within otherwise developed sites. The Fish and Wildlife Service will advise the Corps of Engineers that it may issue permits that comply with the comprehensive plan. Perhaps no one will be totally pleased with the outcome, but both conservationists and developers will have reached a workable compromise.

The story illustrates three points that are broadly applicable to our program and other such endeavors:

1. We cannot save everything and will have to make the most of compromise situations;
2. For the future, because we cannot necessarily protect plants on private land, acquisition of land and interest in land may become increasingly important in our national program;
3. Overall, if we are to accomplish any plant conservation, we must have in hand the best biological information we can possibly obtain and we had better be willing and able to seek imaginative and creative solutions.

References

Endangered Species Act of 1973, Public Law 93–205 (87 Stat. 884).
1978 Amendments to the Endangered Species Act, Public Law 95–632 (92 Stat. 3751).
Smithsonian Institution (1975). *Report on Endangered and Threatened Plant Species of the United States*, House Document Number 94–51, Serial Number 94–A, Government Printing Office, Washington, DC.
US Fish and Wildlife Service (1975). 'Review of status of over 3000 vascular plants and determination of 'critical habitat', *Federal Register*, **40**(127), 1 July, 27824–924.
US Fish and Wildlife Service (1976). 'Proposed endangered status for some 1700 U.S. vascular plant taxa', *Federal Register*, **41**(117), 16 June, 24524–72.
US Fish and Wildlife Service (1980). 'Endangered and threatened wildlife and plants: Review of plant taxa for listing as endangered or threatened species', *Federal Register*, **45** (242), 15 December, 82480–569.

The Biological Aspects of Rare Plant Conservation
Edited by Hugh Synge
© 1981 John Wiley & Sons Ltd.

38
The Nature Conservancy and rare plant conservation in the United States

LARRY E. MORSE *The Nature Conservancy, Arlington, Virginia*

Summary

The Nature Conservancy is a private, non-governmental organization which aims to preserve the natural ecological diversity of the United States. To select reserves and set priorities for conservation, the Conservancy establishes state Natural Heritage Programs which are inventories of the features of the state's natural diversity in terms of species and ecosystems. Emphasis is on the exact localities in which each element occurs. The targets and structures of these programs are explained and the mapping techniques outlined. As it develops, the Heritage data base is used to create state protection plans, to assess both priorities and opportunities for conservation and as an input to general land-use planning. Furthermore the data assist in the management of areas acquired for preserves.

The Nature Conservancy is the largest non-profit land conservation organization in the United States; it was created in 1950 as the successor to the Ecological Society of America's Special Committee for the Preservation of Natural Conditions, established in 1917. The Conservancy's overall goal is to preserve natural ecological diversity, especially in the United States. Although it is a private organization, The Nature Conservancy (TNC) works closely with the conservation efforts of federal, state, and local governments. Its status as a non-governmental organization allows it to take actions more quickly and more flexibly than is usually possible within government agencies. In some cases, the Conservancy acquires lands for transfer to government preserves, while in other cases the organization manages such lands itself.

The Conservancy uses its biological expertise primarily in three areas: inventory, protection planning, and stewardship. Each of these will be discussed briefly below. Further details on the Conservancy's work in rare plant conservation can be found in Jenkins (1981), Moyseenko (1981), and numerous items in *The Nature Conservancy News*, particularly the March/April 1979 issue, devoted to the topic of rare plants. Also of interest is the book *Building an Ark: Tools for the Preservation of Natural Diversity through Land Protection* (Hoose, 1981), and the September/October 1980 issue of *The Nature Conservancy News* on protection planning.

Heritage Programs – Inventory

Initially, TNC preserves were selected by a rather haphazard and opportunistic process typical of early conservation efforts. Inventory of potential preserves has always been important, but by 1974 the need for more systematic procedures led the Conservancy to initiate the first of its 23 state Natural Heritage Programs. These programs are comprehensive, continuing inventories of the places in a state where features comprising the state's natural heritage – the 'elements' of the state's natural diversity – occur. Inventory efforts in Heritage Programs are generally concentrated on extant occurrences of rare, unusual, or declining plant and animal populations and on high quality stands of the more typical plant communities and aquatic habitats that characterize the state. Information on exact localities is emphasized in the Heritage Programs, for it is impossible to conserve a species unless one knows the actual places where its populations occur.

A Heritage Program supplements rather than replaces existing data-collection efforts in the state, serving as a centralized data-base or clearing-house for biogeographical information of conservation importance and promoting co-ordination in setting field-research and conservation priorities within a state. Having all this information at one location gives a basis for planning further research by synthesizing available data and identifying gaps in knowledge. Ultimately, the collective information of the program provides a state-wide perspective on the significance of each feature mapped.

Heritage Programs are conducted state by state, rather than as a single national effort. Generally, a Heritage Program is established by the Conservancy with some mixture of state, federal, and private funds, then transferred after about 2 years to an appropriate state government agency for continued operation and maintenance. Operation of these programs at the state level facilitates data input and review, enhances the opportunity for contact with local researchers, planners, and land managers, and keeps the data base manageable in size. The richest library holdings and museum collections are also usually located within the state. Furthermore, state-by-state implementation allows each program to proceed at its own pace, and adapt itself to the needs and priorities of the state and its region. Also, states have the means and interest to continue the programs, since philanthropy is primarily available at state level, federal funds are often dispersed through states, and the information of the program is especially needed at state level.

Information in a Heritage Program is organized in two major ways. Most general reference material is organized taxonomically, and includes, for example, articles and status reports on particular species. Information on specific localities is organized geographically, plotted to the highest resolution possible on the best available US Geological Survey topographic maps. Information is also maintained on parks, forests, and other managed areas in the state, with their boundaries drawn on the maps used for mapping element occurrences. Files are also kept on interests of specialists on the state's biota and other natural features, and on bibliographic references pertinent to the Program.

Selected kinds of information are systematically indexed on computer to facilitate search, comparison, tabulation, and retrieval. The computer effort, however, is concentrated on the information that will be of greatest general use; instead much of the detailed data is maintained in carefully organized manual files.

The major sources of information for a Heritage Program are museum specimens, published literature, and local naturalists, both amateur and professional. Staff field work is initially of low importance in a Heritage Program since information on individual sites can be more easily developed from secondary sources. Only rarely does such information cover individual localities in sufficient detail for conservation action, so initial field work in a program is concentrated on relocating and evaluating species in previously known sites. This provides up-to-date information on identity, abundance, threats, and protection needs, data rarely available from secondary sources. As a Heritage Program matures and exhausts the available knowledge, *de novo* field inventory becomes the major source of information on new occurrences.

A mature Heritage data base serves two primary roles within a state. On the one hand, it serves as a comprehensive reference on the current conservation status of the rarer or more vulnerable species and communities, thus directing conservation efforts as well as further field inventories. On the other hand, the data of the Heritage Program, especially its set of marked topographic maps, become increasingly valuable references for environmental impact assessments and other planning activities. The site-specific information on the Heritage Program maps is especially useful in fine-tuning proposed plans, for example in laying out natural corridors or setting specific boundaries for various kinds of management. When such data are easily available early in the planning process, it is relatively easy for project sponsors to make relatively minor planning adjustments, such as shifting a pipe-line alignment 100 yards, that cost little money yet avoid destruction of small areas of significant habitat.

Heritage Programs differ from other kinds of natural areas inventories. The emphasis of a Heritage Program is on the specific occurrence as the unit of information, such as the exact locality of a particular plant population. This strategy contrasts with the usual 'natural areas' approach, in which relatively large areas of relatively undisturbed habitat, dozens or hundreds of acres in extent, are identified, sometimes with an incomplete list of species of interest, but usually no information on what is exactly where within the area studied. The Heritage Program point-locality information can always be assembled into lists for specified areas as needed, but the original data are not constrained by the boundaries used at the time of data collection. For example, if a proposed road might cross one corner of a forest preserve, the Heritage maps would show specifically which of the significant features of the area would be directly affected, while the typical natural areas report would be of little use.

Balanced information management is another characteristic of the Heritage Programs. Some of the information is indexed on computer using controlled-value data fields; some is marked by hand on detailed maps; and some is kept in manual files only. Thus, the powerful but expensive computer technology is focused on only the most important information, which in turn serves as an index to further, more specific data on the maps or in the filing cabinets. While a powerful computer graphics capability could undoubtedly be very useful to a Heritage Program, a sufficiently powerful system would not be cost-effective at present levels of technology.

Finally, the continuity of a Heritage Program is another important distinction. A Heritage Program is not a one-time study which becomes outdated within a few years; instead, it provides a dynamic atlas and data base, covering for each element of natural ecological diversity in the state, its characteristics, numbers, condition, locations, and protection status. Additional occurrences are continually added, previously reported occurrences are revised as new information comes to hand, and the working lists of significant species, plant communities, and so forth are themselves revised as scientific knowledge and conservation priorities change. Furthermore, since specific, standardized procedures are used to record, map, index, and document the information in the data base, a Heritage Program does not depend heavily on unwritten staff knowledge, thus providing a resilience to staff change not found in most other projects.

Protection planning

Eventually, a Heritage data base becomes sufficiently mature to be useful in setting conservation priorities in the form of a state protection plan, in which the conservation status of the various species and communities in the state is reviewed comprehensively, considering such factors as their range and distribution, rarity, legal status, degree of threat, existing protection, and whether land protection would be appropriate to their conservation. From this 'status-of-diversity' review, lists are developed of elements most in need of protection. Information on the occurrences of each priority element is then compared to determine which offers the best conservation opportunities.

For example, *Plantago cordata* was determined to be a priority element in Indiana, since it is a sparsely distributed species of restricted range having only two occurrences in Indiana, neither on protected land. If one of these populations is a large stand in a remote area, and the other a few stems in a highly disturbed site, then, other things being equal, the first is the conservation objective.

While drawing upon the Heritage Program data base, protection planning also includes consideration of recommendations of experts as well as of site visits, which evaluate priorities for potential preserves. Factors such as quality, condition, viability, and defensibility of the various sites are reviewed, and efforts are made to locate sites which can be protected and in which a set of significant elements can be preserved.

Stewardship

Stewardship is the third area in which biological data play a major role in the Conservancy's work – here we address the fundamental question of what, if anything, to do to the site once it has been protected from incompatible land-use change. For some areas, a leave-it-alone philosophy is appropriate, but for others, especially tiny sites lacking appropriate buffers, more active management is necessary. Maintenance of prairies, for example, is a current challenge. Also, for some areas, management of human visitation is needed; the educational and aesthetic values of a preserve should be utilized only to the extent acceptable to the long-term conservation of the element(s) at the site.

Currently, The Nature Conservancy is strengthening the biological basis of all three of these aspects of conservation. The Nature Conservancy's national office is conducting the Maryland Natural Heritage Program as a model program in which improvements to inventory procedures and data-processing strategies are being developed and tested. Heritage data are being increasingly integrated into protection planning, with the quality and significance of elements that can be protected as a primary consideration in designing preserves.

Finally, a long-term effort is underway to approach stewardship problems through an element-by-element, site-by-site review of the exact location, condition, and management needs of the special species and natural communities present within established preserves. In all these current efforts, an attempt is being made to handle the various types of data in comparable ways, for example by recording information on plant populations in the same form, although admittedly with different emphases, in Heritage inventories, protection planning processes, and stewardship of established preserves.

References

Hoose, P. M. (1981). *Building an Ark: Tools for the Preservation of Natural Diversity through Land Preservation*, Island Press, Covelo, California.

Jenkins, R. E. (1981). 'Rare plant conservation through elements-of-diversity information', in *Rare Plant Conservation: Geographical Data Organization* (Eds. L. E. Morse and M. S. Henifin), pp. 33–40, New York Botanical Garden, Bronx, New York.

Moyseenko, H. P. (1981). 'Limiting factors and pitfalls of environmental data management', in *Rare Plant Conservation; Geographical Data Organization* (Eds. L. E. Morse and M. S. Henifin), pp. 237–53, New York Botanical Garden, Bronx, New York.

The Nature Conservancy (1979). 'Rare plants', *The Nature Conservancy News*, **29**(2), 1–32.

The Nature Conservancy (1980). 'Protecting the land', *The Nature Conservancy News*, **30**(5), 1–32.

The Biological Aspects of Rare Plant Conservation
Edited by Hugh Synge,
Published 1981 by John Wiley & Sons Ltd.

39
Rare and endangered plant species management: Potential threats and practical problems in US national parks and preserves

SUSAN P. BRATTON AND PETER S. WHITE *US National Park Service, Uplands Field Research Laboratory, Great Smoky Mountains National Park, Tennessee*

Summary

Even in national parks and ecological preserves, anthropogenic modifications and processes of change continue to affect the structure and function of biological systems. In US parks, important and continuing problems in rare plant management include change in the physical environment, impact from exotic species, over-grazing by native herbivores, modification of disturbance regimes, and human trampling and herb gathering. These problems occur in a variety of preserve systems and some, such as trampling and disturbance management, are almost universal. In this chapter botanical management problems in national parks of the southeastern USA are reviewed and compared to those in arid western parks. It is shown that most large US parks have basic floristic data available, but data on rare plant population locations and status have not been consistently collected.

Introduction

Conservationists frequently assume that the key to successful management of endangered species is the prohibition of human exploitation or the inclusion of critical habitat within a nature preserve. Legal protection is, of course, a necessary first step but is just the beginning of sound population management. Even in well-established national parks, human activities may still threaten species, and disturbance and ecological changes continue. The protection phase of rare plant management is commonly executed, but manipulation is less frequent and presents some important philosophical questions. This chapter outlines some of the resource protection problems that are of current importance in managing rare plant species in preserves in the USA.

The opinions presented in this paper are those of the authors and do not represent official US National Park Service policy.

Far too often, preserve ecosystems are thought of as static, representing some ideal state. Even if a site has a history of intensive human disturbance, the hope is usually that it is returning to its prior condition or to some desirable 'climax' community. Viewing 'change' and 'preserve' as contrasting terms may be tempting, but it ignores much of what is known about ecosystem dynamics, disturbance and succession, geologic time, natural selection, population genetics, and human cultural history (White and Bratton, 1980).

Changes in preserves can be initiated by either anthropogenic or natural events. These two factors may sometimes interact, as in the case of a wild fire on logging slash. Although most preserves attempt to curtail or eliminate direct human impacts such as construction or logging, even the most restricted preserves usually allow research and collecting of specimens. In the case of US national parks, recreation, education, and research will continue as part of the legal mandate of the areas.

Human impacts can also be indirect, unintentional, or can act by modifying some physical or chemical property of the preserve environment. The introduction of an exotic species, for instance, or the construction of a dam may affect the native biota of a preserve. In US parks, where human exploitation is carefully regulated, indirect anthropogenic impacts often cause most serious managerial problems, because such impacts are difficult to control through legislation and frequently have distant sources.

Aside from human interference, preserves are subject to a wide variety of natural disturbances such as fires, windstorms, ice storms, floods, droughts, freezes, debris and rock slides, volcanic eruptions, Karst processes, native insect and disease outbreaks, and grazing and trampling by herbivores. Further, long-term environmental changes are related to Pleistocene climatic fluctuations, glacial retreats and advances, and orogenic activities. Evolution, speciation and extinction are ongoing processes in all ecosystems and are influenced not only by conditions in a preserve but also by factors affecting gene pools outside a preserve's boundaries (Bratton and White, 1980).

Ecological change in the Great Smoky Mountains National Park

In the Great Smoky Mountains National Park, for example, changes have varied from anthropogenic (e.g. visitor impacts) to natural (e.g. succession); from detrimental (e.g. drainage changes in a wetland) to beneficial (e.g. landslides that maintain rare species habitat); and from manageable (e.g. fire regime) to unmanageable (e.g. windstorms, droughts, and flash floods). Communities and rare species populations have obviously been affected, as shown by the rare species monitoring program in the park (see White and Bratton, Chapter 22). Changes before the park was declared included succession after agriculture, logging and grazing, and also elimination of large predators and other species which have a big effect on the ecosystem, such as the beaver. Continuing anthropogenic changes influence nearly every part of the park landscape today; Table 1 lists some of the effects on each vegetation type and shows how pervasive is the human impact, even after protection as a national park. These effects include, for example, exotic species problems (Wood and Shanks, 1959; Hay *et al.*, 1978; Bratton, 1975) and changes in fire regime (Harmon, 1980) as well as direct impact from visitors, e.g. legal fishing and exploitation of medicinal and ornamental plants. Even collection of herbarium specimens is implicated; some 60 clumps of *Lycopodium selago* were taken from a single site on a single collecting day – this probably represented over half the population at this site. Recovery has not occurred after 30 years. Management has also led to decline in species populations – examples include the loss of an endemic fish (Etnier, 1978), changes in a sinkhole pond bulldozed to improve recreation, and impacts of historic zone management on natural areas (Bratton, Mathews and White, in press). Human influence, however, has also increased rare species populations – a few endemics to the national park are weedy species growing along trials, in campsites, and in other human-created openings.

Natural disturbances in the park affect communities and rare species populations. Fifty-five per cent of the species in the park are found in open habitats,

Table 1   Anthropogenic change in major vegetation types of Great Smoky Mountains National Park. Direct visitor impacts, recreational developments, air pollution, extirpation of large predators, and past histories of fire, logging, and agriculture are potentially important in all communities and are not listed separately below

Vegetation type	Site moisture	Elevation (m)	Anthropogenic influence
Cove hardwoods and hemlock-hardwoods	Mesic	300–1200	European wild boar; gathering of Panax, Allium, and Orchidaceae
Oak, cove-oak transition and former oak-chestnut stands	Submesic–subxeric	300–1400	Chestnut blight; European wild boar; changes in fire regime; gathering of Orchidaceae
Pine and oak-pine	Subxeric–xeric	300–1400	Changes in fire regime
Northern hardwoods and beech gaps	Mesic	1200–1800	European wild boar
Hemlock	Mesic–submesic	300–1500	
Spruce-fir	Mesic	1400–2000	Balsam woolly aphid
Grassy balds	Various	1000–1800	European wild boar; succession
Heath balds	Subxeric–xeric	1400–2000	

which are in part maintained by natural disturbances. Of the 45 per cent found in closed forests, some species are increased by small-scale disturbance to the forest canopy. In general, natural disturbances maintain habitat heterogeneity and species diversity. The size of the park is large relative to the patch size of natural disturbance; thus a dynamic equilibrium of disturbance patches may have occurred in the pre-human landscape, such that local elimination of populations was balanced by new population establishment (Pickett and Thompson, 1979).

Some rare species, however, exist in small populations that are vulnerable to natural disturbances and natural fluctuations in climate. Particularly vulnerable are small populations of alpine disjuncts which have persisted on cliff faces and seepage meadows long after climatic warming eliminated the natural tree-line. Such species, though their habitats may have been produced by natural disturbance, may nonetheless be vulnerable to specific natural events. Human impacts further the potential effects of natural disturbances. Where human influence (e.g. suppression of fire or trampling) has reduced natural populations, some species may be vulnerable to specific natural disturbances, even if they were once maintained by such processes. Because of the pervasiveness of some human impacts (e.g. air pollution), human-increased vulnerability is likely to be involved even in 'natural' extinctions.

Rare plant management in southeastern parks

As a result of the knowledge of change in Great Smoky Mountains National Park, described above, a table can be constructed to show the human impacts believed to be relevant to the management of the rare plants (Table 2). To broaden the approach and look at rare plant management in relation to changes in a variety of preserve ecosystems, the authors collected information on botanical management (via telephone survey and literature review) for 43 established national parks in the southeastern United States. The results are given in Table 3 which shows the important botanical management problems for a selection of the preserves in the survey.

In all the southeastern parks, past impacts of importance to endangered species management included farming, logging, grazing, burning, and extirpation of native animals. The major threats to endangered plants and native plant communities in southeastern parks are perceived to be at present: (a) changes in the physical environment; (b) exotic species invasion; (c) increase in native herbivore populations; (d) interference with disturbance processes (especially fire); and (e) human trampling or plant gathering

Changes in the physical environment

In two subtropical areas, Everglades National Park and Big Cypress National Preserve, changes in hydrology due to canal building and other construction

Table 2 Botanical management problems of Great Smoky Mountains National Park – their historic and present status and implications for rare plant management. (Ratings are those of the authors and not official US National Park Service)

Impact	Probable aboriginal practice	Now illegal but still practiced	Discontinued almost entirely	Historic and developed zones only	Interacts with natural disturbance	Continuing major eco-system effects	Present effects on rare plants
Extirpation of predators	+	–	+	–	–	+	Indirect
Extirpation of herbivores	+	–	+	–	–	+	Indirect
Hunting of game	+	+	–	–	–	+	Indirect
Gathering of herbs	+	–	–	–	–	–	Serious
Collection of scientific specimens	–	–	–	–	–	–	Moderate
Logging	–	–	+	–	+	+	Recovery
Grazing	–	–	–	+	–	+	Recovery
Farming	+	–	–	+	–	+	Recovery
Burning (arson)	+	+	–	–	+	+	Minor
Fire Suppression	–	–	–	–	+	+	Moderate
Construction of buildings	+	–	–	+	–	–	Minor
Construction of roads	–	–	+	–	–	+	Moderate
Construction of trails	+	–	–	–	–	–	Moderate
Channelization and drainage	–	–	+	–	+	+	Moderate
Trampling	+	–	–	–	–	–	Moderate
Camping	+	–	–	–	–	–	Moderate
Introduction of exotic game	–	–	–	–	–	+	Serious
Introduction of exotic insects and diseases	–	–	–	–	+	+	Serious
Introduction of exotic vascular plants	–	–	–	–	–	+	Minor
Air pollution	–	–	–	–	–	+	Minor

Table 3 Resource management concerns and impacts on native vegetation in selected national parks and monuments with temperate (including upland and coastal) and subtropical climates

Park	Size (hectares)	State	Climate	Important types of rarity		Important impacts on native vegetation						
				Endemism	Disjuncts; range extensions	Exotic animals	Exotic plants	Changing water levels	Shifting substrates	Native grazers	Fire	Human trampling
Everglades NP	556 100	Florida	Subtropical	+	+	—	H	H	M	—	H	L
Big Cypress National Preserve	230 700	Florida	Subtropical			L	H	H	—	—	H	H
Great Smoky Mountains NP	209 100	Tennessee, North Carolina	Upland	+	+	H	L	—	—	M	M	H
Mammoth Cave NP	20 700	Kentucky	Upland			—	L	—	—	H	M	L
Cape Hatteras NS	11 500	North Carolina	Coastal			M	L	—	H	H	M	H
Cumberland Island NS	10 700	Georgia	Coastal			H	L	—	M	H	L	M
Cumberland Gap NHS	8 200	Tennessee, Kentucky, Virginia	Upland			—	L	—	—	—	M	L
Virgin Islands NP	4 800	Virgin Is.	Subtropical	+		H	?	—	—	—	?	?
Gulf Islands NS	3 800	Mississippi	Coastal			M	—	—	H	M	M	M
Chickamauga and Chattanooga NMP	3 200	Georgia, Tennessee	Upland		+	—	M	—	—	—	—	L
Fort Pulaski NM	2 300	Georgia	Coastal			—	L	—	L	—	L	L
Biscayne NM	4 400	Georgia	Subtropical			M	H	—	—	—	L	L

Key: H – high; M – moderate; L – low.

activities outside the parks' boundaries are threatening all major park ecosystems (National Park Service, 1979). Natural disturbances, especially fires and hurricanes, play an important role in these habitats and interact with hydrologic variables. The hardwood hammocks and the pinelands in the Everglades support species endemic to the habitat or disjunct from more tropical areas (Loope and Avery, 1979). Not only are the National Park Service staff working in conjunction with the US Army Corps of Engineers to guarantee that the park receives water, but they practice management burning, which helps maintain endemic herbs in the pinelands.

The temperate coastal parks do not, as a group, support as many rare plant species as do the mountain and subtropical areas, but there are a few species endemic to limited sections of the coast. One of the greatest threats to the vegetation of these sites, most of which are barrier islands, is changes in sand deposition patterns due to offshore dredging, construction of jetties, and other human interference. Not just individual species, but the islands themselves may disappear (Shabica *et al.*, 1978).

An interesting case of past human impacts on the fauna causing a change in the physical environment is the extirpation of the beaver (*Castor canadensis*) from Great Smoky Mountains National Park. The beaver builds dams which create small ponds and wetlands, which in turn provide a habitat for hydrophytes, ordinarily rare in mountainous regions. The demise of the beaver, therefore, may have limited the range of species such as *Campanula aparinoides* Pursh and *Thelypteris palustris* (Salisb.) Schott.

A final anthropogenic impact which is changing both the physical and chemical environments in the parks is air pollution. Concerns vary from climatic warming due to increases in CO_2 in the atmosphere to damage from high levels of ozone (Johnson and Bratton, 1978).

Exotic species invasion

Exotic animals are not an outstanding threat to the mainland subtropical parks, but Virgin Islands National Park contains several exotic species which cause problems; these include feral pigs, donkeys and goats. Several coastal areas are grazed by feral animals; Cumberland Island National Seashore, for example, still supports wild pigs and horses (Hillestad *et al.*, 1975).

Of the upland areas, the Great Smoky Mountains National Park has had the greatest difficulties with exotic animals and diseases but also has the best documentation of impacts, as described above and in White and Bratton (Chapter 22). The European wild boar (*Sus scrofa*), which was originally brought to a game preserve outside the park, invaded after the area was set aside as a preserve (Bratton, 1975). The wild boar roots extensively in mesic forest understories and not only consumes rare plant species such as *Stachys clingmanii* Small and members of the genus *Lilium*, but it disturbs the soil surface and knocks over herbs associated with preferred food items (Bratton, 1979).

Similarly, the balsam woolly aphid (*Adelges piceae*) attacks and kills Fraser fir (*Abies fraseri* Pursh), an endemic tree which grows only on some scattered peaks in the southern Appalachians. The balsam woolly aphid has disrupted canopy structure and initiated secondary succession, this affecting endemic elements in the forest understorey, including *Senecio rugelia* Gray.

In the upland areas, exotic plants are a widespread roadside problem but rarely invade undisturbed forest (Baron *et al.*, 1975). The subtropical parks, however, have more difficulties. Native species and communities are displaced by woody invaders such as *Casuarina equisetifolia* L. and *Melaleuca quinqueneruia* from Australia and *Schinus terebenthefolius* Raddi from Brazil (Loope and Avery, 1979).

Increases in native herbivore populations

In the southeast, problems from over-grazing by native herbivores are largely caused by the expansion in population of the white-tailed deer (*Odocoileus virginianus*). The presence of agricultural land and forest in an early stage of succession increases the food available for deer, and prohibition of hunting and the extirpation of predators before the park was declared reduced annual mortality.

In the Cades Cove historic district of Great Smoky Mountains, for instance, deer graze in hay fields and pastures, but also browse in the surrounding woods, thus threatening some uncommon plants which grow on limestone (Bratton, Mathews and White, in press).

Interference with disturbance

To complicate the issue of human impacts, many preserves have long cultural histories, beginning with aboriginal activities. The American Indians practiced burning and primitive agriculture, thereby modifying much of the vegetation of the southeast. It is not known if many rare plants were dependent on Indian clearing or burning (Bratton, White and Harmon, in press).

The settlers both destroyed and created rare plant habitat. Activities such as logging and drainage of marshes were carried on throughout the southeast, and communities are still in the recovery phase (see Table 2). In Cades Cove in the Great Smoky Mountains, changing agricultural practices have probably modified habitat for species such as *Selaginella apoda* (L.) Spring; *Campanula aparinoides* Pursh, and *Agrostis borealis* Hartman (Bratton, Mathews and White, in press). Yellowwood, *Cladrastis lutea* (Michaux f.) K. Koch, a southern Appalachian endemic, is probably adversely affected by logging outside the park.

Some disturbances, whether anthropogenic or natural, encourage rare plants dependent on canopy openings or disturbed soil. In Great Smoky Mountains, species endangered by natural processes, which include *Glyceria nubigena* W. A.

Anderson and *Prenanthes roanensis* Checkering, are found on grassy balds, small high-elevation openings initiated or maintained by stock grazing, logging, or burning before the establishment of the park. Without interference, these areas are succeeding to forest and will probably lose most of their unusual flora (Lindsay and Bratton, 1979).

In addition, lightning-caused fires occur naturally in the southeast and are presently suppressed by government agencies. This policy has been questioned since fire is probably essential to maintaining pinelands, prairie-like marshes and high elevation meadows. Controlled burning is being tested on a variety of sites and already is integral to rare plant management in the Everglades.

Other natural disturbances, such as landslides and floods, influence rare species distribution but are less frequently controlled by man than is fire.

Trampling and plant gathering

Both the Indians and the settlers established trails and campsites, gathered herbs, and crossed the southeast freely in search of game. These kinds of impact are, in one respect, historic, but the patterns and intensity have changed.

In Great Smoky Mountains, the settlers rarely entered spruce-fir forest prior to the advent of the logging railroads, but today much of the hiking takes place above 1400 m. Not only are many of the important endangered plant records for the park from Mount LeConte and the spruce-fir dominated central ridge, but park visitors find these to be highly desirable areas for viewing scenery. Cliff Tops on Mount LeConte, once accessible only by a difficult trek up a stream, can now be reached by five different trails and may receive as many as 300 visitors a day (Bratton and Whittaker, 1977). Through time, unofficial paths worn in the cliff face have begun to threaten several endangered species, including *Geum radiatum* Gray and *Scirpus cespitosus* Bigelow. Many of the other preserves in the southeast, particularly in the coastal area, have similar trampling problems.

Gathering of herbs, although illegal, is still common in the upland parks. Target species include ginseng (*Panax quinquefolium* L.) and various wild flowers, but the impact of diggers has never been quantified. The hardwood hammocks of the Everglades are famous for their orchids, and despite the enforcement efforts of park rangers, poaching of rare plants continues (Loope and Avery, 1979).

The southwestern parks

In order to compare the management problems found in the southeast with those of preserves from different biotic provinces or ecosystems, the authors selected eight large southwestern parks with arid or Mediterranean climates. Published information is available for vegetation management in all these areas, which were visited in January and February 1980 by the senior author. Comparing Table 3 with Table 4, several common factors may be discerned.

Table 4 Resource management concerns and impacts on native vegetation in selected national parks and monuments with arid or Mediterranean climates

Park	Size (hectares)	State	Climate	Important types of rarity		Important impacts on native vegetation							
				Endemism	Disjuncts; range extensions	Exotic animals	Exotic plants	Changing water levels	Past grazing by stock	Present grazing by stock	Fire management	Mining or construction	Human trampling
Death Valley NM	836 800	California	Arid	+	–	H	M	H	M	L	M	H	L
Grand Canyon NP	493 100	Arizona	Arid	–	–	H	M	M	M	L	H	L	H
Big Bend NP	280 700	Texas	Arid	+	+	L	M	M	H	L	H	L	M
Joshua Tree NM	225 900	California	Arid	–	–	—	L	H	M	L	M	M	L
Saguaro NM	32 000	Arizona	Arid	–	+	L	L	M	H	M	M	L	H
Guadalupe Mountains NP	31 900	Texas	Arid	–	+	L	L	M	H	M	H	M	H
Channel Islands NMP	7 400	California	Med.	+	–	H	H	—	H	—	—	—	H
Pinnacles NM	5 900	California	Med.	–	–	L	L	—	M	L	H	—	M

Key: H – high; M – moderate; L – low; Med. – Mediterranean.

Changes in physical environment

Desert preserves frequently have problems associated with hydrology. Past over-grazing and other human abuses, in combination with what may be a natural drying trend in the climate, probably have caused a decline in the water table and in the number of perpetually flowing springs and streams. The impact of these activities on the floras of various parks is difficult to document, but both over-grazing and a cooling trend in the climate have been implicated in the poor reproduction of the giant saguaro cactus (Steenbergh and Lowe, 1977) in Saguaro National Monument.

Although damming of rivers, like the Colorado upstream and downstream from parks like Grand Canyon, appears to have had a greater impact on rare fishes than on rare plants, changing the flood frequencies and inundating side canyons has modified or eliminated a number of unusual habitats. Since vegetation samp-ling and plant collection have been sporadic in some of the less accessible parts of the US, it is now difficult to assess the changes.

Exotics and native herbivores

Exotic species invasion, coupled with livestock grazing, is a major source of change in the desert communities. Death Valley National Monument, for example, has 11 endemic native plants found only in the monument, and 36 species on the Smithsonian list (National Park Service, 1976). Death Valley National Monument also has a large population of donkeys which intensively graze the range in the western half of the park.

Channel Islands National Park has a sensitive, partially endemic flora, and a host of exotic invaders, European rabbits, are doing well on Santa Barbara Island, for instance. Exotic plants, especially ice plant (*Mesembryanthemum* spp.), are suf-ficiently dominant to characterize some of the major vegetation types (Hochberg *et al.*, 1979).

Tamarisk (*Tamarix* spp.), an exotic plant, is considered a major management problem in several desert parks, particularly Death Valley and Big Bend, where it establishes itself around water sources. Tamarisk not only displaces native plants, but it withdraws water from the soil, causing springs to dry and thus depleting surface water supplies critical for native wildlife (National Park Service, 1976, 1977*b*).

Disturbance and human trampling

Fire management is critically important in the western parks, and burns are an integral part of ecosystem function in most xeric forests and desert grasslands. Parks like Grand Canyon and Saguaro either permit some lightning fires or practice controlled burning.

Human trampling and restriction of hiker impacts are high priority management issues in areas such as McKittrick Canyon in Guadalupe Mountains National Park, where unregulated use could disturb disjunct populations of deciduous forest species such as *Lilium philadelphicum* L., as well as species endemic to the limestone cliffs and unique collections of species on limestone alluvium (Nothington and Burgess, 1979).

Plant gathering affects rare cacti and plants of commercial value, for instance *Euphorbia antisyphilitica* Zucc. in Big Bend (National Park Service, 1977*b*).

Basic management

As can be seen from this brief review, preserves as varied as Death Valley and Great Smoky Mountains not only have rare and endangered species management problems, but they have some problems, such as exotic species invasion, which are similar. Rare plant management is related to the health and functioning of whole park systems as well as to impacts on individual species. In a preserve, sound rare plant management has several phases (see also Bratton and White, 1980, for more detail). The first phase, *Inventory*, includes compilation of a flora checklist for an area and development of the appropriate collections. The second, *Selection*, requires a comparison of lists of species thought to be endangered to the lists of species present in the preserve and a determination of individual species status in the preserve. At this point the preserve should develop their own list of species of special managerial concern. The third, *Monitoring*, includes the location of individual populations, quantification of population condition, and verification of potential threats and disturbances. Maps of rare and endangered plant locations are often constructed after *Selection* by using herbarium data, but mapping is usually best done after thorough field checks for the presence of individual populations. Phase four, *Protection*, includes re-routing roads and trails near rare plant populations, elimination of exotic species, and initiation of other management actions intended to avoid or remove undesired impacts on the species. Phase five, *Manipulation*, includes active modification of ecosystem processes or population structure to encourage or maintain a rare plant population. Examples of manipulation are burning or mowing to encourage disturbance-dependent species, re-introduction of extirpated species, or greenhouse rearing and stocking of young clumps of a faltering species.

The manager of a preserve should recognize that several of these steps may be carried out simultaneously, but that trying to do everything at once could be risky. If dependable maps of species distributions are not available, for instance, manipulation of one species may accidently damage another. Furthermore, if the first three phases are poorly done and rare species lists are not complete, or data are inaccurate, the information base will not be adequate for making managerial policies or decisions.

In the USA many of the larger national parks, Biosphere Reserves, and other conservation areas have completed, or have in progress the first two phases outlined here (White and Bratton, Chapter 22). Floristic inventories are available for most sites, although some inventories are more thorough than others.

Less than half the areas reviewed had the third phase underway. Monitoring tends to be done in areas with their own research staff or in sites favored by university-based scientists. In parks, rare plant monitoring has frequently been carried on in conjunction with other projects, such as construction of a vegetation map or assessment of human trampling damage, and therefore only concerns part of the flora. The techniques are exceedingly variable, and species are often ignored unless there appears to be some immediate threat to their populations (see White and Bratton, Chapter 22).

Since interest in rare plant management is a recent phenomenon, very few US preserves have management plans specifically for rare plants. Although initiation of protection has greatly increased with the development of Environment Impact Statements and park planning teams, an area may or may not do more than check herbarium collections before making decisions.

Concern for rare plants is often an important element in resources management, but it is rarely the primary reason for undertaking a major program.

Throughout the southeast and southwest, resources managers are actively working on the problems described. On Cumberland Island, for instance, the Service has removed hundreds of wild pigs, and at Great Smoky Mountains they are attempting to do the same with somewhat less success. Individual management plans have been developed for single projects, such as control of feral donkeys in the Grand Canyon (National Park Service, 1980). These protection programs are most frequently system-oriented. Although a few efforts, such as a new reviewing procedure for backcountry campsite placement in Great Smoky Mountains are aimed specifically towards rare plants protection, the general trend is towards protecting whole systems. Due to limitations of money and manpower, this may, at the moment, be the most viable strategy.

Manipulation, with the exception of burning, is more commonly used in endangered animal rather than endangered plant management. Restrictions of human interference, including interference by preserve managers, is often the best policy in a natural area, but active management can be necessary to counter or correct past anthropogenic damages and may be the only way to maintain some plant populations.

Manipulation may present a philosophical dilemma if ecosystem or process-oriented actions are favored over those that favor some specific species, or vice versa. Managing for an individual species is more commonly done in wildlife or game-oriented programs, but plant populations can be increased by similar methods.

Re-introduction of rare plant species in native habitat is a new field, as is artificial population expansion. Work by Farmer (1980) on *Parnassia* in Great Smoky Mountains has shown that it is a workable management alternative. Much work remains to be done on manipulation and the population dynamics of rare plants.

The appropriateness of manipulation in preserves as opposed to manipulation in botanic gardens introduces some philosophical dilemmas. Should a park manager burn the way the aborigines burned and thus maintain pre-Columbian disturbance regimes? If the activity of a settler encouraged a rare species, should it be continued? Should a manager re-introduce a species extirpated by a natural event? And perhaps most difficult of all, should a manager try to prevent extinction when it appears to be related to a natural process such as climatic change? Although the goals and mandates of a preserve will largely determine policy, the authors believe that the mechanics and appropriateness of protection and manipulation deserve further research and discussion.

Acknowledgements

We would like to thank Mark E. Harmon for comments on the manuscript, Jay Blowers of the US Department of State for encouragement, and Nicki Macfarland for help with manuscript preparation. Activities reported in this paper are part of the US Biosphere Reserves Program, jointly sponsored by the US Departments of State, Agriculture, and the Interior.

References

Baron, J., Dombrowski, C., and Bratton, S. P. (1975). 'The status of five exotic woody plants in the Tennessee district of Great Smoky Mountains National Park', *US Dep. of the Interior, National Park Service, SE Regional Office, Research/Resources Manage. Rep. No. 28*, 26 pp.

Bratton, S. P. (1975). 'The effect of the European wild boar, *Sus scrofa*, on gray beech forest in the Great Smoky Mountains', *Ecology*, **56**, 1356–66.

Bratton, S. P. (1979). 'Preliminary status of rare plants in Great Smoky Mountains National Park', *US Dep. of the Interior, National Park Service, SE Regional Office, Research/Resources Manage, Rep. No. 25*, 46 pp.

Bratton, S. P., Mathews, R. C., Jr., and White, P. S. (in press). 'Agricultural area impacts within a natural area: Cades Cove, a case history', *Environ. Manage.*

Bratton, S. P., and White, P. S. (1980). 'Rare plant management – after preservation what?', *Rhodora*, **82**, 49–75.

Bratton, S. P., White, P. S., and Harmon, M. E. (in press). 'Disturbance and recovery of plant communities in Great Smoky Mountains National Park: Successional dynamics and concepts of naturalness', in *Proceedings of the 2nd US–USSR Biosphere Reserve Symposium*, Everglades National Park, March 1980.

Bratton, S. P. and Whittaker, P. (1977). 'Great Smoky Mountains National Park: Disturbance and visitation on Mount LeConte', *US Dep. of the Interior, National Park Service, Uplands Field Research Laboratory, Great Smoky Mountains National Park, Rep. for the Superintendent.* 59 + 10 pp.

Etnier, D. A. (1978). 'Report on the search for spotfin chub (*Bybopsis monarcha*) and Smoky madtom (*Noturus baileyi*), on the Little Tennessee River System, North Carolina', *Tech. Rep., Univ. of Tennessee, Dep. of Zoology*, Knoxville, 11 pp.
Farmer, R. E., Jr. (1980). 'Germination and juvenile growth characteristics of *Parnassia asarifolia*', *Bull. Torrey Club*, **107**, 19–23.
Harmon, M. E. (1980). *The Influence of Fire and Site Factors on Vegetation Pattern and Process in the Weston Great Smoky Mountains*, MSc thesis, University of Tennessee, Knoxville, 200 pp.
Hay, R. L., Eager, C. C., and Johnson, K. D. (1978). 'Fraser fir in the Great Smoky Mountains National Park; its demise by the balsam woolly aphid', *Rep. to the National Park Service, US Dep. of the Interior, Southeast Region, Atlanta, Georgia*, 125 pp.
Hillestad, H. O., Bozeman, J. R., Johnson, A. S., Berisford, C. W., and Richardson, J. I. (1975). 'The ecology of Cumberland Island National Seashore, Camden County, Georgia', *Georgia Marine Science Center, University System of Georgia, Skidoway Island, Georgia, Tech. Rep. Series 75–5*, 299 pp.
Hochberg, M., Zunak, S., Rhulbrick, R., and Stimbrook, J. (1979). 'Botany (of Channel Islands)' in *Natural Resources Study of the Channel Islands National Monument, California* (Ed. P. M. Power), pp. 5.1–5.85, Santa Barbara Museum of Natural History, Santa Barbara, California.
Johnson, W. C. and Bratton, S. P. (1978). 'Biological monitoring in UNESCO Biosphere Reserves with special reference to the Great Smoky Mountains National Park', *Biol. Conserv.*, **13**, 105–15.
Lindsay, M. M. and Bratton, S. P. (1979). 'The vegetation of grassy balds and other high elevation disturbed areas in the Great Smoky Mountains National Park', *Bull. Torrey Bot. Club*, **106**, 264–75.
Loope, L. L. and Avery, G. N. (1979). 'A preliminary report on rare plant species in the flora of National Park Service areas of South Florida, *US Dep. of the Interior, National Park Service, South Florida Research Center, Homestead, Florida, Rep. M–548*, 42 pp.
National Park Service (1976). *Environmental Assessment. Management Options for Natural and Cultural Resources, Death Valley National Monument*, US Department of the Interior, Washington, DC., 104 pp. + apps.
National Park Service (1977a). *Environmental Statement: Proposed Colorado River Management Plan*. US Dep. of the Interior, Grand Canyon National Park, Grand Canyon, Arizona.
National Park Service (1977b). *Resources Management Plan for Big Bend National Park*, US Dep. of the Interior, Big Bend National Park, Texas.
National Park Service (1979). *Master Plan, Everglades National Park, Florida*. US Government Printing Office, 66 pp.
National Park Service (1980). *Feral Burro Management and Ecosystem Restoration Plan and Final Environmental Statement*. US Dept. of the Interior, Grand Canyon National Park, Arizona, 65 pp. + app.
Nothington, D. K. and Burgess, T. L. (1979). 'Status of rare and endangered plant species of the Guadalupe Mountains National Park, Texas', in *Biological Investigations in the Guadalupe Mountains National Park, Texas* (Eds. H. H. Genoways and R. J. Baker), US Dep. of the Interior, National Park Service, Proceedings and Transactions Series No. 4.
Pickett, S. T. A., and Thompson, J. N. (1979). 'Patch dynamics and the design of nature preserves', *Biol. Conserv.*, **13**, 27–37.
Shabica, S. V., Brannon, P. P., and Herrmann, R. (1978). 'The extirpation of an island: The dilemma of Petit Bois Island, Gulf Islands National Seashore, Mississippi' in

Proceedings of the Symposium on Technical Environmental Socioeconomic and Regulatory Aspects of Coastal Zone Management, San Francisco, California.

Steenbergh, W. F. and Lowe, C. H. (1977). 'Ecology of the Saguaro: II. Reproduction, germination, establishment, growth, and survival of the young plant', *US Dep. of the Interior, National Park Service, Scientific Monograph Series No. 8*.

White, P. S. and Bratton, S. P. (1980). 'After preservation: philosophical and practical problems of change', *Biol. Conserv.*, **18**, 241–55.

Wood, F. W., and Shanks, R. E. (1959). 'Natural replacement of chestnut by other species in the Great Smoky Mountains National Park', *Ecology*, **40**, 349–61.

The Biological Aspects of Rare Plant Conservation
Edited by Hugh Synge
© 1981 John Wiley & Sons Ltd.

40
The protection of British rare plants in nature reserves

D. A. WELLS *Chief Scientist Team, Nature Conservancy Council, UK*

Summary

A brief account is given of the framework of nature conservation in Britain and of the bodies which own and manage nature reserves. The different criteria adopted for selection of reserves by conservation bodies are discussed. An analysis is made of the numbers of nationally rare species already protected in reserves or by law, which shows the degree of success in conserving rare British plants. From this, some suggestions are made for future research and conservation activity, and the importance of conservation bodies owning rather than leasing their reserves is emphasized.

In Britain, the major factor in achieving conservation of wildlife is the spirited co-operation between the voluntary and official organizations set up to safeguard the nation's wildlife heritage. There are a number of bodies, several voluntary and one official, with a particular remit to acquire and manage nature reserves. The two main voluntary bodies are the Royal Society for Nature Conservation (RSNC) and the Royal Society for the Protection of Birds (RSPB). The RSNC is the co-ordinating body for the 42 Nature Conservation Trusts, which are independently set up and run and now cover every county, whilst the latter has grown from a movement to ban the use of feathers for adornment to a major owner of land for the protection of birds and, incidentally, plants. Members of the public are encouraged to join these organizations and to date they have a com-bined membership of over half a million.

The official government agency is the Nature Conservancy Council (NCC), which was first set up in 1949 as the Nature Conservancy and which assumed its present name following re-organization in 1973. One of the major charges given by government to NCC was the acquisition, establishment and maintenance of National Nature Reserves (NNRs). This term confers crown status to the land so acquired and is a powerful safeguard for wildlife. There are two further nature reserve designations: Forest Nature Reserve (FNR) where the landowner is the Forestry Commission (a government body), and Local Nature Reserve (LNR) designated by a local authority. Both FNRs and LNRs are set up following con-sultation with the NCC. In addition to these designated nature reserves the NCC is also charged with scheduling Sites of Special Scientific Interest (SSSI). The Act of 1949 laid down that,

> where the Nature Conservancy are of the opinion that any area of land, not being land for the time being managed as a nature reserve, is of special interest by reason of its flora, fauna, or geological or physiographical features, it shall be the duty of the Conservancy to notify that fact to the local planning authority in whose area the land is situated.

It should be noted that the safeguards to wildlife of SSSI designation operate through the planning laws and regulations. These only apply when a change of land use is envisaged. Agricultural operations such as drainage, ploughing, fertilizing, etc., do not constitute change of land use and cannot be prevented by the SSSI designation. Nevertheless, with the current awareness for the need to safeguard wildlife the Ministry of Agriculture and other official bodies such as the Water Authorities are made aware of SSSIs and do attempt to pay due regard to the safety of these areas.

Misunderstanding sometimes occurs over the role of the National Trust and the national parks in wildlife conservation. The National Trust, properly the National Trust for Places of Historic Interest or Natural Beauty, is an organization registered as a charitable body under the Companies Act of 1894. Its concern is with preserving historic buildings and scenic beauty and not primarily with wildlife conservation, although among its land holdings are many areas of high biological value such as Wicken Fen in Cambridgeshire. National parks in Britain are not nature reserves, but are areas of scenic beauty, mainly in the north and west, which are set up to enable people to enjoy the countryside without causing undue disturbance to the farming and rural populations. To this end wardens are employed and facilities provided but, as with the National Trust, wildlife conservation, although important, is secondary to enabling public enjoyment of the general countryside.

The above attempts to set out the basic framework of nature conservation in Britain, a subject very ably dealt with in detail by Sheail (1976).

The selection of sites to form NNRs has clearly exercised the minds of scientists from the early days of conservation. Several lists had been drawn up prior to the formation of the Nature Conservancy in 1949 and these formed the basis for the lists presented to parliament as Cmd 7122, 1947 (England and Wales) and Cmd 7814, 1949 (Scotland) – see Sheail (1976). The philosophy behind the selections is stated as,

> To preserve and maintain as part of the nation's natural heritage places which can be regarded as reservoirs for the main types of community and kinds of wild plants and animals represented in this country, both common

and rare, typical and unusual, as well as places which contain physical features of special or outstanding interest. These places must be chosen so far as possible to enable comparisons to be made between primitive or relatively undisturbed communities and the modifications introduced by varying degrees of human interference; typical and atypical physical conditions; distinctive characteristics imposed upon communities and species by differences in geographical position, physiography, climate, geology and soil, both within the main physical regions and in the transitional zones between them; the behaviour of species or communities living within and at the margins of their geographical distribution or their ecological tolerance. The series as a whole should take fair account of the varied requirements and interests of the several different lines of scientific approach: the systematic study of particular groups of species; studies of communities or species in relation to their environment; of the rise and fall in population numbers; of breeding structures of populations and the way in which inherited variations are distributed; of geographical distribution; of plant and animal behaviour; of the climate and microclimatic conditions which so largely govern the distribution of organisms; of soils; of the rocks and the fossils they hold; and of the physical forces which shape the surface of the land; as well as general evolutionary studies.

The current list now considered necessary to cover the range of variability consists of some 750 sites (Ratcliffe, 1977). In his rationale for this list Ratcliffe uses several criteria, among which is rarity, and he has this to say,

> More emphasis has been given to the inclusion of rare communities, habitats or groups of species, and individual rare species have tended to be regarded as a bonus on sites selected for other reasons. The aggregation of several or many rare species to form a group within a single site, as in a plant refugium, is regarded as an important feature and has influenced the choice of certain key sites. Other things being equal, however, the presence of even one rare species on a site gives it a higher value than another comparable site with no rarities.

No NNR has so far been declared on the basis of a single rare plant species and, in my view, this is unlikely to occur. Rare plants seldom, if ever, occur in isolation and most, if not all, act as bonus features to sites already of high quality. This philosophy does not feature as strongly in the voluntary movement, dependent on donations from the general public. Here, the appeal of rarity is very great and Trusts are right to exploit this feeling. Instances of rare species being singled out to substantiate or publicize reserve acquisition are *Ranunculus ophioglossifolius* Vill. in Gloucestershire (see Frost, Chapter 41), *Orchis militaris* L. in Suffolk and *Fritillaria meleagris* L. in Wiltshire.

How successful have these bodies, RSPB, RSNC and the Nature Conservation Trusts, and NCC, been in acquiring reserves? Judged purely in numerical terms the answer must be very successful. To date the RSPB have 78 reserves totalling 35 000 hectares; the Trusts and RSNC 1198 reserves, 40 000 hectares; NCC 164 reserves, 127 000 hectares. In botanical terms one can use the *British Red Data Book* (Perring and Farrell, 1977); this lists 321 species of rare plants in Britain plus 4 non-threatened endemics and 3 species threatened on a European scale but relatively safe in Britain. Using these 328 species we find that even the RSPB reserves, acquired for bird protection, have at least 1 listed species, *Elatine hydropiper* L. The Trust reserves, as shown by the RSNC figures, consist mainly of small reserves but scattered throughout these are a further 36 species. As 48 per cent of Trust reserves are also scheduled as SSSIs it is not possible to give a separate figure for SSSIs, but the combined total for Trust reserves plus SSSIs is 109 listed species. The NNRs range in size from a 2 hectare fen in Oxfordshire to the 26 000 hectare reserve of the Cairngorms in northeast Scotland; 128 listed species occur in NNRs. With 20 species listed as extinct, 71 species are left with at present no form of protection.

Further protection, though not in reserves, is afforded by the 'Conservation of Wild Creatures and Wild Plants Act 1975'. On Schedule 2 of this Act are listed 21 plants which are totally protected from picking, uprooting or destruction; of these 13 occur in NNRs and 7 in SSSIs, leaving only the site of *Diapensia lapponica* L. with no statutory protection.

It is clear that the past reserve acquisition policy of NCC and the voluntary bodies has resulted in many of the species, now classified as rare, being found in nature reserves. This is, of course, not a coincidence as rare species can be divided into two categories: first those which are naturally rare because of their need for very demanding requirements; secondly, those which show man-induced rarity, that is they are restricted to habitats which are grossly exploited by man thus causing the extinction of the habitat together with the species. The sites of the former species would have been considered from the rare habitat concept, for example cliff ledges and mountain tops. The latter will arouse attention once conservationists become aware of the increasing loss of habitats such as wetlands, coppiced woodland and lowland grasslands.

The majority of these species, in common with their associates, require some form of management. We are aware of the many management options open to us for use on communities and of the likely outcome of their use, but our knowledge of the demography of individual species lags behind. The land manager requires this knowledge, not so much to help him directly in management but to calm his fears when he notes a species is declining. This decline may well be temporary and nothing more than an unknown natural factor, totally unconnected with management. To panic and change the management may well precipitate the calamity one is trying to avoid. Monitoring should not be undertaken by the faint-hearted! The knowledge that a particular species has a 10-year cycle of growth and that in years 5–8 it is dormant underground will greatly reassure the manager. With the increased awareness of the possibilities for creating wildlife refugia in barren areas such as worked-out quarries, new roadside verges, country parks, much information is required on seed production, longevity, germination and establishment. This work is also necessary to convince sceptics that at present and in the foreseeable future it is not possible to recreate instantly plant communities such as herb-rich hay meadows or chalk grassland. Research workers and institutions could give invaluable help to hard-pressed conservationists by tackling these two major topics of demography and seedling establishment.

What of the future? Clearly in Britain we have made a reasonable start but much remains to be done. In the long term the security of many of our reserves is at risk as they are held under a tenancy or merely an agreement. Wildlife conservation is forever; therefore the only safe tenure is ownership and this must be the final aim for all our important reserves. In the short term reserves held only by agreement can present almost insurmountable management problems, which at least will cause friction between the owner or tenant and the conservationist, and at worst can lead to loss of interest and possible extinction of certain species. A reserve by agreement may be the only option and certainly this informs all of the importance of the site, but should an opportunity arise to purchase this should always be taken. Buying the freehold and leasing back to the previous owner to continue managing the site under clear terms of reference is increasingly being used. This has advantages to both parties. The original owner has increased capital but still has the produce of the site whilst the conservationist has security of tenure and control of management.

The question of size is often debated. Compared to some animals, plants require much smaller areas and given complete control over management of the site, size is not of great importance for the perpetuation of the species. If conservation is to ensure man's future use of these species, however, it should be remembered that utilization of the site for research, education etc., may require a large minimal area. It could be argued that annuals, requiring to set seed, which in turn may require invertebrates for pollination, may need a larger minimal area than herbaceous perennials which may exist vegetatively for considerable periods of time, or perhaps for ever?

In Britain, we have the knowledge to ensure that no more plant species become extinct as a result of the activities of man. It does require, however, finance and determination to put this knowledge to best use.

Acknowledgements

It is a pleasure to record the help of RSNC and RSPB, and particularly of my colleague Lynne Farrell, who provided much of the raw data on rare species.

References

Perring, F. H. and Farrell, L. (1977). *British Red Data Books: 1. Vascular Plants*, Society for the Promotion of Nature Conservation, Lincoln.
Ratcliffe, D. A. (1977). *A Nature Conservation Review*, 2 vols, Cambridge University Press.
Sheail, J. (1976). *Nature in Trust*, Blackie, Glasgow.

The Biological Aspects of Rare Plant Conservation
Edited by Hugh Synge
© 1981 John Wiley & Sons Ltd.

41
The study of *Ranunculus ophioglossifolius* and its successful conservation at the Badgeworth Nature Reserve, Gloucestershire

L. C. FROST *Department of Botany, University of Bristol, England*

Summary

The purchase in 1932 of a minute nature reserve at Badgeworth for the rare *Ranunculus ophioglossifolius* Vill. led to initial failure as the plant became increasingly a victim of succession. Survey of the literature and studies at the reserve and at Bristol University provided the basis for a management policy whose effectiveness has resulted in the species usually flowering and fruiting in fair quantity each year. The history of the plant in Britain and of the reserve are reviewed, laboratory and field experiments undertaken on the species are described and the present management policy is outlined and its results considered.

My topic is the translation of autecological studies into conservation management as exemplified by Britain's rarest marsh buttercup in one of the world's smallest nature reserves. That is how *Ranunculus ophioglossifolius* Vill. and the Badgeworth Nature Reserve near Cheltenham in Gloucestershire are described in the *Guinness Book of Records*, which is good publicity and helps to foster the interest of ordinary people in nature conservation.

The reserve is owned by the Royal Society for Nature Conservation and in 1962 its management was handed over to the newly founded Gloucestershire Trust for Nature Conservation. A Trust Management Committee was formed with the local naturalist Mrs S. C. Holland as Secretary. At once, we set about the task of managing our rare plant which has rewarded us by flowering and fruiting well or abundantly every year since, except in 1969.

Ranunculus ophioglossifolius was first discovered in the British Isles at St Peter's Marsh in Jersey by Professor Babington in 1838. In about 1885, the marsh was drained and the plant lost. In 1928, it was found on the east side of Jersey at Grouville but never ever seen there again. It was first discovered in England in 1878 on the fringes of a wayside pool near Hythe in Hampshire, but in about 1883 the pool was drained and the plant destroyed. In 1914, it was found on the marshy edge of a meadow near Dorchester in Dorset but a few years later

Figure 1   *Ranunculus ophioglossifolius* at Badgeworth. From a painting by Mary
Grierson, reproduced by kind permission of the Curwen Press

the site was destroyed by road widening. In 1926, it was found at Inglestone Common, now in County Avon, in a marshy area with a pool on lias clay. Commoners still graze their cattle there and, with some conservation management by the Gloucestershire Trust, the buttercup survives at the one site on the common. In 1890, it was discovered at Cold Pool Marsh at Badgeworth, again a marsh with a pool on lias clay. It was not seen there again until 1911 and following the drought of that year appeared in 'vast quantity' in 1912. In fact we have continuous records of the numbers and positions of flowering plants recorded each year by local naturalists and visitors for the past 90 years and this information has proved to be invaluable.

In 1932, the landowner commenced filling in the north side of the marsh in order to sell the site as a building plot. Fortunately G. W. Hedley, one of the authors of the *Flora of Gloucestershire*, saved the plant by purchasing the remainder of the Marsh, one-twelfth of an acre or 290 sq. m, for the large sum in those days of £53, paid out of his own pocket. He handed the reserve to the Society for the Promotion of Nature Conservation, and the Cotteswold Naturalists' Field Club formed a management committee.

Their first effort in 1933, when the whole marsh was full of flowering plants, was to construct a tall, stout fence of barbed wire all round the reserve. This fence has often been quoted as an example of a disaster in management of a reserve, but as we shall see this has fortunately not proved to be the case. Devoid of grazing and poaching (i.e. trampling) by cattle, the buttercup rapidly declined. In five of the years between 1934 and 1962, no plants at all occurred in the reserve; in only two of the years were there 100 or more plants in the reserve. In two other years there were hundreds of plants outside the reserve, but not one plant inside it!

In 1962, when we commenced management, the Nature Conservancy had recommended clearing the site and in the summer of that year, when Mrs Holland and I visited the reserve, we found it like an overgrown wilderness with the soil surface buried beneath a deep layer of acidic decaying vegetation. The evidence available at the time suggested that the buttercup grew in open areas with little competition; remarks in the Reserve Record Books that young plants of one year grew in the tread marks of the previous year's visitors suggested that seed germination occurred on bare, disturbed soil.

Here was, however, a tiny reserve and a declining, rare plant and so we decided to be cautious. Accordingly, in September 1962, a plot about 7 m × 2 m was cleared of all vegetation and decaying litter to expose the underlying lias clay, and the soil surface was trampled. The plot was across the centre of the reserve where no *R. ophioglossifolius* had been recorded as flowering for the past 24 years. Two weeks later Mrs Holland informed me that thousands of the buttercup seedlings had appeared in the plot – so many that she could not count them. Our caution was fully justified, however; the winter of 1962/63 was one of the severest and most prolonged on record. The standing water in the reserve, up to 1 m deep, froze into a solid block of ice and all the young plants were killed. Nevertheless, we persevered with a rotation system of cleared plots (Figure 2), and in both 1964 and 1965 we had over 1000 fine flowering plants in the plots cleared during the previous September.

To appreciate the dynamic nature of the habitat, it is necessary to visit the site at all times of the year. In a typical year, after the autumn rains the marsh becomes filled with standing water, but in spring the *Salix fragilis* pollards, which are cut regularly in rotation but unfortunately sited mostly on the south side of the reserve (Figure 2), assist by transpiration to lower the water level. The buttercup flowers usually in late May when the reserve appears rather overgrown, chiefly by *Glyceria fluitans* which is uprooted by hand and its inflorescences scythed off to

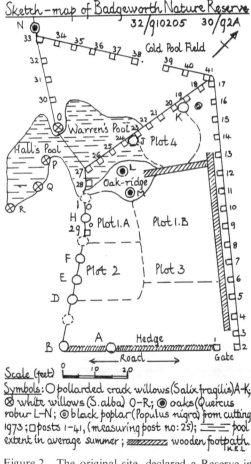

Figure 2   The original site, declared a Reserve in 1933, is 290 sq. m in area, while the extension, acquired in 1975, is 104 sq. m in area

prevent seeding. The site at Inglestone Common is similar, but the grazing and poaching by cattle maintains a much more open vegetation cover although woodland is established on the south side of the site. Both localities dry out during a typical summer.

Accordingly we decided at Bristol University to investigate experimentally the role of temperature and the effects of standing water (Dring and Frost, 1971). In the University's experimental greenhouse, supervised by our technician, Mr M. D. Ames, we soon found this Atlantic Southern species to be certainly a thermophilous one with flowering promoted by a long day-length. With an 18-hour daylength under UV-emitting lights but with night temperatures maintained at a minimum of 15°C, Mr Ames can induce the plant to flower on New Year's Day. Old flowering plants falling over on to the pebble staging, root at the nodes and produce new flowering shoots. This has happened subsequently once at Badgeworth, significantly in the abnormally mild autumn of 1968 when the buttercup continued to flower into November, the latest it has ever flowered there. In fact in the greenhouse, the buttercup becomes a pest; seedlings come up on the staging, in the pots of other experimental plants and even blocking the greenhouse drain.

We also grew young plants out-of-doors at different depths of standing water in miniature, artificial pools. We soon discovered the essential role of the standing water. Seed will not germinate under standing water but young plants will grow well in the autumn under the water, sending up floating leaves. If the leaf blades are encased in ice in winter for a considerable time they are killed but the growing point below in the unfrozen water remains unharmed and produces more leaves in the spring. Only if the growing point is subjected to prolonged freezing is the whole plant killed.

Our pools had to be covered with wire netting to prevent destruction of the leaves by birds. Mallard ducks from the Park at Cheltenham fly to Badgeworth to feast on the leaves there and St Peter's Marsh was nicknamed 'Goose Green' (Syme, 1863) suggesting wild or domestic geese ravaged the plant there. Mud on the webbed feet of these foraging marsh birds, however, may well disperse seeds of the buttercup over long distances. The plants in our small pools flowered much earlier than at Badgeworth, which in turn flower earlier than at Inglestone. Flowering appears to be promoted particularly by increased water and soil temperatures; our pools were in a south-facing sun trap with small volumes of water, whereas Badgeworth is shaded by the *Salix fragilis* pollards and Inglestone even more so by the woodland. There is a positive correlation between the earliness of first flowering at Badgeworth with the onset of high air temperatures recorded at the Cheltenham Weather Station.

Clearly, in the wild a considerable depth of standing water in winter protects the young plants from the lethal effects of prolonged freezing, but the water levels must be lowered in spring to give optimum vegetative growth, flowering and fruiting. In our artificial pools, plants flowered most profusely in shallow water just as

Professor Babington observed in Jersey on 5 June 1838, 'It appears to prefer growing in spots which are just covered in water' (Hooker, 1843). Hence deciduous trees planted on the north side of a locality will not only protect the site from cold but by transpiration in spring assist in lowering water levels and in summer help to dry out the site, which is essential for seed germination in late September.

Accordingly we have devoted considerable time to studies of the conditions favouring high seed germination (Jones, 1978). The following data are based on eight replicates each of 20 seeds. We found that the seeds require an after-ripening period of 3–4 months in a warm, humid atmosphere and a germination temperature of 15°C. The seeds are light-sensitive, giving a significantly increased germination percentage in the light compared with the dark. After-ripened seed, germinated at 15°C in the light on filter paper moistened with distilled water, gave a maximum of 85 per cent germination; the first seeds germinated on the seventh day and the remainder were spread over a further 3 weeks. The addition of 10^{-3} M calcium chloride significantly increased this germination percentage while the addition of 10^{-3} M potassium nitrate gave significantly earlier and more rapid germination. Pre-chilling the seeds at 1.5°C for 7 days also induced earlier germination.

These studies suggest that in the wild, dormant seeds produced in previous years germinate on bare soil moistened by the early autumnal rains and chilled by the first cold nights of the autumn. The dormant seed is brought to the soil surface, and so into the light, by cattle poaching the marsh in summer. A little eutrophication by the cattle and the presence of calcium ions in the soil are both beneficial. Hence, when in 1975 we were able to make a small addition to the reserve of 104 sq. m (Figure 2), we introduced as our experimental studies had indicated a controlled grazing and poaching regime in the extension. Cattle and horses are excluded by means of removable poles in the fence from late September to mid-July after which they graze the lush vegetation and poach the ground. The success of this management regime was demonstrated by the many, fine, flowering plants in the extension in the summer of 1977 after the great drought of 1976.

Now this tiny reserve is very vulnerable to destruction by accident or design. In 1973, it was threatened by pollution from a proposed development of a heavy vehicle park with washing bay only 20 m away. Thanks to the protests by local people and conservationists all over Britain, the support of the mass media, but above all by the concern expressed by our friendly conservationists in Western Europe, planning permission was refused.

Nevertheless, we decided to maintain seed banks of both the Badgeworth and Inglestone strains at Bristol University. An average greenhouse grown plant, usually 35 cm tall, produces 2 gm of seed or about 7000 seeds. Sadly, seeds stored in paper packets at room temperature are all dead after 4 years; there is a dramatic drop to 10 per cent germination in the third year of storage. Accordingly we tested a whole variety of storage methods. The simple expedient of storing the seeds in air-tight sealed containers gives no less than 68 per cent germination after 4 years storage. It appears that storage in sealed containers at 5°C in a domestic refrigerator will be the simplest and most effective method. Time alone will tell how long such seeds will remain viable.

In addition, in order to imitate the overgrown conditions formerly present at Badgeworth, we put known weights of seed in finely perforated polythene bags and sandwiched the bags between two layers of wet sedge peat in containers (Frost, unpub.; Jones, 1978). The containers were either sealed or left open to dry out each summer and then re-moistened each autumn and kept wet through the winter. The containers were stored under a variety of conditions. All of the sealed containers were a disaster; all or most of the seeds rotted away within 2 years leaving only the seed coats under these anaerobic conditions. Badgeworth with its deep layer of rotting vegetation in 1962 must have been close to such a disaster. On the other hand, the open-air, wet/dry regime containers maintained at 20°C in the dark for 4 years gave no less than 93 per cent germination and extremely rapidly – most on the fourth day and the rest within a further week. This 'instant' germination was just like that on the cleared plots at Badgeworth. The addition of calcium chloride and potassium nitrate together with pre-chilling the seeds repeatedly gave 100 per cent germination. Over the 4 years of storage, however, there had been a loss in seed numbers of 33 per cent.

Hence our studies have shown that what we really have in the old, rather overgrown, man-managed reserve is actually a seed bank in the wild. Each year, however, seed numbers in the bank are depleted by natural wastage but by our system of the rotation of cleared plots in a part but not all of the area of the reserve, we have had since 1962, 5 years with over 1000 flowering plants and 6 years with between 100 and 500 flowering plants. As the average Badgeworth plant produces 2500 seeds, we have since 1962 added the order of 16 million seeds to the bank. We hope that this is more than has been lost! At the same time our cleared plots ensure that there is always flowering of *R. ophioglossifolius* in May to June to be seen by the considerable number of visitors who come to the reserve each year. They may have travelled long distances but since we took over management we have not disappointed them, except in 1969, when after a succession of wet summers, the reserve remained full of standing water in 1968 so that no seed germinated for a 1969 display. Visitors must obtain the key to the locked gate from the key-holders and a board walk has been installed so that visitors will not trample on the buttercup (Figure 2).

Outside the north side of the reserve is a small area of marsh with an uncontrolled grazing and poaching regime but considerable numbers of plants may be trampled on and destroyed. This destruction is largely prevented by the controlled grazing regime in the new extension. Se we have in this tiny area, three different management regimes. Now Hall's Pool (Figure 2) would be an ideal site for the buttercup. It is a south-facing sun trap protected on the north side by the *Salix fragilis* pollards. There is a low-lying area around the pool which is not deep enough to collect sufficient standing water but the area could easily be excavated to give a marsh poached and grazed by cattle. While Mr Hall is very co-operative, he is reluctant to let us excavate his meadow. This would be an important experiment especially in view of the fact that when Badgeworth was threatened in 1932, Dr G. C. Druce attempted to establish the buttercup in other pools in the Badgeworth area. These, however, were sharp-sided, cattle-drinking pools with no surrounding marsh and, as our studies have shown, his attempts were bound to be unsuccessful as indeed they were.

Gaining the support of local people is essential to successfully conserve a rare plant site. At the Badgeworth Church Fête held each summer, a Buttercup Queen is selected and crowned with a wreath of buttercups, excluding *Ranunculus ophioglossifolius*! At Inglestone the village shop is close to the marsh and the lady who keeps the shop maintains a close watch on 'The Buttercup' and darts out after any suspicious character seen approaching the marsh. Many young people in both neighbourhoods are members of the Gloucestershire Trust Conservation Corps and do all the hard work in maintaining and managing these two sites.

So both at Badgeworth and Inglestone, the plant is in safe hands and its continued survival reasonably assured. This is important because our studies have also shown that the Badgeworth plants have two pairs of mitotic chromosomes with satellites whereas Portuguese material has only one pair. Our measurements, too, of flower diameter have shown that both the Badgeworth and Inglestone populations are of the large-flowered race (Moss, 1920); the other populations in Britain, now extinct, had smaller flowers. We have then at these two sites a distinct genetic race of *R. ophioglossifolius*. This in turn throws interesting light on the origin of the plant in Britain and the migratory route by which it reached this country (see discussion in Martin and Frost, 1980).

As we have shown, *R. ophioglossifolius* is reasonably safe but I cannot say the same for the unique assemblage of some 30 rare and uncommon plants in the Avon Gorge, Bristol, or yet another extraordinary assemblage of rare plants at the Lizard District, Cornwall. That is why the Vice-Chancellor of Bristol University has put his name to the University's Avon Gorge and Lizard Appeals which were successfully launched in late 1980. The aim is to fund scientific studies in relation to the conservation management of the rare plants in both of these scenically beautiful areas. Plants in the Avon Gorge are threatened by rock blasting and commercial development, while the west coast of the Lizard was polluted by Torrey Canyon oil and the persistently toxic oil dispersants. Today a giant oil-exploration rig can be seen off the east coast. I trust that the delegates to this international conference on rare plant conservation will give our appeals their moral and financial support.

Acknowledgements

I wish to thank Mrs S. C. Holland for much valuable information, my former students M. J. Dring and P. M. B. Jones for their conscientious studies, Mr M. D.

Ames for his technical skill, Miss K. E. Ludbrook for permission to reproduce her sketch map of the Badgeworth Reserve, and the University of Bristol for financial assistance.

References

Dring, M. J. and Frost, L. C. (1971). 'Studies of *Ranunculus ophioglossifolius* in relation to its conservation at the Badgeworth Nature Reserve, Gloucestershire, England', *Biol. Conserv.*, **4**, 48–56.
Holland, S. C. (Ed.) (1977). *Badgeworth Nature Reserve Handbook*, 32 pp., 5 plates and 4 figs. Gloucestershire Trust for Nature Conservation, Standish, Gloucs.
Hooker, W. J. *et al.* (1843). *Supplement to the English Botany of the late Sir J. E. Smith and Mr Sowerby*, Vol. 3, t. 2833, London.
Jones, P. M. B. (1978). *Seed Viability in* Ranunculus ophioglossifolius *Vill.*, BSc thesis, University of Bristol.
Martin, M. H. and Frost, L. C. (1980). 'Autecological studies of *Trifolium molinerii* at the Lizard Peninsula, Cornwall', *New Phytol.*, **86**, 329–44.
Moss, C. E. (1920). *The Cambridge British Flora*, Vol. 3, Pl. 129, Cambridge University Press.
Perring, F. H. (1979). 'Book reviews: Badgeworth Nature Reserve Handbook', *Watsonia*, **12**, 268.
Syme, J. T. B. (Ed.) (1863). *English Botany*, 3rd Ed., Vol. 1, pp. 32–3, London.

Editor's note

A more detailed account of *Ranunculus ophioglossifolius* at Badgeworth is contained in the *Badgeworth Nature Reserve Handbook* (Holland, 1977), which has received many favourable reviews, e.g. Perring (1979). Copies are available from Mrs S. C. Holland, 64 All Saints' Road, Cheltenham, Gloucestershire, England, price 75p including postage within Britain or £1 including postage overseas.

The Biological Aspects of Rare Plant Conservation
Edited by Hugh Synge
© 1981 John Wiley & Sons Ltd.

42
The protection of rare plants in nature reserves and national parks in Yugoslavia

LJERKA GODICL *University of Maribor, Pedagogical Academy of Maribor, Yugoslavia*

Summary

The plant life of Yugoslavia in one of the richest and most varied in Europe. But economic development and industry have destroyed many natural habitats and the need to protect those that remain is urgent. At present about 2.2 per cent of the country is protected in some way. The various forms of protection are described and a short survey of the 16 national parks is given, with notes on their flora and vegetation and lists of prominent rare species.

Yugoslavia is a fascinating country for studying flora and vegetation. Its plant life is one of the richest and most varied in Europe, containing many diverse elements; in the northwest are the Alps where the flora is Central European, to the south is the Karst with a mediterranean flora, to the east stretches the typical Balkan flora with a large endemic element, and the north is part of the large Pannonian Plain, which still contains well preserved relictual steppes where Pannonian and Pontic elements of the flora can be found.

A similar diversity of landscape leads to a wide range of habitats for plants. These include high limestone and siliceous mountains with steep cliffs and deep canyons, big upland woods – over 30 per cent of Yugoslavia is wooded – river plains, and dissected coastline with over 1200 islands and islets. The many lakes and other wetland areas provide good plant and animal habitats, attested by the fact that 508 out of the 666 birds found in Europe occur in Yugoslavia.

Like many other parts of the world, however, economic development and industry have destroyed large areas of natural vegetation. The great economic progress of the last 30 years, such as building roads and factories and urban expansion, has made the protection of the most beautiful and biologically important parts of the country an urgent priority.

The best way to conserve rare plants, in Yugoslavia and everywhere else, is to protect their habitats. In Yugoslav nature reserves many rare and endemic plants and animals are being protected, but unfortunately the list of threatened plants is also long. These plants must be protected, especially from over-eager collectors of medicinal plants and from foreign botanists and horticulturists, who sometimes do not hesitate to collect rarities once outside their own country.

Protected areas also bring economic benefits through farming, forestry and above all tourism. In the national parks (Figure 1) and nature reserves, visitors to Yugoslavia can not only see nature but can also learn about the culture and history of our country. In some national parks, for example, the characteristic way of life has been preserved, with its attractive costumes, art and folklore. So the cultural role of national parks must not be neglected.

No less important is the role of national parks in providing material for scientific research; nature reserves are the best natural laboratories for studying native flora and fauna, especially endemic species, and the plant communities in which they grow.

Protected areas also have great educational importance. Young people must learn about the beauty and biological riches of their country; the first steps of environmental education begin in the pre-school environments – the kindergartens. Nature conservation is included in the biology and geography classes at elementary and secondary school, and is emphasized in teacher training colleges and in some faculties at University level. There is still much to be done in this work.

Yugoslavia is one of the few countries in which the principles of environmental

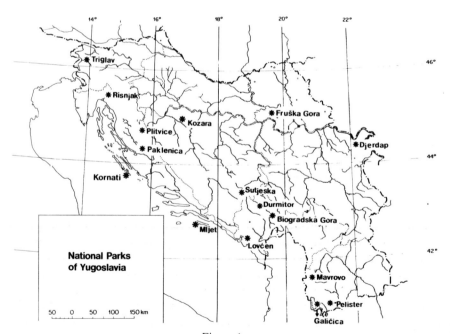

Figure 1

conservation are included in the Constitution. Today about 2.2 per cent of the land is given some form of protection. Plans have been made for this to be raised to about 6 per cent.

There are about 170 nature reserves in Yugoslavia. These are places of extreme natural beauty or the sites of endemic and rare plants and animals or the habitats of representative plant communities. Reserves, for example, include forest plant communities such as the Evergreen Oak forest (*Quercus ilex* L.) on the island of Rab, the Aleppo Pine wood (*Pinus halepensis* Mill.) on Brač, Serbian Spruce habitats (*Picea omorika* (Pančić) Purk.) in the mountains near Drina, old oak forest (*Quercus robur* L.) in Slavonia, birch groves (*Betula pendula* Roth) on Komovi, Sinjajevina and Durmitor, larch forest (*Larix decidua* Mill.) in Mala Pišnica. There are interesting reserves of the Alpine and Illyric flora on the mountains of Snežnik, Črna Prst, Trnovski Gozd and Nanos. Many rare species are protected in the reserves, e.g. *Rhododendron luteum* Sweet at Boštanj and Brusnice, *Primula carniolica* Jacq. at Divje Jezero, Pekel and Iška, *Forsythia europaea* Degen & Baldacci and *Paeonia decora* Anderson at Kosovo. Further rare species in selected reserves are shown in Table 1. Many marshes rich in birds are also protected, such as Hutovo Blato, Skadarsko Jezero, Pelagonija, Dojransko Jezero, Ohridsko Jezero, Obedska Bara.

During the Partisan War there were battles everywhere and many of these sites are now protected as Memorial Nature Reserves; similar sites from earlier history are protected as Commemorative Nature Monuments.

The most important protected areas, however, are the 16 national parks, which cover an area of about 301 700 hectares (excluding Kornati, see below). (In addition five more areas await approval as national parks.) In Yugoslavia national parks are the most stringently protected type of conservation site. They tend to be large areas of natural, little disturbed vegetation, and often include scientific rarities. Usually they consist of a central, strictly protected area and an outer, less strictly protected zone. By law, a national park can only be declared by the highest authority in the land – the Republic's Assembly; it must have its own administration, professional staff and funds for protection to be effective.

The Yugoslav national parks are spread all over the country. They include a wide range of flora and vegetation types for, besides their natural beauty, they represent different biogeographical zones and hence are of great scientific value. Some of the rare plants growing in the national parks are listed in Table 2.

In Slovenia, the Triglav National Park is in one of the most beautiful parts of the Julian Alps and includes the Valley of the Triglav Lakes. The geotectonic structure and the thick strata of the Triassic limestone are among the favourable conditions for Karst development. The flora is extraordinarily varied; besides the Alpine flora there is a strong component of the Illyrian flora with some interesting Tertiary relicts. Among the many plant associations are the subnivean *Potentilletum nitidae* and submediterranean (Illyrian) *Cytisantho-Ostryetum* which represent the two extremes in the vegetation. New proposals have been put

Table 1   Plant species of selected nature reserve types

Location	Pohorje	Podravski peski	nr Deliblatska peščara	nr Subotička peščara
Habitat type	Moorland	Sand Steppe	Sand Steppe	Sand and Salt Steppe
Species	*Andromeda polifolia* L. *Oxycoccus quadripetalus* Gilib. *Oxycoccus microcarpus* Turcz. *Drosera rotundifolia* L. *Carex pauciflora* Lightf. *Gentiana pannonica* Scap.	*Festuca vaginata* W.K. *Corispermum nitidum* Kit. *Tragopogon floccosus* W.K. *Cytisus ratisbonensis* (Schäff.) Rothm. *Corynephorus canescens* (L.) Beauv.	*Artemisia pancicii* (Janka) Ronn. *Astragalus dasyanthus* Pallas *Colchicum arenarium* W.K. *Comandra elegans* (Roch.) Rchb. *Fritillaria degeniana* Wagner *Paeonia officinalis* L. ssp. *banatica* (Roch.) Soó *Paeonia tenuifolia* L. *Rindera umbellata* (W.K.) Bunge *Vinca herbacea* W.K.	*Bulbocodium vernum* L. *Cirsium brachycephalum* Juratzka *Centaurea scabiosa* L. ssp. *sadlerana* (Janka) Aschers. & Graebn. *Colchicum arenarium* W.K. *Dianthus serotinus* W.K. *Iris humilis* Georgi ssp. *arenaria* (W.K.) A. & D. Löve *Iris pumila* L. *Plantago schwarzenbergiana* Schur

Table 2   Some rare, endemic and protected plants in Yugoslav national parks

Triglav National Park
Artemisia nitida Bertol.
Centaurea alpigena Paulin
Centaurea julica (Hayek) v. Soest. (*C. haynaldii* Borbás ex Vuk. ssp. *julica* (Hayek) E. Mayer)
Cerastium austroalpinum Kunz (*C. carinthiacum* Vest ssp. *austroalpinum* (Kunz) Kunz)
Campanula zoysii Wulf.
Gentiana terglouensis Hacq.
Iris illyrica Tommasini f. *vochinensis* Paulin
Papaver julicum Mayer & Merxm.
Pedicularis hacquetii Graf
Scabiosa stricta W.K. (*S. lucida* Vill. ssp. *stricta* (W.K.) Jasiewicz)
Rhaponticum lyratum (Bellardi) Nyman
Gentiana symphyandra Murb.
Leontopodium alpinum Cass.
Nigritella nigra (L.) Rchb.

Risnjak National Park
Genista holopetala (Fleischm. ex Koch) Baldacci
Oxytropis campestris (L.) DC. ssp. *dinarica* Murb.
Eryngium alpinum L.
Gentiana symphyandra Murb.
Lilium bulbiferum L.
Saussurea discolor (Willd.) DC.

The Plitvice Lakes National Park
Cardamine chelidonia L.
Cypripedium calceolus L.
Daphne blagayana Freyer
Lilium bulbiferum L.
Lilium carniolicum Bernh.
Primula kitaibeliana Schott
Primula wulfeniana Schott
Ruscus hypoglossum L.
Paeonia mascula (L.) Mill.

Sutjeska National Park
Achillea lingulata W.K.
Amphoricarpos autariatus Blečić & Mayer ssp. *autariatus*
Aubrietia croatica Sch.N.Ky
Cerastium dinaricum Beck & Szysz.
Daphne malyana Blečić
D. blagayana Freyer
Eryngium palmatum Panč. & Vis.
Hesperis dinarica G. Beck
Geum molle Vis. & Pančić
Gymnadenia frivaldii Hampe ex Griseb.
Iris bosniaca Beck
Knautia sarajevensis (Beck) Szabó
Micromeria croatica (Pers.) Schott
Oxytropis campestris (L.) DC. ssp. *dinarica* Murb.

Table 2 (continued)

Orchis bosniaca Beck
Ranunculus psilostachys Grieseb.
Taxus baccata L.
Teucrium arduini L.

Biogradska Gora National Park
Geranium reflexum L.
Jasione orbiculata Griseb. var. *bosniaca* Stoj.

Durmitor National Park
Daphne malyana Blečić
Carum velenovskyi Rohlena
Edraianthus glisicii Soš. & Černj.
Edraianthus sutjeskae Lakušić
Oxytropis jacquinii Bunge
Saxifraga prenja Beck (*S. sedoides* L. ssp. *prenja* (Beck) Hayek)
Silene graminea Vis. ex Rchb.
Trifolium durmitoreum Rohlena
Verbascum durmitoreum Rohlena
Viola zoysii Wulf.

Lovćen National Park
Amphoricarpos neumayeri Vis.
Berteroa gintlii Rohlena
Campanula hercegovina Degen & Fiala
Centaurea nicolai Baldacci
Dianthus nicolai G. Beck & Szysz. (*D. petraeus* W.K.)
Lamium lovcenicum Rohlena
Viburnum maculatum Pantocsek

Pelister National Park
Crocus pelistericus Pulević
Dianthus myrtinervius Grieseb.
Galium degenii Baldacci ex Degen
Lilium albanicum Grieseb.

Galičica National Park
Aesculus hippocastanum L.
Anthyllis aurea Weld.
Astragalus sericophyllus Grieseb.
Celtis caucasica Willd.
Colchicum macedonicum Košanin
Helleborus cyclophyllus Boiss.
Juniperus excelsa M. Bieb.
Juniperus foetidissima Willd.
Prunus prostrata Labill.
Potentilla speciosa Willd.
Ramonda serbica Pančić
Sibbaldia parviflora Willd.

Fruška Gora National Park
Adonis vernalis L.
Amygdalus nana L.
Crambe tataria Sebeók
Kitaibelia vitifolia Willd.
Notholaena marantae (L.) Desv.
Paeonia officinalis L. ssp. *banatica* (Rochel) Soó
Salvia nutans L.
Sternbergia colchicifolia W.K.
Tragopogon floccosus W.K.
Centaurea sadlerana Janka (*C. scabiosa* L. & ssp. *sadlerana* (Janka) Aschers. & Graebn.)
Dianthus serotinus W.K.

Djerdap National Park
Coronilla elegans Pančić
Erysimum comatatum Pančić
Ferula heuffelii Griseb.
Himantoglossum hircinum (L.) Spreng.
Tulipa hungarica Borb.
Comandra elegans (Roch.) Rchb.

---

forward for expanding and transforming the Triglav National Park into the Julian Alps National Park. According to this plan the Julian Alps would be divided into naturally limited valleys, basins and plateaux with corresponding degrees of protection, reflecting their present and future use. About one half of the total 160 000 hectares under this proposal would form the peripheric area or 'pre-park' zone. The inner part (78 000 hectares) would be divided into the core zone with no economic utilization and into an area with controlled human activities, principally tourism, farming and forestry.

The Risnjak National Park covers 3014 hectares of the most western region of the Dinaric Mountains. Risnjak Mountain, 1528 m high, is made up of limestone and dolomite with magnificent Karstic phenomena and represents a wonderful link between the Alps and the Balkan mountains. During the Ice Ages, many Alpine, Arctic and Boreal plant species migrated over Risnjak to the southern parts of the Balkans. Risnjak mountain also represents a strong climatic and vegetative barrier between the southern submediterranean and the northern continental part of this territory. The southern slopes are covered with typical mediterranean and submediterranean vegetation, rich in relict and endemic elements, whereas on the northern parts there are still elements of the taiga. The Risnjak area has never suffered from strong economic exploitation and its flora and fauna are well preserved with even today unimpaired virgin forests in many places. Therefore the Risnjak National Park has been given the status of a strict scientific reserve.

The Plitvice Lakes National Park is situated in the continental part of the Karst territory and covers 19 172 hectares. The Lakes of Plitvice are a unique Karstic phenomenon. They consist of 16 major and several minor lakes, cascading from terraces and over waterfalls. Most of the area is covered with beech and fir woods, untouched in places.

The Paklenica National Park (3617 hectares) also shows rich Karstic phenomena. It is located on the southern slopes of the Velebit and its vegetation has a more submediterranean character. The most famous features of this national park are the magnificent canyons of Velika and Mala Paklenica deeply cut into the massif of Velebit, surrounded by rocky walls more than 400 m high. The vegetation consists mainly of several types of beech and black pine woods, having survived because of the exceptionally difficult access. The rocky habitats of the region in which the park occurs are known for many rare and endemic plants, as listed in Table 3. A complete collection of the Velebit flora with all the rare and endemic plants can be seen in the Natural Reserve at Rožanski Kukovi, where there is a botanic garden.

The Mljet National Park has a typical Mediterranean character; it covers an area of 3100 hectares on the western part of the south Dalmatian island of Mljet near Dubrovnik. Here are the most beautiful Aleppo Pine and Evergreen Oak woods and an especially well developed formation of evergreen shrubs or maquis.

The Kozara National Park (3375 hectares) in northwestern Bosnia has mainly historical significance. It is a 30 km long Pannonian mountain of serpentine and younger sediments, covered with damp woods with a great abundance of water – a lot of small brooks and rivers.

The Sutjeska National Park also has a great history. It is also remarkable for the virgin forest of Peručica covering 1434 hectares with beautifully developed

Table 3   Some endemic and rare species of the Velebit Mountains, in which the Paklenica National Park is situated

---

Aquilegia kitaibelii Schott
Asperula wettsteinii Adamović
Aubrietia croatica Sch.N.Ky.
Campanula caespitosa Scop.
C. fenestrellata Feer
C. justiniana Witasek
C. velebitica Borbás
C. waldsteiniana J. A. Schultes
Cardaminopsis croatica (Schott *et al.*) S. Jav.
Degenia velebitica (Degen) Hayek
Bunium alpinum W.K.
Edraianthus dinaricus (Kern.) Wettst.
Euphorbia triflora Schott, Nyman & Kotschy
Iberis carnosa W.K.
Knautia pectinata Ehrendorfer
Primula kitaibeliana Schott
Seseli malyi A. Kerner
Sibiraea croatica Degen

mountainous zones of vegetation – from the magnificent oak woods with enormous trunks to the highland areas covered with the dwarfish crooked stems of the Mountain Pine (*Pinus mugo* Turra).

The second largest virgin forest of Yugoslavia is in the Biogradska Gora National Park in the Republic of Montenegro. The forest covers 3400 hectares at an altitude of 830 to 2115 m and includes very well developed montane vegetation zones. The park is covered with mixed woods; the beeches, firs, maples, ashes and oaks attain a height of 60 m or more with the undergrowth about 1.5 m high. Within the national park is one of the most beautiful lakes in Yugoslavia – Biogradsko Jezero – and the woods are full of wild animals.

A highly interesting territory is represented in the Durmitor National Park in Montenegro, covering an area of 32 000 hectares between the Piva and Tara valleys. Durmitor is a large broad mountain, 50 km long and 20 km wide; it is formed of palaeozoic rocks and limestone, descending into the canyon valleys of Piva, Tara and Sušica with steep walls, about 1000 m high. Besides these imposing canyons there are lots of Karstic and glacial phenomena, many lakes, a highly interesting relict and endemic flora and beautifully developed zonation of vegetation.

The Lovćen National Park of 2000 hectares is the smallest national park of Yugoslavia. It is on the top of the 1750 m high limestone mountain of Lovćen arising over the beautiful Adriatic gulf of Boka Kotorska. It is covered with rather degraded forests – the most characteristic tree is *Pinus heldreichii* Christ.

In the most southern part of Yugoslavia, in southern Macedonia, is the Pelister National Park. It covers a territory of 12 000 hectares, from a height of 600 to 2600 m, and includes large forests and alpine pastures. Most characteristic are over 1000 hectares of large endemic Macedonian Pine woods (*P. peuce* Griseb.).

Nearby is the Galičica National Park – a limestone highland between the large Macedonian lakes of Prespansko and Ohridsko Jezero, covering an area of 23 760 hectares. Like the former national park it is known for its most interesting relict and endemic flora. There are about 130 species of trees and shrubs to be found.

One of the largest national parks in Yugoslavia is the Mavrovo National Park. It covers 73 088 hectares and includes many peaks over 2000 m high, deep canyons, small glacial lakes, large areas of beech and fir forests and alpine pastures.

The Fruška Gora National Park covers very different country. It is on the border of the large Pannonian Plain and is known for many rare steppe-plant habitats. The 539 m high mountain is part of the old Pannonian mainland. A big part of Fruška Gora is cultivated – there are about 60 villages and 16 old monasteries, surrounded by large vineyards and orchards, but there are also large territories covered by clear, scattered forest and open dry grasslands with steppe and wood-steppe undergrowth.

The Djerdap National Park includes the longest canyon in Europe where the Danube has cut its way through the Carpathian Mountains. Djerdap is about 150 km long, interrupted by three wide valleys; in the narrowest part of the canyon the river is only 150 m broad and 82 m deep, surrounded by rocky walls about 300 m high. The national park covers 82 115 hectares and spreads over the border into Romania, so representing an internationally protected area. It is known for some rare relict plant communities. The Yugoslav section includes strict nature reserves, historical monuments and over 100 geological, geomorphological or botanical nature monuments.

Proposals for several new national parks have been elaborated. These included the Tara and Zvijezda mountains where near the river Drina there are several sites for the endemic Serbian Spruce; this tree needs strict protection because its wood is used for many purposes; being very decorative and resistant against polluted air, it has been very often planted in parks and private gardens. This area is also known for the habitats of some other rare plants such as *Taxus baccata* L., *Daphne blagayana* Frey., *D. oleoides* Schreber, *Waldsteinia ternata* (Steph.) Fritsch and *Spiraea cana* W.K.

On 16 August 1980 the Kornati Isles National Park was proclaimed. It covers 147 islands and islets with a land area of 69 sq. km. It is rich in marine life but the islands are floristically poor, with only 150 plant species recorded from them.

An important area for rare and endemic plants is the Prokletije territory which has been proposed for a national park; this site includes *Forsythia europaea*, *Dianthus microlepis* Boiss., *Eryngium palmatum* Pančić & Vis., *Euphorbia montenegrina* (Bald.) K. Maly ex Rohlena, *Knautia albanica* Briq., *Narthecium scardicum* Košanin, *Silene macrantha* (Pančić) Neumayer, *Verbascum nicolai* Rohlena and *Wulfenia carinthiaca* Jacq.

Besides the national parks there are also 17 large regional parks or territories of special natural beauty. These are very large areas where less strict measures of protection are introduced. In Slovenia there is a very large regional park in the border region with Austria, covering an area of 180 000 hectares of very picturesque Alpine country. Preparations are being made for declaring other international Regional Parks such as the Julian Alps between Yugoslavia and Italy, the Stara Planina on the Bulgarian border, the Prokletije and Korab massifs on the Albanian border and Kajmakčalan on the Greek border. All these regional parks will, when established, have great significance for international co-operation and for the exchange of experience regarding their establishment.

I hope very much that the efforts of nature conservation, national and international, become stronger and more effective all over the world.

Bibliography

Blečić, V. (1958). 'O nekim karakteristikama flore i vegetacije Crne gore' (Some characteristics of flora and vegetation of Montenegro), *Zaštita Prir. (Beograd)*, **13**, 1–6.

Broz, V. (1963). 'Rad na zaštiti retke i ugrožene flore' (The work on protection of rare and threatened flora), *Zašt. prir.*, **26**, 125–30.

Broz, V. (1965). 'O nekim biljnim vrstama vezanim za ime J. Pančića' (On some plant species rarities associated with the name of J. Pančić), *Zašt. prir.*, **29/30**, 187–94.

Čolić, D. (1972). 'Rad i problemi vaspitanja za pravilan odnos prema okolini u SFRJ' (Work and problems in education for a sound attitude towards environment in SFRJ), *Pos. izd. Republ. Zavoda za zašt. prir. SR Srbije, Beograd*, **2**, 1–32.

Čolić, D. (1974). 'Učešće Jugoslavije u evropskoj saradnji u pogledu regionalnih i nacionalnih parkova' (Yugoslavia's participation in European cooperation concerning regional and national parks), *Pos. izd. Republ. Zavoda za zašt. prir. SR Srbije*, knj. 8, Beograd.

Čolić, D. and Broz, V. (1974). 'Zaštita prirode i zaštita spomenika NOB' (Protection of nature and protection of the monuments of the National Liberation War), *Pos. izd. Republ. Zavoda za zašt. prir. SR Srbije*, knj. 6, Beograd.

Debelak, M. (1974). 'Julijske alpe – slovenski narodni park. "50 let Triglavskega narodnega parka",' *Proteus*, **36**(9/10), 80–6.

Fukarek, P. (1959). 'Neke značajne i rijetke vrste drveća i grmlja u Jugoslaviji' (Some important and rare species of trees and shrubs in Yugoslavia), *Zašt. prir.*, **15**, 19–24.

Fukarek, P. (Ed.) (1969). 'Osnovne prirodne karakteristike, flora i vegetacija nacionalnog parka "Sutjeska"' (The natural characteristics, flora and vegetation of the national park Sutjeska), *Pos. izd. Akad. n. i u. BiH*, knj. *XI*, Sarajevo.

Fukarek, P. (Ed.) (1970). 'Južnoevropske prašume i visokoplaninska flora i vegetacija istočnoalpsko-dinarskog prostora' (The South-European virgin forests and the high mountainous flora and vegetation of the East-Alpine–Dinaric territory), *Pos. izd. Akad. n. iu u. BiH*, knj. *XV*, Sarajevo.

Godicl, L. (1978). *Stepska flora v severozahodni Jugoslaviji* (Steppe Flora of Northwest Yugoslavia), PA Maribor.

Grozdanić, S. (1958). 'Rezervat Stražilovo – Glibovac (Fruška gora)' (The nature reserve Stražilovo – Glibovac (Fruška gora)), *Zašt. Prir. (Beograd)*, **13**, 22–5.

Horvat, I., Glavač, V., and Ellenberg, H. (1974). *Vegetation Südosteuropas*, G. Fischer, Stuttgart.

Jeglič, C. (1963). 'Alpinum Juliana', *Prir. muzej*, Ljubljana.

Kevo, R. (1961). 'Zaštita prirode u Hrvatskoj' (The protection of nature in Croatia), *Zavod za zašt. prir.*, Zagreb.

Marković, J. (1976). 'Priroda Jugoslavije' (The nature of Yugoslavia). *Minerva*. Subotica–Beograd.

Mišić, V. (1980). 'Djerdapski refugijum – jedinstveni prirodni fenomen u Evropi' (The refugium of Djerdap – a unique natural phenomenon of Europe), *IV. simp. biosist. Jugoslavije*, Beograd–Djerdap.

Obradović, M. (1966). 'Biljnogeografska analiza flore Fruške gore' (The plant-geographical analysis of flora of Fruška gora), *Matica Srpska*, Novi Sad.

Peterlin, S. (1976). 'Inventar najpomembnejše naravne dediščine Slovenije' (Inventory of the most significant natural inheritance of Slovenia), *Zavod za spom. varstvo SR Slovenije*, Ljubljana.

Popnikola, N. (1959). 'Nacionalni park "Perister"' (The National Park Perister), *Zašt. prir. (Beograd)*, **16**, 16–23.

Pulević, V. (1976). 'Two new species of the genus *Crocus* from Yugoslavia', *Glas. Republ. zav. zašt. prir. (Titograd)*. **9**, 39–43.

Stajić, S. (1972). 'Nacionalni parkovi Jugoslavije kao šume sa posebnim namenom i njihov značaj za turizam' (Yugoslav national parks as forests predisposed to special purposes and significance for tourism), *Pos. izd. Republ. Zavoda za zašt. prir. SR Srbije*, knj. 3, Beograd.

Stajić, S. (1974). 'Zaštićena priroda Jugoslavije – deo evropskog fonda prirodnih vrednosti' (Preserved nature in Yugoslavia – European natural wealth), *Pos. izd. Republ. Zavoda za zašt. prir. SR Srbije*, knj. 8, Beograd.

Tutin, T. G. *et al.* (Eds.) (1964–1980). *Flora Europaea*, 5 vols., Cambridge University Press.

Wojterski, T. (1971). '*Parki narodowe Jugoslawii*' (The national parks of Yugoslavia), *Zahlad ochrony przyrody polskiej akademii nauk. Ochrona przyrody*, R. 36.

Wraber, T. (1974). 'Botanični sprehod skozi dolino Triglavskih jezer (A botanical walk through the Triglav Lakes Valley). "50 let Triglavskega narodnega parka"', *Proteus*, **36**(9/10), 21–5.

The Biological Aspects of Rare Plant Conservation
Edited by Hugh Synge
© 1981 John Wiley & Sons Ltd.

Appendix 1
Short notes and abstracts of additional papers received

Checklist of the endemic dicotyledons of the Iberian Peninsula and the Balearic Islands

H. SÁINZ OLLERO AND J. E. HERNÁNDEZ BERMEJO *Escuela Técnica Superior de Ingenieros Agrónomos, Universidad de Córdoba, Spain*

A checklist of the endemic dicotyledons of the Iberian Peninsula and the Balearic Islands has been elaborated, based on *Flora Europaea* (Tutin *et al.*, 1964–80) but partly revised. A general review of literature on the Iberian and Balearic flora was made to determine the precise distribution of each taxon. A new classification of phytogeography is proposed and used for analysing distributional data. An evaluation of conservation status in relation to the danger of extinction is also given. The intention of the list is to summarize published information. A new search of herbaria has been started to complete the distributional studies of species in the Iberian and Balearic flora. Recently published endemic taxa will be included. Any future contributions received will be cited and acknowledged. The list itself is now published by the Instituto Nacional de Investigaciones Agrarias (INIA) under the title *Síntesis corológica de las dicotiledóneas endémicas de la Península Ibérica e Islas Baleares*.

Reference

Tutin, T. G. *et al.* (Eds.) (1964–80). *Flora Europaea*, 5 vols, Cambridge University Press.

The biological aspects of rare plant conservation

Endangered plants in central Australia

R. BUCKLEY *Department of Biogeography and Geomorphology, The Australian National University, Canberra*

Poor collecting and uncertain taxonomy hamper the assessment of endangered flora in central Australia very severely. This may be ascribed in part to the lack of interstate communication among taxonomists until recently. Thus *Keraudrenia intergrifolia* Steud. was listed as 'rare' for South Australia by Jessop *et al.* (1975, unpubl.) following Specht *et al.* (1974), but is quite common in the dunefields of Northern Territory and Western Australia. *Frankenia* provides a prime example of imperfect taxonomy: Jessop (1977) listed 17 *Frankenia* species as 'endangered' in South Australia, but there is no consensus on species definition and some may not be valid species at all. A third problem is that of rainfall-linked fluctuations in the abundance of different species: the common species of the dry years are often the rare ones of the wet years, and *vice versa*. In an area where collections are few and far between this can bias the list of putative endangered species in either direction. As a result of further collections and perhaps name changes, not one of the species listed as 'endangered' in northeast South Australia by Jessop *et al.* (1975, unpubl.) remains in the South Australian endangered list compiled by Jessop (1977).

The most recent list is that of Hartley and Leigh (1979), which again is currently under revision. Central Australian species are listed in Table 1. Of these

Table 1   Threatened Species of central Australia (Hartley and Leigh, 1979)

	Distribution	
Species	Type	Range
Acacia peuce F. Muell.	C	A, C
Daviesia arthropoda F. Muell.	A	A
Euphorbia sarcostemmoides Willis	B	A
Goodenia chambersii F. Muell.	A	B
Goodenia helenae Ising	A	B
Helichrysum thomsonii F. Muell.	B	A
Minuria annua (Tate) J. M. Black	B	B
Rulingia magniflora F. Muell.	B	B
Swainsona unifoliolata F. Muell.	B	A
Trachymene gilleniae (Tate) B. L. Burtt	A	A
Wedelia stirlingii Tate	B	A, B
Zygophyllum humillimum Koch	B	B

Key: *Type:* A: restricted endemics, range less than 100 km; B: rare, in small populations, but wider area; C: disjunct, localized.
Range: A: southern Northern Territory; B: northern South Australia; C: southwest Queensland.

I have encountered *Minuria annua, Wedelia stirlingii, Daviesia arthropoda* and of course *Acacia peuce* in restricted but apparently stable populations.

Unpublished threatened plant lists

Jessop, J., *et al.* (1975). Far northeast South Australia.
Lay, B. G., *et al.* (1970–71). Woomera–Coober Pedy area.
Symon, D. E., *et al.* Oraparinna (1971), Mound Springs (1978).
Turvey, F. T. (1966). Ernabella.
Weber, J. Z., *et al.* Lake Frome (1971), northwest New South Wales (1977).

References

Hartley, W. and Leigh, J. (1979). *Australian Plants at Risk,* Australian National Parks and Wildlife Service Occasional Paper 3, Canberra.
Jessop, J. P. (Ed.) (1977). 'Endangered species in the South Australian native vascular flora', *J. Adel. Bot. Gdns,* **1,** 135–9.
Jessop, J. (Ed.) (in press). *Flora of Central Australia.*
Specht, R. L., Roe, E. M., and Boughton, V. H. (Eds.) (1974). 'Conservation of Major Plant Communities in Australia and Papua New Guinea', *Aust. J. Bot.,* Suppl. Ser., 7.
Symon, D. E. (1969). 'A checklist of flowering plants of the Simpson Desert and its immediate environs', *Trans. R. Soc. S. Aust.,* **93,** 17–38.

The coenopopulation as an approach to the conservation of rare plant species

T. A. RABOTNOV *Department of Geobotany, M. V. Lomonosov State University of Moscow*

Abstract

The sum of the individuals of a species in a community may be considered as a phytocoenotic population or coenopopulation. As a rule a coenopopulation consists of a set of individuals in which the number changes from year to year and the individuals differ in age and vitality. To study the spectrum of a coenopopulation, it is necessary to divide the population into groups of individuals at four different 'age states': (a) period of primary dormancy (latent period) in which individuals exist as viable seeds in the soil or on its surface; (b) virginile period from germination up to the formation of generative shoots; (c) generative period in which seed is produced; (d) senile period, a vegetative state as a result of senility.

One can distinguish three types of coenopopulation, reflecting different stages of development from the invasion of a species into a community to its decline and disappearance: (a) coenopopulations of the invasion type; (b) normal coenopopulations in which the species is composed of individuals at different 'age states' and where new individuals arise as old ones senesce and die; (c) regressive coenopopulations which have lost the ability to reproduce.

The age composition of a coenopopulation indicates the vitality of the species in the community. Analysing the structure of a coenopopulation, e.g. by assessing the percentage of seedlings that reach flowering stage, provides an understanding of the position of the species in the community and enables predictions to be made, in particular of the risk of disappearance. As a result, attempts can be made to transform regressive coenopopulations into normal ones, for example by artificial sowing of seeds, by removing predators, by reducing competition from neighbouring plants, and so on. Removing the causes of coenopopulation degradation is a primary aim of species conservation.

The concept of a coenopopulation is considered in more detail elsewhere:

Rabotnov, T. A. (1969). 'On coenopopulations of perennial herbaceous plants in natural coenoses', *Vegetatio*, **19**, 87–95.
Rabotnov, T. A. (1978). 'On coenopopulations of plants reproducing by seeds', in *Structure and Functioning of Plant Populations* (Eds. A. H. J. Freysen and J. W. Woldendorp), pp. 1–26, North-Holland Publishing Company, Amsterdam.

The re-introduction of *Saxifraga cespitosa* to North Wales

D. M. PARKER *University of Liverpool Botanic Gardens, Ness, Cheshire, England*

Saxifraga cespitosa L. is a circumpolar arctic–subarctic species found in open habitats such as recently exposed morainic gravels and, in the south of its range montane habitats. After the last ice age, *S. cespitosa* was common in the British Isles on open immature soils left by the retreating glaciers. As the climate improved and the development of forests and the extension of peatlands took place (particularly during the Atlantic hypsithermal) these open habitats became scarce and mostly confined to mountains and the coast. The open ground tundra species such as the *Saxifraga* became confined to very restricted habitats, mainly in the mountains and usually on cold, high altitude and north-facing calcareous sites, particularly on cliffs.

Saxifraga cespitosa is today a rare species in the British Isles; only about fifteen, mostly small, populations are known. All are in Scotland except for one locality in Snowdonia, North Wales (53° N), where the very small population is in danger of extinction. Many of the Scottish colonies are in very remote places and, apart from those populations with a very low number of individual plants, the species is not endangered at present. Furthermore, the species is given special protection under the 'Conservation of Wild Creatures and Wild Plants Act 1975'.

The Welsh population was discovered in 1796 and collected by botanists from that date until the present day. By 1976, it was reduced to only four plants growing together on a single ledge of 3 × 10 cm. The species cannot normally distribute its seeds over large distances and suitable habitat at the site is very discontinuous; therefore, the extant site would be unable to give rise to new colonies. The Nature Conservancy Council was aware of this and asked Dr H. McAllister of the University of Liverpool Botanic Gardens to try to establish the population in cultivation. Twenty seeds were collected under licence in 1975 and five plants raised in cultivation. These plants were kept in isolated insect-proof enclosures and seed collected from self-pollinated flowers (approximately 30 000 seeds in 1977, 10 000 of which were placed in the Kew Seed Bank) and many further plants were grown on from this seed in 1977 and 1978.

These individuals have been extensively planted on a native plant garden in the University of Liverpool Botanic Gardens creating a feature of both nature conservation value and horticultural interest. A large number of herbarium specimens have been made for distribution to herbaria. Plant material and seed are also available for scientific purposes. It is to be hoped that collecting pressure has now been taken off the wild population.

In the locality, the re-introduction sites were chosen not only to resemble the extant site in terms of all environmental parameters but also to provide a slightly wider range of conditions. The microhabitats themselves, small pockets of soil on large base-rich boulders (of pumice-tuff and basalt), are dominated by bryophytes; angiosperms are scarce and restricted to a few species. Extensive notes were taken of all associated species on all the re-introduction sites.

Four age-classes of plants were used in the re-introduction: (a) small mature plants: 120 planted in groups of 5. These were 'hardened off' single rosette plants of a similar size to the extant plants (i.e. about 1 cm in diameter); (b) seedlings: 150, each with 10 true leaves, planted in groups of 5; (c) seedlings: 150, with cotyledons only, planted in groups of 5; (d) seeds: 30 groups of 50 seeds.

The re-introduction took place on 20–21 May 1978 with the help and permission of the Nature Conservancy Council. The plants were introduced by removing all soil from the roots, parting the bryophytes on the microsites, inserting the plant, and watering in. The seeds were sown on both bryophyte and fine gravel dominated ledges well away from the other introductions.

To prevent genetic erosion the introduced plants had only been through one generation in cultivation and cross-pollination from other closely related species was impossible; the flower is protogynous and has a self-pollination mechanism. Furthermore, the seeds were collected from a small population that had been isolated from other populations of its species probably for several thousand years and no morphological or isoenzyme variation could be detected in cultivation. For this reason, the project can be considered as a valid re-introduction.

All the sites have been visited five times every year and an individual record kept of each plant and all germinating seeds. An exhaustive monitoring of the introduced plants was considered essential, firstly, so that the precise environmental factors required by the species could be determined, and secondly, because work of this kind must be performed with care, especially in a site of national importance for nature conservation.

The results can only be discussed briefly as data for only 2 years are available. About one half of the small mature plants have survived and these have now flowered and set seed. Most of the mortality was in the 2 months following planting and few plants have died during 1979 or 1980. Few seedlings survived the first winter; the main cause of death (in all plants, but especially small seeds) was frost-lift followed by desiccation. This factor was predicted at the outset as the main threat to the success of the programme. The re-introduction therefore took place early in the year to give the plants the maximum possible time to establish themselves by producing a good root system. The re-introduction so far has been very successful and the population of the species in the wild has been restored to somewhere near its earlier, more sustainable level. Full data on the re-introduction are deposited with the Nature Conservancy Council in Bangor, Gwynedd.

It is intended that detailed monitoring of the re-introduced plants will continue for at least 10 years. Apart from assessing the ultimate success of the re-introduction, this will yield valuable information on the phenology, demography and ecology of the species.

This work was performed as part of a PhD project while the author was supported by a 'CASE' Studentship from the National Environment Research Council.

Declining populations of annual *Veronica* species in Britain: Studies on seed production, germination and survival

T. L. WOODINGS AND D. RATCLIFFE *Department of Botany, University of Leicester, England*

Veronica verna L., *V. praecox* All. and *V. triphyllos* L. are today confined in Britain to an area of Norfolk and Suffolk known as the Breckland, which has a more continental climate than the rest of the country. Rainfall is the lowest recorded in Britain (50–60 cm). All of the species occur widely on the continent and may possibly be at their climatic limit in the Breckland. They are winter annuals, which germinate from October to December or January, over-winter in the vegetative state, and start to flower early in the following spring. *Veronica verna* is confined to heavily rabbit-grazed and disturbed grassland on chalk-free soils (pH 4–5); *V. praecox* and *V. triphyllos* are confined to arable fields under crop or fallow (pH 6.1–7.2). The number of localities and the size of the populations within them have decreased in the past 30 years (Table 1). All three species are included in the *British Red Data Book* (Perring and Farrell, 1977), but so far no definite conservation measures have been taken.

The loss of populations may be due partly to a decrease in habitat following an increase in the area and intensity of farming and widespread afforestation. The use of herbicides and other changes in farming practices may have contributed to the decline of *V. praecox* and *V. triphyllos*; winter rye was once the traditional Breckland crop and the life cycles fit well with the rye cultivation programme. Rye, however, has been almost totally replaced by other crops, the cultivation of which occurs either just after germination or prior to seed set so damaging the *Veronica* populations. Nevertheless there remain many apparently suitable sites which are colonized by other, more common, *Veronica* species, i.e. *V. arvensis* L. (ubiquitous in Britain), *V. persica* Poir., *V. hederifolia* L. and *V. agrestis* L.

The study attempted to find out by observation and experiment what were the most important factors which have led to the decrease both in sites and in the populations remaining, and to what extent could the changes be explained by the differences in ecology between the three species and also between them and the other more common but very similar *Veronica* species. Evidence has now accumulated on the factors regulating germination, seedling survival, flowering and seed set, and on short- and long-term variation in population size, although it is not yet known whether the species in question behave as 'typical' ruderal species possessing large seed banks that persist for several years, acting as a stabilizing influence, or less probably whether they lack a seed bank as does *Vulpia fasciculata* (see Watkinson, Chapter 21).

Natural populations of the three species were studied at two sites and the number of individual plants, numbers of capsules and seeds produced recorded for 1979 and 1980 (Table 2). All three species showed surprisingly little difference in population density between the two years. Lower seed production occurred in 1980 owing to an early and severe spring drought which brought flowering to an abrupt end; in *V. verna* and *V. praecox* this was due to a decrease in capsules per plant, but in *V. triphyllos* to a decrease in seeds per capsule.

To avoid disturbing the wild plants, experimental populations were created on the bare soil of a fire-break on a Breckland nature reserve. Four hundred viable seeds (>95 per cent viability using tetrazolium chloride) were added to a series of

Table 1   The sites for *Veronica verna*, *V. praecox* and *V. triphyllos* in Breckland, England

	V. verna	*V. praecox*	*V. triphyllos*
No. of sites 1950–55	18	12	11
No. of sites 1980	9	4	2

Table 2   Performance of representative natural populations of *Veronica verna*, *V. praecox* and *V. triphyllos*

	V. verna		*V. praecox*		*V. triphyllos*	
	1979	1980	1979	1980	1979	1980
Mean capsules per plant	3.8	1.44	13	1.75	2.08	1.83
Seeds (per sq. m)	2100	860	550	79	375	180

0.25 sq. m plots (six per species) in late summer. The plots were examined at fortnightly intervals (more frequently during the germination and flowering periods) for germination, seedling survival, flowering and fruiting. Earliest germination for all three species was mid-November with few recorded after mid-December. During the vegetative period few individuals were lost; most losses occurred during the early spring at the transition from vegetative growth to flowering. The spring drought that caused a decrease in seed production in the natural populations had a similar effect on the plants on these plots causing a sudden 'cut-off' in flowering and capsule production. In a wetter spring flowering and fruiting would be prolonged, leading to higher seed production; thus the occurrence, timing and length of spring droughts may be crucial in determining the size of the 'seed rain' from which the populations of the following autumn are derived. The basic pattern is similar for all the species, varying only in the slightly later and normally more extended flowering period of *V. verna*. The major difference between the species is in the percentage of seeds which germinate – *V. verna* has the highest and *V. triphyllos* the lowest.

Some of the factors governing germination and flowering can be investigated in the laboratory. To simulate the conditions experienced by seeds at or near the soil surface in the field, incubators were used with control of photoperiod and with differing 'day' and 'night' temperatures. Experiments with a range of temperatures on 2-year-old viable seeds (presumed to have lost their post-harvest dormancy) showed that *V. verna* tolerated a wide range of temperatures and photoperiods but did not germinate in conditions corresponding to those of mid-winter. (In the field it germinates throughout the autumn or even earlier.) *Veronica praecox* was less tolerant, corresponding to its more restricted period of germination in the field. All species have a much lower percentage germination in darkness, suggesting that at least deeply buried seeds would not germinate in the field. *Veronica triphyllos* was notable for its low germination both in appropriate photoperiods and in darkness. It was, however, found that a 24-hour pre-treatment of imbibed seeds of this species at 2°C was sufficient to increase germination to 60 per cent. *Veronica verna* and *V. praecox* were not affected in this way. Increasing lengths of cold treatment from 2 to 12 days were decreasingly effective and longer periods were ineffective. It is possible that *V. triphyllos* is stimulated to germinate by the first cold period of autumn.

Similar experiments on freshly harvested seeds enabled the interaction of seed age with changing environmental conditions to be investigated. All three species showed progressive loss of post-harvest dormancy, and changes in germination response to temperature with age. *Veronica verna* has the shortest post-harvest dormancy and *V. triphyllos* the longest.

The results of these germination tests give some insight into possible reasons for the differing declines of the species. *Veronica triphyllos* is clearly the species whose germination requirements are most demanding; is it fortuitous that it is also the most vulnerable of the three to extinction in Britain? *Veronica verna* has the widest tolerance of germination conditions and is in the least danger of extinction. In all germination tests the three species were compared to *V. arvensis*, a widespread species in Britain; *V. verna* closely resembles it, in germination response at least, so that explanations other than germination characteristics must be important.

It would be very unwise to speculate on the causes of decline of the species purely in terms of their germination requirements, as so many other factors must be involved, not least the impact of man in removing those habitats where the species grow best. For small annual species which depend on large seed production in an uncertain environment, however, a species which is tolerant only of a narrow range of conditions for germination may not be well adapted for survival when the environment imposes stress, and the presence, absence or size of its seed bank may be crucial to survival in any one locality. This aspect must obviously be given urgent attention and indeed without information on seed survival in the soil effective conservation measures could not be formulated.

We wish to thank Mrs G. Crompton, University Botanic Garden, Cambridge, for much invaluable help, the Nature Conservancy Council for permission to work on Thetford Heath Nature Reserve and for the assistance of their staff, and Elveden Estates for access to sites on their land. One of us (T.L.W.) is indebted to the National Environment Research Council for financial support.

Reference

Perring, F. H. and Farrell, L. (1977). *British Red Data Books: 1. Vascular Plants*, Society for the Promotion of Nature Conservation, Lincoln.

Appendix 2
Bibliography of Red Data Books and threatened plant lists

CHARLIE JARVIS, CHRISTINE LEON AND SARA OLDFIELD
(c/o) The Herbarium, Royal Botanic Gardens, Kew, England

Introduction

Below is a bibliography of books and papers that list threatened plant species. It has been compiled from the information at the Threatened Plants Committee Secretariat at Kew, using in particular the facilities of the Kew Library. The list is selective: papers about a single threatened species are not included, nor are papers which describe plant conservation activities without a systematic list of threatened species. The authors would greatly appreciate any additions.

The bibliography is designed to complement the accounts of many national programmes to list threatened plants described in Section 1, in particular the lengthy bibliography of state threatened plants lists for the USA given as Appendix V in Chapter 2 by E. S. Ayensu. As will be apparent from this book, many programmes are in a very active state and many lists are in preparation or in press. In this bibliography we include only books and papers which have been published except for brief mentions of TPC lists in manuscript form or in preparation see also Chapter 1). So the picture is soon likely to change dramatically.

A note is relevant here on the term Red Data Book. We believe the first published usage was in 1966 when IUCN issued *Red Data Book 1: Mammalia* by Noel Simon. The book was the brainchild of Sir Peter Scott, then Chairman of IUCN's Survival Service Commission (the Species Survival Commission). This was a loose-leaf book, with a double-sided sheet on each threatened mammal; those pages for endangered taxa were coloured red. The term 'Red Data Book' has stuck, both for the world-wide series continued by IUCN, now covering mammals, birds, amphibians and reptiles, fresh-water fishes, selected invertebrate groups and plants, and for national reports on threatened species.

In 1970–1, IUCN published the first version of *Red Data Book Volume 5 – Angiospermae*, compiled by Ronald Melville. This contained sheets on 118 threatened plants. It has become out-of-print and is now totally recast as *The IUCN Plant Red Data Book* by Gren Lucas and Hugh Synge (1978), (available from the Threatened Plants Committee Secretariat at Kew, price £10). This provides detailed case histories on 250 threatened plants selected from around the world to show the floras most in danger and to highlight the threats to plant life. (An account of the work of the Threatened Plants Committee is provided by the authors in the latter part of Chapter 1 of this book.)

In the lists below, Threatened Plants Committee is abbreviated to TPC throughout. TPC Manuscript Lists are available to botanic institutions and conservation organizations; please write to the Secretariat. The regions used below follow the arbitrary TPC system and are used for geographical convenience only.

Other bibliographies

Miasek, M. A. and Long, C. R. (1978). *Endangered Plant Species of the World and Their Endangered Habitats: A Compilation of the Literature*, Library of the New York Botanical Garden, Bronx, New York, 46 pp. (Mainly US papers.)

General

TPC lists available for threatened cycads and in preparation for palms, cacti, tree-ferns, world-wide.
There are reports on threatened species in various plant groups in:
Prance, G. T. and Elias, T. S. (Eds.) (1977). *Extinction Is Forever*, New York Botanical Garden.
In particular on neotropical Iridaceae, Amaryllidaceae and allied bulbous families (P. Ravenna, pp. 257–66) and palms (H. E. Moore, pp. 267–82, reprinted, see next item.)
Moore, H. E., Jr. (1979). 'Endangerment at the specific and generic levels in palms', *Principes*, **23**(2), 47–64.

Arctic

Polunin, N. (1970). 'Botanical conservation in the Arctic', *Biol. Conserv.*, **2**(3), 197–205.
(Reports on 10 species of vascular plants endemic to the Arctic and 44 species or species complexes which are very rare in the Arctic but widespread elsewhere.)

Greenland

TPC Manuscript list of angiosperms endemic to Greenland; out of 16 species 3 are Rare; most of the rest are listed as Insufficiently Known.

Europe

IUCN Threatened Plants Committee (1977). *List of Rare, Threatened and Endemic Plants in Europe*, Nature and Environment Series No. 14, Council of Europe, Strasbourg. iv + 286 pp.
(Described by Lucas and Synge, Chapter 1; lists c. 2100 species rare and threatened in Europe as a whole; to be revised and updated during 1981.)
IUCN Threatened Plants Committee Secretariat (1980). *List of Rare and Threatened Plants of the States of the Mediterranean Basin*, UNEP/1G.20/INF.10, United Nations Environment Programme.

(Prepared for the Intergovernmental Meeting on Mediterranean Specially Protected Areas, Athens, 13–17 October 1980; provides a more recent version of the above list, but only for states with a Mediterranean coastline.)

Nordic Council of Ministers (1978). *Hotade djur och växter Norden* (Threatened animals and plants in the Nordic countries). Report NU.A. 9, Nordic Council of Ministers, Stockholm.

(Covers Denmark, Finland, Norway, Sweden.)

Austria

Traxler, G. (1978). 'A red list of endangered plants in the Burgenland (Austria)', *Natur und Umwelt im Burgenland*, Sonderheft 1. Eisenstadt (not seen).

Belgium

Delvosalle, L., Demaret, F., Lambinon, J., and Lawalrée, A. (1969). 'Plantes rares, disparues ou menacées de disparition en Belgique: L'appauvrissement de la flore indigène', *Min. Agricult., Service Réserves Nat. Conserv. Nat., Trav.*, **4**, 1–129.

A series of papers occurs in *Bull. Soc. R. Bot. Belg.* by R. D'Hose and J. E. De Langhe, entitled 'New locations of rare plants in Belgium', viz. (1974) **107**(1), 107–14; (1975) **108**(1), 35–45; (1976) **109**(1), 29–41; (1977) **110**(1/2), 20–28.

Bulgaria

Bondev, I., Markova, M., Kozuharov, S., Kuzmanov, B., and Velcev, V. (Eds.) (in press). *Red Book: 2. Plants.* Bulgarian Academy of Sciences.

(Full title not yet received; will cover some 180 species of Bulgarian and Balkan rare and threatened endemics and some 570 species rare in Bulgaria but common elsewhere.)

Dimitrov, D. (1977). 'Rare plant species of the Bulgarian Black Sea Coast', *Priroda (Sofia)*, **26**(3), 95–6.

Kuzmanov, B. A. (1978). 'About the "Red Book of Rare Bulgarian Plants"', *Phytology* (Bulgarian Academy of Sciences), **9**, 17–32 (in Bulgarian).

(150 endemic and rare Bulgarian plants listed; Extract from the English summary quoted in *TPC Newsletter*, (1980), **6**, 13–14.)

Stanev, S. F. (1975). *The Stars are Becoming Extinct in the Mountains: Stories About our Rare Plants*, Zemizdat, Sofia. 129 pp. (in Bulgarian).

(Amusing stories describing searches for rare plants in Bulgaria.)

Stefanov, B. (1978). 'Plants that are very rare in Bulgaria or that have recently disappeared and the cause of their decline', *Gorskostoponska Nauka*, **15**(6), 3–10 (not seen).

Czechoslovakia

Čeřovský, J., Holub, J., and Procházka, F. (1979). 'Červený seznam flóry ČSR' (The Red List of the CSR Flora), *Památky a Příroda*, **6**, 361–78, English summary p. 384.

(First draft list of threatened vascular plants; includes 37 'extinct' and 39 'missing' taxa. 267 'critically threatened' plants, 240 'strongly threatened', 239 'threatened', and 330 taxa 'in need of further study'.)

Holub, J., Procházka, F., and Čeřovský, J. (1979). 'Seznam vyhynulých, endemických a ohrožených taxonů vyšších rostlin květeny ČSR (1. verze)' (List of extinct, endemic and threatened taxa of vascular plants of the flora of the Czech Socialist Republic (first draft)), *Preslia*, **51**, 213–37.

Šomšák, L. (1977). *Ohrozené a zriedkavé taxóny horských a vysokohorských polôh Slovenska* (The Threatened and Rare Taxa of the Mountain Range of Slovakia), Bratislava.

Denmark

Løjtnant, B. and Worsøe, E. (1977). *Foreløbig Status over den Danske Flora*, Rep. Bot. Inst. Univ. Aarhus, 2. 341 pp.
(A detailed survey of the present status of every native vascular plant in Denmark. The English summary analyses the threat to the flora, which contains approximately 1200 species. Approximately 3 per cent of the flora is Extinct, nearly 3 per cent Endangered and nearly 10 per cent Vulnerable.)

Federal Republic of Germany

Anon. (1974). *Rote Liste bedrohter Farn- und Blütenpflanzen in Bayern*, Bayerisches Landesamt für Umweltschultz, München, 44 pp.

Haeupler, H. (1976). 'Die verschollenen und gefährdeten gefässpflanzen Niedersachsens Ursachen ihres Rückgangs und zeitliche Fluktuation der Flora, *Schrift Veg.*, **10**, 125–31.

Haeupler, H., Montag, A., and Wöldecke, K. (1976). 'Verschollene und gefährdete gefässpflanzen in Nidersachsen', in *30 Jahre Naturschutz und Landschaftspflege in Niedersachsen*, Nieders. Ministerium für Ernährung, Landwirtschaft und Forsten, pp. 1–24.

Korneck, D., Lohmeyer, W., Sukopp, H., and Trautmann, W. (1977). 'Rote Liste der Farn- und Blütenpflanzen (Pteridophyta et Spermatophyta) 2. Fassung', in *Rote Liste der gefährdeten Tiere und Pflanzen in Bundesrepublik Deutschland* (J. Blab, E. Nowak, W. Trautmann and H. Sukopp). Naturschutz Aktuell, I. Kilda Verlag, Greven.

Müller, T. *et al.* (1973). *Vorläufige 'Rote Liste' bedrehter Pflanzenarten in Baden Württemberg*, Beihefte zu den Veröffentlichungen d. Landesstelle f. Naturschutz u. Landschaftspflege Baden Württemberg, Beih. 1, 74–96.

Raabe, E. W. (1975). 'Rote Liste der in Schleswig-Holstein und Hamburg von Aussterben bedrohten höheren Pflanzen', *Heimat*, **82**(7/8), 191–200.

Sukopp, H. (1976). 'Rote Liste der in der Bundesrepublik Deutschland gefährdeten Arten von Farn- und Blütenpflanzen (1. Fassung)', *Gärtnerisch-Botanischer Brief*, **48**, 1675–92.

Sukopp, H., Trautmann, W., and Korneck, D. (1978). *Auswertung der Roten Liste gefährdeten Farn- und Blütenpflanzen in der Bundesrepublik Deutschland für den Arten- und Biotopschutz*. Schriftenreihe für Vegetationskunde, Heft 12, Bonn, 138 pp.

Finland

Borg, P. and Malmström, K. K. (1975). 'Suomen uhanalaiset eläin – ja kasvilajit' (Endangered animals and plants in Finland), *Luonnon Tutkija*, **79**(2), 33–43.

Suominen, J. (1974). 'Tuloksia uhanalaisten kasvien tiedustelusta', *Suomen Luonto* (Nature in Finland), **1**, 24, 29.
(Lists over 30 species, English summary on page 52.)

France

Aymonin, G. G. (1974–7). *Etudes sur les régressions d'espèces végétales en France*: Rapport No. 1 – Espèces végétales considérées comme actuellement disparues du territoire; Rapport No. 2 – Listes préliminaires des espèces endemiques et des espèces menacées en France; Rapport No. 3 – Liste générale des espèces justifiant des mesures de protection. Muséum National d'Histoire Naturelle, Paris.

German Democratic Republic

Benkert, D. (1978). 'Liste der in den brandenburgischen Bezirken erloschenen und gefährdeten Moose, Farn- und Blütenpflanzen', *Naturschutzarbert in Berlin und Brandenburg*, **14**(2/3), 34–80.

Jeschke, L., Henker, H., Fukarek, F., Knapp, H. D., and Voigtländer, U. (1978). 'Liste der in Mecklenburg (Bezirke Rostock, Schwerin und Neubrandenburg) erloschenen und gefährdeten Farn- und Blütenpflanzen', *Botanischer Rundbrief für den Bezirk Neubrandenburg*, **8**, 1–29.

Rauschert, S., Benkert, D., Hempfel, W., and Jeschke, L. (1979). *Liste der in der Deutschen Demokratischen Republik erloschenen und gefährdeten Farn- und Blütenpflanzen*, Kulturband der DDR, Berlin. 56 pp.

Rauschert, S. *et al.* (1978). 'Liste der in den Bezirken Halle und Magdeburg erloschenen und gefährdeten Farn- und Blütenpflanzen', *Naturschutz und naturkünkliche Heimatforschung in den Bezirken Halle und Magdeburg*, **15**(1), 1–31.
(Covers 2 provinces; reviewed by S. M. Walters in *TPC Newsletter*, (1978), **3**, 4.)

Greece

Diapoulis, C. (1958). 'Conservation measures for the plants of the Greek flora', in *Proceedings of the IUCN 7th Technical Meeting*, Vol. 5, Brussels, pp. 189–91, IUCN, Switzerland.

Goulimis, C. (1959). 'Report on species of plants requiring protection in Greece and measures for securing their protection', *Proceedings of the IUCN 7th Technical Meeting*, Vol. 5, Brussels, pp. 168–88, IUCN, Switzerland.

IUCN Threatened Plants Committee Secretariat (in press). 'The Rare, Threatened and Endemic Plants of Greece', *Ann. Mus. Goulandris*.

Sfikas, G. (1980). 'Threatened plants of our mountains', *Fusis (Bull. Hellenic Soc. Protection Nature)*, **18**, 42–4.

Hungary

Voross, L. (1976). 'Szársomlyó ritka növényei' (The rare plants of Szársomlyó), *Buvar*, **31**(5), 207–10.

518   *The biological aspects of rare plant conservation*

Italy

Anon. (1972). 'Specie della Flora Italiana meritevoli di protezione (Gruppo di Lavoro per la Floristica, Società Botanica Italiana)', *Inform. Bot. Ital.*, **4**(1), 12–13. List also in *Webbia*, (1974), **29**(1), 361–3.

Corti, R. (1959). 'Specie Rare o Minacciate della Flora Mediterranea in Italia', in *Proceedings of the IUCN 7th Technical Meeting*, Vol. 5, Brussels, pp. 112–29. IUCN, Switzerland.

Filipello, S. *et al.* (Eds.) (1979). *Repertorio delle specie della flora italiana sottoposte a vincolo di protezione nella legislazione nazionale e regionale.* Consiglio Nazionale delle Ricerche, Pavia (loose-leaf).

Malta

Lanfranco, E. (1976). 'Report on the present situation of the Maltese flora', *The Maltese Naturalist*, **2**(3), 69–80.

Netherlands

Mennema, J. (1975). 'Threatened and protected plants in the Netherlands', *Naturopa*, **22**, 10–13.

Mennema, J. (1975). 'Zeldzame Planten Tellen' (Census of rare plants), *Levende Nat.*, **78**(2), 29–31.

Mennema, J., Quené-Boterenbrood, A. J., and Plate, C. L. (Eds.) (1980). *Atlas of the Netherlands Flora 1: Extinct and very rare species*, Junk, The Hague. 222 pp.

Quené-Boterenbrood, A. J. and Mennema, J. (1973). *Zeldzame Nederlandse Plantesoorten in Zuid-Holland* (Rare plant species in southern Holland), The Hague. 110 pp.

There are a series of papers by S. J. van Oostroom, J. Mennema and Th. J. Reichgelt entitled 'Nieuwe vondsten van zeldzame plantent in Nederland' (New discoveries of rare plants in the Netherlands) in *Gorteria* (1967) **3**, 133–47; (1968) **4**, 33–42; (1969) **4**, 167–77; (1970) **5**, 65–74; (1971) **5**, 269–80; (1972) **6**, 41–56; (1973) **6**, 181–98; (1974) **7**, 65–83; (1975) **7**, 185–206; (1977) **8**, 135–56; (1977) **8**, 219–40; (1979) **9**, 208–27; (1979) **9**, 347–64; (1980) **10**, 81–100.

Norway

Halvorsen, R. and Fagernaes, K. E. (1980). 'Sjeldne og såbare plantearter i Sør-Norge: I Kubjelle (*Pulsatilla pratensis*); II Sprikesøtgras (*Glyceria plicata*)' (Rare and threatened plant species in south Norway), *Blyttia*, **38**(1), 3–8; **38**(3), 127–32.

Poland

Jasnowska, J. and Jasnowski, M. (1977). 'Zagrozone gatunki flory torfowisk' (Endangered plant species in the flora of peatbogs), *Chron. Przyr Ojczysta*, **33**(4), 5–14.

Kornás, J. (1971). 'Recent decline of some synanthropic plant species in Poland', *Mater. Zakl. Fitosoc. Stos. U.W.*, **27**, 51–6.

Molski, B. A. (1979). 'The relationship between the national reserves and the activities of botanic gardens in plant genetic resource conservation', in *Survival or Extinction* (Eds. H. Synge and H. Townsend), pp. 54–8. Bentham–Moxon Trust, Kew. (Lists endemic species and protected species.)

Portugal

Tavares, C. N. (1959). 'Protection of the flora and plant communities in Portugal', in *Proceedings of the IUCN 7th Technical Meeting*, Vol. 5, Brussels, pp. 86–94, IUCN, Switzerland.

Spain

Rivas Goday, S. (1959). 'Algunas especies raras o relicticas que deben protejerse en la España Mediterranea', in *Proceedings of the IUCN 7th Technical Meeting*, Vol. 5, Brussels, pp. 95–101, IUCN, Switzerland.

Sáinz Ollero, H. and Hernández Bermejo, J. E. (1980). *Síntesis corológica de las dicotiledóneas endémicas de la Península Ibérica e Islas Baleares*, Instituto Nacional de Investigaciones Agrarias, Spain.
(Described by the authors in Appendix 1 of this book.)

Sweden

See Nilsson, Chapter 8. All species identified as threatened have been studied and written up individually in *Svensk Bot. Tidskr.*

United Kingdom

Perring, F. H. and Farrell, L. (1977). *British Red Data Books: 1, Vascular Plants*, Society for the Promotion of Nature Conservation, Lincoln, 94 pp.
(321 taxa listed as nationally rare or threatened; presently being revised.)

Yugoslavia

Fukarek, P. (1959). 'Arbres et arbustes rares et menacés de la flore de Yougoslavie', in *Proceedings of the IUCN 7th Technical Meeting*, Vol. 5, Brussels, pp. 159–65, IUCN, Switzerland.

Pevalek, I. (1959). 'Sur les plantes rares et menacées de la région Méditerranéenne de la Yougoslavie', in *Proceedings of the IUCN 7th Technical Meeting*, Vol. 5, Brussels, pp. 166–7.

Plašvić-Gojković, N. (1976). 'Rare protected plants of the Croatia Yugoslavia', *Poljopr. znan. smotra*, **36**(46), 61–71.

North Africa and the Middle East

IUCN Threatened Plants Committee Secretariat (1980). *First Preliminary Draft of the List of Rare, Threatened and Endemic Plants for the Countries of North Africa and the Middle East*, Mimeo, Kew.

(List of 967 rare and threatened species, with full lists of endemic species, with conservation categories, for Algeria, Azores, Canary Islands, Cyprus, Egypt, Israel, Jordan, Libya, Madeira, Morocco, Salvage Islands and Tunisia, and partial endemic lists without conservation categories for Lebanon, Syria and Turkey. The lists for Azores, Canary Islands and Madeira were considerably updated in late 1980 for circulation to botanic gardens and are available from TPC. The full list is due for revision and formal publication in 1981. It is outlined in *TPC Newsletter*, (1980) **6**, 9–11.)
See also IUCN Threatened Plants Committee Secretariat (1980), cited under Europe.

Algeria

Faurel, L. (1959). 'Plantes rares et menacées d'Algérie', in *Proceedings of the IUCN 7th Technical Meeting*, Vol. 5, Brussels, pp. 140–55, IUCN, Switzerland.

Canary Islands

Kunkel, G. (Ed.) (1975). *Inventario de los Recursos Naturales Renovables de la Provincia de Las Palmas*, Excmo. Cabildo Insular, Las Palmas de Gran Canaria.

Israel

Dafni, A. and Agami, M. (1976). 'Extinct plants of Israel', *Biol. Conserv.*, **10**, 49–52.
Zohary, M. (1959). 'Wild life protection in Israel (flora and vegetation)', in *Proceedings of the IUCN 7th Technical Meeting*, Vol. 5, Brussels, pp. 199–202, IUCN, Switzerland.

Morocco

Sauvage, Ch. (1959). 'Au sujet de quelques plantes rares et menacées de la flore du Maroc', in *Proceedings of the IUCN 7th Technical Meeting*, Vol. 5, Brussels, pp. 156–8, IUCN, Switzerland.

Tunisia

Pottier-Alapetite (1959). 'Espèces végétales rares ou menacées de Tunisie', in *Proceedings of the IUCN 7th Technical Meeting*, Vol. 5, Brussels, pp. 135–9, IUCN, Switzerland.

USSR

See Beloussova and Denissova, Chapter 6. The principal reference is:
Borodin, A. M. *et al.* (Eds.) (1978). *Red Data Book of USSR*. Lesnaya Promyshlennost, Moscow. 459 pp (in Russian).
(Covers 444 plant taxa with illustrations and maps of each; reviewed in *TPC Newsletter*, (1978) **3**, 3.)
See also:
Takhtajan, A. (1975). *Red Book: Native Plant Species to be Protected in the USSR*, Leningrad. 204 pp (in Russian). (2nd Ed. reported to be in press, p. 104).

Conservation-Requiring Rare and Disappearing Species in the USSR's Flora. Leningrad, Nauka, 1980 (not seen).
Regional Red Data Books (see also Addendum, p. 529):
Akademiya Nauk Arm SSR Botanicheskii Institut (1979). *List of Rare and Disappearing Species of the Flora of Armenia,* Erevan. 27 pp (in Armenian).
Chopik, V. I. (1978). *Rare and Threatened Plant Species of the Ukraine,* Kiev, 211 pp (in Russian).
(Covers over 150 species with descriptions, line drawings, distribution maps and colour photographs.)
Kononov, V. N. and Shabanova, G. A. (1978). *The Rare and Endangered Plants of Moldavia,* Moldavskoe Obshchestvo Okhrany Prirody, Kishinev, 27 pp (in Russian).
Malyshev, L. I. and Peshkova, G. A. (1979). *They Stand in Need of Conservation: Rare and Endangered Plants of Central Siberia,* Nauka, Siberian Branch, Novosibirsk. 174 pp (in Russian).
(Accounts of the progress in compiling regional Red Data Books are given by Beloussova and Denissova, Chapter 6, and by Tikhomirov, Chapter 7.)
Also relevant:
Akademiya Nauk Ukrainskoï SSR. Institut Botaniki im N. G. Xholodnogo (1980). *Ukraine, White Russia, Moldavia: The Protection of Important Botanical Regions,* Kiev (in Russian).
(Pages 332–70 provide lists of threatened plants by region.)
Nikitin, V. V. and Klyushkin, E. A. (1975). 'Plant species of the Turkmen SSR to be entered in the Red Book', *Izv. Akad. Nauk Turkmen SSR, Ser. Biol. Nauk,* **2**, 73–6 (in Russian).
Winterholler, B. A. *et al.* (1976). *Rare plants of Kazakhstan,* Nauka, Alma-Ata. 197 pp (in Russian) (not seen).

China

Sheng Cheng-kui of the Hortus Botanicus Nanjing, China, reports on a preliminary national threatened plant list compiled under the joint auspices of the Environment Protection Agency, the Chinese Botanical Society and the Editorial Commission of the Chinese Floras. There are also threatened plant lists for the Jiangsu, Zhejiang and Anhui Provinces of eastern China (from *TPC Newsletter,* (1981) **7**.)

Middle Asia to Indochina and Japan

India

See Jain and Sastry, Chapter 3. The principal reference is:
Jain, S. K. and Sastry, A. R. K. (1980). *Threatened Plants of India: A State-of-the-Art Report,* Botanical Survey of India, Howrah.
(Short accounts of 134 threatened species, many with colour photographs; reviewed in *TPC Newsletter* (1980) **6**, 15–16.)
See also:
Cook, C. D. K. (1980). 'The status of some Indian endemic plants', *TPC Newsletter,* **6**, 17–18.
(Wetland species.)

Henry, A. N., Vivekananthan, K., and Nair, N. C. (1978). 'Rare and threatened flowering plants of South India', *J. Bombay Nat. Hist. Soc.*, **75**(3), 684–97.
(List of 224 angiosperm species in danger of extinction.)
Kataki, S. K. (1976). 'Indian orchids – a note on conservation', *Amer. Orchid Soc. Bull.*, **45**(10), 912–14.
(List of 35 orchids which are 'found to be scarce or near extinction in their original localities'.)
Pradhan, U. C. (1977). 'Conserving Indian orchids', *Amer. Orchid Soc. Bull.*, **46**(2), 117–21.
(List of threatened orchids.)
Sahni, K. C. (1970). 'Protection of rare and endangered plants in the Indian flora', in *IUCN 11th Technical Meeting Papers and Proc.*, Vol. 2, *3rd Session, Problems of Threatened Species*, IUCN New Series 18, Morges, Switzerland, pp. 95–102.
Santapau, H. (1970). 'Endangered plant species and their habitats', in *IUCN 11th Technical Meeting Papers and Proc.*, Vol. 2, *3rd Session, Problems of Threatened Species*, IUCN New Series 18, Morges, Switzerland, pp. 83–8.
(Includes list of threatened medicinal plants and of orchids in need of protection.)
Subramanyam, K. and Spreemadhavan, C. P. (1970). 'Endangered plant species and their habitats – a review of the Indian situation', in *IUCN 11th Technical Meeting Papers and Proc.*, Vol. 2, *3rd Session, Problems of Threatened Species*, IUCN New Series 18, Morges, Switzerland, pp. 108–14.

Japan

Shimizu, T. and Satomi, N. (1976). 'A preliminary list of the rare and critical vascular plants of Japan (1)', *J. Fac. Liberal Arts, Shinshu Univ., Nat. Sci.*, **10**, 3–16.

Taiwan

Liu, T. and Hsu, K.-S. (1971). 'The rare and threatened plants and animals of Taiwan', *Quart. J. Chin. Forestry*, **4**(4), 89–96 (in Chinese).
Su, H.-J. (1980). 'Studies on the rare and threatened forest plants of Taiwan', *Bull. Exp. Forest Nation. Taiwan Univ.*, **125**, 165–205 (in Chinese) (not seen).

Thailand

Bain, J. R. and Humphrey, S. R. (1980). *A Profile of the Endangered Species of Thailand*, Office of Ecological Services, Florida State Museum, Gainesville, USA.
(Pages 37–55 are accounts and maps of 14 threatened plants.)
Smitinand, T. (1968). 'Some rare and vanishing plants of Thailand', *IUCN Publications, New Series*, **10**, 344–6.

South East Asia

Indonesia

TPC Manuscript list of 22 orchids endemic to Java, most of which are Rare.
Anon. (1978). 'Endangered species of trees', *Conservation Indonesia* (Newsletter of WWF Indonesia Programme), **2**(4).
(Lists 9 Indonesian trees.)

Philippines

H. G. Gutierrez has produced a manuscript list of 242 pages (1974) entitled *The Endemic Flowering Plant Species of the Philippines*, which assigns endemic species to the previous IUCN numerical system (0–4) to indicate degree of threat.
Quisumbing, E. (1967). 'Philippine species of plants facing extinction', *Araneta J. Agric.*, **14**, 135–62.

Australia

See Good and Lavarack, Chapter 5, and Buckley in Appendix 1 (mainly for central Australia). The principal reference is:
Hartley, W. and Leigh, J. (1979). *Australian Plants at Risk*, Australian National Parks and Wildlife Service, Occasional Paper 3.
(List of 2053 taxa annotated by a risk coding system as described in the introduction and by Good and Lavarack; reviewed in *TPC Newsletter*, (1979) **4**, 19–20 and explained by the authors in *TPC Newsletter*, (1980) **5**, 9–11.
The earlier states lists are in:
Specht, R. L., Roe, E. M., and Boughton, V. H. (Eds.) (1974). 'Conservation of major plant communities in Australia and Papua New Guinea', *Aust. J. Bot.*, Suppl. Ser. 7.

New Zealand

See Given, Chapter 4. The principal reference is:
Given, D. R. (1976, 1977, 1978). *Threatened Plants of New Zealand*, DSIR, New Zealand.
(Loose-leaf series of detailed double-paged sheets on selected threatened species; the latest TPC manuscript list derived from this report lists exactly 50 endemic taxa of vascular plants: 5 are endemic to the Kermadec Islands (4 Endangered, 1 Extinct), 8 endemic to the Chatham Islands (1 Endangered, 5 Vulnerable, 1 Rare).)
See also:
Given, D. R. (1976). 'A register of rare and endangered indigenous plants in New Zealand', *N.Z. J. Bot.*, **14**, 135–49.
(Lists 314 taxa under consideration for threatened status.)

Pacific Islands

Galapagos Islands

TPC Red Data Bulletin in preparation (Duncan Porter).
(232 taxa of vascular plants listed as endemic.)
Hamann, O. (1979). 'The survival strategies of some threatened Galapagos plants', *Noticias de Galapagos*, **30**, 22–5.

Hawaiian Islands

Ayensu, E. S. and DeFilipps, R. A. (1978). *Endangered and Threatened Plants of the United States*, Smithsonian Institution and World Wildlife Fund, Inc., Washington, DC.

(Pages 197–224 list 270 'extinct', 646 'endangered' and 197 'threatened' taxa from the state of Hawaii, virtually all of which are endemic.)

Fosberg, F. R. and Herbst, D. (1975). 'Rare and endangered species of Hawaiian vascular plants', *Allertonia*, **1**(1), 72 pp.

(List of 273 'extinct', 800 'endangered' (some protected), 99 'rare', 34 'local', 518 'uncertain' taxa and 8 taxa of 'wider range'.)

Juan Fernandez Islands

TPC Manuscript list of endemic vascular species; out of 117 species, one is Extinct (the famous *Santalum fernandezianum* F. Phil.), 50 are Endangered and 23 are Vulnerable.

Kunkel, G. (1956). 'Über den Waldtypus der Robinson–Insel', *Forsch. Fortschr.*, **30**(5), 129–37.

(Describes some of the above species.)

Marquesas Islands

TPC Manuscript of endemic species. 83 angiosperms are endemic, most of which are rare or threatened.

Ogasawara Islands

TPC Manuscript list of 52 species threatened on the islands, their world status not yet known.

Woolliams, K. R. (1978). 'Observations on the flora of the Ogasawara Islands', *Notes from Waimea Arboretum*, **5**(2), 2–10.

(Reports on 18 species, most of which are threatened.)

Woolliams, K. R. (1979). 'Observations on the flora of the Ogasawara Islands', *Notes from Waimea Arboretum*, **6**(1), 6–12.

Yoshida, A. and Tannowa, T. (1977). 'Endangered plant species of the Ogasawara Islands', *Notes from Waimea Arboretum*, **3**(2), 8–12.

Philip Island (29° 06'S., 167° 57'E.)

Melville, R. (1969). 'The endemics of Phillip Island', *Biol. Conserv.*, **1**, 170 2.

(3 species; 2 Extinct, 1 Endangered.)

Indian Ocean

Several threatened species are included in Hedberg (1968 – see under Tropical Africa, below), in the articles on Madagascar (M. Keraudren, pp. 261–5), Mauritius and Rodrigues (R. E. Vaughan, pp. 265–72), La Réunion (P. Rivals, pp. 272–5) and the Seychelles (C. Jeffrey, pp. 275–9).

Andaman and Nicobar Islands

Subramanyam and Spreemadhavan (1970 – see under India, above) provide a list of species which 'may be considered extinct or very rare' and of Nicobar endemics.

Mauritius, Réunion and Rodrigues

Agence de Cooperation Culturelle et Technique (ACCT) (1978). *La conservation et la valorisation des ressources écologiques dans les îles des Comores, de Maurice, de la Réunion, des Seychelles*, d'après un rapport présenté a l'A.C.C.T. par Michel Baumer. ACCT, Paris. 92 pp.
(Pages 45–52 cover threatened species in Réunion.)

Tirvengadum, D. D. (1980). 'On the possible extinction of *"Randia" heterophylla*: A Rubiaceae of great taxonomic interest from Rodrigues Island', *Mauritius Inst. Bull.*, **9**(1), 1–21.
(Lists 36 endemic species with notes on status and provides map of proposed nature reserves and illustrations; reviewed in *TPC Newsletter*, **7** (1981).)

TPC Manuscript list of endemic species for the 50 angiosperm families revised by 1978 for the 'Flore des Mascareignes' (out of c. 200 families). Out of 106 taxa endemic to one or more of the three islands, 13 are Extinct, 30 Endangered, 9 Vulnerable and 13 Rare.

TPC Manuscript list in preparation for Rodrigues. Out of 34 endemic angiosperms, 32 are Extinct or Endangered.

There is a list of 34 threatened species for Mauritius and Rodrigues by A. W. Owadally in Hedberg (1979 – see under Tropical Africa, below), p. 103.

Seychelles

Procter, J. (1974). 'The endemic flowering plants of the Seychelles: an annotated list', *Candollea*, **29**, 345–87.
(Lists 72 endemic species with the previous IUCN numerical system (0–4) to indicate degree of threat.)

Socotra and Abd al Kuri

TPC Red Data Bulletin in preparation. TPC Manuscript list of endemic species includes 216 endemic angiosperm species of which 85 are Endangered, 15 Vulnerable and 29 Rare, based on 1967 data.

South Atlantic and Southern Ocean

Ascension Island

Cronk, Q. C. B. (1980). 'Extinction and survival in the endemic vascular flora of Ascension Island', *Biol. Conserv.*, **17**(3), 207–19.
(Out of 10 endemic vascular plants, 6 of which are ferns and 2 grasses, 1 is Extinct, 3 Endangered or Extinct, 2 Endangered and 4 Rare.)

Falkland Islands

TPC Manuscript list of endemic species. Out of 13 endemic angiosperm species, 1 is Extinct in the wild but survives in cultivation on one island (*Calandrinia feltonii* Skottsb.), 1 Endangered and 3 Rare.

St Helena

Kerr, N. (1971). *Report on a Preliminary Nature Conservation Project, Island of St. Helena; July–August 1970*, 1BP/4 (71) (mimeo).
(An appendix gives summaries of the status in 1970 of each endemic species.)
TPC Manuscript list of endemics. Out of 32 endemic angiosperm species, 10 are Extinct, 15 Endangered and 7 Rare.

Tristan da Cunha Islands

TPC Manuscript list of endemics. Out of 11 endemic fern species and 24 endemic angiosperm species, 6 are Rare; most are neither rare nor threatened.
This list is based on research described in:
Wace, N. M. and Holdgate, M. W. (1976). *Man and Nature in the Tristan da Cunha Islands*, Monograph 6, IUCN, Switzerland.

Tropical Africa

There are many 'protolists' and reports on lists in preparation in:
Hedberg, I. (1979). 'Possibilities and needs for conservation of plant species and vegetation in Africa', in *Systematic Botany, Plant Utilization and Biosphere Conservation* (Ed. I. Hedberg), pp. 83–104, Almqvist and Wiksell, Stockholm.
(See in particular the accounts for Angola (B. J. Huntley, p. 99), Benin (E. J. Adjanohoun, pp. 91–2), Djibouti (C. Astric, p. 93), Ethiopia (M. Gilbert, pp. 92–3), Ghana (J. B. Hall, pp. 88–91), Kenya (J. B. Gillett, pp. 93–4), Liberia (J. M. Thorne, p. 88), Nigeria (S. O. Oyewole and B. Harris, p. 92), Sudan (G. Wickens, pp. 85–8), Tanzania (R. C. Wingfield, pp. 95–9), Zaïre (F. Malaisse, p. 92) and Zimbabwe (H. Wild and T. Muller, pp. 99–100).)
An earlier volume concentrates on protecting vegetation:
Hedberg, I. and O. (Eds.) (1968). *Conservation of Vegetation South of the Sahara*, Acta Phyt. Suec., 54.
(Threatened species, endemic species, species in need of protection and species from particular sites under threat are mentioned by many authors; see in particular the accounts for Somalia (P. R. O. Bally, pp. 145–8), Cameroun, (R. Letouzey, pp. 115–21), Kenya (G. Ll. Lucas, pp. 152–63) and Tanzania (R. M. Polhill, pp. 166–78).)

Kenya

Mungai, G. M., Gillett, J. B., and Eagle, C. F. (1980). *Plant Species in Kenya: Survival or Extinction*, Bulletin of Wildlife Clubs of Kenya, Nairobi.
(Lists over 20 species as threatened.)

Southern Africa

Several short lists and reports of lists in preparation can be found in Hedberg, I. (1979 – cited under Tropical Africa, above), namely for Lesotho (A. J. Guillarmod, p. 101), South Africa (A. V. Hall, pp. 100–1) and Swaziland (E. S. Kemp, pp. 101–3.)

The region covered by the *Flora of Southern Africa* is treated in:

Hall, A. V., de Winter, M., de Winter, B., and van Oosterhout, S. A. M. (1980). *Threatened Plants of Southern Africa*, South African National Scientific Programmes Report No. 45, Council for Scientific and Industrial Research, Pretoria. x + 244 pp.
(Reviewed in *TPC Newsletter*, 7 (1981).)

The Caribbean Islands

Guadeloupe and Martinique

Sastre, C. (1978). 'Plantes menacées de Guadeloupe et de Martinique I. Espèces altitudinales', *Bull. Mus. Natn. Hist. Nat., Paris*, 3e sér., 519, *Ecol. générale*, 42, 65–93.
(Sheets on 13 rare and threatened species with illustrations and habitat photographs.)

Puerto Rico and the Virgin Islands

Ayensu, E. S. and DeFilipps, R. A. (1978). *Endangered and Threatened Plants of the United States*, Smithsonian Institution and World Wildlife Fund, Inc., Washington, DC.
(Pages 225–32 list 102 'endangered' and 'threatened' taxa from Puerto Rico and the Virgin Islands, both US and British, and provide a valuable bibliography.)
Little, E. L., Jr. and Woodbury, R. O. (1980). *Rare and Endemic Trees of Puerto Rico and the Virgin Islands*, US Dept. of Agriculture, Forest Service, Conservation Research Report No. 27, Washington, DC, 26 pp.
Woodbury, R. O. (1975). *Rare and Endangered Plants of Puerto Rico – A Committee Report*, US Dept. of Agriculture, Soil Conservation Service and Dept. of Natural Resources, Commonwealth of Puerto Rico, 85 pp.

North America

Canada

The principal references are:

Argus, G. W. and White, D. J. (1977). 'The rare vascular plants of Ontario', *Syllogeus*, 14.
Argus, G. W. and White, D. J. (1978). 'The rare vascular plants of Alberta', *Syllogeus*, 17.
Maher, R. V., White, D. J., Argus, G. W., and Keddy, P. A. (1978). 'The rare vascular plants of Nova Scotia', *Syllogeus*, 18.
Maher, R. V., Argus, G. W., Harms, V. L., and Hudson, J. H. (1979). 'The rare vascular plants of Saskatchewan', *Syllogeus*, 20.
White, D. J. and Johnson, K. L. (1980). 'The rare vascular plants of Manitoba', *Syllogeus*, 27.
The report on Saskatchewan was reviewed in *TPC Newsletter* (1980) 5, 11. The three earlier reports (Ontario, Alberta, Nova Scotia) are described by G. W. Argus in *TPC Newsletter* (1978), 3, 13–14. Each report provides an annotated list of species

believed to be rare in that state, with notes on habitat, distribution, etc., but without indication of degree of threat within the state.
See also:
Guppy, G. A. (1977). 'Endangered plants in British Columbia', *Davidsonia*, **8**, 24–30.
Kershaw, L. (1976). *A Phytogeographical Survey of Rare, Endangered and Extinct Plants in the Canadian Flora*, MSc thesis, University of Waterloo, Ontario (not seen).
Kershaw, L. J. and Morton, J. K. (1976). 'Rare and potentially endangered species in the Canadian flora – A preliminary list of vascular plants', *Can. Bot. Assoc. Bull.*, **9**(2), 26–30.

United States of America

See Ayensu, Chapter 2, of which Appendix V is a lengthy list of state threatened plant lists.

The latest version of the Smithsonian list is:
Ayensu, E. S. and DeFilipps, R. A. (1978). *Endangered and Threatened Plants of the United States*, Smithsonian Institution and World Wildlife Fund, Inc., Washington, DC, xv + 403 pp.
(Lists 839 'endangered', 1211 'threatened' and 90 'extinct' taxa for the continental United States, including Alaska; reviewed in *TPC Newsletter*, (1978), **3**, 3.)
The 'Endangered Species Technical Bulletin', issued by the Endangered Species Program of the US Fish and Wildlife Service, Washington, DC, reviews the status of species proposed for listing under the Endangered Species Act, legislation which is outlined by Fay, Chapter 37.
The latest version of the federal US list (species officially designated as 'endangered' or 'threatened' under the Endangered Species Act) is:
Department of the Interior, Fish and Wildlife Service (1980). 'Republication of Lists of Endangered and Threatened Species and Correction of Technical Errors in Final "Rules" ', *Federal Register*, **45**(99): 33768–81. May 20.
(48 'endangered' and 9 'threatened' plants listed.)
The latest list of species being considered for inclusion on the US federal list (protection under the Endangered Species Act) is:
Department of the Interior, Fish and Wildlife Service (1980). 'Endangered and threatened wildlife and plants; Review of plant taxa for listing as endangered or threatened species', *Federal Register*, **45**(242), 82480–569. December 15.

Middle America

Mexico

Anon. (1979). 'Especies en peligro de extinción', *Macpalxochitl, Bol. Bimestral de Soc. Bot. Mexico*, **79**, 3–4.
(24 taxa listed.)
The Instituto de Investigaciones Sobre Recursos Bióticos in Xalapa, Veracruz, maintains a computer file of nationally threatened species using IUCN criteria. This is described with examples by A. P. Vovides and A. Gómez-Pompa in Prance and Elias (1977 – see below), pp. 77–88.

South America

Organización Estados Americanos (O.E.A.) (1965). 'Lista de espécies de fauna y flora en vías de extinción en los estados miembros Argentina, Bolivia y Ecuador', *Conferencia Especializada Latinoamericana Problemas Conservación Recursos Naturales Renovables Continente*, Doc. 16, 1–8 (not seen).
There are many 'protolists' and reports on lists in preparation in:
Prance, G. T. and Elias, T. S. (Eds.) (1977). *Extinction Is Forever*, New York Botanical Garden. vi + 437 pp. See in particular the accounts for Argentina (A. L. Cabrera, pp. 245–7), Chile (C. M. Pizarro, pp. 251–3), Colombia (A. Fernández-Pérez, pp. 117–27), Ecuador and Amazonian Peru (A. H. Gentry, pp. 136–49), Andean and coastal Peru (R. Ferreyra, pp. 150–7) and Venezuela (J. A. Steyermark, pp. 128–35).)

Brazil

Carvalho, J. C. M. (1968). 'Lista das Espécies de Animais e Plantas Ameaçades de Extinção no Brasil', *Fundaçao Brasil. Conserv. Natureza, Bol. Inform.*, **3**, 11–16. (13 plants.)

Chile

Pizarro, C. M. (1973). *Chile: Plantas en Extinction*, Ed. Universitaria, Santiago. 248 pp.

Venezuela

Steyermark, J. A. (1979). 'Plant refuge and dispersal centres in Venezuela: their relict and endemic element', in *Tropical Botany* (Eds. K. Larsen and L. B. Holm-Nielsen), pp. 185–221, Academic Press, London.
(Includes an appendix of endemic and relict species in the Coastal Cordillera and Serrania del Interior.)

Addendum
USSR (Regional Red Data Books)
Malÿshev, L. I. and Sobdeuskaya, K. A. (Eds.) (1980). *Rare and Endangered Plant Species of Siberia*, Nauka, Novosibirsk. 223 pp (in Russian). (Descriptions of over 300 threatened species with line drawings and distribution maps.)
Sytnik, K. M., Grodzinsky, A. M., Topachevsky, V. A., Chopik, V. I. and Fedorenko, A. P. (Edit. Board) (1979). *Red Data Book of the Ukrainian SSR*, Academy of Sciences of the Ukrainian SSR, Naukova Dumka Publishers, Kiev (in Russian). (Covers 151 species of vascular plants with line drawings and distribution maps.)
Tikomirov (Chapter 7, p. 104) reports that *Red Data Book of the Soviet Far East Flora* is in press.

USA
Nelson, B. B. and Arndt, R. E. (1980). *Eastern States Endangered Plants*, US Department of the Interior, Bureau of Land Management, Alexandria, Virginia. 109 pp.

Appendix 3

One theme in this book is the need for an agreed way of assessing the degree of threat to species in danger. Reprinted below is the text of the Threatened Plants Committee booklet which defines and explains the IUCN Red Data Book categories, used for this purpose in TPC's world-wide survey of threatened species (see Chapter 1) and in many national programmes. (Considerable confusion arises from words such as endangered being used in different senses by different authors; in this book such words are shown normally when used in the dictionary sense, in quotes if defined by the author, and with a capital initial if used according to the IUCN scheme outlined below.)

THE IUCN RED DATA BOOK CATEGORIES

The Red Data Book Categories are used by IUCN to indicate the degree of threat to individual species in their wild habitats. They are used for both flora and fauna. Below are given formal definitions of the categories together with additional information and examples to clarify and interpret them for use by botanists.

Extinct (Ex)

This category is only used for species which are no longer known to exist in the wild after *repeated* searches of the type localities *and other known or likely places*. As interpreted by IUCN, this includes species that are extinct in the wild but surviving in cultivation. Our interpretation follows that of the Smithsonian Institution in their 'Report on Endangered and Threatened Plant Species of the United States' (1975).

Endangered (E)

Taxa in danger of extinction and whose survival is unlikely if the causal factors continue operating.

Included are taxa whose numbers have been reduced to a critical level or whose habitats have been so drastically reduced that they are deemed to be in immediate danger of extinction.

This is interpreted to mean including species with populations so critically low that a breeding collapse due to lack of genetic diversity becomes a possibility, whether or not they are threatened by man. An example would be a perennial reduced to 100 specimens occurring on one inaccessible cliff where no man-made threats are likely, but where a land-slide could remove the whole population.

Vulnerable (V)

Taxa believed likely to move into the Endangered category in the near future if the causal factors continue operating.

Included are taxa of which most or all the populations are decreasing because of over-exploitation, extensive destruction of habitat or other environmental disturbance; taxa with populations that have been seriously depleted and whose ultimate security is not yet assured; and taxa with populations that are still abundant but are under threat from serious adverse factors throughout their range.

Rare (R)

Taxa with small world populations that are not at present Endangered or Vulnerable but are at risk.

These taxa are usually localized within restricted geographical areas or habitats or are thinly scattered over a more extensive range.

The categories 'Rare' and 'Vulnerable' have often been confused in the past or thought to be simply stages on a linear scale of increasing degrees of threat to species in danger. This is not the case because they represent the state of plants in fundamentally different situations, both of which can lead to the 'Endangered' category.

The 'Rare' species has a small world population but is under no known or immediate threat. It is not endangered but is simply at risk because of the size of its population. It may have a very restricted distribution, e.g. it may be endemic to a small island or a single mountain. Alternatively it may have a wider distribution but may be severely restricted by its habitat. The difference between risk and threat is best illustrated by an example: *Cyclamen mirabile* is only known at present from areas near Mugla and Isparta in southern Turkey and was not thought to be particularly in danger. Thus, it would have been classified as 'Rare'. However 50 000 corms were recently offered for sale, dug up by local collectors who mistook it for *C. neapolitanum*, a widespread and much cultivated species. No one could have predicted this unlikely fate, but it happened! To use another example, in Brazil there occur two species of plants, *Salvia saxicola* and a new species of *Tripogandra*, which are restricted to a small limestone outcropping near Brasilia. Although under no immediate threat, they could be wiped out by an unusually bad fire or by such development activities as quarrying. The keynote of the 'Rare' species is that they may not need active protection but they do need monitoring to ensure their continued survival.

The borderline between 'Rare' and 'neither rare nor threatened' ('nt' – see below) is a difficult one. Considering the following factors may be helpful.

(1) Area of distribution

Bidens hendersonensis, which is endemic to Henderson Island (about 30 sq. km) in the Pacific, is 'Rare'. The plant is scattered over the island and there is little threat to its survival. On the other hand *Cyclamen creticum*, which is widespread and common on Crete (about 250 km long), and *Crocus cambessedesii*, which is very abundant on the Balearic Islands (one about 90 km long, the other about 40 km long), are 'nt'. None of these three species are greatly depleted.

When considering the area of distribution, the density of the population must also be borne in mind. The *Bidens* is 'Rare'; however, if there was a single endemic tree or shrub species which dominated Henderson Island, providing most of the ground-cover, that species would be considered 'nt' since it would be too numerous to be 'Rare' and of course neither depleted ('Vulnerable') nor in immediate danger of extinction ('Endangered'). There could be literally millions of individuals of a dominant species on an island of 30 sq. km, and this is a much bigger population than that of many species which occur over a wider area but are definitely not considered 'Rare' or 'Vulnerable'. Many of the European orchids are good examples of this form of distribution. Nevertheless, a plant which is restricted to a small area is obviously more at risk than one of a similar population which is more widely spread, and this should be taken into account.

In conclusion, most of the 'Rare' species will not only be endemic to a single mountain range or island but will also be either confined to one part of that area or not be very common throughout their range, unless the island is *extremely* small. An example would be Lundy Island (4 sq. km) off Great Britain where any endemic plant that was not under any immediate threat would be classified as 'Rare', however common or dominant it might be. It is easy to forget how large some islands are – for example Isabela in the Galapagos Islands is nearly 130 km long. When assigning Red Data Book categories to lists of island endemics, 'Rare' should only be used for those species that have *very restricted* distributions and/or *low* population densities, and of course that are under no immediate or known threat to their survival.

(2) Population size

It was once considered that any species with less than 20 000 individuals should be considered 'Rare'. The figure is perhaps in the correct order of magnitude and as such is a useful guide. However, there can be no hard and fast rule since some species have a much greater reproductive capacity than others. The situation is complex and each case must be decided on its own merits.

When a species of such a limited distribution comes under threat and starts to become depleted, it should be transferred to the 'Vulnerable' category if threatened over part of its range, or to the 'Endangered' category if all the population is under threat.

In contrast the 'Vulnerable' species is one that is (or was) more widespread but has become *depleted*. The critical difference between a 'Rare' species and a 'Vulnerable' one is that the former has a relatively stable population while the latter is on the decline. At one extreme of the category 'Vulnerable' are species which have a very wide range but have become massively depleted. They may have been common previously, but will probably have had scattered distributions, usually occurring in small colonies (e.g. wetland species) or as occasional single specimens (e.g. many rain forest trees). At the other extreme are species which have moderately small distributions (e.g. are restricted to an island the size of Crete or Tasmania). *Crocus cambessedesii* was cited above as an example falling into the 'nt' rather than the 'Rare' category. If it becomes depleted, it should then be transferred to the 'Vulnerable' category.

Indeterminate (I)

Taxa known to be Extinct, Endangered, Vulnerable or Rare but where there is not enough information to say which of the four categories is appropriate.

This category is used for species reported as '? Extinct' or 'possibly Extinct' or 'probably Extinct' on the assumption that they are either 'Extinct' or 'Endangered'.

Insufficiently Known (K)

Taxa that are suspected but not definitely known to belong to any of the above categories because of the lack of information.

The key word here is *suspected*. An 'Insufficiently Known' species does not have to be *proved* to be in any of the three categories – 'Endangered', 'Vulnerable' or 'Rare'. Examples of such plants include relict species of limited but uncertain distribution (e.g. Example 25, below) or small annuals known only from a few records but which could be more widespread as they are easily overlooked in the field (e.g. Example 26, below). Also considered as 'Insufficiently Known' may be species of a complex genus, much of which is thought to be in some danger and whose members are not easily distinguished by field characters. An 'Insufficiently Known' species can always be transferred to another category when further information becomes available. It is hoped that listing a species as 'Insufficiently Known' will stimulate others to find out its true status.

The importance of the 'Insufficiently Known' category is that it enables categories to be applied to whole endemic floras where the majority of species are given a more precise category but where a few species are very little known in the field. It is wrong to list 'Insufficiently Known' species as 'Rare' or even 'Indeterminate' simply to be on the safe side. Overestimating the danger often does more harm than good. At present, the Threatened Plants Committee estimates that some 25 000–30 000 species (about 10 per cent of the world's flora) will fall into one of the first four categories.

Out of Danger (O)

Taxa formerly included in one of the above categories, but which are now considered relatively secure because effective conservation measures have been taken or the previous threat to their survival has been removed.

In practice, Endangered and Vulnerable categories may include, temporarily, taxa whose populations are beginning to recover as a result of remedial action, but whose recovery is insufficient to justify their transfer to another category.

Rescued species are put into the 'Rare' category if the threat has been completely averted, or the 'Vulnerable' category if the species is still partly under threat. When deciding on the category, it may be helpful to consider the following:

(1) Is the plant conserved throughout its range or only in one part?
(2) How well is it protected in that part?
(3) What is the status of the reserve in which it occurs?
(4) How permanent is its protection likely to be?

If only a few specimens survive, the species should still be considered 'Endangered'. Some species will in due course recolonize their former habitats and become common, so they will no longer remain 'Rare' or 'Vulnerable'. The category 'Out of Danger' should then be used. Good examples of rescued species in the categories 'Endangered', 'Vulnerable' and 'Rare' are given below (28–30).

For species which are neither rare nor threatened, the symbol 'nt' is used.

Only species in the categories 'Extinct', 'Endangered', 'Vulnerable', 'Rare' or 'Indeterminate' are included in the Red Data Book and on lists of rare and threatened species. (The categories 'Insufficiently Known' and 'nt' are required where full lists of endemic species are given.)

Species only known from old records

These fall into only three categories:

(1) 'Extinct'. As mentioned above, this is only used for plants not found in the wild after thorough and recent searches of their likely habitat.

(2) 'Indeterminate' is the category used for species known only from small areas (e.g. mountain localities) where they have not been recorded for a long time, but where the area has not been thoroughly botanized. However, the area has been botanized to an extent that if the species was refound, it would definitely fall into one of the three categories: 'Endangered', 'Vulnerable', or 'Rare'. In these cases one must be certain that it could not be abundant and widespread enough to be 'nt'. One cannot of course apply the categories 'Endangered', 'Vulnerable' or 'Rare' themselves since the species could turn out to be any one of them, or 'Extinct'.

(3) 'Insufficiently Known' is used when the area from which the plant was recorded has been worked in detail to such a small extent that it is a possibility that the species is 'nt'. Some examples of this situation are given below. Often these areas are under considerable threat (e.g. the Amazon basin) and so it is hoped that more information on the individual species will become available in the near future.

Where full screenings of floras for rare and threatened species are being undertaken, it is felt that 'Insufficiently Known' is the best category for those species that are taxonomically uncertain or whose exact delineation is uncertain. Many of these will be species known only from type collections in which it is uncertain whether or not they are good species. It is best to include such taxa on country lists until they have been definitely shown to be not specifically distinct. However, taxonomically clear species only known from *dubious* records in the country concerned (but obviously occurring elsewhere) are best omitted from such lists as are species predicted to occur in the country but not yet actually found there.

Examples

Extinct

1. *Franklinia alatamaha.* This beautiful, Camellia-like shrub has not been seen in its original habitat in Georgia, USA, since 1802 and is presumed to be extinct in the wild. Fortunately it is successfully cultivated on both sides of the Atlantic but this does not alter the Red Data Book Category which applies to the *wild* population only.

Endangered

2. *Echium pininana.* The Giant Echiums are one of the glories of the Canary Islands – this one is reduced to virtually a single population in the cloud zone on La Palma. It is threatened by goats and by collecting for horticulture. It will obviously not survive unless action is taken to protect it.

3. *Persea theobromifolia.* Once an important source of timber, this member of the Lauraceae is now known only from a highly vulnerable and isolated 0.8 sq. km area of lowland forest at the Río Palenque Biological Center in Los Ríos Province, Ecuador. In the decade between 1960, when a new road was opened, and 1970, most of the plant's habitat was converted to plantations of banana and oil palm. Although the species regenerates readily, the known population is probably no more than twelve reproducing individuals.

4. *Calyptronoma rivalis,* a palm from Puerto Rico, is reduced to a few individuals and could be eliminated by fire or by wood cutting. In 1970 only 20 individuals were seen.

5. *Euphorbia abdelkuri.* An extraordinary succulent which forms forest-like clumps of erect, thornless stems up to 3 m high. Only three such clumps remain, on the barren island of Abd al Kuri in the Socotran Archipelago (Indian Ocean). There appears to be little threat since it is poisonous. However, since the numbers are so low, it must be considered 'Endangered'.

6. *Vepris glandulosa* is a small understorey tree from the Muguga Forest in Kenya where it survives in a 15.5 ha reserve. Only eight trees and a few seedlings are known, and so it is considered 'Endangered' until the population is significantly larger.

7. *Neoveitchia storckii.* In 1972–3 this Fijian palm was reduced to a single population of 150–200 mature trees, occupying an area of less than 2 hectares. Since then it has declined further due to additional felling and clearing of the habitat for banana cultivation.

8. *Iris winogradowii* is much uprooted by gardeners and amateur botanists. Only a few hundred individuals remain in its wild habitat on a single mountain in Georgia, USSR, and it is not yet protected by law.

9. *Areca concinna.* The only known population of this Sri Lankan palm consists of about 1000 individuals and is confined to a swamp of 2–4 hectares where it is at great risk from drainage and subsequent fire.

Vulnerable

10. *Lycaste suaveolens.* This rarely found orchid is largely confined to the middle altitudes of volcanic slopes in El Salvador where large areas of the forest have been cleared for coffee plantations. It is an easy and favourite target for orchid collectors and is likely to become 'Endangered' in the near future if protection is not forthcoming.

11. *Johannesteijsmannia altifrons.* A delicate undergrowth palm scattered in a few parts of Malaysia and Indonesia, only occurring locally. It is confined to primary rain forest. It does not survive clear-felling and is becoming depleted by destruction and exploitation of the habitat for timber.

12. *Myosotidium hortensia.* The Chatham Islands Forget-me-not is a spectacular giant herb formerly abundant along the coasts of the Chatham Islands but now seriously depleted by grazing from introduced animals. It occurs only scattered around parts of the coasts. Whereas most of the less common, coastal endemics from New Zealand (and the Mediterranean) are turning out to be 'Vulnerable', most of the mountain and cliff endemics are 'Rare'.

13. *Cladrastis lutea.* American Yellowweed. A beautiful small tree with a sporadic distribution in ten states of the eastern USA. It is always rare in its localities and some of the sites are threatened by flooding following dam-construction. In other sites saplings of the species are uprooted for use as nursery stock.

14. *Sophora fernandeziana.* Although originally scattered through the lower montane forests which covered Isla Robinson Crusoe (formerly Más á Tierra in the Juan Fernández Group), this species was found to be very infrequent in 1954–5. Although the island has been declared a national park, the forests are still being destroyed by goats, sheep, cattle and even horses, as well as being over-run by introduced plants such as *Rubus ulmifolius*, the South European Blackberry, and *Aristotelia chilensis*, the Chilean 'maqui'. Whereas *Cladrastis lutea* is at the lower, less threatened end of the 'Vulnerable' category, this species is at the top, nearly qualifying as 'Endangered'.

15. *Saxifraga florulenta.* This spectacular endemic to cliffs in the Maritime Alps (France and Italy) has become depleted, partly due to collectors and partly due to natural causes. It is particularly susceptible because it grows very slowly taking at least 10–12 years to flower, and because of its monocarpic habit.

16. *Lodoicea maldivica.* The famous Coco de Mer has the largest seeds in the plant kingdom and is endemic to the Seychelles. It is now scattered on Praslin and Curieuse Islands. It is partly protected on Praslin but there is always the threat of tourists destroying the habitat and local people collecting the seeds to sell to visitors.

17. *Silene diclinis.* A dioecious annual known from one locality in Spain where in 1974 it was reduced to about 500 specimens with little signs of regeneration. Its survival is due to its association with the agricultural system prevailing in the locality, a system which is very different from that of the surrounding area.

This species falls at the borderline of 'Endangered', 'Vulnerable' and 'Rare'. It is not known to be declining but it is likely that the population greatly fluctuates. Because of this, because of its dependence on man-made systems for survival, and because of its dioecious habit, 'Vulnerable' is preferred to 'Rare'; more active conservation measures than monitoring its population are obviously necessary to ensure survival. 'Endangered' is not used since it is suspected that the species may have been in this condition for a long time and so it cannot be said to be in imminent danger of extinction.

Rare

18. *Cupressus macrocarpa*, the Monterey Cypress, is restricted in the wild to two wind-swept sites along the coast of California. The trees occur in a belt 100–200 m wide along the coast, the larger of the two groves being about 4 km long. Both are effectively protected. (The species is common in cultivation but this does not affect its Red Data Book category.)

19. *Saxifraga biternata*. A species only known from two small, mountainous localities in Spain. It is at some risk in one of them from visitors who use the area as a picnic spot, but there is no evidence that the *Saxifraga* is declining. It is still reported to be abundant in both localities. Most of the 'Rare' species are in a position very similar to this one.

20. *Euphrasia campbelliae* is only known with certainty from about nine island localities, difficult of access, in the Outer Hebrides (UK), occurring in maritime grassland. There is no reason to believe these populations are under threat.

21. *Lilium rhodopaeum* is restricted to several mountainous localities on the Bulgarian/Greek border. Its most lovely lemon yellow flowers make it a tempting target for horticulturists but so far it does not appear to be on the decline or under great collecting pressure.

22. *Dionysia mira* is confined to north-facing high limestone cliffs in the mountains of Oman. It tends to occur in low numbers and only in the limited areas of suitable habitat but does extend for around 300 km of mountain range.

Indeterminate

23. *Anthemis werneri* is only known from one locality on one small island of the Aegean (Greece). It must be either 'Rare', 'Endangered' or 'Extinct' but since, to our knowledge, no botanists have visited the island recently to study the species in the wild, it must be considered as 'Indeterminate' for the time being.

24. *Paphiopedilum druryi* is endemic to a single locality in southern India. Excessive collecting and forest fires have virtually exterminated the species and no plants have been seen in the wild since 1972. However it is possible that rhizomes or seedlings still remain. Since it is therefore either 'Endangered' or 'Extinct', the summary category is 'Indeterminate'.

Insufficiently Known

25. *Duckeodendron cestroides.* This plant is only known from two or three records in the Amazon Basin. It probably has a relictual distribution so one *suspects* it may be rare or threatened.

26. *Halophytum ameghinoi* from Argentina has been found only a few times, but as it is a small, weedy plant, it may have been overlooked and may be more common than existing records indicate.

27. *Eriope xavantium* is only known from one gathering in the northern Mato Grosso of Brazil. The area has recently been opened up by a new road and much of the forest has been destroyed.

Rescued species

28. *Tecomanthe speciosa*, the Three Kings Trumpet Flower. This attractive liane is reduced to one plant on Great Island of the Three Kings Group (off New Zealand). The island's goats were destroyed in 1946 and the area is now a reserve, but there is still only one plant so it must be considered as 'Endangered'.

29. *Orothamnus zeyheri*, the famous Marsh Rose of South Africa, is 'Vulnerable' as although rescue measures have increased the population substantially, reaching 1940 individuals in 1977, the species is till partly under threat from low seed set, damage by introduced fungi and native rats, and accidental fire, as well as from habitat destruction at some of its localities.

30. *Cordyline kaspar*, the Three Kings Cabbage Tree, is 'Rare'. It is another example from the small Three Kings Group. The goat population was eliminated in 1946 when the islands were declared a reserve, and the tree is recovering well and regenerating from seed.

Index

541